THE WORKS OF

ORESTES A. BROWNSON

COLLECTED AND ARRANGED

BY

HENRY F. BROWNSON.

VOLUME VI.
CONTAINING THE SECOND PART OF THE WRITINGS IN DEFENCE OF
THE CHURCH.

AMS PRESS, INC.
NEW YORK
1966

AMS PRESS, INC.
New York, N.Y. 10003
1966

Manufactured in the United States of America

CONTENTS.

	PAGE.
TRANSCENDENTALISM, ARTICLE I.,	1
" ARTICLE II.,	50
" ARTICLE III.,	83
PROTESTANTISM ENDS IN TRANSCENDENTALISM,	113
PROTESTANTISM IN A NUTSHELL,	135
THE PRESBYTERIAN CONFESSION OF FAITH, ARTICLE I.,	160
" " " " ARTICLE II.,	211
THE TWO BROTHERS; OR, WHY ARE YOU A PROTESTANT?	
CHAPTER I.,	244
CHAPTER II.,	247
CHAPTER III.,	260
CHAPTER IV.,	267
CHAPTER V.,	282
CHAPTER VI.,	292
CHAPTER VII.,	308
CHAPTER VIII.,	317
CHAPTER IX.,	328
CHAPTER X.,	337
PROFESSOR PARK AGAINST CATHOLICITY,	353
THORNWELL'S ANSWER TO DR. LYNCH, ARTICLE I.,	427
" " " " " ARTICLE II.,	452
" " " " " ARTICLE III.,	485
LITERARY POLICY OF THE CHURCH OF ROME,	520
METHODIST QUARTERLY REVIEW,	550
HOPKINS'S BRITISH REFORMATION,	568

TRANSCENDENTALISM.*

[From Brownson's Quarterly Review for 1845 and 1846.]

ARTICLE I.

WE have nothing to say of the general character of the author of this volume and very little of the volume itself, as a simple literary production, detached from the system in exposition and defence of which it appears to have been written. It is loosely, and even heavily written, in a flippant and affected style, and sins hardly less against grammar and rhetoric than against piety and truth. It bears the marks of haste, and seems to have been hurriedly thrown together, from the author's commonplace-book and the fag ends of his sermons and discourses, and sent forth to the public without his having taken the time or the pains to melt his heterogeneous materials down into a common mass, or to *think out*, so to speak, the principles he had rashly adopted, in their systematic relations, and logical connexions and consequences. It is crude, confused; without method, order, systematic unity, or scientific development. As the production of a vain, conceited pedant and scoffer, it may pass; but as the production of a scholar, a theologian, a man ambitious of contributing to the literature of his country, and establishing a high literary and scientific character of his own,—the less we say of it, the more shall we consult the credit of the author.

But we are not concerned with the author, nor with his book, save so far as one or the other is connected with the system he attempts to set forth, and is to be taken as its exponent. This system we propose to examine,—not simply the author or his book; neither of which, separated from this system, which is not without numerous adherents, both at home and abroad, would deserve any serious attention. But this system, called ordinarily *Transcendentalism*, by Mr. Parker *Natural Religionism,* and not inaptly, by Mr. Andrews Norton *The latest Form of Infidelity*, it is by no means

---
*A Discourse of Matters pertaining to Religion. By THEODORE PARKER. Boston: 1842.

easy to ascertain. Its expounders write on the principle, that "ideas are shy of being expressed in words, and must be suggested rather than stated." They professedly eschew clear and definite statements, and seem to hold that truth can be seen and judged of in its true proportions only as it looms up in the dim and uncertain twilight of vague and indeterminate expressions. This is, no doubt, a convenient theory for them, but it is exceedingly perplexing to readers who would understand what they read, and especially to reviewers who would be just both to themselves and their author. We are not a little perplexed, the moment we undertake to analyze Mr. Parker's book, and reduce it to fundamental propositions which may be clearly apprehended and distinctly stated. It is a book of many pieces. Its author abounds in contradictions no less than in loose and intangible statements, and sometimes brings together in the same sentence not less than two or three mutually contradictory systems. Nevertheless, after much toil and pains, aided by our own familiar acquaintance with the general subject, we believe we may compress what is systematic in the book, what the author most values, what constitute the bases of the transcendental doctrines generally, within the three following propositions ; namely :—

I. Man is the measure of truth and goodness.
II. Religion is a fact or principle of human nature.
III. All religious institutions, which have been or are, have their principle and cause in human nature.

A single glance at these propositions reveals the character of the system. It is sheer naturalism, and Mr. Parker himself calls it "the natural-religious view." Its advocates, however, profess to be religious, to be the especial friends of religion, and to have put a final conclusion to the controversy between believers and infidels, by having discovered a solid and imperishable foundation for religion in the permanent and essential nature of man. Man is religious because he is man, and must be religious or cease to be man. According to them, religion has its foundation, not in supernatural revelation, but in human nature, and rests for its authority, therefore, not on the veracity of God, but on the veracity of man ; and as man can neither deceive nor be deceived, it of course must be eternally and immutably true ! They also affect to discover truth in all religions, and to accept it. But this does not take their system out of the category of naturalism; because, 1, they recognize no religion as having been supernaturally given; and, 2, because they acknowledge in religious institutions, which have been or are, nothing to be truth, which transcends the natural order, or which the natural faculties of man are not adequate to discover, and of whose *intrinsic* truth they are not competent to judge. All the rest they hold to be misapprehension or exaggeration of natural phenomena, or a mere symbolic way of expressing simple truths lying within the reach of natural reason.

This they all admit; but they fancy that they escape the condemnation to which naturalism as ordinarily set forth is justly exposed, by holding that religious institutions depend on what is permanent and essential in man, not on what is accidental and transient. Whence comes the institution of religion? "To this question," says Mr. Parker, "two answers have been given,—one foolish, one wise. The foolish answer, which may be read in Lucretius and elsewhere, is, that religion is not a necessity of man's nature, which comes from the action of eternal demands within him, but is the result of mental disease, so to say; the effect of fear, of ignorance combining with selfishness. . . . . . The wise answer is, that religion comes out of a principle deep and permanent in the heart, ... from sublime, permanent, and universal wants, and must be referred to the soul, to the unchanging realities of life."—pp. 13, 14. But this amounts to nothing; for both the wise answer and the foolish agree in asserting that religion is of human origin, and that it, itself,—not its necessity, merely,—comes out of human nature. Moreover, what Lucretius regards as the result of mental disease, and rejects under the name of religion, the transcendentalists themselves regard as springing from the same source, and also reject under the name of the form, or symbol; and all they hold to be true and permanent, as springing from the permanent and essential nature of man, and which they call religion, Lucretius himself accepts, as well as they, and holds to be eternally true, but is foolish enough to call it "nature." The only real difference, then, between Lucretius and Mr. Parker, between the "foolish" answer and the "wise," is that the former, with all the world, calls what he contemns and discards *religion*, and what he retains and commends *nature*, but the latter is too *wise* to be guilty of such folly.

Whatever, then, the merits of the system under examination, it is naturalism,—nothing more, nothing less. The question, then, between us and transcendentalism is the old question between naturalism and supernaturalism. Is man's natural relation the only relation he sustains to his Creator? Have there been supernatural revelations, or are the so-called supernatural revelations explicable on natural principles? Do man's natural forces—that is, what he is and receives by virtue of his natural relation to God—suffice for the fulfilment of his destiny; or needs he the gracious, that is, supernatural, interposition and assistance of his Maker? These are the real questions at issue; and these questions Mr. Parker and the transcendentalists answer in favor of nature against grace, of man against God. The validity and value of their answer is, then, what we propose to examine.

With these remarks, we proceed to take up, *seriatim*, the propositions themselves. We begin with the first.

1. Man is the Measure of Truth and Goodness.

We do not understand the transcendentalists to assert by this proposition, that man actually knows all truth and goodness, though from many things they say we might infer this; but that man is the measure, the standard, the criterion of all truth and goodness,—the touchstone on which we are to try whatever is alleged to be true and good, and to determine whether it be true and good, or false and evil. Nor do we mean to assert that they are prepared to maintain even this in general thesis; but that they do assert it, that they everywhere imply it, and that without assuming it their whole system would be a baseless fabric, and their doctrines and speculations the sheerest absurdities.

A slight examination of the leading views of transcendentalists on the origin and ground of ideas will sustain our assertion. Transcendentalists may be divided into three classes. They all agree in their antagonism to the doctrines of Locke, as set forth in his *Essay on the Human Understanding*, and in asserting for man the inherent ability to cognize intuitively nonsensible, spiritual, or immaterial facts or realities. We say *intuitively;* for we do not understand Locke himself to deny absolutely our ability to cognize such realities, but simply to deny that we can do it intuitively, and to contend that we can do it only discursively, by reflection operating on sensible *data*. The peculiarity of the transcendentalists is in holding that we cognize them intuitively, immediately, instead of discursively. But in explaining the principle and fact of intuition, and its modes or conditions, they differ somewhat among themselves, and may, as we have said, be divided into three classes.

1. The first class name the *vis intuitiva* reason, and contend that the *νοήματα*, spiritual cognoscibles, or the immaterial realities capable of being known, are really exterior to and independent of the subject knowing, and are simply apprehended on occasion of the sensible phenomena by which they are rendered present. Thus, they contend that the ideas of cause, of cause in general, necessary cause,—in a word, all the Kantian categories,—are entertained by the mind and applied to sensible phenomena, by actual intuition of *the objects* of these ideas,—not merely the ideas themselves —really existing in the non-sensible world. Yet they call this non-sensible world reason, and represent these ideas, objectively considered, that is, as objects existing *in re*, not as mere mental conceptions, to be its constituent elements. Taking ideas in this sense, as the object, reason may be termed the *regio idearum*, or world of absolute and necessary truth. It is impersonal and objective, and operates spontaneously, by an energy not human, but which is the energy of God, whose word or speech reason is. Containing in itself absolute ideas or absolute truth and goodness, reason is a measure of truth and goodness; and as it is divine, it must be an exact measure. Whatever it pronounces true is true; whatever it pronounces beautiful is beautiful; whatever it pronounces good is good.

But this reason, though declared to be impersonal and objective, is also assumed to be a faculty of human nature, a faculty of the human soul, its only light, that by virtue of which it is essentially intelligent, and knows all that it does know, whatever the sphere or degree of its knowledge. Hence, of two things, one,—either man is identical with God, intellectually considered, and it is God that sees in man, which must plunge us, in the last analysis, into absolute pantheism; or reason is human, an attribute, if not of the human personality, yet of man. This class of transcendentalists deny that they are pantheists. Therefore, they must regard absolute reason as a human faculty; and then, since reason is the measure of truth and goodness, man himself, taken in his totality, if not in his simple personality, as the same measure. If, however, it be denied that this reason is human, and it be assumed to be God, as Cousin also contends, then man and God become one; and as God is unquestionably the measure contended for, man must also be it; because it matters not which term you use, Man or God; since, if identical, what may be predicated of the one term may equally be predicated of the other. Therefore, in either alternative, this class of transcendentalists assume that man is the measure of truth and goodness.

2. The second class, in which we are disposed to rank the author of the volume before us, do not, perhaps, differ very essentially from the first class, but they state their views somewhat differently. They hold that the ideas we have mentioned, and others of a like nature, if others there are, are intuitive, indeed, but are intuitions because they are inherent in the soul,—are the soul itself, or its original garniture, endowment, or patrimony. They are the types of the world without us. Hence we cognize the world without us by reason of its correspondence to the type or idea within us. The idea or type of all cognoscibles is in us, and it is by virtue of this fact that we are intelligent and they intelligible. Knowledge is the perception of the correspondence between the inward idea and the external object. "But these [material things]," says Mr. Parker, "are to us only a revelation of something kindred to qualities awakened in ourselves. . . . . . We see out of us only what we are internally prepared to see; for *seeing depends on the harmony between the object without and your own condition within.*"* Hence we know that this or that is true, beautiful, or good, only because it corresponds to the idea or type of the true, the beautiful, or the good in the soul itself. Hence, then, the standard, or criterion, or measure of truth and goodness is assumed to be in the soul. Nothing can be assumed to be naturally in the soul but the soul itself. "By nature," says Mr. Parker, "there is nothing in man but man himself." Man and the soul are identical; at least, the term *man* covers all that can be covered by the term *soul*. Then man is the measure of truth and goodness. Therefore, this second class adopt the proposition in question.

3. The third class, at the head of which stand Ralph Waldo Emerson, A. Bronson Alcott, and several notable women, do the same. These may be distinguished into two subordinate classes. They all agree that the soul knows, and can know, nothing exterior to itself; but the first division of these hold that it knows only by reason of the identity of subject and object, and therefore knows, and can know,

---

*Excellence of Goodness, pp. 3, 4.

only what it is. "What we are," says Mr. Emerson, (*Nature*, p. 92,) "that only can we see." The soul knows not by seeing, apprehending, but by being; and knows all, because it is all. The second division—and these are the majority—hold that the soul knows by *containing*, and that knowledge is the soul protending or projecting itself. "Not in nature, but in man, is all the beauty and worth he sees." —Emerson, *Essays*, 1841, p. 120. Objects are *cognoscibilia*, because they are contained in the soul; and the soul knows all, because it contains all. The outward or sense world is phenomenal, unreal, a shadow without a substance, and we abuse ourselves when we regard it, and the term *knowledge*, when we call perception of it, by that name. Knowledge is *in*science, or science of what is *within*. The true sage never looks abroad, but closes the external apertures of the mind, shuts his eyes, stops his ears, holds his nose, opens the internal aperture through which he looks into the profound abyss of the soul itself. Look not, say they, upon this delusive, this vain show, which men call the world, but into the great soul, which conceals all things in itself, even the infinite and eternal God! "I am God," said Mr. Alcott, one day to the writer of this, "I am God; I am greater than God. God is one of my ideas. I therefore contain God. Greater is the container than the contained. Therefore I am greater than God." With the members of this class, it is a mark of weakness, of littleness, of shallowness, to be intelligible. Light is an enemy. It defines objects too sharply, and presents them in disagreeable outlines. It permits nothing to loom up or spread out in dim and awful infinity,—allows the soul no scope to display its loftier powers and diviner instincts, to stand up and swell out in its sublime proportions into the infinite and eternal God!

These, evidently, in either division, hold that the soul is the measure of truth and goodness; for it must needs be the measure of what it is, and of what it contains. If it be truth and goodness, or if it contain them, it must be their standard or measure. The soul and the man are the same, at least so far as concerns the present question, as we have just seen. Therefore, this third class, as well as the other two, adopts the proposition that man is the measure of truth and goodness.

That all the transcendentalists, of whatever class, do adopt this proposition is still further evident from the rule of faith and practice which they all avow and contend for. This rule, it is notorious, is that of unrestricted private judgment. They reject the authority of the church, the authority of the Bible, of the apostles, of Jesus,—nay, all authority but that of the individual himself.

"Jesus," says Mr. Parker, "fell back on God, on absolute religion and morality,—the truth its own authority ; his works his witness. The early Christians fell back on the authority of Jesus, their successors, on the authority of the Bible,—the work of the Apostles and Prophets ; the next generation, on the Church,—the work of the Apostles and Fathers. The world retreads this ground. Protestantism delivers us from the tyranny of the Church and carries us back to the Bible. Biblical criticism frees us from the thraldom of Scripture, and brings us to the authority of Jesus. Philosophical spiritualism liberates us from all personal and private authority, and restores us to God, the primeval fountain, whence the Church, the Scriptures, and Jesus drew all the water of life wherewith they filled their urns."—p 483.

This is sufficiently explicit; for the concluding remark, about restoring us to God, simply means restoring us to ourselves, to God as he is immanent in each individual soul,—as is evident from what Mr. Parker elsewhere says.

" To obtain a knowledge of duty, man is not sent away outside of himself to ancient documents, for the only rule of faith and practice ; the word is very nigh him, even in his heart; and by this word he is to try all documents whatever."—p. 216. " Jesus is not the author of Christianity, ... its sanction and authority.   *We verify its eternal truth in our soul.*"—p. 280.

The God to whom we are restored is, then, evidently, the God *in* the soul, and in each individual soul. If so, it is God in the soul, either naturally or supernaturally. Not supernaturally, because transcendentalism denies the supernatural. Then naturally. But then identical with the soul; for, as we have found by Mr. Parker's own concession, p. 191, there can be by nature nothing in the soul but the soul itself.

Furthermore, the appeal is always made to the individual reason, conscience, and sentiment. In the individual is the authority before which all must bow, the tribunal before which all claimants must plead. The transcendentalist summons all religions to his private bar, and assumes his right to judge them all. The Bible he holds to be the word of God so far as he judges it to be true, and not his word where he judges it to be not true ; holding that he has the right to decide by his own reason, conscience, and sentiments, what is true and what not. In like manner he summons before him Jesus and the apostles, makes them answer to him, and tells them when they speak wisely, truly, and when falsely and foolishly. Christianity itself is amenable to the same authority. "Christianity, then, is a form of religion..... It is to be judged of as all other forms of religion, by reason and the religious sentiment."—p. 240. But the fact is notorious, and there is no need of proofs. We all know that the transcendentalist denies the authority of the church, of the Written Word, of Jesus, of prophets and apostles, of all inspired messengers, and of the common assent or belief of mankind, claiming for each all that may be claimed for the whole. "What Adam had, what Cæsar could, you have and may do." If they speak respectfully of Jesus, it is as a model-man, because in their view he spoke out from his own mind, acknowledging no external authority, and in this set an example we all should follow. Their leading doctrine is, that each man may and should be a Christ, and speak from his own proper divinity.

But, if our transcendentalists recognize the unrestricted right of private judgment in all cases whatever, they must, in order to have a basis for that right, assume that each man is the measure of truth and goodness. Every judgment involves three terms,—the matter judged, the judge, and the rule or measure by which the judge judges. Now, the rule or measure must be identical with the matter, with the judge, or distinct from both. The first is inadmissible; for, though the matter must needs be the measure of itself, yet its measure is unascertainable, if measured only by itself. The third is denied by the denial of all authority out of the individual reason, conscience, and sentiment, to which the judge is bound to conform his judgments. Then, the second must be adopted, namely, that the individual is his own yardstick of truth and goodness,—not only the judge, but the rule or measure of his judgment; which is what the proposition in question asserts.

This will not be denied. The right of private judgment, as the transcendentalists assert it, is the denial of all rules, measures, or standards, out of the individual reason, conscience, and sentiments, to which he is obliged to conform his judgments. Then either man judges without any rule, measure, or standard by which to judge, or he assumes himself as the standard. The first is absurd; for a judgment which has no rule, which is by no standard, is no judgment at all. Then the last must be assumed, or private judgment is impossible, and the *right* of private judgment utterly baseless.· Rights are not ultimate. They must have some foundation, or they are not rights; and there is no foundation of the right of the individual to judge *for* himself, in all cases whatever, without regard to any external rule, but his right to judge *by* himself; and there is no foundation of his right to judge *by* himself, but in the fact that he himself *is* the rule, standard, or measure of the matter to be judged. The assumption of the right of private judgment, in the sense explained, then, necessarily involves the assumption of the fact, that man is the measure of truth and goodness. But the transcendentalists do assume the right, as is well known; therefore they assume that man is the measure of truth and goodness. This, in fact, is expressly avowed. We quote a few sentences from a pamphlet written in defence of Mr. Parker, by one of his friends, and which has been published since we commenced writing this article. The author is giving, *ex professo*, the views of the sect, and on the very point before us.

"We believe," says the author of the pamphlet, "the truths that Jesus uttered in no degree because of the miracles he wrought; we believe them because our mind recognizes their *intrinsic* truth, ... and this we hold to be good ground of faith for all men . . . . . God has given to all men the power to attain to a religious faith that needs no external evidence to support it . . . . . The deepest, truest religious faith is *not capable* of support from any outward evidence whatever . . . . Men have recourse to outward evidence through the weakness of their faith . . . . . The most deeply religious minds *never*, in any stage of their progress, have any thing to do with such gross outward helps to their belief. To tell them to believe on the evidence of signs and wonders, to offer to prop up their faith by *argument and logic*, is to do violence to all their deepest and most sacred feelings. With hearts overflowing with love, and reverence, and gratitude to God, seeing him in all that is glorious and beautiful around them, feeling him within and about them everywhere, walking in his presence daily, as with a 'Father and a Friend,' —what care such men for logic and cunning reasoning,—what care they for signs and wonders? All around them is wonderful, for they see God in all . . . . . Tell them a deep religious truth, and they cannot but believe it, though all evidence were *against* it. *For truth is native to their souls. God has made them of that nature that they cannot be deceived. Their minds are* TOUCHSTONES *whereon to try all words and thoughts.*"— *Remarks on an Article from the Christian Examiner, entitled,* "*Mr. Parker and his Views*," *pp.* 6, 7.

This is as express as language can well be. Men are so made that they cannot be deceived, and their minds are touchstones on which are to be tried all words and thoughts, Do not imagine that the writer means to assert this only of a few gifted or singularly privileged individuals. No such thing. He intentionally asserts it of all men, for he continues: —

"What these men are all ought to be. What these men are all can be. For God has made men of one nature, and has not left himself without a witness in any heart. It is within the capacity of all men to reach this point of faith . . . . . We have a religious nature, an inborn capacity for receiving truths of God, and heaven, and immortality, and *all unearthly* things. This is not intellect; it is not reasoning. It has nothing whatever to do with these. It cannot depend upon them. It is *faith*, the power of apprehending the unseen and invisible, — the power of rising from earth to heaven. We hold that this [faith] is most peculiarly a faculty of man as man. It is that which makes him man, that which raises him above and separates him from all other creatures." — *Ib.* p. 7.

The fact that the writer calls the power by which we are enabled to affirm the truth in religious matters *faith*, and distinguishes it from intellect and reasoning, affects not our position; for he calls it a faculty of man, the constituent element and distinctive characteristic of man as man. It is therefore human, is man himself, under a given aspect, and inseparable from his nature. His testimony is, therefore, all we could ask. Mr. Parker may not admit his authority, but that is nothing to us. He is a transcendentalist; and it is transcendentalism, not Mr. Parker, we are mainly concerned with.

The writings of Mr. Emerson, who is as high authority on any point of transcendentalism as we can quote without going abroad, contain not a little to the same effect. He teaches expressly that the soul is the source and measure of truth; that a man is never to look abroad, but to consult in all cases only his own soul, the tendencies of his own nature, and in all his judgments of truth and goodness to listen to himself, and to take himself as their rule or standard.

"Whoso," he says, "would be a man must be a non-conformist. He who would gather immortal palms must not be hindered by the name of goodness, but explore if it be goodness. Nothing is at last sacred but the integrity of our own mind. Absolve yourself, and you shall have the suffrage of the world . . . . . . What have I to do with the sacredness of traditions, if I live wholly from *within?* . . . . . But these impulses may be from below, not from above . . . . . They do not seem to me to be such; but if I am the devil's child, I will live from the devil. No law is sacred to me but the law of my nature. Good and bad are but names very readily transferable to this or that ; *the only right is what is after my constitution, the only wrong is what is against it."* — *Essays,* 1841, pp. 41, 42.

"That which I call right or goodness is the choice of my constitution, and that which I call heaven, and inwardly aspire to, is the state or circumstance desirable to my constitution ; and the action which I in all my years tend to do is the work for my faculties." — *Ib.* p. 114. "In the book I read the good thought returns to me, as every truth will, the image of the whole soul. To the bad thought, which I find in it, the same soul becomes a discerning, separating sword, and lops it off. We are wiser than we know. If we will not interfere with our thought, but will act entirely, or see how the thing stands in God, we know the particular thing, and every thing and every man. For the Maker of all things stands behind us, and casts his dread omniscience through us over things." — *Ib.* pp. 231, 232. "Let man, then, learn the revelation of nature and all thought to his heart ; this, namely, that the Highest dwells with him. . . . . . If he would know what the great God speaketh, ... he must greatly listen to himself. . . . . . The soul makes no appeal. The faith that stands on authority is no faith. . . . . Great is the soul. . . . . . It believes always in itself. . . . . . It calls the light its own, and feels, that the grass grows and the stone falls by a law inferior to and *dependent* on its own. Behold, it saith, I am born into the universal mind ; I, the imperfect, adore my own perfect. I am somehow receptive of the great soul, and thereby I do overlook the sun and stars. . . . . Thus viewing the soul, ... man will come to see that the world is the perennial miracle the soul worketh. " — *Ib.* pp, 243 – 245.

These passages, taken almost at random, and to which many others may be added, equally to our purpose, require no comment. The standard is assumed to be in man, to be man, man's constitution ; and all a man has to do, in order to be in conformity with truth and goodness, is to conform to himself, to his own constitution, his own thoughts, tendencies, and impulses. Hence the celebrated maxim of the transcendental school,—" Obey thyself." All this expressly asserts or necessarily implies that man is the measure of truth and goodness.

Mr. Parker also assumes this as the ground of his argument from the existence of the sentiment in man to the existence of the object which it demands, out of man. He defines religion to be a sentiment natural to man, that is, springing from man's nature. But this sentiment, as its object, requires God to love, reverence, and adore. Therefore, God exists. His argument drawn out in form is, whatever natural want man experiences, for that want there is an external supply. Man wants an object to love, reverence, and adore; therefore, such object is. He wants truth, therefore there is truth; God, therefore God is. You may always conclude from the internal want to the external supply. "This general rule," he says, "may thus be laid down;—that for each animal, intellectual, affectional, and moral want of man there is a supply,"—and what may be well to bear in mind,—" a supply set within his reach, and a [natural] guide to connect the two."—pp. 188, 189.

It is on this ground that he holds sentiment to be as authoritative, if not even more so, than reason. Detect in man a sentiment or a want, no matter what, and you may at once say that that which will supply it really exists and is within his reach. Now, this conclusion is valid only on condition, so to speak, of the truthfulness of human nature. It assumes that human nature conforms in all things to eternal and unalterable truth, and is in itself a test or touchstone of what is true and good; that is, as we have said, man is the measure of truth and goodness. Truth is what conforms to his nature. "Right or goodness," says Mr. Emerson, "is that which is after my constitution; wrong, that which is against it." If this does not make man the standard, the measure, we know not what would. Hence, Mr. Parker says again, "the truth of the human faculties [that is, conscience and sentiment, as well as intellect and reason] must be assumed in all argument; and if this be admitted, we have then the same evidence for spiritual facts as we have for the maxims or the demonstrations of geometry."—p. 20, note.

But it may be objected that Mr. Parker does not make man the measure, for he holds up absolute religion and morality as the standard. "Religion," he says, "is the universal term, and absolute religion and morality its highest expression. Christianity is a particular form under this universal term; one form of religion among many others. It is either absolute religion and morality, or it is less; greater it cannot be, as there is no greater."—p. 240. Here evidently the standard is assumed to be not man, but absolute religion and morality.

But the objection is invalid; for Mr. Parker makes man the measure of absolute religion and morality. Absolute religion and morality are declared by Mr. Parker to be "something inward and natural to man," p. 241,—" religion as it exists in the facts of man's soul,"—" the law. God made for man and wrote in his nature," p. 243,—in a word, that which "answers exactly to the religious sentiment, and is what the religious sentiment demands," p. 239. If it be asked, then, What is absolute religion and morality? the answer is, That which answers exactly to the moral and religious sentiments, wants, or *facts* of the soul. Conceding, then, that absolute religion and morality are the standard by which particular forms of religion and morality are to be judged, yet man is himself the standard or measure of absolute religion and morality; which not only answers the objection, but confirms our general assertion, that man is assumed to be the measure of truth and goodness.

That man is assumed to be the measure of absolute religion and morality is also certain from the fact that they are assumed to be matters of intuition. Man is the measure in all cases of intuitive knowledge, as Mr. Parker concedes, p. 263. But the great truths of absolute religion, or absolute religion and morality, (for Mr. Parker uses the two phrases as equivalent,) are declared to be "matters of direct personal experience," "matters of intuition," p. 247. Therefore man is assumed to be their measure.

This conclusion would follow from the ordinary and proper sense of intuition, that of knowing by immediate apprehension of the object known; in which sense it is distinguished from science, which is discursive, and from faith, which depends on testimony. But it follows *a fortiori* from intuition as understood by the transcendentalists. They understand by it, as near as we can seize their sense, the sentiment, feeling, or want of the soul, regarded, not as the characteristic of the subject, but as the intimation or indication of the object which will satisfy it. The sentiments are wants, but wants are indications of something wanted. What is thus indicated is said to be known by intuition, or to be a matter of intuition. The religious sentiment, for instance, is a want; but, as a want, it demands God for its supply. It is therefore in itself an intimation, an indication, of God. Therefore the existence of God is a matter of intuition. To say that any given object is a matter of intuition is, then, simply saying it is what is demanded by an internal want or sentiment, and what answers to that sentiment or want. The intuitions depend, then, entirely on the wants of the soul, and are determined by them. The objects are known to be, not because intellectually apprehended, but because the internal sentiments demand them and are satisfied by them. Ascertain, then, the sentiments or wants, and what will satisfy them, and you have ascertained what is matter of intuition. The sentiments are, then, the measure of the truth and goodness of the objects, that is, the authority we have for saying the objects are, and that they are good. The sentiments are admitted to be facts of the soul, permanent, unalterable, essential; therefore the soul itself; therefore man, under a given aspect. Consequently, the assertion, that absolute religion and morality are matters of intuition, not only invalidates the objection we are considering, but also confirms our assertion, that the transcendentalists hold man to be the measure of truth and goodness.

But we have not yet seized the precise sense in which the transcendentalists hold man to be the measure of truth and goodness. They distinguish, or attempt to distinguish, between man as person, and man as impersonal soul or nature, and predicate the measure of man in the latter sense, not in the former. This is an important fact, and must not be overlooked, if we would attain to a right understanding of transcendentalism.

According to the transcendental view, man is twofold: personal, as Peter, James, or John; impersonal, as simple human nature, a force, or aggregate of forces, underlying the personality. Of the first they make no great account. It is the latter—which they call "Impersonal Reason," "Spontaneity," "Instinct," "Nature," "the Soul," "the great Soul," "the Over-Soul," "the Divine in Man," and which is supposed to enlarge its proportions as it frees itself and recedes from the restrictions and limitations of personality, and to expand at last into the infinite God, the background of all being, the substantiality of all existences, whether material or immaterial—to which they refer when they speak in such lofty terms, and predicate such glorious attributes of man. Man, as mere person, is weak, and falls into the silliest errors, the grossest absurdities, the most degrading and debasing superstitions; but as the impersonal soul, as freed from all personal restrictions and limitations, he is great, grand, noble, sublime, a god, walking the earth in majesty, and the master of all things. If we will but sink our mean and contemptible personality, abandon ourselves to the soul, to its intuitions, spontaneous utterances and suggestions,—to the great unconscious nature that underlies us,—we shall find ourselves one with the Universal Mind, one with the Great Soul of All, whose dread omniscience and almightiness flow into and through us, opening all things to our intuitions, and subjecting all things to our power. Then are we the measure of all things, because one with their Maker, and do contain the source and law of all things in ourselves. Hence, Mr. Emerson says :—

"The heart which abandons itself to the Supreme Mind finds itself related to all its works, and will travel a royal road to particular knowledges and powers. For in ascending to this primary and aboriginal sentiment, we have come from our remote station on the circumference, instantaneously, to the center of the world, where, as in the closet of God, we see causes, and anticipate the universe, which is but a slow effect. . . . . . Persons themselves acquaint us with the impersonal. In all conversation between two persons, a tacit reference is made to a third party, to a common nature. That third party or common nature is not social; it is impersonal; is God." — *Ib.* pp. 228, 229.

All this is express enough; but here is another passage, still more express, if possible.

"It is a secret which every intellectual man quickly learns, that, beyond the energy of his possessed and conscious intellect, he is capable of a new energy (as of an intellect doubled on itself), by abandonment to the nature of things; that beside his privacy of power, as an individual man, there is a great public power, on which he can draw, by unlocking, at all risks, his human doors, and suffering the ethereal tide to roll and circulate through him; then he is caught up into the life of the universe, his speech is thunder, his thought is law, and his words are universally intelligible as the plants and animals. The poet knows that he speaks adequately, then, only when he speaks somewhat wildly, or 'with the flower of the mind;' not with the intellect used as an organ, but with the intellect released from all service, and suffered to take its direction from its celestial life, or, as the ancients were wont to express themselves, not with the intellect alone, but with the intellect inebriated by nectar. *As the traveller, who has lost his way, throws his reins on the horse's neck, and trusts to the instinct of the animal to find the road, so must we do with the divine animal we ride through this world.* For if in any manner we can stimulate this instinct, new passages are opened into nature, the mind flows into and through things hardest and highest, and the metamorphosis is possible. This is the reason why bards love wine, mead, narcotics, coffee, tea, opium, the fumes of sandal-wood and tobacco, or whatever other species of animal exhilaration."—*Essays*, 2d Series, 1844, pp. 28–30.

These quotations sufficiently establish the fact that transcendentalism does distinguish, in man, between the personal and the impersonal, and makes the impersonal, to the exclusion of the personal, the measure of truth and goodness.

What, then, do transcendentalists mean by the impersonal man, the great soul, the unconscious energy, of which they speak with so much awe and emphasis, and to which they exhort us to abandon ourselves without reserve? Whatever they may mean by it, this much, we think, is certain, that they include it in the definition of man, and that the distinction they make is a distinction between what they regard as the personal and the impersonal *in* man, not between man and something not man. They can, then, mean nothing more by it than simple human nature *minus* human personality. Ascertain, then, what in man is constitutive, or the essential characteristic, of personality, eliminate that from the conception or definition of man, and what remains will be at least all they do or can mean by the impersonal soul.

A person, in ordinary language, is a rational being, according to Locke "a thinking and intelligent being"; according to the schoolmen, after Boetius, *rationalis naturæ individua substantia*,—an individual substance of rational nature, and personality is defined by philosophers to be "the last complement of rational nature." A person must be an individual substance or being, because, in the language of the schoolmen, a singular, not a universal,—a whole, not a part,—subsisting in and acting from itself as subject, not in and from another, and incommunicable, not held or shared in common; and of rational nature, because individual substances not rational by nature or essence are never regarded as persons. We may have individual substances not rational by nature, as the stone, the plant, the tree; and even individual substances which are up to a certain degree intelligent, as the dog, the ox, the horse, to which it would be rash to deny at least an imperfect degree, or the rude beginnings, of intelligence, without having personality, because these are not of rational nature. That, then, in man, which is constitutive of personality, its distinctive mark or essential characteristic, is not substantiality, nor individuality,—although, if these, or either of them, be wanting, there is no person,—but the rational nature. The rational nature is expressed by the word reason, therefore the essential characteristic of personality is reason. Where reason is, there is personality, and where reason is wanting, personality is wanting; and, as we shall soon see, where personality is wanting, reason also is wanting.

But personality is the last complement of rational na-

Vol. VI—2

ture, that is, rational nature brought to its terminus, fulfilled, or, if you please, realized. Man, regarded as the genus, as abstract human nature, is, no doubt, rational nature, but without its last complement,—rational nature unfulfilled, a metaphysical rational nature,—a *possible*, but not a *real*, rational nature. It becomes real, is fulfilled, receives its last complement, only in individual men and women, beyond which it has no existence *in re*. It is impersonal, and, properly speaking, void. Hence, we may say human nature attains to personality only in individualization,—is personal only as individualized because it is only as individualized that it receives its last complement, or becomes a real being.

There are, then, three points of view from which we may consider personality, and distinguish the personal from the impersonal. 1. We may consider the person as subject, and wish to note the fact that the person subsists in and operates from himself. In this case, we make, under this point of view, the mark of personality *substantia*, substance. 2. We may wish to denote by person, not abstract human nature, man in general, but human nature as fulfilled, realized, having its last complement; and then, under this point of view, we add *individua*, make the mark of personality *individuality*. 3. But if we wish to distinguish persons from all beings or subsistences not persons, and to express the essential quality of personal natures, we make its characteristic *reason*.

Now it is only from these three, or some one of these three points of view, that it is possible to distinguish between the personal and impersonal. The transcendentalists cannot adopt the first, because the impersonal of which they speak is to be taken as a substantive existence; since they regard it as subsisting in and operating from itself as subject, not as an attribute, a function, an operation, or phenomenon of some other subject on which it is dependent.

Do they adopt the second? They have frequently the air of doing so, and we are not sure but, to a very considerable extent, they really do intend by the impersonal soul the generic man, or man in general, as distinguished from the individual man. This is the most natural interpretation of their language. But, if this is their meaning, if by sinking personality they mean sinking the individual and falling back on human nature as abstract human nature, they require us to fall back on human nature unfulfilled, wanting its last complement, in which sense it is a mere *essentia metaphysica*, and has no real existence, is no entity, and can be the subject of no act or operation : for, as we have said, human nature is real only as individualized in men and women. Out of individuals it is an abstraction, existing, if you will, *in conceptu*, but not *in re*. It is the simple genus; and genera are real, active, operative, only in substance, as they become *substantiæ*, and these, again, only as fulfilled, as they receive their last complement in becoming *subsistentiæ*. To sink individuality and fall back on generic man, or man in general, would be to fall back on a metaphysical abstraction, practically on nothing, and to take a nonentity for our sovereign guide or teacher.

We are not ignorant that the *humanitarian* division of the transcendentalists exhort us to sink the individual and to fall back on our common humanity, and seem to teach that this common humanity is not merely that which each individual man realizes, but that it is, as it were, a mighty entity, a vast reservoir of wisdom, virtue, and strength, which individuals do not and cannot exhaust. We ourselves, especially during the interval between our rejection of eclecticism and our conversion to Christianity, following Plato, the Neo-Platonists, Leroux, and the Saint-Simonians, and some half glimpses of the teachings of the old realists, whose doctrines we did not understand, fell into this absurdity, and sought to make it appear that humanity, not as the collective mass of individuals, but as genus, as out of all individuals, has a real, an entitative existence, and can operate as subject; and that in this sense humanity is not what is common to all individuals, but a somewhat that transcends all individuals, and *makes* all individuals, manifesting itself in various degrees,—in one individual under one aspect, in another under another, and so on. An individual we regarded as a particular manifestation of a particular aspect or phase of humanity, as a particular act of an individual manifests some particular aspect or phase of the individual; and the mission of the individual we declared to be, through his whole life, the realization in his own thoughts, words, and deeds of that particular phase or aspect of humanity he represents. It was in this way we solved the old question of individuation, and found, as we supposed, a basis for the state, and *legitimated*, so to speak, individual liberty. Taking this view, we necessarily held humanity to be greater than the individual, nay, greater than all individuals together. Substantially, all transcendentalists, so far as they admit a human existence at all, do the same. They all say man is greater than men.

The common source of all our errors on this point is easily discovered;—it is in the well known doctrine of the transcendentalists, that the possible exists, not merely as possible, but in point of fact as real, and that what is possible is altogether more perfect than the actual. What you conceive is possible; then it *is*—possible. Then you affirm that it exists, though not yet realized,—is real *in potentia*, and what is real *in potentia* is superior to what is *in actu*. Therefore, regard not the actual, but fall back on the possible. To conceal the absurdity, we gave to the possible the name of the ideal, and then said, live not in and for the actual, but in and for the ideal. All very fine, no doubt, and admirably calculated to make old men see visions, and young men and maidens dream dreams, and, what is worse, tell their dreams.

But what is *in potentia* is no more *in re* than *in actu*, for it is a contradiction in terms to call the *potential* real. Moreover, the ideal, the possible, is always below the real, the actual, because it has never in itself the force to realize or actualize itself. The power to act is below act, because it must receive what it has not, before it becomes act, or is reduced to act. Here is the fundamental error, in denying this, and assuming *potentia* to stand above *actus*,—which is the terminus or last complement of *potentia*. Now, humanity *in abstracto* is at best only man *in potentia*., To assume, then, its superiority over individuals, who are its terminus, or last complement, or that, in sinking individualized humanity and falling back on humanity as abstracted from all individuals, or rather as emancipated from all individuality, we fall back on something higher, broader, and richer, is precisely the error of placing *potentia* above *actus*, the possible above the actual. *Potentia* is void; *actus* is full. Void is therefore superior to full, emptiness to fulness!

Following the old Buddhists and generalizing this important fact into a principle, Leroux, instructed also by the nihilism of the Hegelians, represents God to be infinite void seeking to become full; and since God is *infinite* void seeking to become full, and since the *full* or *plenum* is the actual universe, the universe as a whole and in all its parts must needs be eternally progressive. Hence, a solid and imperishable foundation for the sublime and kindling doctrine of progress, around which gathers "la Jeune France," "das Junge Deutschland," "Young England," "Young Ireland," and "Young America,"—young indeed, and even *green!* But how can void become *plenum, potentia actus,* possibility real, without a reality to realize it? God given as infinite void is given as infinite possibility, that is, merely as a metaphysical existence which no real existence contradicts. But a possibility cannot act, because it is not *in re,*—is a nonentity, and therefore no subject. How, then, can God seek to realize himself in the universe? For the tendency to reality must itself be from a reality, since what is not cannot seek or tend to be or to do. Yet into the absurdity here involved the transcendentalists all fall in raising the ideal over the real, and telling us, as they do, that ideas are potent, active, and take to themselves hands and remake man and the universe to their own image and likeness. Nothing more untrue. What is not cannot act, and ideas existing only *in conceptu* are not and cannot be active. The whole doctrine of progress is an absurdity. Nothing contains in itself the force to be more than it is, and cannot be more than it is, save by the aid of what it is not; for otherwise the stream could rise higher than the fountain, the effect exceed the cause, that is, be an effect without a cause. Man may advance by the aid of his Maker, but is not and cannot be inherently progressive. It will not, then, answer to contend that the possible man is greater than the actual man, humanity in the abstract superior to humanity concreted in individuals.

It may be replied to us, that the transcendentalists do not mean by humanity simply humanity as *abstracted* from all individuals, but as *common* to all individuals. We see no real difference between the one and the other. But if it be humanity as common to all individuals on which they exhort us to fall back, then it is included in each and individualized in each. Each individual, then, has it all to himself, and affirms it in every one of his individual acts; for if wanting, he himself would not be. Hence, the distinction between man as an individual and man as humanity, if this be the distinction contended for by the transcendentalists, can avail them nothing; for, in the first place, to sink the personal and fall back on the impersonal would be to sink the actual and fall back on the potential, the real and fall back on the unreal, on nothing; in the second place, it would be to fall back on what the individual already is, for he is all the human nature there is for him to fall back upon.

There remains, then, the third distinction we pointed out, namely, the distinction between men as persons and existences not personal,—in which sense the essential characteristic of personality is reason. The distinction here is properly a distinction between rational and irrational. The distinction, we must remember, is in man, not out of him, and therefore implies *in man* a personal subject and an impersonal subject. But this is impossible · for man is one subject, one *ego*, one *me*, not two, and human nature in him is one and the same identical nature. He may be affected on one side, so to speak, of his being, by bodily organs, and on the other by God and truth; and he may differ, morally, very widely, as he acts from the one affection or the other; but he is, in either case, always the one identical subject or agent. The distinction, then, in man, of a personal and impersonal subject is impossible.

But we will not now insist on this. The distinction is between personal subject and impersonal subject, and the impersonal is included in the definition of man; therefore as properly man as the personal. What can this impersonal subject be? It can be only what is left after the personal is eliminated. What, in eliminating personality, do we then necessarily eliminate? or rather, on what conditions is the elimination of personality possible? Man must be retained in his substantiality and individuality, because he is to be retained as subject active and operative. But if to man in his substantiality and individuality you add rational nature or reason, he is a person. Then you can possibly remove personality only on condition of removing rational nature, either in itself or in operation. Hence, to sink personality is, practically at least, to sink reason; for the active presence of reason necessarily and *per se* constitutes the personality. This assumed, the elimination of personality is possible only by eliminating reason. The transcendental distinction, then, between the personal and impersonal in man is virtually a distinction between the rational and irrational, and the exhortation to escape from personality is virtually an exhortation to escape from the restraints of reason. To sink our personality is to sink our reason, to refuse to reason; and to refuse to reason is to reduce ourselves, practically, to the condition of brutes,—at the very best, to that of children and the insane.

We can now catch some slight glimpse of the real character of transcendentalism. If it adopts this last view, it represents the irrational as superior to the rational, reverses all our common notions of things, declares the imperfect more perfect than the perfect, that the less of a man one is the more of a man he is, the less he knows the more he knows, that the child is wiser than the adult, the madman more to be trusted as a guide than the sane man,—which, extravagant as it may seem, is actually admitted by our transcendentalists, whom we have often heard contend that the unintelligible is more intelligible than the intelligible, that nothing is less known than the known, that only the unknown is known, that more is to be seen by night than by day, in the dark than in the light. We exaggerate nothing. We have heard all this said, and seriously maintained.

It has been seriously maintained that the child is far wiser than the man. We have, or had quite recently, before us a remarkable book, called *Conversations on the Gospels*, held by a teacher with his children, in which he affects to learn and prove the Gospel, that is, the Gospel according to the transcendentalists, from the mouth of childhood, from what he calls its simple, unconscious utterances. Strange as it may seem, it has actually been maintained by serious persons in our good city of Boston, and, for aught we know to the contrary, is yet, that the teacher is to learn what he teaches from the child; the teaching is merely " tempting forth " what is in the child; in a word, that more wisdom is to be learned by sitting down by the cradle and looking into baby's eyes, than by listening to the profoundest discourses of the sage or the saint. Even no less a man than the poet Wordsworth seems to hold the same :—

> " Heaven lies about us in our infancy;
> Shades of the prison-house begin to close
>   Upon the growing boy,
> But he beholds the light, and whence it flows,
>   He sees it in his joy;
> The youth, who daily farther from the east
> Must travel, still is Nature's priest,
>   And by the vision splendid
>   Is on his way attended;
> At length the man perceives it die away,
> And fade into the light of common day.'

There is no mistaking the philosophy which underlies the whole of the beautiful *Ode, Intimations of Immortality from Recollections of Early Childhood*, from which we have taken this passage,—beautiful, we mean, so far as the mere poetic sentiment and expression are concerned. It is a sort of apotheosis of childhood, as the ballad of *The Idiot Boy* is, one is half tempted to say, that of idiocy. All proceeds from the assumption of the superiority of man *minus* personality over man with the last complement of his nature.

Nor do our transcendentalists shrink from maintaining the superior sanity of the insane over the sane. "The poet," says Mr. Emerson, in a passage already quoted, "knows that he speaks adequately, then only, when he speaks somewhat wildly, ... not with the intellect used as an organ, but with the intellect released from service (that is, from the governance of reason) and suffered to take its direction from its celestial life; . . . . . not with intellect alone, but with intellect inebriated by nectar." And in the following he is still more explicit:—

"The poets are liberating gods. The ancient British bards had for the title of their order, 'Those who are free throughout the world. They are free, and they make free. An imaginative work renders us much more service at first, by stimulating us through its tropes, than afterwards, when we arrive at the precise sense of the author. I think nothing is of any value in books, excepting the transcendental and extraordinary. If a man is inflamed and carried away by his thought, to that degree that he forgets the author and the public, and heeds only this one dream, which holds him like an *insanity*, let me read his paper, and you may have all the arguments and histories and criticism. All the value which attaches to Pythagoras, Paracelsus, Cornelius Agrippa, Cardan, Kepler, Swedenborg, Schelling, Oken, or any other who introduces questionable facts into his cosmogony, as angels, devils, magic, astrology, palmistry, mesmerism, and so on, is the certificate we have of departure from routine, and that here is a new witness. That, also, is the best success in conversation, the magic of liberty, which puts the world, like a ball, in our hands. How cheap even the liberty then seems: how mean to study, when an emotion communicates to the intellect the power to sap and upheave nature . how great the perspective ! nations, times, systems, enter and disappear, like threads in tapestry of large figure and many colors ; dream delivers us to dream, and, while the drunkenness lasts, we will sell our bed, our philosophy, our religion, in our opulence."—*Essays*, 2d Series, pp. 35, 36.

This reminds us of the conversation of a gentleman walking through Bedlam with one of its inmates, with whom he had been previously acquainted. "Ah, Tom, you here! How is this?" "O, I was outvoted." "Outvoted! how so?" "I said the world was mad; they said I was mad, and being the majority, they outvoted me, and sent me here." Tom, according to the transcendentalists, was in the right, the world in the wrong. He had merely broken loose from routine, and made himself "a new witness."

The same philosophy at bottom, though different in form, and apparently less extravagant, runs through our own former writings, and was adopted by us as the basis of our theory of art and of religion. We hope we may be pardoned the egotism of quoting a paragraph or two in this connexion; for it cannot be denied, that, in a history of American transcendentalism, the Editor of the *Boston Quarterly Review* should not be forgotten, pronounced as he was by *Blackwood's Magazine* the Coryphæus of the sect, and by Victor Cousin one who promised to be "a philosophical writer of the first order," &c. In a review of Wordsworth's poetry, we took occasion to bring out a theory of art in general, and of poetry in particular, — a theory which had the good fortune to meet Mr. Parker's entire approbation, if we may credit his personal assurances to the writer, although he differed somewhat from us in its application to Wordsworth's poetry.

"The poet is always a seer; and it is worthy of note that the common-sense of mankind, which makes languages, frequently calls the poet and seer, or prophet, by the same name. Thus, in Latin, *vates* is either a prophet or a poet. The poet is not, strictly speaking, a *maker*, as the Greek name implies. He does not create, — he finds; hence poetry has, with justice, been made to consist in *invention*, in discovering, seeing, finding, that which ordinary men heed not, see not, or do not imagine to exist. He catches glimpses, more or less perfect, of the infinite reality which lies back of the phenomena observed by the senses, or which shines out through them, whether under the aspect of truth, of beauty, or of goodness; and his sensibility is agitated, his soul takes fire, and he utters what he sees in words that burn, in tones which make those who hear him feel as he feels and burn as he burns. This he may do, because the spontaneous reason, by means of which he obtains the glimpses which fill his soul with so much joy, is in all men, and thus lays the foundation of a secret but entire sympathy between him and them, making them capable of recognizing the infinite he recognizes, and of joining their voices with his in sublime chorus to the God of truth, beauty, goodness.

"The poet, we have said, is a seer. He is a spectator. He stands before the spiritual universe, and merely sees what is before him. He does not make that universe; nay, he has not sought to behold it. It has risen in its majesty, or in its loveliness, before him. He does not seek his song; it comes to him; it is given him. He is, to a certain extent, a passive, though not an unmoved, recipient of it. To this fact he always bears witness. It is not he that sings ; it is his Muse :

'Musa, mihi causas memora.'

Apollo, or some God, inspires him. The power he feels, the beauty he sees, he cannot ascribe to himself. The song he sings is a mystery unto himself, and he feels that it must have been given him from abroad, from above. A spirit glows within him, a mind agitates him, which he feels is not his spirit, is not his mind, but the mind of his mind, the spirit of his spirit, the soul of his soul. In this he is right. The spontaneous reason, spontaneity, from which his song proceeds, is, as we have said, the divine in man, and it acts without being put into action by the human will. We may by effort, by discipline, place ourselves in relation with it, bring ourselves within the sphere of its action ; but *it is impersonal and divine* . . . . It follows from the view now taken, that there is always truth in poetry. Of all known modes of utterance, poetry is one of the truest; for it is the voice of the spontaneous reason, the word of God, which is in immediate relation with truth. It is truer than philosophy; for in poetry God speaks, whereas in philosophy it is only man that speaks. The reflective reason, which gives us philosophy, is *personal*, subject to all the infirmities of the flesh, short-sighted, and exclusive; but the spontaneous reason, of which poetry is one of the modes of utterance, is *impersonal*, broad, universal ; embracing, as it were, the whole infinitude of truth. Hence the confidence mankind have universally reposed in their sacred prophets, in the inspired chants of their divine bards, and the distrust they have pretty uniformly manifested for the speculations of philosophers. . . . . . Poetry, if it be poetry, is always inspired. It is inspiration clothing itself in words. And inspiration is never referred to ourselves ; we always refer it to God. 'In inspiration,' says Cousin, 'we are simple spectators. We are not actors; or at best, our action consists merely in being conscious of what is taking place. This, doubtless, is activity, but not a premeditated, voluntary, personal activity. The characteristic of inspiration is enthusiasm; it is accompanied by that strong emotion which forces the soul out of its ordinary and subaltern state, and calls into action the sublime and divine part of its nature. *Est Deus in nobis, agitante calescimus illo.*'"

There is no mistaking this. It is genuine transcendentalism, and differs from it as set forth by others only in the fact, that they make the whole of human nature, *minus* the personality, the measure of truth and goodness; whereas we, in our exposition, take merely a part, the faculty of reason, *minus* its last complement. This, in reality, amounts to nothing, and constitutes no fundamental difference. The theory we bring out is, the more effectually a man abandons himself to spontaneity, to his impersonal nature, and the less he interferes in its operations, that is, the less he exercises reason and volition, the more in accordance with truth are his views, and the more worthy of confidence are his words. This abandonment is, so to speak, a sort of voluntary or premeditated insanity; and the more complete it becomes, the more nearly do we approach the state of insanity. The only difference between a man voluntarily placing himself in the state required and the actually insane is, that the former has the power of resuming the reins, and recovering himself when he chooses, whereas the latter has not. But while in, and so far as in, this state, the resemblance, the identity, is complete. Hence, the nearer we approach to the state of insanity, the more divine do we become, the more open is the universe to our view, and the more trustworthy are our utterances. Mr. Parker, as we shall have occasion hereafter to show, adopts the same general doctrine, and makes the man who comes nearest to God, who stands in the most immediate relation with absolute truth, beauty, and goodness, a sort of maniac.

"There is a new soul in the man, which takes him, as it were, by the hair of his head, and sets him down where the idea he wishes for demands. . . . . . It takes the rose out of the cheek, and turns the man in on himself, and gives him more of truth. Then in a poetic fancy, the man sees visions; has wondrous revelations; every mountain thunders; God burns in every bush; flames out in the crimson cloud; speaks in the wind; descends with every dove; is All in All. The Soul deep-wrought, in its intense struggle, gives outness to its thought, and on the trees and stars, the fields, the floods, the corn ripe for the sickle, on man and woman, it sees its burthen writ. The Spirit within constrains the man. It is like wine that hath no vent. He is full of the God. While he muses the fire burns; his bosom will scarce hold his heart. He must speak, or he dies, though the earth quake at his word. Timid flesh may resist, and Moses say, I am slow of speech. What avails that? The Soul says, Go, and I will be with thy mouth, to quicken thy tardy tongue. . . . . . Then are the man's lips touched with a coal from the altar of Truth, brought by a Seraph's hand. He is baptized with the spirit of fire. His countenance is like lightning. Truth thunders from his tongue; his words eloquent as Persuasion: no terror is terrible; no foe formidable. The peaceful is satisfied to be a man of strife and contention, his hand against every man, to root up, pluck down, and distroy."
— *Discourse*, pp. 223, 224.

This is a tolerable description of a madman, whose frenzy has taken the turn of religious reform. It is designed as the description of an inspired man,—not supernaturally, but naturally inspired, by the "great Soul, wide as yesterday, to-day, and for ever," which seizes and overpowers the man; and is a very good proof that the transcendentalists regard the insane as better measures of truth and goodness than the sane; which is what they ought to do in order to be consistent with themselves.

Something of this same doctrine seems to have spread far and wide. The prevailing notion in our community of the prophet seems to be borrowed from the insane or drunken Pythoness, and the man whom God chooses to communicate his word is looked upon as one possessed. The man is not himself, but beside himself. Thus Washington Allston, in his picture of Jeremiah, seeks to indicate the prophetic character by giving to the prophet the eyes of a maniac. The poet, painter, sculptor, artists of all sorts, it seems to be believed, in order to have genius, to be what their names imply, should be a sort of madmen, doing what they know not, and do not will,—mastered and carried away by a power they are not, and comprehend not; and attain to excellence, gain a right to immortal fame, only by abandoning themselves withous resistance to its direction.

We are not disposed to undertake the refutation of this theory, which may be termed the demoniacal, or madman's theory, for none but a madman will attempt to reason a madman out of his crotchets. The characteristic of the madman is that he has lost the power to reason, and therefore, to be reasoned out of error or into truth. Nevertheless, though not entirely ignorant of the class of facts which are or may be appealed to in support of this theory, we believe every scholar or literary man is able from his own experience to refute it. The man is always greatest, sees the furthest, and produces the most effect on others, when he himself is most self-collected, self-possessed. The most eloquent passages of your most eloquent orators are produced when the orator is intensely active, indeed, but when he has the fullest command of himself, and is the most perfectly conscious and master of his thoughts and words. The orator who would command his audience must first command himself. If he allows them, or his own thought, passion, or imagination, to master him, he fails. So your poets, so far as genuine, write not with "eyes in a fine frenzy rolling," but with a calm, quiet self-possession, perfectly master of what they are saying, and of the mode or manner in which they say it. We need but read Shakspeare to be satisfied of this. Shakspeare inflames your passions, makes you rave, rant, weep, laugh, love, hate, sigh, muse, philosophize, at will; but he himself is in no passion, never loses the command of his verse, nor of his tears, laughter, loves, hates, or musings. You never dream of identifying him with any one of his characters. He is himself no more Macbeth, Hamlet, Othello, than he is Iago, King Lear, or Jack Falstaff. They are his creatures, not himself. And herein is the test of genius, which holds itself always distinct from and above its productions,—sends them forth, yet conceals itself. Great power is always sedate and silent. The ancients represented their gods as asleep, and spread over their features an air of ineffable repose. Real majesty

"Rides on the whirlwind and *directs* the storm."

We feel this in Homer, Dante, Shakspeare, and even Goethe. They are all remarkable for their self-possession, their easy grandeur and simple majesty, and hence the command they have over men. When one loses his self-possession, —loses, as it were, his personality, and suffers himself to be carried away by his thoughts, his passion, or his imagination, —you feel that he is internally weak, that he is but a child, with whom indeed you may amuse yourself for a moment, if in playful mood, but to whom you can surrender neither your heart nor your judgment. Mr. Emerson himself, in his own character, is a striking proof of the falseness of his theory, and the contrast between him and Mr. Parker forcibly illustrates the comparative worth of that theory and its opposite. In the very tempest and whirlwind of his passion, in the very access of his madness, uttering the most incoherent ravings, the wildest extravagances, Mr. Emerson is eminently himself, perfectly cool and self-possessed, and proceeds as deliberately as a mathematician solving his problems, or a stone-cutter in squaring his block of granite. We dissent from his doctrines, we shrink from his impiety and his blasphemy, but we see and feel his intense personality, that he is master of his thought, that he knows what he says, and intends it. No man can listen to the silvery tones of his voice, mark his quiet composure, or read his exquisitely chiselled sentences, and not say,—Here is a man to whom Almighty God has given ability and genius of the first order, and of whom he will demand a large account. No man is more intensely personal, or practises more contrary to the rule he lays down; none can demand of all books, all thoughts, words, deeds, that pass under his observation, a more rigid account of what they are, and of their right to be. And yet he is the first poet of his country, and has written passages unsurpassed for true poetic conception, sentiment, and expression, by any living poet, with whose productions we are acquainted, whether in England, France, or Germany. The man wants but faith, faith in the Son of God, to be the glory of his country, and a blessing to his race. But, alas! wanting this, he wants all. His splendid talents, his keen, penetrating insight, his deep and probing thought, his patient study, and his rich and creative genius avail him nothing. May we not take the wail that now and then escapes him as an indication that he himself is not altogether unconscious of this? O, would that he could bow lowly at the foot of the cross, and consecrate himself, his talents and genius, to the service of the Crucified! May the infinite God, whose goodness is over all, and unto all, bestow upon him the inestimable gift of faith, and enable him to worship the God who in the beginning created the heavens and the earth, instead of seeking to make to himself a god from the unconscious energies of Nature!

Mr. Parker is a very different man from Mr. Emerson. We see that he has read much, that he has a burning thirst for knowledge, that he has wit, fancy, imagination, passion, but that he is not their master. They, each by turns, overpower him, and carry him whithersoever they will. He mounts, indeed, the whirlwind, he rides on the tempest, but he does not direct it; it directs him, and whirls and tosses him as it pleases. He, to no inconsiderable extent, sinks himself, and abandons himself to his instinctive nature. But we feel, as we read him, that he is weak. He has no simple grandeur, no quiet strength, no sedate command. His brow is not imperial. He soars not with ease and grace, as one native to the higher regions, on wings fitted to sustain him, and we fear every moment that they will prove insufficient. His conclusions inspire no confidence, for we see he knows not whence he has obtained them, and has come to them simply as borne onward by the winds and clouds of passion. Never does the man stand above his thought and command his speech. He whirls and tosses with all the whirlings and tossings of his discourse, and we feel that he is not one of those great men whose lives serve to "chronicle the ages."

We think it not difficult now to comprehend the essential character of transcendentalism. It exhorts us to sink our personality, and abandon ourselves to the impersonal soul, the unconscious energy that underlies it. The essential characteristic of personality is reason, and therefore to sink personality is, as we have seen, practically to sink reason itself. If we discard reason, we must also discard will, for will is not simply acting from one's self as subject, nor from one's self as subject *to* an end; but from one's self as subject *propter finem*, to an end and on account of it, which is not possible without reason. Eliminate from man, that is, from what comes properly within the definition of man, reason and will, and nothing remains of man but passion, or, if you will, passion and phantasy, or imagination. At most, then, we have for the impersonal nature, on which to fall back, only passion and imagination; for passion and imagination, together with reason and will, are the whole man, all that can be covered, in any sense, by the word *man*, or by the term *human nature*. But, in order to be as liberal as possible, we will gratuitously suppose, after reason is discarded, will remains; it can remain only as a simple executive force, for that is all it is at any time. Reason discarded, it can remain only as the executor of the suggestions of passion and imagination. The plain, simple transcendental doctrine, then, is, *passion and imagination are superior to reason*. Give loose reins to passion and imagination, and your head will be filled with wilder dreams and stranger fancies than if you subject them to the surveillance and restraints of reason; and these dreams and fancies are to be regarded as superior to the dictates of reason, because these are spontaneous and the dictates of reason are personal!

Passion and imagination, or what remains of man, after the elimination of reason,—are precisely what the schoolmen call the inferior soul, and hold to be the seat of concupiscence. What Christian theology calls the superior soul is the rational nature as distinguished from the sensitive soul, or, as termed by some modern psychologists, internal sensibility, or principle of the sentiments or feelings as distinguished from sensations, or perceptions of sense. It has three faculties,—will, understanding, and memory. To make passion and imagination the superior is simply asserting the superiority of the sensitive nature over the rational. The subject now begins to open, and we approach a territory very well known. The distinction contended for is now quite intelligible, and though not properly a distinction between the personal and impersonal, yet a very real distinction, and one not now noted for the first time. It is the distinction which renders possible and intelligible that spiritual conflict which has been noted in all ages, and which every man experiences who undertakes to live a Christian life. The impersonal soul of the transcendentalists is the "carnal mind" of the Sacred Scriptures, the inferior nature, which, according to Christian faith, has been disordered by the fall, and become prone to evil and that continually,—that "old man of sin," the seat of all inordinate desires and affections,—"the flesh," which our religion commands us to "put off," to "mortify with its deeds," and to bring into subjection to the law of Jesus Christ after the inner man. This is what it is, and all that it is, and under these names it is no new acquaintance.

Now, the peculiarity, we cannot say the *originality*, of transcendentalism consists precisely in declaring the flesh superior to the spirit; this *inferior* soul, or what Christianity pronounces the inferior soul, superior to the rational soul, or what Christianity declares to be the *superior* soul; in giving as its higher nature, noble soul, spirit, instinct, spontaneity, the divine in man, to which we are to abandon ourselves, and which we are to take as the infallible revelation of the will of our Maker, and the measure of truth and goodness, this very carnal mind, flesh, corrupt nature, against which the saint wars, which he mortifies, and through his whole life labors incessantly to subdue, to subject to reason and will, healed of the wounds of the fall, elevated and purified by the infusion of supernatural grace. It makes this struggle not only unnecessary, but wrong; and requires us, as the rule of life, to give up reason, and abandon ourselves to the solicitations of the flesh!

The mist now vanishes; and this transcendentalism, which has puzzled so many simple-minded people, becomes as plain and as unmistakable as the nose on a man's face. It has revealed no mystery, has detected no new facts or elements in human nature, but has simply called *higher* what the Gospel calls *lower*, that true and good which the Gospel calls false and evil, and *vice versa*. It would simply liberate us from the restraints of reason, and deliver us to the license of passion and imagination, free us from the struggle, and permit us to follow nature instead of commanding us to crucify it. It merely gives the lie to our blessed Saviour; and where he says, "Deny thyself," it says, "Obey thyself." It ridicules the notion, that a holy life must be a life of incessant warfare against one's self, and teaches that we are to gain heaven by swimming with the current, not against it; a pleasant doctrine, and, if universally adopted and acted on, would, no doubt, produce some effects.

People who do not believe much in the modern doctrine of progress, and who are not aware that we live in the age of light, may be strongly inclined to believe that we misrepresent the transcendentalists; but they should bear in mind that it was foretold thousands of years ago, that there would come a race of men who would call the churl liberal, evil good, and bitter sweet. The doctrine we charge upon the transcendentalists is but a necessary logical inference from the principles they lay down in the passages we have quoted from their writings. Absolute religion and morality are, we presume, the highest expression of truth and goodness; and absolute religion and morality, Mr. Parker tells us, are "religion as it exists in the facts of man's nature," "what answers exactly to the religious sentiment." By sentiment, we presume also, he means sentiment, for he so calls it, defines it to be a want, and distinguishes it from cognition, discursive reason, and volition; if a sentiment, then a fact of the sensitive or inferior soul, which is the seat or principle of all the sentiments, whether good or bad. If absolute religion and morality answer exactly to the religious sentiment, or if that which answers exactly to the religious sentiment is absolute religion and morality, then the sensitive soul is their measure, and then the measure of truth and goodness.

The transcendentalists, moreover, claim to be *spiritualists*, and they call their doctrine *spiritualism*. Their impersonal soul, it is well known, they term spirit, and distinguish, on the one hand, from reason, and on the other from external sense. They pretend to have detected here an element in man, or a faculty of man's soul, which is overlooked by the rationalists and the materialists, as also by the supernaturalists, whom Mr. Parker classes with the materialists. This element or faculty is the principle of their doctrine, and that which characterizes their school. In their view it *transcends* reason and external sense, and hence their name of *transcendentalists*. They are *pneumatici*, differing from those of the old Gnostic stamp only in claiming for all men what the old Gnostics claimed for merely a select few.

Now strike out reason and external sense, and you have

nothing left of man but this very sensitive soul to which you can possibly apply the term spirit; for these and it are the whole man. Therefore the transcendentalists must mean this, if they mean any thing, by the spirit; for there is nothing else in man they can mean.

That they do mean this is evident enough from the fact that they deny the necessity, nay, the propriety, of struggling against it. There is, as most men know, an internal opposition between the rational soul and the sensitive, and in order to be virtuous, it is generally held that we should make the latter yield to the former; but this the transcendentalists deny.

"In some men," says Mr. Parker, "religion is a continual growth. They are always in harmony with God. Silently and unconscious, erect as a palm-tree, they grow up to the measure of a man. To them reason and religion are of the same birth. They are born saints, the aborigines of heaven. Betwixt their *idea* of life and their *fact* of life there has at no time been a gulf. But others join themselves to the armada of sin, and get scarred all over with wounds as they do thankless battle in that leprous host. Before these men become religious, there must be a change,—well defined, deeply marked—a change that will be remembered. The saints who have been sinners—tell us of the struggle and desperate battle that goes on between the flesh and the spirit. It is as if the devil and the archangel contended. Well says John Bunyan, 'The devil fought with me weeks long, and I with the devil.' To take the leap of Niagara, and stop when half-way down, and by the proper motion reascend, is no slight thing, nor the remembrance thereof like to pass away. The passage from sin to salvation, this second birth of the soul, as both Christians and heathens call it, is one of the many mysteries of man. Two elements meet in the soul. There is a negation of the past; an affirmation of the future. Terror and hope, penitence and faith, rush together, and a new life begins."—*Discourse*, p. 151.

This, though vaguely expressed, is intelligible enough. It evidently recognizes no corrupt nature to be warred against, and by the help of divine grace reduced to subjection. Many never know any struggle at all; and those who are subjected to a momentary struggle, in consequence of past misbehaviour, have to struggle, not against their own nature, but simply against their past deeds. The sin is simply in the fact that there is a gulf between their *fact* of life and their *idea* of life,—that is, a discrepancy between the actual and the ideal. The sinner is one who has not realized his ideals. The wrong is entirely in the fact that his actual conduct does not satisfy or please himself. Let him leap the gulf which separates his actual from his ideal, or let him by a bold effort satisfy his interior longings, and be pleased with himself, recover self-complacency, and the sin is removed, the evil is done away, and the man stands on the mountain-top of life, that is, has got to the top of his ideal. "Absolve yourself," says Mr. Emerson, "and you shall have the suffrage of the world."

"Two elements meet in the soul." What are these two elements? Reason and concupiscence,—the spirit and the flesh? Not at all. They are no elements of human nature, but simply the *fact* of life and the *idea* of life, that is, the actual and the ideal. The man, somehow, one day, as leaping down Niagara at his leisure, and admiring the spray, the current, the rainbow, suddenly comes to see that he is leaping away from his ideal, falling below it, and, comparing one with the other, says to himself, "This will never do," and therefore arrests himself, turns a somerset, and with his proper motion reascends and grasps his ideal. A difficult feat, no doubt, for ordinary mortals; but within the natural power of all men, and quite easy to a transcendentalist, who is thoroughly exercised in all spiritual ground-and-lofty tumbling. But be this as it may, the only struggle is between the man's actual and his ideal. Is this actual the creature of the inferior soul? Nothing says so. Is this ideal the revelation of the superior soul, of reason divinely strengthened or illuminated? Nothing proves it; and, for aught that appears, it may itself be nothing but the longings, cravings, of the inferior soul itself.

A struggle of a different kind Mr. Parker, indeed, admits, and a struggle which the man wages not in becoming a saint, but in being one. But this is not against the inferior or sensitive soul. It is a struggle against old ideas and institutions. The man is to do brave battle, but not against himself,—win immortal victories, but not over himself. He is to stand erect against existing moral, religious, and social institutions, and wage war to the death against whatever may impose a restraint on the soul, or hinder it from acting out itself. So, he says, did our blessed Saviour, whom, in his more compliant moods, he permits to be taken as a model; so did Peter, and Paul, and Stephen, and so all the prophets and sages of all times past, and so should we. But this implies no condemnation of any part of human nature, nor does it require the rational soul to be placed above the sensitive.

Mr. Emerson, the real chief, or sovereign pontiff, of transcendentalism, denies in plain terms the struggle.

"People," says he, "represent virtue as a struggle, and take to themselves great airs on their attainments, and the question is everywhere vexed, when a noble nature is commended, Whether the man is not better who strives with temptation? But there is no merit in the matter. Either God is there, or he is not there. We love characters in proportion as they are *impulsive and spontaneous*. . . . . When we see a soul whose acts are all regal, graceful and pleasant as roses, we must thank God that such things can be and are, and not turn sourly on the angel, and say, 'Crump is a better man with his resistance to all his native devils.'"—*Essays*, p. 109.

This is conclusive. Now, since the transcendentalists avowedly contemn personality, whose basis is reason, and do not condemn in any respect the sensitive soul, and since they call upon us to obey the soul, and since the sensitive soul, after personality is discarded, is all the soul there is left for us to obey, it follows necessarily, that they do, intentionally or unintentionally, raise the sensitive soul over the rational, as we have alleged.

1. It may be objected to this, that the transcendentalists also call their impersonal soul *reason*, and therefore do not intend to distinguish it from the rational nature. They distinguish between reason and understanding. Understanding is the intellectual principle of sensation; reason, of spiritual cognition, and is above understanding. Reason, as understanding, they discard; reason, as the principle of spiritual cognition, of intuition, they do not discard, because it is precisely what they mean by *spirit*. We deny the validity of this distinction, which is supported by no facts alleged, or which can be alleged. Reason is the principle of understanding, and without reason man would cease not only to be rational, but to be intelligent,—for intelligence in man is not the intelligence of animals *plus* reason, but reason itself, as is affirmed when man is affirmed to be of a rational nature. There is not in man an intelligent nature *and* a rational nature; but the intelligent nature in man is essentially and integrally rational nature. The intelligent principle is, then, one and the same, whatever the conditions of its operation, or the sphere or degree of knowledge.

2. But we may be told, again, that the transcendentalists contend that man's *whole* nature should be retained and exercised, and that his supreme good consists in the harmonious development and action of all his faculties; therefore they

cannot assert the superiority of the sensitive soul alleged. We deny the conclusion; for they contend, that, though man's whole nature is to be retained and exercised,—which, by the way, is hardly consistent with what else they say,— yet all is to be retained and exercised *in subordination to the instinctive nature*, which we have identified with the sensitive soul. "We love characters," says Mr. Emerson, "in proportion as they are impulsive and spontaneous." "Absolute religion," says Mr. Parker, "is that which answers exactly to the religious *sentiment*." Instinctive, sensitive nature is evidently, then, placed above personal nature, which is identical, as we have seen, with rational nature,—and this is all our argument asserts.

That all man's faculties, although said to be retained, are to be retained and exercised in subordination to the sensitive or inferior soul is maintained even in general thesis by not a few of our modern speculators and reformers. The Fourierists all place, confessedly, the *passional* nature, which corresponds exactly to the impersonal nature of the transcendentalists, at the summit of the psychical hierarchy, and contend that man's good consists not in controlling his passions, but in harmonizing them, and that they are to be harmonized not by being crucified, but by having all things so arranged as to secure their free and full satisfaction. They expressly make the passional nature legislative, and the rational simply ministerial; and their writings and discourses are filled with tirades against philosophers, moralists, theologians, and legislators, for having sought to make reason legislative, and the passions subservient. Fourierism is nothing but a form of transcendentalism, as may be inferred from the fact that nearly all the transcendentalists are either avowed Fourierists or very favorable to them. Fourierism is simply an attempt to realize in society the leading principles of transcendentalism; and if some transcendentalists reject it, it is not because they question the philosophy on which it rests, but because they doubt its competency, as a practical scheme of social organization, to secure the end proposed.

The same doctrine lies at the basis of the ethical system of the French eclectic school. He must be a tyro indeed in philosophical studies, who does not perceive at a glance that the *instinctive* and *spontaneous* nature of the transcendentalists, the *passional* nature of the Fourierists, and the *primitive facts* or instinctive *tendencies* of human nature, as set forth by M. Jouffroy, are all only so many different names for one and the same thing. In Jouffroy, the tendencies, notwithstanding some pretences to the contrary, reveal and impose the law; reason and will are merely ministerial, and have for their mission simply the realization of the end to which the tendencies aspire; that is, their full and perfect satisfaction. And what is this but raising the instinctive nature, that is, the sensitive soul, over the rational?

Substantially the same doctrine is inculcated by Gall and Spurzheim and their followers. The *primitive faculties* of the phrenologists are, according to M. Jouffroy himself, identical with what he calls the primitive or instinctive *tendencies*; and these every one at all acquainted with such matters can identify, saving some difference of detail and terminology, with the *passional* nature of the Fourierists, and the *impersonal soul* of the transcendentalists. The primitive faculties, according to the phrenologists, are all instinctive and legislative, and reason and will are to accept them, develop and harmonize them by obeying them.

We might go further, and show that every moral code ever promulgated, not resting on positive law, human or divine, rests on the same basis; for, aside from positive law, human or divine, it is not possible, in the nature of things, to find any other basis for a moral code.

If we leave the philosophers, and consult the more popular modern theologians and preachers, we shall find again the same doctrine. The dominant tendency of our age and country is to place the essence of religion in sentiment. The appeal is rarely to reason,—almost always to the feelings. The rational conviction, the firm resolve, count for little. Religion is expressed by the word *theophilanthropy*,—love to God and love to man. So says Dr. Channing, so says Mr. Parker, and Come-outers of all sorts and sizes. And by *love* they mean the natural sentiment of love, a fact of the sensitive soul, not an affection of the will inflamed by supernatural grace, exalting the affection into the supernatural virtue of charity. We know of no popular preacher among *liberal* Christians who contends that man should possess and practise supernatural virtues. With the great mass, religion is not something to be believed, something to be *done*, but something to be *felt*. Its office is to cherish kindly sentiments, humane and generous feelings, to war with whatever restrains the sentiments and hinders the development of the soul, and to harmonize and perfect human nature, by stimulating its faculties and subordinating all to the law imposed by the simple feeling or sentiment of love.

The characters most approved by the transcendentalists are such as appeal with the most success to our sensitive nature. "We love characters," says Mr. Emerson, "in proportion as they are impulsive and spontaneous." Thomas Carlyle, a leading English transcendentalist, who found his earliest and warmest admirers among our American transcendentalists, ridicules without mercy poor Robespierre, not because his aims were bad, his views false, his means unjustifiable and cruel, but because he knew what he was about, had a "formula," and acted after a preconceived plan; but lavishes the warmest praise upon such men as Mirabeau and Danton, because they had large impulsive natures, and acted from natural impulse and suggestion, not from rational design. In his *Heroes and Hero Worship*, he everywhere labors to show that the more a man sinks his personality, and resolves himself into pure nature, makes or suffers himself to be a mere conduit to the stream of natural forces, the more heroic and divine he becomes. In general, the tendency of transcendentalists is to admire characters in whom sentiment or passion predominates. Miss Fuller, in her *Woman in the Nineteenth Century*, patronizes several renowned courtesans; and the chief ground of her complaint against our *masculine* social order seems to be, that it imposes undue restraints on woman's nature, and does not permit her to follow her natural sentiments and affections. A sweet young lady gave us one day as her reason for joining what is now a Fourier community, that she was disgusted with conventionalism, and wished to be free from its galling restraints, and to live in the simplicity of nature. Poor girl! we will not relate her history; nor that of the young Adonis who was willing to aid her in her struggles for freedom. It is not always safe jesting with Nature. She sometimes cracks practical jokes, which are a little too expensive.

In most of our more popular educational schemes we may detect the same doctrine lurking at the bottom. Intellect is cried down, and the sentiments are cried up. The *sentiment* of love is to be always our guide and motive. Duty is an ugly word, and not to be named. We have heard parents in public and private protest against any restraint being laid on children, that the child should never be required to act from a sense of duty; for what is done from a sense of duty is worthless, unmeritorious. We should act, say they, always from love, and never do or exact what love does not prompt. We should leave our children free, and not interfere with their natures. To exact obedience, where they are not inclined to yield it, is to interfere with the free development of their natures,—will mar the beauty of their pure, sweet, and gentle natures, and destroy their integrity;—a pleasant doctrine, no doubt, to the pretty dears, and, judging from the number of graceless urchins one everywhere meets, not seldom acted upon.

These considerations, and many more of the same kind, which could be adduced, may tend to confirm the position we have taken, and satisfy our readers that we have not mistaken or misrepresented transcendentalism, when we have charged it with raising the inferior soul over the superior, and making the sensitive nature, instead of the rational, the measure of truth and goodness.

But can it be possible that men of ordinary capacity, and not without some claims to personal decency and morality, do really advocate such glaring absurdity in doctrine, and what would prove, and is already beginning to prove, such gross license in practice? We own it appears hardly credible, and we are sure would not be possible, if they looked upon the subject as we do, or as do the great majority of our readers. But many of the inevitable consequences which would flow from their doctrine they do not regard as evil, but as good and desirable. We have in our possession a pamphlet written with no mean ability, and brought out from England by some English transcendentalists, which boldly controverts the Christian doctrine of chastity and marriage, and in the sacred name of God and humanity, in the name of morals, "universal brotherhood," and social progress, advocates a promiscuous sexual intercourse, contends that games and amusements should be instituted for the express purpose of inflaming passion, and that our public halls and theatres should be surrounded with private apartments, fitted up in the most luxurious style, and with the most exquisite taste, for the special purpose of affording an easy and speedy opportunity of satisfying desire before it abates. We have met in public and private, we have entertained in our own house, the men who circulate, if they do not write such books, and advocate similar doctrines; and when we have opposed them, have been assured that we opposed them because we had too much of the devil in us to understand them, or to appreciate and relish the pure teachings of the spirit! Nor should this surprise us. These men are no new phenomena. We have known them well in all ages of the world, and especially under the names of Carpocratians, Priscillianists, and Manicheans or Albigenses. They differ not essentially from the pantheistic sect which gathered, in the thirteenth century, around what was called the " Eternal Gospel." Mr. Emerson, a man of great personal purity and rigid morals, does not hesitate to avow the legitimate consequences of transcendentalism. Speaking of the transcendentalist, he says:—" In action he easily incurs the charge of Antinomianism, by his avowal that he who has the Lawgiver may with safety not only neglect, but even contravene, every written commandment."—*Dial*, Vol. III., p. 300.

They cannot avoid this conclusion. They assume nature as the standard; and as in that which is instinctive and spontaneous it is nature that operates, they must conclude that whatever is instinctive and spontaneous, whatever is natural, or prompted by tne permanent and essential nature of man, is true and good, and will be accepted as such by the brave man, let the world say or do what it will.

But whence the evidence that nature is the standard, the measure of truth and goodness? What right have the transcendentalists to make this very important assumption with which they set out? On this point they are far from being explicit, and far from being agreed among themselves. But generalizing their views as much as we can, and premising that what we allege must be understood not in all cases of the whole school, but some portion of one section and some of another, we find them alleging in its support,—

1. That God, who is wise and good, is the author of nature, and must have made nature wise and good,—and therefore the expression or revelation of his will. If the revelation of his will, we have the right to assume it as the standard or measure of truth and goodness.

But they have no right to this conclusion; 1. because none of them admit that God is in reality the author or creator of nature; and, 2. because they call God wise and good only because they hold him to be what their own nature reveals him to be. This last is a plain begging of the question. For, according to their mode of reasoning, their natures must be assumed to be wise and good, as the condition of demonstrating the wisdom and goodness of God. Whence the proof that God is wise and good? In the fact that he is what our natures reveal him to be. On what condition is this a proof of his wisdom and goodness? Obviously, only on the condition that our natures themselves are wise and good. Moreover, 3. because, for aught they show, and as the whole Christian world believes, it may be that nature is not now in its normal state, but has fallen, and is cursed. Admitting nature was wise and good as it came from the hands of its Maker, it must still be shown to be what it was then, before they can have the right to assume it as the standard. But if nature be in its origin wise and good, and there has been no change, no fall, no curse, how will they account for the innumerable evils, the multiplied wrongs, which afflict the human race, and which force even them to become reformers, and to declaim against nearly all that has been or is in human life?

2. But, secondly, the moment man sinks his personality, he becomes absorbed, as it were, in universal nature, which, in the unity of its force, is God. It is, then, God that acts in what is instinctive and spontaneous, and, in obeying our instinctive nature, we are really and literally obeying God. He who obeys God obeys the Highest, and of course what he ought to obey. It is with a view like this, that Mr. Emerson says :—

"His [man's] thought—is the Universe His experience inclines him to behold the procession of facts you call the world as flowing perpetually outward from an invisible, unsounded centre in himself, centre alike of him and of them, and necessitating him to regard all things as subjective and relative to that unknown existence, relative to that aforesaid centre of him."—*Dial*, Vol. III., p. 299.

This is perhaps somewhat enigmatical, but may be grasped if we bear in mind that Mr. Emerson's philosophy recognizes no distinct substantive existences, no distinct natures; but under, within, over, and through all forms or modes of existence, all of which are representative and phenomenal, it asserts one and the same mighty nature, which, as it touches us, he calls Over-Soul, and as it recedes from us and loses itself in the darkness, God, or the Unnamable. We, in our personality, represent it, as the bubble represents the ocean on whose surface it floats. As from the bubble's own point of view the whole ocean underlies it, is its substantiality, so each man, from his own point of view, represents the universal nature, which is his substance, being, force, or whatever of reality he hath. Millions of bubbles may rise, but each has the whole ocean as the centre of itself; so millions of men may be born, but each has the universal centre in himself. This nature, force, substantiality, being of man, strictly and essentially one, is identical in all men and in all phenomena. It is THE ONE (τὸ ἕν) of the Alexandrian philosophers. It works always according to its own laws, and is all that we can conceive of the divine. To sink the phenomenal and rise to the one permanent universal nature is to lose men in man, and to become one with God,—the highest consummation conceivable. All that is real is this one nature. It is the only doer, the only thinker, the only speaker, the only builder. It is the Universal Artist. Hence, in verse worthy of a nobler philosophy Mr. Emerson breaks forth:—

> " Not from a vain and shallow thought,
> His awful Jove young Phidias brought
> Never from lips of cunning fell
> The thrilling Delphic Oracle:
> Out from the heart of nature rolled
> The burdens of the Bible old;
> The litanies of nations came,
> Like the volcano's tongue of flame,
> Up from the burning core below,—
> The canticles of love and woe.
> The hand that rounded Peter's dome,
> And groined the aisles of Christian Rome,
> Wrought in a sad sincerity.
> Himself from God he could not free;
> He builded better than he knew.
> The conscious stone to beauty grew.
>
> ' Know'st thou what wove yon wood bird's nest
> Of leaves, and feathers from her breast?
> Or how the fish outbuilt her shell,
> Painting with morn each annual cell!
> Or how the sacred pine-tree adds
> To her old leaves new myriads?
> Such and so grew these holy piles,
> Whilst love and terror laid the tiles.
> Earth proudly wears the Parthenon
> As the best gem upon her zone;
> And morning opes with haste her lids
> To gaze upon the Pyramids;
> O'er England's abbeys bends the sky,
> As on its friends, with kindred eye:
> For out of Thought's interior sphere
> These wonders rose to upper air,
> And nature gladly gave them place,
> Adopted them into her race,
> And granted them an equal date
> With Andes and with Ararat.

> "*These Temples grew as grows the grass,*
> *Art might obey, but not surpass.*
> *The passive Master lent his hand*
> *To the vast Soul that o'er him planned,*
> And the same power that reared the shrine
> Bestrode the tribes that knelt within
> Ever the fiery pentecost
> Girds with one flame the countless host,
> Trances the heart through chanting quires,
> And through the priest the mind inspires."
>
> *Dial,* Vol. I., pp. 122, 123.

There is no mistaking the doctrine here set forth. It is the identity of all natures with the one nature, of all causes with the one cause, and of this one nature, this one cause, with the impersonal Soul, or God, unfathomed centre and being of each individual.

But, 1. This doctrine is asserted, not proved. No evidence of its truth is adduced, or attempted to be adduced. The transcendentalists must pardon us, if we question their infallibility, and find it not easy to believe on their bare assertion, that all apparent individual substances are but one substance, and all apparently different natures are but one nature, and that that one nature is God. God is the sovereign *cause* of the universe; but where is the proof that he is the *substance,* the *nature,* of the universe?

But, 2. Admitting this, we must either say man is this one nature, or that man as a real being is not. If the latter, there is no further question of man, for it is idle to talk of that which is not. If the former, then God is man, and nothing more nor less than man. Then there is and should be no further question of God.

The attempt, then, to identify impersonal nature with God effects nothing in favor of that nature as a measure of truth and goodness; for, grant its perfect identity, you have gained nothing, for you have nothing but man; and the right to take man as the measure of truth and goodness is the point in question. Man is the same, whether you call him man, or call him God. Call him which you will, your measure remains always the instinctive nature; and that nature is simply what it is, neither less nor more.

Again, if you assume the identity of human nature with all natures, and of these with the one nature, and this one nature with God; and if you assume God to be the universal operator, operative in all phenomena, and operative as essentially true, beautiful, and good; how do you account for evil, for the existence of so much you are obliged to condemn and war against? You cannot ascribe it to personality, because personality, according to you, is purely representative, unreal, unsubstantial, phenomenal, and therefore—though you seem not to be aware of it—necessarily uncreative, unproductive either of good or evil; for what is no substantive existence can be no cause, produce no effect. All force is in nature, and then none in personality. Then you must say one of two things:—1. All that is and all that appears—for what appears depends wholly on what is, as there can be no shadow without a substance—is true, wise, and good; and then you condemn and refute yourselves, for you are warring against almost all that is. This warring is right, or it is wrong. If right, then that which you war against is wrong, and so there is evil; if wrong, then is there evil, because the warring itself is an evil. Or, 2. You must say there is something which has no cause; that is to say, there are effects without causes, which is impossible and absurd.

3. Thirdly, Reason itself has two modes of activity, one personal, the other instinctive or spontaneous. As personal, it is human; as impersonal, spontaneous, it is God, or the word of God. Being absolute, it is one; therefore essentially one in the personality and out of it. If we confine ourselves to its personal modes of activity, which are finite, we are misled, involved in error; if we sink our personality and fall back on it in its spontaneous and impersonal activity, it becomes to us a perennial stream of truth, beauty, goodness, from God himself. This spontaneous activity of reason, Mr. Parker, after Cousin and the Editor of the *Boston Quarterly Review*, makes the principle of inspiration, which, according to him, if we would yield to it, would give us all we need.

This view, in the first place, is only another form of the one just dismissed, and differs from it only in name; and is therefore open to all the objections we have urged against that.

In the second place, *reason has and can have no instinctive, or spontaneous, or impersonal activity;* because reason is the essential characteristic of personality, which is the last complement of rational nature. Instinct or spontaneity is necessarily irrational; for the characteristic of reason is to operate *propter finem*, and, therefore, is possible only in a voluntary or personal agent. Reason is inconceivable without rational nature. Assume rational nature with its last complement, and it is a person; without its last complement, it is impersonal, indeed, but unreal, and gives you no actual reason, at best only reason *in potentia*, which is inactive, for only what is real is active. Therefore reason has and can have no instinctive or spontaneous activity.

Again, if you assume reason as distinct from human personality, you must assume it as a reason above man or as below him. Below him it cannot be, because man's is the lowest order of rational natures; and moreover, if below man, it would not serve the purpose. If above man, it is either actual reason or merely possible reason. If merely possible, it is unreal and inactive; properly speaking, not reason at all. If actual, it is a higher personality, as angel or God, and then separated from man by a difference of order, and incapable of acting instinctively in man; for that would imply the absorption of the higher personality in the lower, which is impossible.

Man has naturally the last complement of his nature, since he is naturally a person. He has, then, naturally all the rational nature, and therefore all the *reason*, that belongs to rational nature of his order. His rational nature is full; therefore his reason is full. Nothing can be more than full. Then man is not naturally susceptible of a higher reason than his own. He can receive even the aid of a higher reason only supernaturally. The higher reason is a higher person. The higher person is incommunicable to him save by hypostatic union, which absorbs his personality in the higher personality, as in the case of the divine Word. For a hypostatic union, as really existing, in the case of all men, the transcendentalists will not contend; 1. because they deny it even in the case of our Saviour; 2. because they deny the supernatural; and 3. because they admit no union of man and the divine Word which absorbs human personality, for they find human personality still existing as the enemy to be warred against.

Beyond the hypostatic union, only two ways are conceivable in which it is possible for the higher reason, even God himself, to instruct the lower, in regard to what lies not within the plane of the lower nature; 1. by supernatural revelation to faith, which takes the truth on the word of the revealer, and believes without seeing or knowing; or 2. by the supernatural elevation of our nature itself, as is looked for in the beatific vision, the reward Almighty God has promised hereafter to them that love and serve him here.

This doctrine of impersonal and instinctive reason is, then, unfounded and impossible in the nature of reason itself. And here is the refutation of M. Cousin's doctrine of spontaneity, and of Mr. Parker's doctrine of natural inspiration, or inspiration by a natural influx of God into the soul, on which his whole system depends for its religious character. Here we may see the source of all Mr. Parker's theoretical errors. He assumes that man and God stand in immediate *natural* relation, and that so much of God flows naturally into man as man's wants demand. This he asserts over and over again; and this is what he means by looking up to God alone, with nothing between the worshipper and the great Father of all; and it is his honest belief of this, we suppose, that has concealed from his view the real character of the doctrine he inculcates.

That man may express his wants to God naturally and directly in prayer, we do not question; and that God will hear and supernaturally answer our prayers, we most firmly believe; but the assumption of a natural communion between man and his Maker is absurd. God may inspire individuals, may inspire all individuals, he may enlarge and elevate their natures so as to take in a higher order of truth than they now can; but he can do it only supernaturally; for naturally there is no communion between beings of a different nature. Man is not a possible God, nor a possible angel. He is man, with a fixed and determinate nature, and tied down to that nature and what it is capable of, save so far as his Maker is pleased to grant him supernatural assistance through faith or the infusion of grace. God is infinite reason, if you will; then he must be infinite rational nature with its last complement, and then infinite personality, that is to say, infinite person. The natural influx of God into human reason demanded by Mr. Parker's theory would, then, be the natural influx into the human reason of the divine personality. Is this possible? The human reason is confessedly finite. Is the finite naturally susceptible of the infinite? Not even Mr. Parker will pretend this. Then this theory of natural inspiration, of a natural "supply of God," as it is called, proportioned to our wants, must be abandoned as untenable.

But it may be alleged that we are reasoning upon a false supposition, namely, that the divine reason and the human are different in kind. This is not admitted. The divine reason and the human are essentially one and the same. "Man," says Dr. Channing, "has a kindred nature with God." If this be so, nothing hinders the divine from flowing naturally into the human, as is contended. We deny that the divine reason and the human are essentially the same. They are essentially different. The human reason is a likeness, or an image, of the divine, we admit, according to the Christian doctrine, that "man was made after the image and likeness of God." But likeness presupposes a difference of nature between itself and that which it is like. The thing imaged and its image cannot be of the same nature; for, if so, the image would be absorbed in the imaged. The child images the father, but only in that wherein he is different from the father. Moreover, God is uncreate, independent, infinite; man is created, dependent, finite, and therefore necessarily of a nature different from the divine nature.

But assume the divine reason and the human are essentially one and the same reason, the rational nature of which this reason is the expression either has its last complement in man, or it has not. If the latter, you deny human personality, the very thing you are fighting against; if the former, you deny the personality of God, therefore, the actual existence of God as divine reason, and therefore make the divine reason itself below that of man; for the smallest *reality* is above the greatest conceivable *possibility*. Assume, then, natural inspiration to be possible, it would be worthless; for it could give less than man is and possesses without it. The in-coming and in-streaming God could bring you nothing you have not already.

Mr. Parker seeks to sustain his theory of natural inspiration by alleging that God is immanent in his works, the *causa immanens* of nature, not merely the *causa transiens;* and being immanent in all, and therefore in man, is necessarily present in man to supply all man's deficiencies. But we must distinguish. If immanent as creator and sustainer of man and all beings, each in the distinctive nature he gives them, we concede his immanence; if immanent in each being as subject, we deny it. To assume that God is immanent in his creatures as the subject which acts in them and produces what are called their acts is Spinozism, a doctrine which admits no existence but God and his modes,—and which, though unquestionably implied by transcendentalism generally, we understand Mr. Parker expressly to disavow. Moreover, it is a doctrine neither he nor the other transcendentalists can admit, without falling into gross contradictions, and refuting themselves; for they find little in the actual world they do not condemn; and yet, if they admit this doctrine, they cannot condemn any thing without condemning God. If they admit God can do wrong, then they gain nothing in favor of the impersonal soul as the measure of truth and goodness by identifying it with God.

If they concede that God is not immanent in his creatures as subject, but simply as cause, creator, and sustainer, then his immanence merely creates and sustains them in their several natures,—that is, each order of being, and each individual being, in its being and distinct nature. In this case, his immanence is no pledge of the natural influx of divinity assumed. For then nothing could be received naturally of God but the nature itself. Whatever more may be received must be supernaturally received, through faith or elevation of nature, which the transcendentalists cannot admit.

Mr. Parker's doctrine on this point seems to be, that man's faculties open on God, and in proportion as he opens them God flows in, and man may thus be strong with the strength of omnipotence, wise with the wisdom of omniscience, and good with the goodness of infinite goodness, and all this as naturally as the lungs inhale the atmosphere, or the stomach secretes the gastric juice. But this is absurd; for it implies that the finite subject may appropriate infinite attributes, the infinite God himself, and live and act with infinite power, wisdom, and goodness. It would imply that the infinite is communicable, and communicable to the finite, without absorbing the finite, leaving it finite still, and a finite personality! The immanence of God in his works is a pledge that they will be upheld, and is a ground of hope, since it implies that he is ever present to afford us the supernatural aid we need, and in a supernatural manner, if we seek this aid in the way and through the channels he has appointed; but this is all, and it is nothing to the purpose of the transcendentalists.

These three different considerations are all we find adduced in support of the proposition, that man is the measure of truth and goodness. They all show that the transcendentalists would fain establish their doctrine if they could, and that they would do it by identifying, in some way, the human and divine natures; for, after all, there is a secret feeling that God is above man, and that truth and goodness are what conforms to God, rather than what conforms to man. Their talk about man's natural relation to God, and the divinity of human nature, &c., may serve to conceal the deformity of their doctrine from their own eyes, but it amounts to just nothing at all; for all the divinity they are able to predicate of man is merely what is constitutive of human nature as human nature, leaving human nature simply what it is,—nothing more, nothing less. Then, when they abandon themselves to this as the only divinity, they abandon themselves to simple human nature, and are obliged to say man is the measure of truth and goodness, just as much as if they said or believed nothing of God at all.

We shall not undertake to refute the doctrine itself, because they who affirm a proposition must bring forward affirmative proofs before they can require us to accept it, or to adduce negative proofs. It is a sufficient refutation to say, as we have shown is the fact, that it is *not proved*. The assertions of the transcendentalists may be very good assertions, but they are not proofs, especially of a proposition denied by the common sense of all men, and affirmed by none but mere theorists, who make little account of reason, and professedly none of logic. Moreover, those who do not see the falsity and danger of the doctrine, on its bare enunciation, are not likely to be reached by any reasoning we could offer. Those who reason at all see what it is; those who cannot or will not reason are not to be reasoned out of error or into truth. We have merely wished to state the doctrine in its true character, and establish the fact that it is a fundamental doctrine of transcendentalism. This we think we have done.

We know now the transcendental rule of faith and practice. We have ascertained its *method;* and knowledge of this rule, of this method, throws no little light over the whole subject of transcendentalism. The more difficult part of our labor is accomplished; we shall be able to dispose of the two remaining propositions with comparative ease. But we must reserve the consideration of these to a future occasion.

ARTICLE II.

In our last *Review*, we established the fact, that the transcendentalists assume, as their rule of faith or method of philosophizing, the truth and rectitude of human nature; that man in his spontaneous or instinctive nature, which we identified with the inferior or sensitive soul, is the measure or criterion of truth and goodness; and therefore, that, in order to ascertain what is proper for us to believe or to do, we have only to ascertain what our nature spontaneously or instinctively approves. We now proceed to consider the second fundamental principle we have charged them with maintaining, namely,—

Religion is a Fact or Principle of Human Nature.

In strictness, perhaps, the transcendentalists do not mean to assert that religion itself is a fact or principle of human nature, but simply, that it has its principle and cause in human nature; and, consequently, this second principle might be resolved into the third principle we enumerated, namely, All the religions which have been or are have their principle and cause in human nature. It is possible that we should have been more strictly scientific in our analysis, if we had omitted the second proposition altogether, and embraced the whole teachings of the school within the first and third. Nevertheless, there is a sense in which the second proposition is true, and includes a portion of the teachings of the school, which we could not, without some inconvenience, discuss otherwise than under a separate head.

The word *religion* may be taken, and is taken by the transcendentalists in several senses. They use the word,—1. To embrace religious institutions; that is dogmas, morals, and worship. In this sense, they do not hold it to be a fact or principle of human nature; but they hold that it grows out of such fact or principle. But, 2. These religious institutions do not constitute what, in their view, is essential in religion. They are not its substance, but its forms and accidents, and we may have all that is essential to it without them, and even in opposition to them. What is essential in religion, if we understand them, is what is invariable and permanent, the same in all ages and nations, and in all individuals,—which is the religious *sentiment* and *idea;* and both of these they make facts or principles of human nature. Yet the teachings of the school are so vague and contradictory on this head, that it is not possible to reduce them to a common principle. It does not appear to have ever distinguished clearly, in its own mind, between the creator and creation, between the active or passive subject and action or passion; nor, again, between intuitive reason and discursive reason. It frequently puts causes for effects, and effects for causes; and just as frequently runs the one into the other, and concludes indifferently from one or the other, without noting any distinction between them. It affirms a proposition to be intuitive, when it is evidently inductive; and tells us that it is given us immediately, when according to its own showing it is obtained only by reasoning. If any one doubts our assertion, we refer him to the first and second chapters of the *Discourse* before us.

In consequence of this contradiction and confusion, and in order to avoid even the appearance of injustice to the school, we shall, for the most part, in what we have to say, treat the proposition under consideration simply as if it stood, Religion originates spontaneously in, and depends upon, a fact or principle of human nature.

We must bear in mind that the transcendental doctrine is not, that from the facts or principles of human nature we may rationally, scientifically, conclude to the objective truths of religion; but that these truths *are given us immediately*, without any reasoning at all, by a special fact, principle, or element of our nature. Religion is natural to us; we are religious by a law of our nature; in like manner as it is by a law of our nature that we breathe, that the stomach secretes the gastric juice, or the liver bile. In a word, religion is a natural secretion of the human soul. That the transcendentalists adhere throughout to this statement we are far from pretending; for it is well known that they are not remarkable for self-consistency, and some of them consider it a mark of littleness for a man to aim at being consistent with himself. Their maxim is, Speak out from the great soul, or, rather, let the great soul speak out, and as it will. Nevertheless, this is their formal, official doctrine, to which we shall insist on our right to hold them.

The transcendentalists begin by distinguishing between religion and religious institutions. Religious institutions are the forms with which man clothes his religious sentiment and idea. They vary according to time and space, and in passing from one individual to another. They are accidental and transitory. They may serve a useful purpose, or they may not; but they are not of the essence or substance of religion. Religion, in its substance, lies back of these, and is their creator, and independent of them. In this sense, as abstracted from religious forms and institutions, religion is, as we have said, sentiment and idea. The sentiment is a special element of human nature, and is defined by Mr. Parker, after Schleiermacher, to be "the *sense of dependence.*" The idea is "an intuition of reason," not obtained by reasoning, whether *a priori* or *a posteriori*, but "is a fact given by the nature of man."—p. 21. Hence religion, in its absolute sense, or what Mr. Parker calls absolute religion, is said to be religion as it exists in the facts of human nature, or "in the facts of man's soul."—p. 243. According to this, we should be justified in insisting, to the very letter, on the proposition, that the transcendentalists hold religion to be a fact or principle of human nature. But it is probable, after all, that they do not mean this, that they in this put the effect in the place of the cause, and really mean only that the origin and ground of religion is in a special element of human nature.

> "We are driven to confess," says Mr. Parker, "that there is in man a spiritual nature, which directly and legitimately leads to religion; that, as man's body is connected with the world of matter, rooted in it, has bodily wants, bodily senses to minister thereto, and a fund of external materials wherewith to gratify these senses and appease these wants,—so man's soul is connected with the world of spirit, rooted in God, has spiritual wants and spiritual senses, and a fund of materials wherewith to gratify these spiritual senses, and to appease these spiritual wants. If this be so, then do not religious institutions come equally from man? Now the existence of a religious element in us is not a matter of hazardous or random conjecture, nor attested only by a superficial glance at the history of man, but this principle is found out, and its existence demonstrated, in several legitimate ways. . . . Thus, then, it appears that induction from notorious facts, consciousness spontaneously active, and a philosophical analysis of man's nature, all lead equally to *some religious sentiment or principle as an essential part of man's constitution*. . . . . It is, indeed, most abundantly established that there is a *religious element in man*."—*Discourse*, pp. 14-19.

The main point asserted in this loosely written passage is the fact, that religious institutions spring from a special religious sentiment, element, or principle of human nature, and "which is an *essential* part of man's constitution." This is the first point to be disposed of. What are the proofs of this? These proofs, so far as we can collect them from Mr. Parker and others, are, 1. The existence of religious phenomena in human history; 2. The universality and indestructibleness of the religious phenomena; 3. The power of religion over our thoughts, passions, and interests; 4. Consciousness; 5. Philosophical analysis of man's nature.

1. The existence of religious phenomena in human history is unquestionable, and this existence proves that they have a principle and cause in man, or *out of him;* but to

infer that this principle and cause are a special element of human nature is a plain begging of the question, — at least, cannot be justifiable, unless it be first established that there is and can be nothing in human history which has not its principle and cause in human nature, — a proposition which may, indeed, be asserted, but not maintained, as we shall show when we come to discuss the third fundamental proposition of the transcendentalists. The history of the human race is inexplicable, save on the supposition of the supernatural intervention of Providence in human affairs.

2. The religious phenomena are universal and indestructible, we admit. Wherever you find man, you find the altar, the priest, and the victim,—at least some sort of religious worship. But this simply proves that religion does not spring from accidental and temporary causes, but from a universal and permanent principle. Yet that principle may be divine as well as human; for God, to say the least, is as universal and permanent a principle and cause as man.

3. The great power of religion in all ages is freely conceded. It is able to control man in his most intimate relations,—to control his thoughts and passions,—to make him forego his strongest desires, his dearest affections, and his most pressing interests,—to make him submit to what is most repugnant to his nature, to glory in being contemned, and to sacrifice himself with joy at its bidding. But this, though conclusive against those who contend that religion is the mere creature of human passion, caprice, fear, hope, ignorance, imagination, or interest, says nothing in favor of its origin and ground in a principle or element of human nature. Indeed, it is rather a presumption that it has its origin and ground in that which is superhuman and independent of man. For it is hard to conceive how that which originates in man, and depends wholly on man, should be able to control him, and make him voluntarily abnegate himself.

4. Mr. Parker alleges that we are conscious of our own insufficiency, and that this consciousness is the consciousness of a religious element in our nature. It is true, he does not say this formally, but this is what he is required to say by the line of argument he is pursuing.

"We feel conscious," he says, "of this element within us. We are not sufficient for ourselves; not self-originated; not self-sustained. A few years ago and we were not; a few years hence and our bodies shall not be. A mystery is gathered about our little life. We have but small control over things around us; are limited and hemmed in on all sides. Our schemes fail. Our plans miscarry. One after another our lights go out. Our realities prove dreams. Our hopes waste away. We are not where we would be, nor what we would be. After much experience, men as powerful as Napoleon, victorious as Cæsar, confess, what simpler men knew by instinct long before, that it is not in man that walketh to direct his steps. We find our circumference very near the centre, everywhere. An exceedingly short radius measures all our strength. We can know little of material things; nothing but their phenomena. As the circle of our knowledge widens its ring, we feel our ignorance on more numerous points, and the unknown seems greater than before. At the end of a toilsome life, we confess, with a great man of modern times, that we have wandered on the shore, and gathered here a bright pebble, and there a shining shell,—but the ocean of truth, shoreless and unfathomed, lies before us and *all unknown*. The wisest ancient knew only this, that he knew nothing. We feel an irresistible tendency to refer all outward things, and ourselves with them, to a power beyond us, sublime, mysterious, which we cannot measure, nor even conprehend. We are filled with reverence at the thought of this power. Outward matters give us the occasion which awakens consciousness, and spontaneous nature leads us to something higher than ourselves and greater than all eyes behold. We are bowed down at the thought. Thus the sentiment of something superhuman comes natural as breath. This primitive spiritual sensation comes over the soul, when a sudden calamity throws us from our habitual state; when joy fills our cup to its brim; at a 'wedding or a funeral, a mourning or a festival'; when we stand beside a great work of nature, a mountain, a waterfall; when the twilight gloom of a primitive forest sends awe into the heart, when we sit alone with ourselves and turn in the eye, and ask, What am I? Whence came I? Whither shall I go? There is no man who has not felt this sensation, this mysterious sentiment of something unbounded."—*Discourse*, pp. 16, 17.

Ergo, we are conscious of a special religious element which is an essential part of man's constitution; *ergo*, again, the religious phenomena depend on a fact or principle of human nature!

We have inserted this passage because it is a favorable specimen of Mr. Parker's style and method of argumentation. In reading it, one is led to ask, Is the writer of this, who allows man the ability only to know that he knows nothing, the same man who sneers at the notion of supernatural revelation,—who assumes to sit in judgment on all ages and nations, on even our blessed Saviour himself,—who contends that man has an intuitive knowledge of God, and bears about with him absolute religion as the standard by which to try even the Christian religion itself,—and who tells us we may and ought "to approach the Infinite One face to face"?—p. 5.

It is a great convenience to be freed from the necessity of maintaining consistency in one's own views.

But this is foreign to our present purpose. The point Mr. Parker was required to establish in this passage was, that we are conscious that the religious element, for which he contends, is an element or principle of our nature. "We feel this element within us." Does he prove this? Not at all. He simply proves that there are facts in all men's experience which prove that we are not sufficient for ourselves, and that, finding we are not sufficient for ourselves, we are very naturally led to ask if there is not a power above us. All this may be very true, but is nothing to his purpose. For, 1. He makes the fact of our own insufficiency a deduction from certain other facts which he enumerates and to which we come by experience; whereas, the fact of our insufficiency should, on his ground, be a fact of immediate consciousness, arrived at without any aid of discursive reason at all. 2. The consciousness of our own insufficiency, according to the paragraph quoted, does not of itself give us religion, or the objects of religion. It does not give us God immediately, but is simply a fact from which we are led to ask if there be not a God, or, at most, from which we *infer* there is and must be something above and beyond us. But his doctrine is not that we may rationally conclude from the facts of our nature to the existence of God and the necessity or propriety of religion, but that religion is given immediately, without any process of reasoning, by a special law, element, or principle of our nature, bearing the same or an analogous relation to spiritual objects that the bodily senses do to material objects. Admit, therefore, that we are conscious of our own insufficiency, and that we may rationally conclude from this insufficiency to the existence of a power that is all-sufficient, this does not prove that we have a special religious element, —far less, that we are conscious of the existence of such element. 3. Even assuming that we are conscious, immediately conscious, which is more than Mr. Parker proves, of our own insufficiency, it does not follow that we are conscious of the religious element; for our insufficiency is not an element or principle of our nature. An element or principle of nature is something positive, constitutive of that nature; but insufficiency is a mere negation, and is not included in what our nature is, but in what it is not. Consciousness of it, therefore, is not, and cannot be, consciousness of an element within us, or an element of our nature, " an essential part of our constitution."

5. According to Mr. Parker, philosophical analysis of man's nature gives us the element in question. This analysis, in his hands, gives us the sense of dependence; and the sense of dependence, in the last analysis, he tells us, is the religious element. But philosophical analysis cannot give us the *sense* of dependence as an element or principle of nature, for the best of all reasons,—because it is not and cannot be such element or principle. The *sense* of dependence is a fact of human life or experience,—not a fact, element, or principle of human nature. That our nature is dependent is a fact, but not an element or principle of that nature, for the same reason that insufficiency is not such element or principle. The word *sense* is, or may be, ambiguous. When we say *sense* of sight or hearing, we mean a principle, or rather power or faculty, of human nature. But we cannot use the word in this sense, when we say *sense* of dependence, any more than when we say *sense* of danger. Sense in this case is not a power or faculty, is not an element or principle of nature, but a simple fact of experience. It means simply, that we mentally apprehend, perceive, or are conscious of the fact that we are dependent. It is an intellectual fact, a product of the activity of the intelligent subject, not an element of its nature. Consequently, it is idle to pretend, that, if the religious element be rightly defined the sense of dependence, it is an element or principle of our nature.

But Mr. Parker, though he officially defines the religious element to be the sense of dependence, tells us that he is not tenacious of that definition. "Others," he says, "may call it the *consciousness of the infinite;* I contend less for the analysis than for the fact of a religious element in man."— p. 18, note. But, dear Sir, how, unless you tell us what you mean by this religious element, are we to determine whether you have proved it to be an element of man's nature or not? We cannot allow you to write thus loosely. You affirm that there is a religious element in man, and that philosophical analysis of man's nature can detect it. If you have not determined what this element is, if you know not its characteristic, how do you know philosophical analysis can detect it? We hold you to your definition, or to the alternative you give us. According, to you it is the sense of dependence, or, at least, the consciousness of the infinite. The first it cannot be, and, if held to that, you are evidently wrong. We will give you the advantage of the second, but we will give you no other advantage. Say, then, the ultimate principle of religion is the "consciousness of the infinite." The infinite is not an element or principle of man's nature, for man's nature is finite. Consciousness is not a principle of nature at all, but simply the act or state of being conscious. It is a fact of life, not an element of nature. Consequently, the consciousness of the infinite, even admitting it to be a fact of our intellectual life, is no more, than the sense of dependence, an element or principle of human nature.

But perhaps we shall be told that it is not contended, strictly speaking, that the consciousness of the infinite is an element or principle of human nature, but that we are conscious of the infinite by virtue of a special principle or power of our nature. This is, we suppose, the real doctrine of the transcendentalists. Hence, Mr. Parker contends that we have spiritual senses, and that the idea of God is an intuition of reason. They question the unity of the intelligent principle in man, and seem to lay down the doctrine, that our knowledge does not differ objectively only, but subjectively also,—that we know one class of objects by virtue of one subjective intelligent power or principle, and another class by another. It is this doctrine which misleads them and involves them in the greater part of their errors and absurdities. But this doctrine we have just refuted as well as on several previous occasions. The faculty of intelligence is not complex, but simple. It may have various degrees and conditions, but in itself is one and the same, whatever the degree or sphere of knowledge. The subjective power, by which we know an object to be a tree or a house, is one and the same with the power by which we know the three angles of a triangle are equal to two right angles, or that we ought to love our neighbour as ourselves. Consciousness is nothing but a peculiar modification of knowing, and is the same subjectively considered, whatever the object of which we are conscious. If, then, we are conscious of the infinite, we are conscious of it by our general power of consciousness, and this consciousness differs from any other consciousness only in so far as its object is different.

Strictly speaking, however, to say we are conscious of the infinite is absurd; for we can be conscious only of ourselves as the subject of our own phenomena, whether voluntary, sentient, or intellectual. The fact of consciousness is restricted by all accurate psychologists to the recognition of one's self, as subject in the intellectual phenomenon to which Leibnitz gives the name of *apperception*. In every act we perform, that is, in every *actus humanus*, we always recognize ourselves as subject or actor, as distinguished both from the act and the object to which we act. This recognition is the fact of consciousness, and the only fact to which the term is ever rightly applied. Consequently, to say we are conscious of the infinite is to affirm our own infinity, which is false and absurd. Instead of saying we are conscious of the infinite, we should say we perceive, or mentally apprehend, the infinite,—that is, the infinite is an object of our knowledge, or, in other words, we know the infinite.

But waiving these remarks on consciousness, which are conclusive in themselves, we deny that the consciousness of the infinite is an element or principle of our nature, for the simple reason, that we have no consciousness of the infinite. The infinite is conceived, but it is no object of knowledge. Knowledge of the infinite would be infinite knowledge, and infinite knowledge is possible only to an infinite subject, which man is not. Man is finite, and his knowledge is necessarily finite, and therefore limited to the finite.

This is a point we commend to the very serious attention of the transcendentalists. They seem on many occasions, and when it suits their purpose, to be duly aware of the limited nature of our faculties, and the littleness and emptiness of our knowledge, as we see in the passage quoted from Mr. Parker, in which he is endeavouring to establish the fact of our own insufficiency for ourselves. Yet, with a consistency purely transcendental, they contend that we may see God face to face, may have intuitive vision of the infinite!

The great endeavour of several of the later German metaphysicians, and of some of our own, as it was with the old Alexandrians, is to find in man's subjective power of cognition a faculty or principle by which he can cognize intrinsically the mysteries of faith. They find mankind believing in certain mysteries, which unquestionably transcend the reach of the ordinary understanding. These are believed, not by the few only,—the *élite* of the race, men of rare genius and cultivation,—but by the simple and uncultivated,— the shepherd watching his flocks, and the rustic following his plough; and often by these more sincerely and more firmly than by the gifted and enlightened few. Whence is this? Surely these simple, unlettered, and unreasoning masses have not demonstrated to their own minds the intrinsic truth of these mysteries, and reasoned themselves into the belief of them; for few, if any, of them can assign even a tolerable reason for their belief, or render any satisfactory account of it. Is this belief a delusion, and is the human race wholly deceived in its faith? We dare not say it. To say so would be to blaspheme humanity, and, in blaspheming humanity, to blaspheme humanity's Maker. To assume that it is a delusion would be to deny all criterion of truth and falsehood, and to plunge into the ocean of universal doubt. Moreover, it would be anti-philosophical to make such assumption, for it would be to assume the reality of an effect, and a most stupendous effect, without conceding it any actual or even possible cause.

This faith, then, must have a solid and imperishable ground somewhere. It must be well founded. Hence, say they, there must be in man some principle or faculty, overlooked by philosophers generally, which takes immediate cognizance of the objects of this faith. These objects all are, or imply, the infinite; therefore man must have the subjective power of cognizing the infinite. Therefore the infinite is cognoscible. Therefore the human race believe in the mysteries, because able, by the inherent faculties of the soul, to apprehend intuitively their intrinsic truth.

But what is this power? It is not sense, it is not intellect, it is not reason in its ordinary acceptation, but a faculty *sui generis*, which may indeed be called reason, but which cannot better be defined than by calling it a spiritual sense, or power of apprehending the invisible, of approaching the inapproachable, of knowing the unknowable, of comprehending the incomprehensible, of measuring the immeasurable! It is a mysterious and incomprehensible faculty, like the matters with which it places us in relation. All very intelligible, no doubt, to those who call darkness light, and finite infinite. But what is the evidence of the reality of such faculty? The only ground, it will be seen from our statement, for asserting the reality of such faculty is the well known fact, that mankind do believe, and always have believed, and, in spite of all obstacles, persist in believing, in mysteries whose intrinsic truth transcends both the senses and the understanding. But how could they believe in such mysteries, if they had no power above that of the senses and the understanding, by which their intrinsic truth is apprehended?

In reply, we may simply ask how a man who has never been in China can believe there is such a city as Peking? Assuredly, he does not perceive the intrinsic truth of the proposition, There is a city in China called Peking. Yet he believes it, and because he has, or believes he has, sufficient *external* evidence of the fact. The philosophers in question assume, that, since mankind believe in the mysteries, the intrinsic truth of the mysteries must be apprehended by them, which could not be, unless we had the subjective power of knowing it. But this assumption is unwarrantable; for faith is to believe what is not intrinsically known. The facts adduced only prove the *faith* of mankind in mysteries; and if it be faith, it is not knowledge. Therefore, the fact, that mankind believe in the mysteries, is itself not proof that the intrinsic truth of the mysteries is cognoscible, but that it is not cognoscible; and therefore the faith of mankind in mysteries which transcend sense and understanding, instead of proving the reality of a subjective power of knowing what transcends sense and understanding, proves, so far as it goes, the reverse; for, if we had such power, our faith would not be faith, but knowledge.

The philosophers in question assume, as their point of departure, that what is believable is intrinsically cognoscible, and that what is believed is intrinsically known,—an evident falsehood; for faith ends where knowledge begins, and what is an object of knowledge is not an object of faith, since faith is belief of what is not known. To establish, then, the fact they contend for, these philosophers must go a step further, and prove that mankind do not merely believe the mysteries, but actually know them. If they prove that the mysteries are intrinsically known by the race, then we will admit in the soul the subjective power to know them. But this the facts they adduce do not prove. These facts only prove that mankind believe them, from which we cannot conclude that they know them.

That this faith of the race has a solid and imperishable foundation we readily admit. But because it must have such foundation, it does not necessarily follow that the foundation is in a special faculty of the soul; for we can conceive the possibility, to say the least, of its being in authority which propounds and evidences them *extrinsically* to the human mind, as religious people contend and always have contended. The philosophers, when they assume the foundation to be in this special subjective faculty, then, merely beg the question. They take for granted the very point the conditions of the argument require them to prove.

Moreover, they reject, in asserting the cognoscibility of the mysteries, the very authority on which their whole reasoning is founded. They infer the solidity of the faith of mankind in the mysteries from the fact, that the race has always believed, and persists in believing in them. But the race, while it has believed the mysteries, has also believed that it did not know their intrinsic truth, and has always confessed that its faith in them *was* faith, not knowledge. Now, if you take the faith of mankind as authority in the one instance, why not in the other? Assuredly, it is worth as much in the latter case as in the former; because no man can know without knowing that he knows, and whenever he really believes he does not know, it is certain that he does not. A man may fancy that he knows when he does not, but he cannot fancy that he does not know when he does. These philosophers, no doubt, are governed by a commendable motive; but they attempt what is not possible to effect. They would fain give a philosophical basis to the religious faith of mankind. They are far from wishing to overthrow or to weaken that faith; their ambition is to legitimate it,—not to *prove* it, indeed, by evidence, but to *demonstrate* it, and to bring it within the province of science. But they should remember that what is of science is not of faith, that faith has its object always in a region into which science does not or cannot penetrate. It rests not on demonstration, but on authority,—and may be proved, but never demonstrated. They would fain find in man an element which bears the same relation to it that the sense of sight bears to colors, or the sense of hearing to sounds, and that we attain to its objects as naturally and as simply as we do by our senses to the objects of the material world. But this element they cannot detect; they assert its reality, but do not and cannot establish it; for, after all they may say, each man knows of himself that to him the objects of his religious faith, however certainly, infallibly, evidenced, are not known. He believes, without doubting, that they are,—but he does not know them.

This is evident from Mr. Parker himself. To know the mysteries is to know the infinite; to know the infinite is to know God; and God, according to Mr. Parker, "is the substantiality of matter."—p. 170. And yet he says, in the passage we have quoted, "We can know little of material things; nothing but their phenomena." That is, the substance of things we cannot know. Yet, since God is this substance, "substantiality," we could know something more than their phenomena, we could know even their substance, if we could know God. Let it not be replied to us, that Mr. Parker has told us elsewhere, that we may know God, that we may approach the Infinite One face to face ; for, if he unhappily contradicts himself, that is not our fault. He says, formally, that we can know nothing of material things but their phenomena,—also that God is the substantiality of matter, and if of matter, of course of material things. To this we hold him. The truth here got the better of his theorizing, and the man had the courage to tell it. It is idle to talk of man's power to cognize the infinite, to behold God intuitively, while you tell us that such is the limited nature of man's faculties, that even in material things he takes notice only of phenomena. In this last, Mr. Parker is right. We know only phenomena; and substances, essences, only as we by reason infer them from the phenomena. Hence, in the Blessed Eucharist, though our senses, our own faculties, show us only the phenomena or the accidents of bread and wine, we are still able to believe, under those accidents, under those phenomena, there is no substance of bread, no substance of wine, but the substance of the body and blood, soul and divinity of our Lord and Saviour.

But, however this may be, it is evident, from what we have said, that, whether we define the ultimate fact in religion to be the sense of dependence, or a consciousness of the infinite, it is not, and cannot be, an element of nature. Neither notorious facts, nor consciousness, nor philosophical analysis of man's nature proves Mr. Parker's position, that religion has its principle and cause in an element of human nature.

But we go still further, and deny the existence of religious phenomena themselves, in the sense in which Mr. Parker and the transcendentalists assert them. They contend that the so-called religious phenomena differ not merely as to their object from all other psychological phenomena, but also as to their subjective principle. This they must do, or else the existence of the phenomena would not warrant the induction of a special element of human nature as their subjective principle. If, for instance, the religious phenomena differ from the other phenomena only as to their object, then their existence would imply no special element in the soul in which they subjectively originate.

Now, we demand the proof of the existence of religious phenomena that are subjectively distinct from other phenomena not denominated religious. Mr. Parker defines the ultimate fact of religion to be a *sense* of dependence, that is, mental perception or apprehension of the fact that we are dependent. Is this sense or apprehension, in so far as sense or apprehension, essentially different from the sense or apprehension of other facts? Or take the other definition, consciousness of the infinite,—is this consciousness, as consciousness, regarded solely in relation to the conscient agent, different from consciousness in any other case? If not, how can Mr. Parker allege that we have in this sense religious phenomena specifically distinct, on the side of their subjective principle, from all other phenomena presented in human history?

In the passage quoted above from Mr. Parker, we find the religious sentiment identified with the sensation we experience " when a sudden calamity overtakes us," " at a wedding or a funeral," " by a mountain or a waterfall," " in the twilight gloom of the primitive forest," or in the solitude of our own self-communings. What is there, then, peculiar in the religious sentiment?

The religious phenomena, under the point of view we are now considering them, may, according to Mr. Parker, be classed under three heads; namely, love, reverence, obedience. But love, on its subjective side, is the same, whatever the object to which it is directed. Love to God, save as to its object, is not essentially different from love to our neighbour. Reverence, as simple reverence, is the same whether directed towards one object or another. Obedience to God, as obedience, differs not from obedience to the magistrate. Indeed, we are aware of no phenomena which are peculiarly religious, save in the intention with which we exhibit them, and the object for the sake of which we exhibit them. We pray to God; we pray also to man. Prayer is simply asking a favor; and we ask favors of man as well as of God. We sing praises to God, so also to the conquering hero, or to the father of our country; and who dares say that we may not with the same power sing the one praises and the other? We offer sacrifice to God, and ought to offer sacrifice to no other being, because sacrifice is the peculiar, the distinctive, act of divine worship; and yet we can offer sacrifice to an idol, if we choose, and the sacrifice in the one case will not differ *psychologically* from what it is in the other.

If this be so, all this talk about a special religious element of man's nature is—talk, and nothing else. By the faculty of loving wherewith we love man, can we love God; and by the same power by which we sacrifice to the Supreme God, may we, if we choose, sacrifice to idols of wood and stone. The religious phenomena are peculiar, distinct from all the other phenomena man exhibits, we admit,—not because they proceed from a peculiar, distinct, special element of human nature, but because they are exhibited for the sake of a peculiar, distinct, and special end, contemplated in the exhibition of no other class of phenomena. With the same tongue we bless God and curse man; with the same power of will we will good and will evil; with the same intellectual power recognize we a man, a horse, an ox, a tree, a mathematical theorem, a metaphysical principle, and a moral precept. There is, then, no need of assuming a special element of human nature to account for the religious phenomena.

So much for the religious sentiment as an element of human nature. We proceed now to the Idea of religion. The idea is the idea of God; and this idea, according to Mr. Parker, is not obtained by reasoning *a priori*, or *a posteriori*, but is a primitive fact given us immediately in our nature. Here we let Mr. Parker speak for himself.

"Now the existence of this religious element of this sense of dependence, this sentiment of something without bounds, is itself a proof by implication of the existence of its object,—something on which dependence rests. A belief in this relation between the feeling in us and its object independent of us comes unavoidably from the laws of man's nature. There is nothing of which we can be more certain. A natural want in man's constitution implies satisfaction in some quarter, just as the faculty of seeing implies something to correspond to this faculty, namely, objects to be seen and a medium of light to see by. As the tendency to love implies something lovely for its object, so the religious sentiment implies its object; if it is regarded as a sense of absolute dependence, it implies the absolute on which this dependence rests, independent of ourselves.

"Now spiritual, like bodily faculties, act jointly and not one at a time; and when the occasion is given us from without, reason, spontaneously, independent of our forethought and volition, acting by its own laws, gives us by intuition an idea of that on which we depend. To this idea we give the name God, or Gods, as it is represented by one or several separate conceptions. Thus the existence of God is implied by the natural sense of dependence in the religious sentiment itself; it is expressed by the spontaneous intuition of reason itself.

"Now, men come to this idea early. It is the logical condition of all other ideas; without this as an element of our consciousness, or lying latent, as it were, and unrecognized in us, we could have no ideas at all. The senses reveal to us something external to the body, and independent thereof, on which it depends; they tell not what it is. Consciousness reveals something in like manner,—not the soul, but the absolute ground of the soul, on which the soul depends. Outward circumstances furnish the occasion by which we approach and discover the idea of God: but they do not furnish the idea itself. That is a fact given by the nature of man. Hence, some philosophers have called it an innate idea; others a reminiscence of what the soul knew in a higher state of life before it took the body. Both opinions may be regarded as rhetorical statements of the truth, that the idea of God is a fact given by man's nature, and not an invention or device of ours. The belief in God's existence therefore is natural, not against nature. It comes unavoidably from the legitimate action of reason and the religious sentiment, just as the belief in light comes from using our eyes, and belief in our existence from mere existence. The knowledge of God's existence, therefore, may be called an intuition of reason, in the language of philosophy; or a revelation from God, in the language of the elder theology.

"If the above statement be correct, then our belief in God's existence does not depend on the *a posteriori* argument, on considerations drawn from the order, fitness, and beauty discovered by observations made in the material world; nor yet on the *a priori* argument, on considerations drawn from the eternal nature of things, and observations made in the spiritual world. It depends primarily on no argument whatever, not on *reasoning*, but *reason*. The fact is given outright, as it were, and comes to the man as soon and as naturally as the belief of his own existence, and is indeed logically inseparable from it, for we cannot be conscious of ourselves except as *dependent* beings."—*Discourse*, pp. 20-23.

This passage is designed expressly to answer the question, How does man come to the idea of God, or how is it that he is in possession of the idea of God, belief in the existence of God, or knowledge of the existence of God? To this question, notwithstanding the looseness of the passage, we may say, two answers are given. 1. The idea of God is a primitive *datum* of our nature, or fact given us in our nature itself. 2 It is an intuitive perception of God,—"given us," as he says in the following page, "by intuition." These two answers Mr. Parker evidently regards as one and the same, and with him a fact given us in our nature and a fact of intuition mean one and the same thing. This shows that he is not far advanced in his philosophy, and that he but imperfectly comprehends the meaning of the words he uses. A fact given us in our nature must, if it mean any thing, mean an essential element or principle of our nature as human nature, the absence of which cannot be conceived without implying the absence or essential change of our nature itself. An intuition is a fact of experience, a simple intellectual act, the immediate perception of an object; that is, perception of an idea or object, without another idea or object as the medium of its perception. An intuition of reason can only mean the immediate perception of an object of reason as distinguished from an object of external sense. Whether in this last sense there are any intuitions of reason, that is, whether we have immediate perception of any non-sensible objects, may be a question, or rather in our mind is no question; but it is certain, that, if the idea of God be an intuition, it cannot be a fact given us in our nature; for since it is an act, it must be subsequent to the nature that acts. The intuitive nature, the intuitive subject, must precede it, be independent of it, and complete without it. It requires very little philosophy to know this. Mr. Parker cannot, then, insist on its being both. Which he will decide in favor of we know not; but we deny that it is either.

1. The idea of God is a fact given us in our nature. By this, we repeat, Mr. Parker does not mean that the idea of God may be merely inferred from a fact or facts of our nature, but that it is itself a fact of our nature; for he tells us it depends on no argument, no reasoning, but is given us outright in our nature. Now, to this we object (*a.*), that no *idea* can properly, in the sense Mr. Parker uses the term, be considered a fact of nature. Idea must be taken either objectively or subjectively. Taken objectively, as it is by Plato, it means the form or essence of the thing in question, that which distinguishes it from all other things, determines it to be what it is, and is that which, in knowing it, must be the real object known. In this case, the idea is simply the object known, and the idea of God would not be a belief or knowledge of the existence of God, but would be the object of such belief or knowledge. But this is not the sense in which Mr. Parker uses the term; for we may learn from the passage quoted, that, what in one place he calls the *idea* of God, he in another calls *belief* in the existence of God, and in still another, *knowledge* of the existence of God. He evidently understands the term in a subjective sense, and designates by it a fact in the mind, not the object of that fact. But, subjectively, idea is simply apprehension, notion, or conception of some object existing, or believed to exist, out of the mind. It is, then, a fact of experience, an act

performed by the intelligent subject, and therefore cannot be a fact or principle of the intelligent nature itself. If Mr. Parker understands the word subjectively, then idea of God is not a fact given in our nature, any more than is the idea of a horse, a mountain, or a book. If he understands it objectively, then the idea of God is God himself, and cannot be a fact of our nature, unless God himself is a fact of our nature, which not even Mr. Parker will dare assert. So, take the word either objectively or subjectively, it cannot designate a fact given us in our nature itself.

(*b.*) According to Mr. Parker's own account of it, the *idea* of God cannot be a fact given us in our nature, for he makes it depend on the sense of dependence. His assertion is, that the sense of dependence implies it. He himself makes it a deduction from the sense of dependence. "The sense of dependence is a proof by implication," he says, "of something on which dependence rests. . . . . . . A natural want in our constitution implies satisfaction in some quarter. . . . . . . As the tendency to love implies something lovely for its object, so the religious sentiment implies its object." Now, admit, what is not true, that the sense of dependence is a fact, element, or principle of our nature,—the idea of God, which Mr. Parker defines to be "an idea of that on which we depend," is only a deduction, a logical inference, from a fact of our nature. It is obtained only by analyzing the idea of dependence, and drawing forth from it what it logically contains. Consequently, the idea of God cannot be said to be given us outright in our nature, prior to, or independent of, all reasoning.

(*c.*) But, even admitting that the idea of that on which we depend is given us in the sense of dependence, explicitly, not merely implicitly,—the idea of that, or of a somewhat, on which we depend is not equivalent to the idea of God. To the idea of this, Mr. Parker says, men give the name God. This is not true; for the idea of God, as the race entertains, and always has entertained it, is the idea of a supreme power from which we spring, to which we are subject, and for which—*propter quem*—we are bound to live, which is more than the mere idea of a somewhat on which we depend, which is merely the complement of ourselves. (*d.*) And, even passing over this, admitting that the idea of a somewhat on which we depend is equivalent to the idea of God, and that it is given immediately in the sense of dependence, it is, nevertheless, not a fact given us immediately in our nature,—for the sense of dependence itself is not a fact of our nature, as we have already proved, but merely a deduction from certain facts of our experience. We find by experience that we are limited, that we cannot do what we will, that we are insufficient for ourselves, and *therefore* infer that we are not self-sustained, but are dependent beings, and therefore, again, that there must needs be something on which we depend, and which does not depend on us.

That this something on which we depend, and which does not depend on us, is God, we, of course, do not deny; but the idea of something not dependent on us, and on which we depend, is yet, considered *in se*, far below the idea of God, and can only by a long chain of induction, to which only a few gifted minds are equal, be shown to imply it. The idea of God is not, we say, therefore, a fact given us in our nature, a primitive *datum*.

2. The same arguments we have used to prove that the idea of God is not a fact given us in our nature, or, at least, all but one of them, prove equally that it is not an intuition. Mr. Parker offers no evidence of its being an intuition, but the fact that it is implied in the sense of dependence, and that men have entertained it before they could have demonstrated it, either by the argument *a priori* or the argument *a posteriori*. Admit the first, and it proves nothing to his purpose; for an idea which is given only as implied in another is not given by intuition, even though that other idea be itself intuitive. An intuitive idea is not an implicit, but an explicit, idea. An implicit idea is merely an idea involved or contained in another, and is obtained through that other as its medium; but intuitive ideas are not given through the medium of other ideas. They are given immediately, or else they are discursive, not intuitive. Moreover, the sense of dependence, assumed to give implicitly the idea of God, is not even itself intuitive, as we have just seen, but a logical deduction from facts of experience. Even admitting, then, that an idea implied in another may be an intuitive idea, the idea of God is not intuitive, since the idea which implies it is not intuitive.

The second proof alleged begs the question. The human race may have entertained, and no doubt have entertained, the idea of God prior to having demonstrated the existence of God; but this does not prove the intuitive origin of the idea of God; for the idea may have been communicated, in the first instance, supernaturally, by God himself, as is alleged by the universal traditions of the race. Mr. Parker must prove that the idea could not have been communicated in this or in any way other than the one he assumes, before, from the fact that the human race has entertained the idea prior to having demonstrated it, he can conclude to its intuitive origin.

But it is unnecessary to dwell longer on this point; for it is evident from what we have already said, that man has, and can have, no intuitive perception of God. Indeed, Mr. Parker concedes this; for he says in a note, p. 24, that the idea of God may be called a judgment *a priori*. Now, if it is a judgment *a priori*, it is not an intuitive perception; for the intuitive idea can never precede, either historically or logically, the actual perception of the object. Consequently, no intuitive idea is or can be a judgment *a priori*, that is, a judgment which logically precedes every real or possible fact of experience.

Nevertheless, we do not admit that the idea of God is a judgment *a priori*; for we do not admit the reality of any judgments *a priori*. A judgment is an act, and always implies an act of discrimination, and therefore, from its very nature, cannot precede intuition of the matter or matters discriminated. The Kantian doctrine on this subject is more specious than solid, and involves us in a new difficulty greater than that from which it proposes to extricate us. What Kant calls judgments or cognitions *a priori* are nothing but the properties, the essential qualities, so to speak, of the subjective faculty of intelligence, — and therefore are not ideas, judgments, or cognitions, but, at best, the subjective ability to form ideas, judgments, or cognitions.

But all this reasoning is unnecessary, for Mr. Parker concedes the whole question in debate. "We can know God only in part,— from the manifestations of his divinity, *seen* in nature, *felt* in man."—p. 160. Even he will not, we think, after this, dare maintain that the idea of God is an intuitive perception; for the existence of a being knowable only through the medium of his manifestations, that is, of his works, is not and cannot be an object of intuitive perception.

The idea of God, Mr. Parker tells us, " is the logical condition of all our other ideas; without this as an element of our consciousness, lying latent, as it were, unrecognized in us, we could have no *ideas* at all." Consciousness is the state or condition of being conscious. An element of consciousness must be a fact of which we are always and invariably conscious, when we are conscious at all. To be conscious is to know, to recognize. If the idea of God be an element or fact of consciousness, it must be a fact of which we are always and invariably conscious when we are conscious at all, and, therefore, cannot lie latent or unrecognized in us.

The *idea* is either subjective or objective. It is not in this case objective, as before proved, and as is evident from the fact that Mr. Parker makes it synonymous with belief or knowledge. It is, then, subjective. Then it is the *notion* or *conception* of the existence of God. Then it is not latent or unrecognized; for no notion or conception exists when not recognized, since its very being is in its recognition. The power to form the notion, but not the notion itself, may lie latent, unrecognized in us; and this is all that Descartes teaches, when he calls the idea of God innate, that is, that we have the innate power to rise to a conception of God's existence.

But we must tell Mr. Parker that he not only fails to prove that the idea of God is a fact given us in our nature, that it is a judgment *a priori*, that it is an intuitive perception, but he does not even show that the existence of God is demonstrable. On his principles of reasoning, from the facts he alleges, we cannot logically even conclude to the existence of God. "A natural want in our constitution," he says, "implies satisfaction in some quarter." If our constitution be assumed to be the work of an all-wise, powerful, and good creator, we grant the conclusion,—otherwise we deny it; for, till it is known that the author of our nature would not or could not implant in us a want for which he makes no provision, the existence of the want is no evidence of satisfaction. It implies the *need* of satisfaction, but not that there is satisfaction. "The tendency to love implies something lovely as its object." *If it is to be satisfied*,—otherwise not. But how do you know that it is to be satisfied? "So the religious sentiment implies its object." If it is to be satisfied,—not otherwise. In itself considered, taken independently of the assumption of a God who has implanted it, and who would not have implanted it without providing satisfaction for it, it merely proves the need of some object,—not that the object really exists. The argument, then, on which Mr. Parker relies is without validity, and is no demonstration of the existence of God.

But we do not stop here. Granting the religious sentiment and the idea of God, that is, the sense of dependence and idea of its object, are facts, elements, or principles of human nature, we deny that religion is a fact or principle of human nature, or that even then there is any thing in our nature in which religion can be assumed to originate.

Mr. Parker's thesis is not, that the principles of religion may be deduced, by reasoning, from the facts of human nature, but that religion originates spontaneously in those facts, independently of our will or foresight. It is, so to speak, a natural production of the essential facts or elements of human nature. This is his thesis, and to this we hold him.

Now, the two facts, sense of dependence and idea of its object, do not authorize, but impugn, Mr. Parker's own definition of religion. Absolute, that is, perfect religion, he tells us (p. 46), is "voluntary obedience to the law of God, inward and outward obedience to the law he has written on our nature." Here is an element very essential, namely, voluntary obedience, not included in the sense of dependence and idea of its object, and which they do not and cannot generate. Doubtless, a man, by reasoning upon all the facts of his nature, by ascertaining that he is a dependent being, and that that on which he depends is God, and that God is his rightful lawgiver, his sovereign, may come very legitimately to the conclusion that he ought to obey God; but this is nothing to the purpose. There can be, according to Mr. Parker's thesis, nothing in religion not spontaneously generated by the two facts of human nature assumed. These operate naturally, independently of will and foresight, from their own inherent force. Voluntary obedience, if essential to religion, must be their spontaneous production, to which volition and reasoning are not necessary, nay, from which they are excluded. But this is impossible; for there is and can be no voluntary obedience, where will and foresight are excluded.

If religion be voluntary obedience, it is not and cannot be a fact of human nature, nor the spontaneous product of a fact of human nature, for it must be a free creation of the human will. If not, the obedience would not be voluntary, but necessary. How, then, obtain the idea of religion as voluntary obedience from the two facts of human nature assumed? But if it is to be regarded as the sense of dependence and idea of its object, or as growing spontaneously out of them, it cannot be voluntary, but must be necessary. By what right, then, does Mr. Parker define religion to be voluntary obedience? And wherefore does he labor to prove that religion is all included in the sense of dependence and idea of its object, when he finds himself obliged to include in its definition an element not even implied by them, and repugnant to them as the essential elements of religion?

But this definition, all too broad as it is for Mr. Parker's thesis, is altogether defective. It has the merit of recognizing the province of the will. In making religion *voluntary* obedience, Mr. Parker makes it a virtue, and therefore rejects the transcendental theory, according to which religion is not a virtue, since it recognizes, as essential to it, no *actus humanus*. This definition shows that he, after all, retains something better than transcendentalism, and has not quite lost all sense of religion. Nevertheless, the definition is defective, and its rejection of transcendentalism more in appearance than in reality. The serpent lies coiled at the bottom, ready, if you penetrate too far, to spring upon you. Religion is defined to be voluntary obedience; but obedience to what? Simply to our own nature. Mr. Parker says, obedience to the law of God; but we must not suffer ourselves to be deceived by his rhetorical flourishes. The law of God is, he himself says, simply the law which Almighty God has written on our nature, which is merely the law of our nature, that is, our nature itself. Hence, religion is voluntary obedience to our nature,—which means, in the last analysis, that it is the surrender of ourselves up to our instinctive nature, to do simply what it moves or impels us to do. This is transcendentalism in full bloom, whether Mr. Parker intended it or not.

Now, Mr. Parker, in using the term religion, is bound to use it in its received sense. Saving his responsibility, he is free to accept or reject that sense, but not free to reject it and still retain the term. If he does not retain, in his definition of religion, all that is essential to religion in its generally received sense, he does not retain religion; if he rejects what is essential to religion, as the term is generally understood by mankind, he rejects religion. That which he retains may be true, may be all he ought to retain, or it may not be; but it is not religion, and he has no right to call it religion. Now, religion, in its generally received sense, is the acknowledgment and worship of the Deity. It may mean more than this, but less it cannot. As Mr. Parker will not quarrel with us about the unity of God, we may say the acknowledgment of the Deity is the recognition of, and expression of our belief in, the existence and providence of God; and the worship of God implies not only the acknowledgment of his being and providence, but the performing certain acts or services, external or internal, believed to be his due and *because* his due. Mr. Parker is familiar enough with the religious history of mankind to know that the race has always meant by religion at least all that is implied in this definition. Then, if what he calls religion does not amount to this, it is not religion. But what he calls religion does not amount to this, and cannot be obtained from the principles which he admits.

In Mr. Parker's definition of religion, not even the being of God is necessarily implied, but simply the *idea* of God, which is alleged to be a fact of human nature. But, in this definition, not only the being of God, but his providence, is implied. Now, the idea of the providence of God, essential to religion, is not included in Mr. Parker's definition of religion; neither when he defines it to be the sense of dependence and idea of its object, nor when he defines it to be voluntary obedience to the law of our nature. Will he tell us how, from the two facts of our nature, or from voluntary obedience, he can then obtain it? The two facts, according to him, ought to generate it spontaneously; for nothing can be essential to religion but these and their spontaneous productions. But will he show us how, even by logic, we can obtain from these the idea of providence? If not,—and he cannot,—they are not themselves religion, nor able to give us religion; for there is no religion, where there is no belief in providence.

Moreover, Mr. Parker nowhere in his book recognizes God's providence. None but a personal being, acting voluntarily, and for the sake of an end, can exercise providence, —that is, care for, watch over, and provide for his creatures. But Mr. Parker expressly denies the personality of God, speaks of the Divinity as an abstraction, applies to him pronouns of the neuter gender, and even refuses to allow him consciousness, save potentially. "God, as absolute cause," he says, "contains in himself"—he should have said *itself*, to have preserved consistency—"potentially the ground of consciousness and personality, yes, and of unconsciousness and impersonality. But to apply these terms to him seems to me a vain attempt to sound the abyss of the Godhead."—p. 165. He denies, by implication, the propriety of prayer (p. 167), though we have heard that he himself goes, at times, through the form of prayer, whether with "his eyes fixed devoutly on himself" or not, our informants do not report. "God," he says (p. 170), "is the substantiality of matter"; p. 182, "as he is the materiality of matter, so is he the spirituality of spirit." We do not suppose he understands the full import of the words he uses; but it is evident, that, so far as he conceives of God at all, he conceives of him not as a free, voluntary being, acting with a purpose, and for the sake of an end, but as a mighty force or energy developing itself through all infinities *ad finem*, it may be, but simply according to its own inherent laws, from the necessity of its own nature, not from freedom of will. He calls him Being, Cause, Knowledge, Love, but never one who is, causes, knows, loves; consequently, never represents him as a being who is capable of exercising a providential care. We may say, then, that his notion of religion does not include the idea of providence, and therefore does not include all that is essential to religion.

Again, the definition of religion, as generally received, involves the idea of *obligation*. We worship God, because we *owe* him a service. In worshipping him, we are simply rendering him his *due*, and we worship him for the sake of paying what we owe. But is the conception of obligation, of a debt due and to be paid, contained in the sense of dependence and idea of its object, or even deducible from them? Of course not. No alchemy can transmute either or both of them into the idea of obligation, nor can either or both of them generate it.

These two facts, if obeyed, cannot lead to the worship of God, because what we do in obedience to them we do *ex necessitate naturæ*, not from reason and will. The acts we should perform would not be acts of worship, because they would not be done for the sake of worshipping God, that is, of rendering him his due. Then, unless they can give us of themselves the idea of obligation, that we owe God a service, they cannot be the essential elements of religion, and we might have them and still have no religion, and nothing able to give us religion. But instinctive, involuntary, themselves, operating without will or foresight, it is evident they do not contain, and cannot give, the idea of obligation, and thus furnish the *motive*, without which no act is or can be religious.

Mr. Parker nowhere, so far as we have discovered, asserts the obligation to worship God. He does not seem to admit that man is *morally* bound at all to worship God. The only obligation he seems to recognize is the obligation of man to obey his own nature,—that is, to cease to be man as rapidly as possible, and descend from a person to a thing. God is nowhere represented as demanding any service of man; man nowhere said to *owe* God any thing; man is merely to study nature and himself,—ascertain and act out his own nature. The law in his nature is all the law there is for him, and religion is nothing but the harmonious action of all his faculties (p. 241). But the ground of *this* obligation is nowhere given, or, if given, is not represented to be the fact that God wills it, and that we are to obey ourselves for the sake of obeying him.

It is, then, false to assume, that the two facts, sense of dependence and idea of its object, include all that is essential to religion. They do not include, and cannot give us, the two essential elements of religion, namely, the idea of providence and that of obligation. They disclose no ground for worship in the providence of God; they suggest no service to God, to be given *because* his due. They are not religion, then, and cannot, of themselves alone, give us religion.

But we are not yet done with Mr. Parker's theory. We have shown that it cannot give us religion; we now assert that it is repugnant to religion, and, if admitted as true, would enable us to account for all religious phenomena without assuming even the existence of God. "Two things," says Mr. Parker, "are necessary to render religion possible; a religious nature in man, and God out of man, as the object of that nature. These two facts admitted, religion follows necessarily, as vision from the existence of a seeing faculty in man, and that of light out of him. Now, the existence of the religious element implies its object. We have naturally a sentiment of God. Reason gives us an idea of him. These are founded in our nature, and are in themselves unchangeable, always the same."—p. 159. This sounds well; but the sentiment of God, the religious sentiment, we must remember, is the sense of dependence, and the idea of God is merely the idea of something on which dependence rests. The sense and the idea are both facts of our nature, facts given us in our nature. Our nature being given, then, both these facts are given. Then man being given, all is given that is essential to religion. Then Mr. Parker is quite too liberal in allowing the existence of God out of man as necessary to religion. The existence of God is quite superfluous, and quite unphilosophically assumed; for philosophy admits no more causes for a fact than are necessary. If religion, then, be the facts of our nature, or their spontaneous production, it requires the admission of no existence but man, and can dispense with God altogether.

But Mr. Parker replies, "The sentiment implies its object." Not if its existence can be accounted for without assuming its object; and this can be done, if it be a fact of man's nature; for, man's nature given, it is given. Moreover, as we have seen, the sentiment only implies the *necessity* of an object to satisfy it, not that the object exists. It implies the necessity of its object, not as the condition of its existence, but simply as the condition of its satisfaction. Here is a point Mr. Parker probably overlooked.

But the sentiment is said to be the sentiment of God, and therefore necessarily implies that God is. The sentiment in question is defined, officially, to be the sense of dependence. Strictly speaking, the object of the *sense* is *dependence*, and therefore, even admitting the sense or sentiment implies its object, it does not necessarily imply God, unless God and dependence are one and the same.

"But reason gives us the idea of God." This amounts to nothing; because reason gives it, not because it sees the object of the idea, or demonstrates from certain *data* that God is. The idea is said to be a fact given in our nature, and therefore antecedently to all exercise of reason. It is simply a fact or property of the rational subject, and is given in the idea of the subject,—consequently, does not necessarily imply God out of the subject. Before you can conclude from the idea to a reality outside of man responding to it, you must estabish the principle, that no idea is, or can be, given in human nature. But establish this, then the idea of God is not given as a fact of human nature. But this is to deny your own assertion. Therefore you have no right to conclude from the idea of God to the existence of God.

It is clear, therefore, that, if you reduce religion to the sense of dependence and idea of its object, and declare these to be facts, elements, or principles of human nature, you have no occasion to assume any existence, in order to account for religion,—to give you all of religion,—but that of man himself. But, if there be no God, all religion is a delusion. Consequently, the attempt to find in human nature a solid and imperishable foundation for religion ends in showing that it has no foundation at all. Alas! man is a poor foundation to build any thing upon. The wise master-builder will seek some other foundation,—even the Rock of Ages.

Again, Mr. Parker has no occasion to assume the existence of God as an object of obedience. When he defines religion to be voluntary obedience, he defines it to be obedience to the law of our own nature. Our nature given, this law is given, and all is given, and contained in it. There is no need, then, of introducing the cumbrous machinery of a God. Man is what he is. He is all his nature is. His nature is all that is essential to it, or essential elements of it. All that is essential to religion is essential in his nature. Man, then, is it all, and all that is essential to religion is given without assuming any existence beyond him. Do not tell us, then, that to religion it is necessary that there should be a God out of man, for to religion, in your sense, it is not necessary. Man is enough for your purpose. With man, therefore, try and content yourself.

This conclusion is inevitable, when the essential elements of religion are made essential elements of human nature. The transcendentalists, we are willing to admit,—for we were ourselves the first in this country to set forth on this point the doctrine we have ascribed to them,—have been governed by good motives, and have really wished to defend religion against the infidel. But they have begun at the wrong end. That man is led by the wants of his nature to seek after some support, and by his reason to recognize a God who has made him and for whom he should live, we do not deny,—though we do not believe, that, as a matter of fact, he first attained in this way to the idea of God; for the belief in the existence of God is too early found, too universal, and too firmly rooted in the human mind, to have originated in so long and so difficult a process. That man's own experience of his own insufficiency, of his nothingness, of the fact that he is everywhere limited, hemmed in, which may be called a sense of dependence, and which all must, to a greater or less degree, experience, is among the first and chief causes that lead him "through nature up to nature's God," we are willing to admit, and much that Mr. Parker says on this head, when not taken in support of his theory, is no doubt true, and even impressive; but the doctrine, that religion is a fact of our nature, or has its origin in our permanent nature, if it mean any thing more than a rhetorical flourish for the fact, that the constantly recurring facts of human experience have a strong tendency to impress us with a sense of our own dependence, and to lead us to look out of ourselves for some independent support,—

which, after all, we suspect, may be what Mr. Parker really means,—is essentially repugnant to the very idea of religion. The sense of dependence and idea of its object are not elements of religion; they are simply facts which lead us to seek religion, and which, perhaps, facilitate its acceptance and observance.

To place religion in these is to deprive it of all moral character, and to render it in itself nothing worth. Mr. Parker may extol the religious sentiment and idea as he will, but, as he defines them, they do not necessarily involve a single moral or religious conception. Man is religious, not by virtue of his *nature*, but of his *acts*. He is placed, not by his *nature*, but by his *Creator*, under a law; and he is religious only in obeying that law, and in obeying it *because* it is God's law. The natural powers by which he obeys, so far as his obedience depends on himself as the obedient subject, are the same as those by which he obeys his parents or the magistrate. He must have reason, by which to perceive the law, and to perceive it as God's law,—and will, by which to will its obedience; but these are not powers brought into play only by religion; they are brought into play in every act which is properly an *actus humanus*.

The transcendentalists, overlooking this fact,—that religion, so far as it depends on man, depends on the rational and voluntary nature,—seek to find its origin in the sensitive nature. Having begun with the principle, that reason and will are to be discarded, and sentiment only retained, and having ascertained that sentiment operates instinctively without will or reason, they have fancied it would afford a more solid and respectable foundation for religion than the inductions of reason and the resolutions of the will. What they really want is to find an origin for religion which is under shelter from human will and reason. This is obvious in all their writings. Thus, Mr. Parker resolves religion into a sentiment and idea both given by our nature, independently of all exercise of will or reason. Placed in the instinctive nature, they really believe religion is raised above us, because, according to them, the instinctive nature is always to be regarded as supreme and authoritative.

But if we examine this doctrine more closely, we find, that, though it adopts, now and then, religious names, it embraces no religious ideas. " The legitimate action of the religious sentiment," says Mr. Parker, " produces reverence."
—p. 44. The religious sentiment is the sense of depend-

ence. Where is the proof that the sense of dependence produces reverence? But suppose it does. What is the quality of this reverence? Like produces like. The reverence that springs from a sentiment must be itself a sentiment. It is a sensible emotion. It may be well enough as far as it goes, but it is not reverence in the religious sense. Religious reverence is not a sensible emotion, though it may be accompanied by such emotion, but an affection of the rational and voluntary nature. Even admitting that the sense of dependence should legitimately produce reverence, it would, then, be only a sensible reverence, possessing in itself no religious character.

But this reverence "may *ascend* into Trust, Hope, and Love, which is according to its nature,—or it may descend into Doubt, Fear, Hate, which is *against* its nature. It thus rises or falls as it coexists in the individual with wisdom and goodness, or with ignorance and vice."—p. 44. A man may be religious, either with wisdom and goodness, or with ignorance and vice! Religion can combine and coexist with either. A very accommodating thing, this religion of yours, and worth writing books about! But let this pass. What is the proof that it is more *against* the nature of reverence to descend into doubt, fear, and hate, than it is to rise into trust, hope, and love, when once it is admitted it *can* so descend without ceasing to be reverence? It would relieve the monotony of Mr. Parker's book, if he would now and then prove an assertion.

But the trust, hope, love, into which reverence *may* rise, what are they? Affections of reason and will? Not at all. They are the products of a sentiment, and belong to the sentimental nature. They are not, then, though Mr. Parker writes their initials in capitals, religious affections. They are sensible emotions, or instinctive affections,—not the result of rational apprehension of their object, and voluntary confidence in him and preference of him. They do not, then, rise to the religious order, and are, taken in themselves alone, worth nothing. But even pass over this. Are they produced *for the sake* of God, and offered to him *because* his due? In trusting, hoping, loving, do we ourselves act, and act *propter finem*, and not merely *ad finem*? According to Mr. Parker's whole doctrine, in them we do not properly act,—we but follow our nature, and therefore really render God no service because his due, and therefore perform no religious act; though the acts of trust, hope, love, when done for the sake of God, are unquestionably among the most acceptable acts we can perform.

Here is apparent the grand defect of transcendentalism. It tries to find a religion which borrows nothing from reason and will, and which will go of itself, requiring us to trouble ourselves no further about it than to leave it alone and let nature do her work. In this they are consistent with themselves. Religion should, on their principles, like every thing else, be reduced to instinct, and, like Dogberry's reading and writing, "come by nature." But they should know, that, however good what thus comes may be, it is not religion, and should never be called by that name. Whether they are right or wrong in commending what they thus get is not now the question. The simple question before us is, whether what they dignify with the name of religion is what we are to understand by that venerated word. We think we have shown that it is not, and, if for no other reason, for the reason that in religion we offer a service to God *because* believed to be his due, and his due from us; whereas, in what they propose as religion, we merely follow our nature, and do what we do, not because we see its justice and will it, but because our instinctive nature prompts it. In their religion we act merely *ad finem*, and our acts are, properly speaking, not *human* acts; in religion as we must understand it, if we retain it at all, we act always *propter finem*, therefore not as instinctive, but as rational and voluntary agents. Here is a broad line of distinction, which separates the transcendentalists totally from the religious world. Religion is a *virtus*, and it demands that we remain and act as *men*. Transcendentalism would sink us from men, from beings of rational nature, that is, persons, to mere *automata*, or, at least, to mere sensitive plants. For ourselves, we prefer to remain as we are, of rational nature, and to act as rational beings. If the transcendentalists do not, if they prefer to sink into the category of mere things, be it so; they have not, if they so prefer, far to sink; nor could their responsibility be great, should they remain even as they are.

In our next *Review*, God willing, we shall close our examination of transcendentalism, and be prepared to enter upon the discussion of open, avowed infidelity. Thus far all we have said, whether against high church or low church, no church or transcendentalism, is merely preliminary to the discussion of the real question for our age. Disguise the matter as men will, the real question of the age is between Catholicity and infidelity. Protestantism, with its Protean forms, would excite only universal derision and contempt, did it not afford a *quasi* shelter for the multitudes who wish to conceal their doubts both from themselves and their neighbours. These multitudes are ashamed of their doubts, have a lurking sense that they are wrong, and that they ought to be believers; they therefore seek to hide their doubts from themselves and from one another. To this end, they catch, as drowning men at straws, at one form of Protestantism or another; but most of them feel that they do catch at straws, and nothing else. Protestantism is incapable of satisfying, for a single moment, a mind that thinks and knows how to reason. It needed not to have been born and bred a Protestant to be aware of this. A few women among the Protestants, who silence their doubts by their gentler affections or their religious dissipation, may fancy that they are firm believers; but the great mass of the world, out of the church, are really at heart, we will not say disbelievers, but doubters. The great question, deny it as they may and probably will, which they want settled, is, whether Almighty God has actually made us a revelation of the supernatural order. We know they will not own this, for, as we have said, they are ashamed of their doubts, and do not like to avow them; but if they lay their hands upon their hearts and answer truly, they will confess that we have stated the real question they want settled. Once recall them to faith in the great fact of the Christian revelation, and it will require no labored arguments to bring them into the church. The only two armies now on the great moral battle-field of the world are those of Catholicity and infidelity, and between these the great battle is to be fought. We have felt this from the first, and have entered into the discussions we have, because we wished to carry all the outworks before attacking the citadel. These we think we have now pretty much carried, and whoever will read fairly the articles we have written against Anglicanism, no-churchism, and transcendentalism, will be troubled to find a single stronghold in which he may intrench himself between the Roman Catholic Church and infidelity.

The next article on transcendentalism will commence the war on infidelity, by showing that the facts, or at least a portion of the facts, of the religious history of mankind are not explicable on any hypothesis which excludes the supernatural intervention of Providence, and, therefore, that, on the plainest principles of inductive reasoning, we must admit the supernatural order, and that God has made us a revelation of it. In the meantime we would say, that we, as Catholics, are too well instructed to rely on argument alone for the conversion of unbelievers. No matter who plants and waters, 'tis God alone who gives the increase. The fervent prayers of the faithful, offered in secret, in the solitude of the closet or the cell, will avail more than all the elaborate arguments ever constructed; and one reason why the conversion of unbelievers is not more rapid is because we rely upon ourselves, upon our wisdom and strength, upon human efforts, rather than on Him without whose aid and blessing all labors are thrown away.

ARTICLE III.

In the analysis we gave of the teaching of transcendentalists, we reduced that teaching to three fundamental propositions, namely:—1. Man is the measure of truth and goodness; 2. Religion is a fact or principle of human nature.; 3. All religious institutions, which have been or are, have their principle and cause in human nature. We have disposed of the first and second of these propositions; and there remains for us now to consider and dispose of only the third and last.

Transcendentalism is virtually the ground on which the enemies of the church, generally, are rallying and endeavouring to make a stand, and the ground on which they are to be met and vanquished. Protestantism, as set forth by the early reformers, is virtually no more. It yielded to the well directed blows of Bossuet, and other Catholic divines, in the seventeenth century. But its spirit was not extinguished. It survived, and, in the beginning of the eighteenth century, reappeared in England under the form of infidelity, or the denial of all supernatural revelation from God to men; and, by the aid of Voltaire, Rousseau, and other French *philosophes*, soon passed into France and Germany, and, to no inconsiderable extent, penetrated even into Italy and Spain. Forced to abandon the form with which it had been clothed by Luther and Calvin, and their associates, it found it could subsist and maintain its influence only by falling back on natural religion, and finally, on no religion. But this did not long avail it. The world protested against incredulity, and the human race would not consent to regard itself as a "child without a sire," condemned to eternal orphanage. Either Protestantism must assume the semblance at least of religion, or yield up the race once more to Catholicity. But the latter alternative was more than could be expected of human pride and human weakness. The reform party could not willingly forego all their dreams of human perfectibility, "the march of mind," "the progress of the species," the realization of what they called "Liberty, Equality, Fraternity," which they had emblazoned on their banners, and in the name of which they had established the Reign of Terror, and drenched Europe in her noblest and richest blood. To abandon these glorious dreams, these sublime hopes, to bow down their lofty heads before priests and monks, to sheathe the sword and embrace the cross, to give up the Age of Reason, and readmit the Age of Faith, was a sacrifice too great for poor human nature. Yet what other alternative was left? The race demanded a religion,—would have some kind of faith and worship. To stand on open, avowed infidel ground was impossible. To return to the elder Protestantism was also impossible, for that had ceased to exist; and if it had not, a return to it would have been only subjecting itself anew to the necessity of going further, and reuniting with Rome, or of falling back once more on deism, and then on atheism. It must, then, either vanish in thin air, or invent some new form of error, which, in appearance at least, should be neither the Protestantism of the sixteenth century nor the unbelief of the eighteenth. The last hope of the party was in the invention of this new form. Germany, mother of the reformation, saw the extremities to which it was reduced, and charged herself with conceiving and bringing it forth, as sin conceives and brings forth death. The period of gestation was brief; the child was forthwith ushered into the world. France applauded; young America hurraed; and even old England pricked up her ears, and calculated the practical advantages she might derive from adopting the bantling.

The bantling is named transcendentalism, and not inappropriately. The name defines the thing. The reform party found itself compelled to avoid in appearance alike the younger infidelity and the older Protestantism, and both without any advance towards Catholicity. It must neither assert nor deny revelation, and yet must do both in the same breath; it must be a believer to the believer, an unbeliever to the unbeliever; appear to the Christian to assert the supernatural order, to the infidel to admit only the natural order; and thus reconcile all repugnances, harmonize all discords, and lay the firm and imperishable foundation of "union and progress." The task was, no doubt, difficult and delicate; but life or death was at stake; and the reform party showed itself equal to the emergency. It boldly faced the difficulty, and solved, it, in general terms, by asserting that the soul is furnished with a transcendental faculty, or power which transcends the senses and intellect, and places us in immediate relation with the world of spirit, as the senses do with the world of matter. This faculty receives various names, but all agree in asserting its reality; some call it instinct, some spontaneity, some consciousness, some the divine in the human, and others reason, distinguishing, or attempting to distinguish, between reason and understanding. These last suppose understanding to be in the centre of the human subject; on one side the five senses, through which the material world flows into it,—and on the other, reason, through which flows in the spiritual world, or world of absolute and necessary truth. But, as all admit the reality of a faculty transcending the understanding and senses, however diversely named or defined, they are all denominated transcendentalists, and their doctrine, transcendentalism,—that is, a doctrine founded on that which transcends or surpasses sense and understanding.

According to Mr. Parker, this transcendental faculty is a sort of pipe, or conduit, through which the Divinity flows naturally into the human soul. The soul has a double set of faculties, one set on each side. Each at the terminus is furnished with a valve, which the soul opens and shuts at will. If it opens one set, the external world flows in, and it lives a purely material or animal life; if the other, the Divinity flows in, it becomes filled to its capacity with God, and lives a divine life. As the pipe or conduit through which the Divinity is let in is a natural endowment essential to the soul, and as we open or close its valve, and let in or shut out God at will, the "supply of God" obtained is said to be obtained *naturally*, and as it is really God who runs in and fills the soul, the influx is said to be *divine*, or *divine* inspiration. As it is of God, and received through a natural inlet in a natural manner, it is *natural* inspiration, and distinguishable, on the one hand, from the mere light of nature, and on the other, from *supernatural* inspiration, and may be termed, if you will, natural supernaturalism, natural spiritualism, or "the natural *religious* view."

Religious institutions are constructed by the human intellect and passions, on the ideas of God furnished the soul through this natural channel. They are the more or less successful efforts of men to realize outwardly as well as inwardly the ideas and sentiments of God, of spirit, of the true, permanent, eternal, and absolute, which are supplied by this natural influx of God. Considered in their idea and sentiment, all religious institutions are true, sacred, divine, immutable, and eternal; but considered solely as institutions, they are human, partial, incomplete, variable, and transitory. They may even, as institutions, in relation to their time and place, when they are in harmony with the actual intelligence of the race and respond to the actual wants of the soul, be useful and legitimate. They spring from, at least are occasioned by, what is purest and best in the human soul, and do, then, really embody its highest conceptions of what is highest and holiest.

It is not necessary to denounce the race for having formed to itself religious institutions, nor even to denounce religious institutions themselves, regarded in relation to their legitimate time and place. We should rather view them with indulgence and seek to explain them, to ascertain their real significance, the great and eternal ideas they are intended to symbolize. It is foolish, for instance, to unite with the unbelievers of the last century in their denunciations of the Bible. We should accept the sacred books of Christians; ay, and of all nations,—the Veda, the Zendavesta, the writings of Confucius, the Koran, and the Book of Mormon. All are the sincere and earnest efforts of the soul to utter the Divinity with which it is filled, and each in its degree, and after its manner, is authentic Scripture. Every sincere utterance of an earnest soul is a divine word; for every sincere soul is filled with God, with an elemental fire, and is big with a divine message. Hence the worth of sincere souls; hence the importance of studying individualities, what is peculiar, exceptional, without regard to what is common to men in general. If you are a true man, you can make us a new revelation of God. What can you tell us? Under what new and peculiar phase can you show us the Universal Being? In what new tone are you able to speak?

As all religious institutions have a common origin in the soul, and do, in their degree and after their manner, shadow forth the same idea and sentiment, they are all, as to their idea and sentiment, identical. Mumbo-Jumbo of the African, or Manitou of the North American savage, is, at bottom, the true God, as much as the Zeus of the Greeks, the Jupiter of the Romans,—and either of these as much as the Jehovah of the Jews, or God the Father of the Christians. One or another is nothing but the form with which, in different ages and in different nations, men clothe the eternal and immutable idea of the highest and best, which is the same in all ages and nations and in all individuals. The difference is all in the form; there is none in the idea. Mumbo-Jumbo is to the African all the Father is to the Christian; save that he marks a lower stage of civilization, a less advanced state of moral and intellectual refinement, in his worshippers. So far as concerns his worshippers, the service he receives is as sincere, as pure, as available, as acceptable, as that rendered by a Bossuet, a Fénelon, a St. Bernard, a St. Francis, a St. Benedict, or a St. Theresa. Foolish men talk of idolaters bowing down to idols of wood and stone, to images rudely or cunningly carved or painted, adoring creeping things and fourfooted beasts, the elements of nature, or the hosts of heaven; but these idolaters, as they are called, adore what to them is highest and best, and we only adore what is highest and best to us; and we fall as far short of the infinite reality in our conceptions, as they do in theirs. The only idolatry is in substituting the eidolon for the idea, the symbol for the symbolized, in attaching ourselves to obsolete institutions, and refusing to advance with the race.

The unbelievers were unwise in making war on Christianity. The Christian religion is, no doubt, the sublimest product of man, the least inadequate form with which he has thus far clothed his conceptions of the true, the beautiful, and the good, and as such should be respected. The elder Protestantism is inexcusable for its hostility to Catholicity. The Catholic Church was in its day the highest expression the world could appreciate of the lofty and ennobling ideas which Jesus of Nazareth taught and lived. All honor to those by whose toils, sufferings, prayers, tears, fastings, watchings, and blood, it was established; but none, indeed, to the stupid Catholic of to-day, pouring over the legends of dead saints, and foolishly imagining, that, because his church was once beautiful and holy, it must needs be so now, or that, because it could once produce saints, heroes, martyrs, it must needs produce them through all time to come. Poor man! he gazes so intently on the glory that was, that he is stark blind to the glory that is, or is to be. Foolish man! he sees not that he is left behind, and that the race goes on without him. O dear brother, why lingerest thou amongst the tombs? The Lord has risen, and goes before thee into Galilee. Seek not the future in the past; the living among the dead; but go on with humanity, live its life, and share its progress. The world is not superannuated; it is still in the heyday of youth, and has a long career before it. Behold, new prophets and new messiahs arise in long succession. Each man may be for his age a new and worthier messiah; for each, did he but know it, is an incarnation of the living God.

After all, religious forms, institutions, though inevitable and perhaps even useful, for a time and under certain circumstances, are not essential to religion. They are inevitable and natural, when the human race has not advanced far enough to perceive that all which is really essential is the divine idea and sentiment, which are the same in all men. Weak and ignorant men naturally imagine that the idea and sentiment must be inoperative and inefficacious, unless clothed with positive institutions. The African no sooner becomes conscious of the divine idea and sentiment of religion, than he supposes he must embody them. Hence, he proceeds forthwith to locate them, and to clothe them with the attributes of his own humanity, as he has ascertained them. Hence Mumbo-Jumbo and his service. The conception of pure spirit transcends the African's stage of progress, and he fancies ideas must needs want substance, reality, unless materialized, and fixed in a local habitation. But the race has now advanced far enough to correct this mistake. Jesus saw the mistake, and his superiority lies in his having risen superior to all forms, and asserted the sufficiency of the idea and sentiment alone, that is, of *absolute religion*. He discarded all forms, all institutions, all contrivances of men, and fell back on absolute religion, on the naked idea and sentiment, and taught his followers to do the same. Here was his transcendent merit. Here he proved himself in advance of his age,—nay, in advance of all ages since. Unhappily, the world knew him not. His immediate disciples did not comprehend his divine work. They foolishly imagined that he came to introduce a new form, or to found a new religious institution, which, like Aaron's rod, should swallow up all the rest; and even to this day the great mass of his professed followers have supposed, that, to be Christians, they must sustain some formal institution, believe certain formal dogmas, and observe certain prescribed rites and ceremonies. Nevertheless, in all ages, a bold few, branded as heretics by the orthodox of their time, have had some glimpses of the real significance of the Christian movement, and have stood forth the prophets and harbingers of the glory hereafter to be revealed. In our day the number is greatly augmented. Catholics and old-fashioned Protestants may call them heretics, and fear they will deprive the world of its Maker, and man of the Spirit in which he lives and moves and has his being; but this need not disturb us; for these are the Scribes and Pharisees of our time, and do but reproduce the rage of the old Jews and pagans against the early Christian missionaries. Opposition from them we must expect. All who will live godly in Christ Jesus shall suffer persecution. We must be prepared for the malice of those who see the world escaping from their tyranny. But what of that? The brave spirit quails not, and will on its way, though earth and hell oppose. Brave spirits now there are. Germany, classic land of reform, teems with them; France, the land of beautiful prose, teems with them; England, staid and haughty England, land of deeds and not of ideas, feels their quickening impulse; and young America, daughter of Freedom, and promised land of the future, leaps with joy to receive them. The mighty *Welt-Geist*, the world-spirit, is on their side, moves in them, and fights and conquers for them; and we may trust that the time draws near, when, in this country at least, we can dispense with all religious forms and institutions, and carry out the sublime thought of Jesus, for proclaiming which, a corrupt and formal age crucified him between two thieves. Then men will be satisfied with absolute religion; then the noble spirit of man will be emancipated, and the godlike mind that would explore all things, and rise to its primal source, will spurn all formal dogmas, all contracting and debasing forms, and scorn to seek the living word of God in the dead petrifactions of crafty priests and besotted monks. Then God himself will be our teacher, and the soul nestle in the bosom of the All-Father; then man will be man, dare act out himself, and bow to no authority but that of the invisible Spirit, to whom gravitation and purity of heart, a man, a maggot, a mountain, a moss, are all the same; and then the human race will——what?

Such, in general terms, is transcendentalism in its most religious aspect,—virtually, if not formally, the view taken by all who to-day represent and continue the reformers of the sixteenth century. By asserting the influx of God into the soul, they have the appearance of recognizing divine revelation and assistance; and by asserting this influx to be by a natural channel and in a natural manner, they escape the supernaturalism they abhor and know it would be suicidal for them to admit. They have, then, apparently, in transcendentalism, all that is necessary to meet the present emergency. In it the party seem to have all the advantages of both belief and unbelief, without the responsibilities of either. By this means they can contradict themselves on principle, without incurring the charge of inconsistency; make any assertion they find convenient, without the necessity of proving it; reason against unreason, and take refuge in unreason against reason; appeal from feeling to argument, and from argument to feeling, from reason and feeling both to the soul's transcendental faculty, and laugh at their puny assailants. When all fail, and no subterfuge is left, they can refuse to reply, and make their silence a merit. It is unworthy the prophet to engage in controversy, in repelling personal attacks. It is nobler to be silent. Jesus, when accused, opened not his mouth; why should we? We only say our say, and you are free to say yours. We throw out our word; take it for what it is worth. If worth something, as every sincere word must be, take it and be thankful; if worth nothing, let it go; why dispute about what is worthless? It can be but a worthless dispute, and, *ernst is das Leben*, life is too serious to be wasted in worthless disputes. Evidently, transcendentalism is the very thing for our present reform party.

A peculiar excellence of transcendentalism is, that it permits its advocates to use the consecrated words of faith and piety in impious and infidel senses, and with so much speciousness as to deceive men and women, not centemptible either for their intelligence or their motives. All religious institutions are symbolical, and shadow forth, or *conceal*, real facts. Every rite, every ceremony, every dogma of religion has its root in the soul, and conceals some truth of the soul. This truth *is* a truth, and therefore not to be rejected; but this truth, or fact, is all that in the symbol is valuable, or that it is essential to retain. Penetrate the symbol, then, ascertain this fact, and you have its real meaning, all that it has ever *meant*, even for the race.—Thus, the human race believes in divine inspiration. Very well. Then divine inspiration is a fact. But the human race believes that divine inspiration is the supernatural communication, through chosen individuals, of truths pertaining to the supernatural order. But this is not the fact; it is only the form with which, through craft, ignorance, or credulity, the fact has been clothed; not the fact itself, but its symbol. The real fact is, that every man's soul is furnished with a pipe through which God runs into it as it wills, in any quantity not exceeding its capacity.—The church asserts the Incarnation,—that the human nature and the divine nature were united in Jesus in one person. Very true. She also asserts that the two natures were so united in him and in no other. There she is wrong; for there she gives not the fact, but its symbol. The real fact is the union of the human and divine in all men, or that no man need look out of his own nature to find God, who is one with the nature of each man. I and my Father are one.—The Christian life is a combat, a warfare; we must take up the cross, and fight constantly against the world, the flesh, and the devil. All very true. But *the* world, flesh, and devil against which we are to fight are not what stupid ascetics dream; but low and debasing views of religion, attachment to obsolete forms, and unwillingness to receive new light. The real devil is the conservative spirit. At one time it is the church; at another, civil government; among Protestants, it is the Bible; among Christians generally, the authority of Jesus. In a word, the devil is always that particular thing, institution, or party which restrains the free action of the soul, and confines it to a prescribed formula, whether of religion, politics, or morals, or whatever would subject the soul to any law or authority distinguishable from itself. Against this, in our own time and country, be it what it may, we must take up arms, fight the good fight, regardless of what may be the consequences to ourselves.—In this way, transcendentalists appropriate to their own use all the sacred language of religion, and utter the foulest blasphemy in the terms of faith and piety. If we accuse them of rejecting religion, they smile at our simplicity, and ask us what sacred terms we have they cannot and do not use. But you use them in a false sense. Be not the dupe of words; we use them to designate the real facts in the case, what you yourselves mean by them, if you mean any thing real by them. Not quite so fast, good friends, if you please. How do you know that it is not we who state the real fact, and you who misstate it, or substitute your interpretations of the fact for the fact itself? We, by your own admission, are your equals, have all the faculties you have, even the transcendental faculty itself, if it be a faculty. Wherefore, then, are not our assertions as good as yours? And why is not the fact that we differ from you as strong a proof that you are wrong, as your difference from us that you are right?

It is evident from the mode in which transcendentalists interpret the symbols, notwithstanding some appearances to the contrary, that they hold that religious institutions, regarded as institutions, originate in the human element of religion rather than in the divine. In fact, they are the peculiarly human element itself. In this they show their descent from the Protestant world. Protestants, with the exception of a few high-church men, hardly worth counting, agree that our Lord, though he may have revealed formal doctrines, founded no formal church, but simply deposited in the hearts of his followers certain principles, which, fecundated by our faith and love, lead to the establishment of such forms of ecclesiastical government and discipline as in human prudence are judged to be most convenient. Many go further, and say he revealed no formal faith or worship, and that his revelation consists solely in placing in the hearts of men certain great "seminal" principles of action. These, warmed into life by our love and obedience, tend naturally to expand and purify our affections, and gradually to extend and clarify our views, and thus enable us to form sounder judgments than we otherwise could of the attributes of God, the nature, relations, and destiny of the human soul, and therefore of moral and religious duties. These judgments, moulded into form, become respectively dogmas, precepts, and rites, and approximate absolute truth of doctrine, morals, and worship, in proportion to the love and fidelity with which we cultivate the principles, or, more strictly, our own intellectual and moral powers. The first class reduce all forms of ecclesiastical government to the same level, and, so far as the form is concerned, find the true church alike under the papal, episcopal, presbyterian, or congregational form. The second class not only reduce all forms of ecclesiastical government to the same level, but also all forms of faith and worship, and thus place all professedly Christian sects and denominations, how widely soever they may differ from one another, on the same broad platform, and render it a matter of indifference to which of them one may be attached. Transcendentalists only follow in the same direction, and, by a little broader generalization, bring all religions within one and the same category, whether Pagan, Jewish, Christian, Mahometan, or Mormon. The great majority of Protestants agree with them that all forms of religion, whether ecclesiastical, doctrinal, moral, or liturgical, that is to say, all religious institutions, are purely of human origin, and spring from human prudence, or from human weakness. If there is any difference, it is that the Protestant holds that he is *moved* to their creation by the supernatural principles deposited in his heart, while the transcendentalist holds that he is moved to their creation by what is purely human. The Protestant makes them a human work, but on a divine principle; the transcendentalist makes them human in both their cause and their principle. This may seem to be some difference, but it amounts practically to nothing.

The transcendentalist restricts all that he acknowledges to be divine in religion to the simple idea and sentiment. These are what he calls the permanent in religion, absolute religion, all that is needed, or in fact admissible. This is evident from Mr. Parker everywhere. He professes to reverence Jesus because he proclaimed the sufficiency of absolute religion. He himself holds that all forms of religion are not only not necessary, but mischievous. They tend to hide absolute religion, and to generate idolatry by inducing us to mistake the symbol for what is symbolized, the shadow for the substance. Their existence through all ages and in all countries is a proof of the universal and permanent presence of absolute religion; but they are not it, nor does it need them, or of itself move us to create them. It occasions, but does not cause them. Undoubtedly, if man had no religious idea or sentiment, he would form no religious institutions; but the principle of the institutions is in his own nature,—in his natural tendency, when he is conscious of an idea, to conceive it under some form, to measure it, determine it, and fix its value, give it a location,—that is, an institution,—and to take his conceptions for the idea itself, to imagine that to reject them is to reject it, and, therefore, to seek always to impose them on himself and on others. But if he only knew that the idea is of itself sufficient, and would, or could, distinguish between it and his conceptions, and refrain from imposing his conceptions as it, he would never form any religious institutions, would be satisfied with absolute religion itself, and never seek to go beyond it. It is clear, then, that transcendentalists hold that forms or institutions have their principle and cause, not in the religious idea and sentiment themselves, but in human nature as distinguished from them.

But if this be questioned, and it be alleged that the institutions have their principle and cause in the religious idea and sentiment, it will still be true that transcendentalists teach that they have their principle and cause in human nature; for they teach that the idea and sentiment are not only natural, but essential elements of human nature, as is proved by their second fundamental proposition, namely, Religion is a fact or principle of human nature, and from the whole drift of their writings and speculations. It is on this assumption that they rest their whole defence of religion against the incredulity of the last century. It is the grand discovery which entitles them to the admiration and gratitude of mankind. The unbelievers of the last century held religion to be an accident in human history, originating in local and transitory causes. This was their primal error; and it is precisely this error transcendentalists profess to correct, by showing that religion, reducible in the last analysis to the simple idea and sentiment, is a permanent and indestructible fact of man's nature, an essential element of his very being as man. Grant, then, that the institutions originate in the idea and sentiment, which would seem to be their natural genesis, it is still true that they have their principle and cause in human nature.

But, it may be asked, if the idea and sentiment, or absolute religion, be constitutive principles of our nature, how can they be divine? The answer to this question is in the identity of the divine nature and the human. In a former article, we proved that transcendentalists deny all distinct natures, and assert the unity and identity of one and the same nature under all forms of existence,—material in matter, spiritual in spirit, mineral in minerals, vegetable in vegetables, animal in animals, rational and moral in man,—changing through all, and yet in all the same,—nature, substance, being, of all that is or appears. Besides this one nature, identical under all forms, there is no reality. Forms are phenomenal, variable, unsubstantial, evanescent. This one nature, considered in itself, detached from all forms or phenomena in which it appears, or through which it manifests itself, is God. Hence, nature is divine; and as this one nature is the particular nature of each specific form of existence, the nature of each is divine, and therefore the nature of man. Then whatever is constitutive of the nature of man is divine, and therefore the religious idea and sentiment.

This, it may be alleged, is only saying, in other words, that they are human; and then what is gained by calling them divine? At bottom, so far as he is real being or substance, that is, in his nature, man is, indeed, identical with God, and it matters not which term, man or God, is used; for one is the equivalent of the other. In this sense we are indistinguishable from God; for in him we live and move and have our *being*. Hence, to know God, one has only to know his nature,—hence the profound significance of the ancient inscription on the portals of the temple, KNOW THYSELF; and to obey God, one has only to obey his own nature; hence the maxim of the ancients, *Follow nature*, and of the transcendentalists, OBEY THYSELF. But man may be considered in his form, as a particular form of existence; and in this sense he is *formally*, though not really, distinguishable from God. The form is the humanity (*humanitas*), and is in itself empty, limited, transitory. It is, properly speaking, what is meant by personality, which is not the last complement of rational nature, as schoolmen dream, but its limitation, that which individualizes, renders the nature determinate, particular, and then, of course, as predicable of a tree, a stone, an ox, a maggot, as of man. It is not predicable of God at all; for to call God personal would be to deny his universality and his infinity, and to make him particular and limited. Hence transcendentalists are accustomed to say, We believe in God, but not in a *personal* God. All individual things, all particular existences, are indeed God as to their nature, so far as they have real being, and can be said to *be;* but so far as individual, particular, they are distinguishable from him, and are merely individual, particular, specific forms of him. When we speak of any one of these, we are accustomed to call by its name, not only the form, but the one nature, or God as under that form, or manifesting himself through it. We ordinarily think and speak of man as an individual or personal existence, and do not take note of the fact that his nature is God, or is nothing but God under the form of humanity. Thus we are led to content ourselves with the human form, and to neglect the divine nature. When we content ourselves with the form, which as form is empty, we live an empty and godless life; but when we lose sight of the form, and fall back on the great nature under it, we live a divine life, the life of God himself. Here is the advantage of knowing that our nature is one with God, and of calling it divine rather than human.

This answer may be very clear and satisfactory to transcendentalists, but to us it is not free from embarrassment. To distinguish man from his nature, in which is his whole substance, being, reality, active force,—and yet to conceive him, when so distinguished, therefore as mere unsubstantial form, as capable of acting, confining himself to his personality, or sinking his personality and falling back on the great nature underlying him, decidedly *transcends* our ability. The transcendentalist evidently struggles to keep clear of pantheism, and perhaps, for the most part, fancies that he succeeds; but, having begun by denying substantial forms, or all real differences of nature, and by affirming the reality of only one and the same nature under all forms, however numerous or diversified they may appear, he has rendered success impossible, save in appearance, and hardly even in appearance. If man has no substantive existence distinct from the universal substance, no nature of his own distinguishable from one universal nature, he has in himself, in his distinctive character, no active force, is no active force, and therefore can perform no act, can be the subject of no predicate. If you assume that his personality, his individuality, is a mere limitation, an empty or unsubstantial form, you must concede that he as personal or individual is really nothing, and therefore can neither sink his personality nor confine himself to it. The *vis activa*, or *vis agendi*, is not man as personal, as an individuality, but man as nature, in which sense you assume him to be not distinguishable from God. Consequently, whatever you predicate of him is predicated of God, and what you disapprove in him and what you approve are alike the work of God; for God is the only active or productive force you acknowledge; and to acknowledge no active or productive force but God is to profess pantheism.

But passing over this, we are still embarrassed. We understand, indeed, how transcendentalists can call the religious idea and sentiment divine, even while making them constitutive of human nature. But they go further, and make the sentiment and idea the *whole* of religion, define them to be absolute religion, and, as religion, all-sufficing. These we have always and everywhere; the same and in the same degree; for they are invariable, permanent, and indestructible facts of nature. Assuming this, our difficulty is to understand the significance and office of inspiration. Here the oracle grows mysterious, and utters only a vague and uncertain response, and, after all our consultations, gives us nothing satisfactory. We confess ourselves at a loss, and altogether unable to discover any good reason why transcendentalists should recognize the fact of inspiration at all.

In order to throw what light we can on this intricate question, we must observe that transcendentalists do not all adopt precisely the same ontological views. The American and English transcendentalists, best represented by Bronson Alcott, and the late J. P. Greaves, take the view we have given, and hold that God is the one universal and indeterminable nature of all particular existences, which particular existences, in fact, are nothing but mere phenomena, or modes in which the universal being manifests itself. But the German and French transcendentalists, the former represented by Hegel, and the latter by Pierre Leroux, though perhaps coming at last to the same result, take a somewhat different view. They undertake to construct God and the universe from the analysis of human thought, which they reduce to three terms, translatable in plain English by the terms *Possibility, Ideality, Reality*. These three terms, then, comprise the universe of being, in all its actual, conceivable, or possible modes of existence or manifestation. We have, then, first, *possible* being,—second, *ideal* being,—and last, *real* being. The possible—called by Hegel *das Seyn*, as identical with *das Nicht-Seyn*,—by Leroux *le Ciel*, the *Tien* of the Chinese, the *Void* of the Buddhists, and the *Bythos* of the Gnostics—may be defined the infinite possibility of being. The real, *das Wesen*, is the *plenum*, or so much of the possible as has been filled up or become actual being. The ideal is the mediator between the possible and real, or that by which they are made one.

Now, we may contemplate the universe of being under the three points of view respectively, of the possible, the ideal, and the real. If, under the first point of view, we ask, What is God? the answer is, He is infinite possibility. If under the second, He is the infinite ideal. If under the third, He is the actual universe, or sum total of real beings. The possible tends always to the ideal and the real; the real seeks always its own ideal and possible, and in this consists universal *life*. The possible realizing itself through the ideal is the fact we mortals term *creation*. God as possible, realizing himself through the ideal in actual beings, or in creation, becomes *das Wesen*, real or *living* God. He lives a real life in the life of living beings, and only in their life. Thus we may say God lives and moves and has his being in us, instead of our living, moving, and having our being in him. God, or Being, realizes itself progressively,—not perhaps as to time, but as to order,—and passes successively through all the grades of real beings, till arriving at personality and self-consciousness in man, the highest form of real being. He is everywhere, and everywhere infinitely active; but he is conscious activity, activity that knows itself, knows that it is, only in man, that is, in man's consciousness; and man, therefore, is his *Thought*, his *Word*,—in the language of theology, his Son, his first-born and only begotten Son, the image and likeness of himself.

Each particular being is God, or the entire universe, in miniature, and therefore at once possible, ideal, real; and its life or *living* consists in realizing its ideal and possible. As real, it is limited, finite; as ideal and possible, unlimited, infinite. Hence, there is always room for it to continue and extend its realization. Man's life consists in realizing his own ideal and possible. Ever does the ideal, the form under which the possible is revealed, stretch out beyond him, hover over and float before him. By means of the transcendental faculty of the soul, he apprehends this ideal and aspires to it. Contemplating it, he perceives that his real being is not full, that it contains a void not filled up, that he may be more and better than he is,—better because more. His soul is quickened, his heart inflamed, his whole being moved, by the view of the ideal ever floating before him, the revelation to him of the infinitely possible; and he is urged on by an all but irresistible power to seize it, appropriate it, realize it, and thus augment his being, fill up its void. Here is the fact of inspiration. This ideal is God, from the point of view of the ideal, and therefore the inspiration is *divine;* it is also man's own nature as ideal, and therefore the inspiration is *natural*. It is literally an aspiration, or effect of an aspiration, to the ideal; and by obeying it we realize God, take up more of God into our being, augment our own real being and that of God.

No comments are necessary to show that this theory, which is at present so highly esteemed in Germany, is really nothing but another form of stating what the world has known under the name of French philosophy, or French atheism. At bottom, it is simply the doctrine we find in the *Système de la Nature*, attributed to Baron d'Holbach, as M. Leroux, though virtually adopting it himself, has very clearly shown, in one of the numbers of his *Revue Indépendante* for 1843. This sublime doctrine does not seem to be wholly unknown to our American transcendentalists, and we find decided traces of it in *The Present*, a periodical lately published in New York, and edited by a man of whom we had the right to hope something better, and of whom, if God preserve his reason, we dare yet hope something better, for he seems to us a man of singular purity and ingenuousness; and we also not unfrequently find traces of it in Mr. Parker. But whether Mr. Parker adopts its view of inspiration we are not able to say. He has read much, but digested little. He brings together scraps from Plato, Plotinus, Proclus, Julian, Spinoza, Leibnitz, Kant, Hegel, Goethe, Schleiermacher, De Wette, Schelling, Coleridge, Jacobi, Locke, Cudworth, Voltaire, Cousin, George Fox, Benjamin Constant, and Tom Paine, but throws them together in such singular confusion, that, with the best intentions in the world to do him justice, we find it all but impossible to determine what is the precise view he would be willing to have us take as his own. But systematizing his general views as well as we are able, and making him as coherent and consequent as possible, we take him to hold inspiration to be the spontaneous activity of the universal and impersonal nature of which we have so often spoken. This impersonal nature, which in itself considered, is God, is, as to its essential qualities, power, wisdom, and goodness, and therefore its action is always the action of wisdom and goodness, or, from the point of view of reason, truth, of the affections, goodness, and the sentiments, beauty. Being power or *vis activa*, it is necessarily active, and from within by its own inherent laws. As its nature never varies, its quantity of action and the direction of its action must be always the same. It is a sort of machine fixed in immensity, immovable under all forms, and generating and supplying to each the quantity of inherently wise, good, and beautiful power each needs, or has the capacity to receive. It is always there, and the particular being has but to raise a gate, and it flows in, to the measure of the particular being's capacity. This flowing in is *inspiration*.

But this flowing in is not from abroad. To be inspired, we need not receive any thing not already in ourselves. The source of the inspiration is our own nature. But this is what embarrasses us. How our own nature can inspire us, or we from our nature receive more than we receive in having our nature, puzzles us, and we cannot solve the mystery. But, be this as it may, it is certain man is not required to go out of himself for inspiration.

"The word is nigh him, even in his heart......As God fills all space, so all spirit; as he influences and constrains unconscious and necessitated matter, so he inspires and helps free and conscious man......There are windows towards God, as towards the world. There is no intercessor, angel, mediator, between man and God; for man can speak and God can hear, each for himself. He requires no advocate to plead for man, who needs not to pray by attorney. Each soul stands close to the Omnipresent God; may feel his beautiful presence, and have familiar access to the All-Father; get truth at first hand from its Author. Wisdom, righteousness, and love are the spirit of God in the soul of man; wherever these are, and in proportion to their power, there is inspiration from God."—pp. 216, 217.

That is, in proportion as a man is inspired, he *is* inspired. There is no gainsaying that. But

"*God's action on matter and on man is perhaps the same thing to him,* though it *appear* differently modified to us. But it is plain, from the nature of things, that there can be but one *kind* of inspiration, as of Truth, Faith, or Love; *it is the direct and intuitive perception* of some truth of thought or of sentiment;—there can be but one *mode* of inspiration; *it is the action of the Highest within the soul,* the divine presence imparting light; this presence, as of truth, justice, holiness, love, infusing itself into the soul, giving it new life; the breathing in of Deity, the in-come of God to the soul, in the form of truth through reason, of right through conscience, of love and faith through the affections and religious sentiment. Is inspiration confined to theological matters? Is Newton less inspired than Simon Peter?—p. 218.

Why not? And, if inspiration be taken not in its authorized sense, how are Mr. Parker's readers to decide the question he asks? Suppose they should deny Newton's inspiration, how would he prove it? And what absurdity is there in asserting that St. Peter was inspired, and that Sir Isaac Newton was not?

"If God be infinitely perfect he does not change; then his modes of action are perfect and unchangeable. The laws of mind, like those of matter, remain immutable and not transcended. As God has left no age nor man destitute of reason, conscience, religion, so he leaves none destitute of inspiration. *It is, therefore, the light of our being; the back-ground of all human faculties; the sole means by which we gain a knowledge of what is not seen and felt, the logical condition of all sensual knowledge;* our highway to the world of spirit. Man cannot exist without God, more than matter. Inspiration, then, like vision, must be everywhere the same thing in *kind*, however it differs in *degree*, from race to race, from man to man. The degree of inspiration must depend on two things: first, on the natural ability, the particular intellectual, moral, and religious endowment, or genius, wherewith each man is furnished by God; and next, on the use each man makes of that endowment;—in one word, on the man's *quantity of Being*, and his *quantity of Obedience*. . . . . A man of noble intellect, of deep, rich, benevolent affections, is by his endowments capable of more than one less gifted. He that perfectly keeps the soul's law, thus fulfilling the conditions of inspiration, has more than he who keeps it imperfectly; the former must receive all his soul can contain at that stage of its growth. Thus it depends on a man's own will, in great measure, to what extent he will be inspired."—pp. 219, 220.

All this is clear enough, as to the fact, that inspiration is the action of the impersonal nature, which is our real self; but it is not unencumbered with difficulties. "God's action on matter and on man is perhaps the same thing to him, though it *appear* differently modified to us." This action is inspiration. Then the stone, the moss, the tree, the maggot, is inspired in like manner, and in the same sense, as man, and the effect differs only in its *appearance* to us. The action is always the same. God does his best to inspire one as much as another; and if one is not as much inspired as another, it is because one has a less quantity of being, or because it makes a less faithful use of its faculties. But he tells us, again, that "inspiration is the *consequence* of the faithful use of our faculties; each man is its subject [he might have added, each block or stone], God its source, truth its only *test.*"—p. 220. Here we are thrown out, quite off the centre of gravity; for we have just been told, that inspiration is "the light of our being; the back-ground of all human faculties; the sole means by which we gain a knowledge of what is not seen and felt, the logical condition of all sensual knowledge." Hence, it follows necessarily, that without inspiration we have no sensual knowledge, that is, knowledge by the senses, no light, and no faculties; and yet inspiration is the *consequence* of the faithful use of our faculties! Decidedly this is too bad. To compel us, without knowledge, without light, without faculties, to use our faculties, and to use them faithfully, and thus gain inspiration, is worse than the tyranny of Pharao, in compelling the Israelites to make brick without straw, for they *could* wander over the fields and gather up stubble. Furthermore, truth is the only *test* of inspiration. Then the inspiration is not the communication of truth, for truth is something we must be already in possession of, as a criterion by which to test it.

"He that has most of wisdom, goodness, religion, the most of truth in its highest modes, is the most inspired."—*ib.* Either the inspiration and these are identical, and then the sense is, He who is the most inspired is the most inspired; or the inspiration is the effect of these, and then the possession of wisdom, goodness, religion, truth in its highest modes, is the condition of inspiration, which we suppose to be the author's meaning,—and not it the condition of possessing truth, wisdom, goodness, religion. But as the possession of these, not inspiration, is the end we should aim at, and if these are attainable without the inspiration as a means, what is the office or use of inspiration? Really, we do not know, and we confess we cannot understand why transcendentalists assert it at all, unless because they think it would not *appear* religious to deny it. Perhaps it is the homage they pay to truth; perhaps the "pear," as Luther called the Christian miracles, which they throw to children. At any rate, the matter is left quite in the dark.

Having done our best to explain away the difficulties likely to embarrass our *un*transcendental readers, we are led very naturally to ask, what are the proofs by which transcendentalists attempt to sustain their position, that all religious institutions have their principle and cause in human nature? But transcendentalists regard this question of proofs as a delicate one, and are apt to look upon the demand for proofs as a decided breach of politeness, a downright piece of impertinence. They do not reason; they affirm, and we should take their simple assertion as sufficient. They are not reasoners, but *seers;* and will we not believe them, when they tell us what they see? Their doctrine rests not on discursion, but on intuition. The intuition is, indeed, possible to all, but not to all states of the soul. The soul must be prepared, and its vision purged by regimen, and strengthened by exercise. We must, by strict regimen and exercise, rise to the pure empyrean, and then we shall see and know for ourselves. Then no proofs will be needed; and before then none can be appreciated. Proofs offered to one still in the low regions of the logical understanding are pearls cast before swine. What avails it to reason with a blind man on colors? Couch his eyes first. So couch the eyes of the soul, open "the windows towards God," and you will want no proofs; you will see as we see, and all we see. Moreover, you must take the proper attitude to see. The transcendental attitude is to turn the eyes upside down, and look at things through your legs.* You and the objects you see will then be reversed; and the essence of transcendentalism is not in seeing what others do not see, but in seeing what all the world sees,—but with the *seer* and the *seen* reversed.

But if, by a rare condescension to our *rationality*, transcendentalists deign to discuss the question of proofs with us, they refer us to their doctrine of the unity and identity of the one nature, which surges under all forms, and which, out of courtesy to the religious world, they are pleased to call God. What we foolishly imagine to be distinct natures are, as distinct from this one nature, mere forms, mere phenomena, and therefore unproductive. But there can be no phenomenon without being, any more than a shadow without a substance. The being of each particular phenomenon is the one identical nature, universal in all, particular in each. But this nature is named always from the particular phenomenon or class of phenomena in which it manifests itself. Manifesting itself in the phenomenal man, it is called *man* or *human nature*, and is precisely what is meant by man considered as real instead of phenomenal. But as the phenomenal is in itself unproductive, all in the history of man must proceed from this nature, which we term human nature. Religious institutions are facts in man's history; therefore they proceed from, or have their principle and cause in human nature.

Moreover, if you consider the matter, your demand for proofs is exceedingly foolish. There can be nothing in history which has not its principle and cause in nature. But all natures are really one and the same nature, however diversified the forms of its manifestation, and this one nature is the nature of all men and of each man, is in all and in each; for no man can *be* without a nature. Then you need but study your own nature, look into yourselves, in order to see and know the truth of our position. All truth is in nature, and all nature is in each man. Each man contains all the facts of history in himself, and can ascertain them from

---

*"Turn the eyes upside down, by looking at the landscape through your legs, and how agreeable is the landscape, though you have seen it twenty times!"—R. W. EMERSON, *Nature*, p. 64.

the analysis of his own consciousness. Nature is essentially intelligent, and therefore each man must needs know all that has been, is, or is to be, and therefore all phenomena past, present, and to come. We have, then, a universal intuitive power, and therefore may have the particular intuition of the fact in question. This universal intuitive power is the transcendental faculty of the soul which we assert, and from which we derive our name of transcendentalists. Having this faculty, we can of ourselves know all things. Hence our Mr. Parker is a perfect master of all history, corrects the statements of Moses, and gives us a full and authentic account of the creation, the primitive condition of man, and of all that has befallen or is to befall him in his pilgrimage through the ages; and he could, if he were so disposed, tell us the precise number, age, size, and color, whether blue or ringstreaked, of the dogs that licked up Jezabel's blood. Why not? He has but to sink the phenomenal man, the *Parkeritas*, which is mere form and in reality nothing, and fall back on the impersonal soul, on his real self, and he is universal nature, the omnipresent, omniscient, and omnipotent God, in which sense he assists at the birth of all phenomena, not as spectator only, but also as creator. He was present when the stars were set in their course; he beheld when the earth was fashioned and poised on nothing; he heard the song of the sons of the morning, and to him, as creator, rose the exulting hymn of praise. What we say of Mr. Parker we may say of all men and of each man; for each is in all, and all are in each. All, then, in and of themselves, may know all things. What need, then, of proofs? Why carry coals to Newcastle?

This established, the transcendentalist can have no further trouble. He carries in him the measure of all things, as he asserts in his first fundamental principle, namely,—Man is the measure of truth and goodness. Nay, not the measure only, but the source of all things. He wills, and it is; commands, and it stands fast. All historical facts adjust themselves to his standard, and his explanations of all phenomena are final. What beyond his simple assertion can the most captious or the most *rational* demand? What he asserts is asserted on the highest conceivable authority. The world believes in the fact of inspiration. So far, so good. It believes, or supposes it believes, inspiration to be a supernatural fact,—the communication, in a supernatural manner, of facts pertaining to the supernatural order. If by *super-*

natural it means supersensual, all very well; but if more, it is wrong, for there is no supernatural, since there is but one nature, and nature cannot transcend or surpass itself. The world has fancied that Almighty God has not only inspired particular individuals, but that he has established positive religious institutions, which must be accepted and obeyed as the essential condition of pleasing him; but in this it only gives form to the great fact, that it always seeks to embody its conceptions of what is highest and best, and to impose on itself its embodiment as law. It obeys in this, indeed, its highest conceptions, but nevertheless blunders. The world has adored Jesus as the incarnate God. All right, for he was the incarnate God, and so is every man. Jesus was only the type of what all men may and should be, the most perfect model of the true man—always excepting Mr. Theodore Parker—the world has as yet beheld. The world has said Jesus was the *only* incarnate God. In this it has been wrong, through ignorance or craft, has listened to priests and monks, instead of its own great nature. In this way transcendentalists survey all religious institutions, and tell us, *ex cathedra*, what is true, what is false, where we are right, and where we are wrong. They do it all by virtue of their inherent godship. They cannot possibly err; for they are themselves the infallible criterion, are in themselves the Great Soul, the Universal Soul, Impersonal Nature, the Eternal and All-perfect God.

But, dear friends, you forget yourselves. On your own principles, we are God as well as you, and have the same Great Soul underlying us that you have. If you plant yourselves on your godship, we must plant ourselves on ours. Ours, as you yourselves assert, is the equal of yours; why, then, are we to yield to you, rather than you to us? If you are right, our godship is one and identical with yours. Why, then, is not its voice as authoritative, when in us and the race it condemns you, as when in you it condemns us? In the race and in us, it testifies alike to what you concede and what you deny. In the race and in us, it positively rejects your interpretations of the facts of religious history, and pronounces you—*Transcendentalists*. If it is the voice of God always and everywhere the same, how can it testify to one thing in us and to another in you, and why is its denial in you paramount to its affirmation in us? Is it because you look at things with the eyes turned upside down, and through your legs, and we do not? This is something, we own; but it can hardly avail you. How do you establish the fact that your mode of looking is preferable to ours? Nay, it cannot be so good. Ours is unquestionably the most *natural* mode, as well as the easiest and least constrained. On your own principles, all truth is in nature, and the more in conformity one is with nature, the more natural his mode of looking, the truer and more trustworthy is his intuition. Decidedly, then, we and the race, who look at the landscape with our eyes in their normal position, have altogether the advantage of you who look at it with your eyes upside down, through your legs, and, in case of difference, must trust our godship in preference to yours.

The primal error of transcendentalism, as must be obvious to the philosophic reader, is in the denial of substantial forms or distinct natures, and the assertion of the unity and identity of all natures in one and the same universal nature. Granting this denial and assertion, the greater part of their system follows as a necessary logical consequence. But the absurdity of the consequence is the refutation of the principle. Any principle which compels us to assert that there is no difference between gravitation and purity of heart, between the nature of a stone and the nature of man, and between the nature of man and the nature of God, thus making God the nature of the stone, and therefore stone itself, is refuted by that figure of logic termed *reductio ad absurdum*, and may be dismissed without further comment.

Transcendentalists have probably been led *philosophically* to the adoption of this error, by attempting to reduce the categories of reason to the single category of being and phenomenon. Aristotle gave us ten categories, which he made forms of the object, or at least forms of the reason, with their foundation in reality; Kant has given us fifteen, which he makes purely forms of the subject; transcendentalists, following Schelling, Hegel, and Cousin, attempt to identify the subject and object, and to resolve all the categories into one. Cousin, indeed, professes to recognize two, substance and cause; but he resolves that of cause into that of substance, by defining substance, in the last analysis, after Leibnitz and some of the schoolmen, to be *vis activa*, or acting force; and, by resolving the effect into the reaction of the cause, he really retains only the category of substance, or being and phenomenon,—which, as Schelling himself has admitted, is sheer Spinozism, or downright pantheism,—the abyss in which all modern philosophy is rapidly losing itself. M. Cousin prides himself on this reduction of the categories, and regards it as his chief claim to originality as a metaphysician; but, though we own we were simple enough to be taken with it, we consider it the rock on which he split, and the source of his failure. Kant was wrong in making the categories forms of the subject, without any foundation in reality, and thus falling into pure conceptualism, the old error of Abelard, but which may be rejected without falling into the error of either the realists or the nominalists; but his list of the categories is probably complete and exact, admitting neither of enlargement nor of reduction.

If being or substance, in the last analysis, be *vis activa*, or acting force, it is causative and productive of effects; and if infinite, it must be capable of producing diversified effects, and effects, in their sphere and degree, themselves productive of effects. Then each of these effects, inasmuch as productive of effects, will be a being, and, as productive of effects diverse from those of others, a being of a distinct and different nature. Transcendentalists admit the category of being as *vis activa*; they also admit infinite being. Then they must concede the possibility of distinct and different natures. Then they cannot assert *a priori*, that there is only one and the same nature under all forms of existence; and as they do not pretend to be able to assert it *a posteriori*, to establish it by positive proofs, they have no right to assert it at all.

Transcendentalists have been led also into the same error, by misapprehending the true doctrine of God's immanence in creation. God, say they, is not merely *causa transiens*, but also *causa immanens*, and therefore must be immanent in all his works; which is true. He must be immanent in his essential character. True again. He is essentially being; then he must be immanent as being; then immanent as the being of all and of each. He is essentially cause; then he must be immanent as cause; then he is the causativeness of all and of each. But the conclusions do not follow. He is, indeed, immanent in all as being, not as the being *of* all and of each, but as *that which creates and sustains* the being of all and of each. He is immanent as cause, not as the causativeness of all and of each; but as *that which creates and sustains* the causativeness of all and of each. He is immanent, not as the subject, but as that which creates and sustains the subject, and distinguishable from it as the cause from the effect. *Non implicat*, then, to suppose that he creates and sustains different subjects, different beings, distinguishable *by nature*—or their inherent power or quality of producing diverse effects—both from himself and from one another, as all the world believes, as is implied in every speech or language of men, and which must be assumed, or it is impossible to reason a single moment, or even to make a single intelligible proposition. This last consideration is of itself sufficient to convict the transcendentalists, and ought to silence them forever. The authority of the human race is for them the highest conceivable authority; for it is, on their principles, the authority of God. Then, since the race never confounds itself with any other race,—since it believes, and always has believed, there is some real difference between the nature of a stone and a loaf of bread, between a maggot and a man, between man and God,—and as it never gathers grapes of thorns, or figs of thistles,—transcendentalists are bound to admit the reality of distinct natures, by an authority they cannot gainsay, without abandoning their whole theory.

Assuming the reality of distinct natures,—that God has made and sustains all beings, each after its kind,—that there are real genera and species, substantial forms,—and that each race of beings has its specific nature, then what comes within the scope of that nature is *natural*, pertains to the natural order, and what transcends it is *super*natural, pertains to the supernatural order. Each specific nature, by the fact that it is specific, is limited, finite; and then an infinite distance between it and God, who is infinite. Then necessarily an infinite order above the highest specific or created nature, that is to say, an infinite supernatural order, of which the highest conceivable created nature knows and can conceive nothing by virtue of its natural powers. If there is a God, then there is and must be a supernatural order. The transcendentalists profess to believe in God. Then they must admit that there is a supernatural order, of which they neither have nor can have any knowledge by any natural means. Nothing, then, hinders God, if he chooses, from revealing supernaturally more or less of this supernatural order to such of his creatures as he has made naturally intelligent. It may be, that the end for which he intended man, when he made him, lies not in the plane of his natural powers, but in this very supernatural order. If so, our true end is attainable by no natural means, and is, and must be, unattainable without supernatural aid. Then either God has made us for an unattainable end, which would implicate his power, his wisdom, or his justice ; or he furnishes us the supernatural aid by which it is attainable, and without which it is not attainable. If he furnishes this aid, he may, if he chooses, furnish it through positive institutions, to the observance of which he attaches the grace needed. But whether he has made us for a supernatural destiny, for an end which transcends the natural order and pertains to the supernatural order, whether he has furnished us the supernatural means of attaining it, and whether he has furnished these means through positive institutions, and, if so, through what or which institutions, are all questions of fact, and must be decided as questions of fact, not of reason. The human race believes that he has made us for a supernatural end, and that he furnishes us the necessary aid through positive institutions, and Catholics believe through the positive institutions which we call the Catholic Church. Transcendentalists believe, or at least assert, the contrary. Here are the parties, and here is the issue. The issue is obviously one of fact, and can be decided only by an appeal to the proper documents and monuments in the case.

If the documents and monuments be authentic, it has been generally conceded the decision must be in favor of the supernaturalists. So have thought believers; the unbelievers of the last century thought the same, and therefore frankly denied their authenticity. The advocates of religion met this denial, and proved the documents and monuments to be authentic, and by all the rules of evidence to be admissible and conclusive. Transcendentalists saw this, and thus saw that it would be of no avail to attempt to impeach the testimony. But could they not admit it, and even turn it against the supernaturalists ? The thing, if it could be done, would be capital; it would be overthrowing religion by means of religion. Why can it not be done? Protestantism has conquered for us the glorious right of private interpretation. It is done. We will accept the documents, but interpret them in our own way, and show the religionists that they have never understood them. What they have applied to the supernatural order we will apply to man's natural relations, powers, and destiny, and our cause is won.

The documents are authentic. Conceded. Then their testimony must be referred to the natural order, since *there is no supernatural order.* Then, if you attempt to interpret them in favor of a supernatural order, you attempt to impeach them by making them testify in favor of what is not. If you believe them, you must believe with us; if you disbelieve them, you must still believe with us,—for then, according to your own principles, you have no authority for believing otherwise. You, as well as we, are bound to presume the documents are authentic; then they must receive a transcendental interpretation, and then they prove transcendentalism, and you must be transcendentalists on their authority, if on no other. Would you be guilty, or have us guilty, of the absurdity, of the blasphemy, of making them testify to what is false or absurd? This is a fair specimen of the mode in which the author of the work before us reasons in regard to the Bible, and is but a simple statement of the exegetical canon he adopts in its interpretation. The force of the argument lies solely in the assumption that there is no supernatural order, which is false, if there be a God; and its beauty consists in assuming the truth of transcendentalism, and then gravely concluding that the Scriptures, for instance, if authentic, must be so interpreted as to teach it, and, if they teach it, those who believe them must believe it. This is what may be called *transcendental* logic, and certainly transcends all the author of the *Organon* ever thought of commending.

But, after all, transcendentalists must sustain their interpretation of the documents and monuments of religion either by an appeal to the divine and supernatural, or by an appeal to the human and natural. If by the former, they concede what they deny and wish to disprove; if by the latter, they are refuted by the very authority to which they appeal. The human and natural must be collected from their operation; for, so far as inoperative, they are, so far as their authority is concerned, as if they were not. Then, after the divine and supernatural, the assent of the race must be the best and most authoritative exponent of what is human and natural; for it is only in the race that we have a full view of the human and natural in operation. But the race does not sustain the transcendentalists; it agrees, whether believing or not believing, that the sense of the documents and monuments relates to the supernatural. Then the transcendentalists must abandon their interpretation, as contradicted by the only authority on which they can rely for sustaining it. Then they must admit the supernatural order; then supernatural revelation; then positive religious institutions; and then the Catholic Church; or impeach the documents. This latter alternative is out of the question, as they themselves admit, by their effort to explain them in accordance with naturalism. Then nothing remains for them, if they do not wish to write themselves down what Dogberry wished to be written down, to confess that they have been chasing their own shadow, and to beg God to forgive their folly and absurdity, and to receive them as humble postulants at the door of his church.

We have now gone through with what we proposed to say on *Transcendentalism, or latest form of Infidelity.* We have said all we have judged to be necessary to enable our readers to understand its essential character, and all that can be requisite for its refutation. It can hardly be expected that what we have said will have much influence on confirmed transcendentalists themselves; but we trust in God that it may serve to put those who are as yet unbitten on their guard, and make our readers generally more suspicious of the novel principles of modern literature and philosophy. The danger is not, that any man with his eyes open will espouse transcendentalism, when fully developed, and dressed in its own robes; but that specious principles which imply it may be imbibed by well-meaning individuals before suspecting the fatal consequences they involve. In fact, all modern philosophy and literature are more or less tinctured with transcendentalism, and we find not unfrequently traces of it where we are not only sorry to find them, but where we little expected them. The enemy has sown its principles broadcast over the modern world, and they rarely fail to spring up, and flourish, and bear their poisonous fruit. One hardly knows when he is safe in accepting any view or doctrine of a more recent date than the reformation. Let no man fancy, because he can laugh at the absurdity of transcendentalism, when full grown, and displaying itself in all its deformity, absurdity, and impiety, that he is in no danger of countenancing it. Even while laughing, he may find that he is sustaining principles which logically imply it.

But, after all, what is the real sum and substance of transcendentalism, this latest and noblest birth of Time, as its friends regard it, and from which we are promised the universal *palingenesia* of man and nature,—what is it, when reduced to its simple, positive teachings? We have been led through tomes of metaphysical lore; we have been allured by brilliant promises of a recovered Eden; we have been flattered by glowing descriptions of our godlike powers, affinities, and tendencies; we have been transported by the assurance that we may dispense with priests, prophets, intercessors, and mediators, and of ourselves approach the Infinite One face to face, and drink our supply at the primal Fountain of Truth itself; but now, having lingered till the ascending sun has exhaled the dewdrops and exhausted the gems and precious stones which sparkled in rich profusion at our feet, what is the real and positive value of what has so long detained and charmed us? Things are what they are; man is what he is, and by a right use of his faculties may be, do, and know all he can be, do, and know. So far as we are wise, good, and loving, so far we have and know wisdom, goodness, love; and so far as we have and know wisdom, goodness, love, we have and know God, in so far as he is wisdom, goodness, love. He who knows more of these knows more than he who knows less. If the possession of wisdom, goodness, love, be inspiration, then he who has the most wisdom, goodness, love, is the most inspired,—and to be more inspired, he must get more wisdom, goodness, love. To be more inspired, he must be more inspired. If white be white, then white is white; if black be black, then what is black is black; if two be two, then two are two. Or, in two grand formulas from Mr. Parker, "Goodness is goodness," and "Be good and do good," and—you will be good and do good! If this is not the whole of transcendentalism, when divested of its denials, its blasphemy, and its impiety, and reduced to its simple dogmatic teaching, then we have given days, weeks, months, and years, to its study to no purpose. Stated in plain and simple terms, it is the veriest commonplace imaginable. It is merely "much ado about nothing," or "a tempest in a teapot." Dressed up in the glittering robes of a tawdry rhetoric, or wrapped in the mystic folds of an unusual and unintelligible dialect, it may impose on the simple and credulous; but to attempt to satisfy one's spiritual wants with it is as vain as to attempt to fill one's self with the east wind, or to warm one's freezing hands on a cold winter's night by holding them up to the moon. Yet its teachers are the great lights of this age of light, before whom all the great lights of past times pale as the stars before the sun. Men and women, through some mistake not in a lunatic hospital, run after them with eagerness, hang with delight on their words, and smack their lips as if feeding on honey. Our Protestant populations, on whom the sun of the reformation shines in its effulgence, are moved, run towards their teaching, and are about to hail it as the Tenth Avatar come to redeem the world. Wonderful teachers! Wonderful populations! Wonderful age!

In conclusion; while surveying the mass of absurdities and impieties heaped together under the name of transcendentalism, and which attract so many, and even some of our own friends, whose kindness of heart, whose simple manners, and whose soundness of judgment on all other subjects command our love and esteem, we have been forcibly struck with the utter impotence of human reason to devise a scheme which reason herself shall not laugh to scorn. As often as man has attempted of himself alone to build a tower which should reach to heaven, or to connect by his own skill and labor the earthly with the celestial, and make a free and easy passage from one to the other, the Lord has derided his impotent efforts, confounded his language, and made confusion more confused. Uniform failure should teach us the folly of the attempt, and lead us to ask, if it be not the highest reason to bow to the divine reason, and the most perfect freedom to have no will but the will of God. "O Israel! thou destroyest thyself; in *me* is thy help."

PROTESTANTISM ENDS IN TRANSCENDENTALISM.*

[From Brownson's Quarterly Review for July, 1846.]

WE have no intention of reviewing at length the book the title of which we have just quoted. Indeed, we have read it only by proxy. We have heard it spoken of in certain literary circles as a remarkable production, almost as one of the wonders of the age. The Protestant lady who read it for us tells us that it is a weak and silly book, unnatural in its scenes and characters, coarse and vulgar in its language

---

Margaret, a Tale of the Real and Ideal, Blight and Bloom, including Sketches of a Place not before described, called Mons Christi. Boston: 1846.

and details, wild and visionary in its speculations; and, judging from the portions here and there which we actually have read, and from the source whence it emanates, we can hardly run any risk in endorsing our Protestant friend's criticism. The author is a man not deficient in natural gifts; he has respectable attainments; and makes, we believe, a tolerably successful minister of the latest form of Protestantism with which we chance to be acquainted; though, since we have not been introduced to any new form for several months, it must not be inferred from the fact that we are acquainted with no later form, that none later exists.

So far as we have ascertained the character of this book, it is intended to be the vehicle of certain crude speculations on religion, theology, philosophy, morals, society, education, and matters and things in general. The *Mons Christi* stands for the human heart, and Christ himself is our higher or instinctive nature, and if we but listen to our own natures, we shall at once learn, love, and obey all that our Blessed Redeemer teaches. Hence, Margaret, a poor, neglected child, who has received no instruction, who knows not even the name of her Maker, nor that of her Saviour, who, in fact, has grown up in the most brutish ignorance, is represented as possessing in herself all the elements of the most perfect Christian character, and as knowing by heart all the essential principles of Christian faith and morals. The author seems also to have written his work, in part at least, for the purpose of instructing our instructors as to the true method of education. He appears to adopt a very simple and a very pleasant theory on the subject,—one which cannot fail to commend itself to our young folks. Love is the great teacher; and the true method of education is for the pupil to fall in love with the tutor, or the tutor with the pupil, and it is perfected when the falling in love is mutual. Whence it follows, that it is a great mistake to suppose it desirable or even proper that tutor and pupil should both be of the same sex. This would be to reverse the natural order, since the sexes were evidently intended for each other. This method, we suppose, should be called *learning made easy, or nature displayed*, since it would enable us to dispense with school-rooms, prefects, text-books, study, and the birch, and to fall back on our natural instincts. These two points of doctrine indicate the genus, if not the species, of the book, and show that it must be classed under the general head of transcendentalism. If we could allow ourselves to go deeper into the work and to dwell longer on its licentiousness and blasphemy, we probably might determine its species as well as its genus. But this must suffice; and when we add that the author seems to comprise in himself several species at once, besides the whole genus humbuggery, we may dismiss the book, with sincere pity for him who wrote it, and a real prayer for his speedy restoration to the simple genus humanity, and for his conversion, through grace, to that Christianity which was given to man from above, and not, spider-like, spun out of his own bowels.

Yet, bad and disgusting, false and blasphemous, as this book really is, bating a few of its details, it is a book which no Protestant, as a Protestant, has a right to censure. Many Protestants affect great contempt for transcendentalism, and horror at its extravagance and blasphemy; but they have no right to do so. Transcendentalism is a much more serious affair than they would have us believe. It is not a simple "Yankee notion," confined to a few isolated individuals in a little corner of New England, as some of our southern friends imagine, but is in fact the dominant error of our times, is as rife in one section of our common country as in another; and, in principle, at least, is to be met with in every popular anti-catholic writer of the day, whether German, French, English, or American. It is, and has been from the first, the fundamental heresy of the whole Protestant world; for, at bottom, it is nothing but the fundamental principle of the Protestant reformation itself, and without assuming it, there is no conceivable principle on which it is possible to justify the reformers in their separation from the Catholic Church. The Protestant who refuses to accept it, with all its legitimate consequences, however frightful or absurd they may be, condemns himself and his whole party.

We are far from denying that many Protestants, and, indeed, the larger part of them, as a matter of fact, profess to hold many doctrines which are incompatible with transcendentalism; but this avails them nothing, for they hold them, not as Protestants, but in despite of their Protestantism, and therefore have no right to hold them at all. In taking an account of Protestantism, we have the right, and, indeed, are bound, to exclude them from its definition. Every man is bound, as the condition of being ranked among rational beings, to be logically consistent with himself; and no one can claim as his own any doctrine which does not flow from, or which is not logically consistent with, his own first principles. This follows necessarily from the principle, that of contradictories one must be false, since one necessarily excludes the other. If, then, the doctrines incompatible with transcendentalism, which Protestants profess to hold, do not flow from their own first principles, or if they are not logically compatible with them, they cannot claim them as Protestants, and we have the right, and are bound to exclude them from the definition of Protestantism. The man cannot be scientifically included in the definition of the horse, because both chance to be lodged in the same stable, or to be otherwise found in juxtaposition.

The essential mark or characteristic of Protestantism is, unquestionably, *dissent* from the authority of the Catholic Church, in subjection to which the first Protestants were spiritually born and reared. This is evident from the whole history of its origin, and from the well known fact, that opposition to Catholicity is the only point on which all who are called Protestants can agree among themselves. On every other question which comes up, they differ widely one from another, and not unfrequently some take views directly opposed to those taken by others; but when it concerns opposing the church, however dissimilar their doctrines and tempers, they all unite, and are ready to march as one man to the attack. As dissent, Protestantism is negative, denies the authority of the Catholic Church, and can include within its definition nothing which, even in the remotest sense, concedes or implies that authority. But no man, sect, or party can rest on a mere negation, for no mere negation is or can be an ultimate principle. Every negation implies an affirmation, and therefore an affirmative principle which authorizes it. He who dissents does so in obedience to some authority or principle which commands or requires him to dissent, and this principle, not the negation, is his fundamental principle. The essential or fundamental principle of Protestantism is, then, not dissent from the authority of the Catholic Church, but the affirmative principle on which it relies for the justification of its dissent.

What, then, is this affirmative principle? Whatever it be, it must be either out of the individual dissenting, or in him; that is, some external authority, or some internal authority. The first supposition is not admissible; for Protestants really allege no authority for dissent, external to the individual dissenting,—have never defined any such authority, never hinted that such authority exists or is needed; and there obviously is no such authority which can be adduced. In point of fact, so far from dissenting from the church on the ground that they are commanded to do so by an external authority paramount to the church, they deny the existence of all external authority in matters of faith, and defend their dissent on the ground that there is no such authority, never was, and never can be.

But some may contend, judging from the practice of Protestants, and what we know of the actual facts of the original establishment of Protestantism in all those countries in which it has become predominant, that it does recognize an external authority, which it holds paramount to the church, and on which it relies for its justification. Protestantism, as a matter of fact, owes its establishment to the authority of the lay lords and temporal princes, or, in a general sense, to the civil authority. It was, originally, much more of a political revolt than of a strictly religious dissent, and its external causes must be sought in the ambition of princes, dating back from Louis of Bavaria, and including Louis XII. of France, rather than in any real change of faith operated in the masses; and its way was prepared by the temper of mind which the temporal princes created in their subjects by the wars they undertook and carried on ostensibly against the popes as political sovereigns, but really for the purpose of possessing the patrimony of the church, and of subjecting the church, in their respective dominions, to the control of the secular power. The reformers would have acomplished little or nothing, if politics had not come to their aid. Luther would have bellowed in vain, had he not been backed by the powerful Elector of Saxony, and immediately aided by the Landgrave Philip; Zwingli, and Œcolampadius, and Calvin would have accomplished nothing in Switzerland, if they had not secured the aid of the secular arm, and followed its wishes; the powerful Huguenot party in France was more of a political than of a religious party, and it dwindled into insignificance as soon as it lost the support of great lords, distinguished statesmen and lawyers, and provincial parliaments. In Denmark, Sweden, and Norway, the reform was purely the act of the civil power; in the United Provinces, it was embraced as the principle of revolt, or of national independence; in England, it was the work, confessedly, of the secular government and was carried by court and parliament against the wishes of the immense majority of the nation; in Scotland, it was effected by the great lords, who wished to usurp to themselves the authority of the crown; in this country, it came in with the civil government, and was maintained by civil enactments, pains, and penalties. We might, therefore, be led, at first sight, to assert the fundamental principle of Protestantism to be the supremacy in spirituals of the civil power. But this would be a mistake, because it did not recognize this supremacy unless the civil power was anti-catholic, and because the assertion of this supremacy of the civil power in spirituals was itself a denial of the authority of the church, and therefore could not be made without making the act of dissent. There is no question but the Protestants did, whenever it suited their purpose, assert the supremacy of the state in spiritual matters; and it must be conceded that it is very agreeable to its nature to do so, as is evident from the fact, that even now, and in this country, it opposes the Catholic Church chiefly, and with the most success, on the ground that Catholicity asserts the freedom of religion, or, what is the same thing, the independence of the spiritual authority. Still this cannot be its ultimate principle. The church taught and teaches, that, though the independence of the civil power in matters purely temporal is asserted, its authority in spirituals is null. To deny this is to deny the church, and as much to dissent from her authority as to deny her infallibility, her divine authority, or any article of the creed she teaches; and this must be denied before the supremacy of the civil power in spirituals can be asserted. Therefore, if Protestantism did openly, avowedly, assert the Erastian heresy of the supremacy of the civil power in spirituals, it would not justify her dissent by an external authority, unless she could make this assertion itself on some external authority acknowledged to be paramount to the church. But for this she has no external authority, since the church denies it, and the authority of the state is the matter in question. She can, then, assert the supremacy of the state only on the authority of some principle in the individual dissenting, and therefore only on some internal authority. Whatever authority, then, Protestantism may ascribe to the civil power, it is not an external authority, because the authority asserted is always of the same order as that on which it is asserted, and can never transcend it.

Others, again, may think, since Protestants, and especially those among them denominated Anglicans and Episcopalians, occasionally appeal to Christian antiquity and talk of the fathers, and sometimes even profess to quote them, that they have, or think they have, in Christian antiquity an authority for dissent, virtually, at least, external to the individual dissenting. But Christian antiquity, unless read with a presumption in favor of the church, save on a few general and public facts manifestly against Protestants, decides nothing. Understood as the church understands it, and it evidently *may*, without violence to its letter or spirit, be so understood, it condemns Protestantism without mercy. To make it favor Protestantism even negatively, it is necessary to resort to a principle of interpretation which the church does not concede, and the adoption of which would, therefore, involve the dissent in question. If we take with us the canon, that all the Christian fathers are to be understood in accordance with the church when not manifestly against her, Christian antiquity will be all on the side of the Roman Catholic Church; if we take the canon, that all in the Christian fathers is to be understood in a sense against the church, when not manifestly in her favor, Christian antiquity may, on some important dogmas, leave the question doubtful; though even then it would, in fact, be decisive for the *authority* of the church, and therefore implicitly for all special dogmas. But, be this as it may, it is undeniable that it is only by adopting this latter canon that Protestantism can derive any countenance from Christian antiquity. But on what authority do they, or can they, adopt such a canon? Protestants call themselves reformers; they are accusers, dissenters, and therefore all the presumptions in the case are manifestly against them, as they are against all who accuse, bring an action or a charge against others; and they must make out a strong *prima facie* case, before they can turn the presumptions in their favor. This is law, and it is justice. Till they do this, the presumption is in favor of the church; and then it is enough for her to show that the testimony of antiquity *may*, without violence, be so understood as not to impeach her claims. Till then, nothing will make for Protestants which is not manifestly against her, so clear and express as by no allowable latitude of interpretation to be reconcilable with her pretensions. That is to say, the Protestant must impeach the church on *prima facie* evidence, before he can have the right to adopt that canon of interpretation without which it is manifestly suicidal for him to appeal to Christian antiquity. Take, as an illustration of what we mean, the testimony of St. Justin Martyr to the

Catholic doctrine of the Real Presence. It is clear to any one who reads the passage, that the words in a plain and easy sense confirm the Catholic doctrine; and yet, if there were an urgent necessity for interpreting them otherwise, we are not certain but, without greater deviation from the literal sense than is sometimes allowed, they *might* be so understood as not to be inconsistent with the views of the Blessed Eucharist which some Protestant sects profess to entertain. But by what authority, because they *may* be so interpreted, are we to say they *must* be? In truth, it is nothing to the Protestant's purpose to say they *may* be, till he establishes by positive authority they *must* be, for it is obvious they also *may* not be. Now, what and where is this positive authority? Manifestly not in Christian antiquity itself; and yet it must be had, before Christian antiquity can be adduced as authorizing dissent from the Catholic Church. This authority, as we said before, must be either external to the dissenter or internal in the dissenter himself. It cannot be external; for, after the church, there is no conceivable external authority applicable in the case. It must, then, be internal. Then the authority of Christian antiquity, as alleged against the church, is only the authority there is in the dissenter himself, according to the principle already established, that the authority asserted is necessarily of the same order as that on which it is asserted.

Finally, it will, perhaps, be alleged, inasmuch as all Protestants did at first, and some of them do now, appeal to the written word, or the Holy Scriptures, in justification of their dissent, that they have in these a real or a pretended authority, external to and independent of the dissenter, distinct from and paramount to that of the church. But a moment's reflection will show, even if the Scriptures were not in favor of the church, that this is a mistake. The Holy Scriptures proposed, and their sense declared, by the church, we hold with a firm faith to be the word of God, and therefore of the highest authority; but, if not so proposed and interpreted, though in many respects important and authentic historical documents, and valuable for their excellent didactic teachings, they would not and could not be for us the inspired, and, in a supernatural sense, the authoritative, word of God. To the Protestant they are not and cannot be an authority external to the dissenter; because, denying the unwritten word, the church, and all authoritative tradition, he has no external authority to vouch for the fact that they are the inspired word of God, or to declare their genuine sense. If there be no external authority to decide that the Bible is the word of God, and to declare its true sense, the authority ascribed to it in the last analysis, according to the principle we have established, is only the authority of some internal principle in the individual dissenting; for, in that case, the individual, by virtue of this internal principle, decides, with the Bible as without it, what is and what is not God's word, what God has and has not revealed; and therefore what he is not bound to believe, what he is and what he is not bound to do.

It is, moreover, notorious that Protestants do really deny all external authority in matters of faith, and hold that any external authority to determine for the individual what he must believe would be manifest usurpation, intolerable tyranny, to be resisted by every one who has any sense of Christian freedom, or of his rights and dignity as a man. Even the Anglican Church, which claims to herself authority in controversies of faith, acknowledges that she has no right to ordain any thing as of necessity to salvation, which may not be proved from God's word written; and by implication at least, if she means any thing, leaves it to the individual to determine for himself whether what she ordains is provable from the written word or not; and, therefore, abandons her own authority, by making the individual the judge of its legality. No one will, furthermore, pretend that Protestants even affect to have dissented from the Catholic Church, in which they were spiritually born and reared, in obedience to an external authority; that is to say, another church, which they held to be paramount to the Roman Catholic Church. If they had admitted that there was anywhere an authoritative church, they would have agreed that it was this church, and could have been no other. In denying the authority of the Roman Catholic Church, they denied, and intended to deny, in principle, all external authority in matters of faith; and the chief count in the indictment of the church, which they have drawn up, and on which they have been for these three hundred years demanding conviction, is, that she claims to be such authority, when no such authority was instituted, or intended to be instituted. We may, then, safely conclude that the affirmative principle on which Protestantism relies for the justification of its denial of Catholic authority is not some authority external to the individual dissenting, and held to be paramount to that from which he dissents.

Then the principle must be internal in the individual himself and this is precisely what Protestantism teaches; for by her own confession, nay, by her own boast, her fundamental principle is, *private judgment.* This was the only principle which, in the nature of the case, she could set up as the antagonist of Catholic authority; and it is notorious the world over, that it is in the name of this principle that she arraigns the church, and commands her to give an account of herself. We see, even to-day, emblazoned on the banners borne by the motley hosts of the so-called "Christian Alliance," this glorious device,—*The Right of Private Judgment.* This is their battle-cry, as *Deus Vult* was that of the Crusaders. It is their *In hoc signo vinces.* "We want no infallible pope, bishops, or church, to propound and explain to us God's word, to lord it over God's heritage, and make slaves of our very consciences. No! we are freemen, and we strike for freedom, the glorious birthright of every Christian to judge for himself what is or what is not the word of God; that is, what he is or is not to believe." There is no mistake in this. If there is any thing essential, any thing fundamental, in Prøtestantism, any thing which makes it the subject of a predicate at all, it is this far-famed and loud-boasted principle of *private judgment.*

In saying this, we of course are not to be understood as asserting that Protestants always, or even commonly, respect, in their practice, this right of private judgment. Practically, every Protestant says "*I* have the right to think as I please, and *you* have the right to think as I do; and if you do not, I will, if I have the power, compel you to do so, or confiscate your goods, deprive you of citizenship, outlaw you, behead, hang, or burn you; at least, imprison you, flog you, or bore your ears and tongue." In point of fact, Protestants, we grant, have very generally violated the principle of private judgment, and have practised, in the name of religious liberty, the most unjust tyranny over conscience,—unjust, because, on their own principles, they have received from Almighty God no authority to dictate to conscience, and because they also concede, what is unquestionably true, that conscience is accountable to God alone. Every attempt of any man, set, or class of men, not expressly commissioned by Almighty God,—so expressly that the authority exercised shall be really and truly his,—to exert the least control over conscience is a manifest usurpation, an outrageous tyranny, which every man, having a just reverence for his Maker, will resist even unto death. The Catholic Church, indeed, claims plenary authority over conscience; but only on the ground, that she is divinely commissioned, and that the authority which speaks in her is literally and as truly the authority of God, as that of the representative is that of his sovereign. If, *per impossibile*, she could suppose herself not to be so commissioned, and therefore not having the pledge of the divine supervision, protection, and aid which such commission necessarily implies, she would concede that she has no authority, and should attempt to exercise none. We cheerfully obey her, because in obeying her we are obeying not a human authority, but God himself. In submitting to her we are free, because we are submitting to God, who is our rightful sovereign, to whom we belong, all that we have, and all that we are. Freedom is not in being held to no obedience, but in being held to obey only the legal sovereign; and the more unqualified this obedience, the freer we are. Perfect freedom is in having no will of our own, in willing only what our sovereign wills, and because he wills it. If the church, as we cannot doubt, be really commissioned by God, the more absolute her authority, the more unqualified our submission, the more perfect is our liberty, as every man knows, who knows any thing at all of that freedom wherewith the Son makes us free. But in yielding obedience to a Protestant sect, it is not the same. When any one of our sects undertakes to dictate to conscience, it is tyranny; because, by its own confession, it has received no authority from God. It is tyranny, even though what it attempts to enforce be really God's word; for it attempts to enforce it by a *human*, and not by a *divine* authority. It would still tyrannize, because it has no right to enforce any thing at all. It may say, as our sects do say, it has the Bible, that the Bible is God's word, and that it only exacts the obedience to God's commands which no man has the right to withhold. Be it so. But who has made it the keeper and executor of God's law? Where is its commission under the hand and seal of the Almighty? It is, doubtless, right that the civil law should be executed,—that the murderer, for instance, should be punished; but it does not *therefore* follow that you, as a simple citizen, have the right to execute them, and to inflict the punishment. That may be done only by the constituted authorities, and is not your business; and it is a sound as well as a homely adage, Let every one mind his own business. Protestants, on this point, fall into grievous errors. The simple possession of the Holy Scriptures does not constitute them *keepers* of the word,—even supposing the Scriptures to contain the *whole* word,—and give them the right to dictate to conscience, as they imagine, any more than the fact of your having in your possession the statute-book constitutes you the guardian and administrator of the laws of the commonwealth. Protestants, whenever they interfere with the right of private judgment, convict themselves, on their own principles, of practising on what, in these days, is called "Lynch law"; and Lynch law is to the state precisely what Protestantism, in practice, is to the church.—This is a fact which deserves the grave consideration of those sects which contend for creeds and confessions, and claim the right to try and punish as heretics such as in their judgment do not conform to them. Even Dr. Beecher himself came very near, a few years since, being *lynched* by his Presbyterian associates; and if it had not been for an extraordinary suppleness and marvellous skill in parrying blows, hardly to have been expected in one of his age, it might have been all up with him. Our Presbyterian, Dutch Reformed, Puritan, and Anglican friends should lay this to heart, and never suffer themselves to complain of the practice of "Lynch law," or to find the least fault with the commission of Judge Lynch himself,— for it emanates from the same authority as their own, and is as regularly made out and authenticated. But this is foreign from our present purpose. It is enough for our present purpose, that Protestants assert, in theory, as they unquestionably do, the right of private judgment, and make it the principle of their dissent from the authority of the Catholic Church.

But all men, at least as to their inherent rights, are equal. The right of private judgment, then, cannot be asserted for one man, without being at the same time, and by the same authority, asserted for all men. Then Protestants cannot assert private judgment as their authority for dissenting from the Catholic Church, without erecting it into a universal principle. We may assume, then, that Protestantism begins by laying down as its principle the right of *all men* to private judgment.

But the right of all men to private judgment is in effect the *unrestricted* or universal right to private judgment. This may not have been clearly seen in the beginning, and there is no question but Protestants intended in the commencement to restrict the right of private judgment to the simple interpretation of the written word. But every one, whatever may be his intentions, must be held answerable for the strict logical consequences of the principles he deliberately adopts; for if he does not foresee these consequences, he ought not to take upon himself the responsibility of adopting the principles. The right of private judgment, once admitted, can no longer be restricted. If restricted at all, it must be by some authority, and this authority must be either external or internal. If internal, it is private judgment itself, and then it cannot restrict, for it would be absurd to say that private judgment can restrict private judgment. It cannot be an external authority, because Protestants admit no external authority, and because we cannot assert an external authority to restrict private judgment, without denying private judgment itself. Either the authority must prescribe the limits of private judgment, or private judgment must prescribe the limits of the restriction; if the first, it is tantamount to the denial of private judgment itself, for private judgment would then subsist only at the mercy of authority, by sufferance, and not by right; if the latter, the *authority* is null; for private judgment may enlarge or contract the restriction as it pleases, and that is evidently no restriction which is only what that which is restricted chooses to make it. It is impossible, then, to erect private judgment into a principle for all men, and afterwards to restrict it to the simple interpretation of the Holy Scriptures.

If we assert the right of private judgment to interpret the Holy Scriptures, we must assert its right in all cases whatsoever; for the principle on which private judgment can be defended in one case is equally applicable in every case. Will it be said that private judgment must yield to God's word? Granted. But what is God's word? The Bible. How know you that? Do you determine that the Bible is the word of God by some external authority, or by private judgment? Not by some external authority, because you have none, and admit none. By private judgment? Then the authority of the Bible is *for you* only private judgment. The Bible does not propose itself, and therefore can have no authority higher than the authority which proposes it. Here is a serious difficulty for those Protestants who set up such a clamor about the Bible, and which shows them, or ought to show them, that, whatever the Bible may be for a Catholic, for them it can, in no conceivable contingency, be any thing but a human authority. *The authority of that which is proposed is of the same order as that which proposes, and cannot transcend it.* This is a Protestant argument, and is substantially the great argument of Chillingworth against Catholicity. Nothing proposes the Bible to Protestants but private judgment, as is evident from their denial of all other authority; and therefore in the Bible they—not we, thank God!—have only the authority of private judgment, and therefore only the word of man, and not the word of God. If the authority on which Protestants receive the word of God is only that of private judgment, then there is for them in the Bible only private judgment; and then nothing to restrict private judgment, for private judgment can itself be no restriction on private judgment.

Moreover, if we take the Bible to be the word of God on the authority of private judgment, and its sense on the same authority, as Protestants do and must, then we assume private judgment to be competent to decide of itself what is and what is not the word of God, what God has revealed and what he has not revealed, has commanded and has not commanded,—and therefore competent to decide what we are to believe and what we are not to believe, and what we are to do and what we are not to do. But this is to assume the whole for private judgment, and therefore to assume its unrestricted right. We may, then, assume, in the second place, that Protestantism not only lays down the principle of the right of all men to private judgment, but the right of all men to the universal or unrestricted right of private judgment.

But private judgment itself is not, strictly speaking, ultimate, and therefore, though it be the principle of Protestantism, is not its ultimate principle. The ultimate principle of Protestantism lies a little further back. Rights are never in themselves ultimate, but must always, to be rights, rest on some foundation or authority. The right of private judgment necessarily implies some principle on which it is founded. Every judgment is by some standard or measure; for when we judge it is always *by* something, and this, whatever it is, is the principle, law, rule, criterion, standard, or measure of the judgment. In every act of private judgment this standard or measure is the individual judging. The individual judges by himself, and to judge by one's self is precisely what is meant by private judgment. In it the individual is both measurer and measure, —in a word, his own yard-stick of truth and goodness. But rights, to be rights, must not only be founded on some principle, but on a *true* principle; for to say they are founded on a false principle is only saying in other words, that they have no foundation at all. The right of all men to unrestricted private judgment, then, necessarily implies that each and every man is in himself the exact measure of truth and goodness. In laying down the principle of private judgment as the principle of its dissent from the Catholic Church, Protestantism, then, necessarily lays down the principle, that each and every man is in himself the exact measure of truth and goodness,—the very fundamental proposition of transcendentalism. The identity in principle is, then, perfect; and no Protestant, as we began by saying, can refuse to accept transcendentalism, with all its legitimate consequences, without condemning himself and his whole party.

This conclusion is undeniable, for the acutest dialectician will find no break or flaw in the chain of reasoning by which it is obtained. We, then, may assume this very important position, that transcendentalism is the strict logical termination of Protestantism; and if some Protestants, as is the case, refuse to admit it, it is at the expense of their dialectics; because they cannot, or dare not, say, Two and two make four, but judge it more prudent to say, Two and two make five, or to compromise the matter and say, Two and two make three. There are few things which are more disgusting than the cowardice which shrinks from avowing the legitimate consequences of one's own principles. The sin of inconsequence is, as the celebrated Dr. Evariste de Gypendole justly remarks, a mortal sin,—at least, in the eyes of humanity; for it is high treason against the rational nature itself; and he who deliberately commits it voluntarily abdicates reason, and takes his place among inferior and irrational natures. If your principles are sound, you cannot push them to a dangerous extreme; and if they will not bear pushing to their extreme consequences, you should know that they are unsound, and not fit to be entertained; for it is always lawful to conclude the unsoundness of the principle from the unsoundness of the consequences.

Taking this view of the case, we confess the transcendentalists appear to us the more respectable, and indeed the only respectable because the only consistent, class of Protestants. Consistent as Protestants, we mean, not as men; for transcendentalism is the *ne plus ultra* of inconsistency and absurdity; but as Protestants they are consistent in so far as they carry out with an iron logic the Protestant principle to its legitimate results; and in doing this, in the providence of God, they are rendering no mean service to the cause of truth. They are a living and practical *reductio ad absurdum* of Protestantism. They strip it of its disguises, expose it in its nakedness, and subserve the cause of truth as the drunken Helotæ subserved the cause of temperance in the Spartan youth by exposing to them the disgusting effects of drunkenness.

It is of great practical importance that Protestantism should be exhibited by its followers in its true light as it really is in itself. Thus far Protestants have owed their success and influence, in the main, to the fact, that the mass of them have never seen and comprehended Protestantism in its simple, unadulterated elements. It has always been presented to them in a livery stolen from Catholicity. The great mass of the Protestant people, seeing it only in this livery, have supposed that it appertained to the household of faith, and that they had in it all that is essential to the Christian religion. Unable to penetrate its disguises, unable to distinguish between what was genuinely Protestant and what was surreptitiously taken from the church, they could not understand the force or truth of the Catholic accusations against them. It seemed to them utterly false to say that they had no faith, no church, no religion, and that their Protestantism necessarily involved the denial of the whole scheme of revealed religion, and left them in reality nothing but mere naturalism. Had they not something they called a church? Had they not places of worship modelled after Christian temples? Had they not the Holy Scriptures, pastors, and teachers, hymns, prayers,—all the exterior forms of worship? Did they not profess to believe in God, the Holy Trinity, the Incarnation, the Atonement, the necessity of grace, the endless punishment of the wicked, and the eternal beatitude of the just,—all that even Catholic doctors have ever taught that it is necessary *ex necessitate medii ad salutem* to be explicitly believed? Did they not try to lead holy and devout lives, spend much time in prayer and praise, seek earnestly to know and do the will of God, and actually, in many instances, attain to a moral elevation which would more than compare favorably with that of many Catholics? How say, then, that we have no religion, that our principles are at war with Christianity, and lead necessarily to the destruction of all faith, of all Christian morality? Have we not in our Protestantism, as we hold it, a living lie to your unjust charge, your foul aspersion? It must be confessed, that appearances to the Protestant, were much against the Catholic, and it required considerable insight and firmness of logic to establish the charges which the Catholic, from the principles of an infallible faith, was fully warranted in preferring. But time and events have now made clear and certain to all who can see and reason, what then seemed so doubtful, not to say, so unfounded. In transcendentalism, which is both the logical and historical development of Protestantism, it may now be seen that the Protestant, not the Catholic, was deceived; that not the Catholic was unjust in his charges, but the Protestant was carried away by his delusions. This is an immense gain, and by showing this, by stripping Protestantism of its disguises, by compelling it to abandon what it had attempted to retain of Catholicity, and to restrict it to its own principles, transcendentalism is subserving in no ordinary degree the cause of religion and morality. Three hundred years of controversy have resulted in simplifying the question, and in making up the true and proper issue. If the true and proper issue could have been made in the beginning, Protestantism would have died in its birth. The mass of those who have followed the Protestant standard have done so because they supposed *they* had in the Holy Scriptures a divine authority for their belief. Here was their mother delusion. Catholics have really in the Holy Scriptures a divine authority, because they receive them on the proposition of the church expressly commissioned by Almighty God to propose the truth revealed; but Protestants, as we have seen, since they take the Holy Scriptures only on the authority of private reason, have in them only the authority of private reason,—a merely human authority. It is now seen and understood that the Scriptures, if taken on human authority, have only a human authority; and therefore, as Catholics always alleged, Protestants, with all their pretensions, have only a human authority for the dogmas they profess to derive from them, and therefore are not, and never have been able to make that act of divine faith without which, if they have come to years of discretion, they possess no *Christian* virtue, and do nothing meritorious for eternal life. If Christianity be a supernatural life, the life which begins in supernatural faith and contemplates a supernatural destiny, it is now clear that Protestants cannot and never could claim to be truly within the pale of the Christian family, but do reject and always have virtually rejected the Christian religion itself.

This being so, it becomes necessary now either to deny the supernatural character of the Christian life, and therefore the necessity of divine or supernatural faith, or to give up Protestantism as having no claim to be called Christian. This is becoming a general conviction among Protestants themselves, and therefore the tendency to reject Christianity, as a supernatural religion, is manifesting itself all over the Protestant world. Even Bishop Butler, the great Anglican light of the last century, declares the Gospel to be only " a republication of the law of nature;" and we have rarely met with a Protestant, whatever might be his unintelligible jargon about the New Birth, that did not hold, substantially, that the Christian life is merely the continuation and development of our natural life. The old modes of speech, adopted when Christianity was held to be a supernatural religion, are, we admit, in some instances, retained and insisted upon; but they have lost their former significance. *Supernatural* is defined to be *supersensuous*, as if spiritual existences could not be natural as well as material existences. It is thus Coleridge defines supernatural; it is thus, also, the *supernaturalists* of Germany, of the school of Schleiermacher and De Wette, understand it, while the rationalists deny it in name as well as in reality. In no higher sense do we find the word recognized by the mass of Swiss and French Protestants. "What did Almighty God make us for?" said we, the other day, to a worthy Protestant preacher, not without note in this community and the councils of his country. "To develop and perfect our spiritual natures," was the ready reply; that is, to finish the work which Almighty God began, but left incomplete; and this is the reply which, in substance, is almost universally given by those Protestants who plume themselves on having pure and ennobling spiritual views of religion. Thus it is, men everywhere lose sight of their supernatural destiny, and then deny the necessity of a supernatural life, and then the necessity of grace. Thus, in substance, if not in name they reject the doctrines of the Trinity, the Incarnation, the miraculous conception and birth of our Saviour, original sin, the Atonement, remission of sins, the plenary inspiration of the Scriptures, and, finally, all that is incompatible with the principle of man's sufficiency for himself, as so many reminiscences of Popery, or traditions of the Dark Ages, and as interposing between the human soul and its Creator, and hindering its freedom and growth. It is idle to deny, that all over the Protestant world the tendency to this result is strong and irresistible, and that it is already reached by the more thinking and enlightened portion of Protestants. The true and proper issue, then, cannot be really any longer evaded. Protestants must meet the simple questions of naturalism or supernaturalism, of transcendentalism or Catholicity, of man or God.

No doubt, a certain class of Protestant doctors do, and will, for some little time to come, struggle to stave off this issue, but in vain. Matters have proceeded too far. It is too late. The internal developments of Protestantism are too far completed, the spirit at work in the Protestant ranks is too powerful, to prevent the direct issue from being made. Transcendentalism, under one form or another, has struck its roots so deep, has spread out its branches so far, and finds so rich a soil, that it must ere long cause all the other forms of Protestantism, as the underbrush in a thick forest, to die out and disappear. The spirit of inquiry which Protestantism boasts of having quickened, the disposition to bring every question, the most intricate and the most sacred, to the test of private judgment, which she fosters, and which it would be suicidal in her to discountenance, will compel these doctors themselves either to give up their vocations, or to fall into the current and suffer themselves to be borne on to its termination. Resistance is madness. The movement party advances with a steady step, and will drive all before it. Whatever Evangelical doctor throws himself in its path to stay its onward march is a dead man and ground to powder. There is no alternative; you must follow Schlegel, Hurter, Newman, Faber, back into the bosom of Catholic unity, or go on with Emerson, Parker, and Carlyle. Not to-day only have we seen this. Think you that we, who, according to your own story, have tried every form of Protestantism, and disputed every inch of Protestant ground, would ever have left the ranks of Protestantism in which we were born, and under whose banner we had fought so long and suffered so much, if there had been any other alternative for us?

The "No Popery" cry which our *Evangelicals* are raising, and which rings in our ears from every quarter, does not in the least discompose us. In this very cry we hear an additional proof of what we are maintaining. We understand the full significance of this cry. The Protestant masses are escaping from their leaders. The sectarian ministers, especially of the species *Evangelical*, are losing their hold on their flocks, and finding that their old petrified forms, retained from Luther, or Calvin, or Knox, will no longer satisfy them,—have no longer vitality for them. Their craft is in danger; their power and influence are departing, and *Ichabod* is beginning to be written on their foreheads. They see the handwriting on the wall, and feel that something must be done to avert the terrible doom that awaits them. Fearfulness and trembling seize them, and, like the drowning man, they catch at the first straw, and hope, and yet with the mere hope of despair, that it will prove a plank of safety. They have no resource in their old, dried-up, dead forms. They must look abroad, call in some extrinsic aid, and, by means of some foreign power, delay the execution of the judgment they feel in their hearts has already been pronounced against them. They must get up some excitement which will captivate the people and blind their reason. No excitement seems to them more likely to answer their purpose than a "No Popery" excitement, which they fancy will find a firm support in the hereditary passions and prejudices of their flocks. Here is the significance of this "No Popery" excitement.

But this excitement will prove suicidal. Times have changed, and matters do not stand as they did in the days of Luther, and Zwingli, and Henry, and Calvin, and Knox. The temper of men's minds is different, and there is a new order of questions up for solution. The old watchwords no longer answer the purpose. What avails it to prove the pope to be antichrist, to populations that do not even believe in Christ? What avails it to thunder at Catholicity with texts which are no longer believed to have a divine authority? Protestantism must now fall back on her own principles, and fight her battles with her own weapons. She must throw out her own banner to the breeze, and call upon men to gather and arm and fight for progress, for liberty, for the unrestricted right of private judgment, or she will not rally a corporal's guard against Catholicity. But the moment she does this, she is, as the French say, *enfoncée;* for she has subsisted and can subsist only by professing one thing and doing another. Let our Evangelical doctors, in their madness, rally, in the name of progress, of liberty, of private judgment, an army to put down the pope, and the matter will not end there. Their forces, furnished with arms against Catholicity, will turn upon themselves, and in a hoarse voice, and if need be, from brazen throats and tongues of flame, exclaim, "No more sham, gentlemen. We go for principle. We do not unpope the pope to find a new pope in each petty presbyter, and a spy and informer in each brother or sister communicant. You are nothing to us. Freedom, gentlemen; doff your gowns, abrogate all your creeds and confessions, break up all your religious organizations, abolish all forms of worship except such as each individual may choose and exercise for himself, and acknowledge in fact, as well as in name, that every man is free to worship one God or twenty Gods, or no God at all, as seems to him good, unlicensed, unquestioned, or take the consequences. We will no more submit to your authority than you will to that of the pope."

This is the tone and these the terms in which these "No Popery" doctors will find, one of these days, their flocks addressing them; for we have only given words to what they know as well as we is the predominant feeling of the great majority of the Protestant people. The very means, in the present temper of the Protestant public, they must use to insure their success, cannot fail to prove their ruin. They will only hasten the issue they would evade. Deprived, as they now are, for the most part, of all *direct* aid from the civil power, the force of things is against them, and it matters little whether they attempt to move or sit still. They were mad enough in the beginning to take their stand on a movable foundation, and they must move on with it, or be left to balance themselves in vacuity; and if they do move on with it, they will simply arrive—nowhither. They are doomed, and they cannot escape. Hence it is all their motions affect us only as the writhings and death-throes of the serpent whose head is crushed.

Regarding it of the greatest importance that the whole matter should be brought to its true and proper issue, and believing firmly, that when the real alternatives are distinctly apprehended and admitted, that many Protestants will choose "the better part," we are not displeased to witness the very decided tendency to transcendentalism now manifesting itself throughout the Protestant world. It is a proof to us that the internal developments of Protestantism are not only bringing it to its strictly logical termination, but, what is more important still, to the *term of its existence.* The nations which became Protestant rebelled against the God of their fathers, the God who had brought them up out of the bondage of ignorance, barbarism, idolatry, and superstition, and said they would not have him to reign over them, but they would henceforth be their own masters, and rule themselves. He, for wise and merciful but inscrutable purposes, gave them up to their reprobate sense, left them to themselves, to follow their own wills, till bitter experience should teach them their wickedness, their impiety, their folly and madness, and bring them in shame and confusion to pray, "O Lord, in thy wrath remember mercy; save us from ourselves, or we perish!" To this desirable result it was not to be expected they would come till Protestantism had run its natural course, and reached its legitimate termination. They would not abandon it till they had exhausted all its possibilities, and till it could no longer present a new face to charm or delude them. In this transcendental tendency, we see the evidence that it has run or very nearly run its natural course, and in transcendentalism reaches its termination, exhausts itself, and can go no further; for there is no further. Beyond transcendentalism, in the same direction, there is no place. Transcendentalism is the last stage this side of *nowhere;* and when reached, we must hold up, or fly off into boundless vacuity. In its prevalence, then, we may trust we see the signs of a change near at hand; and any change must certainly be in a better direction.

PROTESTANTISM IN A NUTSHELL.*

[From Brownson's Quarterly Review for October, 1849.]

WE have seen few works written with a more just appreciation of our age than the one before us, or so well adapted to the present state of the controversy which we are always obliged to carry on with the enemies of the church. Its author understands well the essential nature of Protestantism, and clearly and distinctly points out the proper method of meeting it under the various forms it at present assumes, and of imposing silence on its arrogant and noisy pretensions. He does not confine himself to the field of theological controversy, properly so called, but he meets Protestants on their own chosen ground, on the broad field of European civilization, and shows them that, under the point of view of civilization, of liberty, order, and social well-being, Protestantism has been a total failure, and that, even in reference to this world, Catholicity has found itself as superior to it as it claims to be in regard to the world to come. He does not merely vindicate Catholicity, in relation to civilization, from the charges preferred against it by the modern advocates of liberalism and progressism, but by a calm appeal to history and philosophy, he shows that the opposing system has interrupted the work of civilization which the church was prosecuting with vigor and success, and has operated solely in the interest of barbarism. In doing this, he has done a real service to the cause of truth, and we learn with pleasure that one of our friends in England has translated his work, and rendered it accessible to the great body of English and American readers.

Such a work as this was much needed in our language. We have, indeed, many able controversial works,—works admirable for the learning, ability, and skill of their authors; but we have comparatively few which are adapted to the present state of the controversy with Protestants. The greater part of those accessible to the mere English reader

---

*El Protestantismo comparado con el Catolicismo en sus relaciones con la civilizacion Europea. Por Don Jaime Balmes, Presbítero. Paris: 1849

are well adapted only to the few individuals whose hearts the grace of God has already touched, and whose faces are already set towards the church. Truth is one and invariable, but error is variable and manifold. It is always the same truth that we must oppose to error, but it is seldom the same error for two successive moments to which we must oppose it. We must shoot error, as well as folly, "as it flies," and we must be able to shoot it under ever-varying and varied disguises. The works we have, excellent as they are in their way, and admirably fitted to guard the faithful against many of the devices of the enemy to detach them from the church, and to aid and instruct persons in heretical communions who are virtually prepared to return to the church, do not hit the reigning form of Protestantism; they do not reach the seat of the disease, and are apparently written on the supposition of soundness, where there is, in fact, only rottenness. The principles they assume as the basis of their refutation of Protestantism, though nominally professed or conceded by the majority of Protestants, are not held with sufficient firmness to be used as the foundation of an argument that is to have any practical efficacy in their conversion. They all appear to assume that Protestants as a body really mean to be Christians, and err only in regard to some of the dogmas of Christianity and the method of determining the faith; that Protestantism is a specific heresy, a distinct and positive form of error, like Arianism or Pelagianism; and that its adherents would regard themselves as bound to reject it, if proved to be repugnant to Christianity, or contrary to the Holy Scriptures. This is a natural and a charitable supposition; but we are sorry to say, that, if it was ever warrantable, it is not by any means warrantable in our times, except as to the small number of individuals in the several sects who are mere exceptions to the rule. Protestantism is no specific heresy, is no distinct or positive form of error, but error in general, indifferent to forms, and receptive of any form or of all forms, as suits the convenience or the exigency of its friends. It is a veritable Proteus, and takes any and every shape judged to be proper to deceive the eyes or to elude the blows of the champions of truth. It is Lutheran, Calvinistic, Arminian, Unitarian, Pantheistic, Atheistic, Pyrrhonistic, each by turns or all at once, as is necessary to its purpose. The Protestant as such has, in the ordinary sense, no principles to maintain, no character to support, no consistency to preserve; and we are aware of no authority, no law, no usage, by which he will consent to be bound. Convict him from tradition, and he appeals to the Bible; convict him from the Bible, and he appeals to reason; convict him from reason, and he appeals to private sentiment; convict him from private sentiment, and he appeals to scepticism, or flies back to reason, to Scripture, or tradition, and alternately from one to the other,—never scrupling to affirm, one moment, what he denied the moment before, nor blushing to be found maintaining that of contradictories both may be true. He is indifferent as to what he asserts or denies, if able for the moment to obtain an apparent covert from his pursuers.

Protestants do not study for the truth, and are never to be presumed willing to accept it, unless it chances to be where and what they wish it. They occasionally read our books and listen to our arguments, but rarely to ascertain our doctrines, or to learn what we are able to say against them or for ourselves. The thought, that we may possibly be right, seldom occurs to them; and when it does, it is instantly suppressed as an evil thought, as a temptation from the devil. They take it for granted, that, against us, they are right, and cannot be wrong. This is with them a "fixed fact," admitting no question. They condescend to consult our writings, or to listen to our arguments, only to ascertain what doctrines they can profess, or what modifications they can introduce into those which they have professed, that will best enable them to elude our attacks, or give them the appearance of escaping conviction by the authorities from tradition, Scripture, reason, and sentiment which we array against them. Candor or ingenuousness towards themselves even is a thing wholly foreign to their Protestant nature, and they are instinctively and habitually cavillers and sophisticators. They disdain to argue a question on its merits, and always, if they argue at all, argue it on some unimportant collateral. They never recognize—unless it is for their interest to do so—any distinction between a *transeat* and a *concedo*, and rarely fail to insist that the concession of an irrelevant point is a concession of the main issue. They have no sense of responsibleness, no loyalty to truth, no mental chastity, no intellectual sincerity. What is for them is authority which no body must question; what is against them is no authority at all. Their own word if not in their favor, they refuse to accept; and the authority to which they professedly appeal they repudiate the moment it is seen not to sustain them. To reason with them as if they would stand by their own professions, or could or would acknowledge any authority but their own ever-varying opinions, is entirely to mistake them, and to betray our own simplicity.

Undoubtedly, many of our friends, who have not, like ourselves, been brought up Protestants, and have not to blush at the knowledge their Protestant experience has given them, may feel that in this judgment we are rash and uncharitable. Would that we were so. We take no pleasure in thinking ill of any portion of our fellow-men, and would always rather find ourselves wrong in our unfavorable judgments of them than right. But in this matter the evidence is too clear and conclusive to allow us even to hope that we are wrong. There is not a single Protestant doctrine opposed to Catholicity that even Protestants themselves have not over and over again completely refuted; there is not a single charge brought by Protestants against the church that some of them, as well as we, have not fully exploded; and no more conclusive vindication of the claims of Catholicity can be desired than may be—nay, than in fact has been—collected from distinguished Protestant writers themselves. This is a fact which no Protestant, certainly no Catholic, can deny. How happens it, then, that the Protestant world still subsists, and that, for the last hundred and fifty years, we have made comparatively little progress in regaining Protestants to the church?

We may, it is true, be referred to the obstinacy in error characteristic of all heretics; but, in the present case,—unless what is meant is obstinacy in error in general, and not error in particular,—this will not suffice as an answer; because, during this period, there has been no one particular form of error to which Protestants have uniformly adhered. No class of Protestants adheres to-day to the opinions it originally avowed. In this respect, there is a marked difference between the Protestant sects of modern times and the early Oriental sects. The Jacobite holds to-day the same specific heresy which he held a thousand years ago; and the Nestorian of the nineteenth is substantially the Nestorian of the fourth century. But nothing analogous is true of any of the modern Protestant sects. Protestants boast, indeed, their glorious reformation, but they no longer hold the views of its authors. Luther, were he to ascend to the scenes of his earthly labors, would be utterly unable to recognize his teachings in the doctrines of the modern Lutherans; the Calvinist remains a Calvinist only in name; the Baptist disclaims his Anabaptist original; the Unitarian points out the errors he detects in his Socinian ancestors; and the Transcendentalist looks down with pity on his Unitarian parents, while he considers it a cruel persecution to be excluded from the Unitarian family. No sect retains, unmodified, unchanged, the precise form of error with which it set out. All the forms Protestants have from time to time assumed have been developed, modified, altered, almost as soon as assumed,—always as internal or external controversy made it necessary or expedient. Here is a fact nobody can deny, and it proves conclusively that the Protestant world does not subsist solely by virtue of its obstinate attachment to the views or opinions to which it has once committed itself, or in consequence of its aversion to change the doctrines it has once professed.

This fact proves even more than this. Bossuet very justly concludes from the *variations* of Protestantism its *objective* falsity, because the characteristic of truth is invariability; but we may go further, and from the same variations conclude the *subjective* falsity of Protestantism, or that Protestants have no real belief in, or attachment to, the particular doctrines they profess,—not only that Protestants profess a false doctrine, but that they are insincere, and destitute, as a body, of real honesty in their professions. If they believed their doctrines, they could never tolerate the changes they undergo. New sects might, indeed, arise among them, but no sect would suffer its original doctrines to be in the least altered or modified. The members of every sect, if they believed its creed, would, so long as they adhered to it, be struck with horror at the bare idea of altering or modifying it; for it would seem to them to be altering or modifying the revealed word of God. This is a point of no slight importance in judging the Protestant world, and seems to us to deserve more attention than the great body of Catholics even are disposed to give it. These variations prove, at least, that Protestantism is something distinct from the formal teachings of Protestants, and something that can and does survive them.

That we are neither rash nor uncharitable in our judgment of Protestants, severe as it unquestionably is, may be collected from facts of daily occurrence. The great body of

Protestants, it is well known, labor unceasingly to detach Catholics from the church, and to this end use all the means the age and country will tolerate. It was to combine their forces against Catholicity, that, a few years since, under the pontificate of Gregory XVI., the Protestant ministers held their World's Convention in London; that they formed Protestant alliances in England, Germany, France, Switzerland, and this country, devised a plan in concert with the Italian refugees in these several countries for effecting a civil revolution in every Catholic state, especially in the Papal States, and called upon the Protestant people everywhere to contribute funds for carrying it out,—a plan, even to minute particulars, which the well-known ministers, Bacon, Coxe, Beecher, Kirk, and others, forewarned us of in a meeting of the Protestant Alliance in this city in 1845, and which we have seen to a great extent realized during the last two years, much to the joy of thousands of nominal Catholics, who little suspected themselves to be the dupes of miserable demagogues on the one hand, and of hypocritical Protestant ministers on the other. But while Protestants, in season and out of season, by means fair and by means foul, by means open and by means secret and tortuous, seek to detach Catholics from the church, they appear quite indifferent as to which of the thousand and one Protestant formulas they are led to embrace, or whether, indeed, they are led to embrace any one of them. Excepting, as we always do, here and there an individual, they are satisfied with the simple fact, that those drawn off from the church are no longer Catholics. Whatever we lose, they count their gain, and although they are well aware that the majority of those they gain from us turn out rank apostates, infidels, and blasphemers, they nevertheless rejoice over them, and claim them as so many accessions to their ranks. If Protestants had any sincerity in their professions, if they had any sense of religion, how could they regard themselves as triumphing in proportion as they succeed in detaching miserable wretches from us, and sinking them in religion even below the ancient heathen,—especially since none of them dare pretend that we do not embrace all the essentials of the Christian religion, or that salvation is not attainable in our church? They profess to be Christians, but they would rather make us infidels, apostates, atheists, blasphemers, than suffer us to remain Catholics. What more conclusive proof can you ask of their insincerity,—of the fact that their professions afford no clew to the real state of their minds, and ought to count for nothing?

Doubtless, we are not to be understood to imply that Protestants are always distinctly conscious of their own want of strict honesty and sincerity. No man knoweth whether he deserveth love or hatred. Knowledge of one's self is hard to acquire; self-deception is one of the easiest things in the world, and few there are who are certain that they have a *good* conscience, or are sure of the motives which govern them. No doubt, Protestants gloss over their conduct, and have some method of justifying it in their own eyes; no doubt, they persuade themselves that they are sincere,—at least as sincere as they can afford to be, as honest in their belief as people generally are; but they know not what manner of spirit they are of, and as that spirit is inherently a lying spirit, as Catholics well know, it must needs lie unto themselves as well as unto others. Probably every heresiarch dupes himself before he dupes others, and holds the post of leader only because a greater dupe than his followers. That kind of honesty and sincerity compatible with a false spirit and gross delusion, we are not disposed to deny to Protestants; but we should remember that no really sincere and truthful mind ever is or ever can be deluded. No man ever is or ever was strictly honest and sincere in the profession of a false doctrine,—for no false doctrine can ever, in the nature of things, be so evidenced as to exclude doubt; and he who professes to believe what he doubts professes what he knows he does not believe, and therefore professes what he knows is not true. A man may be honestly in doubt as to what is or is not the truth on certain points; but no man can honestly *profess* faith in a false doctrine,—for in a false doctrine no man can have faith.

A sort of honesty and sincerity we certainly concede to the generality of Protestants; but as to the end for which they profess their doctrines, rather than as to the doctrines themselves. The principle common to them, and the only one we can always be sure they will practically adhere to, is, that the end justifies the means. The end they propose is, neither to save their souls nor to discover and obey the truth, but to destroy or elude Catholicity. The spirit which possesses them maddens them against the church, and gives them an inward repugnance to every thing not opposed to her. To overthrow her, to blot out her existence, or to prevent her from crushing them with the weight of her truth, is to them a praiseworthy end, at least a great and most desirable end; directly or indirectly, consciously or unconsciously, it becomes the ruling passion—after money-getting—of their lives,—a passion in which they are confirmed and strengthened by all the blandishments of the world, and all the seductions of the flesh. Any means which tend to gratify this passion, to realize this end, they hold to be lawful, and they can adopt them, however base, detestable, or shocking in themselves, with a quiet conscience and admirable self-complacency.

That the ruling motive or dominant instinct of Protestants, in their character of Protestants, is, at least under a negative point of view to destroy or elude Catholicity, is evident from the character of the variations which their Protestantism has undergone, and is daily and hourly undergoing. Examine these variations, and you will find that they each and all tend to remove Protestantism further and further from the Catholic standard, and to shelter it from the blows of Catholic assailants. Each successive reformer eliminates from his sect some Catholic doctrine which it may have retained, or modifies some element of which he sees the Catholic controversialist can take advantage. The tendency of the Protestant world, collectively and in each of its divisions and subdivisions, has been steadily in the direction from the church against which it protests, and the progress which Protestants so loudly boast, has consisted, and still consists, in getting rid of what they originally retained in common with Catholics. The Protestant vanguard, which announces that the main body is at hand, has advanced very far, and retains less of Christian principle than was retained by the old heathen world in the times of the apostles. Take your fully developed transcendentalist, the last word of Protestantism, and you will find him divested of every Catholic principle, and, under the point of view of religion, reduced, not only to nudity, but to nihility. The poor man retains nothing, not even so much as a shadow. He is a Peter Schlemil, and has sold his shadow to the man in black. What can have reduced him to such straits,—driven him to such extremes? Love of truth, force of conviction? Nothing of the sort. Be not so simple as to pretend it. He assigns, and attempts to assign, no authority, no reason, for his nihilism. He even acknowledges that he has no reason to assign, and tells you that he only throws out what he thinks, without pretending to prove it. He is a seer, and utters what he sees, and you must take him at his word, or not at all. Why, then, does he rush into nihilism? Simply, because he is seer enough to see, that, if he admits that any thing exists, he will be driven ultimately to acknowledge the truth of Catholicity. Rather than do that, he will sell his soul, as well as his shadow, to the man in black, and consent to deny his own existence. Almost every day, we meet intelligent Protestant gentlemen who frankly acknowledge tnat there is no alternative but Catholicity or no-religion, and yet who just as frankly tell us that they will not be Catholics. Not long since, a Protestant minister of respectable standing in this city assured us, in all seriousness, that he "would rather be damned than become a Catholic." We of course informed him he could have his choice, for Almighty God forces no one to accept the gift of eternal life. This worthy minister is, no doubt, very ready to embrace the truth that does not convict him of error, if such truth there be; but if we may take him at his word, he is prepared to resist, at all hazards, the truth that would indict him. Is it truth, or his own opinion that he loves?

The mistake of our popular controversialists seems to arise from their supposition, that Protestantism can be learned from the symbolical books and theological writings of Protestants. Undoubtedly we can thus learn that Protestantism which is put forth to elude Catholicity, or to lure Catholics from their church, and therefore a Protestantism highly important, for the sake of Catholics, to be studied and refuted; but not thus can we learn the Protestantism which lies in the Protestant mind and heart, and which it is necessary to refute for the sake of Protestants themselves. This Protestantism is not learned from symbolical books or theological writings, and but comparatively few Protestants themselves can give us a clear and distinct statement, much less a just account of it. We can seize it only in the historical developments and manifest tendencies of the Protestant movement, and explain it only by means of a thorough knowledge of human nature on the one hand, and of Catholic faith and theology on the other.

It appears to us, that our controversialists are mistaken, also, in regarding the more reputable sects—that is, the sects which, in their symbols and professions, have departed the least from the Catholic standard—as better exponents of the Protestant mind than the less reputable, and as those whose views it is the most important to study and refute. Nearly all the controversial works we have, originally written in the English language, are directed against the Anglican and Protestant Episcopal sects. We are not aware of a single Catholic work, written expressly against the so-called Evangelical sects, Presbyterians, Baptists, Methodists, or what we may call Pietism. And, with the exception of the profound and scientific work of Father Kohlmann, against Unitarians, —too profound and scientific to be intelligible to those for whom it was written,—we have in English not a single work against rationalism, which, in reality, has a larger number of adherents, in both England and this country, than either Anglicanism or Evangelicalism. This indicates a serious defect in our controversial literature, and seems to us to be owing to a false estimate of the relative importance of the several Protestant sects. There are, no doubt, many individuals included in the more reputable sects, who, if compelled to choose, would sooner return to the church than follow the Protestant movement to its natural terminus; but they are only a small minority, and would hardly be missed in the sects to which they respectively belong. All the sects are on the move, tending somewhither. Not one of them is stationary. This they make their boast; and one of the most frequent and most effective charges they bring against the church is, that she is not progressive, but remains immovable, insisting that we shall believe to-day the very doctrines which she taught and believed in the Dark Ages. The dominant tendency of any given sect is the tendency which the great majority of its members obey. Ascertain, then, the dominant tendency of each sect, and you have ascertained the direction in which the great majority of its members are moving, and will continue to move, if diverted or arrested by no foreign influence. But what, in fact, is the dominant tendency of each and every Protestant sect? Is there a single one whose successive developments, modifications, and changes tend to bring it nearer and nearer to the Catholic standard, and to prepare it for communion with the church? Nobody can pretend it. Everybody knows that every sect is moving in the opposite direction, and that the dominant tendency of the Protestant world, a few individuals excepted, is towards rationalism, transcendentalism, and therefore towards pantheism, atheism, nihilism. This is decisive, and proves that those sects which have departed furthest from Catholicity are the truest representatives of the Protestant spirit, and the best exponents of genuine Protestantism, as the fully developed man is a better exponent of humanity than the new-born infant. What it is most important, then, to study and refute, must be the principles of these more advanced sects, not those of the sects who remain behind, or are still rocking in their cradle, and therefore transcendentalism, rather than Anglicanism.

Undoubtedly we see, from time to time, a conservative, perhaps a retrograde, movement in the bosom of the several sects. But this movement is the result, in most cases, of alarm for the credit or prosperity of the sect, rather than of any deep or sincere attachment to the principles or doctrines the sect threatens to leave behind. Besides, the movement is ever but a mere eddy in the stream, or a slight ripple on its surface. It reaches never to the bottom of the sect, and arrests or diverts never its main current. This is evident from the late Oxford movement, one of the most important movements of the kind which have recently been witnessed. There was a time when timid Protestants feared, and many good Catholics hoped, that it would restore England to Catholic faith and unity; but no sooner did it become manifest to all the world that its tendency was to communion with Rome, than it was arrested. A few individuals became reconciled to the church, but the majority of those at first favorably disposed towards it avowedly or tacitly abandoned it, lapsed into the ordinary channel of their sect, and suffered themselves to be borne onward with it towards its natural term,—no-religion, or nihilism. So it is in every sect in which a similar movement takes place. As soon as it is clear that its tendency is anti-protestant, that is, towards Rome, it is arrested, and only here and there an individual dares henceforth avow his adherence to it.

It may be thought by some, that the more reputable sects are the real bulwarks of Protestantism, and that, if we refute them, the less reputable sects will fall of themselves. Doubtless this is one reason why our English and American Catholic controversialists direct their attacks so exclusively against Anglicanism and Protestant Episcopalianism. But we are disposed to believe that the real supporters of Protestantism, if not in themselves, at least in their views and influence, are the sects which are furthest removed from Catholicity. If there was nothing below Anglicanism to which Anglicans could descend, we should have short work with it, and the Anglican and Episcopal sects would soon disappear. The more reputable sects, comparing themselves with the immense Protestant world below them, look upon themselves as substantially orthodox, and are more disposed to dwell on what they retain that others have given up, than on what they themselves lack which we have. They form, too, a sort of aristocracy, a *haute noblesse*, in the sectarian world, and are pleased with their rank, and unwilling to forego the importance it gives them in their own eyes. Moreover, the sects below them, all Protestant, and of their own race, smooth the descent for them in proportion as they are driven from their more elevated position, and enable them to descend by an easy gradation, by almost imperceptible steps, to the lowest depths of error. If the High-churchman is defeated, he can descend to Low-churchism; if the Low-churchman is defeated, he can descend to Evangelicalism; if the Evangelical is defeated, he can descend either, on the one hand, to rationalism, or, on the other, to transcendentalism,—for, in point of fact, Evangelicalism is nothing but a loose combination of rationalism and transcendentalism. It is far easier for a High-churchman to become a Low-churchman than it is for him to become a Catholic, and always is the next step in the descending scale far easier to take than the next step in the ascending scale.

> "Facilis descensus Averni:
> Noctes atque dies patet atri janua Ditis;
> Sed revocare gradum superasque evadere ad auras,
> Hoc opus, hic labor est."

As long as there is a lower step that can be taken without abandoning the essential element of Protestantism, the defeat of the more reputable sects, on the ground they profess to occupy, will do little for their conversion; for they will never acknowledge, even to themselves, that they are defeated, so long as there is any conceivable Protestant ground from which they are not actually driven. It is owing to the fact that Protestants now claim as Protestant all the territory between the ground occupied by Dr. Pusey and that occupied by M. Proudhon, and thus have a larger field for advance or retreat, that we find their conversion in our times so much more difficult than it was formerly. St. Francis of Sales, Bishop of Geneva, himself alone regained seventy-two thousand Protestants to the church; we are aware of no bishop in the present age, however zealous, learned, able, or saintly, who has the consolation of recovering any thing approaching a like number. We cannot, therefore, but regard the views and tendencies of the more advanced sects as those which it is now altogether the most important to study and refute.

Not only does Protestantism, as our divines have from the first maintained, logically lead to the denial of all religion, to atheism, and therefore to nihilism,—for to deny that God exists is to deny that any thing is,—but it is now clear to all who have examined the subject, that the great body of Protestants are really prepared, as occasion may require, to follow it thus far. The majority of the Protestant world are really, if not avowedly, transcendentalists to-day, as every one knows who is acquainted with recent Protestant literature; and Strauss, Feuerbach, Bauer, Parker, Emerson, Michelet, Quinet, and Proudhon have more sympathizers than Hengstenberg, Pusey, Seabury, Nevin, Alexander, Beecher, and Kirk. Proudhon is nothing but a consistent red republican; and where is the Protestant, in case he is not restrained by his temporal interest, who does not sympathize with red republicanism? Have not Protestants very generally, in England and this country, sympathized with Mazzini and his Roman Republic? Nay, was it not in concert with, and by aid even of, the more reputable Protestant sects, that he expelled the Sovereign Pontiff, and established his Reign of Terror? Is not Protestant sympathy very generally enlisted in favor of the infidel and socialistic revolutions in Europe, all of which have been stirred up and helped on by Protestants, under the lead of their ministers, in the name of liberty, but really for the purpose of overthrowing and annihilating the church? Evident is it, then, that they will go, as a body, to all lengths which they find necessary to accomplish their purpose of hostility to Catholicity; and as they never can even logically overthrow the church, so long as the existence of any thing is admitted, they must deny every thing, and rush into nihilism.

It is necessary, then, if we wish to arrest the Protestant movement, and do what in us lies to save the souls of Protestants, that we reason with them, not as if it were a sufficient refutation of them to prove that they are tending to atheism, but as men who believe nothing, and build up our argument against them from the very foundation. Prove to them that their doctrines are anti-christian, and they will only beg you to inform them wherefore that is a reason for not believing them; prove Christianity to be true, and they will merely beg you to prove your proofs, and thus demand of you an infinite series of proofs. They are, under the point of view of religion and philosophy, wholly rotten, and from the sole of the foot to the crown of the head there is no soundness in them. Nothing will answer for them that does not descend as low as the last denial that it is possible for the human mind to conceive, and drive them from position to position, till there is no position remaining outside of the church which they can even affect to take.

Protestantism as we now find it, and even as it was, virtually, in the sixteenth century, is not merely the denial of certain Catholic dogmas, is not merely the denial of the Christian revelation itself, but really the denial of all religion and morality, natural and revealed. It denies reason itself, as far as it is in the power of man to deny it, and is no less unsound as philosophy than it is as faith. It extinguishes the light of nature no less than the light of revelation, and is as false in relation to the natural order as to the supernatural. Even when Protestants make a profession of believing in revelation, they discredit reason. In regard to reason, they are, even when professing to believe, very generally Pyrrhonists. The Evangelical sects, for instance, do not merely deny the sufficiency of reason as our only guide, but they deny its trustworthiness altogether, and assert that we must take for our guide the Scriptures, not as interpreted by an authority accredited to reason, nor as interpreted by reason itself, but as interpreted by the private illuminations of the spirit. They thus supersede, as it were, annihilate, reason, and reduce themselves to the condition of irrational beings, virtually declare man incapable of receiving a supernatural revelation, and then call upon him to believe the Bible, and to walk by the supernatural light of faith. As long as their enthusiasm lasts, as long as they can keep up a sort of unnatural excitement, they may half persuade themselves that they are supernaturally illuminated; but as soon as their fever abates, and they sink to their ordinary level, they experience the most painful misgivings, the supposed supernatural light fades away, and, having no reason on which to fall back, they can believe nothing, and either openly avow themselves infidels, or, merely keep up a show of piety, seek relief by devoting all their energies to worldly distractions or pleasures. They begin by proposing revelation, not as the complement, but as the substitute, of reason; and when revelation fails, as fail it must if not supported by motives of credibility addressed to reason, and satisfactory to it, nothing remains for them but universal scepticism.

The formalistic sects, as the Anglican and Episcopalian, reach the same result though by a different process. Building on sham, taking the shadow for the substance, and denying both the substance and the light the shadow necessarily implies,—or, in other words, refusing to draw from their premises their logical consequences, afraid to make a complete proposition, to say two and two make four, and stopping short with saying two and two, lest they lose the *via media*, and roll over to Rome, or fall off into Dissent,— they destroy reason by mutilating and enslaving it, and find themselves without any thing by or to which a supernatural revelation can be accredited. The rationalistic sects, seeing the errors of Evangelicals and formalists, think to save reason by resolving the supernatural into the natural; but in doing this they lose revelation, and therefore reason,—because no man can deny revelation without denying reason, and because reason without revelation is insufficient for herself, inadequate to the solution of the great problems of life which she herself raises. Beginning by asking of reason more than she can give, they end by discarding her and falling into universal scepticism, the ultimate term of all Protestantism.

Protestants, it is well known, are able to keep up the self-delusion that they are believers only by obstinately refusing to push their principles to their legitimate consequences, and by shutting their eyes to the objections which may be suggested or urged against them. The condition of a Protestant wishing to retain his Protestantism, and yet keep up the appearance of being a believer, is most pitiable. The poor man has no mental freedom, no intellectual courage, but is a cowardly slave, with all the weakness and meanness characteristic of slaves in general. He never dares trust himself to his principles, and follow them out to their remotest logical consequences, and is doomed, turn which way he will, to be inconsequent, and to submit to a most tyrannical and capricious master; for otherwise he would find himself, on the one hand, approaching too near Catholicity to remain a Protestant, or, on the other, too near to nihilism even to pretend to be a believer. Alas for the poor man! He hugs his chains, and, by the strangest infatuation imaginable, fancies his slavery is freedom. All who have studied the subject know well that Protestants are Protestants, not by virtue of reason, but in spite of reason,—not because they reason, but solely because they do not, will not, and dare not reason. The rejection of reason is their fundamental vice. Reason is our natural light, and, though of no value out of its sphere, in its sphere is inerrable. It does not suffice of itself for all the wants of the human soul, but its annihilation reduces us below the condition of men, and renders us incapable of receiving even a supernatural revelation. Revelation does not abrogate or supersede reason; it restores it and supplies its deficiencies. Grace supposes nature. Christianity is a system of pure grace,—is, in fact, a supernatural creation, but a supernatural creation *for* the natural, designed to repair the damage nature has incurred by guilt, and to enable man to attain the end to which his Creator originally appointed him. Man is not for the sacraments, but the sacraments are for man. The first office of grace is to restore nature, or to heal its wounds; having restored it to health, it elevates it, indeed, but always retains it, and uses it. Here is the grand fact that Protestant theologians always overlook. They, in reality, always present nature and grace as two antagonistic powers, and suppose the presence of the one must be the physical destruction of the other. Luther and Calvin, weary of the good works, and shrinking from the efforts to acquire the personal virtues enjoined by Catholicity, began their so-called reform by asserting the total depravity of human nature, and maintaining that original sin involved the loss of reason and free-will, reducing man physically to the condition of irrational animals, and superadding the penalty of guilt. Here, in the very outset, they denied natural reason, all natural religion, and all natural morality, and consequently asserted for man in the natural order, left to his natural powers and faculties, universal scepticism and moral indifference; for without reason there can be no belief, and without free-will no moral obligation, no moral difference of actions.

The Arminians, indeed, saw this, and sought to remedy it by reasserting the natural law; but as they still held to total depravity, the reassertion amounted to nothing; or, if they sometimes abandoned total depravity, they rushed to the opposite extreme, and reasserted Pelagianism or semi-Pelagianism, and restricted the office of grace to enabling us to do more easily what, nevertheless, we are able to do without it. If they succeeded in escaping the peculiar error of Luther and Calvin, they fell into rationalism. As Luther and Calvin annihilated reason and free-will, the whole spiritual nature of man, and made man purely passive in the work of regeneration and Christian perfection, the Arminians, become rationalists, disregarding the necessity of grace, made the natural law sufficient, and asserted only a natural morality. But experience proving the inadequacy of the natural law, when taken without its revealed complement and sanction,—of natural morality, when not elevated by supernatural Christian virtue,—they, like the others, lapsed, of necessity, into the same scepticism.

The error of each class is avoidable only by understanding that grace always supposes nature, and that grace without nature would be as a telescope to a man without eyes. Revelation supposes reason, and we as effectually deny Christianity when we deny reason as when we deny revelation; both must be asserted with equal firmness and emphasis, each in its own sphere, in relation to its appropriate office, or nothing is asserted. To deny reason is, *a fortiori*, to deny revelation, and to deny revelation is virtually to deny reason; because the evidences of the fact of revelation are amply sufficient to satisfy reason, and because reason, without revelation, being undeniably insufficient to solve the problems which torture the mind without faith, and to satisfy the craving of our nature for something above itself, cannot maintain itself practically in credit, and necessarily loses its authority. Philosophy, undoubtedly, rests for its basis on natural reason, otherwise we should be unable to distinguish it from Catholic theology, or to draw any intelligible distinction between the natural and supernatural; but without the light of revelation, we shall never be able, in our fallen condition, to construct a sound and adequate philosophy. So, on the other hand, without a sound and adequate philosophy, we can never possess a true and adequate theology; for as revelation is necessary as an instrument in the construction of philosophy, so is philosophy necessary as an instrument in the construction of theology,— that is, theology as a science, and as distinguishable from faith. Hence, in all courses of Catholic instruction, the student makes his philosophy before he proceeds to his theology.

It is clear enough, from what we have said, that the most pressing want of Protestants, under the intellectual point of view, is a sound philosophy, which, so to speak, shall rehabilitate reason, and restore them to natural religion and morality. They have lost reason, and have fallen below the religion or morality which lies in the natural order, and which all revealed religion and morality presuppose. The philosophy needed is nowhere to be found in the Protestant world, and cannot possibly be created by Protestants, for the reason that the revelation which must serve as its instrument they have not, or at best only some detached fragments of it. The only respectable school of philosophy to be found among Protestants is the Scottish School of Reid and Stewart; but this school dogmatizes rather than philosophizes. It very justly assumes that all philosophy must proceed from certain indemonstrable principles, and it does not err essentially in its inventory of these principles; but it fails to establish them, or to show us that they have scientific validity. It calls them the constituent principles of human belief, and says, very truly, that they must be admitted, or all science, all philosophy, is out of the question. But this is no more than Hume, whom it aims to refute, himself said. Is science or philosophy possible? is the precise question to be answered. Without the conditions you assert, we grant it is not possible; but what then? Therefore your alleged principles are sound? Why not: Therefore all science, all philosophy, is impossible? No doubt, the Scottish School has protested vehemently against the scepticism of Hume, but its refutation of that scepticism is a mere paralogism, a simple begging of the question, and therefore, scientifically considered, worthless.

But, after all, we cannot place our chief reliance on philosophy as an instrument in the conversion of Protestants. Philosophy is too indirect and too slow in its operations to meet their wants. They are too far gone, too restless, too impatient, too averse to calm reflection and continuous thought, to listen to us while we set the true philosophy before them, or to submit to the labor absolutely requisite to comprehend and appreciate profound philosophical science. An age of balloons, steam-cars, and lightning telegraphs is not exactly the age for philosophers. Moreover, Protestant perversity would find in the necessity of the long and patient thought, and close and subtile reasoning, demanded by philosophy, an objection to our religion itself.

Your religion, they would say, if true, is intended for all mankind, and therefore should be within the reach of every capacity. The thought and reasoning necessary to create or understand the philosophy you insist upon, transcend the capacity of all but the gifted few, and therefore, if necessary to establish your religion, prove that your religion is not true. We might, indeed, reply, that the thought and reasoning objected to are necessary to refute the errors of Protestants, not simply to establish our religion; but that would amount to nothing in practice. The nature of the Protestant is to devise the most subtile errors in his power, and to find an objection to our religion in the very labor he makes necessary for their refutation. When he objects, he may be as subtile and as abstruse as he pleases; but when we reply, he insists that we shall be popular, and never go beyond the depth of the most ordinary capacity,—that we shall answer the objection not only to the mind that raises it, but to the minds of all men. Only the candid among Protestants would acknowledge the justness of our reply, and these would fail to comprehend it; for if you find a candid Protestant, you may safely conclude that he lacks intelligence, as when you find an intelligent Protestant you may be sure that he lacks candor. There must, then, be some briefer and more expeditious way of dealing with Protestants than that of philosophy, if we wish to affect them favorably.

We have defined Protestantism to be hostility to the church, and virtually nihilism, because Protestants in general, sooner than return to the church will push their hostility to its last consequence, which is the denial of God, therefore of all existence and existences. But this is not all that we have to say of the matter. No man loves error for its own sake, or wills what does not appear to him to be good. The natural heart of every man recoils instinctively from atheism; and it is seldom, if ever, that one without a fearful and even a protracted struggle abandons all faith and piety, resigns all hope of an hereafter, and consents to place himself in the category of the beasts that perish. Hatred, no doubt, will carry a man to great lengths; but even hatred must have its cause, real or imaginary. Hatred is love reversed, and intense hatred of one thing is the reverse action of intense love of something else. Protestants hate the church. Wherefore? Because they love truth? Nonsense. Because they believe her false, and destructive to the souls of men? Nonsense again. We hope there is no Catholic so stupid as to believe it. Their hatred of the church has nothing to do with concern for truth or for salvation. A large portion of them believe in no truth, in no salvation; a larger portion still are of opinion that all men will be saved, and that truth is whatever seems to a man to be true; and the remainder hold that the church is substantially orthodox, and that salvation is attainable in her communion, as well as in their own. Whatever, then, the cause of their hatred of the church, it is a cause unconnected with considerations of another world, or with truth as such.

We need not look far for this something which Protestants love and the church condemns, and for condemning which they are full of wrath against her. It is nothing very recondite, or very difficult to seize. We make quite too much of Protestantism, which is, in reality, a very vulgar thing, and lies altogether on the surface of life. Protestantism is nothing more or less than that spirit of lawlessness which leads every one to wish to have his own way,—very common in women and children, and perhaps not less common in men, only they have, generally, a better faculty of concealing it. Objectively defined, it is expressed in the common saying, "Forbidden fruit is sweetest;" and subjectively, it is a craving for what is prohibited, because prohibited. It imagines that the sovereign good is in what the law forbids, and opposes the church because she upholds the law,—hates the law because the law restrains it, duty because duty obliges it; and since, as long as it admits the existence of God, it must admit duty, it denies God; and since, as long as it admits the existence of any thing, it must admit the existence of God, it denies every thing, and lapses into nihilism. Here is the whole mystery of the matter,—Protestantism in a nutshell.

The source of this impatience of restraint, and this desire to have one's own way, is the pride natural to the human heart, the root of every vice and of every sin. "Your eyes shall be opened, and ye shall be as gods, knowing good and evil," said the serpent to Eve; and she reached forth her hand, plucked the forbidden fruit, ate, and sin and death were in the world. Pride is, on the one hand, a denial of our dependence, and, on the other, the assertion of our own sufficiency. Here you may see the origin and the essential characteristic of Protestantism, which is as old as the first motion of pride or of resistance to the will of God. Protestantism, after all, is more ancient than we commonly concede. Dr. Johnson, in his Dictionary, would have been as correct if he had said the devil was the first Protestant, as he was in saying that he was "the first Whig." It offends pride to be compelled to acknowledge our own insufficiency, to admit that we cannot be trusted to follow our own inclinations, that we must be subjected to metes and bounds, and placed under tutors and masters, who say, Do this, Do that; and we are galled, and we resolve we will not endure it; we will break the withes that bind us; we will stand up on our own two feet, and assert our freedom in face of heaven, earth, and hell. Hence we see Protestants, in every age, mounting the tallest pair of stilts they can find or construct, and with more or less vehemence, with more or less *éclat*, according to the circumstances of time and place, magniloquently asserting the "inborn" rights of man, proudly swearing to be free, to stand up in their native dignity, in the full and resplendent majesty of their own manhood, and making such appeals and forming such alliances as they fancy will best secure their independence, relieve them from all restraints, and give them the opportunity to live as they list.

Such is the general and essential characteristic of Protestantism; its particular character or form is determined by, and varies with, the circumstances of time and place. In itself, as Balmes well shows, it is a phenomenon peculiar to no period of history, but whatever it has that is peculiar it borrows from the character of the epoch in which it appears. It is always essentially the spirit that works in the children of disobedience, but the form under which the disobedience manifests itself depends on exterior and accidental causes. What it resists is what it finds offensive to human pride, to pure, unmitigated egotism, and what it asserts is always asserted as the means of securing free scope to its independent action. In the sixteenth century, pride found itself galled by submission to the church, for the church could not tolerate its wild speculations and its theological errors. It then denied the authority of the church; and in order to make a show of justifying its denial, it asserted the supremacy of the Scriptures, interpreted by private reason, or by the private Spirit. Soon it found that the assertion of the supremacy of the Scriptures, so interpreted, limited its sovereignty, and that it was as galling to its sense of independence to submit to a dead book as to a living church, and then it denied the Scriptures, and, to justify its denial, asserted the supremacy of reason. But reason, again, galled it, reminded it of its dependence, and would not suffer it to live as it listed. Then it cried out, Down with reason, and up with sentiment!—a transcendental element paramount to reason,—and thus reached the jumping-off place. In order to resist effectually the pope, it at one time, as in England, proclaims the divine right of kings; and then, in order to get rid of the divine right of kings, it proclaims the divine right of the people, or, to speak more accurately, of the mob; and finally, in order to get rid of the authority of the mob, it proclaims the divine right of each and every individual, and declares that each and every individual is God, the only God,—thus resolving God into men, and all men into one man, which implies the right of every man to take the entire universe to himself, and possess it as his own property. You laugh at its absurdity? Upon our conscience, we invent nothing, we exaggerate nothing, and say nothing more than is asserted, in sober earnest, by men whom the Protestant world delights to honor.

Turn Protestantism over as you will, analyze it to your heart's content, you can make nothing more or less of it than mere vulgar pride, and the various efforts pride makes from time to time and place to place to secure its own gratification, to realize the assertion of the serpent, "Ye shall be as gods knowing good and evil,"—that is, ye shall know good and evil of yourselves, as God knows them of himself, and shall be independent, and act as seemeth to you good, even as God is independent and doth according to his will, not as subject to a power above himself, and in obedience to another will than his own. Just see the proof of this, in the sympathy now universally given to every revolt against established authority. All your modern literature is satanic, and approves, and teaches us to approve, every rebel, whether against parental, popular, royal, or divine authority. The Protestant readers of *Paradise Lost* sympathize with Lucifer, in his war against the Almighty, and if they had been in heaven, as one of our friends suggests, would have sided with him. Our friend, J. D. Nourse, defending himself against our strictures on his book, boldly asserts that God is a despot, and his government a despotism,—nay, that all authority is despotic.

Finding the essence of Protestantism to be mere vulgar

pride, that it is a moral disease rather than an intellectual aberration, it is evident that we are to treat it as a vice rather than as an error, and Protestants as sinners rather than as simply unbelievers or misbelievers. This may not be very flattering to their pride, nevertheless, it is the only way they deserve to be treated, and the only way in which they can be treated for their good. We honor them quite too much when we treat them as men whose heads are wrong, but whose hearts are sound. The wrongness of the head is the consequence of the rottenness of the heart. The remedy must be applied to the seat of the disease, or it will be wholly ineffectual ; and as the disease is in the will rather than in the intellect, we must, as we do with sinners in general, avail ourselves of motives that tend to persuade the will, rather than of those which tend primarily to convince the understanding. Get the heart right, and the intellect will soon rectify itself.

Now it is certain, that, so far as the great body of Protestants are concerned, it is of no use to appeal to any love of truth or regard for salvation they may be supposed to have. They are very generally prepared, with Macbeth, "to jump the world to come," and think only how they shall manage matters for this world. They are worldly, and their wisdom is earthly, sensual, devilish ; even their virtues, their honesty, their uprightness of conduct, have reference, not to God, but to their justification, either in the eyes of the world, or in the eyes of their own pride. They are too proud or too vain to do this or that act which is contrary to good manners. We must therefore approach them as men who are wedded to this world, who are Protestants for the sake of living for this world alone, and refuse to be Catholics because Catholicity enjoins humility, detachment from the world, and a life of self-denial and mortification, lived for God alone. As long as it is conceded, or as long as they believe it true, that their Protestantism is more favorable to man, regarded solely as an inhabitant of this world, than Catholicity, we cannot get them to listen to what we have to say for our religion. If they hear, it will be as if they heard not.

But it is a fact, as clearly demonstrable, in its way, as any mathematical problem, that Catholicity enjoins the only normal life for man, even in this world, letting alone what it secures us in another. Human pride just now takes the form of socialism, and socialism is *the* Protestantism of our times. It is human pride under this form that we must address, and show to the socialists, not—as some silly and misguided creatures calling themselves Catholics, and sometimes occupying editorial chairs, are accustomed to do—that Catholicity favors them by accepting their socialism, but that it favors the object they profess to have at heart,—that it is the true and only genuine socialism, the basis of all veritable society, and the only known instrument of well-being, either for the individual or for the race. We must show, that, under the social point of view, under the various relations of civilization, Protestantism is an egregious blunder, and precipitates its adherents into the precise evils they really wish to avoid. That it does so is evident enough to all who have eyes to see, and is proved by the very complaints Protestants make of their own movements. Their own complaints of themselves show, to use a vulgar proverb, that they always " jump from the frying-pan into the fire," in attempting to better their condition. They could not endure the authority of the church; they resisted it, and fell under the tyranny of the sect, even in their own view of the case, a thousand times less tolerable. They rebelled, in the name of liberty, against the pope, and fell under the iron rule of the civil despot; in England, they could not endure the Lord's bishops, and they fell under the Lord's presbyters, and from Lord's presbyters under the Lord's brethren, and from Lord's brethren under the capricious tyranny of their own fancies and passions. In political and social reforms it has fared no better with them. In France, the *Constituante* were more oppressive than the old monarchy, the *Gironde* than the *Constituante*, the *Mountain* than the *Gironde ;* and the present French government, in order to save society from complete destruction, is obliged to adopt measures more stringent than ever Charles X. or Louis Philippe dared venture upon. The overthrow of one tyranny leads to another of necessity more heartless and oppressive, because weaker and possessing a less firm hold on the affections of the people. A strong government can afford to be lenient. A weak government must be stringent. Yet the wise men of the age rush on in their wild-goose chase after worldly felicity, while it flies ever the faster before them. Like the gambler, who has played away his patrimony, his wife's jewels, and pawned his hat and coat, but keeps playing on, they insist on another throw,—though losing all, fancy they are just agoing to recover all, and make a fortune equal to their boundless wishes. If they could but see themselves as the unexcited bystanders see them, they would throw away the dice, and rush with self-loathing from the *hell* in which they find only their own ruin.

The principle on which Protestants seek even worldly felicity is false, and we can say nothing better of them, than that they prove themselves what the sacred Scriptures would term fools in following it. When was it ever known that pride, following itself, did not meet mortification, or that any worldly distinction, or good, sought for its own sake, did not either baffle pursuit, or prove a canker to the heart? Did you ever see a man running after fame that ever overtook it, or a man always nursing his health that was ever other than sickly? Have you no eyes, no ears, no understanding? Fame comes, if at all, unsought, greatness follows in the train of humility, and happiness, coy to the importunate wooer, throws herself into the arms of him who treats her with indifference. All experience proves the truth of the principle, "Seek first the kingdom of God, and his justice, and all these things shall be superadded unto you." Take it as inspiration, as the word of God, or as a maxim of human prudence, it is equally true, and he who runs against it only proves his own folly. "Live while you live," says the Protestant Epicurean. Be it so; live while you live, but live you cannot, unless you live to God, according to the principles of the Catholic religion. Live now you do not, and you know you do not; you are only *just agoing*, and not a few of you fear that you are never even agoing to live, as all your poetry, with its deep pathos and melodious wail, too amply proves.

Here comes in to our aid the excellent work before us. It exactly meets the present state of the Protestant world, and makes the only kind of appeal to which, in their present mood, they will listen. Its author makes no apology for Catholicity, he offers no direct argument for its truth; he simply comes forward and compares the respective influences of Protestantism and Catholicity on European civilization, and shows, that, while Catholicity tends unceasingly to advance civilization, Protestantism as unceasingly tends to savagism, and that it is to its hostile influences we owe the slow progress of European civilization during the last three centuries. He shows that Protestantism is hostile to liberty, to philosophy, to the higher mental culture, to art, to equality, to political and social well-being. He shows it, we say; not merely asserts, but proves it, by unanswerable arguments and undeniable facts. If any one doubts our judgment, we refer him to the work itself, and beg him to gainsay its facts, or answer its reasoning, if he can. The Protestant who reads it will hardly boast of his Protestantism again.

THE PRESBYTERIAN CONFESSION OF FAITH.*

[From Brownson's Quarterly Review for 1846.]

ARTICLE I.

A REVIEW of the Constitution of the Presbyterian Church, confined chiefly to its Confession of Faith, may not present that degree of interest or attraction which might be found in that of some of the *new works* which are daily poured upon our book-devouring community; but it has seemed to us that it might, nevertheless, be highly useful, inasmuch as it will give us an opportunity of showing the venom of error at its fountain-head, and of exposing in a strong light the frail fabric of Protestantism, by laying bare the weakness and instability of its foundations. Even on the score of novelty, the Constitution of the Presbyterian church may, after all, not be devoid of interest. It is true, its substance is old, we might add antiquated, made up, as it is, from shreds taken from Calvin, Knox, and others, but Presbyterians, as Protestants in general, can always affix a character of novelty to their church constitutions and doctrinal opinions, for they hold it to be the inalienable privilege of freemen to change their articles of faith and methods of church government so as to suit the times and follow the *onward march of mind.* Hence, the editors of the work before us are very particular in stating all the improvements, modifications, amendments, corrections, additions, and subtractions, which the said constitution underwent at the period of its publication; and we find on the title page a solemn declaration of

* *The Constitution of the Presbyterian Church in the United States of America, containing the Confession of Faith, the Catechisms, and the Directory for the Worship of God; together with the Plan of Government and Discipline, as ratified by the General Assembly at their Sessions in May, 1821, and amended in 1833.* Philadelphia: 1838.

a committee of Presbyterian divines, that the present edition "is a correct and authentic copy of said Constitution, as *amended*, ratified, and in force *at the present date*" (1834). As the Constitution of the Presbyterian Church changes, very much like the Paris and London fashions, it is probable that there is one more recent than this now before us; but this must suffice for our present purpose, and the more so, because it is the one adopted by both the *Old* School and the *New* School Presbyterians before their schism in 1837.

Some may think that it is altogether useless to discuss the inconsistencies and errors of the Presbyterian Constitution, and that any attempt at argument against them would be only time and labor lost, since Presbyterians and Calvinists, from their intense hatred to every thing Catholic, seem to be inaccessible to reason and argument, when presented by Catholics; and we confess that this to a great extent is true, and has almost decided us to desist from our present ungrateful undertaking. We know there is a sin for which St. John said, "*Non pro illo dico, ut roget quis*"; we know there is a spiritual pride which renders men as headstrong and insensible as old Satan himself; and we fear that no small portion of it has fallen to the lot of the followers of the sour, morose, selfish, hating, and hateful Calvin. Still, the fear that some may not profit by the truth is no good reason for concealing it, or for refusing to advocate and support it by arguments. The ways of God are mysterious, and he can, even from stones, raise up children to Abraham. Moreover, had we no other reason for undertaking a review of the Presbyterian Church Constitution and Confession of Faith than a simple sense of justice to ourselves, it would be amply sufficient. The Calvinistic pulpits and press resound with hardly any thing but declamatory and incendiary invectives against the Catholic Church. The General Assembly never meets, without appointing a preacher to deliver, *ex-officio*, a solemn address against Catholicity, and it has been customary for it to proclaim hypocritical fasts for the downfall of *Popery*. This propagandism against us may be met with everywhere, not only in the pulpit and lecture-room, but even in the railroad-car and the steamboat, where, orally or by tracts, the most insipid and absurd tales against our institutions and people are circulated. The virulence of this Calvinistic opposition to Catholicity shows itself chiefly in the Presbyterian newspaper press. It is there— we are sorry it has been our duty to look into such disgusting trash—Calvin still disgorges, in filthy streams, the venom and rancor with which his disappointed ambition and revengeful pride filled him. These attacks, constantly repeated, demand always a new resistance. This unholy warfare against the true church we must try to put down,—not by calumny, insult, vituperation, and the like, but by solid argument, by discussions based on sound logic, by the exhibition of that brilliant aureola of sanctity, unity, miracles, and other irresistible evidences which must for ever encircle the brows of truth; and by unravelling the contradictions, inconsistencies, paralogisms, sophisms, misrepresentations, and other tortuous arguments, which must always form the hideous train of error.

Nothing appears to us more likely to effect this end than the critical examination and discussion of the formularies which the most numerous sect of Protestants present us, as containing the foundations of that religious system which they would substitute for the dogmas, doctrines, and government of the Catholic Church, with their reasons for rejecting the latter and embracing the former. We propose, therefore, in what follows, to discuss the plan of religious doctrines and ecclesiastical government, as understood by Presbyterians. We shall confine ourselves chiefly to the *Confession of Faith*, the first and most important piece in the work we have quoted, that from which all the rest is deduced, and on which the whole fabric of Presbyterianism rests.

Before entering upon our main subject, it may be well to premise, that, if but one point of doctrine contained in a confession of faith be unfounded, and unsupported by any motive of belief,—much more, if but one point be evidently false and reprobated by Scripture, good sense, and whatever else must serve as the vouchers of the truth,—it follows, immediately and inevitably, that the confession is an imposition, the work of men who either were deceived or meant to deceive, and that the church or society admitting it as its standard of belief is not the church of Christ, or the true church; for a religion that contains one plain falsehood is not a religion of heaven, but of men, rather of Satan himself; since a confession of faith in which there is one error can have no ground for admitting firmly any of the articles it may contain. Any society proposing such a confession betrays its human origin. No matter what good things may be found in such a symbol or formulary of faith, it is deprived of the seal of Heaven, which is incompatible with the least error; and the society imposing it on its members is only a human, not a divinely constituted society, —therefore, not the society founded by Christ, and consequently not the church of Christ. If not the church of Christ, then not that society in which salvation is to be found. This is only the expression of reason and common sense. All Christians, for instance, agree, that, if *one* error were found in the Bible, the Bible could not be the work of God. So, also, if a church enjoin any one article of faith which is a falsehood, it is not and cannot be the church of Christ. Thus, the Catholic Church would consider *all* her titles to divinity and truth forfeited, if a single error had crept into her creeds, and formed one, even the least, of her articles of faith. But if only one error professed by a religious society destroys all its titles, what shall we say, if the confession, instead of containing only one error, contains scarcely a single truth, and is nothing but a tissue of false reasoning, unwarranted assertions, palpable contradictions, wilful misrepresentations, and gross corruptions of the word of God and divine traditions? This last is the fact with regard to the Confession of Faith now under consideration; and we trust to make good to every unprejudiced mind, before we close, that it has no other support than that of the authority of the prince of that empire where no order but "everlasting horror dwelleth."

Still further, as preliminary to our main design, it will not be amiss to state summarily the history of the introduction of the Presbyterian Confession into the world. During the civil anarchy in which ended the reign of the unfortunate Charles I., the Scotch Presbyterians having obtained a decided ascendency, there was convened by order of parliament an assembly of divines, who for many years held theological sessions at Westminster, and, with a view to obtaining a "thorough Godly reformation," concocted there that precious code of doctrine, government, and discipline, which was to unfetter the whole world, and carry out fairly the principles of the glorious reformation, which had almost sunk under the mitigated *Papism* of Elizabeth and James I. It belongs to the history of England to record the disputes, quarrels, tricks, frauds, and various manipulations which characterized the sittings of these divines; but, after a protracted and stormy discussion, at last came out the Confession of Faith, and other formularies of Presbyterian orthodoxy, which received, in 1649, the full sanction of the parliament of England,—the great judge of English Protestant controversies.

The confession of faith given by the Westminster divines, and hence often called the *Westminster Confession*, is nearly the same with the Scotch confession of faith which appeared in 1560. The immediate lineage of the Presbyterians from the goodly Calvin thus clearly appears; for John Knox, whom the Presbyterians represent as having "lighted his torch at the candle of God's word," was the friend and pupil of Calvin, and he was the master spirit who, *per fas et nefas*, introduced the reformation into Scotland, and determined its confession. Of the character of this apostate priest it is not necessary to speak; for, if it be a disgrace to humanity to have produced a Nero or a Robespierre, Presbyterianism is not to be envied the glory of having produced a John Knox.

The Confession of Faith framed by the Westminster divines is the standard of the various hues of Presbyterians found in the United States,—the *Old School* Presbyterians, who perhaps justly claim the unenviable privilege of being the true, lawful, and uncompromising children and successors of Calvin and John Knox, the *New School* Presbyterians, the *Associate Presbyterians*, the *Associate Reformed Church*, and the *Cumberland Presbyterians*. It is also implicitly, if not explicitly, the confession of faith of the *Congregationalists* and of the *Dutch Reformed*, who are strong Calvinists in doctrine. The population adhering to it the world over may, perhaps, be set down at fifteen millions; the Catholic population over the whole globe, we may add by the way, is not much below two hundred millions.

The Confession opens with a chapter on the "Holy Scriptures," no doubt to make the doctrine given in that chapter the foundation of what is to follow. But the subject of the authority of Scripture is beset with insuperable difficulties for Protestants; and although they continually boast of following the Scriptures, although they wish to have the name of receiving the Bible above all men, and of making the Bible a voucher for all they say, still it is impossible for them, on their own principles, to come at any thing positive concerning its authority. They cannot prove its inspiration; so, with all their pretended respect for it, they have undermined its authority, and are compelled, on their own principles, to view it merely as a human book which may be correct on the whole, but only after the manner of other human books written on human subjects by judicious authors.

We begin with the first paragraph of this chapter, which runs thus:—

"Although the light of nature, and the works of creation and providence do so far manifest the goodness, wisdom, and power of God as to leave men inexcusable, yet they are not sufficient to give that knowledge of God, and of his will, which is necessary unto salvation; therefore it pleased the Lord, at sundry times and in divers manners, to reveal himself, and to declare that his will unto his Church; and afterwards, for the better preserving and propagating of the truth, and for the more sure establishment and comfort of the Church against the corruption of the flesh and the malice of Satan and of the world, to commit the same *wholly* unto writing, which maketh the Holy Scripture to be *most necessary;* those former ways of God's revealing his will unto his people being now ceased."

The doctrine laid down in this paragraph it is then attempted to support by arguments; but what kind of argument can be given in an introduction to the belief of Scripture, and in support of its authority? Common sense tells us that it cannot be Scripture itself; else, one might as well quote the authority of the Koran to prove the Koran, and the forger of a will might adduce the very will itself as a proof of its genuineness. Yet, notwithstanding this plain dictate of common sense, the framers of the Confession quote Scripture all at once, and thus open the way to that long string of false, inconsistent, and absurd proofs with which the book abounds. The plainest rules of logic seem to have been quite beyond the reach of these powerful geniuses. Faith must be reasonable,—that is, founded on reasonable motives, or motives capable of forcing the assent of a judicious mind; for if not, it becomes fanaticism, superstition, credulity, downright nonsense. It is this reasonableness of motives which makes the distinction between Christianity and Mahometanism or paganism.

But waiving this want of logical strictness and propriety, and taking up the Scripture proofs adduced, we shall find that the Scripture says nothing at all of what it is made to say. We select from the passage quoted the three following propositions which it contains, and which we maintain are unsupported by Scripture, utterly false, and even contradicted by others in the same passage. 1. That what the Lord revealed at sundry times and in divers manners *was committed wholly to writing.* 2. That this makes the Holy Scripture *most necessary.* 3. That the former ways of God's revealing his will unto his people *are now ceased.*

1. The first position assumed, that "it pleased the Lord to commit the same (that which he had revealed at sundry times, and in divers manners) *wholly* unto writing," is attempted to be proved by the following Scriptural quotations, which we scrupulously transcribe.

"Luke i. 3, 4. It seemed good to me also, having had perfect understanding of all things from the very first, to write unto thee in order, most excellent Theophilus, that thou mightest know the certainty of those things wherein thou hast been instructed. Rom. xv. 4. For whatsoever things were written aforetime were written for our learning ; that we, through patience and comfort of the Scriptures, might have hope. Isaiah viii. 20. To the law and to the testimony : if they speak not according to this word, *it is* because *there is* no light in them. Rev. xxii. 18."

Now, we ask, is there any thing in those passages to prove the peculiar position assumed in the text, namely, that the revelations of God were committed *wholly* unto writing? These quotations suppose that things were written, and written for our instruction and comfort; but where is the passage proving that *all* was written? There is none; and hence these quotations are nothing more than a vain display of Scriptural erudition, or rather, a petty theological trick, and dialectical sleight of hand, by which evidence is brought for only a *portion* of a proposition, and still the *whole* proposition is confidently asserted. As if one were to say, *Something* was written, therefore *all* was written; which is a form of argument too obviously false to need refutation.

We will, however, go rapidly over these texts, and show that they have no bearing on the question. The last, from Revelations, or the Apocalypse, xxii. 18, is not expressly cited, which shows, perhaps, that little reliance is placed on it in support of the position assumed. The text is, "I testify to every one that heareth the words of the prophecy of this book ; if any man shall add to these things, God shall add upon him the plagues written in this book." This reference, then, is intended to convey the impression, that, if any one adds any thing to Scripture, he will incur the wrath of God, and consequently that all has been written. But what an abuse of Scripture is not such an interpretation ! For any reader that will take up this chapter will see that the meaning of the writer of the Apocalypse is, that no one should either add any thing to, or subtract any thing from, that Apocalypse, as is most obvious and expressly stated in the very passage. Here is, then, the queer argument used by the writers of the confession: St. John, at the conclusion of his Apocalypse, threatens with the vengeance of Heaven the one who shall either add to or subtract from his book, or the one who shall interpolate and corrupt his book; therefore all things are written in Scripture!

The text taken from Isaias,—" To the law and to the testimony: if they speak not according to this word, it is because there is no light in them,"—is not more to the purpose. These words of the prophet have long been the cant of Scotch fanatics; and this is strange enough; for the "testimony" there mentioned naturally leads to the notion of *tradition*, which it is their great object to discard. Any one who will read the passage will find it somewhat obscure; but the meaning which will present itself to his mind will be, that the prophet inveighs against those who consulted pythons and wizards, and exhorts them to have recourse rather to the law and to the testimony. But no powers of imagination can draw from it the conclusion that every thing is written, even that which was revealed by Christ; for Isaias speaks of a law written hundreds of years before Christ.

The text from St. Paul to the Romans says merely, that what was written was written for our learning; but it does not say that the *whole* of God's revelation was committed to writing. In fine, the passage from St. Luke is brought forward with no better grace. The passage states, that the writer, after having received full information from eyewitnesses, wrote for the purpose of giving to Theophilus a full certainty in regard to the matters of which he wrote. But it does not say that he wrote *all* that was revealed. It is true, the passage states that the writer had "perfect understanding of all things from the very first," and, without entering into a discussion as to the propriety of the translation used by Protestants, we say, it is perfectly evident St. Luke does not mean that he wrote absolutely every thing which Christ did or taught; for if so, he would have been guilty of a barefaced lie, in the very first line of his Gospel, since St. Matthew, St. Mark, and St. John say a great many things which he does not record; therefore he must mean merely that he was fully informed of all the things which he wrote about. Now, we hope, all can see the difference between the assertion, I vouch for the truth of *every thing* I write, and this other assertion, I write with truth *every thing* that can be written upon the subject. These remarks show, with absolute evidence, that none of the texts adduced by the Presbyterian Confession of Faith prove that the revelations of God were committed wholly unto writing. This is sufficient to prove to the Presbyterians that their tenets are totally ungrounded, that their faith has no foundation, and that they believe without any motive or reason capable of making any impression on a reasonable man. But their doctrine is not only purely gratuitous; we can even prove, by the most obvious arguments, that it is absolutely false, and clearly at variance with Scripture itself, and with common sense.

St. John concludes his Gospel with the following declaration:—"There are also many other things which Jesus did, which if they were written every one, the world itself, I think, would not be able to contain the books that should be written." Who, in the face of this declaration, will dare assert that every thing is written? Here, as a manifest proof that it never was the plan of divine Providence that all should be written, the evangelist closes his account with the avowal, that he knows many things more that Christ did, many more words that he uttered, and many more examples that he gave, than he commits to writing. The same apostle concludes his last two Epistles with a declaration which seems to have been written purposely to contradict the assertion of Presbyterians. "Having many things to write unto you, I would not by paper and ink; for I hope that I shall be with you, and speak face to face." The apostle had many things to write, and consequently these things were necessary, or at least useful, and still he declines writing them. Who will, in the face of this declaration, maintain that every thing pertaining to the revelation of God is written? Again, St. Paul, no doubt, made important regulations concerning the Lord's Supper, as he asserts in those words,—"The rest I will set in order when I come."—1 Cor. xi. 34. Can Presbyterians point out the place where these regulations are found? Furthermore, the same apostle, writing to the Thessalonians, tells them,— "Remember you not, that, when I was yet with you, I told you these things? and now you know what withholdeth, that he may be revealed in his time."—2 Thess. ii. 5, 6. The Thessalonians, then, had learned *orally* from St. Paul, and knew what withheld Antichrist. What is that thing? Is it written anywhere? There is, then, a revelation which certainly was not committed to writing.

The first chapter of the Acts of the Apostles expressly states that Jesus Christ employed the forty days which elapsed between his resurrection and ascension in teaching his apostles,—"for forty days appearing to them, and speaking of the kingdom of God."—verse 3. And now where are those heavenly instructions given by Christ, risen from the dead, to his apostles, who were now, in a great measure, freed from that carnal sense and those grovelling ideas which had besotted their hearts during their former intercourse with him? Those instructions which lasted forty days take up only a few lines in the Scriptures; whereas, the discourse of our Lord on the eve of his death, a discourse which could have lasted but a few hours, takes up five chapters. No doubt, these discourses for forty days were of the greatest importance, since the sacred writer says they related to the *kingdom of God;* and who can doubt but that the necessity of giving those instructions was one of the great objects of the stay of the Man-God among mortals? Scarcely anything of these discourses is written; not that the apostles had forgotten them, but because it was not deemed proper to write them. This fact, taken in connection with another, shows how absurd and untenable is the Protestant theory about the sufficiency of Scripture. History represents to us the Christian Church springing from its cradle with dogmas, rites, practices, fasts, feasts, sacraments; and yet there is no direct mention of many of those things in Scripture, at most only a remote or obscure allusion to a few. Who, then, can resist the conclusion, that the apostles received upon those points instructions which they delivered orally, and which they *wrote*, not with ink on paper or parchment, but in a more substantial, imperishable, and authentic way, in the habits and practice of the faithful? Many things, in particular concerning the sacred rites of divine institution which we call sacraments, are not mentioned in Scripture; but such rites were unquestionably written in the practice and habits of Christians; which was a safer way to propagate them than writing them in a book, especially as the latter way had many inconveniences, since the pagans should not be allowed a free access to those peculiar rites which they would understand but imperfectly from a book, and which they would disfigure; and hence we find in the very first ages of Christianity, frequent allusions to the fact of the rites and mysteries of Christians being made a subject of secrecy, so as to conceal them from the knowledge of the pagans. And this law of secrecy, which history proves most clearly, was nothing but the continuation of the plan alluded to in the Scriptures themselves,—not to write every thing, but to transmit much by the belief, practice, and habits of the Christian people.

To descend to particulars corroborating these general remarks, we ask, where is it written that children can be validly and lawfully baptized? Where is it written that immersion is not necessary in baptism, and that aspersion and infusion are lawful modes of administering that sacred rite? Where is it written that the sacraments of the church are validly administered by sinners, and by wicked ministers? We say, it is written nowhere in Scripture. But all this was written in the practice of the Christian Church, and hence is admitted not only by Catholics, but by Presbyterians also. A proof that these points are not clearly set down in Scripture is, that the largest body, perhaps, of Protestants in the United States, the Baptists, deny the validity of baptism conferred on children, or on adults by infusion. We know, too, that laymen can administer baptism validly; and though Presbyterians deny it, they show only their inconsistency, or their *heresy*,—a word which means *choice;* for among traditions they choose those which suit them, and reject the others. But as the traditions all stand on the same ground, they should either be admitted in their totality, or rejected in their totality. Furthermore, how do we know that baptism can be administered but once? By tradition alone. For if one says that Scripture does not order its reiteration, it is equally certain that neither does it forbid it. And hence, at most, we could only conclude that the Scripture says nothing about it; and then something held as true and essential by Presbyterians themselves is not written in Scripture; and then the assertion, that all the doctrine of Christ is written, goes by the board. Scripture says not that baptism conferred by a layman is null; still, Presbyterians hold it null, against the tradition of the church. Scripture says nothing about the repetition of baptism, and Presbyterians hold, with the tradition of the church, that it cannot be repeated,—a good exemplification of that spirit of contradiction by which they admit just enough of tradition on some points to put a whip into the hands of their opponents, while they reject it on others.

We have mentioned several points about which the Scriptures say nothing, though the Presbyterians themselves hold them to be revealed. But we are far from having exhausted the list of those points which were revealed, but which were not written in the Scriptures. To mention a very striking example, we find it written in Scripture that it is forbidden to eat blood and things strangled. "It hath seemed good to the Holy Ghost and to us, to lay no further burden upon you than these necessary things; that you abstain from things sacrificed to idols, and from blood, and from things strangled, and from fornication."—Acts xv. 28, 29. Here, then, the Scripture, or the Holy Ghost, declares it a *necessary* thing to abstain from blood; and still, all Christians, from time immemorial, have held it a thing lawful to eat blood or things strangled, and we have no doubt that the strictest Presbyterian would make no scruple to eat blood-pudding, if he relished it. Where is it written, we ask, that this prohibition to eat blood was to cease? Where is the passage of Scripture that says, that after a certain time required to *bury the synagogue with due honor*, as theologians say,—that is, after there should be no danger of scandalizing the Jews, to whom blood and strangled things were an abomination,— the eating of blood and of strangled things would become a thing indifferent in its nature, and consequently lawful? The assumption, then, that every thing is written in Scripture, is evidently unwarranted.

Again, what part of Scripture declares that the washing of feet prescribed by our Lord, in St. John xiii., is only of a spiritual nature? "If I, then, being Lord and Master, have washed your feet, you also ought to wash one another's feet. For I have given you an example, that, as I have done to you, so you do also." Hence, among the thousand and one Protestant sects which have arisen since Luther, we have one taking the modest title of "Church of God," though its existence is not of an earlier date than 1820, that believes firmly in *feet-washing*. "She believes that the ordinance of feet-washing, that is, the literal washing of the saints' feet, according to the word and **example** of Christ, is obligatory upon all Christians, and ought to be observed by all the Churches of God."* These sectarians are unquestionably right, if we have Scripture only for the rule of faith; for no text more positive could be brought forward to prescribe feet-washing; but the apostles who were present, and knew what our Lord said better than we can, wrote, not in a book, but in the practice, and rites, and habits of the churches they founded, that this washing was spiritual; and hence we know with equal certainty that this washing is a spiritual one, and that all is not recorded in Scripture that Christ revealed to his apostles. To obtain another clear instance of the silence of the Scriptures on many points which were revealed and known at first, we have only to read the two genealogies of Christ, the one in St. Matthew, and the other in St. Luke. The reader of Scripture will be in a real dilemma as to the meaning and agreement of these genealogies; and the fact is, that they have exhausted the ingenuity of commentators. The commentators propose many solutions of the difficulty; but with the avowed conviction, that it is impossible to tell which is the true one. Now a few words, added to either, or both, of these genealogies, would have cleared up for us the whole difficulty. But these words were not added, because the thing was clear at the time the genealogies were written, when all the circumstances of time, place, and persons were fully understood. The loss of these circumstances has rendered the enigma insolvable,—an evident proof that all was not written.

But on no subject does it more clearly appear that the Almighty never intended that all things pertaining to religion should be written in the Scriptures, than by their complete silence on the Christian festivals. That these festivals are essential to religion is sufficiently obvious to all from reason alone, and is admitted, at least for the celebration of Sunday, by all shades of Presbyterians. The conduct of God in relation to the chosen people, who had so many festivals commemorative of the great events of his mercy to them, together with the historical documents of the early Christian Church, must convince every one who is not determined to be a sceptic, that Christ left powers and orders to the apostles and to the church to institute feasts and anniversaries, so that, besides Sunday, there have always been in

---

**History of the Religious Denominations in the United States*, p. 180.

the church other festivals, such as the commemoration of the death of Christ by humiliation and fast, the anniversary of his resurrection, or Easter, of the descent of the Holy Ghost, &c. Now, where is mention made in Scripture of these festivals, including the weekly festival, Sunday? Nowhere. We find, indeed, express mention made of the *abolition* of the Jewish Sabbath. St. Paul solemnly declared that Jewish festivals, new moons, and Sabbaths were all gone. "Let no man judge you in meat, or in drink, or in respect of a festival day, or of the new moon, or of the sabbaths." —Colos. ii. 16. But we see nowhere that Sunday was to replace the Judaical Sabbath, or Saturday. *Allusions* to Sunday are found in the Scripture, it is true; but Scriptural allusions prove nothing, unless interpreted by tradition. The fact, that there are only *allusions*, which prove nothing when detached from tradition, shows that it never was intended that all the Christian doctrine and practice should be committed to writing. But there is no allusion to the Christian fast of Lent, or to the Christian Easter, and other Christian festivals; nevertheless, who can reasonably deny their institution and observance in the very time of the apostles, when he reads in authentic history, that Polycarp, who had long lived and conversed with the Apostle St. John, went from a remote province of the East to Rome, for the purpose of conferring with the bishop of that city, the successor of Peter, not indeed upon the keeping of Easter, which was instituted both in the East and the West, but upon the particular and *proper* day at which Easter should be kept,—a question which was partly astronomical? *
Who can doubt that the festivals kept in memory of the principal events of Christ's life were either appointed formally by the apostles, or at least instituted in conformity with their teaching and practice? Let us take Christmas as an example. This day is not spoken of in the Gospel. Still it is kept by the Christian world on the 25th of December. It is true that Presbyterians reject this as unscriptural, and we read there was at one time a fine of five shillings, in Massachusetts, on every one who kept Christmas. But this only shows the folly of rejecting every thing not found in Scripture. What does it matter whether we find it written on paper, that Christ was born on a certain day of December, and that Christians ought to keep

---

* Hier. *De Script Eccles.*, Cap. xvii.

that day as one of joy and gratitude, or whether we find the same written in the practice and the customs of a whole people? The latter is by far the most substantial way of transmitting the event. What does it signify, for instance, that the constitution of the United States does not mention that George Washington was born on the 22d of February? Every one knows this to be a fact, from the festivities usual on that day; and to one who now would venture to deny this fact, on the ground that the constitution does not mention it, no answer would need to be returned. No one, then, can doubt that Christians have always kept, and should keep, days in commemoration of Christ's birth, death, and resurrection.* The fact, that nothing is said of such festivals in Scripture, shows, then, that the Scriptures were never intended to record every thing.

In fine, the most irrefragable argument that all is not written in Scripture, is that the canon, or list of Scripture books, is nowhere given in Scripture, so that it is impossible for Presbyterians to prove their inspiration and divinity. But more of this hereafter, when the Confession brings this subject more directly before us. We will not, however, dismiss this subject without quoting the positive testimonies of Scripture to show that all was not written, but much left to be transmitted by tradition. St. Paul writes to the Thessalonians, 2 Thes. ii. 15,—" Therefore, brethren, stand firm, and hold the traditions which you have learned, whether *by word*, or by our epistles." No clearer statement of our doctrine can be imagined. If any should object that what is here called tradition *by word* was afterwards written in

---

* The *Martyrology* for the 25th of December has the following account. " In Nicomedia, the martyrdom of several thousand Christians, who, being assembled on Christmas day to celebrate the holy mysteries, were shut up in the church by order of the Emperor Diocletian, who caused a fire to kindled all around, and a stand with a censer to be placed before the door, whilst a herald cried out with a loud voice, that all those who wished to save themselves from the fire should come out and offer incense to Jupiter; they all answered, that they preferred dying for Christ, and, the fire being kindled, they were all consumed in it, and thus deserved to be born in heaven that day that Christ was born on earth for the salvation of the world." Here the reflection forces itself irresistibly upon the mind,—we must believe witnesses who die for what they assert. The death of those thousand Christians on Christmas day will render Christmas dear to us, although Presbyterians would impose fines on us for keeping it, as unscriptural; though a plain and unprejudiced man will conclude that if any refuse to commemorate the birth, death, and resurrection of Christ, such do not acknowledge Christ as their father.

the other Epistles of St. Paul, because this to the Thessalonians was among the first he wrote, we would ask, where is the date of the Epistle to the Thessalonians written? It is written nowhere, and certainly not in the Scripture. But where does the apostle say that he will on some other occasion write those discourses, or *traditions by word*, which he commands them to keep? This silly objection, however, will not apply to the Second Epistle of St. Paul to Timothy, the one which he wrote a short time before his martyrdom, and the same in which (iv. 6) he says that he is ready for sacrifice, and that the time of his dissolution is at hand. Now in that Epistle he charges his disciple in the following words:—"The things which thou hast heard from me, before many witnesses, the same commend to faithful men who shall be fit to teach others also." Here the apostle alludes, not to what he has *written*, but to what he has *said*, and which Timothy had *heard* before many witnesses; and he directs Timothy, not merely to *write* the same, but to *intrust* and *commend* it to others, who will be fit to teach others;—thus establishing a tradition of holy doctrine quite distinct from Scripture. Here it is evidently asserted, that St. Paul had taught Timothy, that Timothy was to teach faithful men, and these faithful men, other men. Thus is the Christian doctrine transmitted; and it is transmitted in all its purity through these successive teachings, because the Holy Ghost is promised to the body of pastors who teach in the church. The same Epistle, i. 13, 14, has the following no less conclusive passage, containing also a promise of the Holy Ghost to watch over the sacred deposit of holy doctrine intrusted to pastors:—"Hold the form of sound *words* which thou hast heard from me in faith, and in the love which is in Christ Jesus. Keep the good deposited in trust to thee by the Holy Ghost who dwelleth in us." Here the apostle charges him to keep, not writings, but words,—not what he has read, but what he has *heard;* and the Holy Ghost is said to dwell in us to accomplish this holy purpose. We could easily add numerous and evident testimonies of all Christian antiquity, to show that all was not written in the Scripture; but we think we have dwelt enough upon this first false assertion of the first article of the Confession, and have shown sufficiently that Presbyterians fail in proving their position, that the whole revelation of God was committed to writing, and that the contrary assertion is incontrovertibly established by every sort of positive and conclusive argument.

2. But it is time to pass to the second assertion we have taken exception to, namely, that the Scriptures are *most necessary;* and we begin by discussing the proofs of this necessity adduced by the Confession, which we transcribe in full.

"2 Tim. iii. 15. And that from a child thou hast known the Holy Scriptures, which are able to make thee wise unto salvation, through faith which is in Christ Jesus. 2 Pet. i. 19. We have also a more sure word of prophecy; whereunto ye do well that ye take heed, as unto a light that shineth in a dark place, until the day dawn and the day-star arise in your hearts."

Here are, then, the mighty, the all-convincing proofs of the absolute necessity of Scripture, which our Presbyterians adduce. The Presbyterians must count largely on the simplicity of the readers of the Confession, to have the courage to offer them such proofs as these. As for ourselves, we can of course smile on them. To begin with the text of St. Paul to Timothy; what is there in that passage that has any the least bearing on the *necessity* of Scripture? No doubt the Presbyterians mean in their Confession, that, if any Scripture be most necessary, it is the New Testament. But this passage speaks of the Old Testament only; for the Old Testament was the only Scripture Timothy could have learned in his childhood, since it was the only one which was then in existence. This passage, therefore, could not in any manner prove the necessity of the New Testament. But it does not, in the least, prove the necessity of even the Old. It contains not one word about the *necessity* of the Scriptures. From the fact, that Timothy had known the Sacred Scriptures from his infancy, we can no more conclude that the Scriptures are necessary, than we can conclude that Latin or Greek are necessary because we have known them from our childhood. It is said in the text, that the Scriptures are *able* to make one wise; but if we are to draw any conclusion from this, it is not that the Scriptures are necessary, but useful. If we say that mathematics are *able* to sharpen one's intellect and judgment, we imply, that there are other methods besides mathematics, and that mathematics are not absolutely necessary.

The text from St. Peter is equally defective as a proof of the necessity of Scripture. St. Peter is speaking of the prophecies of the Old Testament, and if what he says proves the necessity of any Scripture, it is that of the prophecies of the Old Testament, and of nothing more. But the apostle says nowhere that the prophecies even are necessary; he simply says that they are a firm and sure word. He adds, that Christians *do well* to attend, but does not say that it is *most necessary* that they should attend, to this word of prophecy. Hence, these proofs of the necessity of Scripture are totally unworthy a serious refutation, and prove only one thing, that the compilers of the Confession considered it their duty, by means of Scripture texts, to throw dust into the eyes of their readers. They would, doubtless, have brought forward better proofs, if they had had them to bring; and we need no better evidence that it is impossible for Presbyterians to make up a confession of faith from the Scriptures alone, than these *pretended* Scriptural proofs themselves.

Having shown that there is no Scripture proof of the *necessity* of Scripture, we will now go further, and prove by very conclusive arguments that the Scriptures are *not* absolutely necessary; for true religion was for a long time preserved and propagated without them, and the teaching of the pastors of the church is adequate to preserve and propagate the religion of Christ, even independently of them. The Scriptures were not given to supersede this teaching of the pastors, but chiefly to afford them a greater facility in the discharge of their trust. The teaching of the pastors may suffice without Scripture, but the Scriptures cannot suffice without that teaching.

The assertion, that the Scriptures are most necessary, is at variance with two indisputable facts:—1. That God never left the world without the true religion; and 2. That he did leave it without any Scriptures at all for over two thousand years, namely, from Adam to Moses. Adam, Noe, and many in the time of Noe, of whom St. Peter speaks (1 St. Pet. iii. 20), Abraham, Isaac, Jacob, Melchisedech, and innumerable others, followed the true religion, were acceptable in the eyes of God, and obtained salvation, and yet they had no Scripture. But as they had a revealed religion, we must conclude that even a revealed religion can be propagated without Scripture. That they had a revealed religion, we know from positive facts, and it may be collected from the very text of the Confession already quoted, where, on a new perusal, the reader will find it stated that reason alone cannot give that knowledge of God which is necessary unto salvation. If those men—as Abraham, Isaac, and Jacob, who are certainly of the number of the elect, since God calls himself the God of Abraham, Isaac, and Jacob—obtained salvation, and salvation cannot be obtained by the light of nature or of reason alone, they must have had the light of revelation; and since they had not Scripture, Scripture cannot be " most necessary." So that we find on this point a plain contradiction in the very first article of the Presbyterian Confession, and this first contradiction is speedily followed by another, in which Scripture is stated to be, on the one hand, *most necessary*, and, on the other, to have been resorted to, only as the means of " *better* preserving and propagating the truth!"

The truths which were preserved and propagated during more than two thousand years anterior to the law of Moses were both very numerous and very important. The unity of God, supreme arbiter and creator of all things, formed the first and most important of these truths. Then came the attributes of God, which were known during that period, as will appear to those who read Genesis; then the creation of man after the image and likeness of God; the fall of man and original sin, which was known from the history of the human race, and is alluded to by holy Job; also, the immortality of the soul, which must have been revealed, since we find it established and believed everywhere; and certainly, after the fall of Adam, man could not know by reason alone that he was immortal. Another point revealed, and not written, was the redemption of man, and the promise of a Redeemer or Messiah. Another revelation still was that of the practice of offering sacrifices, and for the most part bloody sacrifices, which we find existing long before Moses. Also, long before any Scripture was written, God gave to Abraham and his posterity the precept of circumcision, which was faithfully transmitted for several centuries. We see, in fact, a complete system of religion, including important revealed truths, composed of dogmas and precepts, faithfully preserved without Scripture for more than two thousand years; and it is therefore supremely absurd to assert, as a general proposition, that the Scriptures are " most necessary."

If the Scriptures are most necessary, the first thing the apostles should have done, before separating to spread themselves over the world, would have been to compose them; but every one at all conversant with history knows that this is precisely what they did not do. For many years the primitive church was without the New Testament, and the different parts of that sacred volume were not all written at once, but on accidental occasions, as the circumstances of places and persons seemed to require; precluding, therefore, the idea, that the apostles intended to leave in their writings a complete system of religious instruction. We know that St. Thomas, the apostle, went to the East long before the greater part of the New Testament had been written. Could he have left to the Christians in the East the Gospels and Epistles written in the West? If the Scriptures are most necessary, the apostles, by separating before having composed them, exposed themselves to the danger of leaving the nations they converted without that which, according to the Presbyterian Confession, was most necessary. Can we believe this? The conduct of the apostles, then, in respect to the composition of Scripture, shows conclusively that they did not deem Scripture to be most necessary, as Christianity could be, and actually was, established and propagated by the preaching of the word, without it. Hence, St. Irenæus, who had *almost* conversed with St. John, and is more likely to know what the apostles said and did than are the Presbyterians who met at Westminster sixteen hundred years after Christ, tells us that there were nations fully Christian, who nevertheless were without the Scriptures. "What!" says he, "even if the apostles had left no Scriptures, should we not follow the order of tradition which they delivered to those with whom they intrusted the churches? A state of things found among many barbarous nations, who believe in Christ without paper or ink, but have salvation written in their hearts by the Holy Ghost, and carefully preserve the ancient tradition, believing in one God, creator of all things through Jesus Christ his Son."*

It must be a matter of surprise, that the doctrine of the *necessity* of written, divine laws, or a written religion, should have found a foothold in countries like England and America, where there are so many unwritten laws by which the most common and important relations of life are governed more universally and effectually than by the ponderous volumes of the *written laws* composed every year at Washington and elsewhere. What is the *common law* which here and in England governs the most important transactions of life, but a law written originally only in the customs of our Saxon ancestors? How do we know that by marriage the husband becomes possessed of all the personal property of

---

Contra Hær., Lib. III., c. 4.

his wife? How do we know that husband and wife form but one person before the law? How do we know that parents are entitled to the earnings of their minor children? Or a thousand other very important features of our legislation, which become so apparent to us when we travel in other countries, where different customs obtain? We know all these things from the *common law*, which is called even by jurists themselves the "unwritten law." The common law is said to be "unwritten," because it never was the result of a written or printed legislation made by any prince or court of England; for it preceded every statute or written legislation, and it was written in the customs and habits of the people, before it was written in books. Hence, to the present day, no one can point out any code or legislative enactment by which those articles are found to have been introduced and become obligatory, but their existence is proved by the doctrine of jurists and by the decisions of courts; but courts have no right to make laws; and hence a recourse to their decision is nothing else than an appeal to a witness of a law made before. The state of English countries as to the common law is a good representation of the polity of the Christian Church as to divine and ecclesiastical laws, and their enforcement. Courts of justice make their decisions from written laws or statutes, and unwritten laws or the *common law;* so does the church make her decisions from the whole word of God, both written on paper and parchment, and unwritten on parchment, but written in the practice and habits of the Christian people; with this difference, however, that courts of justice are only a *human* authority, whereas the Christian court is one gifted with assistance from above. "I am with you all days to the end of ages." The similarity here indicated runs through another important feature of the two sorts of laws. The common law, although unwritten in its nature, is still written equivalently, because it has been a frequent matter of written discussion among jurists, and because the *cases decided* by courts are written. So also the points of the Christian doctrine, not written originally, are written equivalently in the works of the fathers, and in the decisions of the councils. We may conclude, then, that, if human laws can be preserved and have been preserved without writing, by human societies with the influence of nature and reason only, much more so can unwritten divine laws be preserved and kept faithfully with the supernatural influence of Heaven; and therefore it is a glaring absurdity to make the Scriptures most necessary, and a still greater one to make them contain every thing, and to constitute each individual the judge of their meaning.

All Christian dogmas and precepts are *facts* which can be preserved and transmitted by testimony and tradition, as other facts; hence, the fact, that America is a newly discovered continent, and since settled by Europeans, is plain and evident independently of any written account of the voyages of Columbus and others. All books might be destroyed, and this fact nevertheless be faithfully transmitted for centuries. But with regard to the divine and religious facts which constitute Christianity, there is a peculiarity which greatly facilitates their faithful transmission by tradition, and renders changes and alterations impossible. Those religious traditions are tangible and permanent practical facts. The fact of the newness of our continent has nothing practical; but take a Christian traditionary dogma,—say, that laymen can baptize in case of necessity. This is a practical fact, because at all times there are and there have been cases where, recourse being impossible to the regularly appointed minister, and where, there being danger of death, laymen have performed this duty. No change, then, could occur in this fact, any more than in that other practical traditionary fact, that the day which we call Sunday is truly the weekly commemoration of Christ's resurrection. Religious traditions have another advantage, that of having been spread over a wider extent of country; for, from the origin of Christianity, the whole world received this sacred deposit; hence, if the tradition be found at very distant points, there is every evidence of its truth. Again, no tradition is kept with greater fidelity than the divine instructions which form that sacred deposit which Timothy was charged by the apostle to keep so preciously; and as the importance of those traditions is greater than that of any other, innumerable persons would step forward to oppose any change that would be contemplated by innovators. The history of the church is but one illustration of these remarks. Hence, tradition alone can preserve religion; and if, humanly speaking, we could come to this conclusion, what an additional strength will it not receive from the positive assurance of Christ to be all days with the pastors of the church to enable them to *teach* right, and with the faithful to enable them to *believe* right! We must, then, conclude, that the assertion of the Presbyterians, that the Scriptures are most necessary, is not only unfounded and left unproved by them, but is positively disproved by every kind of argument appropriate to the case. But if Scripture be not *most necessary*, what is it then? It is most useful and most beneficial; it is a sweet pledge of divine mercy; it is a treasure of infinite value. Hence, no one has ever entertained a greater respect and a greater love for the Scriptures than the Catholic Church, and no one has ever shown a greater assiduity in meditating on the sacred writings than the Catholic clergy. This is not, however, at present, the point at issue; and we pass to the third assertion contained in the first article of the Presbyterian Confession of Faith, that the "former ways of God's revealing his will unto his people are now ceased."

3. Presbyterians, then, gravely inform us that the former ways by which God revealed his will unto his people are now ceased. The assertion is not, perhaps, as clear as it might be, but, as it is, what proof do they give of it? Perhaps the proof will throw some light on their meaning. What is, then, O learned divines! the proof of your assertion, that God ceases to reveal his will unto us as he did formerly? Here is the sole and whole ground of the assertion, as found in the Confession:—"Heb. i. 1, 2. God, who at sundry times and in divers manners spake in times past unto the fathers by the prophets, hath in these last days spoken unto us by his Son, whom he hath appointed heir of all things, by whom also he made the worlds." We have read this passage over and over again, to ascertain what bearing it can have on the assertion. But we have racked our brains to no purpose. We can discover nothing leading at all to the learned conclusion of the Westminster divines. Truly there must be a peculiar logic for "Presbyterian heads"; and they should have appended it as a valuable and indispensable supplement to their confession. God spoke in times past by the prophets; he has lately spoken to us by his Son; therefore the former ways of God's revealing his will have now ceased. This is admirable. The following argument would be in keeping with it: Calvin and Knox promulgated and established Presbyterianism; the Westminster divines improved it, talked, and wrote much about it; therefore modern Presbyterians have nothing more to say about it, and the best thing they can do is to shut their mouths altogether. If this conclusion be not contained in the premises, it nevertheless indicates their wisest policy; for the more they talk of Presbyterianism, the more do they expose its nakedness.

The peculiar absurdity of the proof adduced by Presbyterians is, that it implies that God, after our Lord had spoken and risen to heaven, ceased to reveal his will to men as formerly; which makes the apostles themselves common men, and deprives them of the ability to use any of those "former ways" by which the prophets could reveal the will of God. This conclusion, fairly and fully accepted, destroys the inspiration of the New Testament; for it was written many years after "God had spoken by his Son."

If we go to the very foundation of the assertion of the Presbyterian divines, we shall find it to be totally at variance with the text of Scripture they quote, and one which they were unwilling publicly to confess. The following is implicitly the course of reasoning which led them to the conclusion they adopted. We Presbyterians, of course, form the true church, the spouse of Christ, the saints of God. But we see among us no sign of a vivifying influence of heaven; we see no extraordinary display of the power and mercy of God by signs and wonders; we see no *miracles* performed among us, and dare not even dream of them; we see among us no supernatural virtues, but every thing common, trivial, and worldly; quarrelling about Scripture, uncertainty and doubt as to the most fundamental articles of Christianity, are the leading traits of our religious system; we see the clergy sighing for "filthy lucre," and making it the basis, the measure, and the end of their preaching, and the laity entertaining a profound contempt for the clergy; we see in our church no other unity than the privilege granted to each one to construct his creed differently from the others,—no other sanctity than that of cursing the pope and hating every body,—no other apostolicity than a descent from Simon Magus through all the heretics that have disfigured the church in the lapse of ages,—no other catholicity than the narrow limits of the General Assembly, annual or triennial, both confined to a very small corner of the globe; we see among us nothing but human passions, worldly views, ambitious projects, satanic pride, and hearty hating;—and *therefore* we conclude that God's former ways of revealing himself to his people have long since ceased. Certainly the conclusion is eminently and undeniably true, when confined to the Presbyterian Church, in which, assuredly, the former ways of God's revealing his will unto men have ceased, long ceased, or, to speak more properly, have never existed. It is well to record this tardy avowal of Presbyterians; for in it they concede that neither Luther, nor Calvin, nor the other innovators, had any *extraordinary* call from Heaven to reform the church; and as they had not the *ordinary* one, it follows necessarily that they were sent by nobody, and consequently that they were intruders,—a set of ambitious, proud, stubborn, and rebellious men, who stamped upon the very face of their enterprise a seal of condemnation and reprobation. " I did not send these prophets, yet they ran; I have not spoken to them, yet they prophesied."—Jer. xxiii. 21.

Not so with the Catholic Church; she has kept, ever since the time of the apostles, the marks of a supernatural influence and agency,—marks as extraordinary and miraculous, nay, much more remarkable, than those by which God revealed himself to men under the law of nature or the Jewish dispensation. We do not pretend that she has received new revelations of articles of faith; for this would suppose that Christ left his work imperfect, when founding the church. But we maintain that Christ has not " left himself without testimony,"—Acts xiv. 17,—even miraculous testimony, of his presence, and of his influence on her. This is no more than what is clearly promised to her. " I am with you all days." " These signs shall follow them that believe; in my name they shall cast out devils." " Keep the good deposited in trust to thee by the Holy Ghost *who dwelleth in us*."—2 Tim. i. 14. It is true, there has been no Scripture added since the apostles; but the solemn decisions of the church, chiefly in her general councils, have the same certainty as Scripture, though not inspired in the same way; and hence, a great pope, St. Gregory, said he received and revered the definitions of general councils as the four Gospels; and so hath God spoken also through the last general council assembled in Trent; indeed, it is nothing short of a miracle, that all those councils, and the latter in particular, have been admitted without a dissenting voice by so many millions of Christians, among whom are numbered so many eminent scholars and profound philosophers. Had the authority of those councils been merely human, they would have met with a very different fate. The heroic sanctity of so many of the children of the church has been a perpetual miracle in her bosom. *The Lives of the Saints* are a proof of it, and it is only in her communion that such a book can be found. In fine, miracles and prophecies have always illustrated the church, from the time of the apostles. He who wishes to be satisfied of this has only to read the history of the church, where at each page he he will find proofs of celestial agency transcending the ordinary course of nature; he will find that the prophets of the new law have been greater than those of the old,—that St. Augustine in England, St. Boniface in Germany, St. Francis, St. Dominic, St. Bernard, St. Francis Xavier, St. Ignatius, St. Francis Regis, St. Vincent de Paul, are, in point of miracles and other extraordinary effects of divine power, incomparably superior to Isaias, Jeremias, Jonas, and others who have written portions of the inspired volumes. As an incontestable proof of God's revealing himself by miracles in the Catholic Church, we merely mention that in every century since the rise of Protestantism many saints have been canonized. Now, according to the rules of the Roman court, no saint is publicly proposed to the veneration of the faithful, unless at least three miracles be proved by evidence superior to every sort of objection. The objections which are stated against those miracles are far more severe, more precise, more subtle, than Protestants ever would think of. We admit, it is easy to laugh at the idea of miracles; but it is easy also to be an infidel; and we confidently assert that any one who will take the trouble of examining the authenticity of those miracles must admit them, or be an incorrigible sceptic.

So far we have disposed of the first article of the first chapter of the Presbyterian Confession of Faith, and have pointed out three gross errors which it contains, besides other minor contradictions. We are now ready to take up the second article, which runs thus:—

"Under the name of Holy Scripture, or the Word of God written, are now contained all the books of the Old and New Testament, which are these, Genesis......Revelation, all which are given by inspiration of God, to be the rule of faith and life."

We find in the notes the following Scriptural authority.

"Eph. ii. 20. And are built upon the foundation of the apostles and prophets, Jesus Christ himself being the chief corner-stone. Rev. xxii. 18, 19. For I testify unto every man that heareth the words of the prophecy of this book, if any man shall add unto these things, God shall add unto him the plagues that are written in this book; and if any man shall take away from the words of the book of this prophecy, God shall take away his part out of the book of life, and out of the holy city, and from the things which are written in this book. 2 Tim. iii. 16. All

Scripture is given by inspiration of God, and is profitable for doctrine, for reproof, for correction, for instruction in righteousness."

This second article is not less important than the first, nor less abundant in false proofs. It is an equally good specimen of Presbyterian logic. We pass over the assertion, that *Scripture is the rule of faith and life;* for we do not construe it as meaning the *sole* rule of faith and life, —a point which we shall have occasion hereafter to examine. The present article sets forth the inspiration and canon of Scripture, excluding, of course, from the canon some books, of which mention is made in the following article. Upon this important topic we unqualifiedly assert, that it is an utter impossibility for Protestants to establish that there are inspired books, and especially which they are.

But let us first examine the proofs adduced by the Confession of Faith. They are reduced to the following masterly enthymem. *We read in Scripture that Scripture is inspired; therefore, the Scripture is inspired.* Now it so happens, that the first assertion is false in its generality; but, admitting it to be true, the conclusion would still be gratuitous and unsupported. Admit, then, that the Scripture says that the Scripture is inspired; what will this avail you, unless you know from some other quarter that the Scripture is infallible? White paper will bear any thing. Is it enough to write at the beginning or end of a book, *Inspired by the Holy Spirit,* to make it so? Then the book of Mahomet is inspired, and, to come nearer home, so also is the book of Mormon. Hence, unless there be some infallible authority, and some evident and irrefragable proof independent of Scripture, to establish the inspiration of Scripture, it is perfect folly to adduce Scripture as a proof of its own inspiration. For let it be carefully remarked that the inspiration of Scripture is not an *external,* but a *purely internal* fact; consequently, not admissible on the same ground which would compel any man who is not a sceptic, even an infidel, to admit the *public* facts recorded in the Old and New Testaments, merely as points of authentic history. There is but one way in which the book of Scripture can prove itself inspired, and that is by exhibiting the great seal of Heaven, namely, miracles. Hence, if a Presbyterian, on taking his Bible, were to hear, not in his imagination, but in reality, a voice proceeding from the book itself, and telling him, *Every thing found here is given by the inspiration of God,* or if this book applied to a dead man by the one who inquires into its inspiration were to raise him to life, then might its authority be established from its intrinsic merits, but not otherwise; or else any impostor, by writing that he is inspired, might compose Scripture.

But do the Scriptures in reality say that they are inspired? The Presbyterians adduce three testimonies to prove it. The first asserts that we are built upon the foundation of the apostles and prophets, Jesus Christ being the corner-stone. But how Presbyterians can conclude from this that Scripture is inspired is a mystery to us, and especially how they find in it the name of all the books inspired. This text, viewed in relation to the New Testament, with which we are more particularly concerned, would support the assertion of Presbyterians only on the supposition, 1. That none but apostles wrote the New Testament; 2. That the apostles were inspired in every thing they wrote; 3. That we know with certainty that all the parts of the New Testament bearing the name of apostles come truly from them. But these three positions are either false, or at least teem with insuperable difficulties for Protestants. It is false that none but apostles wrote the New Testament. St. Luke and St. Mark were not apostles, but merely disciples of the apostles, like Barnabas, Clement, Hermes, and Ignatius, whose writings are not a portion of Scripture. Now the writings of St. Luke and St. Mark form over a third of the New Testament. That the apostles were *inspired* in every thing they wrote is not clear or demonstrated. The most that one is bound to admit is, that they were infallible in their solemn teaching; but this differs from inspiration. Lastly, how do Presbyterians know that a portion of the New Testament comes from an apostle, merely because it bears the name of an apostle? How do they know that the Epistle of James, that of Jude, the Epistle to the Hebrews, and the Apocalypse, come from the apostles? We ask them in reference to those portions of the New Testament, because all who have a slight acquaintance with antiquity and Biblical criticism know that many sincere Christians, in the very first ages of Christianity, doubted the authenticity and inspiration of those and other portions of the New Testament, and the question can be set at rest only by the infallible assistance promised to the church in deciding doubts which arise. It is indeed exceedingly strange and anomalous, that Presbyterians should make up their minds with certainty, that the Epistle to the Hebrews, or that of James, come from the apostles, and that the *Symbol of the Apostles* does not come from them. If they were built upon the foundation of the apostles, as the text now under discussion has it, this Apostles' Creed would have been found at the head of their Confession. The truth is, however, that the Confession does not say a word about it; and though it is found in the book whose title heads this article, it seems to have been thrown in at the end of the Shorter Catechism as a kind of outwork, and is given there simply as the Creed, and not as *the Apostles'* Creed. Hence, the text, that "we are built upon the foundation of the apostles," does not prove the inspiration of the New Testament. To found an argument on this text, the author of the last portion of Scripture should have been an apostle, and he should have drawn up a list of the inspired writings, and have closed his book with the solemn assertion, that his own book, together with all those mentioned in the list, are inspired, and all that are inspired. But such is not the fact. The Scriptures say not a word about the one who wrote the last portion of the New Testament, so that from them we do not know whether he was an apostle or not, while we know with certainty that he mentioned no catalogue of inspired writings.

The second text adduced by the Westminster Presbyterians is taken from the last lines of the Apocalypse, and is neither more nor less than a threat to the rash copyist who should either add to or take from the Apocalypse. But that book does not say that its author was inspired. Moreover, it does not say that he was an apostle. Protestants call his book the Revelation of John the Divine; and though the tradition of the Catholic Church attributes it to St. John the Apostle, it is nothing to their purpose, for Presbyterians reject tradition. It is well known, too, that some commentators have doubted whether John the Divine was the same with John the Apostle; and Beza, a celebrated Calvinist, attributes it to another John, namely, John Mark,—Acts xii. 25. In fine, there is nothing in this text from the Apocalypse which asserts that all the books mentioned in the Presbyterian catalogue, from Genesis to Revelation, are inspired.

But we pass to the third testimony, adduced from St. Paul. This testimony is at least a little more to the purpose; but it wholly fails to establish the Presbyterian catalogue of inspired writings. The Protestant version says, "All Scripture is given by inspiration, and is profitable," &c. But the Vulgate, and others say, "All Scripture given by inspiration is profitable," &c., omitting the *and*. Which is the true reading? Only St. Paul himself could tell us whether he used that *and* or not. Certain it is, that the Greek Testament, such as the common edition has it, is not free from errors,—by no means to such a degree as to be the one St. Paul wrote, without the variation even of a single *and*. Certain it is, also, that St. Paul could not say, and surely did not say, that all Scripture ($\gamma\rho\alpha\phi\eta$), that is, *all writing*, is given by inspiration of God; for this would make the *Holy Scriptures* quite too voluminous. But waiving this remark, which we give only to show the straits to which those who make Scripture alone the rule of faith are reduced, and; admitting that St. Paul is speaking of the *Sacred Scripture*, that he declares it to be divinely inspired, there are still several difficulties which occur. How shall we know, and this with infallible certainty, that this Epistle is truly from St. Paul, and that St. Paul was infallible in teaching Timothy? For a letter to an individual does not bear on its face sufficient guaranties of authenticity to set such an important point at rest. How do we know that St. Paul was an apostle? From the *Acts?* But the *Acts* were not written by an *Apostle;* and hence, for one who wants to build upon the foundation of the apostles, this leaves a link in his chain of certainty missing. Will it be said, these objections are only cavils, and that they savor of scepticism? We grant they are cavils for a Catholic, for whom all these points are decided by a higher authority; but they are no cavils for Protestants, and they show that those who wish to remain Protestants, and who possess logical heads and sound dialectics, must become sceptics, and throw Christianity to the winds, or at least Unitarians, and consider the Scriptures as *probably* written by the authors whose names they bear, and as a good and moral, but merely a *human* book. However, we grant all of the above remarks on the text of St. Paul are not *absolute* difficulties, but only *relative;* here is, however, one which is most obvious and absolute, and which must reduce Presbyterians to complete silence. The Scriptures of which St. Paul speaks can be no other than those of the Old Testament; for the text, taken in its totality, says, that Timothy from a child had known the Holy Scriptures, and it is of those Holy Scriptures known by Timothy from his infancy that St. Paul says they are inspired. Now it is obvious that those Holy Scriptures, which Timothy, yet a child, had known, were the Old Testament; for these were the only Scriptures then in existence; since all the New Testament was not written at the time when St. Paul wrote, and none of it when Timothy was yet in his infancy. This argument will not and cannot be denied by Protestants, and hence they must confess that this text proves at best only the inspiration of the Old Testament.

But here is another difficulty not less formidable than the foregoing. St. Paul says the Old Testament is inspired; but what constitutes the Old Testament? Of this he says nothing, and of this no sacred writer says any thing,—a clear proof that the Scriptures do not contain all that is necessary, and that by them alone no one can form his belief; for while we are told the Old Testament is inspired, we are not told which are the books composing the Old Testament, so that the enumeration given by Protestants is purely *human*, not Scriptural. Besides, they fail in the main point, which is to establish the inspiration of the New Testament, the portion of Scripture in which we are evidently most intimately and vitally interested; and the difficulty is increased ten-fold by the fact advanced by Protestants themselves, that one-third of the New Testament was written, not by the apostles themselves, but by their disciples. But before we proceed any further, we conceive it to be required by the thread of the discussion to state here the process by which Catholics come to the knowledge of the inspiration of Scripture. The method is plain, obvious, and free from every vicious circle and false dialectics; it is conclusively and eloquently expressed by the great light of the church in the fourth and fifth centuries, St. Augustine:— "I would not believe the Gospel, if I were not moved by the authority of the Catholic Church. If, then, I obey them when they tell me, Believe in the Gospel, why should I not obey them when they tell me, Believe not in Manicheism?"* Hence, the church teaches us the inspiration of Scripture, and we believe it. But now what evidences to us the authority of the church? The church evidences herself to us to be the spouse of Christ, the representative of Heaven, the ambassador of the Almighty, and the organ of

---

Contr. Epist. Manichæi, c. 5.

God, by that mass of moral and historical proofs which scepticism or blindness alone can reject, when duly proposed. The church is composed of innumerable witnesses, who, for ages linked in unbroken succession, unanimously and firmly attest and certify to us, that, 1846 years ago, a heavenly personage appeared, who performed innumerable miracles, and commissioned men, called apostles, to preach his doctrine, promulge the true religion, and establish a church, or religious society, in which, and in which alone, the doctrine of salvation should be taught to the end of time. That society attests to us that God inspired some men to write more at length the plan of that divine religion, and the circumstances of its establishment; and we believe the testimony of that society, because it consists of men who were not deceived, could not have been deceived, were not deceivers, and could not have been deceivers; because the testimony of that immense mass of witnesses we perceive to be sealed with the blood of innumerable martyrs; because, in fine, *miracles*, the usual *seal* of Heaven, have at all times borne out the testimony of that society. Hence, as that society claims to have received from divine inspiration these volumes, together with the right of interpreting them, and as she hurls her anathemas against gainsayers, these pretensions and privileges of the church must be real, or else Heaven would sanction fraud and imposture by its miracles. The testimony of that church is further corroborated by the eminent sanctity of thousands of her members, who have always held all the doctrines taught by that church as absolutely necessary to salvation; which, together with so many other considerations we might adduce, proves that church to be in possession of the true doctrine descended from heaven; and consequently, upon her testimony, we admit as inspired all the books for which she claims inspiration. The perfect agreement of the doctrine of those books with what she teaches us is another argument of the divinity and truth of the system of religion which she holds. Our method of reasoning is, therefore, that of sound dialectics. The church and Scripture stand with regard to one another, as the heir and the will constituting him heir. The will must be proved to come from the testator by other modes besides a mere assertion to that effect found in the will; but thus proved, the heir may investigate and define his rights from the will itself. Hence, Catholics may quote the Bible to prove the church, not only by an argument *ad hominem* against those who admit it to be infallible, but also as the explanation and development of the will of Him whom they prove by invincible arguments to have dictated it.* We believe the Scripture to be inspired, because the apostles and their successors have so taught the church, and have taught us to believe in the church, having made this belief in the church one of the articles of their creed; and we believe the teaching of the apostles, because they proved their doctrine by their miracles. The fact, that the church has always believed in the inspiration of Scripture upon this testimony of the apostles, and that she teaches it as an essential doctrine, is too obvious, and too generally admitted, to stand in need of proof. We conclude, then, that Catholics have the highest evidence of the inspiration of Scripture, while for Protestants the question is involved in darkness which nothing can dissipate. Hence, it is not surprising to hear that many Protestants, especially in Germany, reject the inspiration of Scripture altogether.

But it is time to pass to the third article of the Presbyterian Confession of Faith. It runs thus:—

"The books commonly called apocrypha, not being of divine inspiration, are no part of the canon of Scripture, and therefore are of no authority in the church of God, nor to be any otherwise approved, or made use of, than other human writings."

We subjoin likewise the Scripture authority.

"Luke xxiv. 27. And beginning at Moses and all the prophets, he expounded unto them in all the Scriptures the things concerning him-

---

* This illustration must not be pushed too far. So far as it concerns the special argument in the text, it is apposite and unobjectionable; but it must not be interpreted to favor the notion, that the church in teaching is restricted to the office of simple interpreter of the Sacred Scriptures; or that she has no rights but such as are contained in, or may be deduced from, the written word. The church received the *whole* revelation of God, irrespective of the written word, and would possess, and could teach, the whole, even if there were no written word. She has the will and all its contents, in her divine traditions, and therefore does not necessarily depend on the written word for a knowledge of what they are. Moreover, the whole revelation was not written; or, in other words, the church has received more than is recorded. The whole, then, of what she is commissioned to teach is not deducible from what is written. Her authority and her doctrine remain complete without the written word, and to us, as her children, it is no question what the Scriptures teach, but simply what the church teaches. Nevertheless, after the church has established the fact of the inspiration of the Scriptures, then she may appeal to them, as we allege in the text, in explanation and development of her rights.

self. Ver. 44. And he said unto them, These are the words which I spake unto you, while I was yet with you, that all things must be fulfilled which were written in the law of Moses, and in the Prophets, and in the Psalms, concerning me. 2 Peter i. 21. For the prophecy came not in old time by the will of man, but holy men of God spake *as they were* moved by the Holy Ghost."

This article is a thrust at the Catholic Church, which admits, besides the books mentioned in the Presbyterian canon of Scripture, in the Old Testament, the following: namely, Tobias, Judith, some chapters of Esther, Wisdom, Ecclesiasticus, Baruch, fragments of Daniel, and two books of Maccabees.

Now we ask Presbyterians, how they know that these books, in spite of the belief of the Catholic Church, are not of divine inspiration. Is it because they are commonly called apocrypha, as the text seems to insinuate? But who calls them apocrypha? Presbyterians? But is this a proof that they are apocrypha? And if Unitarians call all apocrypha, is it a proof that they are all apochrypha? The Confession, however, hints that such books are *commonly* called apocrypha. This is false; they are commonly called inspired books. Let us count the votes. These books are called inspired Scripture by the two hundred millions of Catholics spread over the globe; they are called inspired Scripture by the Greek Church, though separated from the Catholic Church; and that church alone outnumbers all the Protestant denominations put together. Those books are held to be inspired Scripture by all the other oriental Christian sects. Hence, there are at least four or five Christians calling these books inspired Scriptures to one calling them apocrypha. At the rise of Protestantism, all editions of Christian Bibles contained the books now called apocrypha by Protestants. The Latin version, the Septuagint, the Syriac version of the Scriptures, contain them all. In fact, these books have always been *commonly* called Scripture, and had the authority of prescription in the church by long continued possession, when it came into the heads of Protestants to deny their authority.

However, the Westminster divines pretend to give a better proof of the want of inspiration in these books, than a mere name given them by the interested party. They offer Scripture authority; and the proofs they adduce are at least amusing. The first is, that Christ, after his resurrection, "beginning at Moses and all the prophets, expounded to them in all the Scriptures the things concerning himself." This is the mighty argument by which Presbyterians show that Baruch, Judith, Tobias, &c., are not inspired. But that text says nothing of them; how, then, can Presbyterians conclude they are not inspired? They will answer, perhaps, that Moses and all the prophets constitute the whole of the Sacred Scripture. Be it so, if you choose. But what is meant by the word *prophet?* and, this definition being settled, how do you prove that Baruch, Judith, Tobias were not prophets? *Prophet* may mean only an inspired man. If you say that *prophets* means those who have announced future things, then the writer of the book of Proverbs and Ecclesiastes, the writers of several of the historical books, the books of Kings, for instance, and the Paralipomena, or Chronicles, as Protestants call them, have no claim to prophecy, since they either relate past events, or give moral lessons. This is a primary difficulty for Protestants. Another and a greater one is, that Baruch, Judith, and Tobias were prophets, properly so called; for they announced things to come, as we see by reading their books, which must, at least, be considered as *human* books of great merit and reputation. So those personages were prophets, and received miraculous gifts from heaven. If, then, this text of the New Testament quoted in the Confession proves any thing, it proves the inspiration of these books; and if it destroys the authority of the Maccabees, as a merely historical book, it destroys also that of the Paralipomena; if it destroys the authority of Wisdom and Ecclesiasticus as moral books, it destroys also that of the Proverbs and Ecclesiastes. The text adduced, then, either proves nothing, or too much; if it favors either side, it favors the Catholics; for Christ speaks of *all* the prophets and of *all* the Scriptures, and since these books were known in his time, they are rather included in *all* the prophets than excluded.

The second text adduced by the Presbyterians is not more happy than the first; for in this new enumeration of Scripture are mentioned the law, the prophets, and the Psalms. Here Christ adds the *Psalms* to the other parts, but this demands no material change in the remarks we have just made; on the contrary, it shows that Christ did not intend to make a complete enumeration of the parts of the Bible; and we say that the word *prophets* includes all the books rejected by Presbyterians, or else it excludes many admitted by them. In fine, the last text adduced by Presbyterians, from 2 Pet.

i. 21, is ridiculous in the highest degree to prove the want of authority in Baruch, Judith, Tobias, &c.; it says that the prophets spake not of themselves, but as moved by the Holy Ghost; but it does not say, that prophets *only* can write Scripture, or that Baruch, Judith, and Tobias were not prophets.

Not only is there no passage of Scripture against those books, but we may safely assert that the text adduced above to prove the inspiration of the Old Testament applies to these books. "All Scripture is given by inspiration of God, and is profitable for doctrine." St. Paul says, generally, that *all* Scripture is inspired by God. Now we say that this term *all* includes the books rejected by Presbyterians. To establish this, we have only to remark that St. Paul in the text speaks of the Scripture or Bible, as it was found in the celebrated Greek version of the Septuagint; for St. Paul wrote to Timothy in Greek, and it is likewise an evident fact that the apostles used and quoted the Septuagint. St. Timothy, to whom he writes, was born in Lyconia, a Grecian province, of a heathen father and a Jewish mother; and a proof that he was not over-Jewish is, that he had not been circumcised at an advanced age, when St. Paul circumcised him for the greater advantage of the Jews for whose conversion he was to be employed. All this shows sufficiently that the Greek edition of the Bible was the one which Timothy had read from his infancy, and the one which St. Paul recommended as divinely inspired. Now the Septuagint edition of the Bible contained these books, and consequently they come under the name, *all* Scripture, used by St. Paul. A convincing proof of the fact of the Greek version of the Bible, or the Septuagint, containing these books is, that the old Latin version of the Bible, made from the Septuagint in the first century, as also the Syriac version, made in the same century, and which is one of the most esteemed by the learned, contains these books. The Arabic, Armenian, and many other versions, also contain them, having been made from the Septuagint. This argument is absolutely unanswerable. The Greek Church has never used any other Bible than the Septuagint, and, as she admits these books, they must always have been in that version. But this fact is so well established, that it is clear St. Paul must have included these very books under the name "*all* Scripture." These books were held sacred by those who adopted the Septuagint, and, having quoted this version, and knowing that they were in it, St. Paul could not have said all Scripture is given by inspiration, if these books had not been inspired. If they were not, it was his duty to have warned his disciple Timothy and others against ascribing to them divine authority. Since, then, we do not find in his Epistles that Tobias, Judith, Baruch, &c., are not inspired Scriptures, we must conclude he did not wish to prevent the faithful from believing them to be inspired Scripture, and consequently, if we are wrong in so believing them, we are wrong because the apostles themselves have deceived us.

But the texts quoted do not contain the real grounds on which Protestants reject the books in question. Their true reasons for rejecting them are to be found elsewhere. They had, in rejecting them, two objects in view: the first, to contradict the Catholic Church on a point which could be maintained with some show of argument; the second, to escape the inferences drawn by Catholics from those books against doctrines which they had broached. The pleasure and gratification of contradicting the church was the chief reason for rejecting the "so-called apocrypha." The Jews did not admit them into their catalogue of Sacred Scriptures, and hence the Hebrew Bibles of the present day do not contain them. Moreover, some fathers of the church have doubted their canonicity. Protestants, then, and Presbyterians especially, could not but seize with avidity this occasion of calumniating the church, as if she admitted human books among the inspired writings. This reason, which Presbyterians are ashamed or unwilling to acknowledge in their Confession, is, however, the true one why they reject what they call the apocrypha. But that they are exceedingly unfortunate and unlucky in this, as in other quarrels with the Catholic Church, is evident from what we have already said, and have yet to add. To understand this matter fully, it must be borne in mind that before Christ there were two divisions of Jews,—some who remained in Palestine and continued to use the Bible written in Hebrew, and others scattered through the various parts of the Grecian empire, and particularly in Egypt, who were better acquainted with the Greek than the Hebrew; for the Greek was then the predominant language of the world. For the use of this latter division of Jews, numerous in Alexandria and other parts of Egypt, the Scriptures were translated into Greek several centuries before the coming of our Saviour. These were they who used the Greek version of the Septuagint, and, having been scattered through the different provinces of the civilized world, were those to whom the apostles chiefly preached the Gospel; so that the translation of the Bible into Greek, and the dissemination of Hellenist Jews through the various parts of the world, were among the means which Providence employed to facilitate the diffusion of the Gospel. It was these Hellenist Jews who, even before Christ, placed the books under consideration in the rank of Scriptures, for they associated them to the other canonical books of the version of the Septuagint. As to the Jews of Palestine, they did not put the same books among the Scriptures, because either they were not written in Hebrew, or came too late to be put authoritatively in the canon, which was closed by Esdras. But the fact of the Jews of Palestine not associating these new books with the other parts of Scripture is no argument against them, provided they were afterwards put into the canon by lawful authority. One thing, however, is certain; the Palestine Jews respected these books, and the Talmud and the Rabbins generally quote them. Judith and Tobias especially, and even Baruch, were publicly read on a certain appointed day.

If it be said that the practice of the Hellenist Jews in placing these books among the canonical Scriptures proves nothing, we may grant that in strictness it does not; but what proves conclusively and without the possibility of cavil that they are canonical is, that the apostles took the Scriptures from them in the Septuagint, which is the edition of the Bible they quote, and their testimony and their authority are amply sufficient to entitle these books to the rank of Scripture; for, as they were infallible, they must know whether such books were inspired or not, were the word of God or the word of man. If they had been only the word of man, the apostles would have expunged them from the Greek edition; they would have warned the faithful against the use of such forged word of God; and as they have not done so, but on the contrary retained the Septuagint, and since all the editions of the Bible used by their immediate disciples, the Latin version and the Syriac, contain these books, we must hold them to be Scripture, not indeed on the testimony of the Hellenist Jews, but on that of the apostles. Moreover, the Jews who embraced Christianity read the Scriptures for the most part in Greek, and this was an occasion or pretext for the other Jews who rejected Christianity to adhere with greater pertinacity and zeal to the Hebrew Bible; hence, through a spirit of hostility to the Greeks, they went so far afterwards as to appoint a day of fasting and humiliation for the pretended misfortune of the translation of the Scriptures into Greek, as we read in the Talmud. As those Jews who read in Hebrew were the only ones that retained a sort of nationality among other nations, they, of course, kept in their edition of the Scriptures only the Hebrew books; and this circumstance occasioned the doubts which arose among some fathers of the church, as to the canonicity of those books, though they always respected and quoted them. There has never been, however, any real interruption in the tradition of the church concerning their inspiration, and the Roman Church founded by Peter and Paul has always had them in its Latin version, and they have always been venerated as the word of God. If some fathers, those particularly who knew Hebrew, and lived among the Jews, not finding these books in the canon of the Hebrews, have expressed doubts of their canonicity, it was not a tradition, but a personal notion of theirs, arising, perhaps, from not using their science according to prudence; and it is not the sole instance in which a certain science has been an impediment to the simplicity of faith. But even those fathers who made that concession of the non-canonicity of those books to their science, or to the prejudices of the Jews among whom they lived, in practice were carried away by the torrent of tradition; for they quoted those books; and St. Jerome in particular, who declares positively in some places that they are out of the canon and are unfit to prove dogmas, believed Judith to have been placed among the Scriptures by the great Council of Nice, gives the name of Scripture to the books of Wisdom and Ecclesiasticus, and is to be understood, when discarding them from the canon, as he himself wrote in his defence against Rufinus, as having spoken after the opinion of the Jews, who reject them; so that he meant only that they cannot be used to confirm dogmas against the Jews, because they reject them; and in this way are all those fathers to be understood who seem to deny the authority of these books.

To show now the tradition of the church with regard to those books, we may quote among the councils one of Hippo in the year 393, the third of Carthage in 397, and the Epistle of Innocent the First in 405, the first Council of Rome in 494, the General Council of Florence, which preceded the Protestant schism by nearly a century, and in which the Greek Church was represented, and lastly the Council of

Trent, which only copies the canon of the Council of Florence. We may add, also, the testimonies of some of the earliest and most celebrated doctors of the primitive church. Some will think it, perhaps, a waste of paper and ink, to quote the fathers against the Presbyterians; for these mighty geniuses think themselves far above the fathers, and despise them as a set of superstitious and ignorant fools. But we cannot allow such a notion, entertained by Presbyterians, and which betrays no less ignorance than pride, to deter us. If Presbyterians laugh at our quotations, we will claim the privilege, not of laughing at them, but of pitying them. We think it self-evident that men who lived almost in the age of Christ and of the apostles, and who had all the writings we have, and many we have not, should be believed upon a matter of fact, namely, what Christ and the apostles have taught, in preference to self-made doctors who arose sixteen hundred years after the event. We are invincibly disposed to attribute more weight to the testimony of a Clement, an Irenæus, a Cyprian, &c., who sealed their faith with their blood, than to the unsupported assertions of mercenary teachers, who changed theirs that they might secure to themselves the riches of the ancient church, and who never knew what it was to suffer for it. We own we are not ashamed to follow for our guides men whose sanctity, science, prudence, and Christian virtues were the object of the veneration of their contemporaries and of succeeding generations, in preference to these Westminster divines, who, in the turmoil of public life and agitating scenes of revolution and political struggles, broached and set forth a confession of faith with the same hand with which they signed the death-warrant of their sovereign. If we are wrong in this, we must plead in excuse that indomitable instinct of nature, which prompts all not utterly depraved to choose virtue, knowledge, modesty, and self-sacrifice, before pride, presumption, cupidity, and self-love.

St. Clement, pope and martyr, lived in the time of the apostles, and is mentioned in St. Paul's Epistle to the Philippians. We have of him an Epistle to the Corinthians, which must be viewed as one of the most venerable monuments of antiquity. In this he quotes the book of Wisdom, "Who shall say to thee, What hast thou done?"—xii. 12; and also, "Who shall resist the strength of thy arm?"— xi. 22. St. Irenæus had conversed with the immediate disciples of the apostles, and he shed his blood for the faith.

In the fifth book, chapter 35, *Against Heresies*, he quotes at full length a beautiful passage which is taken from the end of the fourth and the beginning of the fifth chapter of Baruch,—"Look about thee, O Jerusalem," &c. St. Cyprian sealed likewise his testimony with his blood, towards the middle of the third century. Nothing is more frequent in his writings than quotations from those books which have been branded as apocrypha by Protestants. We have taken the trouble of counting twelve quotations from Wisdom, and twenty-nine from Ecclesiasticus; others in the same proportion. St. Athanasius (Cont. Arian. 17, 1) quotes as Scripture the following maxim of the book Ecclesiasticus, ch. xv. 9 : " Praise is not seemly in the mouth of a sinner"; and he adduces this testimony together with one of about the same import borrowed from Psalm xlix. 16. Now St. Athanasius is one of those who apparently reject the books which are not found in the Hebrew Bible, and this proves the truth of what we have said above, that those fathers who in theory rejected the books in question, admitted them in practice. St. Augustine, whom at least Presbyterians and Calvinists must respect, if they respect their patriarch Calvin, condemns in positive and most emphatic terms those who, with the Westminster divines, discard the book of Wisdom from the Sacred Scriptures. "No one," says he, " can reject a passage taken from the book of Wisdom, which has been read in the church for so many years, and which, from all Christian bishops, to the lowest of the faithful among the laity, penitents, and catechumens, is listened to with the respect due to *divine* authority."* We might swell our quotations to a volume; but if what we have adduced does not suffice for our Presbyterian friends, one would rise in vain from the grave to convince them.

Having disposed of this question, we will add a true list of the apocrypha, that is, of those writings which, though some may have regarded them as Scripture, yet are not held by the church to possess the authority of the word of God. The word *apocrypha*, a Greek word, means simply *unknown ;* hence, a book is said to be apocryphal, when its authority as Sacred Scripture is not acknowledged. It may be an excellent book, and perfectly authentic,—that is, truly written by the one whose name it bears,—or it may not be. The apocryphal books of the Old Testament are the third

---

* *Lib. de prædestinatione Sanctorum C.* xiv.

and fourth of Esdras, the third and fourth of the Maccabees, the book of Henoch, the prayer of King Manasses, and the One Hundred and Fifty-first Psalm; those of the New Testament are the book of Hermas, quoted by some as Scripture, because Hermas was a disciple of the apostles, and is mentioned in the Epistle to the Romans, xvi. 14; the Epistle of St. Barnabas, which, though truly his, and though his name is found in the Acts in connection with that of St. Paul, is not Sacred Scripture,—for all the disciples of the apostles were not inspired; the First Epistle to the Corinthians by St. Clement, whose name is also in the Sacred Scriptures (Phil. iv. 3),—a genuine and authentic epistle, but, though quoted by not a few, is not Sacred Scripture; the letter of Christ to Abgarus in answer to a letter from that king, as related by Eusebius; the Apostolic Canons, or canons made by the apostles, of which the first fifty, though not Scripture, are received by the Roman Church; and, in addition, a large number of Gospels, to some of which St. Luke alludes, when he says, in the preface to his Gospel, "Forasmuch as *many* have taken in hand to set forth," &c. Many of these Gospels have perished; fragments of others have come down to us. These are properly termed apocryphal.

In connection with this subject, we take the liberty of proposing some queries to Presbyterians, and of requesting them to explain what appear to us glaring contradictions in their conduct. When they drew up their catalogue of the Scriptures, on what authority did they take this or that book to be Scripture? assuredly they did not see the books they receive falling from heaven, or Jehovah's throne. Was it on the authority of the Jews, or on that of the Christians? If on the authority of the Jews, then they should reject the New Testament, since the Jews reject it; if on the authority of Christians, they should receive all the books which the Christians received, and as the Christians received all the books which Catholics now receive, even the so-called apocrypha, they should also receive them. Why, then, do they receive a part, and reject the rest? Will they answer, that they receive those books which were received by the primitive church? But how do they know that? how do they know what the primitive church taught? Moreover, if they are obliged to have recourse to the primitive church, tradition becomes necessary and indispensable, at least to enable us to distinguish the inspired from the non-inspired books. But they reject tradition. Again, if they rely on the authority of the primitive church, they must admit the apocrypha which are rejected only by the Jews. For Clement, Irenæus, the authors of the Itala and Syriac versions, belonged to that church, and are unanimous in receiving them as Scripture. If they discard Tobias, Judith, &c., because some fathers have doubted their inspiration, then why do they admit the Epistle to the Hebrews, that of St. James, and, above all, the Apocalypse; for many fathers, as Protestants themselves confess, have doubted the divine authority of these? Will they say that these writings come from the apostles, who were infallible? But this is precisely what those fathers doubted; and if it be enough to have the name of an apostle on the title-page, why do they not receive all the Gospels which bear the name of some apostle? At least, as many fathers have doubted the canonicity of the Apocalypse as that of the Maccabees; why, then, acknowledge the authority of the one, and reject that of the other? "A weight and a weight are an abomination before the Lord."—Prov. xx. 23. But are Presbyterians candid and sincere? If they admit the Apocalypse, is it not because they can so interpret it as to make it countenance their aspersions and condemnations of the pope and the church of Rome? Finally, will they say they admit the New Testament on the authority of the apostles who wrote it? But was St. Luke an apostle? Was Mark an apostle? Certainly not. They were only disciples of the apostles, as were Barnabas, and Clement, and Hermas. Why, then, do they admit as Scripture the writings of Luke and Mark, and not those of Barnabas, Clement, and Hermas? To be consistent, they must admit all, or reject all; for the apostles themselves are equally silent respecting all. What proof have they that Mark was inspired, and that Clement was not? No reason can be assigned, save the testimony of the apostles, made known by tradition. But if tradition is necessary in this case, wherefore is it to be rejected, as the fundamental tenet of Presbyterians asserts? If tradition be good for one thing, why not for others? If in this case, why not in that of prayers for the dead, the distinction between bishops and priests, the real presence of Christ in the Eucharist, the intercession of saints, &c.? Assuredly, on all these points Protestants are entangled in difficulties, from which they can extricate themselves only by consenting to swallow innumerable absurdities, and inscribing on their standard, CONTRADICTION, INCONSISTENCY, and FALSEHOOD.

The fourth article of the Presbyterian Confession of Faith, which we have now reached, is, that

"The authority of the Holy Scripture, for which it ought to be believed and obeyed, dependeth not upon the testimony of any man or church, but wholly upon God (who is truth itself), the author thereof; and therefore it is to be received because it is the word of God."

Since we have thus far objected to every article, it may be thought that we are hard to please, if we also object to the present. When we read a law of Congress printed in the newspaper, we assuredly admit the law, because it comes from Congress, and not because the editor, who may be deserving of no credit, places it before his reader. When a constable serves an execution, it is the authority of the court we respect, not that of the constable. Nevertheless, this fourth article can find no more favor with us than its predecessors. It is a shaft at St. Augustine, whose assertion we have already quoted, and at the Catholic Church, on whose testimony we receive the Scriptures. It, however, need not detain us long, for a very obvious distinction will at once disclose its sophistry. The doctrines taught in the Scriptures are one thing, and the genuineness of the book itself is another. The doctrines are believed because revealed or taught by God himself; but why is the Bible believed to have come from God? It does not, in a miraculous manner, proclaim to all that it is the word of God. What is it, then, that makes you believe it to be his word? The Catholic answers, The testimony of the church, for which God himself vouches by miracles and other marks of his authority. The Protestant has nothing, at least, as we shall soon see, nothing reasonable, to answer. In a word, if God speaks, we believe on his authority, and it would be ridiculous and blasphemous to believe God because Peter or James assures us that what God says is true. But in order to believe that God hath spoken, we must have motives of credibility, or reasons sufficient to convince a sound understanding that he has really spoken; otherwise, faith would be only superstition and credulity. Hence, it is absurd to reproach Catholics with attributing a greater authority to the church than to the word of God. When Mary believed that she should conceive and bring forth the Son of God, without any detriment to her virginity (Luke ii.), she believed in God, and made an act of heroic faith, as Elizabeth said afterwards, "Blessed art thou that hast believed." But on whose testimony did she believe? On that of the angel Gabriel, who brought her the message. Would she have believed without the testimony of the angel? Assuredly not. Did she reverence the angel more than God? By no means; but the apparition and declaration of the angel were the motives of credibility on which she believed the message to be truly from God, and without which her belief would have been only fanaticism or pride. In this way St. John, in the Apocalypse, gives clearly the motives of credibility for the revelation which it contained. "The revelation of Jesus Christ which God gave . . . . and signified sending by his angel to his servant John, who hath given testimony to the word of God."—i. 1, 2. As John gave testimony to the word of God, that is, that God spoke it, so does the church now; and as the testimony of John was proved true by incontestable evidence, so also is that of the church. As the testimony of John did not derogate from the majesty of the word of God, or the respect due to it, nor suppose any pride in him, neither does the testimony which the church bears to Scripture imply the least irreverence, or pride, or arrogance, on her part.

The fifth article of the Confession, the last we shall now consider, will confirm, from the mouth of the Presbyterian divines themselves, all we have asserted concerning the impossibility of Presbyterians arriving at the inspiration of Scripture, besides presenting a few more of those glaring contradictions with which, as so many bright stars, they intersperse and adorn their creed.

"We may be moved and induced by the testimony of the church to a high and reverend esteem for the Holy Scripture; the heavenliness of the matter, the efficacy of the doctrine, the majesty of the style, the consent of all the parts, the scope of the whole (which is to give all glory to God), the full discovery it makes of the only way of man's salvation, the many other incomparable excellences, and the entire perfection thereof, are arguments whereby it doth abundantly evidence itself to be the word of God; yet, notwithstanding, our full persuasion and assurance of the infallible truth and divine authority thereof is from the inward work of the Holy Spirit bearing witness by and with the word, in our hearts.

"1 Tim. iii. 15. But if I tarry long, that thou mayest know how thou oughtest to behave thyself in the house of God, which is the church of the living God, the pillar and ground of the truth.

"1 John ii. 20, 27. But ye have an unction from the Holy One, and ye know all things.—But the anointing which ye have received of him abideth in you, and ye need not that any man teach you; but as the same anointing teacheth you of all things, and is truth, and is no lie, and even as it hath taught you, ye shall abide in him." &c.

The doctrine embodied in this article is, that the testimony of the church renders the inspiration of Scripture probable; the internal excellences of Scripture demonstrate that inspiration; still, we believe Scripture to be the word of God, because we hear the Spirit of God in our hearts telling us it is his word. A more monstrous accumulation of absurdities, of sophisms, of fanaticism, it would be difficult to condense within the same number of lines. The assertion, to be true, should run: The internal excellences of Scripture render its inspiration somewhat *probable*; the testimony of the church renders it *certain*; the Holy Ghost by his divine grace makes us assent, in a *supernatural* manner, and in a way *conducive to salvation*, to the inspiration of Scripture and the doctrine it contains. Stated in this way, the assertion would be correct. But the Westminster divines, after having disclaimed all human testimony in Art. IV., now tell us that the testimony of the church moves us to a high and reverend esteem of Scripture. Then they should at least have "a high and reverend esteem" for the books of Tobias, Judith, &c., which had, at the time of the rise of Protestantism, the testimony of the whole church both in the East and in the West. But does not the passage you quote to inculcate this high and reverend esteem for the Holy Scripture say more than you make it say? You conceive a high and reverend esteem for Scripture from " the church, which is the pillar and ground of the truth."—1 Tim. iii. 15. But if the church be the *pillar and ground of the truth*, and if the church tell you that these books or those are the word of God, you must not only *esteem* them, but believe them to be the word of God; otherwise, the church would cease to be "the pillar and ground of the truth," by telling you to receive as inspired by the Holy Ghost writings which have only a human authority. The church evidently would then be the herald and the basis of error. Presbyterians therefore adduce here a text which, fairly considered, overthrows the whole fabric of their belief in Scripture. The church is the pillar and ground of the truth: they admit this. Then, as a matter of course, they must admit what the church teaches, and admit it not only as probable, but as the very truth of which the church is the pillar and ground. By adducing this text, then, they *cut their own throat*; this text, if it prove any thing, proves not only that Scripture must be esteemed, but also believed, on the testimony of the church. It proves that not only Genesis and the Gospels are Scripture, but also Tobias, Judith, &c. Calvin, who seems to have been a little keener than the Westminster divines, found himself not a little troubled to explain this text of St. Paul, that the church is the pillar and ground of the truth; and was compelled to assert that the church is the pillar and ground of the truth, not because she teaches the truth, but because she keeps the Scriptures, which are the word of God. But on this principle every man who has a Bible in his pocket is a pillar and ground of the truth, and booksellers will become not only the pillar and the ground of the truth, but its citadels, and fortresses, and spiritual Rocks of Gibraltar, because they keep in their shops hundreds and thousands of copies of the word of God, with romances and obscene books. To state such an absurdity is to confute it.

But let us pass to the consideration of the arguments by which Presbyterians contend that Scripture abundantly evidences itself to the word of God. The first is, "the heavenliness of the matter." But is every book that treats of *heaven* an inspired book? and what will become of the inspiration of some books, if tried by this Presbyterian touchstone? The Songs of Songs,—can you determine that to be inspired from the heavenliness of the matter? If you admitted tradition and the testimony of the church, you might, perhaps, find that its subject is heavenly; but with Scripture alone, you cannot; for not even the name of God is mentioned in the whole book. The book of Ruth, from the heavenliness of its matter, will hardly produce a conviction that it is inspired, and so of some other historical books of the Old Testament. This test, applied to the Epistle of Paul to Philemon, or to the Second and Third Epistles of St. John, might give very unsatisfactory results. Hence, this test of the inspiration of a book may be a conjecture, but it will never amount to a demonstration. But if inspired books are to be tested by this mark, we say that Tobias, Judith, Wisdom, and Maccabees are far more heavenly in the matters they treat of, than most of the other books of the Old Testament. In these books we find the clearest allusions to heaven and eternal life, and the brightest examples of heavenly virtue. Is there any thing more heavenly than the conduct of Tobias?—any thing more heavenly than this maxim, "We are the children of saints, and look for that life which God will give to those that never change their faith from him"?—Tob. iii. 18. Is there any thing more beautiful and heavenly in the whole Testament than the martyrdom of the seven brethren and their heroic mother? 2 Macc. vii. We say it, then, confidently, if the heavenliness of the matter be a test of inspiration, those books which Protestants stigmatize as "apocrypha" must have the first place in the canon of Scripture. So is it with error; when its advocates try to cover one side opened to attack, they are forced to uncover another which they have equal interests in protecting; the present and the other tests of inspiration assigned by Protestants apply as well, and perhaps better, to those which they brand as spurious, than to those which they choose to retain.

The second test of inspiration is "efficacy of doctrine." The Bible is inspired because its doctrine is efficacious. So do our modern doctors think. But we should rather contend that the Bible is efficacious because it is divine. Will an unprejudiced man say a book is inspired because it persuades to the adoption of the doctrine it teaches? If so, immoral books would be the most certainly inspired of all; for their doctrine is terribly efficacious. The Koran also would be inspired; for it has been tolerably efficacious; and the Book of Mormon threatens to be the same. This mark of inspiration will not answer, even admitting a book to contain the best doctrine in the world. A man may write eloquent pages on the practice of virtue, and persuade others to adopt it, and we have still no voucher for his inspiration. Otherwise, all good and pious ministers of God would be inspired; which is somewhat more than anybody is prepared to admit.

"The majesty of the style" is the next evident mark of inspiration adduced by the Westminster divines,—a queer test, we must confess. This test we take to be applicable to the original languages in which the Scripture was written; for otherwise the majesty of the style would prove the inspiration of the translator rather than that of the author; and we know of very clumsy translations of the Bible. The appreciation of this test would, then, require the full knowledge of the Hebrew and Greek languages; for a smatterer in those languages would scarcely venture to decide upon the merits of the style. How many are competent to the task may be a delicate question; but we hardly think it would be excessive rashness on our part to doubt if the Westminster divines themselves were altogether competent judges. It is not among people involved in political turmoils, it is not in our parliaments, our houses of representatives or senate-chambers, that we find such eminent Greek and Hebrew scholars. Moreover, a portion of the Presbyterians themselves—the Cumberland Presbyterians—will reject this test, since they separated themselves from the main body chiefly because they would not subject their ministers to the necessity of learning Greek and Hebrew. We may also remark that St. Paul did not insist very strenuously on this proof of his inspiration; for in his Second Epistle to the Corinthians, xi. 6, he says,—"Though I be *rude in speech*, yet not in knowledge." And when we reflect that many books, having no claim to inspiration, have a fine and majestic style, and that the appreciation of style presents so many difficulties, and varies so with different individuals, we can set very little, if any, value upon this test of inspiration.

Another evident mark of inspiration, according to the Westminster divines, is "*the consent of all the parts.*" Taking this test of inspiration, we venture to say, that, assuredly, the Confession of Faith is not a work *inspired*,—that is, from above; for, whatever else it may claim, it can claim nothing like a "*consent of all the parts.*" We have gone over only the first five articles, and it would puzzle the reader to count the many contradictions we have found in it. If the Bible be inspired from God, surely there can be no contradictions in it. But the fact, that there are no contradictions in a book, does not prove that it is inspired; it proves, at most, only that the author speaks the truth, and is a man of sound judgment. Who ever thought of ascribing inspiration to our mathematical treatises, because there is in them a consent of all the parts? But it cannot be denied that there are in the Bible many *apparent* contradictions, which it often requires no small amount of learning and research to remove or reconcile; and it is this fact that supplies infidels with their arguments against our holy religion. That all these apparent contradictions are cleared up, and very satisfactorily too, we cheerfully and loudly acknowledge; but we say, that, if we did not know from other independent and infallible sources of information that the Bible is inspired, this character of the consent of all the parts could never lead to a firm assent to its inspiration.

The other means of arriving at the inspiration of Scripture, such "as the scope of the whole (which is to give all glory to God), the full discovery it makes of the only way of man's salvation, the many other incomparable excellences, and the entire perfection thereof," are all as little conclusive as those we have just considered. When we once know, by some positive, undeniable fact, that the Scripture is the word of God, we may find all these excellences, but not before; and to found the inspiration of Scripture upon such tottering motives is to deliver it up to the contempt of unbelievers. We say, then, that the external motives of credibility in the inspiration of Scripture assigned by Presbyterians are altogether illusory, and that the point can be settled only by recourse to the testimony and declaration of the church, whose doctrine has always received, and continues to receive, the stamp and approbation of Heaven.

But it is chiefly upon the internal motives of credibility that Presbyterians rely. They believe in Scripture because the Holy Spirit bears witness in their hearts. A man, when driven to this last resource of fanatics, visionaries, and impostors, the resource of Mahometans and Mormons, should at once own himself vanquished. This pretense is exceedingly convenient, for it supplies the place of argument and logic. *I remain a Presbyterian, because God tells me in my heart that I am in the true religion.* We do not think it worth while to undertake seriously to confute this assertion. All reasonable persons have an irresistible inclination to laugh at this peremptory mode of settling a controversy. Pity, disgust, or merriment, if the subject were not so grave, would be the only answers suitable to be given. We know of a deluded lady, who, fearing she had "sinned the day of grace away," staid on her knees some hours, and at last obtained full forgiveness, because she felt her heart as "big as a hat." When the Lord speaks in an extraordinary manner, he gives *external* miraculous signs of his presence, as one may read in so many different passages of Scripture, especially in the call of Moses, Gideon, and Samson. The ordinary operation of divine grace in the hearts of the just, though supernatural, can never be a foundation for any assertion or discovery; and this divine grace is never given as the ground for believing or maintaining any thing contrary to the doctrine held and proposed by the church of Christ, which doctrine is founded, not upon internal and invisible revelation accessible to nobody, but upon facts performed in the face of the whole world, and of a brilliancy greater than that of the sun. Nor do we need to dwell upon the passage of St. John, with which visionaries would try to uphold their delirious notions,— "Ye have an unction from above, and ye know all things." For such persons as bring forward their own visions and imaginations, on the strength of this text, should prove first that this is said of them, and not rather the following: —" Thou sayest, I am rich, and made wealthy, and I have need of nothing; and thou knowest not that thou art wretched, and miserable, and poor, and blind, and naked." Yes, they have the best reasons for applying to themselves the following passages. " If one will not hear the church, let him be to thee as a heathen and publican." " O senseless Galatians! who hath bewitched you, that you should not obey the truth?" " The animal man knoweth not the things that are of the Spirit of God." Hence, it is not to every one that opens the Epistle of St. John, that this is said,—" You have an unction from above, and ye know all things"; it is to such as love God with all their heart, are docile to their pastors, and revere in them the authority of Christ; for St. John immediately adds, " I have not written to you as to such as know not the truth, but as to such as know it." He who does not acknowledge thoroughly and sincerely the church to be the ground and pillar of truth, to be the rock against which the gates of hell shall not prevail, has no share in those words of St. John, but rather in these of St. Jude :—" These are they who separate themselves, sensual men, having not the Spirit."

But we must conclude here, for the present, our review of the Presbyterian Confession of Faith. We have found it full of false reasoning, of arbitrary and absurd applications of Scriptural passages, of obvious and strongly marked contradictions, of shallow views, and false conclusions. We have conclusively established, we think, that Presbyterians have in no respect whatever any reason or argument to offer in defence of the inspiration of Scripture, and that there is for them no rational ground on which to believe it to be the word of God. We have also shown, that, on every principle, even on their own, they cannot refuse to admit as Scripture some books which they choose to reject. We may, then, conclude that Presbyterianism precludes the very possibility of making an act of faith, of believing any thing reasonable this pretended Confession of Faith may contain, undermines Christianity, and leaves men with empty shadows and sonorous words instead of religious truth. It is not a *confession*, it is a real, stanch, bold, and blasphemous *negation* of faith.

ARTICLE II.

In the foregoing article, we disposed of only the first half of the first chapter; we hope to be able in this to dispose of the remaining half, and present our readers a complete view of the tenets, or rather inconsistencies and contradictions, which the Westminster divines have contrived to compress within their preliminary chapter, "Of the Holy Scripture." In reality, the controversy should be regarded as ended with the fact we have already established, that Presbyterians are utterly unable to prove the inspiration of the Scriptures; for, since they profess to found their doctrines on the Scriptures as inspired, it is evident, that, by failing to establish the fact of inspiration, they cannot proceed a single step in the argument, and that their whole fabric falls to the ground, and is only ruins and rubbish, if even so much. But waiving this, and granting them the inspiration of the Scriptures,—not, indeed, on their grounds, but on the testimony of the Catholic Church, which has all the marks of credibility the most captious can ask,—we resume the discussion, and admire anew the beauty and vigor of logic, the marvellous concatenation of conclusions, the acuteness of judgment, the felicitous application of Scriptural texts, which they display throughout their formulary, and which they offer us as their *credentials*.

We have already examined the first five articles of the first chapter; we commence now with the sixth, which is as follows:—

"The whole counsel of God, concerning all things necessary for his own glory, man's salvation, faith, and life, is either set down expressly in Scripture, or by good and necessary consequence may be deduced from Scripture; unto which nothing at any time is to be added, whether by new revelations of the Spirit, or traditions of men. Nevertheless, we acknowledge the inward illumination of the Spirit of God to be necessary for the saving understanding of such things as are revealed in the word; and there are some circumstances concerning the worship of God, and the government of the Church, common to human actions and societies, which are to be ordered by the light of nature and Christian prudence, according to the general rules of the word, which are always to be obeyed."

The proofs of the three parts of the article are,—

"1. 2 Tim. iii. 16, 17. All Scripture is given by inspiration of God, and is profitable for doctrine, for reproof, for correction, for instruction in righteousness ; that the man of God may be perfect, thoroughly furnished unto all good works. 2. Gal. i. 8. But though we or an angel from heaven preach any other gospel unto you than that which we have preached unto you, let him be accursed. 2 Thess. ii. 2. That ye be not soon shaken in mind, or be troubled, neither by spirit, nor by word, nor by letter as from us, as that the day of Christ is at hand. 3. St. John, vi. 45. It is written in the prophets, And they shall be all taught of God. Every man therefore that hath heard, and hath learned of the Father, cometh unto me. 1 Cor. ii. 9, 10, 12. But as it is written, Eye hath not seen, nor ear heard, neither have entered into the heart of man, the things which God hath prepared for them that love him. But God hath revealed them unto us by his Spirit ; for the Spirit searcheth all things, yea, the deep things of God. Now we have received, not the spirit of the world, but the spirit which is of God, that we might know the things that are freely given to us of God. 1 Cor. xi. 13, 14. Judge in yourselves: is it comely that a woman pray unto God uncovered ? Doth not even nature itself teach you, that, if a man have long hair, it is a shame unto him? 1 Cor. xiv. 26, 40. How is it, then, brethren? when ye come together, every one of you hath a psalm, hath a doctrine, hath a tongue, hath a revelation, hath an interpretation. Let all things be done unto edifying. Let all things be done decently and in order."

This article is designed to establish the sufficiency of the Scriptures, and to reject the traditions of the Catholic Church, and we should undoubtedly be bound to admit it, if Presbyterians could show conclusively that all was written, and that all not written is necessarily tradition of men. But this, we proved in our former article, by undeniable facts and even by Scripture itself, they do not and cannot show. We also showed that the Scriptural texts which they adduced to prove that the *whole* word was written prove no such thing, and when adduced for such a purpose are mere mockery, or rather, an imposition attempted on the people. It is not necessary to go anew over the ground we then surveyed ; it is enough for us now simply to examine the additional texts which the Presbyterian divines quote in support of the sufficiency of the Scriptures, and against Catholic tradition.

We remark, in passing, the palpable contradiction which the article just quoted bears on its very face. Its authors evidently felt themselves in an awkward position. They were under the necessity of making the article say, The Scriptures are sufficient, yet something is wanting in them; they contain every thing, yet still something must be added. For, after asserting that the Scriptures contain the whole counsel of God, every thing necessary unto faith and life, they suppose that "good and necessary consequences" are still to be drawn from them, as the condition of obtaining what is truly necessary for faith and life. Is not this asserting and denying the sufficiency of the Scriptures in the same breath? If the Scriptures had been intended by Almighty God to contain his whole counsel, and to furnish us with all things necessary for his glory, and man's salvation, faith, and life, would they not of themselves draw these good and necessary consequences, and not leave a matter so important to the discretion and judgment of our Presbyterian divines? To draw good and necessary consequences from given principles is far from being an easy matter, and is not unfrequently quite impossible. In science, for instance, the law of gravitation contains all the motions of the planets and comets, and he who could draw all the good and necessary consequences it involves would be the paragon of astronomers. This drawing of good and necessary consequences is, in fact, the real difficulty. What more absurd than to assert, that nothing must be added to the law of gravitation in astronomy, or that he who knows that law knows the whole of astronomy? The whole of civil and municipal law is contained in the principle, Give to every one his due. Is every man able to deduce the whole, by "good and necessary consequences," from this principle? and are all works on law to be condemned and reprobated, on the ground, that every man knows the principle, and the principle is all that needs to be known? The immense number of volumes on jurisprudence have been written solely because, in the various cases which arise, it is not always easy to determine what really are the good and necessary consequences to be drawn, and applied to each particular case.

Is it different in religious matters? Take, as an example, carrying the Lord's Supper to the sick. This is not expressly commanded in Scripture. But it is expressly stated, that the Lord's Supper is to be celebrated, and that, unless one eat the flesh of the Son of Man, and drink his blood, he shall not have life in him. Now, what are the "good and necessary consequences" to be drawn from these two statements as to carrying the Lord's Supper to the sick? Catholics draw one consequence, Presbyterians another; which proves that it is difficult to draw "good and necessary consequences" from Scripture *alone*. In point of fact, the Scriptures neither expressly command nor forbid the practice, and it must therefore be impossible from them alone to come to any *certain* conclusion respecting it, since the practice depends on the will of Christ, and they, in this instance, tell us nothing particularly of that will, one way or the other. Presbyterians consider the practice superfluous and even superstitious; while the Catholic Church, the Church of England, and all the oriental sects, are solicitous to impart this sacrament to the dying Christian, and believe this to be not only the most plausible consequence of the words of Scripture, but a positive institution of the apostles and of our Lord himself. Who dares assert that "good and necessary consequences" from Scripture forbid it? especially since they say nothing expressly about it, and it has been observed, from the time of the aposles down, by so many millions of Christians, as an apostolic practice,—not indeed written in a book, but intrusted to living men, who continually observed it, and could not possibly mistake or forget it? This is one example among a thousand equally clear and conclusive. It is, then, perfectly idle to tell us that the Scriptures are sufficient, and yet tell us that "good and necessary consequences" remain to be drawn from them, without which they would be insufficient. The great difficulty is in drawing the consequences, and it is in the consequences they draw that men chiefly differ one from another, and fall into their dangerous errors and heresies. No book could be sufficient which should not itself draw and set down expressly all the good and necessary consequences requisite to God's glory, and man's salvation, faith, and life; and as the Bible does not, by the confession of Presbyterians themselves, do this, it is evidently insufficient, and they confess it to be insufficient, even while insisting on its sufficiency.

The article contains, also, another contradiction, not less palpable. It affirms the Scriptures to be sufficient for all that concerns God's glory, and man's salvation, faith, and life, and yet asserts, that, besides them, "the illumination of the Spirit of God is necessary to a saving understanding of the word." There is more in this apparently modest and pious assertion of the necessity of inward illumination to the saving understanding of the Scriptures than may at first appear. It leaves the Scriptures open to every visionary or enthusiast, and wholly destroys their credibility as a monument of our faith. The meaning of a book is to be made out from the natural sense of the terms and expressions it employs, as understood by the community which uses them. If something interior and invisible is necessary to determine that meaning, the book is a mere scrawl or riddle, and utterly unfit to serve any purpose for which written documents are needed or used among men. The words, "this is my body," have a meaning of themselves, which must be sought in the religious community for which the book containing them was written. If, then, a Presbyterian comes forward and tells us that these words mean "this is *not* my body, but bread," and grounds his assertion on the assumed fact, that he has the Spirit and we have not, we can only treat his assertion as a like folly would be treated in a civil court. The assertion of the necessity of the inward illumination to the saving understanding of the Scripture is, then, a flagrant contradiction of the assertion of the sufficiency of Scripture. It makes the Bible, in itself considered, virtually a sealed book, or a book of riddles, whose sense, if sense it have, only a few adepts can make out. Nothing could be more hostile to that sufficiency of the Holy Scriptures which Presbyterians profess to assert as their fundamental principle.* These contradictions can surprise no one at all acquainted with sectarians. Iniquity and error must ever of necessity contradict themselves. Only justice and truth can be always consequent and self-consistent.

But let us pass to the examination of the Scripture testimony by which the Presbyterian divines attempt to prove that the written word contains every thing necessary and is the sole rule of faith and practice. The passage adduced is the same which was previously brought forward, and which we examined in our former article, namely, "All Scripture

---

*The Christian reader will readily understand we here neither deny nor mean to deny the necessity of divine *grace*, to enable one to make an act of faith *meritorious* in the sight of God. But an act of faith is one thing, and ascertaining the meaning of a text of Scripture quite another thing.

is given by inspiration of God," &c.; only it is now produced with the addition of the words, "that the man of God may be perfect, thoroughly furnished unto all good works." What more inapposite or inadequate to their purpose could they possibly allege? The holy apostle is here instructing his disciple Timothy, not giving directions to Christians generally. He speaks, moreover, of the Old Testament, the only Scriptures Timothy could have known from his childhood, since a great part of the New Testament was not written till after St. Paul wrote this Epistle, and the part which was written had, most likely, not yet been collected into a volume. If, then, the text quoted proves any thing to the purpose, it proves too much; for it proves that the Old Testament *alone* is sufficient, which Presbyterians would be as loath to admit as we. Such a conclusion might, indeed, be acceptable to Jews; but even Presbyterians must reject it at once. Then, again, the text by no means asserts or maintains the *sufficiency* of the Scriptures of the Old Testament, or of the New, or of both together. It simply indicates the Scriptures, and especially those of the Old Testament, the only Scriptures the holy apostle is then speaking of, as an excellent means of perfecting *the man of God*,—that is, the clergyman, the bishop, or pastor of souls,—of thoroughly furnishing him for every good word and work. All this is true, and does not in the least suppose that the Scriptures contain every thing necessary and are of themselves alone sufficient for every purpose. It simply supposes that the clergyman will acquire perfection by the perusal and study of the Sacred Scriptures. If we exhort a young orator to study Demosthenes, and tell him that this study will *perfect* him as an orator, and furnish him with proper models for every species of composition, we by no means assert or imply that Demosthenes will absolutely suffice for every thing, that there will be no need of Greek grammar and lexicon, without which, perchance, Demosthenes might be a sealed book. Hence, this text, adduced by Presbyterians to prove that the Scriptures alone are sufficient for every thing, and are the sole rule of faith and practice, proves nothing to their purpose. It is one of those illusory and nugatory proofs with which this Confession of Faith abounds, and merely proves either the want of ingenuousness and strict integrity on the part of its framers, or the great difficulty they found in drawing "good and necessary consequences" from the words of Scripture.

But, leaving this text, we turn to the consideration of the Scriptural authorities adduced for rejecting Catholic traditions. The pertinency and force of these authorities consist in a species of trick, which is any thing but ingenuous, and is altogether unworthy the character, we were about to say, even of Presbyterians. We are told that the Scriptures are so complete, that nothing is to be added to them "by the traditions of *men*,"—just as if any Catholic held that traditions of *men* were to be taken as the word of God! If the question turned on traditions of *men*, traditions broached and set up, after the apostles, by men who gave out their own visions, fancies, or excogitations for the word of God, we should be as ready, to say the least, to discard them as Presbyterians are. We grant, nay, earnestly contend, that all such traditions are to be discarded, and this is one reason why we do and must discard Presbyterianism itself,—palpably a mere tradition of men, first concocted full fifteen hundred years after Christ and his holy apostles. These are not the traditions Catholics assert and contend for. Catholics say Christ and his apostles taught men, *viva voce*, many things which were not committed to writing, but which have been preserved faithfully in the doctrine and practice of the church, according to the admonition of the holy Apostle Paul:—" Stand firm, brethren, and hold the traditions you have learned, whether *by word* or by our epistle." 2 Thess. ii. 14. These traditions are not the traditions of *men*, but an integral part of the revealed word,—the revelations and teaching of God (*tradited*) transmitted by men, who can and do transmit many things without writing, as they transmit language, and various practices and habits, which no one finds first, if at all, in books, but which every one learns long before opening a book.

If the Presbyterians had the candor to acknowledge these facts, or if their readers were aware of them, they would see, at a glance, that the passages adduced do not in the least impugn Catholic traditions. Those passages simply condemn traditions of *men*,—not traditions transmitted by men, but traditions which are of human origin, and which Catholics have always been, and are, the first and most strenuous to condemn. The first text adduced is from St. Paul. " Though we or an angel from heaven preach any other gospel unto you than that which we have preached unto you, let him be accursed." The Presbyterian divines bring forward this passage as expressly condemning all traditions; but no selection could be more unfortunate for them. It not only says nothing against traditions, but is an awful denunciation of Presbyterianism, and an express command to all who would adhere to the Gospel of our Lord to hold it accursed. These divines would represent this text to mean, If anybody holds any doctrine to be divinely revealed not written in the Scriptures of the Old and New Testaments, let him be accursed: therefore, let Papists, who hold traditional doctrines, be accursed. Yet there is no scholar but would be ashamed to pretend that this is the real meaning; and even Presbyterians themselves, if they would examine the context, would, on this point, agree with us. The Galatians had been converted to Christ by the Apostle St. Paul, who had taken great pains to make them understand that the Mosaical ceremonies were not only unnecessary, but, if observed in a Jewish spirit, and considered a *necessary* part of Christianity, even superstitious. Some Jewish teachers went among them, and persuaded them to embrace these same ceremonies as necessary, and thus caused them to turn again to the weak and poor elements of the Law. They observed days, and months, and years, and wished again to come under the Law. (iv. 9, 10, 21.) On learning this, the apostle wrote to them in terms of mingled holy indignation and burning charity. " I wonder that you are so soon removed from him who called you to the grace of Christ, to another gospel, which is not another, only there are some who trouble you, and would pervert the Gospel of Christ. But though we or an angel from heaven preach any other gospel to you than that which we have preached to you, let him be anathema." The meaning of St. Paul is clearly, If anybody, even an angel, come and preach to you the necessity of Jewish observances, let him be accursed; and, in a more general sense, If any one, even an angel, preach to you any doctrine *contrary* to that which we have preached, let him be accursed. That this is his meaning, and that the one given in the Confession is absurd, must be manifest to all who reflect that St. Paul says nothing here of a gospel *written*, but speaks simply of a gospel *preached*, —that the Four Gospels were not then written,—certainly not that of St. John, which was not written till many years afterwards,—and that many other portions of the Scriptures were also as yet unwritten, as learned Presbyterians are themselves aware and admit. If the Presbyterian interpretation of the text were admitted, we should be required to reject every writing of the apostles posterior to the date of the Epistle to the Galatians, even many of the Epistles of St. Paul himself, as another gospel than that which he preached to the Galatians,—a conclusion which even Presbyterians must shrink from with horror. But, if many things were added to the New Testament, containing doctrines not found in the parts written prior to the Epistle in question, every one must see that St. Paul could have meant only what we have alleged, that is, If any one hold any thing *contrary* to the Christian traditions which you have received from us, let him be accursed. The Gospel preached to the Galatians must have been, to a great extent, if not exclusively, a traditional one. Consequently, the meaning of St. Paul must have been, If any one hold any doctrine contrary to that which has been given to you, whether in writing or orally, it matters not whether in the one mode or the other, let him be accursed. So far, then, from asserting that there must be no traditions, this text, as far as it goes, presupposes and teaches to the contrary.

The church has always cherished this maxim of the great apostle, written far more efficaciously in the convictions and practices of Christians than it can be on paper. If any one comes forward preaching any doctrine unknown before him, or irreconcilable with the dogmas already received, the language of Catholics has been from the first, Let him be anathema. On this ground any doctrine which is new is rejected as false: for, if new, it cannot be a doctrine of the apostles, but must be the offspring of the human intellect or fancy. There is no need of discussion, no need of a long course of reading. Is the doctrine contrary to what has been taught? Then it is false. If, *per impossibile*, an angel from heaven were to preach it, still it is false and to be rejected; for we know that the doctrines taught by the apostles are from God, and so confirmed by miracles, that it would be absurd not to receive them. We know, also, that God protects his church against even hell, whose gates can never prevail against it. We know this latter point from innumerable proofs, among which we reckon as not the least this very text of St. Paul, which commands us, if even an angel should come preaching any novelty contrary to the doctrine preached in the church, not to listen to him.

But what will become of Presbyterianism, if tried by this test,—the touchstone furnished by the great apostle, the Doctor of Nations? What, in fact, is it itself, but a naked, undisguised, and undisguisable novelty? What is it, but a doctrine undeniably contrary to that of the apostles and which has been received in the church through every age? That it was a novelty at the time when John Calvin and John Knox broached it is so evident, that Presbyterians themselves cannot seriously undertake to deny it. They themselves tell us that they left the Catholic Church in consequence of its *old* errors, *old* superstitions, *old* corruptions, *old* traditions of men. Calvin and Knox gave themselves out as the preachers of *new* and pure doctrines, the propagators of a *new* light, and the authors of a *new* era for the religious world. What was this, but setting aside the ancient doctrine, and substituting a modern one? But the apostle solemnly declares, that, if even an angel comes preaching a doctrine different from what has been preached before, he is to be accursed. Alas for Presbyterianism! even if it had been preached by an angel from heaven, we are commanded by the very text which Presbyterians adduce, and are ambitious of engraving on their escutcheon, to hold it accursed; how much rather, then, since it was preached by no angel, but by such men as John Calvin and John Knox, certainly no angels,—unless of darkness! This text of St. Paul, then, instead of militating against Catholic traditions, is evidently a direct and irrevocable condemnation of Presbyterianism itself, indeed of all modern sects, among which Presbyterians, we admit, are entitled to the first rank. Decidedly, they should not quote this text. The Philistines flattered themselves that they had achieved a glorious victory, when they took captive the Ark of Israel, and carried it in triumph to their own country; but when they beheld their god Dagon mutilated and their cities depopulated by the divine justice, they were even more eager to restore it than they had been to possess it. Presbyterians, perhaps, will be as eager hereafter to restore this text to its rightful owners, as the Philistines were the Ark.

The second text the Confession quotes against Catholic traditions is, "Be not soon shaken in mind, or be troubled, neither by spirit, nor by word, nor by letter, as from us, as that the day of Christ is at hand." This is a singular text to prove that Scripture is sufficient, and that Catholic traditions are traditions of men, and to be discarded.

> "Sharp optics he must have, I ween,
> Who sees what is not to be seen."

So sharp logicians are our Presbyterian divines, who find proofs where proofs there are none. St. Paul writes to the Thessalonians not to believe the *Millerites* of their time; *therefore* the Scriptures alone are the sole rule of faith and practice; *therefore* Catholic traditions are traditions of men, and to be discarded! There is no refuting such reasoning. But, seriously, if Presbyterians adduce this text as evidencing an instance of false tradition, how happens it they fail to perceive, that, in their haste to pluck out their neighbours' eyes, they most effectually pluck out their own? St. Paul refers to tradition not only by *word*, but also by *letter*. If Presbyterians say, Therefore there have been false traditions, and therefore *all* traditions are to be discarded; we retort, Therefore there have been false Scriptures, and therefore all Scripture is to be discarded.

If the subject were not so serious, one could not help being amused with the zeal of Presbyterians against the traditions of men, when their own Confession and Constitution show us with what admirable docility and tameness they submit to doctrines and practices which have and can have no origin but in the pride of innovators; when we are able to point out the very year of the birth of the founder of Presbyterianism, fifteen hundred years after our Saviour, the year in which he separated himself from the church, the exact date of the Calvinistic inoculation of John Knox, the year and the month of the various enterprises of Calvinism in the several parts of Europe, and, in fact, of the origin of all their religious practices. Here we have unquestionably an example of traditions of men held as the pure word of God by Presbyterians themselves, although the year and day can be pointed out when they sprang from the head of Calvin and Calvinistic leaders. How, then, can they have the hardihood, nay, how can they be so suicidal as to speak against traditions of men? What can be more supremely ridiculous than to discard as human tradition the celebration of Easter, the solemn commemoration of the death of Christ by a season of penance and fasting, when the death and resurrection of Christ are both mentioned in the New Testament, when the Old Testament abounds with festivals divinely instituted in commemoration of great events, and these two yearly commemorations are found to have been observed in the church from the earliest ages,— and yet to admit as Scriptural a mode of ecclesiastical government by congregational, presbyterial, and synodical assemblies, of which there was no example at the time of Calvin's birth, and of which there never had been an example in the world? What more undeniably a human tradition than the name, office, functions, and mode of election and ordination, of a Presbyterian *ruling elder?* Surely, Presbyterians are the last people in the world to speak disrespectfully of human traditions. Deprive them of human traditions, and they would be in the sad plight of the man of Mount Ephraim, who ran after the Danites with his piteous wail, and when asked why he cried, answered, "Ye have taken away my gods which I have made me, and the priest, and all that I have, and do you say, What aileth thee?"—Judges, xviii. 24.

After all, it is only in theory and by way of boasting, that Presbyterians assert the sufficiency of the Scriptures alone as the sole rule of faith and practice. They really hold the Bible alone to be quite inadequate to the formation of a system of religious doctrine, and are in this respect remarkable among all modern sects; or else why the volume before us? If the Scriptures alone be sufficient, if they are the sole rule of faith and practice, why the Westminster Confession of Faith, the Larger and Shorter Catechisms, the Directory, the Form of Government and Discipline, and other valuable appendages? Is it not solely because Presbyterians fear that people will not find in the Bible this mode of government by ministers, ruling elders, and deacons, the three grades of the Presbyterian hierarchy? Is it not because they have a suspicion that people will not, without the help of the Confession of Faith, the Larger and Shorter Catechisms, find out that God in the beginning made some men with the design of beautifying and glorifying them, and others with the design of making them the prey of eternal fire? Is it not because they are afraid that the dogma, that God leaves sinners, and sometimes even just men, without the gracious assistance necessary to enable them to keep his law, will not be ferreted out by the reader of Scripture, unless it is propounded to them in the Confession and Catechisms, since Presbyterians or Calvinists are the only ones who find out that this and the other articles of the Calvinistic creed are clearly taught in Scripture? They hold their Confession of Faith, their Directory, their plan of government, their catechisms, and their discipline to be *necessary;* hence, they ordain that no one shall be licensed "as an elder or a minister, unless he adopt the Confession of

Faith, and approve of the government and discipline of the Presbyterian Church." If these be necessary, and Scripture alone contains every thing necessary, how happens it that it does not contain these, and in the precise form in which they are to be adopted and approved by the candidates for license? Did the Holy Ghost forget himself, and hence the necessity of the Westminster divines to supply his deficiency?

There are some Protestant sects who are far from being guilty of the particular species of hypocrisy chargeable upon Presbyterians; sects which do not uphold the sufficiency of Scripture with one hand, and demolish it with the other by imposing creeds and confessions drawn up by men, which discard all creeds, even the Apostles' Creed, every discipline and directory as a curse, and hold up the Scriptures alone as sufficient, as the sole rule of faith, without gloss, note, or comment. In one sense these *do* admit the sufficiency of Scripture, for this is all they admit; since they do not agree on a single article taught by the Scriptures, as must be the case with all who assert the sufficiency of the Bible alone;—another and a conclusive proof to Catholics, that Scripture alone is not sufficient, and that Christ and the apostles did not intend to write every thing necessary, but left every thing in the hands of a *living* body subsisting always unto the consummation of the world, always supernaturally assisted and able to transmit both what was written, with its true interpretation, and what was not written. Hence the command and the promise,—" Going, teach all nations, ... teaching them to observe all things *whatsoever* I have commanded you; for, behold, I am with you all days unto the consummation of the world." St. Matt. xxviii. 19, 20.

But we come now to another point in the Protestant creed, namely, the *clearness* of Scripture. Here the Presbyterians seem to surpass even themselves in mystification, and in that peculiar skill in deducing proofs from Scripture, which reminds us of the etymology of *lucus* from *non lucendo*. We quote the article, entire, with its proofs.

"Art. VII. All things in Scripture are not alike plain in themselves, nor alike clear unto all; yet those things which are necessary to be known, believed, and observed, for salvation, are so clearly propounded and opened in some place of Scripture or other, that not only the learned, but the unlearned, in a due use of the ordinary means, may attain unto a sufficient understanding of them.

"2 Pet. iii. 16. As also in all *his* epistles, speaking in them of these things; in which are some things hard to be understood, which they that are unlearned and unstable wrest, as *they do* also the other Scriptures, unto their own destruction. Ps. cxix. [cxviii.] 105, 130. Thy word is a lamp unto my feet, and a light unto my path.—The entrance of thy words giveth light; it giveth understanding unto the simple."

The hypothesis on which this article was framed is, since the Scripture contains every thing, is of itself sufficient, without tradition or any thing else, and the *sole* rule of faith and practice, it must, of course, be clear and open to all; but there is an unlucky text of St. Peter which states boldly and uncompromisingly that there are things in the Scriptures hard to be understood, and Catholics do not fail to urge this text, with advantage, against us. We must, then, lay it down in our Confession, that in things not necessary Scripture is indeed obscure, but in things necessary it is clear even to the unlearned. This article opens a wide field of inquiry, but we must confine ourselves to a few points. What, we ask, are those things which are necessary, and about which Scripture is clear? The Presbyterians evidently mean their doctrines, as contained in the Confession of Faith, the Larger and Shorter Catechisms, &c. Be it so. But unhappily, as blind men seeking to avoid one danger fall into another, they assert this without proof, and may be met by stricter logic with the reply, that those things are necessary which are clear, and not the reverse; and then, that it is necessary for salvation to believe there once lived a man called Methusalem,—for this is so clearly stated in Scripture that no one, believing the Scriptures, ever did or ever can call it in question; and, on the contrary, that it is not necessary to believe in the divinity of our Lord,—for this is not clear in the Scriptures, since there were many who questioned it in the fourth century, and there are many who do not believe it now, and deny that it is taught in the Scriptures at all. But granting the necessary articles may be settled by some other process, let us look at the proofs which Presbyterians adduce to establish their position, that Scripture is obscure only on matters which are not necessary. These proofs are in the text from St. Peter. But this text proves the very reverse. It says there are things hard to be understood in the Scriptures, which some wrest *to their own destruction*. If they can wrest these things hard to be understood to their own destruction, they must be necessary to salvation; for if not, no misapprehension of their sense could involve destruction. The things, then, of which St. Peter speaks, are not unnecessary things, but necessary, and which it is necessary for salvation rightly to understand. The Presbyterians, therefore, prove on Scriptural authority the opposite in their notes of what they assert in the text, as is usual with them.

Nothing but pride and ignorance could ever induce any one to deny that there are things in the Bible obscure and hard to be understood. That the obscurities and difficulties pertain to things important and most essential is obvious from daily experience, and from St. Peter, who would not have spoken of them, if they concerned neither faith nor salvation. Suppose an ordinary reader, on finding in the Bible that the eyes of our first parents were opened, imagines that they were previously blind, or had an additional eyelid; that one commentator thinks the forbidden fruit was an apple, and another that it was an orange, and still another that it was a fig; that one believes that the fish which swallowed Jonas was a shark, and another that it was a whale, or some other kind of fish now extinct; that this one, when he reads St. Paul's declaration, "A night and a day I have been in the deep," concludes that he was on a plank *upon* the water, and another, that he was *under* the water; will it be necessary to conclude that one or the other of these wrests the Scriptures to his own destruction, and must necessarily be lost? Nobody can believe it. Then it cannot be of such interpretations as these, or the misapprehension of such matters as these, St. Peter speaks; but we must understand him to speak of such matters as Christians generally, and Presbyterians particularly, hold to be necessary. For instance, St. Paul tells us, "Abraham believed and it was reputed to him for justice"; are we, therefore, to hold ourselves secure, if we only believe, but are careless about every thing else? So of innumerable other questions which immediately concern religion and morality.

Presbyterians, then, evidently fail to make out that the obscurities of Scripture are confined to things which are not necessary; let us see if they succeed better in making out that it is clear in things necessary,—clear not for the learned only, but also for the unlearned,—and not by extraordinary means or helps from above, but by the due use of the ordinary means. Their whole proof of this rests on the texts from the Psalmist, "Thy word is a lamp unto my feet, and a light unto my path," "The entrance of thy words giveth light; it giveth understanding unto the simple." David, writing his Psalms under the influence of divine inspiration, says the word of God is a lamp to his feet, a light to his path, and therefore every Presbyterian, in case he has the written word, is to conclude that he is equally privileged! David says in the same Psalm, "I rose at midnight to give praise to Thee." Shall we, therefore, conclude, forthwith, that all Presbyterians rise at midnight to sing psalms? But admitting the text to be applicable to all Christians, nothing proves that David spoke of a word known to him by his own reading of the Bible, or even by the common tradition of the Jews; and consequently, the text proves merely that knowledge of the law of God, when once obtained, however obtained, whether by reading the Bible or from oral tradition, is a lamp and and a light. It does not say this knowledge is obtained or obtainable from reading the Bible, much less does it say the Bible by the due use of ordinary means is clear even to the unlearned in all necessary things. Any man, knowing the true religion, might and would apply the words to himself, even though unable to read a syllable. The text, moreover, makes no reference to the distinction between things necessary and things unnecessary. If, then, it prove the necessary facts of the written word to be clear, it proves the unnecessary facts to be equally clear. Finally, it is presumable that St. Peter knew the psalms of the royal prophet, and the particular passage in question, at least as well as modern Presbyterians know them, and yet he expressly and solemnly asserts that there are things in the Scriptures "*hard to be understood*, which the unlearned and unstable wrest to their own destruction." But it is unnecessary to say more on such proofs as these. Presbyterians cannot be supposed to place any confidence in them themselves.

There is no need of dwelling longer on the fact that the Scriptures are not clear in every thing necessary. It is altogether silent on many points of great consequence, as we proved in our former article, and it barely alludes to others no less important. After what we have said, we may conclude the discussion of the clearness of Scripture with the remark, that Presbyterians must have an unenviable share of assurance to assert, as they do, and apparently without blushing, notwithstanding these words of Scripture, "If any man be sick among you, let him bring in the priests of the church, and let them pray over him, annointing him with oil," &c., or these other words, "Take ye and eat, this is my body, ... Wherefore, whosoever shall eat this bread, or drink the chalice of the Lord unworthily, shall be guilty of the body and blood of the Lord," that it is clear there is no such thing as the Real Presence in the Eucharist, and that Extreme Unction is a Popish imposition; or to assert, as they also do, in the face of the declaration of St. Paul, " He that is without a wife is solicitous for the things which belong to the Lord ; but he that is with a wife is solicitious for the things of the world, how he may please his wife ; and the unmarried woman thinketh on the things of the Lord, that she may be holy both in body and in spirit," 1 Cor. vii, 32–34. that it is, nevertheless, clear from Scripture, that monastic vows of perpetual celibacy are superstitious and sinful snares. While they reject Catholic dogmas and practices so unequivocally expressed in the Scriptures, we can only smile at their simplicity, or grieve at their impudence, in asserting that they find clearly stated in Scripture all the rules enjoined for keeping Sunday, and all the impediments to marriage originating in consanguinity or affinity. They can quote long Scripture passages upon these points, it is true ; but these passages are from the law of Moses, which everybody admits to have been abrogated by Christ, yet this is nothing to Presbyterians. They are bent upon finding Scripture authority for the practice they have determined to adopt, and they can hardly be expected not to succeed—in some way; especially since their people are blest with a plentiful share of ignorance and credulity. We would, however, since they insist on quoting the law of Moses, when it suits their predeterminations, recommend them to go the whole length of the thing ; and, if they will quote the Old Testament for the keeping of Sunday, let them keep also the " Sabbath of years," and leave their land fallow every seventh year, Lev. xxv. 4. Let them also keep all the laws of Moses on marriage ; and in particular the law in Deuteronomy xxv. 6–10. They would then preserve, at least, some show of consistency. But enough on this branch of the subject.

We have now reached the eighth article, which will detain us a little longer.

"The Old Testament in Hebrew (which was the native language of the people of God of old) and the New Testament in Greek (which at the time of the writing of it was most generally known to the nations), being immediately inspired by God, and by his singular care and providence kept pure in all ages, are therefore authentical, so as in all controversies of religion the Church is finally to appeal unto them. But because these original tongues are not known to all the people of God, who have right unto and interest in the Scriptures, and are commanded in the fear of God to read and search them, therefore they are to be translated into the vulgar language of every nation unto which they come, that the word of God dwelling plentifully in all, they may worship him in an acceptable manner, and through patience and comfort of the Scriptures have hope.

"Matt. v. 18. For verily I say unto you, till heaven and earth pass, one jot or one tittle shall in no wise pass from the law, till all be fulfilled. Isa. viii. 20. To the law and to the testimony, &c. Acts xv. 15. John v. 46. John v. 39. Search the Scriptures, for in them ye think ye have eternal life ; and they are they which testify of me. 1 Cor. xiv. 6–28. Col. iii. 16. Let the word of Christ dwell in you richly, " &c. Rom. xv. 4.

Before proceeding to consider the real merits of the questions involved in this article, we must say a word or two on the marvellous appositeness of these Scriptural authorities. We have so often been compelled to notice the peculiar beauty and force of Presbyterian logic in the application of Scriptural texts, that our readers may be wellnigh surfeited, as we confess we are ourselves. Too much of a good thing, says the proverb, is good for nothing. Nevertheless, we must sit yet longer at the feast. Christ said, " One jot or one tittle shall not pass from the law till all be fulfilled "; *therefore* the Hebrew and Greek copies of the Scriptures which we now have are authentical, and have been kept pure in all ages! It is not easy to surpass this. But add, for the greater edification of pious Presbyterians, *therefore* the Bible of King James is authentical, correctly translated, and perfectly pure ! The marvellous appositeness of this proof is in the well known fact, that St. Matthew, from whom it is taken, wrote his Gospel in Hebrew, and that Hebrew text is lost, and we have only a translation of it ! Again. " To the law and to the testimony "; *therefore*, if we have a religious controversy to settle, we must run and learn Hebrew and Greek, for it is only by appealing to the Hebrew and Greek copies that we can have a reasonable hope of arriving at the truth. Wonderful logic ! Who but Presbyterians could ever have compassed it ? St. Paul found fault with certain primitive Christians, who, having received the gift of tongues, were eager to speak in the church in unknown languages. He wishes them to show more moderation, and to speak in them only where there is an interpreter. *Therefore* the Scriptures are to be translated into the vulgar tongues, distributed everywhere to all, and in every language ! But, if so, why did not the apostles themselves draw this conclusion, so "good and necessary" in the view of our learned and acute Presbyterian divines, and give us from their own hands a Latin, a Syriac, an Arabic, a Gallic New Testament ? It is singular how much superior as logicians our Presbyterian divines are to the apostles, and how inconsistent the neglect of the apostles must appear to them. But the Presbyterians live in modern times, have the advantages of modern progress, and therefore must naturally be supposed to surpass the apostles, who lived a long time ago, and had only the lights of divine inspiration.

We shall restrict what we have to say on the article under consideration to three questions, namely : 1. Are the Hebrew copies of the old Testament and the Greek copies of the New, *which we now possess*, more "authentical" than the Latin Vulgate ? 2. Is there a positive obligation upon all men to read the Scriptures? And 3. Is the distribution of the Scriptures to all indiscriminately in the vulgar tongues an effectual way of making *the word of God dwell plentifully in all*, and of attaining the end for which it was given ?

1. The Latin Vulgate, put by the side of the Hebrew and Greek copies of the Scriptures we now have, will not suffer by the comparison; and our Douay Bible, made from it with remarkable accuracy, is superior to the version of King James, though this last purports to be made from the original tongues, since the Latin Vulgate is at least as good a representative of the word of God as the modern copies in the original tongues now in our possession, and the English version made from it is a far better performance than that of the translators appointed by the royal theologian. If we possessed the autographs of Moses and the other Jewish writers in Hebrew, and those of the apostles themselves in Greek, no one would be found, of course, to contest their superiority ; though, after all, they would be found to agree substantially with our modern Bible. But the autograph is lost, and the manuscripts or printed copies of Hebrew and Greek Bibles are only transcriptions of other copies which are also lost, and which themselves were only transcriptions. To tell the number of transcriptions there have been, in ascending from a modern Hebrew Bible to Moses, would puzzle greater men than even Westminster divines. This being un-

derstood, it will not be disputed that our present copies of the Hebrew Bible may and must have mistakes and errors, unless indeed it be contended that God has by a continual miracle directed the hand of every copyist. These errors and mistakes, it is true, do not affect the substance of the text, or prevent it from representing the substance of the dogmas, morals, and history recorded by the sacred penman; but they are blemishes, and blemishes which place the Hebrew and Greek text as low as, and even lower than, an early translation, in which there must have been fewer chances of accidental variations, and in which such as did occur were more likely to be corrected. Such a translation is the Latin Vulgate, at least in the view of Catholics, who respect, indeed, the Hebrew and Greek copies, but are far from considering them the only or even the most authentic monuments we now have of divine revelation.

Presbyterians seem, in their Scriptural quotations, to intimate that every thing, even to a single jot or comma, in the Hebrew and Greek copies is correct; but this, it is well known, is not the fact. The several Hebrew and Greek manuscripts extant are known to differ from one another by something more than jots and commas. Which of these manuscripts is the one Presbyterians declare to be genuine, the one immediately inspired? Open Griesbach's edition of the New Testament, and you shall find scarcely a page which does not present various readings, all of which are supported by Greek manuscripts, and with no possible means of determining in all cases which is the genuine reading. Who, in the face of this fact, can unblushingly assert that God by his providence has so watched over the Hebrew and Greek copies of the Bible, that they are absolutely pure, and in nothing differ from the autographs themselves? Every one who can read a word of Hebrew and Greek, and compare editions, knows such an assertion to be false. The simple fact, then, that the Old Testament was written in Hebrew, and the new in Greek, is not, then, in itself a reason for preferring our present Hebrew and Greek copies to authentic versions, possessing the requisite qualities. The Latin Vulgate may, then, represent the word of God as well as the received Hebrew text, and we hesitate not to say that in many things it actually does represent it even better. Not to enter too far into Biblical criticism, we select a couple of examples from many others we might adduce. Genesis, iv. 8, we read in the Vulgate, " And Cain said to his brother

Abel, Let us go forth abroad. And when they were in the field, Cain rose up against his brother Abel and slew him." In the Hebrew the words *let us go forth abroad*, are wanting, and hence the royal theologians in the Protestant version translate, " And Cain talked with Abel, his brother; and it came to pass, when they were in the field, that Cain rose up against his brother and slew him." The Vulgate here is far preferable to the Hebrew, and Moses must have written as in the Vulgate, and not as in the modern Hebrew. The proof of this is in the fact that the Septuagint has these words, " Let us go forth abroad," the Targum of Jerusalem has them, and so has the Pentateuch of the Samaritans; and this last must be for the learned high authority. Hence St. Jerome, who had the Samaritan Pentateuch under his eyes, was induced to retain the reading which we have in the Vulgate. The context itself confirms this reading. The modern Hebrew says that Cain spoke to Abel, but, unless, we add the words in the Vulgate, he is made to speak without saying any thing. Moreover, if we admit that Cain said, " Let us go forth abroad," the following words, " And when they were in the field," &c., come in naturally, and with perfect propriety. Here are sufficient considerations for preferring the reading of the Vulgate to that of the modern Hebrew.

The other example we select is Ps. xxi. 17, " They have dug my hands and feet," said in reference to Christ on the cross. The modern Hebrew text, however, has, instead of " they have dug," the words " like a lion." But so untenable is this latter reading, that Protestants generally, and even the Westminster divines themselves, notwithstanding they found out that the Hebrew text is absolutely pure, because not a jot or a tittle of the law was to pass away, reject it and adopt that of the Vulgate and other versions. There is no need of multiplying examples in support of a point which no learned Protestant disputes. The rule to be laid down is, that the best reading is not always that of the Hebrew or Greek, but is to be determined by a cautious and judicious comparison of the texts of ancient manuscripts and versions.

The merits of the Vulgate, as a translation, far exceed those of any modern version. It was chiefly the work of St. Jerome, whose reputation for learning and skill in the oriental languages stands unrivalled, and who had far better opportunities than we now have of obtaining the best Hebrew and Greek manuscripts, since he lived at the time when the great Alexandrian library was still in its glory. Moreover, he was admirably well acquainted with the country, the usages, the laws, and the history of the Jews, and he spent a great portion of his life in the conscientious performance of his task. Hence his translation was soon adopted by the whole church, and acquired from this fact a higher stamp of authenticity than could be obtained by the mere skill of a translator; because divine Providence could not suffer any but an authentic copy of the precious deposite of divine revelation to become current in the church. This consideration weighed with the fathers of the Council of Trent, in declaring the Vulgate to be an authentic copy of the word of God, and their judgment has been confirmed by the most learned and impartial Protestants. English translations of the Bible, purporting to be from the original tongues, are often wretched performances, and sometimes shameful corruptions of the word of God. The version of King James, though freed from many wilful corruptions and alterations, yet contains many unwarrantable errors, and pernicious additions and mutilations, as our authors easily establish. We refer the reader on this point to Ward's *Errata,* and also to Campbell's *Preliminary Dissertations.*

2. But we pass to our second question, namely, Is there a positive obligation upon all men to read the Bible? Our Presbyterian divines say authoritatively that there is, but without satisfying us that they are right. No obligation should be assumed to be binding on all men, unless established by irrefragable proofs, and, in the present case, unless established by clear and undeniable Scriptural authority. Presbyterians hold that the Scriptures alone are the sufficient and the sole rule of faith and practice, and that they clearly and sufficiently expound all the duties of Christians. Then they cannot assume that all men are bound to *read* the Scriptures, unless they can prove it by a clear and undisputable command from the Scriptures themselves. But where is the Scriptural text which declares it to be the *duty* of all men to read the Bible? The Confession of Faith relies on the passage from St. John, "Search the Scriptures; for in them ye think ye have eternal life; and they are they which testify of me;" but this in reality proves nothing to the purpose. By reading the chapter from which this text is taken, it will be seen that our Lord, by the cure of an in-

firm man at the pond Probatica, on the Sabbath day, incurred the displeasure of the Jews, who even thought of putting him to death. Against these Jews, against these envenomed enemies, he argues to prove the divinity of his mission, and refers them to the Scriptures, and bids them study them attentively, for they bear testimony for him. Now, how from this can it be inferred that it is positively obligatory upon Christians, and especially upon all men, to read the Bible? In the first place, the Presbyterian who reads this passage in the original tongue must find that the word *search* may be in the indicative mood, as well as in the imperative, and that the translation might have been, without any impropriety, " Ye search the Scriptures, for in them ye think ye have eternal life; now they are they which testify of me." St. Cyril, who was at least as good a Greek scholar as were King James's translators, so interprets it, and some modern Protestants do the same. In this case, the words of our Lord do not contain even the shadow of a command. Now, a Presbyterian has no possible way to determine whether the inspired writer used the indicative mood or the imperative; and here is a *clear* proof of the obscurity of Scripture on a duty which Presbyterians must hold to be of paramount importance.

But suppose the verb to be in the imperative mood, still no obligation upon all Christians to read the Bible can be deduced. The words quoted were addressed to the Jews, who denied the mission of Christ,—not to Christians at large, for the purpose of enjoining a precept; they were said, moreover, only in reference to the Old Testament, the only Scriptures then in existence, and merely imply, that, if the Jews had attentively read the Old Testament, they would have been brought to a knowledge of Christ's authority. As much as to say, If ye were acquainted with the Scriptures, in which ye think ye have eternal life, ye would not reject me, for they bear witness to me. Suppose a Christian, arguing against a Mahometan, should say, Read attentively the Koran, and you will find a splendid testimony in favor of Jesus Christ; who could thence conclude that he intended to assert that there is an obligation upon all Christians to read the Koran? How, then, is it possible from the words in question to conclude that there is a positive obligation upon all men to read the Bible? Presbyterians hold that all obligations are clearly expressed in Scripture. Then, on their own grounds, if all men are under obligation to read the Bible, it must be clearly expressed in the Scriptures,—say, as clearly as the obligations contained in the ten commandments. But it is not so expressed; and therefore, on their own ground, we have the right to conclude the obligation does not exist.

We have here disposed of the only text which Presbyterians adduce in support of the obligation in question. Other texts might have been adduced, but none which prove anything beyond the *utility* of reading the Scriptures,—a point which, when coupled with the proper preparation and disposition on the part of the reader, we by no means contest. The precept of St. Paul to Timothy, " Attend to reading," 1 Tim. iv. 13, might perhaps be alleged; but it is obvious that St. Paul in that epistle is pointing out the duties of a clergyman, not of each individual Christian; and we grant that reading in general, but especially the Scriptures, is not only useful, but necessary, for a clergyman.

What we have said is sufficient to disprove the positive obligation or *duty* of all men to read the Bible; but we go further, and say that the admission of such an obligation is altogether at variance with the conduct of the apostles, and the paternal and merciful providence of God in the government of men. If it had been obligatory upon all men to read the Scriptures, the apostles would have written them in, or at least translated them into, all languages, which they did not do; and we learn from St. Irenæus, that whole nations embraced Christianity, among whom not a copy of the Scriptures was to be found. The apostles, indeed, composed a symbol or creed, and directed that every one should learn it by heart before baptism; but the creed is short, and to learn it is comparatively an easy task; whereas the Bible is a large volume, and it is no trifling labor to commit it all to memory. Moreover, for fifteen centuries, to obtain a Bible was not a little difficult, and few could go to the labor and expense of copying it. Who can calmly assert that there is a strict moral obligation upon all men even to learn reading? To admit the assertion, that to read the Bible is strictly obligatory upon all, would be to transform the great mass of men into a set of prevaricators, and to impeach the goodness of God, who for fifteen hundred years left the world without that easy means of producing and obtaining books at cheap rates which we now possess.

Finally, reading the Scriptures can be maintained to be obligatory upon all men, only on the supposition, that without them it is impossible to attain to a knowledge of Christian faith and morals. But this supposition is inadmissible. Universal experience, from the times of the apostles who gave us the creed, proves that men do and can come to a knowledge of the duties and the mysteries of faith more easily, and more surely, by learning their catechism and listening to their pastors, than by reading the Bible, which does not and never was intended to contain a clear and succinct summary of Christian doctrine. "There is," says St. Francis de Sales, "the same difference between the word of God as contained in the Scriptures, and the same word as contained in the catechism and the instructions of the pastor, that there is between a nut covered with its hard shell, and the same nut broken and laid open before you." For the mass of mankind, at least, the nut must be broken and laid open, before they can perceive and eat its delicious contents. The real obligation, the real necessity, is to learn, not the Bible so called, but the Christian doctrine, which can be done, and effectually, without ever handling a book. Moreover, as a matter of fact, what the various Protestant sects call Christian doctrine is not learned from reading the Bible. The Presbyterian child learns Presbyterianism, not from the Bible, but from his Sunday-school teacher, his manual, and the instructions of his parents and his pastor. Even Unitarians, who discard all creeds and confessions, have their catechisms and manuals, through which they indoctrinate their children in their dogmas against dogmas, their creed against creeds. No sect relies on reading the Bible alone as the means of obtaining or of imparting what it holds to be Christian doctrine. We say truly, then, universal experience is against the supposition in question, and the universal practice of all those who insist that reading the Bible is strictly obligatory on all Christians affords ample evidence, that, however convenient they may find it to make such a profession, they in reality believe no such thing.

3. We are now led to the third and last question, namely, Is the distribution of the Bible to all indiscriminately an effectual way of making the word of God dwell plentifully in all, and of attaining the end for which it was given? We unhesitatingly say that it is not, and that mankind have witnessed no greater folly, since the reformation, than the rage which has obtained, more especially from the early part of the present century, for distributing Bibles every-

where, in all places, to all sorts of persons, and in all languages. This rage, this mania, is merely an impeachment of our Lord and of his blessed apostles. The apostles, the heralds of evangelical doctrine, never dreamed of a distribution of Bibles as a means of establishing and propagating Christianity. We have a detailed account of the missions of St. Paul throughout nearly the whole known world, yet nowhere do we find that he was anxious to procure copies of the Bible, and that he distributed them at random. The same blessed apostle in his Epistles enters into many minute details of Christian life, but never does a syllable escape him about copying and distributing Bibles. The apostles taught and instructed the heathen and the faithful, not by books, but *viva voce*, or by preaching; because they had received from their divine Master the solemn injunction to "*preach* the Gospel to every creature," and because the great work of the conversion and sanctification of men, in the ordinary state of things, can be successfully performed only by *living* men, and not by a dead book. Hence, the general maxim of St. Paul was, "Faith comes by *hearing*,"—*fides ex auditu*,—not by reading. This is the process and economy of nature. It is little less than folly to suppose that science can be communicated and diffused without living teachers. The practice and common sense of mankind are opposed to the plan of learning without a teacher, from books alone; and if sometimes adopted by a few through necessity, it is only at great expense and trouble. Those who do adopt it never become thoroughly learned; their knowledge is never complete and exact; and they constantly expose themselves to disappointments and blunders, from which those who have had the benefit of the more usual and less defective methods are free. Only a few, again, can learn any thing by this method; the bulk of mankind can learn nothing by it. Yet the difficulty of learning any thing positive in religion from the study of a book, especially of a book never intended to be a summary of doctrine, or a clear and appropriate introduction to religious truth, is much greater.

If the whole secret of propagating Christian doctrine consisted in the multiplication and distribution of copies of the Bible, and not in the oral teaching of divinely appointed instructers, would the apostle have ever referred us to these stages in the Christian ministry,—" And some Christ gave to be apostles, and some prophets, and others evangelists, and others pastors and teachers, for the perfection of the saints, for the work of the ministry," Eph. iv. 11, 12 ? Would he not have said, And some Christ gave to be *colporteurs*, or distributors of Bibles, others buyers and sellers of Bibles, others transcribers or printers of Bibles, others paper or ink makers, others rag-merchants, and others rag-collectors? for in this strange system, these are all valuable and necessary members of the sacred hierarchy.

It is not the mere hearing or reading of the word of God that avails us, but the proper understanding of it, and especially the fruit we gather from it. Scripture itself asserts, " Not the hearers of the law, but the doers thereof, shall be blessed before God." And there was more Christian virtue, piety, humility, disinterestedness, contempt of riches, Christian heroism, in those ages in which Bibles had not become as common as stones, than there is now. We read often reports of committees who congratulate themselves, that, within a year, or a shorter period, there have been more Bibles distributed than were ever transcribed or printed prior to the present century; but we find none to read which speak of a corresponding growth in the Christian virtues. Paper-makers, printers, and booksellers may find cause of gratulation in this multiplication and distribution of Bibles, but the Christian none, unless he sees men in the same proportion becoming meek and humble, charitable and self-denying, rising above the world while in it, and living only for God and heaven. We regret to say that there is little reason for supposing that a moral reformation at all keeps pace with the multiplication and distribution of Bibles. There are too many who can subscribe to the moral of what we know in one instance to have occurred. A pious Protestant lady offered a Bible to a plain commonsense man. " Begone with your Bibles," was his indignant reply. "Before you began distributing them, the boys would jump over my fence and steal my peaches ; now they break the fence down to steal more freely."

The Bible mania, indeed, makes " the word of God dwell more plentifully in all," but it is in the shape of dead letters, covered in ink, and buried in paper. If this be the " dwelling of the word " which the blessed apostle meant, we have undoubtedly reached the last degree of perfection; but if he spoke of another dwelling of the word of God, we may, for aught that appears, have fallen back not a little. We do not find among these Bible-maniacs any who seem inclined to renounce every thing on earth, to deny themselves, take up their cross, and follow Christ. We have not heard of many who have sold all they had, that they might buy the pearl of evangelical poverty. We read of St. Anthony, that, on hearing these words, "Go sell all thou hast, and give to the poor," he immediately put this lesson of evangelical perfection in practice. We have yet to learn of similar instances as the effect of the distribution of Bibles. One thing we know, that many there are who seldom or never take a Bible in their hand, who yet have constantly in their minds, in their hearts, and in their daily life the words of St. Paul, "Whether you eat or drink, or whatsoever ye do, do all things for the glory of God"; and we hazard nothing in saying that these are they in whom the word of God dwells plentifully, even though they know not how to read; and we cannot be blamed for preferring these to the proud and wordly-minded, though able to boast of a house full of Bibles.

It were well if sterility of good works were the only consequence of the promiscuous distribution of the word of God. But this distribution is not only inadequate to the production of good, but it has been and cannot fail to be the occasion, if not the direct cause, of serious and enormous evils. A thing may be in itself good and holy, and yet not be fitting for all, —nay, even be most prejudicial to those who are only prepared to abuse it. Hence, the church, while revering the word, and preserving it with an affection and fidelity of which Protestants can form no conception, has yet always protested against this Protestant mania, for mania it is. She obeys the words of Christ, "Give not that which is holy unto dogs, neither cast ye your pearls before swine"; and this distribution of the Bible indiscriminately to all sorts of persons, whether prepared to receive and read it with the proper dispositions, with due reverence for the word of God, or not, is a flagrant violation of the precept contained in these words of our Lord. The Scriptures are holy, a treasure of infinite value to the Christian church; but they are profitable only to such as are initiated into and well grounded in Christianity; to others, they are in general poisonous and destructive. From the reading of the Bible by those not prepared to profit by it has resulted the wildest and maddest fanaticism; and the "thousand and one" sects which have afflicted the Christian world since Luther, and which every right-minded man must deeply deplore, owe their origin to no other cause.

People reading the Bible have, as St. Paul complains, 1 Tim. i. 7, learned to assume the title of Doctors of the Law, though "understanding neither the things they say, nor whereof they affirm." Many by this reading have lost their faith; and, indeed, if the apparent contradictions found in the Bible give no little trouble even to the learned, and have been the occasion of voluminous commentaries, what temptations must they not offer to a mere sciolist? Voltaire thought there was no more effectual way of speading infidelity than by the Bible explained in his own way; and the grand means on which unbelievers of our day rely for spreading their creed of unbelief is the same. Deprive them of these *apparent* contradictions and inconsistencies, of the difficulties and objections which they find or suppose they find in the Scriptures themselves, and they would have very few arguments with which to perplex the unlearned and captivate the conceited and vain. And what shall we say of the imminent danger young persons particularly must run of shipwrecking their purity and chastity, when they read the impure actions related in the Old Testament in all the simplicity of primitive manners? Alas! they need not so much to inflame their passions, and it will be well if they escape without approving even in theory some crimes which they find to have been committed by persons eminent, in general, for their good qualities and deeds! We could easily enlarge on this topic, but forbear, lest we fall into the very inconvenience we are speaking against. It is, however, a topic well worthy the serious consideration of those who affect to be so shocked with certain passages in our *Moral Theologies*, not intended for general reading, but simply to prepare the moral physician for treating the moral diseases which, unhappily, he is but too sure to encounter in the practice of his profession. Looking to the little good and the enormous evils which result from this indiscriminate distribution of Bibles, to the character of the book itself, and its utter unfitness to serve as the summary of Christian doctrine or as the introduction to religious truth, its obscurities and acknowledged difficulties, many of which baffle the skill of the ablest and most learned commentators, and the ease and readiness with which the unlearned and unstable wrest it to their own destruction, we are forced to conclude that a more ineffectual and absurd way of making the word of God dwell plentifully in all, and to answer the end for which it was designed, than this proposed by Protestants, could not easily be devised.

But we come at length to the last two articles of the chapter on the Scriptures. We give them together, for they both mean the same thing, and together form a suitable keystone to the arch of Presbyterianism. They are as follows:—

"Art. IX. The infallible rule of interpretation of Scripture is the Scripture itself; and therefore, when there is a question about the true and full sense of any Scripture (which is not manifold, but one), it may be searched and known from other places that speak more clearly. X. The Supreme Judge, by whom all controversies of religion are to be determined, and all decrees of councils, opinions of ancient writers, doctrines of men, and private spirits are to be examined, and in whose sentence we are to rest, can be no other than the Holy Spirit speaking in the Scriptures.

"Acts xv. 15. And to this agree the words of the prophets, as it is written. John v. 46. For had ye believed Moses ye would have believed me, for he wrote of me. Matt. xxii. 29, 31. Ye do error, not knowing the Scriptures nor the power of God. Eph. iv. 20. Acts xxviii. 25."

Singular articles these! Reduced to plain English, they are simply, Scripture interprets itself, and God is the supreme judge of religious controversies. The proofs in the notes are in keeping with the assertions in the text. They have, however, the merit, if not of proving the assertions, at least that of disproving them. They show us our blessed Lord reasoning from the Scriptures against the Jews, and in his own person giving them an example and establishing the necessity of a *living* tribunal, a speaking judge, for the interpretation of Scripture and the determining of controversies of religion. So far as the example of our Lord and the occasion he found for correcting the Jews in their understanding of the Scriptures can count for any thing, they establish the contrary of what they were brought to prove. It is remarkable how difficult it is for Presbyterians to quote any Scriptural authority in their defence which does not make against them. There is a providence in this, cheering to the faithful, but which should make Presbyterians fear and tremble.

But, in these articles, we have the secret arrived at by our Presbyterian divines as the result of their long and laborious researches. It is now laid open before us. Come, ye men of the Old School, of the New School, Cumberland and all other species of Presbyterians, ye Congregationalists, Baptists, Methodists, Unitarians, Universalists, and hearken to this lesson of profoundest wisdom! Why in vain dispute and quarrel, why worry and devour each other, about the various matters which separate you one from another? Let the Bible decide. Call forthwith a "world's convention" of all the sects; let them assemble; let the Bible be placed reverently on a stand; let all keep silence; the book will open its mouth, utter a sentence, and all your controversies will be settled, and ye will all bow down in meek and humble submission. How simple and easy! What a pity men should not have discovered this admirable method of settling controversies, before the Westminster divines! Alas! the controversy between sectarians is precisely as to what the decision of the Bible is!

Presbyterians, however, have been driven to adopt this rule by the necessity they were under of steering between two formidable sand-bars. If they acknowledged in the church an always living and divinely instituted tribunal for the determination of controversies, it was all over with them; for that tribunal existed at the birth of Presbyterianism, and had condemned it; and on the other hand, they were ashamed to avow, in just so many words, that every one interprets the Bible as he thinks proper. If the first, they condemned themselves, and must, to be consistent, return to the church; if the second, then they must adopt an absurdity too gross even for them to swallow. What, then, could they do? Mystify themselves and others with high-sounding words, meaning nothing. They must say, Scripture interprets itself, and the Holy Ghost is the supreme judge of controversies. But as the Holy Ghost decides, according to them, only as *speaking in the Scriptures*, and as the Bible has never been heard to utter a single syllable, they gain nothing, but are ultimately reduced to the rule, Each one understands the Scriptures as he chooses,—the great fundamental principle of Protestantism, and nearly the only one in which all Protestants are able to agree. So, after all, in trying to avoid one sand-bar, they stick fast on the other, or as one of our former legislators would express it, "In keeping clear of *Skiller*, they run foul of *Charybogus*."

We do not intend, on this occasion, to give the various and satisfactory proofs of the necessity or of the fact of a living tribunal in the Christian Church for determining religious controversies. But we may say, the tribunal alleged by Presbyterians is obviously no tribunal at all; and the fact, that they are ashamed to avow it, and seek in every possible way to disguise it, is a sufficient refutation of the principle of private interpretation, or, if not, it has already been several times and amply refuted in the pages of this journal, as well as elsewhere. It will suffice for our present purpose to adduce a couple of edifying commentaries on the Presbyterian rule, supplied by the very volume before us.

In the *Form of Government*, p. 364, we read,—" To the General Assembly belongs the power of deciding in all controversies respecting doctrine and discipline, of reproving, warning, or bearing testimony against error in doctrine, or immorality in practice, in any church, presbytery, or synod, ... of suppressing schismatical contentions and disputations;" and on page 378, that the Presbyterian minister who preaches at the ordination of a candidate is to propose to him the following questions:—" Do you believe the Scriptures of the Old and New Testaments to be the word of God, the only infallible rule of faith and practice? Do you sincerely receive and adopt the Confession of Faith of this Church as containing the system of doctrine taught in the Scriptures? . . . . . Do you promise *subjection to your brethren* in the Lord?" To all these questions the candidate answers in the affirmative.

Well done, O ye learned divines! These lessons of submission given to the candidate are admirable; these enactments to enforce obedience to the decisions of the General Assembly are truly edifying! But, dear friends, how could you so soon and so completely forget and abandon your cherished and favorite doctrine? How could you write one thing in the beginning of your book, and give it such a flat denial in the end? How could you establish one principle in the *Confession*, and a contrary principle in the *Form of Government?* Indeed, most amiable doctors, you hardly treat us fairly. Which are we to believe, the *Confession* or the *Form of Government?* In one place you tell us the Scripture and the Scripture alone can interpret itself; and now in another, instead of the Scriptures, you give us the decisions of the General Assembly. You told us that the supreme judge in controversies can be none other than the Holy Spirit; and now, when controversies arise among you, instead of having recourse to "the Holy Spirit speaking in the Scriptures," you modestly invest the General Assembly with "the power of deciding all controversies." In the *Confession* you solemnly assert that "the decrees of councils, the opinions of ancient writers, the doctrines of men, and private spirits," are to be brought only before the bar of the supreme judge, "the Holy Spirit speaking in the Scriptures"; and now you summon us before the bar of the General Assembly, that is to say, before a couple of hundred of Presbyterian ministers, and a like number of Presbyterian *elders!* You were telling us, a moment ago, that the Holy Spirit speaks only through the Scriptures; and now you tell us, that he speaks through the Presbyterian elders of the United States! Really, gentlemen, this obliviousness on your part is too bad, altogether too bad. Alas for the poor candidate! How deplorable is his fate! After having received the assurance of having no other interpreter of Scripture than Scripture itself, and no other judge but the Holy Spirit speaking in the Scriptures, he now finds that all was a delusion, and that he must tamely promise subjection to his brethren, and follow their decision, or be ignominiously dismissed and branded for life.

Alas! how many lies does that first lie render necessary! Thus it is that error must necessarily stamp all its proceedings with contradiction and lie. *Mentita est iniquitas sibi.* Protestants, and Presbyterians in particular, were at first most obstreporous against all authority; for this was necessary in order to be able to wrest a portion of the faithful from their legitimate pastors. But having done this, and finding that no shadow of government or society was possible on the principles they at first set up, they turn round, and with admirable coolness deny and reject those very principles without which they had never existed, and institute in their novel and self-constituted tribunals the most intolerable tyranny, in the place of the paternal authority they threw off, and which had received the traditions of all Christian nations, and the promise of the divine protection and guidance. But it was not to be supposed that such tribunals, such supreme judges, would command any respect, or much submission. Dissent breeds dissent. The first dissenters authorize by precept and example the new dissenters. What right had you to dissent from the authority to which you were born subject, which we have not to dissent from you? Hence, the decisions of these tribunals and judges are followed only so long as force, or self-interest, money, or social position are present to back them; when not supported by such or like considerations, they are mere cobwebs. Hence, Protestantism is everywhere cut up into divisions sects, parties, and factions, too numerous to count, and which serve only to worry and devour each other, and to place in bold contrast the majestic and compact unity of the Catholic Church.

THE TWO BROTHERS; OR, WHY ARE YOU A PROTESTANT?

[From Brownson's Quarterly Review for 1847—8.]

CHAPTER I.

My old master, Jeremiah Milwood, as I have told you, had but two children, both sons, and with only about two years' difference in their ages. They were his pride, and he spared no pains or expense in their education. He was a stanch Presbyterian; and his highest ambition for his two sons was, that they should become earnest, devoted, and distinguished Presbyterian ministers. He seemed likely to be gratified. Both were of a serious turn, studious and piously inclined. Before the elder had completed his seventeenth year, both became subjects of grace, and both, on leaving college, entered the seminary.

During the second year of their residence in the seminary, their mother, a woman of great strength of character and sweetness of disposition, fell ill and died. From that moment, a striking change was observed in the tone and manner of John, the elder brother. He was his mother's favorite, and shared especially her confidence. At her request, he had spent several hours with her alone just previously to her death, and, though none of us knew what transpired to affect him, it was subsequently surmised, from one or two words which escaped him, that she had expressed, in that trying moment, to him, as the only member of her family she could hope to influence, or to whom she felt able to open her heart, some misgivings as to the truth of Presbyterianism, and had begged him, by his love of her and his regard for the welfare of his soul, to examine thoroughly its foundations before entering the ministry. However this might be, it is certain he was never again what he had been. He returned, after the obsequies, to the seminary, and even remained there several months; but he lost his relish for the prescribed course of studies, and became unwilling to attend the services in the chapel. Finally, he wrote to his father, informing him that he did not wish to become a Presbyterian minister, and, indeed, could not, without binding himself to profess what he did not then believe and in all probability never should believe, and begging permission to return home and take some other calling. My old master, you know, was never remarkable for his sweetness and amiability, and the recent affliction he suffered in the loss of his wife had rendered him doubly sour and morose. His wrath was terrible. His son had disappointed him, disgraced him, and he replied to him, that, unless he continued at the seminary and returned to his original faith and resolution, he was henceforth no son of his, and must seek a home, father, and friends where he could find them. John, knowing explanation or expostulation would be vain, took the only alternative left him, and suffered himself to be exiled from his home. James, the younger brother, who in many respects resembled his father, remained at the seminary and completed his course.

John withdrew to a distant part of the country, assumed his mother's name, and supported himself for three or four years by teaching at an academy. While teaching he contrived to study law, in the practice of which he subsequently engaged, distinguished himself, and, in a few years, amassed a fortune adequate to his simple wants and tastes. Having done this, he retired from business and went abroad. James, on completing his course, was licensed to preach, and in a few months was called and ordained to the pastoral charge of a wealthy and influential congregation in one of our principal Atlantic cities, and was soon known and esteemed as one of the leading ministers of his denomination. About a year after his settlement, his father died and left him the bulk of his estate, which was considerable; and a year later he married the beautiful and accomplished daughter and heiress of his richest parishioner, who brought him a still more ample fortune, and became the mother of five children, two sons and three daughters. Every thing prospered with him, and he had all that heart could wish. But, after a while, the tide of prosperity began to ebb; death visited his home, and his children, one by one, all, save the youngest, who was deformed, sickly, and partially idiotic, were taken from him, and at length his wife followed them. He bore up with stoical fortitude against these repeated blows, but he felt them,—was forced to reflect on the certainty of death, the uncertainty of life, and the perishable nature of all earthly goods, more seriously than he had ever done before, and to some extent his heart was softened and his spirit bowed.

Time had hardly worn off the wire-edge of his grief and begun to heal the wound in his heart, when he was surprised by a letter from his brother, whom he had neither seen nor heard from for nearly thirty years. The letter offered him such sympathy and consolation as befitted the occasion, and brought him the intelligence that its writer was about to revisit his native land, and, following the yearnings of his heart, would hasten to embrace the brother he had never for a moment forgotten, or ceased to love. James received the letter with mixed emotions, but upon the whole without displeasure, and looked forward even with interest to his brother's return. In a few weeks after sending his letter, John embarked, and, favored with a short and pleasant voyage across the Atlantic, landed in the city in which James was settled, and without delay drove with his baggage to his brother's residence. The brothers met; but so altered in appearance was each, that it was with difficulty that either could recognize his brother in the other. The meeting was frank and cordial on the part of the elder, and less cold and restrained on the part of the younger than could have been expected from his general character. Perhaps he had recently had some compunctious visitings of conscience for having so long forgotten even to think of one he was bound by the ties of nature to love; perhaps he had a vein of tenderness in his nature which had not hitherto been observed, and that early scenes and early recollections revived, and for the moment half subdued, the sectarian and minister. But be this as it may, he was not displeased to meet his brother. They were soon seated in a well-furnished apartment, engaged in free and familiar conversation. They recalled their boyish days and boyish frolics, spoke of their college life and college companions, and finally of their mother and her lamented death. The tone of both was subdued, and they turned their conversation upon death, sin, redemption, the resurrection, and immortal life. While speaking on these awful and sublime topics, John referred to the change which early came over him with regard to his religious views, and stated that he was, and for years had been, a member of the Roman Catholic Church. This was unexpected as well as unwelcome news to James. If his brother had told him that he had become a Socinian or even an unbeliever, he would not have been surprised, and could have borne it; but to be told that he, the principal mover of the Protestant league for the conversion of the pope and the overthrow of popery, had himself a brother who had turned Papist, was more than he could bear. He was thunderstruck, and seemed for some minutes as one bereft of thought and sense. Never had he been known to be so overcome. At length, he partially recovered, and said to his brother,—" Mr. Milwood, your room is ready; I must wrestle with God in prayer for you before I can speak to you again." John bade him good night, and quietly retired to his room. It was already late in the evening, and, offering a prayer for his brother, another for the repose of the soul of his mother, and commending himself to his heavenly Father and the protection of our Lady and all the saints, he composed himself, with a subdued but serene mind, to rest.

CHAPTER II.

THE brothers met again in the morning in the breakfast-parlor. James was exteriorly composed, and greeted his brother in his blandest tone; but a careful observer would have suspected that he intended to play the part of the civil and courteous host, rather than that of the warm and affectionate brother. Breakfast passed pretty much in silence. John was disposed to wait the motions of his brother, and James was undecided whether to broach the Catholic question or not. But he could not converse freely with his brother on indifferent matters; he felt that sooner or later he must discuss the question, and perhaps the sooner the better. Revolving the matter for some time in his mind, he at length, throwing aside the morning paper he had been pretending to read, broke the silence by remarking to his brother:—

"So it seems the result has been that you have turned Papist?"

"I am a *Catholic*," replied John, with a slight emphasis on the last word, intended as a quiet rebuke to his brother for employing a nickname.

"It is strange! What in the world could have induced the son of a Presbyterian father, piously brought up, well instructed in the Protestant religion, and not wanting in natural ability, to take a step so foolish, not to say so wicked?"

"Let me rather ask my brother why he is a Protestant?"

"Why I am a Protestant?"

"Yes; I am much mistaken, or that is the harder question of the two to answer."

"I am a Protestant because the Romish Church is corrupt, the Mystery of Iniquity, the Man of Sin, Antichrist, the Whore of Babylon, drunk with the blood of the saints, a cage of unclean birds, cruel, oppressive, tyrannical, superstitious, idolatrous——"

"But you are simply telling me why you are not a Catholic; my question is, Why are you a Protestant?"

"Protestantism is a solemn protest against Rome, and my reasons for not being a Catholic are my reasons for being a Protestant."

"Jews, pagans, Mahometans, deists, atheists, protest as earnestly as you do against Rome; are they therefore Protestants?"

"Protestantism is, indeed, a protest against Rome; but it is also a positive religion."

"Unaffected by supposing the Catholic Church to have never been or to have ceased to be?"

"Yes; Protestantism is independent of Romanism."

"A Protestant is one who embraces Protestantism in this independent, positive sense?"

"Yes, if we speak properly."

"Before telling me why you are a Protestant, it will be necessary to tell what, in this sense, Protestantism is."

"It is the religion of the Bible;—the Bible is the religion of Protestants."

"And the religion of the Bible is——?"

"The truths revealed in the Bible."

"And these are——?"

"The great evangelical doctrines asserted by the reformers against the false and corrupt doctrines of Rome, and which we commonly call the doctrines of grace."

"These doctrines are Protestantism?"

"They are."

"So Protestantism is the religion of the Bible, and the religion of the Bible is Protestantism!"

"There is nothing absurd or ridiculous in that. Protestantism, Sir, *is* the religion of the Bible, of the whole Bible, the Bible alone,—that precious gift of God to man,—the word of God, the charter of our liberties, the source of redemption, the ground of the Christian's hope, carrying light and life, the blessings of truth, freedom, and civilization, wherever it goes; and which you Papists, with characteristic cunning, lock up from the people, because you know full well, that, were they once to read it for themselves, they would make short work with the pope and his minions, break their covenant with death and hell, and put an end to their blasphemies, idolatries, and oppressions."

"I suspect, brother, you have accommodated that from the speech you made at the last anniversary of the American Bible Society. It may do very well to address to the mob that collects on 'anniversary week'; but can you not give me a clear, distinct, and precise statement of what Protestantism really is?"

"Protestantism is the great truth asserted by the reformers against Rome, that the Scriptures of the Old and New Testaments contain all things necessary to salvation, and that they are the sole and sufficient rule of faith and practice."

"If I believe the Scriptures are sufficient, and are the sole rule of faith and practice, do I believe the whole of Protestantism?"

"No; you must also believe the word of God as contained in the Scriptures."

"And this word consists of certain *credenda* or propositions to be believed?"

"It does; and these may all be summed up in the text,—'Believe on the Lord Jesus Christ, and thou shalt be saved.'"

"To believe *on* the Lord Jesus Christ is to believe——?"

"The truths he has revealed, whether of himself, or other things."

"These truths are——?"

"The great evangelical doctrines asserted by the reformers."

"That is, they are Protestantism. Therefore, Protestantism is—Protestantism! But can you not be a little more particular, and tell me what these truths or doctrines are?"

"You will find an excellent summary of them in the Westminster Confession of Faith, and the Larger and Shorter Catechisms."

"That is, they are Presbyterianism? Protestantism, then, is Presbyterianism."

"What else, from my profession as a Presbyterian minister, should you infer to be my belief?"

"I am rather slow to infer a Presbyterian minister's belief from his profession. But, if Protestantism be Presbyterianism, none but Presbyterians can be Protestants. Is this your belief?"

"Not exactly; for there are Protestants who are not Presbyterians."

"These, of course, differ more or less from Presbyterians, or else they would be Presbyterians. Consequently Protestantism must differ more or less from Presbyterianism."

"In non-essentials, but not in essentials. All who embrace the essentials are Protestants."

"Do Catholics embrace the essentials?"

"According to the general opinion of Protestants, they do."

"Then, according to the general opinion of Protestants, Catholics are Protestants?"

"But I think differently, and our General Assembly will soon, I hope, solemnly declare that Rome does not retain even the essentials of the Christian faith."

"That will be a sad day for Rome, no doubt; but what, in your judgment, are the essentials?"

"They are the great evangelical doctrines of the reformation, embraced by all orthodox Protestants."

"And *orthodox* Protestants are―――?"

"All who agree in accepting the sufficiency of the Scriptures, and the great essential doctrines of revelation."

"Which means that the essential doctrines are the essential doctrines, and orthodox Protestants are orthodox Protestants."

"The essential doctrines are substantially what is held by Presbyterians."

"Those orthodox Protestants who are not Presbyterians differ from Presbyterians only in relation to non-essentials?"

"That is all."

"Presbyterianism, or, what is the same thing, the orthodox faith, then, is made up of two parts, one essential, the other non-essential?"

"All parts of the orthodox faith are not alike essential. But there may be differences which are not differences of faith. The Congregationalists, Evangelical Episcopalians, Dutch Reformed, the Calvinistic Baptists, &c., differ from us in matters of discipline and church government, while they embrace substantially the same faith we do."

"Is infant baptism a matter of faith?"

"Not strictly."

"Then you do not baptize infants because you believe Almighty God commands you to baptize them?"

"We do; but the point is not so essential, that those who differ from us must needs err essentially."

"One may, then, reject a positive command of God, without essential error?"

"We think our Baptist brethren err grievously; but, as they hold the great cardinal doctrines of the Gospel, we do not think their error is absolutely essential. In the present state of the religious world, it is the duty of God's people to make the platform of Christian union as broad as possible, to discountenance theological wranglings, to seek to heal sectarian divisions, and to follow after the things which make for peace."

"But if you had no fears of popery, and felt that your own sect had the power to make converts, I suppose you would regard the Baptists as of the number of those who bring in 'damnable heresies.'"

"You are ungenerous; I regret the unsoundness of my Baptist brethren, but I do not consider them as essentially wrong."

"Not even when they deny you the Christian character, by denying that your baptism is baptism,—and when they refuse to commune with you, on the ground that you are unbaptized persons; that is, infidels, in the proper sense of the word?"

"There they are wrong; but still not essentially so, because baptism itself is a non-essential."

"Then you do not agree in opinion with our Lord, who says, 'Unless a man be born again of *water* and of the Holy Ghost, he shall not enter into the kingdom of heaven?'"

"Christian doctrines are distinguishable into fundamentals and non-fundamentals. The fundamentals are the essentials, the non-fundamentals are the non-essentials. All who believe the former are substantially orthodox, though they may differ about the latter."

"The non-fundamentals are either revealed truths, or they are not. If they are not, your distinction of fundamentals and non-fundamentals is simply a distinction between what is revealed and what is not revealed, between the word of God and the words of men or of devils; and, on this supposition, the essentials will be what God has revealed, and the non-essentials what he has not revealed. If they are revealed truths, you imply that a portion of the revealed word is unessential, and may be disbelieved or rejected without essential error. Which do you say?"

"Suppose we say they are no portion of the revealed word?"

"You cannot say that, because you have declared them to be revealed truths, by asserting that *Christian* doctrines are distinguishable into fundamentals and non-fundamentals. But pass over this. If you say the non-fundamentals, that is, the non-essentials, are not revealed truths, you imply, by making the fundamentals essential to be believed, that the *whole* revealed word is essential to be believed, and therefore deny that there can be any differences of opinion as to any portion of what is revealed, without essential error, which renders your distinction between fundamentals and non-fundamentals of no avail; since no one, unless a Protestant, is likely to contend that any thing more than what is revealed is essential to be believed. Is it not so?"

"So it appears."

"Then again, you say, men, though differing about the non-essentials, that is, about what is not revealed, are substantially orthodox, if they believe the essentials, that is, what is revealed. Now they may differ about the non-essentials, by believing, some, that they are, and some, that they are not, revealed truths, or portions of the word of God, as we see in the case of you and the Baptists concerning infant baptism; you believing it to be revealed and commanded by God himself, they believing it not revealed and implicitly forbidden. Now, if men may believe the non-essentials to be revealed, they may, according to you, without essential error, believe that to be the word of God which is the word of men or of devils. Do you admit this?"

"Of course not. 'Cursed is every one that addeth to the words of this book.' The condemnation of Rome is not so much that she denies the essential truths of the Christian religion, as that she overlays them by her corrupt additions, and renders them of none effect through the traditions of men. It is as much an error to add to the word as to take from it."

"Then you abandon this supposition, and take the other, —that the non-essentials are revealed truths, portions of the word of God?"

"Be it so, for the present."

"Then you must say, since you allow men to believe or reject them, without essential error, that a portion of the word of God, of the truth Almighty God has revealed, may be denied without essential error. Do you hold that one can be substantially orthodox, and yet deny a portion of God's word?"

"Even your own doctors distinguish between fundamentals and non-fundamentals, and teach that faith in the fundamentals suffices for salvation."

"This, even if true, would not avail you; for our doctors are no authority for you, and you cannot urge them against me in this discussion, since I am not defending the church. But it is not true. Our doctors distinguish between the articles of the creed which are logically fundamental or primary, and those which are secondary, I admit; but they do not teach that faith in the primary alone suffices for salvation. They teach that the *whole* must be believed, either explicitly or implicitly, and simply add, that *explicit* faith in the primary articles, with implicit faith in the secondary, is all that is necessary, *necessitate medii.*"

"That is all I ask. He who believes explicitly the primary believes implicitly the secondary; for the primary imply the secondary."

"So, on the other hand, he who explicitly *dis*believes the secondary, implicitly disbelieves the primary; for the secondary presuppose or imply the primary. No man believes implicitly what he explicitly denies. But you hold the non-fundamentals may be explicitly denied without essential error; therefore, you cannot assume that they are implicitly believed."

"But do you pretend that every thing, however unimportant or insignificant, is essential to be believed?"

"Your faith, not mine, is the matter in question."

"As a Catholic, you are bound to hold that the book of Tobias is the word of God. In that book I read that Toby had a dog, and that the dog came to his master, wagging his tail. Is it essential to your salvation, that you believe with a firm faith that Toby really had a dog, and that the dog actually did wag his tail?"

"That is not precisely the question. Assuming the inspiration of the book, can you *deny* the fact without essential error?"

"Why not? Common sense teaches us that the fact is not and cannot be in itself essential."

"And do you hold that there can be essential error only where the matter denied is in itself essential?"

"How can there be?"

"What, in *religious* or divine faith, is the immediate object believed?"

"The truth of the particular proposition, whatever it may be."

"Not exactly; for the faith is *religious* only where the proposition believed is a *revealed* proposition."

"The truth of the particular *revealed* proposition, then, whatever it may be."

"In believing, does the mind perceive the truth of the proposition believed, or only the proposition itself?"

"Explain yourself."

"What is faith, as distinguished from knowledge or science?"

"Faith is the substance of things hoped for, the evidence of things not seen."

"Or, as says St. Augustine,—*Fides est credere quod non vides*,—Faith is to believe what you do not see. But you must see or mentally apprehend the proposition, or you cannot assent to it. What, then, is that in the proposition which you assent to, but which you do not see?"

"The truth of the proposition."

"As in the proposition, 'God exists in unity of essence and trinity of persons,' you distinctly and immediately apprehend the proposition, but not its truth; otherwise, it would be a proposition, not of faith, but of knowledge or science,—knowledge, if perceived intuitively; science, if perceived only by means of discursion. Hence, rationalists, when they refuse to believe the mysteries of faith because they cannot immediately perceive their truth, deny, virtually, the possibility of faith, and fall into the absurdity of contending that they cannot have faith, unless it be knowledge or science; that is, they cannot have faith unless faith be impossible! Where there is sight, there is not faith. Hence we say, faith will lose itself in sight, hope be swallowed in fruition, but charity abideth for ever. I immediately perceive the propositions of faith, or the *credenda*; but not their intrinsic truth. Therefore, the *truth* of the revealed proposition cannot be that which is *immediately* believed or assented to."

"So it would seem."

"If it is not *immediately* believed, it must be *mediately* believed; that is, must be believed *in* some thing else, *on* or by some authority at least formally distinct from itself."

"That must be true; for faith is always by some authority distinct from the believer and the proposition believed."

"Then the *immediate* object believed will be, not the intrinsic truth of the proposition, but this authority in, on, or by means of which it is believed?"

"Be it so."

"Now, in *religious* faith, what is this?"

"The Bible, as all Protestants contend, in opposition to Romanists, who say it is the church."

"Catholics do not say the church is the authority for believing the *truth* of the revealed proposition, but simply for believing it is a revealed proposition; and, if you reflect a moment, you must admit that the Bible is at best only authority for believing this or that is revealed, not authority for believing that what is revealed is true."

"We recognize no authority above the Bible."

"Then you place the Bible above God himself, which I own is what you who call yourselves Protestants often have the appearance of doing; but this cannot be your meaning. All you can mean is, that, in determining what God has revealed, the Bible is the highest authority you recognize. But the Bible, although assumed to be the highest authority for determining what God has revealed, is yet no authority for saying what he reveals is true. Why do you believe what God reveals in or through the Bible is true?"

"Because it is his revelation, his word."

"That is, you believe it because God says it. But, in believing it because God says it, what is it you *immediately* believe?"

"God himself."

"That is, you believe the proposition because it is God's word, and you believe his word because you believe him. But why do you believe him?"

"Because it is impossible for him to lie."

"That is, because he is infinitely true, is truth itself, and can neither deceive nor be deceived?"

"I have no objection to that."

"Then the object immediately believed, in believing a revealed proposition, is the infinite truth or veracity of God who reveals it."

"Be it so."

"Which, in religious faith, then, shall we say is the more

essential point to be believed,—the matter revealed, or the infinite veracity of God who reveals it?"

"What is the difference?"

"The difference, perhaps, will appear, if you tell me what it is that makes the faith *religious* faith, or distinguishes it, as *religious* faith, from all other kinds of faith."

"It is religious faith because the proposition believed is a *revealed* proposition."

"If I believe the proposition, 'God exists in unity of essence and trinity of persons,' because you teach it, or because I think I have discovered and demonstrated it by my own reason, is my belief religious belief?"

"Why not, since the proposition in either case is the same? What difference can it make, if it be believed, for what reason or on what ground it is believed?"

"If I believe it because you teach it, I believe you, and what I immediately believe is that you are a man of truth and worthy of credit. Is there any thing religious in my believing you?"

"Not necessarily."

"If I believe it because I think I have discovered and demonstrated it by my own reason, I simply believe my own reason. Is to believe my own reason religious belief?"

"Certainly not."

"For, if it were, every belief, whether intuitive or scientific, would be religious, and the belief of falsehood as much as truth; since, in every act of belief, whether the belief be well founded or not, I believe my reason. But if I believe the proposition, not because you teach it, not because I discover or demonstrate it by my own reason, but because God says it, and therefore because I believe him, and that he is infinitely true, and can neither deceive me nor be deceived, and, furthermore, because he commands me to believe it, is my act now religious?"

"It is."

"Then it would seem that it is believing and obeying God, which makes the belief *religious* belief?"

"That appears to be so."

"Then the more essential point in *religious* belief is not simply belief of the matter revealed, but of God who reveals it?"

"Very well, let it be so."

"In every proposition, be it what it may, which I believe because God reveals it, I do believe him, do I not?"

"So it follows from what we have said."

"But if the more essential point is to believe God, the more essential error must be to disbelieve him, must it not?"

"Certainly, to disbelieve God is the most heinous offence of which man can be guilty. The grossest insult we can offer even to a fellow-mortal is to call him a liar; and we call God a liar, whenever we disbelieve or refuse to believe him."

"But do I not disbelieve or refuse to believe God, and therefore make God a liar, whenever I refuse to believe a proposition because I have only his word for it?"

"You do, and are guilty of the sin of infidelity."

"Then, if God has told me, no matter for what reason, that Toby had a dog and the dog wagged his tail, and I refuse to believe it, do I or do I not err essentially?"

"You err essentially, as it appears from what we have said."

"Then there may be essential error, where the matter or proposition denied is not in itself essential?"

"So it would seem."

"Then you will concede what you call the non-fundamentals, if revealed truths, can no more be denied without essential error than the fundamentals themselves?"

"Not at all. Doubtless, where the matter is clearly and manifestly revealed, refusal to believe is essential error; but it does not therefore follow that it is essential error to refuse to believe, where it is not clearly and manifestly revealed, where it is uncertain that God speaks, and, if he does, what is the exact meaning of what he says."

"This uncertainty, not the fundamental or non-fundamental nature of the matter in question, then, is that which saves the refusal to believe from being essential error?"

"That seems to follow."

"If the same uncertainty existed with regard to what is fundamental, the refusal to believe it would, then, no more be essential, than the refusal to believe the non-fundamentals?"

"That seems also to follow."

"In order, then to determine what are the essentials, that is, what must be believed, and cannot be denied without essential error, and what are the non-essentials, that is, what without essential error may be either believed or denied, it will be necessary to inquire, not what are the fundamentals and what the non-fundamentals, but what is or is not clearly and manifestly revealed."

"Since the fundamentals are all clearly and manifestly revealed, I have no objections to saying so."

"Whether the fundamentals are all clearly and manifestly revealed or not, you must so say, or abandon the ground you have taken. The essentials, then, are what is clearly and manifestly revealed?"

"Be it so."

"The non-essentials what is not clearly and manifestly revealed?"

"Agreed."

"He who believes all that is clearly and manifestly revealed believes all the essentials, is free from essential error, is substantially orthodox?"

"Agreed, again."

"He who rejects any truth clearly and manifestly revealed errs essentially?"

"He does."

"But he who rejects only the non-essentials does not err essentially?"

"Stop there a moment. Men may differ as to the non-essentials without essential error; but to differ in opinion about a point is not necessarily to deny it; for both parties may intend to believe it, and would, if they could only ascertain the truth involved."

"But individuals may differ in some respects, even as to matters of faith, from Presbyterians, without erring essentially?"

"I do not deny it."

"The points on which they differ must be non-essentials, otherwise the difference would be essential. In regard to these points they must differ from Presbyterians, either by holding some things to be revealed truths which Presbyterians do not, or by denying some things to be revealed truths which Presbyterians believe are revealed truths?"

"They may also differ from them by simple ignorance."

"That is true; but then they differ only negatively, not positively. Presbyterians in this respect must differ from one another; for some are better informed as to what Presbyterianism is than others are or can be; but they are, nevertheless, all alike Presbyterians. So I, as a Catholic, may be ignorant of some points of the Catholic faith, and in this respect *differ* from the one who knows them all; but I am as true a Catholic as he, because I intend to believe all the Church teaches, because I am ready to believe all as soon as explicitly propounded to me, and because the points on which I am ignorant I believe implicitly, since they are implied in what I believe explicitly. This is, therefore, a mere negative difference, and amounts to nothing. The differences in question are positive differences, and these must consist, either in believing things to be revealed which you deny to be revealed, or in denying certain things to be revealed which you believe to be revealed."

"I do not see how that follows."

"The differences we are considering concern matters of faith; and nothing, I suppose you will grant, is or can be matter of faith which is not a divinely revealed truth. Or, rather, no man can hold any thing to be matter of faith, unless he holds it to be matter of revelation, that is, a revealed truth."

"I do not know about that."

"But you do; for the faith we are speaking of is *religious* faith, and we have agreed that there can be *religious* faith only where the proposition believed is a *revealed* proposition."

"Very well, proceed."

"If, then, you admit differences as to matters of faith may exist without essential error, you must admit that the non-essentials may be either believed or *dis*believed without essential error, unless you choose to admit that you yourselves are in essential error."

"How so?"

"You certainly deny some things, which you call non-essentials, to be revealed truths; such, for instance, as the divine institution of the episcopacy, which is asserted by Protestant Episcopalians. But, if the non-essentials cannot be denied without essential error, then you err essentially in denying it. On the other hand, you assert infant baptism to be a divine command, which your Baptist brethren deny. Infant baptism, you say, is a non-essential; if, then, non-essentials cannot be positively denied without essential error, your Baptist brethren err essentially, and are not, as you have admitted, substantially orthodox. Moreover, unless you admit the non-essentials may be either believed or disbelieved without essential error, your distinction between essentials and non-essentials avails you nothing, and you must come back and assert that none, who differ positively in any matter from Presbyterians, have or can have the essential faith; and then you must recall your denial, and say that Presbyterianism and Protestantism are one and the same thing, and that Presbyterians are the only Protestants."

"Very well, I will not insist on the point. Say the non-essentials are matters which one may either believe or disbelieve without erring essentially."

"We now seem to be in a fair way of determining what Protestantism is. It is, you say, the essentials, and the essentials are all the truths clearly and manifestly revealed in the Scriptures of the Old and New Testaments. Tell me what these truths are, and you tell me what Protestantism is, and take the preliminary step towards answering my question, Why are you a Protestant?"

CHAPTER III.

MUCH to the relief of James, while he was considering what he should reply to John's last demand, the conversation was suspended by the entrance of Mr. Wilson, a brother Presbyterian minister, settled over the oldest Presbyterian congregation in the city. He was of Scottish descent, and upwards of seventy years of age,—a man of antiquated notions, with little respect for the younger ministers of his denomination. Presbyterianism, in his view, had nearly lost its original distinctive character. Wesley and Whitefield, by their appeals to heated passion and mere animal excitement, instead of reason and voluntary affection, had well nigh ruined it. Presbyterians were now Methodists, Arminians, in all except name and outward organization and government; and the new methods and measures lately adopted for the conversion of sinners appeared to him likely to prove in the end its total destruction. He saw with pain the lecture-room and rostrum superseding the pulpit, strolling evangelists and revival preachers the regular pastors, and "inquiry" and "anxious" meetings the orderly ministrations of the word.

Between him and James there was little sympathy. James was a man of his times. He understood the tendencies of his age and country, and held that it was the part of wisdom, if not indeed of duty, to yield to and obey them. To have power over the people, he held it to be necessary to consult them, to change with them, to take the direction they indicate, to be always just in advance of them, and never to lag behind them. He availed himself of their passions and tendencies as the readiest way of occupying the post of leader, and, if he could only occupy that post, the direction he followed or the final goal he might reach was comparatively indifferent. He was adroit, shrewd, unscrupulous, but he did not know that he who leads the mob only by yielding to them leads them only by being their slave. The true leader is he who makes the multitude follow him, not he who follows them. He who has principles and will stand by them, though he stand alone, or be hewn down by the maddened multitude for his fidelity to them, is by many degrees superior to him who sacrifices his principles, if he have any, to popularity, or who has no principles but to ascertain and yield to the passions and tendencies of the age or country. But of all this James knew, at least, cared, nothing. He lived in an age and country of demagogues, and he did not aspire to be thought superior to his age and compatriots. The greatest modern achievement in the state, he was accustomed to hear it boasted, had been to establish the rule of demagogues; and why should it not be as glorious to establish this rule in the church as in the state?

Little as James sympathized ordinarily with Mr. Wilson, he welcomed him in the present instance with great cordiality, and introduced him to his brother. After some commonplace remarks, he told him he had just learned that his brother, who had been absent for many years, had become a Catholic. He recapitulated the conversation they had just had, stated the point at which it had arrived, and begged Mr. Wilson to answer the question they were debating. Mr. Wilson was not pleased with the course adopted by James, and replied:—

"If I had had the management of this discussion from the beginning, I should have given it another direction. Your brother has, doubtless, been under the training of the Jesuits, is versed in all their scholastic refinements and subtilties, and a perfect master of all the sophistical arts by which they entrap and bewilder the simple and unwary. When you dispute with such a man, mind and keep the management of the argument in your own hands. Consent to ply the laboring oar yourself, and you are gone. The great secret of dialectics is in knowing how to put your questions. You gentlemen of the modern school are far abler demagogues than logicians, and much better skilled in exciting the passions of the mob than in managing a discussion. I have often told you the folly and madness of neglecting severer studies. You have studied only to conform to the multitude; you have made the mob supreme, and taught them to lord it over their pastors, loosened them from their old moorings, set them adrift upon a stormy and tempestuous sea, without helm or helmsman, or rather with the helmsman bound to obey the helm. Their passions are a favorable gale for you to-day; but what certainty have you that they may not make the port of Rome, or be stranded on the rocky beach of popery, to-morrow? Attempt to guide or control them, cross in any thing their prejudices or their wishes, and where are they,—where are you? How often must I tell you, it is hard making the port of the Gospel with the devil for pilot? If you had had a grain of common sense, you would have insisted on your brother's answering your question, why he had become a Catholic, instead of consenting, as a great fool, to answer his question, why you are a Protestant. If you had been acquainted with the old Protestant controversialists, you would have seen that they leave Protestantism to take care of itself, while they reserve all their forces for the attack upon Rome."

"Never mind that now, Brother Wilson. I could hardly foresee the turn the conversation would take, for those Catholics I have known have generally contented themselves with replying to the charges brought against their church, without going far in their attacks upon Protestantism; and besides, it is no more than right, since Protestantism is a positive religion, that they who profess it should define what they mean by it, and give their reasons for believing it."

"If the old Protestant masters of whom Mr. Wilson speaks," interposed John, "had thought of that, and, before attacking Catholicity, had defined and established a religion of their own, my brother would have had an easy task now, if indeed any task at all."

"The true polemical policy is always to keep yourself and party on the offensive; but if you imagine that Protestantism, as a positive religion, is indefinable and indefensible, you are very much mistaken."

"The readiest way to convict me of that will be to define it, and give me good and valid reasons for believing it."

"In becoming a Catholic you abjured Protestantism. Am I to infer that you abjured you knew not what?"

"Mr. Wilson pays me but a sorry compliment, if he supposes I shall voluntarily surrender what he terms the true polemical policy. The question is not what I may or may not know of Protestantism, what I may or may not have abjured, on becoming a Catholic, but what Protestantism is, as understood by those who profess it?"

"But, if you were not fully informed as to what Protestantism really was, how could you know that in abjuring it you were not abjuring the truth?"

"He who has the truth has no need of knowing the systems opposed to it, in order to know that they must be false. But suppose you proceed with your definition. You profess to be a Protestant, and so able, experienced, and learned a man cannot be supposed to profess to believe he knows not what. If you know what it is, you can easily tell me."

"I will give you Dr. Owen's definition. I dare say your brother James has never read Owen's works, nor Boston's, nor those of any other man who was in breeches fifty years ago. It is a shame to think how the old worthies are neglected. Nobody reads them now-a-days. The study of school divinity is wholly neglected. Our theologians are frightened at a folio, tremble at a quarto, can hardly endure even an octavo. The demand is for works, 'short, pithy, and pungent.' It is the age of petty Tracts, Penny Magazines, Peter Parleys, Robert Merrys, trash, nonsense, and humbug."

"And yet it is the glorious age on which the glorious sun of the glorious reformation beams in all its effulgence. If the reformers were here, they would exclaim, *Et tu, Brute!*"

"I hope Mr. Wilson will not heed my brother's sneer," interposed James; "but proceed with his definition."

"Brother Milwood, have you Owen's works? No? No, I dare say not. But I presume you have Dowling, D'Aubigné, and the last new novel."

"I do not read novels."

"The best thing you have said for yourself yet. Well, I see I must quote from memory. Protestantism,—remember I quote the *great* Dr. Owen, one of those sound old English divines who cared as little for prelacy as for papacy, and would no more submit to king than to pope. They were the men. It will be long before we shall look upon their like again. They were God's freemen. The pomps and vanities of the world could not dazzle or blind them. They cared not for crown or mitre, and the blood of a king was to them as the blood of a common man. They went straight to their object. England was not worthy of them. The Lord directed them here. Here they laid the foundations of a noble empire. This is their work; this land is their land, and their children's after them, and a crying shame is it, that a miserable, idolatrous Papist should be suffered to pollute it with his accursed foot."

"But you are thinking of the Independents, rather than of the Presbyterians. The Presbyterians were for king and covenant, and pretend to have disapproved of the execution of Charles Stuart."

"No matter. The Independents only completed what the Presbyterians began, and soon sunk into insignificance when left to struggle alone. In the glorious war against prelacy and papacy they were united as brothers, as I trust will always be their children."

"But the definition."

"Remember, I quote the words of the great Dr. Owen, great and good, notwithstanding he left the Presbyterians and became a Congregationalist;—excepting in matters of church government, rigidly orthodox, and as much superior to the degenerate race of ministers in our day, as a huge old folio is to a modern penny tract, and whose works I recommend to both of you to read. Protestantism is,—'1. What was revealed unto the church by our Lord and his apostles, and is the whole of that religion which the Lord doth and will accept. 2. *So far as* needed unto faith, obedience, and salvation of the church, what they taught, revealed, and commanded is contained in the Scriptures of the New Testament, witnessed unto and confirmed by the Old. 3. All that is required, that we may please God, and be accepted with him, and come to the eternal enjoyment of him, is that we truly and sincerely believe what is so revealed and taught, yielding sincere obedience unto what is commanded in the Scriptures. 4. If in any thing they [Protestants] be found to deviate from them, if it [what they teach] exceed in any instance what is so taught and commanded, if it be defective in the faith or the practice of any thing so revealed or commanded, they are ready to renounce it.' What do you ask more clear, brief, comprehensive, and precise than that?"

"Did our Lord and his apostles reveal any religion which they did not reveal to the church, or which God doth not and will not accept?"

"Of course not."

"Then Mr. Owen might have said simply, Protestantism is what was revealed by our Lord and his apostles unto the church."

"Perhaps he might."

"What was so revealed is the true religion, is it not?"

"It is."

"Then he would have said all, if he had said, Protestantism is the true religion."

"Be it so."

"If you will now tell me what is the true religion, you will tell me what Protestantism is."

"Mr. Owen tells you in his second article."

"I beg your pardon. He tells me in that *where* the true religion is, so far as needed; but not *what* it is."

"In his third article, then."

"Not in that; for in that he simply tells me, that, if I believe and obey the true religion, so far as contained in the Scriptures of the New Testament, I have all that God requires of me."

"Well, in the fourth."

"But that simply informs me, that, if Protestants have mistaken the true religion, if they contend for more or for less than is contained in the Scriptures, they are ready to renounce *it;* although whether by *it* is to be understood true religion, the mistake, the excess, or the defect, he does not inform me. So, you perceive, I am not as yet told what Protestantism is."

"But you are told *where* it is, and that is enough."

"That may or may not be. The cook knew *where* the teakettle was when it fell overboard, but nevertheless he could not get it to make the captain's tea."

"It is in the New Testament, witnessed unto and confirmed by the Old. You can go there and find it for yourself."

"Has it any mark by which I may recognize it when I see it?"

"If you seek, you shall find. Our Lord himself says that, and I hope you will not dispute him."

"Does he say, if you seek *in the Scriptures of the New Testament*, you shall find?"

"Not expressly."

"Do all who seek in those Scriptures find?"

"All who faithfully study them and rightly understand them."

"Do all who attentively read them rightly understand them?"

"No; some wrest them to their own destruction, and bring in damnable heresies."

"You have faithfully studied and rightly understand them?"

"I think so."

"Lest I should be one of those who wrest them to my own destruction, suppose you tell me what is the true religion which they contain, or which I ought to find in them."

"If you are one who would wrest the Scriptures to your own destruction, you would do the same with my statement of what they contain. I should do you no good by complying with your request. If you believe not Moses and the prophets, neither will you believe me."

"How, then, am I ever to know certainly what this thing you call Protestantism, and say is the true religion, really is?"

"Read your Bible, Sir, with humble submission, without any reliance on yourself, with sincere and earnest prayer to the Holy Ghost to enlighten you, and you will be led into all truth."

"Perhaps so. But our question is not, What is truth? but, What is Protestantism?"

"Have I not told you Protestantism is the true religion? He, then, who is led to the truth must needs be led to Protestantism."

"I stand corrected. But since some do wrest the Scriptures to their own destruction, and bring in 'damnable heresies,' how do you determine infallibly that you may not yourself be one of them?"

"I am accustomed, Sir, to being treated with respect, and I trust you mean me no insult."

"They who are accustomed to be treated with respect are, in general, slow to think themselves insulted. If Mr. Wilson does not know infallibly that he rightly understands the Scriptures, he cannot deny that it is possible he may be wresting them to his own destruction."

"Through God's distinguishing grace vouchsafed to me, for no worthiness of mine, I have been enabled to see and know the truth."

"Is that same grace vouchsafed to all?"

"To all whom God has preordained unto everlasting life; but those whom he has from all eternity reprobated to everlasting death, for the praise of his vindictive justice, he leaves to their reprobate sense, to their own blindness, and even sends them strong delusions, that they may believe a lie and be damned."

"And these never had it in their power to come to the knowledge of the truth and be saved?"

"If they had willed."

"Were they ever able to have willed?"

"Naturally, yes; morally, no."

"But actually?"

"No. Those whom God ordains to everlasting death he ordains to sin, that they may be damned justly."

"That is a hard doctrine, Brother Wilson. It was taught indeed by the great Calvin, whom God so highly favored, but it is not now generally taught by Presbyterians. The doctrine of God's decrees is, indeed, full of sweet comfort to the elect, but it needs to be handled with great prudence, and is to be meditated in our closets rather than made the basis of our instructions to others. Sinners do not and cannot understand it. They only make a mock of it, and it proves to them the savor of death unto death."

"There it is! The time has come when the people will no longer hear sound doctrine, when it is *imprudent* to declare the whole counsel of God. Hence the race of weak and puny saints, who must be fed on milk, and that diluted. Very well, I must leave you to manage the discussion in your own way; but be on your guard. The time is not far distant, if things proceed as they have done for a few years back, when you will have no Protestantism to define or defend, but each man will have a gospel of his own. Good morning, gentlemen."

CHAPTER IV.

THE conversation was not resumed for several days. James found it a less easy task to define Protestantism than he had imagined. He had been accustomed to take the word in a very loose and indefinite sense. As chief of the Protestant League, he had meant by it little else than the denial of Catholicity; in his warfare against Socinians, rationalists, and transcendentalists, he had made it stand for doctrines and principles which logically imply the Catholic

Church; in his own pulpit, addressing the people of his charge, he had understood by it simply Presbyterianism, with a slight leaning, perhaps, towards Arminianism. But he had never given the term a clear, distinct, and uniform meaning, which he was willing to stand by in all places and on all occasions. He saw that to define it in a negative sense, and make Protestantism merely a protest against Rome, was not necessarily to distinguish it from paganism, Mahometanism, Judaism, deism, or even atheism; and to restrict it to simple Presbyterianism, if not against his conscience, was in the present state of the world, bad policy. It would be tantamount to saying that Protestantism is an empty name; that there are indeed Presbyterians, Episcopalians, Baptists, Methodists, &c., but no Protestants; that there is a multitude of sects, indeed, sometimes arranged under one common name, but without any common faith or principles, except that of hostility to the church. It would, moreover, too openly expose his weakness to the enemy, and confess that the great and mighty Protestant party, which had begun by assuming such lofty airs, and threatening to become commensurate with Christendom, had dwindled down to the little handful of Presbyterians in Great Britain and the United States,—those on the Continent having pretty generally lapsed into Socinianism, rationalism, and transcendentalism,—divided into four or five separate, if not hostile, communions, and their numbers every day relatively diminishing, which would create mirth rather than dread at Rome, against whom he wished to carry on a war of extermination. On the other hand, to extend its meaning so as to embrace all the so-called Protestant sects, from Dr. Pusey down to Theodore Parker, from Oxford to the Melodeon, was hardly less inconvenient. He would never march through Coventry at the head of such a motley company. Rome would declare that all motleydom and all devildom had broken loose. He should never hear the last of it. But to find a definition which should extend beyond the narrow boundaries of Presbyteriandom without including all sectariandom was the difficulty. *Hoc opus, hic labor est.*

James spent several days in meditating on this problem, and without hitting upon a solution quite to his mind; but having obtained a few hints from some of the earlier Protestant controversialists, and trusting to the chapter of accidents, he took occasion, finding himself in his library alone with John, to renew the discussion.

"I think," said he, addressing his brother, "that, if you review our former conversation, you will own, my last answer to the question, What is Protestantism? is all that you have any right to demand."

"I have no wish to make any unreasonable demands," John replied. "What I want is to find out precisely what, in its distinctive features, this thing or this no-thing which you call Protestantism really is. If your answer tells me what it is, and distinguishes it, or enables me to distinguish it, from what it is not, it is unquestionably sufficient."

"Protestantism is the essentials, and the essentials are all the truths clearly and manifestly revealed in the Scriptures of the Old and New Testaments."

"If to believe the essentials be all that is necessary to constitute one a Protestant, then all who believe all the truths clearly and manifestly revealed in the Scriptures must be Protestants."

"Certainly."

"If Catholics, as is very supposable, to say the least, believe all that is clearly and manifestly revealed in the Scriptures, then Catholics are Protestants."

"But Catholics do not believe all that is clearly and manifestly revealed in the Scriptures."

"They profess to do so, and they say with you, all that is clearly and manifestly revealed is essential to be believed, and no point of it can be disbelieved without essential error."

"But they hold that other things than those clearly and manifestly revealed in the Scriptures are also essential to be believed."

"That is, they believe all that you define to be the essentials are essentials, but do not believe that these are all the essentials. But this does not hinder them from being good orthodox Protestants; for your definition excludes only those who believe less, not those who believe more, than the essentials."

"Say, then, Protestantism is to believe all the essentials, and that what, and only what, is clearly and manifestly revealed in the Scriptures is essential, or, without essential error, can be believed to be essential. That excludes Catholics, by asserting the sufficiency of the Scriptures, which they do not admit."

"But besides the essentials, are the non-essentials, which may without essential error be either believed or disbelieved, to be the word of God?"

"That is what I contend."

"But they who believe them to be the word of God must believe them to be essential."

"Why so?"

"Remember Toby and his dog. He who believes a thing to be the word of God must either believe it essential to be believed, or else believe that it is no essential error to disbelieve God. Can I, without essential error, believe it is no essential error to disbelieve God?"

"No, for that is tantamount to making him a liar, since there is no essential difference between believing that it is no essential error to disbelieve God, and actually disbelieving him."

"Then they who believe the non-essentials to be the word of God must believe them to be essential, or else virtually make God a liar?"

"That follows."

"But it is essential error to believe any thing to be essential which is not essential?"

"So I have implied."

"Then it follows, does it not, that he who believes any of the non-essentials to be the word of God errs essentially?"

"So it would seem."

"All who differ from Presbyterians differ from them either by believing some things to be the word of God which Presbyterians deny to be his word, or *vice versa?*"

"True."

"If the latter, they err essentially, assuming Presbyterians to be right, by not believing all the essentials."

"Agreed."

"If the former, they err essentially by believing some things to be essential which are not."

"That also follows."

"Then all who differ from Presbyterians in matters of faith err essentially. Therefore, none who differ from them as to matters of faith can be essentially orthodox. If, then, you say none can be essentially orthodox who believe any of the non-essentials to be essential, you exclude all who differ from Presbyterians, make Presbyterianism and Protestantism equivalent and convertible terms, and declare none but Presbyterians are Protestants, which I understand you to deny."

"I do deny it; for Presbyterians are not the only essentially orthodox Protestants."

"How, then, can you say that Protestantism is to believe the essentials, and that only the essentials can, without essential error, be believed to be essential? Do you insist on saying this still?"

"I do."

"Is infant baptism an essential or a non-essential?"

"A non-essential, as I have told you more than once."

"But Presbyterians believe it to be a revealed command?"

"They do."

"Therefore believe it to be the word of God."

"Certainly."

"Then they believe it essential, and therefore err essentially by believing a non-essential to be essential. Hence, if you insist on saying that they who believe any thing but the essentials to be essential err essentially, you will exclude Presbyterians themselves from the number of essentially orthodox Protestants."

"But I have just told you Presbyterians hold infant baptism to be a non-essential."

"Then they hold it is no essential error to disbelieve God, which is itself a most essential error, for it virtually makes God a liar, as you have conceded. In either case, then, Presbyterians are excluded; in the one case, by believing a non-essential to be essential; and in the other, by believing it no essential error to make God a liar. Do you still insist that it is essential error to believe any thing in addition to the essentials to be essential?"

"I do."

"Then you abandon your distinction between the essentials and non-essentials?"

"Not at all."

"You still say, there are portions of the revealed word which may be either believed or disbelieved to be the word of God without essential error?"

"I do. To deny this would be to place myself in opposition to the whole Protestant world, from the time of the reformation down to the present moment. It is by means of this distinction that we have met and repelled the charge which Papists bring against us, that there is no unity of faith amongst us. In non-essentials we have always admitted we do not agree; but in essentials we have always contended we do agree; and, therefore, that there is among us substantial unity as to faith."

"These non-essentials, as to which Protestants have differed and still differ, have they been held to be non-essentials alike by those who believed and those who disbelieved them to be the word of God?"

"They have."

"All have agreed, then, that there is a portion of the word of God which it is no essential error to disbelieve?"

"Such is the fact."

"Are you not mistaken?"

"I think not."

"Then you hold that the whole Protestant world, from the time of the reformation down to the present moment, have believed it no essential error to disbelieve God, that it is no essential error to make God a liar; in a word, you hold that all Protestants always have been, and still are, virtual infidels. Will you still insist on the distinction between essentials and non-essentials?"

"I tell you I cannot surrender that distinction without placing myself in opposition to the whole Protestant world."

"You still say that there are portions of the word which are not essential?"

"I do."

"And these may be believed to be the word of God?"

"They may."

"And some who are essentially orthodox do so believe them, or at least some of them, to be the word of God?"

"They do."

"Yet no one is essentially orthodox who believes any thing but the essentials to be essential?"

"No one."

"And no one can believe any thing to be the word of God without believing it to be essential, as we have proved in the case of Toby and his dog?"

"Unless it be no essential error to disbelieve God."

"Some essentially orthodox Protestants believe, then, the same thing at the same time to be both essential and not essential?"

"That is not possible."

"Then it will be convenient to drop the distinction between essentials and non-essentials, and say that all who believe any thing to be the word of God, except what is clearly and manifestly revealed, err essentially, will it not?"

"No; for all that is revealed in the Scriptures evidently is not clearly and manifestly revealed, and it would be absurd to say that a man can err essentially in believing, when what he believes is the word of God."

"Then you will take the ground, that all essentially orthodox Protestants are, and always have been, virtual infidels, believing it no essential error to make God a liar?"

"Not that, by any means."

"You fall back, then, on your former ground, and say Protestantism is the essentials; he who believes these, whatever else he believes or disbelieves, to be the word of God, is essentially orthodox."

"Very well."

"But the non-essentials, or matters it is lawful to believe or disbelieve to be the word of God, are not the words of men or of devils, but revealed truths, as we agreed in our former conversation?"

"Certainly."

"But to believe the words of men or of devils to be the word of God is, as you have said, essential error."

"True."

"Then, after all, we cannot say that he who believes the essentials is essentially orthodox, whatever else he believes or disbelieves to be the word of God; for this would imply that it is no essential error to add to the word of God the words of men or of devils."

"Say, then, he who believes the essentials is essentially orthodox, whatever else he believes or disbelieves to be the word of God, provided he believes nothing to be the word of God which is not his word."

"Then none of those who believe any thing to be revealed which Presbyterians deny are essentially orthodox."

"I do not see that."

"What they believe which exceeds what you believe, you hold to be either revealed or not revealed. If revealed, *you* are guilty of the sin of infidelity in not believing it; if not revealed, you must hold they err essentially, for you hold they believe that to be the word of God which is not his word. The last is what you do hold, and therefore you cannot hold that they are essentially orthodox Protestants."

"Be it so."

"You must also deny those to be essentially orthodox who believe less than you do. If the matters you believe which they do not are not revealed truths, you err essentially in believing them to be revealed; if they are revealed, you must believe they err essentially in disbelieving them; since in disbelieving them you must hold they disbelieve God."

"That seems to be so."

"Then you exclude from the essentially orthodox all who believe more or less than yourselves; that is, all but yourselves. If, then, you insist on the proviso you have adopted in your definition, and say no one can be essentially orthodox who believes any thing in addition to the word, you must either give up your distinction, as I have said, between essentials and non-essentials, or else say it is no essential error to disbelieve God; which will you do?"

"Neither."

"But you either believe the non-essentials to be revealed truths, that is, the word of God, or you do not. If you do not, your distinction between them and the essentials avails you nothing, as we have seen. Hence you have insisted that they are revealed truths. But if you hold them to be revealed truths, you must hold them to be not non-essential, but essential, as Toby and his dog have proved to us, since to disbelieve them would be to make God a liar. This you admit, do you not?"

"I have admitted it over and over again."

"Then on no ground whatever can you admit any portion of revealed truth to be unessential, and, willingly or unwillingly, you must abandon your distinction between the essentials and non-essentials, and either say Protestants have been and are virtual infidels in teaching that it is no essential error to disbelieve God, or else that they have never meant that any portion of the revealed word, clearly and manifestly revealed or not, can be disbelieved without essential error. Which alternative do you elect?"

"If either, the latter."

"Presbyterians, then, are the only essentially orthodox Protestants."

"Very well."

"Presbyterians are fallible, liable to be mistaken?"

"We do not, like Romanists, set up a claim to infallibility."

"If they are fallible, it is possible they take that to be the word of God which is not his word, or deny that to be his word which is his word. In either case, they will be guilty of essential error. Consequently, it is possible that Presbyterians themselves are in essential error, and therefore impossible for them to say with certainty that they are essentially orthodox, and therefore they must admit that it is uncertain whether there are any essentially orthodox Protestants at all!"

"But you forget that the essentials are clearly and manifestly revealed, and therefore may be known with all necessary certainty."

"You also forget that we have just agreed that *all* revealed truth is essential, and that you have surrendered the distinction between essentials and non-essentials. You assumed, as you were obliged, the non-essentials to be revealed, for otherwise they would be simply the words of men or of devils, which it is not lawful to believe to be the word of God; but the moment you admit them into the category of revealed truths, you must either concede them to be essential, or else that it is no essential error to disbelieve God; that is, to be an infidel, and make God a liar. This last you could not do; therefore you were obliged to say all that is revealed is essential. But, if you say this, you must say, either that the essentials are not restricted to what is clearly and manifestly revealed, or else that nothing but what is clearly and manifestly revealed is revealed at all. Which will you say?"

"For the present, that nothing is revealed but what is clearly and manifestly revealed. Almighty God is good, and natural reason suffices to prove that he cannot have made that necessary to be believed which is obscure or doubtful. If he has made his whole word necessary to be believed, the whole must be clearly and manifestly revealed, and what is not so revealed can be no part of his word."

"His word, being clear and manifest, cannot be mistaken, or, at least, there can be no difficulty in determining what it is?"

"None."

"But clear and manifest are relative terms. A thing may be clear and manifest to you, and not to me. To whom, then, do you say the word is clearly and manifestly revealed?"

"What is clear and manifest *is* clear and manifest, and can be honestly mistaken by no one."

"That is, what is alike clear and manifest to all men."

"But I mean what is alike clear and manifest to all men."

"The word is revealed in the Scriptures, and in the Scriptures alone, and these alone are sufficient?"

"Yes; that is what all Protestants assert."

"The word is revealed in these alike clearly and manifestly to all men?"

"Yes."

"To those who cannot read, as to those who can?"

"There should be none who cannot read."

"But nineteen-twentieths of mankind, at the lowest calculation, cannot read, and nearly as large a proportion of those who can read cannot read so as to understand what they read. Do you say the revealed word is clearly and manifestly revealed to all these?"

"Of those to whom little is given little will be required."

"That is to say, Almighty God does not require faith in his word of the immense majority of the human race?"

"I say not that. Those who cannot read he instructs by his pastors and by his Holy Spirit."

"But if the instructions of pastors and the direct revelation of the Holy Spirit are necessary in the case of the larger part of mankind, how can you say the Scriptures are sufficient?"

"The Scriptures *are* sufficient."

"That is, for whom they suffice, and when and where they are not insufficient! That can hardly be questioned. But let us confine ourselves to those who can read, and who claim to be teachers among Protestants, so called. These all admit the Scriptures contain the whole revealed word?"

"They do."

"That they are the sole and sufficient rule of faith and practice?"

"Certainly."

"And that the word revealed in them is clear and manifest?"

"Unquestionably."

"And that only what is clear and manifest is revealed?"

"Be it so."

"Then they all agree as to what the word is?"

"No; I am sorry to say they do not."

"There is disagreement, then,—some saying the word is one thing, others saying it is not that, but something else?"

"But there is no *honest* disagreement; for the matter is clear and manifest, and none who do not wilfully close their eyes to the truth can mistake it."

"Are all parties dishonest?"

"No."

"Which is the honest, which the dishonest party?"

"The orthodox party is the honest party."

"Which party is that?"

"The one which believes what, and only what, is clearly and manifestly revealed."

"So say all parties; but which is that party?"

"The Scriptures must decide."

"But the dispute is as to what the Scriptures teach. They, by the very terms of the supposition, have already been appealed to, and each party has obtained a decision in its own favor. The question now is, Which is the true answer? What is the decision of the court?"

"Let the Scriptures be appealed to again."

"That avails nothing; for they decide always in precisely the same terms, and the dispute remains always the same."

"But the dispute is not honest."

"Be it so. But who is honest, who dishonest, you or your opponents? You charge them with dishonesty, and say the matter is clear and manifest as you believe; they retort and say it is clear and manifest as they believe. Which am I to believe?"

"Neither; but read the Scriptures and decide for yourself."

"And suppose I decide against both of you? There will then be three sects instead of two. Why shall I be counted the honest party rather than you or your opponents, they rather than you, you rather than they, either of you rather than I?"

"But the matter is clear and manifest to all who do not wilfully close their eyes to the light."

"With all my heart; but who are they who wilfully close their eyes to the light?"

"The Scriptures——"

"They have given their decision, and nothing is decided, for the dispute is as to what they decide."

"Evidently they cannot be good orthodox Protestants who teach doctrines repugnant to those of the Protestant reformation."

"Do you abandon the sufficiency of the Scriptures, then, and call in the aid of Protestant tradition?"

"I do not abandon the sufficiency of the Scriptures, but I maintain that what is clearly and manifestly repugnant to the doctrines of the reformers cannot be clearly and manifestly revealed in the Scriptures."

"Your rule of faith, then, is the Scriptures understood according to the reformers?"

"I hold the Scriptures alone are the rule of faith, but I compare my understanding of the Scriptures with the teachings of the reformers."

"And if it coincide with what they taught, you hold that you rightly understand the Scriptures, and believe what is clearly and manifestly revealed?"

"Very well."

"If the Scriptures alone are the rule, this appeal to the reformers is, if admissible, unnecessary; if it is necessary, and you cannot say that you rightly understand the Scriptures till you have brought your understanding of them to the test of the reformers, you cannot say the Scriptures alone are sufficient, or are alone your rule of faith. You then make the reformers, not the Scriptures, the test of the word."

"I do not make the reformers the test of the word. I love, honor, and revere the reformers as great and good men, raised up by God in his providence to deliver his people from the bondage of Rome, to arrest the tide of papal corruptions, roll back the darkness which was gathering over the world, restore the preaching of the word, and save the Christian religion from utter banishment from the face of the earth; but they were men, subject to the common frailties of our nature, and I follow them only so far as they follow Christ, who bids me call no man father upon earth, for one is my Master in heaven."

"In order to ascertain when and where the reformers follow Christ, you bring the reformers to the test of the Scriptures?"

"Precisely. I am to obey God rather than men."

"So you subject your understanding of the Scriptures to the test of the reformers, and the reformers to the test of your understanding of the Scriptures. If you agree with them, you are right; if they agree with you, they are right. Thus you prove your understanding by theirs, and theirs by yours!"

"I do no such thing. The Bible is the religion of Protestants, the Bible alone, and I am not obliged to consult the reformers in order to ascertain what is clearly and manifestly revealed."

"Then you have nothing to do with the reformers, and may at once dismiss them to their own place."

"That is, you would say the reformers, those great and godly men, are gone to hell?"

"If that is their own place, not otherwise."

"This is too bad. You know I love, honor, and revere the reformers, and it is no more than what you owe as a gentleman, not to say a Christian, while conversing with me, to treat them and my own feelings with some little respect."

"Very well said, my most courteous and gentlemanly brother. Happy is he who practises as well as preaches. You know I love and revere the Holy Catholic Church, the immaculate spouse of the Lamb, and the joyful mother of all the faithful; and yet you have not hesitated to call her the 'Mystery of Iniquity,' 'Antichrist,' 'the Whore of Babylon,' 'a cage of unclean birds,' &c. Where was your regard for *my* feelings? And what right have you to complain, if there be meted to you the measure you mete? But you will not receive such measure from Catholics, for they have studied in the school of Christ, and learned, when reviled, not to revile again. I said nothing against the reformers, offered no opinion as to their final doom. It is not mine to judge them. But if they, Judas-like, betrayed their Master, rebelled against the church of God, and refused to obey the pastors the Holy Ghost had set over them, and died unrepentant, I need not tell you what is and must be their doom, or that of all who partake in their evil deeds, if they die unreconciled to God. It is no pleasant thought, but you called it up, not I."

"So Catholics send all Protestants to hell!"

"All good Catholics do all in their power to prevent their Protestant friends and neighbours from sending themselves there. But suppose we waive questions of this sort for the present. We shall be better able to discuss them after we have determined what Protestantism is, and when inquiring whether it is true or false, from heaven or from hell,—is a safe way of salvation, or only the way that leadeth to perdition. It is no idle question, my brother, we are discussing. It involves eternal consequences. If Protestantism be not of God, if it be not that one, true, holy religion which he revealed from the beginning, which he has commanded to be taught to all nations, and which he has promised to be with, to protect, and to bless all days unto the consummation of the world, I need not tell you what must inevitably be your doom, if living and dying where and as you are, or what you have but too much reason to fear is the doom of those you have nursed in your bosom, so tenderly loved, and for whom your tears are still flowing."

"Are you a priest? You talk like one."

"Perhaps nearly as much of one as yourself."

"Singular! I never thought of that before. Upon my

word, I believe you are a Romish priest, perhaps even a Jesuit."

"If either, you must believe me able to keep my own counsel. It is enough at present for you to see in me plain Jack Milwood, your elder brother, who, may be, knows a great deal more about you than you do about him."

"I wish, John, you would give me the history of your life since you left home. It must be full of interest, and I should really like to hear it."

"Rather than exert all your wit and skill in defining Protestantism? But when we have disposed of Protestantism, perhaps,—but at present we must return to the question."

"No, no, I insist on the life and adventures of John Milwood, eldest son of the late Jeremiah Milwood——"

"And brother of the distinguished James Milwood, the Reverend pastor of ——, and chief of the Protestant League for the conversion of the pope and the suppression of popery, and who, when questioned, could not tell what he meant by Protestantism. No, no, brother, let us finish our definition of Protestantism first."

"I have given you definitions enough and more than enough already, and you ought to be able to suit yourself with some one of them."

"But it is not what suits me, but what suits you. Which of these numerous definitions do you finally settle down upon?"

"Protestantism is what and only what is clearly and manifestly revealed."

"And what is that? Is it what you teach or what Mr. Silvertone teaches?"

"Mr. Silvertone is a Socinian."

"What then? Does he not believe all that is clearly and manifestly revealed?"

"No, he does not."

"He says he does; and why am I to believe you rather than him?"

"Read and decide for yourself."

"Then the word is what is clearly and manifestly revealed to *me*; but why what is clearly and manifestly revealed to me rather than to you, or to you rather than to Mr. Silvertone?"

"Mr. Silvertone, I tell you, is a Socinian, and denies what have always and everywhere been held to be the great fundamental doctrines of the Gospel."

"If you say that, you appeal to Catholic tradition. Is your rule of faith incomplete without Catholic tradition? But if you allege Catholic tradition against Mr. Silvertone, he alleges it against you; for the same tradition that condemns him condemns you. You cannot say he errs because he teaches what is repugnant to Catholic tradition, without condemning yourself and all Protestants."

"But the points on which he is condemned are fundamental points; those on which we are condemned, if we are condemned, are not fundamental."

"You forget Toby and his dog."

"No more of Toby and his dog."

"Honestly, brother, have so-called Protestants ever been able to agree as to what is clearly and manifestly revealed?"

"In truth, they have not."

"And are as far from agreeing as ever?"

"Apparently so."

"Then, in point of fact, they have never been able to agree among themselves as to what Protestantism really is?"

"Such, it must be owned, is the fact."

"The great reason, then, why you have found it so difficult to tell me what it is, is that what it is has never yet been determined?"

"Possibly."

"Since I would rather relieve than aggravate your embarrassment, allow me to suggest that you define Protestantism to be what all who assert the sufficiency of the Scriptures, and maintain them to be the sole and sufficient rule of faith and practice, agree to accept as clearly and manifestly revealed. This would make agreement the test of clear and manifest, and then you can say the word is that which is clearly and manifestly revealed, and which nobody disputes, which never has been disputed, and is not likely to be disputed."

"There is, undoubtedly, a tendency among those commonly regarded as orthodox Protestants to say this, and several distinguished actors in the recent movement against Rome have proposed that we should say this and make it the basis of our alliance. It has, I own, some plausibility, and one would naturally say what is disputed cannot, while what is not disputed must, be clear and manifest. But though I am far from being a bigot, and would encourage the largest liberty compatible with essentially religious faith, I cannot accept your suggestion. It is the Socinian ground, and would place all sects who profess to be Christians on the same level. The Unitarian, who denies the Holy Trinity and Incarnation, would be as orthodox as he who believes them; and the Universalist, who denies future rewards and punishments, would be as sound in the faith as they who believe the righteous will enter into life eternal, but the wicked will go away into everlasting punishment. Nor is this all. I am unable to find any distinctively Christian doctrines which all, who would in such a case be rallied under the Protestant banner, really agree in accepting; for I am not aware of a single one which some professed Protestant has not controverted. So, were we to adopt the suggestion, there would be no revealed truth which would not be abandoned as non-essential, and nothing above mere natural religion to be held to be essential."

"So the various Protestant sects, taken altogether, have denied the whole Gospel, and left nothing but mere natural religion undisputed."

"Not even that, in fact, for German and American transcendentalists question essential portions of even natural religion."

"It is a hard case, brother, and I do not see that I can help you."

CHAPTER V.

PROTESTANT controversialists are well hit off in Lessing's Fable of the *Poodle and Greyhound*. "'How our race is degenerated in this country!' said one day a far-travelled poodle to his friend the greyhound. 'In those distant regions which men call the Indies, there is still the genuine breed of hounds,—hounds, my brother, (you will not believe it, and yet I have seen it with my own eyes,) who do not fear to attack the lion and grapple with him.' 'Do they overcome him?' asked the prudent greyhound. 'Overcome him! Why as to that I cannot exactly say; but only think, a lion attacked!' 'But,' continued the greyhound, 'if these boasted hounds of yours do not overcome the lion when they attack him, they are no better than we, but a great deal more stupid.'" Only think, the church attacked! Attack her boldly, with or without success, and you are sure of the admiration of all—the poodles.

When the infamous Danton was asked by what means the pitiable minority he headed were able to maintain their

Reign of Terror and paralyze the millions opposed to him, he answered,—" By audacity, *audacity*, AUDACITY." Protestant leaders understand very well the advantages of audacity, and that, if one is only bold and unprincipled enough to throw out grave charges against the purest and noblest cause which ever existed, he will not fail of multitudes to credit him. Groundless objections, if not susceptible of an easy or a popular refutation, are as much to their purpose as any. They serve to attack the lion, to put Catholics on their defence, and that is the same as a victory. A child may start an objection which the ablest and most learned divine cannot answer—to the child. A very ordinary man may urge an objection to some article of faith which will demand, in him who is to receive the answer, as well as in him who is to give it, for its refutation, the most rare and extensive erudition, and familiarity with the deepest principles and nicest distinctions of scholastic theology and philosophy. No small part of the objections urged against the sacred mysteries of the Trinity, the Incarnation, the Eucharistic Sacrifice, the Real Presence, and Transubstantiation, are objections which an ordinary mind may understand, but which it is impossible to answer to the general reader,—especially if the general reader be a Protestant. Such objections are exactly to the purpose of the Protestant controversialists, and gain them the applause of—the poodles.

These controversialists it is not to be presumed are ignorant that all the objections of past and present times to the church have been refuted, and unanswerably refuted ; but, from the nature of the case, they have, in numerous instances, been refuted only to the professional reader. The nature of the objection, though itself popular, precluded a popular reply. In all such cases, Protestant controversialists have only to deny that any reply has been given, or to assert that the one given is inconclusive, and they come off triumphant. This is their common practice. Nothing is more common than to meet, in Protestant controversial works, objections, which have been refuted a hundred times, reiterated without a hint that any reply has ever been even attempted, and urged in a tone of confidence, as if Catholics themselves conceded them to be unanswerable. The impudence of Protestant polemics in this respect is notorious and undeniable.

That this method of conducting a controversy, on matters in which no one has any real interest in being deceived or in deceiving, is fair, honorable, or just, it is not presumed any Protestant is silly enough to pretend; but, filled with an inveterate hatred of the church, and having decided that it is the church of Antichrist, Protestant leaders, apparently, regard themselves at liberty to make use of any means for its overthrow which promise to be successful, and have no scruple in resorting to artifices which would shock the moral sense of an ordinary heathen. The Catholic writer who should give a faithful account of their nefarious conduct in their war on the church, would find it harder to sustain himself with his friends than against his enemies; and he would hardly fail to be condemned by his own communion as a calumniator. Their conduct is so foreign to all the habits and conceptions of a simple-minded, honest Catholic, that one needs to have been a Protestant a great part of his life to be able to conceive it possible for beings having the human form, and pretending to some respect for religion and morals, to be guilty of so wide a departure from all that is true, just, and honorable. Hence the great tenderness and forbearance with which Catholics usually treat Protestants, and the undeserved credit they are accustomed to give them for a partial degree, at least, of fairness and candor.

At first view, one is at a loss to account for the sudden rise and rapid spread of the Protestant rebellion in the sixteenth century. Knowing by infallible faith, that the church is of God, the immaculate spouse of the Lamb, and that she has truth, wisdom, justice, sanctity, reason, evidence, on her side, the Catholic is astonished at so singular a phenomenon; but as he penetrates deeper into that mystery of iniquity, and becomes familiar with the character of the rebel chiefs, and the means they adopted, his astonishment ceases, and his wonder is, not that the success was so great, but that it was not greater,—that the revolt was so soon arrested and confined within limits that it has not as yet been able to overleap. He sees nothing marvellous in the success of these rebel chiefs, but he is struck with the manifest interposition of divine Providence to confound their language, to divide their counsels, to defeat their plans, to arrest their progress, to protect his church, to show his unfailing love for her, and to augment her power and glory. Protestantism, as relates to Europe, is actually confined within narrower limits than it was fifty years after the death of Luther, while the church has gone on enlarging her borders, and never at any former period was the number of the faithful so great as it is now.

They who attack existing institutions, especially if those institutions are wise and salutary, may always count on the admiration and applause of all the poodles. Fixed and authoritative institutions are offensive to the natural man. They are a restraint, and no man, save so far as assisted and subdued by grace, loves restraint; and there is no one that has not a natural repugnance to whatever curbs his lawless desires and licentious passions, or interposes an obstacle to his living as he lists. In every community,—because in every natural man,—there is always a predisposition, more or less manifest, to rebel against the existing order, and to welcome and adhere to those who are prepared to war against it, especially to credit whatever may be advanced to its prejudice. They who attack the existing order, appealing to this predisposition, have the appearance of attacking tyranny and oppression, and of being champions of freedom and justice. This fact renders them respectable, almost sacred, in the eyes of the multitude. Their position, moreover, permits them to assume a bold and daring tone, to make broad and sweeping assertions, and to forego clear and exact statements, and close and rigid logic. They can declaim, denounce, be impassioned, and affect all the eloquence of virtuous indignation. The eloquence of denunciation is the easiest thing in the world to command; for it appeals directly to those elements of our nature which lie nearest the surface and which are the most easily moved, and weak men prefer it and excel in it.

But he who defends authority labors always under a disadvantage. He has an unpopular cause. To the superficial,—and they are always the great majority,—he is the advocate of tyranny, the enemy of liberty, warring against the best interests and true dignity and glory of his race. He can appeal to no popular passion, use no burning words, and pour forth no strains of indignant eloquence. He cannot speak to the multitude. He must speak to sober sense, to prudent judgment, and aim to convince the reason, instead of moving the sensibility, or inflaming the passions. His words, to all but the few, are cold and spiritless, tame and commonplace. For the foaming tankard or sparkling goblet, with which the popular declaimer regales his auditors, he has only simple water from the spring. He must be subdued in his tone, measured in his speech, exact in his statements, rigid in his reasoning, and few only will listen to him, and fewer still can appreciate him. He who for-years has been on the side opposed to authority, and by his bold and daring declamation roused up a whole ocean of popular passion, and at every word brought an echo from the universal heart of humanity, no sooner finds himself on the other side, than all his marvellous eloquence is lost, and he is pronounced, by the very public which had hailed him as a second Cicero or Demosthenes, cold and weak, a Samson shorn of his locks and grinding in the mill of the Philistines. No matter how true and just his thought, how deep and searching his wit, how wise and prudent his counsel, how lucid and exact his statements, how clear and cogent his reasoning, he can excite no passion, move no sensibility, and bring no popular echo. The spell is broken; his magic is over, and his power to charm is gone for ever. He is no Indian hound, fearing not to attack the lion, and the poodles see nothing in him to admire.

Then, again, the poodles regard the lion attacked as the lion vanquished. They hold every objection boldly and confidently made to be true, till it is proved to be false. In this fact, in the tendency of the great majority to regard every objection made to existing authority as well founded till the contrary is shown, lies the secret of the Protestant reformation. To this the reformers owed their brilliant success. They well understood that their objections to the church would be credited by multitudes, till refuted. It was a matter of little importance, so far as their success was concerned, whether their objections were true or false. What they wanted was simply objections easily made, but not easily refuted,—susceptible of being proposed in a popular form, but not susceptible of a popular answer. Such objections they employed their wit in inventing, and their skill and activity in circulating. A lie, happily conceived, adroitly told, and well stuck to, was in their case hardly, if at all, inferior to the truth; and it must be conceded that they had a marvellous facility in inventing lies, and in adhering to them when they had once told them. Whoever coolly examines their objections to the church will readily perceive that they are all framed with respect, not to truth, but to the difficulty of refutation, and on the principle that a lie is as good as the truth till it is contradicted. Gloriously did they chuckle, we may fancy, when the "Father of lies" helped them to a popular objection, to which no popular answer could be returned. Boldly, or with brazen impudence, they threw it out, sent it forth on its errand of mischief, and then laughed at the heavy answer which, in process of time, came lumbering after it. The objection was made in a few words, on a loose sheet, and wafted by the wind of controversy through every land, town, village, and hamlet, to every door, and became universally known; the answer followed in a ponderous quarto or folio, all bristling with scholastic formulas and scholastic distinctions, formidable even to the professional reader. Its circulation was necessarily limited; few only heard of it; fewer read it, and still fewer were able to appreciate it. The authors of the objection safely ignored it, or, if they could not, they misrepresented it, denied its conclusiveness, and even made it the occasion of a new triumph with their followers. Or, when they could neither conceal the fact of the answer nor its conclusiveness, they could still count on all the poodles, who would insist that there must have been something in the objection, or else it would not have required so elaborate and so learned a refutation. The lion had been attacked,—and that was something.

"Where there is much smoke, there is some fire," says the popular proverb. Surely there must be something wrong in the church, or so much would not, and could not, be said against her. Whether, therefore, the objections actually urged be precisely true or not, it is evident the church is not unobjectionable, and if not unobjectionable, we are justified in rejecting her. So reason the poodles,—forgetting that our blessed Lord himself was everywhere spoken against, was called a glutton and a drunkard, the friend of publicans and sinners, a blasphemer, a seditious fellow, a fool, said to be possessed of the devil, and finally crucified between two thieves as a malefactor. Here was smoke enough,—was there also some fire? Here were objections enough raised, charges enough preferred,—was there also some truth in them? Where is the blasphemous wretch that dare think it? If they have called the Master of the house Beelzebub, how much more them of his household! If so they have accused the Lord himself, how much more his church? To one competent to reason on the subject, the grave character and multiplicity of the objections alleged against the church are an evidence that she is God's church. "Will you tell me what books I may read to become acquainted with the Catholic faith?" said, the other day, an intelligent Protestant to the writer. "I am wholly ignorant of the Catholic Church, but I hear, everywhere, so much said against it, that I cannot help thinking there must be something good in it, and that possibly it is the true church." This lady, brought up a rigid Calvinist, through God's grace, had learned to reason far more justly than she had been taught by her Protestant masters, and, if true to the grace she has received, will ere long be admitted into the "Communion of Saints." But she is not one of the poodles; and the reformers preferred, and their successors prefer, the admiration of these to the approbation of the sober and prudent greyhounds.

The policy of the reformers was indicated by Luther, when he took the discussion of theological questions out of the schools and from the tribunal of professional theologians, and brought it before the unprofessional public. I picked up, the other day, in a steamboat, a flaming quack advertisement. It appeared that the advertiser had, as he alleged, discovered an entirely new medical system, which placed all the regular mediciners, from Æsculapius down, quite in the wrong. He had challenged the regular practitioners to a discussion of the merits of their respective systems. The challenge had been accepted, but on condition that the discussion should be before a jury of medical men. The advertiser scorned this condition. It proved that the "regular doctors" had no confidence in their own system; for if otherwise, they would not shrink from a public discussion. It was an insult to the public, and he would not submit to it. He was ready and anxious to discuss the question; but he would do it before no prejudiced jury of professional men; he would do it openly before his free and enlightened fellow-citizens, who were the only proper tribunal. He trusted his fellow-citizens, the free and enlightened public, would appreciate his motives in refusing to be a partner in offering so gross an indignity to their intelligence and impartial judgment, and would be at no loss to understand why the regular practitioners had annexed to their acceptance of his challenge so insulting a condition.

Now here am I, said I to myself, throwing down the advertisement, at least a fair average of the popular intelligence. I have even studied, with considerable attention, several branches of medical science; and yet how utterly unqualified I should be to sit as judge on the respective merits of rival systems! I might listen to the statements of either party, but I am too ignorant of the general subject to be able to perceive the bearing and real value of the statements of one or the other. I might, indeed, if such should happen to be the case, perceive that this pretended discoverer silenced his opponent; but I could draw no inference from that, for nothing is more common than for a man to triumph through impudence, or because too ignorant to be refuted. The proper judges of a controversy like the one here proposed are medical men themselves, as lawyers are the proper judges of law questions. Indeed, the very fact, that this advertiser refuses to argue his case before an audience of professional men, and appeals to the unprofessional public, is to me full proof that he is a quack, and sufficient to decide me, without further examination, against him. If I need medical advice, I am sure I shall not call him in, any more than I would a miserable pettifogger in an important and intricate law case. I can confide my health and that of my family to no practitioner whose science and skill are not superior to my own, and vouched for by those who know more of medical matters than I do, and are far better judges of medical systems than I am.

Just so would I have reasoned, if I had been present, when Luther made his appeal to the unprofessional public. Why did he make such appeal? Because the public at large are the proper tribunal for professional questions? Because they can really judge better, discriminate more accurately, and decide with more wisdom and justice, than they who by their profession are at least somewhat acquainted with the matters in controversy? Because he really believed them the best qualified to be judges? No one can be so simple as to believe it, so senseless as to pretend it. Luther knew that loose statements, confident assertions, bold allegations, and impassioned appeals would avail him nothing before a jury of theological doctors. He knew that there he could not lie with impunity, and that his " bellowing in bad Latin" would win him no laurels. He may have persuaded himself, or suffered the devil to persuade him,— and if we may believe his own statements, his colloquies with the devil were frequent, and intimate—that the church was wrong; but he must have known that the particular objections he brought against her were groundless, and that it was only by disregarding the established rules of reasoning, and resorting to falsehood and sophistry, confident assertions and bold and daring denunciations, that he could sustain himself or his party. And these could avail only with the unprofessional public, who could never understand the exact points in question, perceive the bearing, or feel the force, of strict logical arguments. With them eloquence would pass for reason, and invective for argument. This he knew, and hence his appeal from the schools to the public at large. Hence have his followers continued to appeal to the multitude, and to leave truth and justice to take care of themselves.

This policy, however, is not without certain drawbacks. It answers admirably while the party adopting it have nothing of their own, and are mere Bedouins of the desert, free to attack when and where they please. But when and where they have acquired a partial success, and wish to abandon their wandering life and predatory warfare, and settle down in fixed dwellings, with something established and permanent of their own, they find it unavailing. Men, as Carlyle remarks, cannot live without clothes, and surely in this bleak, wintry world it is not convenient to go naked. They must and will have something to cover their nakedness,—some sort of institutions for their protection. They will cover themselves with aprons of fig-leaves, and build them a hut with broken branches, seek out a cavern in the rocks, or a hole in the earth, if they can do no better. They must and will have something they call religion, some established mode of communion, real or not real, with the Invisible. Even the atheist fabricates to himself a god of nature, and renders it a species of worship, and the sceptic seeks to convert his scepticism into a creed. It is horrible to feel one's self alone in the world, abandoned to the blind workings of the elements, with no Father in heaven, no brothers on earth, standing on a mere point, surrounded by a universal blank. We cannot endure it. Nature recoils from herself, and the soul shrieks out, "O thou Great Unknown, save me from myself! leave me, O, leave me not to the solitude of my own being!" There is a God, and a God to be worshipped, is written in golden letters on all nature, and engraven as with the point of a diamond on every heart. In vain would man tear himself away from his Maker. Go where he will, be and do what he will, sleeping or waking, the God that made him and seeks his heart wooes him with his love, or pursues him with his justice. The boldest recoil from his justice, and quake before the undefined dread of his vengeance, and seek some medium of yielding the love, or of providing a substitute for the love he solicits.

Protestants went on gloriously, while they aimed at nothing but to attack the existing ecclesiastical order. The means they had chosen were just fitted to their purpose. But when a large number had been seduced from their allegiance, and found themselves homeless, and shelterless, and naked in this bleak world, a new class of wants sprung up to be provided for. Some substitute for what had been thrown away in their madness was to be sought out. Their old arts and methods were useless now. As soon as they had something with which they were unwilling to part, something, in a word, to defend, the weapons which they had forged were no longer adapted to their purpose, and could be turned against them with murderous effect. Thus short-sighted and self-destructive is iniquity ever.

Poor James experienced the truth of this, the moment he was called upon to answer why he was a Protestant. The question was a novel one, and he soon found that he was wholly unprovided with a satisfactory answer. He had sought long and earnestly for specious objections to the church, but he had entirely neglected to furnish himself with arguments for Protestantism as distinguishable from Socinianism or infidelity. Nay, he was unable even to tell, save in a negative sense, what he meant by Protestantism. Adopt what definition he would, it would include either too much or too little. It was too bad. Yet his natural pride would not permit him to yield to the obvious truth, that he must either be a Catholic or reject all revealed, if not all natural, religion. With the multitude he might, indeed, sustain himself. There his audacity and his eloquence would serve him, but they were lost upon his cool and logical brother. John was no poodle, that was certain, and could never be made to regard the lion attacked as the lion overcome, or even to admire the rashness of an attack where there could be no victory. What was to be done? Give up the point? That would never do, and he the virtual chief of the Protestant league for the conversion of the pope and the suppression of popery! What then? Surely he was the equal of his brother in acquirements, and he had always, in their school days, been regarded as his superior in natural gifts. He would not believe that he had the weaker cause. His failure, thus far, must be owing to his yielding the management of the argument to his brother, and his not having been sufficiently on his guard against his sophistry and Jesuitical cunning. Could he not correct this? Could he not contrive to change the issue, and throw the burden of proof on the Catholic? He pondered the matter for several weeks, and finally concluded, that, if he could not define and establish Protestantism, he might at least disprove Catholicity, and thus justify the reformers in separating themselves from the church.

CHAPTER VI.

As soon as James had come to this sage conclusion, an opportunity was found of renewing the discussion. This time it was John who opened it.

" Well, brother, he said, have you succeeded in finding a definition of Protestantism to your mind?"

" I wish to consider Protestantism, now, only as a protest against the errors and corruptions of popery. Here you affirm and I deny, and consequently the laboring oar is in your hands."

" Not exactly, my prudent brother. You affirm Catholicity is corrupt. You are, then, the accuser, the plaintiff in action, and must set forth your charges and sustain them. The principle of law is, every man is to be presumed innocent till proved guilty. The church must, therefore, be presumed innocent till the contrary is made to appear."

" The church claims to be an ambassador from God, and to have the right to command me in his name. She must bring credentials from God, before I can be held to hear or obey her. I demand her credentials."

" All in good time. But not too many things at once. You shift the question before you get it fairly stated. You begin by charging the church with being corrupt, and, without offering any proofs of her corruption, you proceed immediately to demand her credentials as the ambassador of God. This will not do. Corruption implies integrity; and the plea that the church is corrupt concedes her credentials, and merely charges her with exceeding her authority, or with having abused it. This plea concedes her authority; but the demand for credentials denies it. You cannot, therefore, plead, at one and the same time, want of authority, and corruption or abuse of authority. You must elect one or the other, and confine yourself to the one you elect."

"I am no lawyer, and do not understand special pleading."

"But you are an educated man, and are to be presumed to understand, at least, the ordinary rules of logic, and therefore that the same thing cannot be both conceded and denied in the same breath. You cannot say that the church is corrupt, has abused or misused her authority, and yet deny her authority. When you deny that she has ever received authority from God, you declare her, *in quantum Ecclesia*, a nullity from the beginning, and to allege the corruption of a nullity is absurd."

"Be it so. The Romish Church never received authority from God, or, in other words, was never divinely commissioned."

"Possession is in law *prima facie* evidence of title. The church is in possession, and has been so from time immemorial. The presumption is, therefore, in her favor, and you must admit her title, or set forth good and valid reasons for contesting it."

"Prescription does not apply in the case of the church."

"It is admitted in law, and therefore, by the reason of mankind, as a general principle. If you deny its application in the case of the church, you allege an exception to the general rule, and must show a reason for it."

"Prescription does not give an absolute title, but simply a presumptive title against adverse claimants. It presupposes the existence of the estate to be conceded, the title of which is vested in some one, and presumes it to be in the possessor, unless the contrary is shown. But where the existence of the estate is the matter in question, it is idle to plead possession or prescription. What is not cannot be possessed. The estate, in the present case, is the divine commission. Supposing it conceded that such a commission has at some time been issued, possession may, I grant, be pleaded as *prima facie* evidence of title in the possessor. But I deny that such a commission as the Romish Church claims to have received has ever been issued. You must prove, therefore, the fact of such commission, before you can plead possession or prescription."

"Possession implies the object possessed. Evidence of the possession is, therefore, evidence of the existence of that which is possessed. Consequently, just in proportion as there is evidence that the church has possessed, or claimed and exercised, with the general consent, the commission in question, and as her having claimed and exercised it with this consent is presumptive proof of title against adverse claimants, is there presumptive proof that the commission has been issued."

"*Quod nimis probat, nihil probat.* Your argument, if it prove any thing, proves too much. A pagan or a Mahometan may say as much."

"If either paganism or Mahometanism claims a similar commission, and can, as the church, be said to be in possession, the fact is, in like manner, presumptive evidence of title till the contrary appears, I both concede and contend. Nothing can generate nothing. The claim to a divine commission must have had some origin, and, on the principle of law, that every man must be presumed innocent till proved to be guilty, must be presumed to have had a good origin till the contrary is proved. False religions imply the existence of the true religion, as counterfeit coin implies the genuine. The claim to divine commission, if it be really made by either paganism or Mahometanism, is therefore *prima facie* evidence that at some time, to somebody, a divine commission has issued. If no such commission had ever been given, it is not conceivable that it could have been claimed. No one would ever have falsely claimed to be an ambassador from one court to another, if no genuine ambassador, or nothing in the same order, had ever been known or heard of; and the sending of ambassadors must have become a general custom, before any one, not duly commissioned, could have conceived the project of palming himself off as one, or could have hoped for any success in the attempt to do it. The fact of possession, where it could be pleaded, would be a presumption of title in the Mahometan or the pagan, in like manner as it is in the case of the Catholic. Hence the church, where she has never been in possession, when presenting herself as an *adverse claimant*, always produces her credentials, and gives good and valid reasons why the present occupant should be ousted and she placed in possession. I admit, therefore, all that the argument implies, and deny that it proves too much."

"But admit it, and every mad enthusiast who claims to be divinely commissioned must be presumed to be so till the contrary is shown."

"Not at all. His claim to a divine commission is, if you will, a presumption that at some time, to somebody, a divine commission has issued; but not that it has issued to him; for he is not and never has been in possession. He must show a reason for *his* claim, before it can be admitted."

"At least, the principle applies to Protestants as well as to pagans and Mahometans, and you can no more plead prescription against us than against them."

"I have admitted the plea of prescription, in the case of paganism and Mahometanism, on the supposition that they are really in possession,—a fact, however, which I let pass, but do not concede. But Protestants cannot plead prescription, because they are not and never have been in possession, and because they do not even claim to be, since you, in their name, deny that the commission in question has ever issued."

"But conceding that there was a presumption in favor of the church at the epoch of the reformation, and that the reformers were not at liberty to separate from her without cause, this cannot be said now. The church is not now in possession. The reformers gave good and valid reasons for separating from her communion, and she has been condemned as a usurper by the judgment of mankind. The question is not now on ousting her from a possession which she has held from time immemorial, but on reversing the judgment rendered against her, and readmitting her to a possession from which she has been ejected by due process of law."

"When was the judgment you speak of rendered? and where is the record of the court?"

"The fact is one of public notoriety, and all the world now laughs at the ridiculous pretensions of Rome."

"Do you include in *all the world* the pagan and Mahometan worlds?"

"Why should I not?"

"It may be doubted whether the question has really ever come before them in such a shape that they can be said to have pronounced judgment upon it; and as they reject Protestantism, whenever it pretends to be Christian, no less than Catholicity, they might possibly be as unsafe witnesses for a Presbyterian as for a Catholic,—perhaps even more so."

"Let them go. I mean by *all the world* all the Christian world, Christendom so called."

"You mean to assert, then, that Christendom has pronounced judgment against the Catholic Church?"

"Yes, against the *Romish* Church."

"You distinguish without a difference. The church in communion with the church of Rome, acknowledging its pontiff for its supreme head on earth, is the only church which, by the consent of mankind, is or ever has been denominated the *Catholic* Church."

"She should be denominated the mother of harlots."

"So that Protestant communions might claim to be her daughters. But no more of this. Have Catholics, who remain in her communion, pronounced judgment against the church?"

"Perhaps not."

"And they are as two, if not three, to one of all who bear the Christian name."

"I am sorry to say they are."

"And I am not sorry, and would to God there were none but Catholics on the earth!"

"That is, you would, if you could, exterminate all Protestants."

"Yes, if making them sincere and humble Catholics were exterminating them. But if Catholics are the great majority of Christendom, how can you tell me that Christendom has pronounced judgment against the church?"

"I do not reckon Papists among Christians."

"And I regard what you call Papists as the only true Christians; and I have, to say the least, as much right to my reckoning as you have to yours. You mean, then, by Christendom those who protest against the church?"

"You may have it so."

"Then your position is, the church is condemned by all by whom she is condemned! This may be granted. But these are a small minority, a mere handful, of those who bear the Christian name. By what right do you pronounce their judgment the judgment of mankind?"

"Protestant nations are the more enlightened and advanced portion of mankind."

"Is that a conceded fact?"

"Is it not?"

"Do Catholics concede it?"

"Perhaps not."

"They are the great majority, and, as they deny it, how can you put it forth as generally conceded?"

"The denial of Catholics amounts to nothing,—the fact is as I allege."

"In whose judgment?"

"In the judgment of all who are competent to judge in the premises."

"Who says so?"

"I say so."

"On what authority?"

"The fact is evident, and cannot be questioned."

"But it is questioned and denied by Catholics, who are as five to one to your Protestants."

"They will swear to any thing their priests tell them. Their denial is not to be counted. They are not to be permitted to testify in their own cause."

"As much as you in yours. Their denial is as good as your assertion, till you show some reason why your assertion is to be preferred."

"I tell you Protestant nations are the most enlightened and advanced portion of mankind, as is well known."

"Well known to whom? To themselves?"

"Yes, if you will."

"By what right are they both witnesses and judges in their own cause?"

"By the right of being the most enlightened and advanced portion of mankind."

"What is it to be truly enlightened and advanced?"

"Those nations are the most enlightened and advanced that are the most enlightened and advanced in what is of the greatest importance and utility to man."

"And what is that?"

"Religion, the 'one thing needful.'"

"True religion, or false?"

"True religion, of course."

"The most enlightened and advanced nations are, then, those who are the most enlightened and advanced in the requirements of true religion?"

"They are; and therefore I claim Protestant nations as the most enlightened and advanced."

"And therefore beg the question. If Protestantism be the true religion, you are right; if Catholicity be the true religion, you are wrong. Consequently, you must determine which is the true religion, before you can determine which are the more enlightened and advanced nations."

"But it cannot be denied that Protestant nations are more intelligent, more industrious, and better instructed in the science and art of government."

"What you say may be questioned; but even conceding

it, it amounts to nothing. Because a man is a good cobbler it does not follow that he is a good sculptor. Because a nation is enlightened in mere earthly matters, it does not follow that it is in religious matters. It would be a solecism to say the Athenians were a more enlightened and advanced nation than the Jews, or that a Socrates is better authority on religion than David, Solomon, or Isaias."

"But I have always considered it undeniable that Protestant nations are in advance of all the others."

"If to advance consists in shaking off Christian civilization and in returning to that which is superseded, you may have been right; otherwise, the probability is, that you have been altogether wrong. You must prove Protestantism to be true religion, before you can claim Protestant nations as the more enlightened and advanced nations; and till you can so claim them, you cannot claim their judgment as the judgment of mankind, even if you could then; and till you can claim their judgment as the judgment of mankind, you cannot say the judgment of mankind has condemned the church. This you have not yet done. Consequently, you cannot say the church has been ejected from her possession by the judgment of mankind. She is, as it appears, from the fact that the overwhelming majority of those who bear the Christian name continue, as they have always continued, to adhere to her, still in possession. She has lost nothing, and you have gained nothing, by the lapse of three hundred years. The question stands to-day as it did in 1517, and she may plead the *olim possideo*, as she could then, and with even additional force; and you must set forth in your declaration good and valid reasons for ejecting her, before you can compel her to plead any other title than that of prescription."

"But you forget that the reformers did set forth such reasons."

"I cannot have forgotten what I never knew. But whatever reasons they set forth, the presumption is that they were insufficient; for they have been so regarded by Christendom generally, since the church continues in possession, and the great majority of all who are called Christians still adhere to her communion."

"But they were in reality sufficient, and ought to have been so regarded."

"That is a point to be proved. What were those reasons?"

"The first in order, if not in time, was, that our Lord founded no authoritative church such as the Romish claims to be."

"We have seen she was in possession, and the presumption was in her favor. What you state was an allegation which needed to be proved."

"The reformers proved it."

"By what evidence?"

"By the word of God."

"Had they the word of God?"

"They had."

"Did the church concede that they had it?"

"They had the Holy Scriptures, and she admitted that they were the word of God."

"That the mere letter was the word of God, or the sense in which the Holy Ghost dictated them?"

"The sense, of course; for words are nothing without their sense."

"Did she admit that the reformers, in having the letter of Scripture, had its sense, which is the word of God?"

"She did not."

"Was, according to her, the Holy Scripture the word of God, if understood in any sense different from hers?"

"No; she claimed the right to declare its sense."

"Did the reformers adduce the words of Scripture, in support of their allegation that our Lord had founded no such church as she pretended to be, in the sense she gave them?"

"They did not; for she explained them in her own favor."

"Then she did not admit that what they adduced in support of their allegation was the word of God. Then, as the burden of proof was on them, they were bound to prove that it was his word."

"They quoted the Scriptures, and they were the word of God."

"In the sense of the church, not otherwise. The reformers pleaded the word of God in support of their allegation. The church replied by denying that what they set forth as the word of God was his word. Her reply was sufficient, unless they proved that it was his word."

"But their plea was evident on its face, for they alleged the very words of Scripture."

"That they alleged the very words of Scripture may be

denied, for in point of fact there are no words of Scripture which say that our Lord did *not* found such a church as the Catholic Church claimed and claims to be; but let that pass for the present. They pleaded the word of God, and the word of God is not the words, but the sense, of Scripture. To adduce the words, therefore, availed them nothing, unless they proved that the sense of the words, as intended by the Holy Ghost, was what they pretended; for till then they could not assert that they had adduced the word of God."

"But the matter was so plain, that there could be no question as to the genuine sense of the words adduced."

"But there was a question as to the sense, by your own admission. The church attached to them one sense, and the reformers another."

"But the words themselves necessarily mean what the reformers asserted."

"We cannot go into that question at present. The right to declare the word of God is included in the possession of the church, and the fact that she denied the reformers' sense is *prima facie* evidence in her favor and against them."

"I do not admit that."

"You have admitted it; for you have conceded that prescription was in favor of the church, and is *prima facie* evidence of title. You must, therefore, admit the word of God as the church declares it, till you can assign a good and valid reason for not doing so."

"The fact that the express words of Scripture are against her is such a reason."

"The express words of Scripture you cannot allege; because, as a matter of fact, no such words are to be found; and because, if there were such words, they still could not be adduced against the church, for the Scriptures are in her possession, and denied to have authority save as she understands them."

"That would be to deny that the Scriptures are legitimate evidence in support of an allegation against the church."

"That is not my fault. The reformers could not, of course, legitimately quote the Scriptures as the word of God against the church, save in the sense she authorized, unless they succeeded in removing the presumption she derived from prescription, and in getting themselves legal possession of them."

"I do not admit that. The Scriptures were the law, to which the church and all were accountable."

"As declared by the church, *transeat;* but that they were the law in any other sense the reformers were bound to prove."

"But the reformers had the word of God as well as the church, and therefore were not bound, even presumptively, by the sense she declared."

"Had they *legal* possession of the word of God?"

"I care nothing about that. They had the Scriptures, and that was enough; for they had in them the rule of faith, both for them and for the church."

"But you must care for that; for it is conceded that the church was in possession, and, being in possession, she had the presumptive right to declare the law; and they were bound to take it from her, unless they could prove that they had legal possession of the word."

"They received the Scriptures from God himself."

"They were, then, the legal depositaries of the word?"

"Yes, as much as the church."

"Had they the right to declare its sense?"

"Why not?"

"If you say that, you concede the point you dispute. You allege against the church, that our Lord founded no such church. The essential character of the church, so far as concerns the present controversy, is, that she has the word of God, and is its legal keeper and expounder. If, then, you say the reformers had legal possession of the word, and were authorized to keep and expound it, you make them essentially such a church as you assert our Lord did not found. You contest the claims of the church on the ground that our Lord founded no church with the authority she exercises; you must, then, unless you would concede what you deny, disclaim that authority on the part of the reformers."

"I do disclaim it on their part."

"Then you grant, in the outset, that they had no legal possession of the word, and were not its authorized keeper and expounder; therefore, that they had no word of God which they had authority to quote against the church. What they had not they could not adduce. Consequently, they did not, for they could not, adduce the word of God in support of their allegation."

"But they had the Scriptures, as a matter of fact, and could read and understand them for themselves."

"They had the Scriptures as a private citizen has the statute-book, it may be; but as they were not the authorized keeper and expounder of the word of God, their understanding of it was without authority, and not to be entertained."

"They had the right from God himself to read and understand the word for themselves."

"Then they were authorized to keep and expound it, at least for themselves."

"They were."

"But I understand you to deny that any body was authorized to keep and expound the word."

"I do not say so. Almighty God, in revealing his word, has authorized every one to keep, read, and expound its sense."

"Then, so far from its being true, as you have alleged, that our Lord has founded no church with the authority the Catholic Church claims, he has constituted each individual a church with the same authority. Decidedly, brother, you must give up this, or withdraw your allegation. If you admit that our Lord has anywhere authorized any body, individual or collective, to keep and expound the word of God, you admit that he did found, essentially, such a church as your allegation denies. You cannot deny such authority to the church on the ground that no such authority was ever given, and then claim it for each and every individual."

"Be that as it may, I do claim it for each and every individual."

"That is a bold stand for a Presbyterian, but necessity sometimes compels us to be bold. But did the church admit this?"

"No, she denied it."

"Then the reformers were bound to prove it."

"They did prove it."

"By what authority?"

"The word of God."

"By what the church admitted to be the word of God?"

"No matter what she admitted. They proved it by the word itself."

"Who says so?"

"They said so."

"On what authority?"

"On the authority of God's word."

"On what authority did they say that that was the word of God which authorized them to say so?"

"The word itself."

"But by what authority did they prove the word itself?"

"The word of God *is* the word of God, and is in all cases supreme. Would you deny the word of God?"

"But as the church denied what they adduced as the word of God to be his word, they were then bound to prove that it was his word."

"What did Almighty God give us his word for, if it was not that we should read and understand it for ourselves?"

"Your first business is to prove that he has given *you* his word. The church asserts that he has given it to *her*, and that she permits the faithful to read the Scriptures for their edification, but always with submission to her authority, and the reservation that no doctrine is to be deduced from them which she does not authorize."

"There she is wrong."

"That is for you to prove."

"God proposed to teach mankind by writings, not by a body of men."

"That, also, is for you to prove."

"It is evident from the word itself."

"You must prove that *you* have the word, before you can introduce it as evidence."

"No one can read the New Testament and believe otherwise."

"Not true in fact; for the great mass of all who do read the New Testament actually believe otherwise. But you must get legal possession of the New Testament, and establish your right to interpret it, before you can quote it in a sense the church denies. Till then, the denial of your assertion by the church is *prima facie* evidence against you."

"I do not care for the church. I deny her authority."

"I know that; but her authority is to be presumed, till reasons are set forth for denying it. You are not at liberty to deny it without a reason."

"I have given a reason."

"What is it?"

"Why, I tell you she is condemned by the word of God."

"You *tell* me so, but that is not enough. You must *prove* that it is so."

"You do not suffer me to do so. You will not suffer me to quote the Bible against her."

"No such thing. *When you have proved that the Bible, in the sense you adduce it, is the word of God,* you may quote it to your heart's content."

"Why, I have told you again and again that the church herself admits the Bible to be the word of God, and therefore it is not necessary, in arguing against her, to prove that what I adduce from it is the word of God."

"The Bible in the sense she authorizes, she admits to be the word of God, I grant; in any other sense, she denies it to be the word of God. Consequently, since you would adduce it in a sense she does not authorize, if you adduce it at all, she denies what you would adduce is the word of God. You must, then, prove that it is, before you can legally adduce it."

"But you will not let me prove it."

"I do not hinder you."

"I offer to prove it by the word itself."

"That is not logical; for it would be to assume the word to prove the word."

"Not so. Here are the Scriptures, admitted by the church, when taken in their genuine sense, to be the word of God. I simply propose from them and by them to show what is their genuine sense; and if I do so, I prove by an authority which she herself concedes all that I am required to prove."

"You cannot do that, because in doing it you assume that the church is not the authorized interpreter of the word, which is the point you must prove; and that you are the authorized interpreter, which is also a point you must prove. The church simply admits that the Scriptures, taken in the sense she authorizes, are the word of God. This is the full extent of her admission. But taken in another sense, she denies them to be the word of God; for the word of God, as we have agreed, is not the words, but the sense, of the Scriptures. Consequently, before you can allege them in a sense contrary to hers, nay, before you can go into any inquiry as to their sense, you must, on the one hand, dispossess her of her prescriptive right to declare their sense, and establish your own authority as their interpreter. Till you have done one or the other, the sense of Scripture is not an open question, and you cannot open it without assuming the point in dispute."

"That denies absolutely my right to quote the Scriptures against the church."

"Not absolutely. You may quote them in her sense against her, if you can; and in your own sense, when you have proved it to be the word of God."

"But the first would be of no avail, because she has taken care to explain the Scriptures in her own favor; and I cannot prove them to be the word of God in any other sense, unless I am at liberty to explain them by themselves."

"That is, you cannot prove your point, unless you are at liberty to prove the same by the same! Prove that you are authorized to declare the sense of Scripture, and then you will have no difficulty."

"But I cannot prove that I am, save from the word itself."

"That is to say, unless you are at liberty to assume and exercise the authority to declare the sense of Scripture, as the condition of proving that you have such authority! That will not do, brother. It would be proving *idem per idem*, the same by the same, which is bad logic."

"How, then, am I to proceed?"

"That is your affair, not mine."

"The church spreads her claim over every thing, and leaves me, according to your principles of logic, no possible means of adopting any line of argument against her, which does not, in some sense, assume the point to be proved. So subtle and crafty in her tyranny, that it leaves absolutely nothing to those who would resist it. This to me is only another evidence of her wicked origin and pernicious influence."

"So you are of opinion, that, if Almighty God should establish a church, he would take good care to leave it open to attack, to give its enemies a fair and solid ground on which to carry on their operations against it! I am of a different opinion, and predisposed to believe the Almighty to be more than a match for the devil, and that, if he should establish a church, he would so constitute it that no attack could be made upon it which should not recoil upon those who made it,—no argument be framed against it which should not serve to demonstrate the folly and absurdity of its framers. It is unquestionably a very difficult matter to make an action lie against the church, or to find a court in which an action can be legally commenced against her; but I have yet to learn that this is her fault. The church is in possession of universal and supreme authority under God, has a *prescriptive* right to that authority, and must be presumed to have a *valid* right to it till the contrary is shown. You cannot *assume* the contrary, but are bound to *prove* it. Now you must prove it without authority, or with authority. Without authority you cannot prove it; for proofs which are sustained by no authority prove nothing. You must, then, prove it with authority, or not prove it at all. That it is difficult to find any authority whose assertion does not assume the nullity of the supreme authority which is to be presumed, is undoubtedly true. You wish to arraign the actual possessor of the supreme authority, but you cannot do so unless you have some court of competent jurisdiction. But any court which should claim authority to issue a precept against the possessor of supreme authority, and summon him to answer at its bar, would assume authority over him, and by so doing prejudge the case. This is in the nature of things, and cannot be avoided; but whose is the fault? The reformers, if they had been lawyers, would have seen that what they attempted was against law, and a *prima facie* crime on their part, for which they were liable to suffer the full vengeance of the law. If they had been even tolerable logicians, they would have seen that they could urge no argument which did not assume what was in question. But surely the church is not to be censured, because they were miserable pettifoggers and shallow sophists."

"But there is a court competent to institute proceedings against the church."

"What court?"

"The court of conscience."

"You must prove that conscience is supreme, before you can say that; for the church, as the vicegerent of the Almighty, claims and possesses jurisdiction over conscience, and is supreme judge *in foro conscientiæ*. This is an integral part of her possession to which she has a prescriptive right. You must dispossess her, before you can compel her to plead at the bar of conscience."

"But she is at least bound to answer at the bar of the Bible, interpreted by private reason."

"Not till you dispossess her, or place the Bible interpreted by private reason in possession; for she possesses jurisdiction over them."

"At the bar of reason, then."

"Reason has and can have no jurisdiction in the premises; for the question turns on a supernatural fact, lies within the supernatural order, and therefore out of the province of reason."

"The general sense of mankind."

"That is against you, and in favor of the church, as we have already seen, and is conceded in the fact that the church is allowed to plead prescription."

"Then to the written word, interpreted and its sense declared by the Holy Ghost."

"Establish the fact of such a court, and she will not refuse to appear and answer. But she claims to be that court herself, and is in possession as that court; you must dispossess her by direct impeachment of her claims, or by establishing, before a competent tribunal, the rights of an adverse claimant, before you can allege such a court."

"The reformers were aided by the private illumination of the Holy Ghost, and what they did, they did in obedience to his commands."

"That was for them to prove."

"They did prove it."

"How?"

"From the written word."

"But they could prove nothing from the written word, for they had no legal possession of it."

"They had legal possession of it. The Holy Ghost gave them legal possession of it."

"What and where was the evidence of that fact, if fact it was?"

"In the Scriptures."

"That is, they proved by the Holy Spirit that they had legal possession of the Holy Scriptures, and by the Holy Scriptures that they had the Holy Ghost! But this was to reason in a *vicious circle*."

"The reformers set forth other and conclusive reasons for rejecting the church, which I will reproduce on another day; but you must excuse me now, for I have some parochial duties to which I must attend."

"So you give up the first reason, namely, our Lord founded no such church as the Catholic?"

"Not by any means. I may have erred in bringing that forward before the others. I ought not to have departed from the example of the reformers. They did not allege that reason first, and I see now that they were wise in not doing so. They first proved that the church had forfeited her rights, by having abused her trusts. Having thus ejected her, they took possession of the word, and easily and clearly demonstrated that she had been null from the beginning, by showing that our Lord never contemplated such a church."

"That is, they dispossessed themselves by acquiring possession. Very good Protestant law and logic."

"You may spare your sneer, for perhaps it will soon be retorted with seven-fold vengeance."

"O, not so bad as that, I hope."

"We shall see. I will, God willing, prove that the reformers were rigid reasoners, and sound lawyers."

"An Herculean task. Clearing the Augean stables was easy compared with it."

"The reformers were great and glorious men, rare men, the like of whom will not soon be seen again."

"Some consolation in that."

"To call such men miserable pettifoggers and shallow sophists is——"

"To use soft words, which turn away wrath."

"To outrage common sense and common decency."

"Why, would you censure me for not calling them by harder names? I might have easily done so, but I wished to spare your prejudices as much as possible."

"I tell you, John, that, in becoming a miserable idolatrous Papist, and drunk with the cup of that sorceress of Babylon, the mother of every abomination, you seem to have lost all sense of dignity, all self-respect, and all regard for the proprieties of civilized life."

"Because I do not rave and rant, every time I have occasion to allude to the chiefs of the Protestant rebellion?"

"No; you know that is not what I mean. You degrade yourself in speaking so contemptuously of the glorious reformers."

"And what does my most excellent, amiable, polite, and sweet-spoken brother do, when he calls God's Holy Church the sorceress of Babylon, &c., and brands the members of her holy communion with the name of idolaters?"

CHAPTER VII.

ONLY a few days elapsed before John, finding his brother apparently at leisure, pressed him to redeem his promise.

"You are prepared, brother, by this time, I presume, to undertake your vindication of the reformers, and to prove that they were sound lawyers and rigid reasoners."

"The church has so spread out her claims over every thing, that it is hard to construct an argument against her, which does not apparently take for granted some point, which she contends is the point to be proved; but the devil, though cunning, can be outwitted."

"What! by heretics?"

"Protestants are not heretics."

"The church is in possession; and since Protestants break away from her and contend for what she declares to be contrary to the faith, they are at least presumptively heretics, and are to be treated as such, unless they prove the contrary."

"The church is in possession *de facto*, not *de jure*. She is a usurper."

"Possession *de facto*, we have agreed, is *prima facie* evidence of title. The reformers were, therefore, as we have seen, bound either to admit it, or show good and valid reasons for questioning it."

"True; but they showed such reasons."

"So you have said, but you have not told me the reasons themselves."

"I gave you as one of those reasons, the fact that our Lord founded no such church as the Romish."

"But that was a reason you could not assign, because the simple fact of the existence of the church in possession was *prima facie* evidence to the contrary."

"I offered to prove my position from the word of God."

"But could not, because the church was in possession as the keeper and interpreter of the word, and you could not adduce it in a sense contrary to hers without begging the question."

"I have the word as well as she, and it interprets itself."

"That you have the word, or that it interprets itself, you were not able to prove. Moreover, the argument may be retorted. The church has the word as well as you, and the word interprets itself. She alleges that the word is against you, and her allegation, at the very lowest, is as good against your position as yours is against hers."

"I deny her infallibility."

"Do you claim infallibility for yourself?"

"I claim infallibility for the word of God."

"That is what logicians call *ignorantia elenchi*. But do you claim infallibility for your own private understanding of the word?"

"No."

"Then you are fallible, and may fall into error?"

"I do not deny it."

"The church, at the very worst, is only fallible, and therefore, at the very worst, is as good as you at the very best, for at the very best you are not infallible. Consequently, your allegations of what is the word of God can never be a sufficient motive for setting aside hers. Nothing, then, which you can adduce from the Scriptures, even conceding you all the right to appeal to them you claim, can be sufficient to invalidate her title. As she, at worst, stands on as high ground as you can even at best, her simple declaration that the word of God is in her favor is as good as any declarations you can make to the contrary. The proof, then, which you offered to introduce, would have availed you nothing, even if you had been permitted to introduce it."

"I do not admit that. I offered to prove, and I am able to prove, from the Holy Scriptures, that our Lord founded no such church as the Romish."

"It is certain that you can introduce no passage of Scripture which expressly, in so many words, declares that our Lord founded no such church. If, then, you can prove it from the Scriptures at all, you can prove it only by means of the interpretations you put upon the sacred text. But, at any rate, and on any conceivable hypothesis, the church has as much right to interpret the sacred text as you have, and her interpretations have, to say the least, as high authority as, granting you all you ask, yours can have. But she interprets the word in her favor, and, according to her interpretations of the word, it is clear and undeniable that it is in her favor, and that our Lord did found such a church as she claims to be. Since, then, your interpretations can never be a sufficient motive for setting aside hers, for they at best can be no better than hers at worst, it follows necessarily that you can never, under any hypothesis, prove from the Scriptures against her, that our Lord did *not* found such a church as she assumes to be. All this I could say, even waiving the argument from prescription. But I do not waive that argument. You have conceded that the church was in possession. She is, then, presumptively what she claims to be. Then her interpretations are presumptively the true interpretations, and yours against her presumptively false. For you to say, then, that no such church was ever instituted, is a plain begging of the question, and so is every argument you can construct against her, drawn from the Holy Scriptures."

"But I may disprove the claims of the Romish Church by

proving positively that some other church is the one actually founded by our Lord."

"Unquestionably; but you cannot plead at one and the same time an adverse title, and that no such title was ever issued. If you plead that there was no such church ever instituted, you are debarred from pleading an adverse title; for you plead that the church has no title, because none was ever issued. If none was ever issued, there can be none in an adverse claimant. On the other hand, if you plead an adverse title, you concede, what you have denied, that our Lord did institute such a church as the Catholic Church claims to be; that the title she possesses has been issued and vests somewhere. This changes the whole question. There is no longer any controversy between us as to the fact whether our Lord did or did not found a church in the sense alleged, but simply a question whether it be the Roman Catholic Church or some other."

"Grant that our Lord did found such a church as is pretended,—and I believe in the Holy Catholic Church as well as you,—still I deny that it is the Romish Church."

"You join a new issue, then, and plead now, not no title, but an *adverse* title?"

"Be it so, for the present."

"And what is the adverse claimant you set up against Rome?"

"The church of which, by God's grace, I am an unworthy minister."

"That is to say, the Presbyterian?"

"Yes. The Presbyterian Church is the visible Catholic Church, out of which there is no ordinary possibility of salvation."

"So says the Westminster Confession of Faith. But which Presbyterian church do you mean?"

"I do not understand you."

"There are, you know, brother, quite a number of Presbyterian churches, for instance, in Scotland, the Kirk by law established, the Free Kirk, and the Seceders; in this country, the Old School, the New School, and the Cumberland Presbyterians; in England, the Presbyterian Dissenters, for the most part Unitarian; and on the Continent, the Dutch Reformed, the Reformed German, the Genevan, and the French Huguenots, all virtually Presbyterian churches, and very generally fallen into Socinianism, rationalism, deism, or transcendentalism. Which of these, not to mention several others, is the one you mean?"

"It is not necessary to particularize; I mean the Presbyterian Church in general."

"Do you include even those who have become Socinian, rationalistic, deistical, transcendental?"

"It is to be regretted that in many of the old Presbyterian churches grievous, and, as I hold, damnable, errors have crept in."

"But are those which have lapsed into these damnable errors still integral portions of the Presbyterian Church? Do you claim the English Presbyterians, the Genevan, and French?"

"The church is never free from error, taken as a whole, but there are always in the church a remnant who are faithful, and somewhere in it there is always the pure preaching of the word, as well as the maintenance of the true ordinances of God's house."

"You forget that you have just conceded that our Lord did found such a church as the Roman Catholic claims to be; but the Roman Catholic Church claims to have authority from God to teach, and to teach everywhere, and at all times, one and the same doctrine, free from all admixture of error."

"I do not forget what I have conceded. I say, in the language of the Westminster Confession of Faith, that 'the purest churches under heaven are subject both to mixture and error; and some have so degenerated as to become no churches of Christ, but synagogues of Satan. Nevertheless, there shall be always a church on earth to worship God according to his will.'"

"But this does not relieve you, for it says positively the purest churches under heaven are subject to mixture and error. Then there is no church not liable to error and corruption. Then, whatever your Presbyterian Church may claim, it does not claim, even as the church, to be able to teach infallibly; therefore does not even claim to be such a church as the Roman Catholic Church claims to be. Consequently she cannot be set up as an adverse claimant. The title she claims is not the title the Catholic Church claims, and therefore, if established, does not necessarily negative hers. If, then, you concede that our Lord did found such a church as the Roman Catholic Church claims to be, you must concede that it is not the Presbyterian."

"Not at all; for does not the Confession say, 'Nevertheless, there shall be always a church on earth which shall worship God according to his will?'"

"True; but this either amounts to nothing, or it contradicts what you have just alleged. If it means that there shall always be on earth a church which teaches God's word infallibly, then it is false to say that the purest churches under heaven are subject to mixture and error; but if it means that the church which worships God according to his will is not free from mixture and error, it amounts to nothing, for it proposes no church claiming to be what the Catholic Church claims to be, since it is undeniable that she claims to teach without the least mixture or error."

"But one may be subject to error, and yet not err in fact. The church is not exempt from the liability to err, but there is always a portion of it which, as a matter of fact, does not err."

"What prevents it?"

"The grace of God; for God will not suffer the gates of hell wholly to prevail against his church."

"Very well; but is the church, what your Confession calls the 'visible Catholic Church,' herself always preserved by this grace from error? and if so, can she be said to be subject to error?"

"The visible Catholic Church consists of all those persons throughout the world who profess the true religion, together with their children. There is always a portion of these who are, though grace, preserved from error; and therefore there is always a church or body of worshippers who worship God according to his will. In some periods the number of these is very small, in others it is large."

"But you do not answer my question. Individuals may err, particular branches of the church may fail; but does the church, the teaching and judging authority of the church, in matters of faith and morals, ever err?"

"Individual members and particular churches may err, but God always preserves some individuals who do not err, who are witnesses for him in the darkest and worst of times. Consequently, the whole church never falls into error."

"But your Confession declares the visible Catholic Church to be a *kingdom*. Jesus Christ, it says, 'hath erected in this world a *kingdom*, which is his church.' Now to a kingdom it is essential that there be a supreme authority. There may be provincial and communal governments with local authority, customs, and usages, but they must all be subordinated to one supreme central authority, or else you have not one kingdom, but as many separate kingdoms as you have separate local governments. The kingdom erected by our Lord is one, not many, and therefore must have somewhere, somehow constituted, a supreme central authority, from which all the subordinate authorities derive their authority, and to which they are responsible. This supreme central authority is, in the case of the church, the church teaching and governing, and is what is specially meant by *the church*, when speaking of its fallibility or infallibility. Now my question is, whether the church herself, that is, the supreme central authority from which all the particular and local authorities are derived, is subject to error, or by grace rendered infallible."

"I know no such authority as you speak of but that of Jesus Christ himself, who is the head and husband of the faithful, and he of course cannot err."

"You admit that the church is a *kingdom?*"

"Yes."

"And a kingdom erected in *this world?*"

"I do."

"And that where there is no supreme central authority there is no kingdom?"

"There must be such authority, but it may be in Jesus Christ, who is the invisible head of the church."

"It is the authority that constitutes the kingdom, not the kingdom the authority for prior to the authority, the kingdom is not. The authority and kingdom must be in the same order. If, then, the kingdom is in the visible order, the authority which makes it a visible kingdom must be in the visible order, and therefore itself be visible. You could not call Great Britain or France a visible kingdom, if one or the other had no visible supreme authority The most you could say would be, that there is an invisible kingdom in Great Britain or France, not that either is itself a visible kingdom. So of the church. If it is a visible kingdom, it must have a supreme visible authority; if not, it is not a visible, but an invisible kingdom. The individuals might be visible as individuals, but not as members of the church, or subjects of the invisible authority. In such case, the distinction your Confession makes, and which you contend for, between the visible church, and the invisible, would be a distinction without a difference. When, therefore, you tell me, as you do in your Confession, that the visible church is *a kingdom in this world*, you necessarily tell me that it has in this world a supreme visible central authority. And in point of fact, Presbyterians themselves do recognize such authority; for they regard their church as a polity, and it has its constitution, its officers, its supreme legislature, and supreme judicatory. If not, what means the General Assembly, which 'represents in one body' all the particular churches of the Presbyterian denomination, and to which belongs 'the power of deciding in all controversies respecting doctrine and discipline; of reproving, warning, of bearing testimony against error in doctrine, or immorality in practice, in any church, presbytery, or synod; of erecting new synods when it shall be judged necessary; of superintending the concerns of the whole church; . . . . . of suppressing schismatical contentions and disputations,' &c., and to which every candidate for ordination must promise obedience and subjection?"

"There is a supreme visible government of the church, *under God*, I admit."

"*Under God;* and who ever dreamed of a supreme government of the church *over* God?"

"The Papists."

"Nonsense! Do you not know that Catholics hold Jesus Christ to be the supreme invisible Head of the church, and that they call the pope his vicar? If the pope is the *vicar* of Jesus Christ, how can he be above him? God is supreme, the sovereign of sovereigns, and there is no power not from him and subject to him. So no more of this nonsense. But you hold the church to be a kingdom or polity, do you not?"

"I do."

"And as such it has its government, its supreme authority; for if not, it is no kingdom or polity."

"Be it so."

"Now, what I ask is, Does this supreme authority, such as it is in the Presbyterian Church, claim to be infallible in all that concerns faith and morals?"

"It does not."

"Then your plea of an adverse title amounts to nothing; the title you allege is not the negative of that claimed by the church. The title she claims is that of an infallible teacher of God's word, the title you set up is that of a fallible teacher, which you may well be without prejudice to her claim; for you can claim to teach *fallibly* without denying her claim to teach *infallibly*."

"But were I to grant this, it would not follow that the claim of Rome must be conceded."

"Not from this fact alone; but as you have conceded that the title was issued, and must vest somewhere, in some one, it follows necessarily that it vests in the Roman Catholic Church, if it vests in no one else. And as she is in possession, you must concede it to her, unless you can produce and establish an adverse title."

"The Greek Church has as good a title as the Romish."

"That is not to the purpose. The Greek Church has either a valid title, or none at all. It is not enough to say that she has as good a title as the Roman Church; you must say she has a perfect title, or say nothing."

"I say, then, she has a perfect title."

"Then she is the church of God. Why, then, are you not in her communion?"

"That is neither here nor there. You have no right to conclude any thing to her prejudice from my practice. I may be inconsistent. What then?"

"But she condemns you, and has solemnly anathematized every one of your doctrines, with a single exception, in which you depart from the teachings of the Roman Church."

"Be it so; what then? That may prove that we Protestants are wrong, but not that she is wrong, or you right."

"Moreover, she does not even claim to be the One Holy Catholic Church, and to have the supreme central authority over the whole body of the faithful throughout the world. She does not pretend to unchurch the church of Rome, or even that the Roman Church does or ever did owe subjection to her. She admits, even to this day, the Roman Catholic Church to be truly the church of Christ in what was originally the patriarchate of the West, that the pope is the legitimate patriarch of the West, and rightfully exercises patriarchal authority over that patriarchate. She does not claim and never has claimed for herself the title she denies to Rome. She denies the supreme authority over the whole church claimed and exercised by the pope, not because she claims the supremacy for herself, but because she denies that any such supremacy was conferred on any one in the original constitution of the church. She is, then, no adverse claimant, and in all essential respects, except this one, she concedes virtually, if not expressly, the title claimed by Rome, at least so far as it is now in question. So you cannot get an adverse claimant in the Greek Church. Indeed, when you have once conceded that our Lord founded such a church as the Roman claims to be, you must concede that the Roman is that church, for there is no other that even claims to be it."

"That is hardly true The Anglican Church claims to be it."

"The Anglican Church, as well as your own, puts on lofty airs, and she now and then tells us gravely that she is Catholic,—not *Roman,* but *Catholic,*—and lets off her double battery of popguns on the one hand against Rome, and on the other against Presbyterians, Baptists, Congregationalists, Methodists, &c.; but she has not courage enough to claim to be the Catholic Church in its unity and integrity. She claims, at most, to be only a branch of it, which implies that the root and trunk are elsewhere; and she does not even pretend that the supreme visible central authority she obeys or exercises is the supreme visible central authority of the whole church of Christ. Moreover, she confesses that she is fallible, that she has heretofore erred grievously in doctrine and manners, and may err again. Her claim, therefore, is not the same as that of the Roman Church, and her title is not, strictly speaking, an adverse title. So you can succeed no better with her than with the Greek Church, or than with your own."

CHAPTER VIII.

"But you told me the other day," replied James, after a short pause, "that the essential character of the Romish Church is, that she claims to have received a divine commission or authority to teach, or to keep and declare the word of God."

"To keep and expound or teach the word of God, I grant; but I conceded this only so far as concerned the special controversy in which we were engaged, as I then told you. Nevertheless, I admit now that the essential claim of the church is, that she has been divinely commissioned or authorized to teach the word of God."

"Then you must concede that any other church claiming to be divinely commissioned is an adverse claimant."

"Divinely commissioned *to teach,* granted."

"Then it is not true that there is no adverse claimant against Rome, as you so confidently assert; for, in point of fact, the Greek Church, the Presbyterian, and the Anglican each claims for itself to be divinely commissioned."

"The Greek Church claims the commission for herself in

no sense in which she does not concede it to Rome, and therefore is not an *adverse* claimant. The Presbyterian and Anglican Churches do not in reality claim it at all; for both deny the fact of a divine commission in denying the infallibility of the church."

"But to deny the infallibility is not necessarily to deny the divine commission of the teacher; and, therefore, not to claim the infallibility is not to fail to claim the commission."

"The commission in question is the commission to teach, and must be the warrant of infallibility in the teacher, unless God can authorize the teaching of error."

"That proves too much. All the teachers of your church, you hold, are divinely commissioned; but you cannot hold that each is infallible; for, if you should, you would be obliged to hold that Luther himself did not err, since, as is well known, he was at first a Romish doctor."

"The teachers of the church are all divinely commissioned to teach in communion with and in subordination to the sovereign pontiff, the successor of St. Peter, I admit, and so long as they so teach, they teach infallibly; but when they break away from that communion, and assume to be independent teachers, they are fallible; for then they have no divine commission."

"Is there any of these teachers, taken individually, who may not break from that communion, and assume to be an independent teacher?"

"No one except the pope himself."

"What, then, is your warrant that your particular teacher does not err?"

"The fact that he teaches in communion with and in subordination to the sovereign pontiff."

"So the pope is his voucher?"

"Communion with the pope."

"Who vouches for the pope?"

"The divine commission, which gives him, as the successor of St. Peter, plenary authority to teach and declare the word of God."

"If the pope should fail, your whole church might fall to the ground."

"Not necessarily; but the pope cannot fail, because he is divinely commissioned. As the successor of St. Peter, he inherits the authority of St. Peter, and the promise made to him,—' Upon this rock will I build my church, and the gates of hell shall not prevail against it.' The pope, there fore, since he has the promise of God, cannot fail, unless God himself can fail, which is not supposable."

"But your argument, nevertheless, proves too much; for all legitimate civil governments are divinely commissioned, and yet no man can pretend that they are infallible."

"Commissioned to govern, but not to teach or declare the word of God. There is a difference between the commission to govern and the commission to teach. Teaching has reference to the conscience, to the internal act of the man; government only to external acts. The teacher is commissioned to teach the truth; government is commissioned simply to control and direct the external acts for the general good, according to the rules of prudence; and to attain its end, it is not essential that it should be able to propose measures which are absolutely in all and every respect the wisest and the best; nor is it necessary, in order to believe it for the general good, and to obey all its commands, that the subject should believe it infallible, or that it can never err in any one of its measures. He can obey an unwise order, and it may be for the general good that sometimes he should do so. But the end of teaching is the proposition and belief of the truth. All teaching is in order to truth. If the teacher be fallible, the end of teaching is not secured; for he may propose, and I may believe, on his proposition, what is not true. The commission is authority from God to teach, and a command to those the teacher is commissioned to teach to believe as the truth, and nothing but the truth, what he teaches. If fallible, then, he may propose and I believe, on *divine authority*, what is false ; and then God may authorize the teaching and the believing of falsehood,—which cannot be; for he is infinitely true, and can neither be deceived nor deceive, which would not be the fact, if he could authorize the teaching or the believing of falsehood. Therefore, the divine commission to teach— and it is only of the commission to teach that I speak— must necessarily be the warrant of infallibility in the teacher."

"Though the divinely commissioned teacher be assumed to be infallible, the commission is not itself necessarily and essentially a warrant of his infallibility."

"To the full extent of the matter covered by the commission it is, you yourself do and must admit."

"I do not admit it. A commission, by the simple fact that it is a commission, does no such thing; for a government may commission an ambassador, and yet that ambassador may misrepresent its will and intention."

"Commissions in general may not, but the divine commission to teach does. Human governments have no power to secure the infallibility of their ministers; but you cannot say this of God. He can make his ministers infallible."

"He can; but it does not therefore follow that he does."

"I have shown that he must, because he cannot authorize either the teaching or the believing of error, without contradicting his own nature, which is infinitely and essentially true; and that he does, to the full extent of their commission to teach, you yourself do and must hold, or give up all belief in external revelation."

"Not at all."

"Why do you believe our Lord was the Son of God?"

"Because he himself so declared."

"Why do you believe his declarations?"

"Because he was the Son of God, and could not lie."

"A good reason, after it is proved that he was the Son of God; none at all before."

"I believe him because the miracles he performed proved that he was from God; for no man could do the miracles he did, unless God were with him."

"Was *from* God, that is, sent or commissioned by God as a teacher, but not that he was God."

"The miracles proved him to be God. He raised the dead, and none but God can raise the dead."

"None but God can raise the dead as *efficient* cause; but men as *instrumental* cause may raise them, as is shown by the fact that the apostles and many of the saints have raised the dead. How, then, from the miracle alone conclude that our Lord raised the dead, not as instrumental cause, but as *efficient* cause?"

"The efficient cause was the divine power."

"Granted. But the divine power inherent in Jesus, as his own proper power, or the divine power merely displayed on the occasion of his saying to the dead, Arise? Moses smote the rock, and the water gushed out. Was it Moses, or God who stood behind Moses, that caused the water to flow from the rock?"

"God who stood behind him."

"So, for aught the miracle itself says, it may have been, not Jesus himself, but God who stood behind him, that caused the dead to live. The miracle does not prove the proper divinity of our Lord. It only proves that he was sent from God, and that God was with him, and displayed his almighty power at his word."

"Very well."

"The miracles having proved that our Lord was from God, that God sent him and was with him, you *therefore* believe what he said. He said he was the Son of God, and therefore you believe he was the Son of God, and therefore God himself."

"Be it so."

"The miracles, then, simply proved his divine commission, that is, accredited him as a teacher sent from God. But how from the fact of his commission conclude the truth of what he said, if the divine commission be not the warrant of infallibility? If one who is divinely commissioned to teach, notwithstanding his commission, may err, how can you say that our Lord himself did not err, and that you do not err in believing him to be the Son of God? Indeed, it is only on the ground that the divine commission is the warrant of infallibility, that your profession of faith in the Bible as the infallible word of God is not ridiculous and absurd."

"The sacred writers were inspired, but the divinely commissioned teachers you speak of are not. Being inspired, they could know the truth of what they affirmed; and being honest and godly men, they would not affirm what they did not know."

"That is nothing to your purpose. The inspiration was nothing more nor less than God simply telling or communicating to them what they were to teach, and they have in this respect no advantage over the church, in case she be fully instructed as to what she is to propose as the word of God. If instructed, it matters not, as to her ability to teach, whether instructed by immediate inspiration to herself, or only mediately through that of the prophets and apostles. She claims to have been fully instructed, for the commission under which she professes to act was, 'Going, teach all nations; . . . . . teaching them to observe *all things whatsoever I have commanded you.*'—St. Matt. xxviii. 19. The alleged defect of immediate inspiration in her case, or its presence in the case of the sacred writers, can, therefore, of itself, be no reason for believing one in preference to the other. The real reason for believing the sacred writers is, that God authorized them to teach; and you have the same reason for believing the church, if you have equal reasons for believing her authorized by God to teach his word. The commission is a warrant of infallibility in her case, as much as it was in theirs."

"But you forget that I gave as my reason for believing the sacred writers, that they were honest and godly men, and would not affirm what they did not know."

"You, then, consider the personal character of the teacher better authority than the divine commission? This is a common Protestant blunder, and hence the worthlessness of the greater part of your treatises on the evidences of Christianity. God's authority for believing is not sufficient till man indorses it! The best men are fallible, and may be deceived. If we had nothing but the personal characters of the sacred writers on which to rely, honest and godly as they certainly were, we should have no sufficient reason for believing what they wrote to be the Word of God. Their personal character may be important when the question turns on their credibility as witnesses to the facts they record, but does not enter into the account when the question is on their authority as teachers of revealed truth. No man's personal character is a sufficient warrant for believing that any thing he asserts to be a doctrine of revelation is really and truly a doctrine of revelation. If it were, we should be obliged to believe whatever any man, whose character, so far as we know, is honest and irreproachable, chooses to teach as the word of God. How, then, can you maintain that the personal character of the teacher is a surer warrant of infallibility than the divine commission?"

"The simple fact that the sacred writers were honest and godly men may not be alone a sufficient reason for believing them, yet, if they had been bad men, that would alone have been a sufficient reason for *not* believing them. For God does not and will not speak by bad men."

"That is not so certain. Balaam, the son of Peor, was a bad man; yet God spoke by him, and caused him to utter a glorious prophecy. Do you believe his prophecy on his personal character, or because divinely commissioned teachers have told you that it was not he who spoke from himself, but the Lord who spoke by him?"

"I believe the sacred writers because God authorized them to teach his word, and the Holy Ghost was with them to enable them to teach it, and to preserve them from error in teaching it."

"Is not the assistance of the Holy Ghost, so far as needed, necessarily implied in the commission or authority to teach?"

"If the commission were the warrant of infallibility, it would be so implied; but that is precisely what I deny."

"No man can teach infallibly without it?"

"No."

"But with it any man can teach infallibly?"

"Perhaps so."

"No *perhaps* about it. It must be so positively, or you cannot assert the infallibility of the sacred penmen."

"God leaves the will free; any one who has the assistance may teach infallibly, if he chooses; but it does not therefore follow that he must and will so teach."

"In what concerns personal morality, natural or Christian, the will is free; but in teaching at the command of God, it is not. The individual speaks not as moved by his own will, but as moved by the Holy Ghost. Thus, Balaam was forced against his will to bless Israel, and to utter a prophecy he did not intend, and which he was unwilling to utter; for it was against his interest, and he loved the wages of iniquity. Thus, too, the prophet Jonas sought to run away from the Lord, and not to preach as commanded to the Ninevites, but the Lord brought him back by a miracle, and forced him to utter his word. Moreover, if the matter depended on the human will, the teachings of no human teacher, however authorized and assisted by the Holy Ghost, could ever be regarded as infallible; because no one could ever know whether the teacher spoke as moved by the Holy Ghost, or merely from his own proper motion. In vain, then, would you claim to have in the Bible the *infallible* word of God. Nay, you have yourself just said, the Holy Ghost enables the teachers to teach the word, and *preserves* them from error in teaching it."

"In the case of the sacred writers, not of all men."

"For all men have not the assistance of the Holy Ghost to teach the word of God, nor are all commissioned to teach it; but if it be what you define it, any one who has it must be able to teach, and be preserved from error in teaching, and therefore must teach the word infallibly."

"Be it so."

"But the divine commission does not necessarily imply this assistance?"

"No, it does not; therefore, I admit the infallibility of the sacred writers specially, and not of divinely commissioned teachers in general."

"What is the significance of the divine commission to teach the word of God?"

"It authorizes the one who receives it to be a teacher of God's word, but does not necessarily enable him to teach it infallibly."

"So one may have authority from God to teach his word, and yet not have the ability to teach it in the only sense in which God can authorize it to be taught! What, then, means the authority?"

"Why, it is authority to teach."

"Unquestionably, but what is that?"

"He who has it is authorized to speak or teach in the name of God."

"That is, to propound the word of God, not in his own name and on his own authority, but in the name and on the authority of God?"

"Yes, it means that he is empowered to teach with divine authority."

"Can any thing but truth be taught with divine authority?"

"No."

"God cannot authorize the teaching of error?"

"No; for that would be the same as to teach it."

"Then no one not able to teach the truth, and not preserved from error in teaching it, can be said to teach by divine authority?"

"So it would seem."

"You say that for God to authorize the teaching of error would be the same as for him to teach it?"

"I do."

"And on the principle that what is done by another's authority, it is virtually that other that does it? Thus, what the agent does by the authority of the principal is held to be done by the principal himself, who is responsible for it. What an ambassador does by the authority of his government is done by his government. Consequently, what one does by the authority of God is done by God himself, and the responsibility rests on him, and not on his agent. So what one teaches by divine authority is taught by God himself, and God is responsible for it. No one can, then, be divinely commissioned to teach what God may not himself teach immediately, and for which he will not hold himself responsible."

"I do not deny it."

"Can God teach or be responsible for error, or for any thing but truth?"

"He cannot."

"Then he can authorize no one to teach any thing but truth?"

"He cannot."

"Then he who is divinely commissioned can teach nothing but truth?"

"Apparently so."

"He who can teach nothing but truth is infallible, is he not?"

"So it would seem."

"Then the divine commission is, as I have said, the warrant of infallibility, and as one cannot be infallible without the assistance of the Holy Ghost, it necessarily implies that assistance. Consequently, the claim to the divine commission to teach the word of God is necessarily and essentially the claim to infallibility in teaching, and therefore to the assistance of the Holy Ghost, so far as needed to enable the teacher to teach the word, and to preserve him from error in teaching it. Is it not so?"

"I have been accustomed to think differently, but let it pass."

"Then my position, that the essential claim of the church is that she teaches the word infallibly, is not different from the one I assumed the other day, when I declared it to be the claim to the commission to teach, or that she had the word of God and was its legal keeper and expounder?"

"Be it so."

"Then you produce no adverse claimant, since you produce none that even pretends to be able to teach the word infallibly."

"Very well."

"But in pleading an adverse title, you conceded that the title was issued, and vests somewhere; or, in other words, that there is and must be somewhere such a church as the Roman claims to be. Now, as you do not and cannot produce an adverse claimant, you must concede that she is what she claims to be; therefore the church of God; and therefore that you and all who make war upon her are rebels and traitors to God. Is it in this way you propose to vindicate the reformers?"

Poor James was misled by his Protestant theology, which

makes every thing pertaining to religion a sham. Thus, justification is with it, not making one just, but *reputing* him just,—a forensic, not an inward, intrinsic justification. It is no real justification at all, but a mere make-believe justification,—to say nothing of the blasphemy of representing God as accounting or reputing a man just who is intrinsically unjust,—for it leaves the man as foul a sinner as he was before he was justified. So in the matter of the divine commission to teach, this same theology teaches that one may have the commission, be authorized by God to teach, and yet not teach infallibly, as if God could authorize the teaching of a lie! A queer thing is this Protestant theology! Well may its authors and adherents boast themselves the lights of the age!

This notion, that the authority does not necessarily imply the ability to teach, is the source of much of that prejudice which exists in the Protestant community against all claims to authority from God to teach his word. There is a general feeling among the great majority of intelligent Protestants, that there can be no divine authority to teach where there is not the ability to teach; and seeing nowhere among themselves any teacher who has the ability, they very naturally conclude that no one has the authority. It is absurd, say they, to suppose that God authorizes a man like ourselves to teach, a man who knows no more than we do, and is no better able to teach than the rest of us. When the Catholic speaks to them of the commission of his church to teach, and that God gives her authority to teach all nations, they turn up their noses, and ask us, if we suppose they are such fools as to believe that God, the common Father of us all, has given to mortals like ourselves authority to teach us, and commanded us to yield up our own reason and judgment to our fellow-men!

Now, probe the matter to the bottom, and you will find that these people object by no means to the idea that God may authorize men to teach his word, but simply to the notion that the authority can exist where the requisite qualifications to teach are wanting. Their real objection is to the doctrine which Mr. James Milwood attempts to maintain, that teachers confessedly fallible as teachers may nevertheless be divinely commissioned to teach. They object, not to the Catholic doctrine of authority, but to the Protestant. To really God-commissioned teachers, that is, teachers who, in their judgment, have the intrinsic ability to teach truly and infallibly the word of God, they do not object, as is evident from their tendency to hero-worship, and their common remark that he who is able is divinely commissioned. Read Carlyle, Emerson, the transcendentalists generally, and you will find that it is always to the notion of authority without the intrinsic ability that they object, and that wherever they fancy the ability they are ready to concede the commission. They err in making the ability the warrant of the authority, instead of making the commission the warrant of the ability; yet they are right against Protestantism, and perceive a great and essential truth which old-fashioned Protestantism denies, namely, that the authority and the intrinsic ability to teach are inseparable, and that any authority separate from the ability cannot be conferred by God, and is therefore a usurpation. To one who is familiar with the Protestant community, and who comprehends its more recent developments of thought, it is evident that Protestants are very generally growing tired and sick of sham and shamming. They are rapidly becoming unable to satisfy themselves with a religion which is no real religion, but a mere make-believe religion. They cry out from the depths of their hearts for something real, for something which *is*, not merely *seems*. They see that the reformers built on mere *seeming*, and taught and acted a lie,—gave them hollow appearances, and no solid realities,—at best, the mere hull without the kernel,—a symbol symbolizing nothing,—a mere pretence; and they grow indignant, turn away in disgust, and say, "Give us something real, something that is, if it be but the devil; for any thing that *is* is better than nothing seeming to be something. If your religion is a mere sham, call it a sham and away with it; for the oldest gospel is, that a lie is a lie, and no truth. Stop lying, stop seeming, and begin to be." So deep is this feeling of the hollowness of all Protestant pretensions, and so strong is the craving for something real, that it has almost become one of the cants of the day.

It is true, that, knowing no religion but the Protestant, they to whom we refer conclude rashly that Catholicity is also a sham, also a mere hollow pretence, and that no religion is real but that of nature. But in this they draw a conclusion quite too broad for their premises. The church detests Protestantism as heartily as they do, and, in most cases, for like reasons. She detests it because it is outward, lifeless, empty, and no living reality; because it contains nothing solid, substantial, has no bottom, but is bottomless, like the pit from which it is an exhalation, and into which, as the religious atmosphere clears up, it subsides. She condemns with all her energy whatever is mere pretence or make-believe. She tolerates no empty forms, no insignificant rites, no vain ceremonies. She will and can approve nothing which is not real, solid, substantial. She teaches the doctrine of the REAL PRESENCE, and always presents the very reality she symbolizes. She can call no man justified who is not intrinsically just, and recognize no teacher as teaching by divine authority who does not teach God's word infallibly. If these people would turn their attention to her, they would soon find the truth and reality for which their hearts cry out; for, to say the least, grace is not less true and real than nature.

CHAPTER IX.

"UNQUESTIONABLY," at length James replied, "there is no other church which makes the same specific claim as the Romish, and if my plea of an adverse title is to be taken as a concession that God has founded such a church, I of course must concede that she is it, and that the reformers cannot be justified."

"I have not confined you to her *specific* character; I have only restricted you to her *generic* character, to what she must absolutely be, if a church at all, with divine authority to teach."

"Well, let that pass. I made the concession, not absolutely, but provisorily; since, as you well know, I do not and cannot, as a Presbyterian, admit that our Lord ever founded, specifically or generically, such a church as the Romish claims to be, and which is no church of Christ, but a synagogue of Satan."

"Then you retract your plea of an adverse title, and revoke your concession?"

"I do."

"Very well; as I have no wish to take advantage of your mistakes, you may do so. What do you plead now?"

"The Romish church is corrupt, and by her corruptions has forfeited her title to be the church of God."

"That is your original plea, which you withdrew for the sake of pleading that no title was ever issued, or, in other words, that our Lord had founded no such church as she claims to be. You will remember that you cannot plead at one and the same time the forfeiture of title, and that no title ever existed. A title which never existed cannot have been forfeited. The allegation, that the church has forfeited her title, concedes, then, that the title originally existed, and was hers. Am I to understand you as meaning to concede that our Lord did originally found such a church as the Roman claims to be, and that she was originally that church?"

"Not at all. I do not admit that such a title as she claims ever existed."

"You deny, then, that our Lord ever founded such a church as she claims to be, that is, a church with authority from him to teach."

"I do."

"But she is in possession as such a church, and possession is *prima facie* evidence of title. If, then, you allege that no such title ever existed, the burden of proof is on you. But you cannot prove that no such title ever existed, as you learned in our conversation the other day. Moreover, you have just alleged forfeiture of title, which concedes that the title originally existed and was vested in the church of Rome. You cannot now deny that it ever existed."

"I admit *a* title once existed, and was vested in her, though not such a title as she claims; and when I say that she has forfeited her title, I mean not that she has forfeited such a title as she now claims, but such a title as she originally had."

"That is nothing to the purpose. But what was that title?"

"I have told you already, in declaring that she has forfeited her title to be the CHURCH OF GOD. I do not deny that the church of Rome was once a pure church, but I contend that she is now corrupt, and no longer God's church, or any portion of it."

"But the pure church, the church of God, is either such a church as the Roman claims to be, or a different church."

"It is widely different."

"Is the church of God one, or many?"

"Properly speaking, there is but one church, although the one church may be composed of many particular churches."

"But such must be the character of the particular churches as not to detract from the real unity of the whole?"

"Granted."

"And this one church composed of many particular churches is *the* church and the *only* church our Lord founded?"

"It is."

"And it is widely different from such a church as the Roman claims to be?"

"Certainly it is."

"Then you simply deny that our Lord ever founded such a church as the Roman claims to be, and merely reiterate the plea you have withdrawn."

"I do not care for that; I am not to be tied down by your arbitrary rules of special pleading. The church of Rome was once pure. She then belonged to the church of God; she is now corrupt, and has forfeited her title. I do not say her title to be such a church as she pretends to be, but to be an integral part of the church of God."

"She has degenerated from her original purity, and is now a corrupt church?"

"That is what I allege."

"But she is in possession as the pure and authoritative church of God, and the burden of proof that she is corrupt is on you."

"I accept it, and am ready to prove her corruption."

"Corruption implies a change from a former or primitive state. You must know that state, or you cannot know that she is corrupt."

"She has corrupted the word of God; she teaches the commandments of men for the pure word; and has so disfigured the original gospel of our Lord, that it can be no longer recognized in her teachings."

"That is for you to prove."

"I am ready to prove it. Indeed, it needs no proof. It is notorious. The world admits it. She has become a sink of corruption; is full of all manner of uncleanness and filth."

"Words, brother; mere words. Pause a moment and take breath, and then proceed to the proof. When you tell me the Catholic Church is corrupt, has degenerated, you assume a primitive state from which she has fallen; and it is only by comparing her present state with that primitive state, that you can determine that she has fallen from it. What, then, was that primitive state?"

"I can show what it was from the Scriptures."

"They are not in your possession. You are not their legal keeper, and have no authority to expound their sense. You can therefore make no appeal to them against the church who is in possession, and has, presumptively, the sole right to interpret them. She interprets them in her favor, and you are bound to presume her interpretations to be correct, till you can prove by a competent authority to the contrary. This competent authority you are not; for, on any conceivable hypothesis, at the very worst her authority is as good as yours can be at the very best. You must get a commission, or at least a *presumptive* commission, from Almighty God, as the legal keeper and expounder of the Sacred Scriptures, before you can prove any thing from them but your own arrogance and impudence."

"I can prove from the early fathers that the primitive church was essentially different from the present Romish Church."

"That is, you can prove it from early tradition?"

"Yes."

"But the church is in possession as the keeper and expounder of primitive tradition, as well as of the Sacred Scriptures. She interprets it in her own favor, and from it proves that she conforms perfectly to the primitive model."

"But she misinterprets the fathers."

"As a matter of fact, it is undeniable that the fathers may without violence be interpreted as she interprets them, and that she rightly interprets them is to be presumed, till the contrary is shown. Moreover, as her authority as the interpreter of primitive tradition, or of the fathers, is at the worst equal to yours at the best, you have and can have no sufficient authority for setting her interpretation aside. So the appeal to primitive tradition will avail you no more than the appeal to the Scriptures; and the fact that you have no authority to declare the sense of either debars you from all right to appeal to either against what she declares to be their sense."

"But she has corrupted the primitive faith."

"You cannot say that, unless you are authorized to say what the primitive faith was. She has presumptively the right to declare that faith, and she declares that it was what she now teaches, and therefore she declares that she has not corrupted it. You are bound to presume that she has not, and must prove that she has, before you can use an argument which *assumes* that she has. But what was the original faith which she has corrupted?"

"There is a great number of doctrines which she has corrupted. It is not necessary to mention all. Take, for instance, the doctrine of justification. The primitive doctrine was, that man is justified by faith alone; the Romish doctrine is, that man is justified by works."

"The Catholic doctrine is, that man is justified by faith and works, meaning thereby works done through grace purchased for us by the merits of our Lord; but on what authority do you assert that the primitive doctrine was, that man is justified by faith alone?"

"The Holy Scriptures."

"On what authority do you assert that the Holy Scriptures teach it?"

"Why, they teach it."

"You either have authority for saying so, or you have not. But you have not, as is certain from the fact that you have no authority to keep and expound the Scriptures. Then you say it without authority. An assertion made without any authority is worthless, and not to be entertained. Here is the answer to every instance of corruption of doctrine you do or can allege. In confessing the fallibility of your sect, you have confessed that you have no authority from God to teach his word. Then you have no authority for declaring what was the primitive faith, and then none for saying that the church has corrupted it."

"But the Romish Church has forfeited her title to be considered the church of God by authorizing superstition and idolatry, for evidently no church that authorizes these can be the church of God."

"That is something to your purpose, and you will be entitled to a judgment, if the evidence sustains you. You take now the only ground from which you can legitimately frame an argument against the church. Every previous ground you have taken has been untenable, because it required the authority to maintain it which you were contesting, and which you had not, and were obliged to presume to be in the church herself. You undertook to prosecute her under the law of grace, and failed for the want of a court of competent jurisdiction. As she is presumptively the supreme court, under the law of grace, you could under that law institute no process against her; for to every allegation you could make she had only to plead want of jurisdiction. The only possible way of prosecuting her is under the law of nature, and it is only by proving her to have violated some precept of that law, that you can obtain judgment against her. The law of nature falls, to some extent, under the jurisdiction of reason, and reason, to that extent, is its legal keeper and judge, and has the right to sit in judgment on its infractions. As the law of nature and that of grace both have the same origin, are enacted by the same sovereign Lawgiver, and as the latter confessedly presupposes the former and confirms it, it can never authorize what the former prohibits, any more than the former can authorize what the latter prohibits, unless we may suppose, what is not supposable, that God may be in contradiction with himself. The law of grace transcends the law of nature, but does not and cannot enjoin what it forbids. As superstition and idolatry are undeniably forbidden by the law of nature, if you prove that they are authorized, or in any sense sanctioned, by the church, you prove that she is not and cannot be the church of God. But she does not authorize or sanction them; she strictly forbids them. Thus, in her catechism for children she teaches the child to ask and answer:—

" ' *What is forbidden by this* [the first] *commandment?*

" ' To worship false gods or idols; or to give any thing else whatsoever the honor which belongs to God.

" ' *What else is forbidden by this commandment?*

" ' All false religions; all dealings with the devil; and inquiring after things to come, or secret things, by fortune-tellers or superstitious practices.

" ' *What else?*

" ' All charms, spells, and heathenish observation of omens, dreams, and such like fooleries.

" ' *Does this commandment forbid the making of images?*

" ' It forbids making them so as to adore them; that is, it forbids making them our gods.

" ' *Does this commandment forbid all honor and veneration of saints and angels?*

" ' No, we are to honor them as God's special friends and servants; but not with the honor which belongs to God.

" ' *And is it allowable to honor relics, crucifixes, and holy pictures?*

" ' Yes; with an inferior and relative honor, as they relate to Christ and his saints, and are memorials of them.

" ' *May we, then, pray to relics and images?*

" ' No, by no means; for they have no life or sense to hear or help us.'

Here is evidence enough that the church denies your charge. The burden of proof is on you, and you must prove her guilty of superstition and idolatry."

"And I am ready to prove it. The reformers charged her with idolatry, and we have never ceased from their day to reiterate the charge."

"But a lie, though a million of times repeated, is none the less a lie. Nobody disputes that Protestants have accused the church of idolatry, but that is not to the purpose. You must prove your allegation."

"Why, you might as well ask me to prove that there is a sun in the heavens. All the world knows that the church of Rome is sunk in the grossest idolatry and the foulest superstition."

"Words, words, brother; give me the proofs."

"Proofs! you need no proofs. The fact is undeniable, and nothing but the grossest impudence on the part of the Romish Church could ever dream of denying it."

"No advance in the argument, brother. Have you yet to learn that the unsupported assertions of a man who admits that he speaks without authority are not proofs? Here is the church, on the one hand, teaching her children, in the very first lessons she teaches them, to abhor idols and all superstitious practices; and here are you, on the other, accusing her of superstition, and that worst and most abominable species of superstition, idolatry,—she in possession and to be presumed to be the church of God, and you presumptively a rebel against God, and a calumniator, till you make good your charge. Prove, then, the charge, or withdraw it."

"The reformers proved it, the greatest and best of our writers have asserted it; it is a question settled, *res adjudicata*. Has it not entered into history? Do you not read it in the very elementary books for children? Look at the great and enlightened State of Massachusetts! she prohibits by law all sectarianism in her admirable system of schools, and the introduction into them of any books which show any preference for one religious denomination over another; and yet she does not hesitate to permit the introduction of books which teach that Papists are idolaters and image-worshippers. Have we not, in every land where we have had the power, prohibited the Romish worship? Why have we, the only friends of religious liberty, why have we who have poured out our treasure and our blood to redeem the world from papal tyranny and superstition, why have *we* done this, but for the reason that we have not dared tolerate superstition and idolatry?"

"Why did the Jews, God's chosen people, through whom the Messiah was to come, and who were hourly expecting him and praying for his coming, crucify him between two thieves when he did come, but on the pretext that he had a devil and was a blasphemer? Did the fact that they falsely accused him, and then crucified him on that false accusation, supported by false witnesses, render them the less guilty?"

"Do you mean to say that so many great and good men, so many pure and holy men, the glory of their age, their country, and their religion, have all conspired to bear false witness against the Romish Church? The thing is incredible."

"More so than that the Jewish nation conspired to crucify their God? I know nothing about your great and good men, your pure and holy men; but I know that whoever accuses the church of idolatry, or any species of superstition, utters as foul a lie as did the wicked Jews who told our Lord he had a devil, and that he blasphemed. No doubt, it is an easy matter to prove the church guilty, if all you have to do is to bring a false accusation, assume your own sanctity, and then conclude it must be well founded or you could not have made it. But your logic would be more respectable, if from the falsity of your accusation you concluded your want of sanctity. If the character of Protestants is a presumption against their conspiracy to bring a false accusation, the character of Catholics is a still stronger presumption against their having conspired to uphold and practise idolatry; for the great and pure and holy men who have lived and died in the Catholic faith, granting you all you can pretend to, are as a thousand to one to those of Protestant communions. But you forget that I was brought up a Protestant, and that to talk to me of Protestant sanctity is ridiculous. I am acquainted with Protestants, and with what they facetiously call their religion. Our dear mother, too, was brought up a Protestant, a Presbyterian, and yet what did she tell me on her deathbed?"

"What did she?"

"No matter now; but she did not die a Presbyterian."

"Did not? What mean you?"

"Some day, I may tell you, but you are not now worthy to hear."

"Did my father know?"

"As much as you, and no more."

"Did anybody know, but yourself?"

"Yes."

"Do you mean to insinuate that a Popish priest was smuggled into our house?"

"O my wise brother, you do not know all things. Angels of mercy, messengers of grace, are sometimes sent even where the ministers of Satan fancy they do and can find no admission. All things are possible with God, and nothing is too good for him to do for those who are obedient to his grace."

"Am I to understand that my mother on her death-bed renounced Presbyterianism, and became a Papist?"

"She did not die a Presbyterian. You may recollect, that during the last week of her life she refused to see Mr. Grimface, her old Presbyterian pastor."

"True, and my father and I thought it strange; but as we had no doubt of her being one of the elect, it gave us no great uneasiness. But there was no Romish priest within two hundred miles of us."

"I have no doubt that my mother died in a state of grace; but more I will not tell you, till you prove or withdraw your charge against the church."

"But why did not our mother tell us all, as well as you, of her apostasy?"

"She knew both your father and you, and that, if she had told you, she would have been denied the last consolations of religion; and after she had received them, there was no opportunity, till she became unable to do so. But your charge,—prove or withdraw it."

"I will prove it, but you must excuse me now. Our conversation has been long, and I am fatigued. But to-morrow, God willing, I will prove that the Romish Church is an idolatrous church."

"Be it so. But remember and prove it, or I shall require you to own that Protestantism——"

"Is of the devil. I accept the alternative. If I fail to establish the charge of idolatry and superstition against the Romish Church, I will consent that the reformers be branded as calumniators, and that Protestants are and have been from the first acting under the delusion of Satan."

"See that you keep your word."

The brothers separated for the remainder of the day, and James, though pleading fatigue, betook himself to his library to look up his proofs and prepare for the morrow. He felt that all depended on the issue he had joined, and that, if he failed to justify his charge, he could no longer pretend to uphold the reformers. Hitherto his brother had kept him discussing the law of the case; but now he thought he saw a chance of entering upon its merits, and of introducing his witnesses. How he succeeded will be related in the next chapter.

CHAPTER X.

"You will bear in mind, James," remarked John, on resuming the conversation the next day, "that you have pledged yourself to prove that the Catholic Church authorizes superstition and idolatry."

"And if I do not prove it," replied James, "I will abandon the reformers and the reformation."

"Since you prefer the charge, it devolves on you to prove it."

"That is not difficult. The fact is notorious."

"Assertions are easily made by the unscrupulous, my brother; but I ask for *proofs*."

"Proofs, proofs! I have them in abundance. What else are your prayers for the dead,—your invocation of saints,—your worship of Mary,—adoration of crucifixes, pictures, images, relics of dead men and women? What is all this, but the most abominable idolatry and superstition? What else is your adoration of the mass, and all the vain and empty ceremonies of your church? O, it is frightful to think to what horrible lengths idolatry and superstition are carried among you! What more besotted, than for a full-grown man to believe that the priest can make his God at will, to fall down and adore a bit of bread, or to imagine that he is worshipping God by kissing the crucifix and telling his beads? I hope, John, you, at least, avoid the superstitious practice of telling your beads."

"I say my beads daily for your conversion."

"That is enough; my charge is proved. When a man like you can do that, there is no need of other evidence to prove that your church favors superstition."

"It requires strong faith, no doubt, to be able to regard your conversion as possible; but all things are possible with God, and he has never been known to deny his holy Mother any request, for she can request nothing not in accordance with his will. If she intercedes for you, your conversion is certain."

"Worse and worse. You confess all I need to prove my charge."

"Did you ever read the record of the trial of our Lord?"

"Why do you ask that?"

"Because you remind me of his accusers, who pretended to convict him of blasphemy out of his own mouth. Yet it is nothing strange or uncommon for children to resemble their parents. You say the church is superstitious?"

"The *Romish* Church, yes; and I prove it."

"What is superstition?"

"A spurious religion or false worship; a false system of religion, credulity, vain observance."

"You would hardly be able to convict the church, or to attempt to convict her, of superstition, under that definition, without assuming that you have authority to determine, or by which you can determine, what is true religion; which we have seen is not the fact. Allow me to suggest a definition a little more to your purpose. Superstition is a vice opposed to true religion, as the schoolmen say, by way of excess, as irreligion is opposed to it by way of defect, and consists in rendering worship to an object to which it is not due, or an undue worship to the object to which it is due. It is, on the one hand, the worship of false gods, and, on the other, the false worship of the true God, and includes all you mean by both superstition and idolatry."

"Very well; I say the Romish Church is guilty of superstition in the sense in which you have defined the term."

"Superstition, in this sense, divides itself into the worship of false gods, and the false worship of the true God. It will be well to consider each division separately. Let us begin with the first, that is, *idolatry*, or giving the worship due to God alone to that which is not God; or, in other words, worshipping as God what is not God."

"The Romish Church worships as God what is not God."

"The proof?"

"She pays divine worship to the Virgin Mary."

"The proof?"

"She authorizes prayers to her."

"Nonsense! prayer is nothing but a request or a petition, and may without sin or impropriety be addressed by one man to another. You might as well say, the constitution of the United States authorizes idolatry, because it recognizes the right of petition, and forbids congress to make any law prohibiting the people from peaceably assembling and petitioning for a redress of grievances. As well say, every subject who petitions the king, or citizen who petitions the court or the legislature, is an idolater. Try again, brother."

"Your church honors her, a mere woman, as the mother of God."

"Well, if she is the mother of God, where is the harm in that, since it is only honoring her for what she is?"

"But she is not the mother of God."

"That is for you to prove. You must remember, however, that you are to convict the church of idolatry by the light of nature, and you can in your argument deny nothing the church teaches, unless it is forbidden by the natural law. Assuming the Blessed Virgin to be the mother of God,—as she must be, if Christ is God,—does the law of nature forbid her from being honored as such? This is the question."

"The law of nature, which, as you have agreed, forbids idolatry, forbids her being honored as God."

"Unquestionably; but does it forbid her being honored for what she is?"

"But Catholics worship her as divine, and pay her the worship which is due to God alone."

"The proof?"

"They call her our Advocate, our Mediatrix, and thus rob Christ of the glory which is his due; for he is the only Mediator between God and men."

"The only mediator and advocate, in his own right; but, for aught the law of nature says, his mother may be an advocate and a mediatrix under him, by his will and appointment; for she would then advocate or mediate only by his authority, and he would still be our only advocate and mediator,—since that which I do mediately by another, as my minister or delegate, I do myself as much as if I did it immediately. These terms, applied to the Blessed Virgin, no doubt imply that she is exalted above every other creature; but as her exaltation is that of a creature, and an exaltation not by her own natural right, but by grace, it by no means places her in the same rank with her Son, who is exalted above *every* creature, by his own right, the right of his own proper divinity which assumed humanity."

"But Catholics pray to her much more than they do to God."

"That may be questioned; but if so, it is nothing to your

purpose. You must prove that they pray to her as God, ask of her what may be rightfully asked only of God, and that they pay her honors which are due to him alone."

"They pray to her to have mercy on them, and mercy is the prerogative of God alone."

"Mercy, in the sense of pardon or forgiveness of sin, is the property of God only; and in this sense, Catholics never ask the Blessed Virgin to have mercy on them. But mercy, in the sense of pity or compassion, belongs to human beings. Thus we say, 'The merciful man is merciful to his beast.' To ask the Blessed Virgin to have compassion on us, and to intercede with her divine Son for us, to obtain his pardon for us by her powerful intercession, is nothing more than we may lawfully ask of our pastors,—nothing more than what the Scriptures say the Lord commanded the three friends of Job to do."

"The worship which Catholics pay to the saints in general is idolatry."

"The highest form of worship we pay to any saint is that which we pay to the holy Mother of God. If that is not idolatrous, then, *a fortiori*, not that which we pay to the other saints."

"But you honor the saints."

"And what do you conclude from that? Does not the law of nature command us to give honor to whom honor is due? What authority have you for supposing that we pay *undue* honor to the saints?"

"To honor them as God, in the place of God, is to give them an honor which is not their due, and is idolatry."

"Granted; but who so honors them?"

"Catholics."

"The proof?"

"Catholics may not honor them as the Supreme God; but they honor them as a species of inferior gods, as the *Dii Minores* of the heathen."

"The proof?"

"The fact is evident of itself."

"Not by any means. The honors the heathen paid to their inferior gods were different in kind from those which we pay to the saints, and, moreover, were paid as due them in their own natural right, and not as due only to what they became through grace. The heathen offered sacrifices, and therefore paid *divine* honors, to their inferior gods. Catholics offer no sacrifices and pay no divine honors to the saints; they venerate them for what, through grace, they became, and they ask their prayers and intercession, which is no more than we may ask of the living, and is no more than your parishioners not unfrequently ask of you,—no more than you sanction whenever you pray God for your congregation, or for an individual who has requested to be remembered in your prayers."

"But you have no warrant in Scripture for praying to the saints."

"That were nothing to the purpose, if true. You bring your action on the law of nature; and when you find that under the law of nature you have no cause of action, you are not at liberty to plead some other law. If praying to the saints is not idolatry by the law of nature, you cannot allege it under the head of idolatry, against the church."

"But, unless the church has a warrant in the word of God for praying to the saints, she has no right to pray to them."

"And unless it is forbidden by some precept of the law of nature, you cannot deny her right."

"The Romish Church worships crosses, dead men's bones, locks of their hair, their finger-nails, and shreds of their garments."

"What then?"

"Then she is idolatrous; for we must worship God, and him only."

"*Worship* is a word of more than one meaning; it may mean paying divine honors, and also simply paying a civil respect, honoring or acknowledging worth wherever we find it. In the former sense, it is due to God alone, and is by Catholics paid to him alone, and never to the objects you enumerate. In the latter sense, it may be paid, and the law of nature requires that it should be paid, to kings, judges, magistrates, to our parents, and to whosoever by rank or worth is entitled to honor. In this sense, the law of nature not only does not forbid, but commands us to honor or to treat with respect such objects as are related to eminent worth. To honor crosses and relics of the saints, for the worth to which they are related, is, then, in accordance with the law of nature, and it is only in this sense that we honor, respect, or, if you please, *worship* them."

"But you do not honor them merely as memorials of a worth which was real; you pay them divine honors."

"False!"

"Not false. Witness the Holy Coat of Treves."

"What of that?"

"Multitudes, in the recent pilgrimage to it, prayed to it, saying, 'O Holy Coat, have mercy on us!'"

"The evidence of what you assert?"

"It is said so."

"By whom, and on what authority?"

"Do you deny it?"

"Deny it? Do you suppose Catholics are so besotted as to pray to what has no life, no sense, no power to help them, and that, too, when their church, as I showed you yesterday, positively prohibits praying to relics? The thing is impossible; no Catholic ever did, or ever could, utter such a prayer. You must not judge our people by your own. We preserve, and we honor, the relics of departed saints; they remind us of the worth of the saints; and when they do so, we pray to the *saints* to pray God for us, and procure for us the graces and favors we need. What precept of the law of nature does this violate?"

"Why not pray directly to God?"

"That question is out of place. Why do you ask a fellow-mortal to pray for you? Why do you pray and intercede for your congregation?"

"But you are idolaters, for you worship images."

"If by *worship* you mean paying divine honors, your assertion is false."

"Your houses and churches are full of images and pictures, and you kneel and pray to them."

"Kneel and pray *before* them, I grant; kneel and pray *to* them, I deny. There is a difference between praying *before* an image and praying *to* it, which I should suppose even a Protestant might understand."

"But you break the second commandment; and that your deluded followers may not detect the fact, you have expunged it from the Decalogue."

"We do not expunge what you call the second commandment; we only reckon it as a part of the first commandment."

"Nevertheless you break it, for it says, 'Thou shalt not make unto thee any graven image, or any likeness of any thing that is in heaven above, or that is in the earth beneath, or that is in the water under the earth.'"

"Graven *thing*, not graven *image*, is the correct translation, and more to your purpose; otherwise the precept would not forbid making statues of Jupiter, Neptune, and other purely fictitious beings. But do you understand that precept to forbid absolutely the making and keeping of images, statues, or pictures?"

"Of course I do; I am not wise above what is written."

"Nobody asks you to be wise above what is written; the question is, What *is* written? Then I am to understand you to maintain that Moses broke that commandment when he made and set up the brazen serpent in the wilderness; that Solomon broke it when he placed the brazen sea in the temple on twelve brazen oxen; that it was broken by the images of the Cherubim, who spread out their wings over the mercy-seat where God promised to meet his people; that our stern Puritans of Massachusetts break it by suspending the image of a codfish in their State House; that Congress break it in ordering a statue of Washington; and that it is broken by that dog's head carved on your cane, and those lion's claws on the feet of your table?"

"No, I do not say all that."

"Well, what do you say?"

"Why, that the commandment forbids the making and keeping of images, &c., as objects of religious veneration."

"That is, 'Thou shalt not adore them, nor serve them,' or, as the catechism says, 'It forbids making them, so as to adore and serve them; that is, it forbids making them our gods.'"

"But the Romish Church commands, you cannot deny, supreme religious worship to be paid to what you call the sacred Host."

"What then?"

"Then she is idolatrous; for she commands her children to pay divine honors to a bit of bread."

"False! She commands no such thing. She commands us to worship Jesus Christ, who is God and man, entitled in his own right to supreme worship, and who veils his divinity and his humanity both under the sacramental species. It is not the bread, for she teaches there is no bread there, but the Son who is consubstantial to the Father, and whom we are to honor as we honor the Father, that she commands us to adore. There is, then, no idolatry in the adoration."

"But her teaching is false,—the Host is nothing but bread."

"That is a matter which you, by the light of nature, cannot decide."

"But she must prove to me that it is not bread, before I can be bound to adore it."

"Undoubtedly; but you must prove that it *is* bread, before you can pronounce the adoration idolatrous."

"But I have the evidence of my senses that it is bread."

"You have the evidence of your senses that the species of bread are there, and that the church asserts; but that, under the species of bread, there is the *substance* of bread, you have *not* the evidence of your senses; for the senses never, in any case whatever, take cognizance of substances. You have, therefore, the evidence of your senses against nothing the church asserts. Consequently, by the light of nature alone, you can neither affirm nor deny what she asserts; and unless you can deny it, you cannot say that the adoration of the Host is idolatrous. If what she teaches be true, the adoration is due, and commanded by the natural law, which commands us to give to every one his due. Have you any thing more to adduce in support of the charge of idolatry?"

"Perhaps it is true that Catholics worship, in the strict sense of the word, only God; but, though they may worship the true object, they render him a false worship."

"That is, they worship him in an undue manner."

"Yes, that is what I mean."

"To be able to say that, you must first determine the *due* manner of worshipping him. But you cannot do this without authority, and you have, as we have seen, no authority, except the light of nature. Are you able by the light of nature alone to determine what is the due worship of God?"

"I am able, in some cases, at least, by the light of nature, to say what is *not* due worship."

"Be it so; what is there, then, in Catholic worship forbidden by the law of nature?"

"All her peculiar worship,—her saint-worship, her veneration of relics, her beads and crucifixes, her fasts and feasts, her empty forms and idle ceremonies."

"Her empty forms and idle ceremonies? By what authority do you pronounce her forms empty, and her ceremonies idle?"

"Do you deny that her whole worship consists of empty forms and idle ceremonies?"

"Of course I do. But be so good as to specify what you call an empty form, or an idle ceremony."

"The light of nature teaches us that God is not worshipped by mere show, by vain pomp and parade, and that no worship can be acceptable to him which is not real, in spirit and in truth."

"Granted; proceed."

"Your bowings and genuflections, your fasts and your feasts, are a vain mockery, if merely external, and the heart be far from God."

"No doubt of it; proceed."

"Confessions to a priest, external acts of penance, the repetition of *paters* and *aves*, and even the giving of alms, are vain illusions, and have no power to purge the conscience, if there be not genuine repentance, deep and pungent sorrow for sin."

"Nothing in the world more true; proceed."

"The heart must be right; there must be internal holiness, or all our outward worship will avail us nothing."

"As true as preaching. Go on."

"This is enough. In conceding this much, you condemn your church."

"How so?"

"Because all she enjoins is outward, formal, mechanical, addressed to the senses and imagination, requiring no internal purity and holiness in the worshipper."

"And where did you learn that?"

"Is it not so?"

"What proof have you that it is so?"

"It is what the reformers and we have always alleged against her."

"If they have called the master of the house Beelzebub, how much more them of his household! I have not asked what you allege, but the proof of what you allege, against the church."

"Do you mean to call all Protestants false witnesses and calumniators?"

"Is it more unreasonable to believe them to be such, than it is to believe that the overwhelming majority of all who bear the Christian name, or have borne it, have, for eighteen hundred years, or from the very age of the apostles, been sunk in superstition, and guilty of the abominable sin of idolatry? It seems to me much easier to believe that a Protestant can calumniate than that a Catholic can be an idolater; and in so believing, I believe nothing worse of you than you profess to believe of us."

"What else can one see in your worship than mere outward form?"

"What else should you expect to see in external worship but external worship? External is by its very nature external; and I am unable to comprehend how the church should have an external worship, and yet not an external worship. But if you had ever taken the least pains to inform yourself, you would have known that the church teaches all her children that no external act, which does not proceed from internal justice and sanctity, is, or can be, meritorious."

"You rely on the sacraments."

"Well, what then?"

"Are they not outward?"

"Are they not inward?"

"Does not the church teach that the child is regenerated in baptism?"

"She does."

"And it is no superstition to believe that a little water poured upon the head of the child, and a few words muttered over him by the priest, can regenerate the soul?"

"If you make the water and the words the efficient cause of the regeneration, it is unquestionably superstition, for none but the Holy Ghost can regenerate the child; but if you understand by the water and the words simply the medium through which the Holy Ghost is pleased to communicate the grace which regenerates, there is no superstition; for the cause assigned is adequate to the effect. The church teaches the latter; the former is the vain fancy of her calumniators."

"If it is the Holy Ghost that regenerates, why can he not regenerate without the water and words as well as with them?"

"That is a question which does not fall within the jurisdiction of the law of nature. You and I have no right to call Almighty God to an account, and to ask him, Why do you so?"

"But how does the church know that the Holy Ghost regenerates in baptism?"

"That is a question which pertains to positive revelation, and not to the natural law. The revelation is her authority for what she asserts, concerning which, if it do not contradict natural reason, the natural law enacts nothing."

"There are other sacraments."

"Certainly; but all are founded on the same principle, and are not the efficient cause of grace, but the media through which the Holy Ghost communicates the graces which our Lord, by his own infinite merits, has purchased for us."

"But anybody can receive the sacrament, whatever his internal disposition; and the efficacy of the sacrament does not depend on the recipient."

"Anybody can receive the sacrament externally; but nobody can receive any spiritual benefit from it, unless he receives it with proper internal dispositions. He who should approach the sacrament of penance, for instance, without all you understand by *repentance*, would, instead of receiving the fruits of the sacrament, only profane it, and add to his guilt. In the sacrament of the Eucharist, he who eats or drinks unworthily eats and drinks condemnation to himself. The efficacy of the sacrament does not, indeed, depend on the recipient; but that the recipient may experience its effects, or that it may operate its effects in him, he must take care that he interpose by his malice no obstacle to its operation."

"But what is the use of your saint-worship?"

"That is not precisely the question."

"The worship, if useless, is idle or vain, and therefore superstitious. You must, then, prove that it is not useless, or you do not clear your church of the charge of superstition."

"You must prove from the light of nature that it *is* useless, or you do not sustain your charge against her. You bring the action, and the burden of proof is on you."

"I accuse the church of superstition; and I adduce as proof of my accusation the worship of the saints, which she authorizes."

"But you cannot adduce your accusation in proof of your accusation. The *cultus sanctorum* is conceded to be authorized by the church, and the very point in dispute is, Whether that is or is not superstitious. It is only on the assumption that it is, that you can conclude from it that the church is superstitious. To assume that it is superstitious is to assume what is in question, which you are not permitted to do. You must, therefore, since the point is denied, prove that the *cultus sanctorum* is useless."

"Reason can see no use in it."

"That, if conceded, were not enough. You can conclude nothing against the church from the inability of reason.

Reason must be able to affirm its inutility, or it can affirm nothing to your purpose."

"But I must have affirmative proof that it is useful, before I can reasonably assent to it."

"Nothing more true; but the authority of the church suffices for that, unless you can divest her of her authority. You are attempting to convict the church of superstition, in order to be able to conclude against her authority. You must, then, prove that she authorizes superstition, as the condition of setting aside her authority, and, therefore, that what she authorizes is superstitious, as the condition of proving that she authorizes superstition. It is, therefore, not for me to prove that the *cultus sanctorum* is useful, but for you to prove that it is useless, and therefore superstitious."

"It is an undue worship."

"That is the point you must prove."

"Any worship which God forbids, does not exact, or approve, is an undue worship, and therefore superstition."

"Granted; what then?"

"What is your authority for saying that God does exact or approve what you term the *cultus sanctorum?*"

"Your memory is apparently very short. Let me ask you by what authority you assert that God forbids it, or does not exact or approve it."

"I find no authority for it in the Scriptures."

"That is not certain; but you cannot appeal to the Scriptures, for you have no legal possession of them and are not authorized to interpret them, and because you bring your action, not on the revealed, but on the natural law. Besides, the fact that you find no authority for the *cultus sanctorum* is not sufficient for your purpose; you must have authority *against* it, and you can conclude nothing against it, unless you find it prohibited by the law of nature."

"I know, by the light of nature, that God does not exact or approve, but forbids, all idle and vain worship."

"Undoubtedly; but what *is* idle and vain worship?"

"The Romish worship of the saints."

"That is begging the question, or making your accusation the proof of the truth of your accusation,—the ordinary Protestant method of proving what they assert against the church. But proceeding in this way, we shall never be able to come to any conclusion. Is not any worship superstitious in which the worshipper looks for effects from inadequate causes?"

"Perhaps so."

"Thus it is superstition to fear bad luck because we have seen the new moon over our left shoulder, or because we have begun a piece of work, put to sea, or commenced a journey on Friday; to expect to discharge what we owe to God by paying divine honors to what is not God, to please him by vain observances, or to obtain blessings by means of prayers to inanimate or senseless objects,—objects which can neither bestow the blessings nor intercede with God for them; for in these, and all similar cases, the causes are inadequate to the effects. On the contrary, in all cases in which the effects feared or expected are feared and expected from adequate causes, although there may be error, there is no superstition."

"Be it so."

"Then in order to convict the *cultus sanctorum* of superstition, you must show that the effects we expect from it are expected from inadequate causes."

"That can easily be done. The saints cannot atone for our sins, and be our mediators."

"Granted; nor do we expect any thing of the sort from them. All we ask of them is their prayers."

"Even that is superstitious, because the saints have no power to hear your prayers or to pray for you."

"How know you that?"

"They are no longer living."

"In the flesh, conceded; but the church assures us that they still live in the presence of God, and if they do, they can hear our prayers in him, and do for us all we ask of them; and how can you, from the light of nature, say they do not so live?"

"Your veneration of relics is superstitious, for you acknowledge that they have no life or sense to help you."

"We do not expect them to help us."

"Then the veneration is idle, and therefore superstitious."

"In the respect we pay to the relics of a saint, it is the saint we honor; and whatever we expect, we expect from the intercession of the saint, and through that intercession from God, who is honored in his saints, and who himself delights to honor them."

"But the superstition is in supposing that honoring the relics is honoring the saint."

"The law of nature teaches the reverse; for that teaches

us that honor to what belonged to another, because it belonged to him, is a pious and affecting mode of honoring him. Hence the universality of funeral ceremonies, the marks of respect which all men show to the relics of their deceased friends, especially to the remains of those held to be deserving of honor for their rank, their virtues, their services, their heroic deeds; and surely none are more deserving of honor than the saints of God."

"Your feasts, fasts, and external observances are all superstitious."

"How do you prove that?"

"They are all external and mechanical; and to expect spiritual effects from them is to look for effects from inadequate causes."

"The law of nature commands us to worship God externally as well as internally, and an external worship must needs be external. The fact, that what you object to is external, is, therefore, no ground of objection. Feasts or festivals are merely days set apart for public thanksgiving to God for his mercies and favors to us, in becoming man for us, in suffering and dying for us, in rising again for us, in sending us the Holy Ghost, in raising up and giving to us such or such a saint, &c. If kept according to the intent of the church, internal as well as external thanks are rendered by each worshipper, and therefore the observance of the festival is not and cannot be mechanical. The law of nature commands the giving of thanks to God; and perhaps even the mere external observance of appointed seasons for public thanksgiving is better than no observance at all. Fasts are for the mortification of the body; they are admirably adapted to that end; and the light of nature teaches us that the mortification of the body is wholesome for the soul. Moreover, to fast, as required, is also to fast with proper interior dispositions. You cannot, then, say, either that in them there is only a mechanical action, or that we look for effects from inadequate causes."

"But the idle ceremonies and vain observances of your public worship are superstitious."

"If idle and vain, superstitious of course; but how do you know that they are idle and vain? Our public worship consists of the holy sacrifice of the Mass, prayers, and singing the praises of God. These you have no right to pronounce idle or vain. Our sacrifice we hold to be a real sacrifice, in an unbloody manner, of a real victim; and prayers and the singing of praises have, by the common consent of mankind,—the authority for determining what is the law of nature,—always been held to be appropriate parts of public worship. Much of what you call idle ceremony and vain observance is integral in the worship itself; and what is not absolutely essential is adopted for the sake of decency, solemnity, and the edification of the faithful."

"I am not edified by it."

"Because you are not one of the faithful, and do not worship. Satan, no doubt, could himself bring the objection to our worship which you do. Our worship is adapted to the edification of those who worship, not of those who do not."

"But your worship is calculated to lead the weak and ignorant into idolatry and superstition."

"It will be time to consider that objection when you have shown that a Catholic, by practising what the church enjoins or permits, is rendered superstitious."

"Your worship is exceedingly offensive."

"To whom? To Protestants? Then let them become Catholics,—especially since they have no warrant from Almighty God to be any thing else."

"Your church is exceedingly impolitic. The practices to which we object may have been very well in dark and superstitious ages; but men in this enlightened and scientific age demand a more pure and spiritual worship."

"The policy you would recommend to the church, then, is, to be superstitious with the superstitious, and irreligious with the irreligious? If her practices could have a superstitious tendency, it is precisely in a dark and superstitious age in which they would be dangerous, and when it would be least proper to insist on them. If this age be what you suppose, it is precisely now that they are most appropriate, as being in opposition to dominant tendencies. But the church is not reduced to the necessity of taking the advice of those who despise her, and very possibly the age is not so enlightened as it appears to those whose eyes are accustomed only to the twilight. Have you any thing more to add?"

"There is no use in continuing the discussion. Let me say what I will, you will dispose of it by declaring it irrelevant, or by a sophistical distinction."

"Do you keep your word, and give up the reformers and the reformation?"

"You have not made me a Romanist."

"I have not attempted to do that; I have simply demanded of you a reason why you are a Protestant."

"I have given you reasons which satisfy me, and that is enough. Each of us must answer for himself, and not for another."

"You pledged yourself, if you failed to convict the church of idolatry and superstition, to give up the Protestant cause. Do you regard yourself as having made out your case?"

"There is no use in multiplying words. My mind is made up."

"You have no right to make up your mind without reason."

"My choice is made. I was born a Protestant; I have lived a Protestant; and I will die a Protestant."

"If you choose death, you, no doubt, can have it. Almighty God forces no man to enter into life."

"I take the responsibility; and nothing shall move me."

Here the conversation ended, and the two brothers separated. John entered a religious house, where he resides, devoting himself wholly to religion; James remains the minister of his congregation. He has recently married again, and he appears to have forgotten his domestic afflictions. He continues at the head of the "Protestant League," is louder than ever in praise of the reformers and the glorious reformation, and more violent than ever in his denunciations of Catholics and Catholicity. Humanly speaking, there is no hope of his conversion. It is to be feared that James Milwood is the type of a large class of Protestant ministers. I would judge no individual, but it seems to me that the notion many people have that Protestants are generally in good faith, and ready to embrace the truth, if presented to them, rests on no adequate authority. So far as I have known Protestants, they are ready to say, as said a Protestant minister to me the other day, "I would rather be damned than be a Catholic."

PROFESSOR PARK AGAINST CATHOLICITY.*

[From Brownson's Quarterly Review for October, 1845.]

THE periodical here introduced to our readers is a quarterly review, somewhat larger than our own, published at Andover, Massachusetts, and "edited by B. B. Edwards and Edwards A. Park, Professors in Andover Theological Seminary, with the special co-operation of Dr. Robinson and Professor Stuart." It is the most elaborate, erudite, and authoritative organ of the Puritan or Calvinistic denomination of Protestants we are acquainted with, though it wants the lively and interesting character of *The New Englander*, another organ of the same denomination, which is published at New Haven, in Connecticut. It is able, but, upon the whole, rather heavy. It appears to be made up, in great part, from translations, learning, and ideas from the modern rationalists, supernaturalists, and evangelicals of Germany, and its pages bear very unequivocal evidence that its contributors have made considerable proficiency in "High Dutch."

But our present concern is not with the journal, but with the third article in the number before us, on the *Intellectual and Moral Influence of Romanism*,—a Dudleian Lecture, delivered before the University of Cambridge, last May, by Professor Edwards A. Park, of Andover Theological Seminary, and one of the editors of the *Review* itself. We have heard Professor Park spoken of as a profound thinker, an able reasoner, and an eminent scholar, and been assured that he holds a high rank among his brother professors. His Lecture has evidently been elaborated with great care, and, considering the importance of the question it discusses, and the distinguished body before whom it was prepared to be delivered, we may reasonably presume it to be a fair specimen of what he is able to accomplish. He has done here, probably, the best he could. If so, we cannot help thinking that it requires no extraordinary abilities or attainments to be a distinguished professor in Andover Theological Seminary; for

---

*Bibliotheca Sacra and Theological Review, No. VII., Andover. August, 1845.

the Lecture, though it makes some pretensions to a philosophical appreciation of principles and tendencies, is characterized by no remarkable depth or acuteness of thought, force or justness of reasoning, extent, variety, or accuracy of scholarship, novelty of view, originality of illustration, clearness of method, precision, strength, or beauty of expression. From a commonplace lecturer against "Popery" it would be respectable; but we are not able to discover in it any thing to indicate the distinguished professor, or that in the seminary in which its author *can* be a distinguished professor there prevails any but a low tone of thought and feeling.

In a community accustomed to close, vigorous, and just reasoning,—accustomed to demand a reason before believing, and not to believe without a tolerable reason for believing, and in which the real principles and history of Catholicity were passably known,—this Lecture could only excite a smile at the author's simplicity or temerity, and would deserve and receive no answer. But, unhappily, ours is not such a community. Our *enlightened* community has a remarkable facility in disbelieving against reason, and in believing without reason. It will believe any thing against Catholicity, on the bare assertion of an individual whose oath, in a case involving property to the amount of five dollars, it would not take,—and not believe any thing in its favor, though sustained by evidence the most conclusive. Consequently, we have heard this Lecture, in which there is nothing from beginning to end but bare assertion, unsustained by the least fact or argument, highly commended, as a masterpiece of philosophical investigation and of logical argument,—a triumphant refutation of the claims of the Catholic Church; and one of our editors, a most malignant enemy of Catholicity, goes so far as even to intimate in one of his papers, that, if its reasoning should be fairly met and refuted, he would almost or quite turn "Romanist" himself. We hope, however, in this the editor is joking; for we should be sorry to gain a convert on such easy terms,—fearing he would hardly be worth having, and that he would be one in whom the word would soon wither away. Nevertheless, this indicates the state of our community, and shows, that, however intrinsically undeserving a serious reply the Lecture may be, it yet, under existing circumstances, requires to be refuted, so far as what is without principle can be refuted.

The design of the Lecture, as the author himself tells us

(p. 452), is to "attempt to show that the *essential* tendencies of Romanism [Catholicity] are injurious to the mind and heart of man." Its design is not to show, that in the history of the Catholic Church, reference being had to the conduct of churchmen, and not to what the church officially teaches and commands, there has been much evil,—many depravities of mind and heart, justly deplorable, justly censurable,—but that the *essential* tendencies of Catholicity are injurious; or that the injurious effects the author thinks he has discovered are not merely *accidents* of the system, growing out of the ignorance of the human mind and the depravity of the human heart, against which the church always struggled, though unable at once to overcome them, —but that they are essential in her very nature, necessarily inseparable from her very existence and action. In proof of this, he alleges that Catholicity, 1. Discountenances the investigation of first principles; 2. Checks the instinctive longings of the soul for progress in the science of divine things; 3. Exalts the traditions of antiquity above our own perceptions of truth, and degrades the mind by communion with triflers; 4. Authorizes a worship which presents a low standard of thought and feeling; 5. Is deficient in candor, in truth, and in eminent philosophers and preachers; 6. Holds doctrines which have a peculiar tendency to be perverted; 7. Adopts mystical machinery, or asserts that the efficacy of the sacraments is *ex opere operato*; 8. Has a tendency to separate religion from good morals, or undervalues morality as distinct from religion, and thus gives a false idea of religion itself; 9. Is austere; 10. Engenders an exclusive and persecuting spirit; 11. Founds religion on faith instead of reason; 12. Is fascinating to all classes; and, 13. Is peculiarly injurious to a republic.

Here is a formidable list of charges, and some of them rather queer ones to come from a theological professor, who himself has a fixed creed, and is a professor in a seminary in which the professors are obliged to subscribe to a creed imposed, not by the church even, but by the lay-founders of the professorships, and to renew their subscriptions every five years. But this is of small moment. It will be seen by the Catholic reader at a glance, that the professor proceeds throughout on what logicians call a *petitio principii*, or begging the question. Set aside all those charges which are false in fact, and those which can be urged only by an unbeliever, take only those which have some foundation in truth, and not one of them is or can be injurious to the mind, if the church be what she claims to be. They could be injurious only in case the church were a human institution, fallible, and unable to teach with authority. When, therefore, he assumes them to be injurious, he assumes that the church is a mere human institution, which we do not grant him, and which is the very point he should first establish.

Moreover, before proceeding to the direct consideration of these charges, we must demand of the professor, by what authority he determines what is injurious to the mind and heart of man. He says the tendencies of the church are injurious. We deny his assumption; for the church is infallible, and her teachings and commands are the infallible standard of what is true or false, right or wrong, good or evil, and therefore her tendencies cannot be injurious. Prove, then, the church authorizes what you allege against her; you do not prove to us that she is in fault, but you prove to us, infallibly, that what you allege is not evil, but good. But the professor replies, that he denies the infallibility of the church, and adduces these very facts to prove that she is not infallible. Very good. But he must prove that the tendencies he alleges are false and injurious tendencies, before from them he can conclude any thing to the prejudice of the infallibility of the church. Now, we demand of him, by what authority he pronounces this or that tendency injurious. He must do it by some authority or by no authority. If by no authority, then he has no authority for what he says, and we are under no obligation to entertain it. If by some authority, that authority must be fallible or infallible. If fallible, it will not answer the purpose; because it may turn out that he calls good evil. It cannot set aside the authority of the church, for, at best, it is only a fallible authority against a fallible authority, and, for aught the professor can say, the mistake may be on his side, instead of being on the side of the church. If infallible, what is it?

The professor says (p. 451), "The character of a religious system may be known, first, from the relation of its principles to the standard of reason and Scripture; secondly, from its influence on the soul of man." The second method is the one he adopts. The character of Catholicity may be learned by its influence on the soul of man. The essential tendencies of Catholicity are injurious to the soul. From this he concludes against the church. We grant the church must be bad, if her tendencies are injurious to the soul. But here is a previous question to be disposed of, namely, By what authority does he pronounce her tendencies, admitting even that they are what he alleges, injurious to the soul? He assumes that he is able to say what is or is not an injury to the soul. He must have, then, a standard by which he determines what is good or evil to the soul. Now, what is this standard? Suppose he declares a given tendency injurious to the soul, and the church declares it wholesome to the soul,—where is the authority to determine which is right? He and the church are at issue. Which are we to believe? Professor Park against the church, or the church against Professor Park? If the two authorities be equal, there can be no decision. If one is paramount, which is it? Is the professor fallible? Then his authority is not of itself a sufficient motive for setting hers aside, for hers is only fallible, and is probably, at worst, as good as his, and may be better. Is he infallible, and is it impossible for him to err in his judgment, and mistake the character of a tendency? If so, he must establish this infallibility in the outset; for it is not a self-evident fact, to be taken for granted. We demand, then, once more his authority for pronouncing an essential tendency of the church injurious to the soul.

Will the professor appeal to reason? The appeal is good, if reason have jurisdiction in the case; but we deny that reason has jurisdiction in the case. An influence may be injurious to the soul, on the supposition that it has only a natural destiny or is to perish with the body,—and not be injurious, but wholesome, on the supposition that the soul has *no* natural destiny and is to live for ever. Reason, by her own light alone, has jurisdiction only in questions relating to the natural destiny of man, for she cannot go out of nature. She can pronounce concerning good or evil to the soul, if its destiny be, as our religion teaches us, not natural, but supernatural, only as she borrows her light from revelation. The good of the soul is in realizing the end for which it was made; the injury of the soul is in being hindered or diverted from realizing that end. Before, then, you can say any particular influence is injurious to the soul, you must be able to say for what end the soul was made, and that the influence in question tends necessarily to divert it from the realization of that end,— two facts, which you must obtain, if you obtain them at all, not from reason, but from supernatural revelation. Therefore, we say, reason has not jurisdiction in the case. If, then, the professor summons us, on this question, to plead at the bar of reason, we shall plead want of jurisdiction in the court.

But may we not, from the tendencies of a religious system, conclude to the character of the religious system itself? Yes, *if you are able to determine the real character of the tendencies by an authority to which both the system and its tendencies are bound to answer,—not otherwise.* Here is the fact the professor forgets. He assumes to judge the tendencies of the church, and then assumes his judgments of these tendencies as the standard by which to try the church. We call upon him to go a step further back, and establish the validity of these judgments, by showing us the authority on which they are founded, and that that authority is sufficient to authorize us to receive them as infallible. In assuming them as the standard by which to try the church, he forgets that the church denies his ability to form valid judgments in the premises, and therefore that he must begin by showing that he can, and showing it, too, by an authority which the church, as well as he, must acknowledge to be ultimate. Till he does this, his judgment of what is or is not an injurious tendency is of no authority, and his conclusion from it for or against the church is deserving of no attention; for it is a mere *petitio principii.* This is a fact which all our Protestant doctors overlook, and which proves that they themselves have made less proficiency in the investigation of first principles, at least of logic, than they flatter themselves.

Will the professor fall back now on his first-named method; namely, the principles of reason and Scripture? Not on reason alone, for we have just precluded him from that. On reason *and* Scripture? Well; will he fall back on them as the court, or as the law which is to govern the decisions of the court? Not as the court, for they are not a court, and cannot be, any more than the statute-book is, or can be, a court. Then as the law? Very good. But the law authoritatively declared, or declared without authority? Without authority? Then we deny it to be law. With authority? Then what authority? The authority of reason? Then, whose reason? Yours or ours? Not ours; for, if so, we should be both defendant and judge of the law; and to this you cannot be required to assent. Not yours; for, if so, you would be both plaintiff and judge of the law; and to this we cannot be required to assent. Whose reason, then? The reason of the court? But where and what is the court, if the church is set aside?

Here we come back to the question with which we started,—On what authority does the professor assume his judgments of the tendencies of the church to be valid against hers? If his own, he only pits his infallibility against hers, and we know beforehand that he is not infallible. If he says some other body, he only predicates of another body the infallibility he denies to her; and then comes up the question of the infallibility of that other body. We may deny it as we do his, and then nothing is decided. Infallible authority there must be somewhere, or there is no decision of the question. We demand of the professor, what and where is this authority?

If the church be from God, and infallible in her teachings and commands, we know that none of her essential tendencies can be bad; for her teachings and commands constitute the rule of truth and falsehood, right and wrong, good and evil. It is no matter what you prove she teaches and commands; for, if it be clear that she teaches and commands it, we will maintain that it is true, right, and good, against all gainsayers, even to the dungeon, exile, or the stake, if need be. Nay, you are precluded from calling it false, wrong, or injurious; and if you so call it, you arraign Almighty God himself, and charge him blasphemously with falsehood and evil. It matters nothing in this case, that her teachings run athwart your prejudices, or that her commands shock your sensibilities; for her authority is higher, more ultimate, than yours. What more contrary to our ordinary notions of justice and humanity than the command given to the Israelites, through Moses, to conquer and possess the land of Canaan, and to extirpate by the sword its inhabitants,—men, women, and children? Yet the Israelites were justifiable in obeying it,—nay, were bound to obey it; for it was the express command of God, and the commands of God constitute right and create obligation. Yet, without such command clearly given, the Israelites would not have been justified in doing what they did. So, many things the church commands would not be right or obligatory, if commanded by any other body,—as the execution of a criminal is an act of justice, if commanded by the sovereign authority, but a murder, if done without such authority. This is all clear and undeniable, if you concede the church to be from God, to be authorized by him to speak in his name,—or, rather, if she be as she claims, and as all Catholics believe, the organ through which he himself speaks, teaches, and governs. If this be conceded, you have nothing to do but to submit, receive the command, and obey it, on peril of rebellion against God and your own damnation.

Now, this conceded, as it must be, the professor, before going into the investigation of the essential tendencies of the church, must deny the authority of the church; for, till the authority of the church is set aside, the character of her tendencies is not an open question. In concluding from the character of the tendencies to the authority of the church, he is guilty, as we have said of a *petitio principii.* Thus,—

This is an essential tendency of the church; but this tendency is injurious, therefore the church is injurious. But, if injurious, she cannot be from God, and infallible. Therefore, the church is not from God, and infallible.

But to this we reply, by denying the minor; no essential tendency of the church can be injurious, because the church is from God, and infallible; but this is an essential tendency of the church; therefore, this tendency is not injurious.

Now, the professor, it will be seen, in his minor begs the question in dispute. In it he does not disprove our major, but simply assumes it to be false; and if he concedes our major, his minor cannot possibly be true. He must, then, disprove our major, that is, the infallibility of the church, before he can proceed to the proof of his minor. We suppose the professor is well enough acquainted with logic to understand this; if so, he will see the question between him and us cannot turn on the character of the tendencies of the church, but must turn on the authority and infallibility of the church; and this, in fact, is the only question there is or can be between Catholics and Protestants; for the infallibility of the church closes all debate on the other questions they may raise. The debate is all in the question, Is the church from God, the organ through which he himself teaches and governs? If yes, all is settled. If no, all remains *in statu quo,* and the Protestants must show us some such organ, or we must grope our way along in the darkness as well as we can, by the feeble ray of reason, which only serves to make the darkness visible. Doubtless, the church must vindicate her own claims, and prove, by sufficient evidence, that she is the organ of the divine Word; for the law does not bind till sufficiently promulgated, that is, so promulgated that by the prudent exercise of reason there can be no uncertainty as to what it is. But this she does, and we are ready to show that she does it, whenever the question shall be fairly raised.

But having made these observations by way of protest against the method of argument, if argument it can be called, which the professor pursues, and in order to show that he merely begs the question, we proceed to the direct consideration of his list of charges. We, of course, within our limited space, cannot consider them at so great a length as might be desirable, and must content ourselves with brief replies; but we will endeavour to make them, if brief, conclusive.

1. Catholicity is injurious to the mind, because it "discountenances the investigation of first principles."—p. 453. If this means, that Catholicity discountenances the investigation of first principles of science, in so far as they come within the legitimate province of science, we deny the assertion; for whoever knows any thing of the principles or history of the church knows that it is not true. If it mean, that Catholicity discountenances the investigation of first principles, as principles or articles of faith, so far as to ascertain what they are, and the extrinsic motives of receiving them as principles or articles of faith, we also deny the assertion. If it be meant, simply, that the church discountenances the investigation of the principles or articles of faith, for the purpose of ascertaining their intrinsic truth, we admit the charge, but deny that it is injurious; and furthermore allege, that, if it be an injury to the mind, it is an injury which must be objected not to Catholicity alone, but to all divine revelation, to be received as authority; and therefore an objection to which the professor, unless he is an infidel, is himself as obnoxious as the Catholic.

The articles of faith are received on the authority of God revealing them, and are to be taken as first principles; this we admit and contend. But the question, whether God has revealed them or not, is open to investigation. Here Catholicity discountenances no investigation, of first principles. The question, whether they are intrinsically true or not, is not an open question; because, 1. The articles of faith are mysteries, and their intrinsic truth lies out of the range of investigation; and because, 2. If they are revealed by God himself, there can be no question of their intrinsic truth; for God cannot reveal what is not intrinsically true, since he is *prima veritas in essendo, in cognoscendo*, *et in dicendo.* Once ascertained to be articles of faith, that is, God's word,—and if not God's word, they are not articles of faith,—they of course cease to be subjects of investigation, and are to be taken as first principles, as primitive *data* from which we are to reason, and to which we are to conform in our reasonings, as the geometrician must reason from, and conform to, the axioms and definitions of his science. But this we deny to be an injury to the mind.

1. Nothing can be an injury to the mind that does not deprive it of some one or more of its natural rights. But over the articles of faith reason has no natural rights, never had any, never can have any; because they lie out of her province, and belong to the supernatural, where her authority does not extend. In denying her the right to investigate the truth of these, we do not restrict her rights, nor in any sense abridge her domain or her authority. She is left in possession of all her territory and of all her original sovereignty.

2. The articles of faith are not taken from the dominions of reason, but they are certain grants made gratuitously to her, extending, instead of abridging, her authority, and therefore serve, instead of injuring her. By their means, she can extend her authority over an immense region, where without them she could have no authority at all. They enlarge her power, and therefore cannot injure her. They furnish her with first principles for the science of theology, without which the science of theology could not exist. Is this an injury to the mind? Why not say it is an injury to the mind to have first principles at all? Are his axioms an injury to the geometrician? Is there any science that supplies its own first principles? Is it an injury to the mind to be able to cultivate the science of theology? But as the science cannot exist without these articles of faith as first principles, and as it cannot of itself furnish its first principles, since no science supplies its own first principles, how say it is an injury to the mind to have them furnished?

But admitting that it is an injury to the mind to be debarred from investigating first principles, that is, from investigating the intrinsic truth of God's word, and ascertaining whether God speaks the truth or not, it is an injury which is done, not by Catholicity alone, but by every system which admits divine revelation at all. If we admit divine revelation at all, we must admit it as ultimate on all matters which it covers. No matter in what symbol that revelation is to be found,—in the decrees and canons of the church, in the Apostles', the Nicene, or the Athanasian Creed, in the Old and New Testaments, in the Thirty-nine Articles, the Augsburg, Helvetic, or Westminster Confession, the Five Points of the Synod of Dort, the Saybrook Platform, or the New England Primer,—if admitted to be divine revelation, it is final, held to be infallible, and no investigation into its truth can be permitted; for it is not permitted to go behind the word of God, and ask if the word be true, since that would be asking, Does God tell the truth?—a question no one can ask without blasphemy. The professor, if he admits divine revelation at all, condemns himself if he brings this as a charge against Catholicity, and must contend that not Catholicity only, but the very idea of divine revelation to be received in any case as ultimate authority, is injurious to the mind of man. If his objection, then, has any force, it is only in the mouth of an infidel that it has it. Is it on infidel ground that our theological professor wishes to take his stand? If so, let him avow it, and perhaps he will find he has a question to settle nearer home,—unless Andover Theological Seminary is prepared to put down Catholicity at the expense of Christianity itself.

But the real gist of the professor's objection we suppose to be, that such is the state of the question with regard to the evidences of religion, that no articles of faith can rightfully be imposed or received as first principles. "Our Maker," he says (p. 452), "intended to leave the evidences of religion such as . . . . . to sharpen the intellect. He designed to invigorate the reason . . . . by allowing arguments of *real* weight to exist in favor of what may be proved, upon the whole, to be false, and in opposition to what may be proved, upon the whole, to be true. But the Romish idea of the infallibility of the church is, in itself and in its results, at variance with the nature of moral reasoning, and incompatible with a due regard to the evidence which exists for and against the truth." This passage, if analyzed, will be found to contain four assumptions: 1. To sharpen the intellect, or, what is the same thing, invigorate the reason, is, in itself considered, a good. 2. That the mind is really invigorated, not by the possession of truth, but by the search after it and difficulty of finding it. 3. That arguments of *real* weight may exist in favor of falsehood and against truth. And, 4. That faith rests on moral reasoning, which does not, and cannot, exclude uncertainty as to its truth or falsehood. The first three are evidently false, and the last begs the question, and denies the possibility of faith.

1. The cultivation and improvement of the mind in the service and for the sake of God is a good, but not in or for the sake of itself, as the professor assumes, when he makes sharpening the intellect or invigorating the reason an end which Almighty God himself contemplates in adjusting the evidences of religion. God is good, and can contemplate, in what he does, no end, as an end, which is not good in and for the sake of itself. Such must be sharpening the intellect, if he contemplates it as an end. But it can be a good only on condition that the development and perfection of our faculties is in itself good, and this can be good only on condition that the development and perfection of our faculties is the end for which we were made; which is false. That this is a good cannot be sustained from the Sacred Scriptures, the only authority beside reason to which the professor can appeal; for they nowhere assert it, but the contrary. They are not the acute in intellect, the vigorous in reason, but the pure in heart, who shall see God. The Sacred Scriptures never commend mere sharpness of intellect, mere vigor of reason; for, if they did, they would commend, by implication, Satan himself, who, probably, in acuteness of intellect and vigor of reason is an over-match for even our able and learned professors of Andover Theological Seminary themselves. The Scriptures do not commend the merely intellectual, the subtle reasoners,—men ever disputing, doubting, learning, never able to attain to the knowledge of the truth,—but the simple, the docile, who with meekness and humility receive the ingrafted word, and obey it with all fidelity and alacrity. We recommend the professor to read and meditate 1 Cor. i. 19–31. If he will do so, he will, perhaps, not be ambitious of repeating this first assumption.

2. So far as the mind is really improved, invigorated, in the sense in which to sharpen the intellect, or invigorate the reason, is not an evil, but a good, it is not done by the search after truth and the difficulty of finding it, but by the possession of truth. Truth is the appropriate food of the mind; and as well say the body is sustained and invigorated by the search after food and the difficulty of finding it, instead of eating and digesting it, as say that the mind is invigorated by the search after truth and the difficulty of finding it, and not by possessing it. The mind does not suffer in presence of truth, but in its absence,—in the darkness of doubt, and

the hell of falsehood. There it loses its vigor, its acuteness, becomes enslaved, bound hand and foot. It is the truth that liberates it,—*veritas liberabit vos*,—that restores it its strength, sanctifies it, and secures its free and healthy action.

The professor reasons on the supposition, that the mind, as soon as it comes into possession of truth, loses its motive to exertion, relaxes its energy, and sinks into inanity and death. He concludes from what is unquestionably the effect of false doctrines on the mind, which it is compelled by authority to embrace, and forbidden to examine, to the effect of truth. But his conclusion is evidently false; for truth has a vivifying, strengthening, and sanctifying influence on the mind that receives it; or else how sad must be the condition of the saints in heaven, who are to see the truth as it is, in itself, and spend an eternity in its immediate possession and contemplation! The professor probably forgot himself, when he undertook to show that doubt, uncertainty, and falsehood were more beneficial to the mind than truth; or rather, he chose to assume principles on which it would be easy to overthrow Catholicity and defend Protestantism. When a man has the making of his own first principles, he must be an unskilful workman indeed, not to make them to suit his purpose.

3. Arguments of *real* weight are solid arguments, founded in truth, therefore true; for what is not *true* is not *real*. The professor's third assumption is, then, that truth may exist in favor of falsehood, and against truth; for he says arguments of *real* weight exist in favor of falsehood and against truth! This looks very much like contradicting the first principle of all philosophy, namely, the same thing cannot both be and not be,—called, by metaphysicians, *the principle of contradiction*. Did our professor make his theology before his philosophy? He must be on his guard, lest he raise a suspicion that even Protestantism does not exert a remarkably wholesome influence in sharpening the intellect and invigorating the reason.

4. The fourth assumption of the professor is, 1. A *petitio principii;* for it asserts that the evidence for and against the truth is such that the articles of faith cannot be affirmed with infallible certainty, that is, so as to preclude all room for doubt whether they are the word of God or not. But this the church denies; for she alleges they can be so affirmed, and that she so affirms them. We have here merely the professor against the church, and the church against the

professor; and our old question comes up, Which are we to believe?

But, 2. There is an assumption here that the articles of faith are exposed to uncertainty. But, if so, they cannot be articles of faith; for faith is not compatible with uncertainty, since the property of faith is to exclude all uncertainty. Admit the professor's assumption, then, and it excludes faith. His objection to the church, then, is that she asserts the possibility of faith. Is this the objection of a believer in divine revelation, or of an unbeliever? Does the professor mean to deny the possibility of faith in the word of God? If so, his objection lies against all who contend for faith in God's word, no less than against Catholicity. The professor should beware what arguments he uses, lest he find himself in the condition of Sir Hudibras, whose gun,

> "Aimed at pigeon, duck, or plover,
> Recoiled, and kicked its owner over."

Again, the professor's reasoning is based on the supposition, that faith rests on moral reasoning, and that moral reasoning does not exclude all uncertainty. But, in the first place, faith rests, not on moral reasoning, but on the veracity of God. God has said; therefore we believe. In the second place, the authority on which we take the word to be the word of God does not rest on moral reasoning, but also on the veracity of God. The church declares it to be the word of God; therefore we believe it to be the word of God. God has commissioned the church in his name, and promised to speak in her speech; therefore we believe the church. The fact, that God has so commissioned the church and given this promise is the only question to be settled by moral reasoning; and here moral reasoning may give as high a degree of certainty as we have of our own personal existence or identity, as we proved in our essay on *The Church against No-Church*,* and are ready to prove again, when properly called upon. Therefore, we may be as certain what the church propounds to us is true, as we can be that God cannot lie, or as we are of our own existence or identity. Deny this, and you deny the possibility of faith; for faith is not a balancing of probabilities, and the conclusion that upon the whole, all things considered, *this* is most probable, most likely to be true, therefore we *think* it is true, though of that we are not *quite*

---

*Vol. V. p. 331.

certain; for if it be not absolute certainty, a certainty which leaves no reasonable ground for doubt, it is not faith, as we see by the definition of faith itself. The whole question, then, resolves itself into this:—Is the evidence which exists for and against the truth such as to warrant faith? If you say yes, your objection falls to the ground; if you say no, you are an unbeliever, and therefore have a quarrel to settle not only with us, but with all who profess to have faith in Christianity as the word of God.

Lastly, the professor speaks of the dogmatic spirit the idea of the infallibility of the church encourages. Encourages in what or in whom? In the church? If she be infallible, she has the right to speak with dogmatic authority, and you must set aside her infallibility, before you can bring that as an objection to her. In individual Catholics? We deny the assertion. For, in admitting the infallibility of the church, they necessarily deny to themselves the right or even the disposition to dogmatize. How can we dogmatize, when we are bound to take our faith from the church, when we confess both her right and her ability, and her exclusive right and ability, to propound the faith, and find our merit in obedience to her? If any thing does or can check the spirit of dogmatism in individuals, it is this. The charge against Protestantism of encouraging a spirit of dogmatism in individuals would come with much more grace and truth from us; for the very nature of Protestantism—since it has no ultimate authority from which all are bound to take their faith, and since it proclaims the principle of private interpretation—is to encourage almost every man, woman, and child to dogmatize, to say, "This is the word of God, and you must believe this or be damned; no, that is n't the word of God, this is the word of God; believe what I say is the word of God, or you 'll be damned." This is the spirit of dogmatism, and the history of Protestantism is little else than a history of this spirit, and its deplorable effects. The professor knows this, and, if he understands any thing of the relation of causes and effects, he knows wherefore it is so, and wherefore there cannot be, and never is, any spirit of dogmatism among Catholics. The Catholic never dogmatizes; he but teaches what he is commanded by his church to teach; and you will rarely, if ever, find a Catholic writer, who lays down a proposition, without attempting, at least, to sustain it by competent authority or appropriate evidence. "Catholic theologians compare," says the professor (p. 543), "the evidences for their theology to those for their personal existence and identity." If he means theology, as he says, this is false, utterly false; for no Catholic theologian pretends this, since every purely theological question is open to discussion. If he means *faith*, when he says theology, we ask the professor if he is prepared to maintain the negative of what he condemns,—that the certainty afforded by the evidences there are for the word of God is a less degree of certainty than that we have of our own existence and identity? What the professor says, on the same page, about "the deadness and corruption which come from an unthinking reception of a *human* creed," we cheerfully accede to, and could find in the history of our beloved New England much to confirm it; but who told him the creed enjoined by the Catholic Church is a *human* creed? Does he not see that he begs the question? A humanly imposed creed, we admit, is destructive; a divinely imposed creed is not destructive, but wholesome, and essential to the life of faith Does the professor suppose we do not condemn all man-made and man-imposed creeds as much as he does, ay, and more too? Does he not know that we strenuously maintain that nothing but God's word is or can be an article of faith? We will spare him all necessity of reasoning against *human* creeds. Show us our creed is imposed by human authority, and it suffices; we abandon it at once. But no begging of the question. You are trying to prove our religion is hostile to the mind; be sure, then, you vindicate the wholesome effects of your own, by reasoning clearly, honestly, and justly.

II. The second allegation is, that Catholicity "checks the instinctive longings of the soul for progress in the science of divine things." "The spirit of the reformation is that of improvement; the principle of the Romanists is that of hyper-conservatism."—p. 453. We thank the professor for this. We have hitherto heard it urged that the fault of Rome was that of departing from the faith, corrupting it by her innovations, adopting new articles of faith, new sacraments, and imposing new conditions of salvation, unknown in the primitive ages of Christianity; and that the glory of the reformers was not in attempting improvements in the Christian system, in undertaking to perfect what Almighty God had left incomplete, but in reviving primitive faith and worship, which had been lost through the usurping and innovating spirit of Rome. Sure are we that we have read all this in Luther, in Calvin, in Zuingli, in Melancthon, in Œcolampadius, in Bucer, in Beza, in all the fathers of the reformation whose writings we have chanced to look over, and we do not remember ever to have stumbled upon a single passage, in any one of them, that even intimates that the sin of Rome was that of nostility to progress in the science of divine things. Even in later times, when we read in Owen, and Robinson, and others, passages which urge a progress on Luther and Calvin, it is always a progress in restoration, or, as the militia captain has it, an "advance backwards," a progress in throwing off more and more of Babylonish error and corruption, and recovering more and more of the primitive truth long hidden beneath the rubbish of Rome. Sure, we had seen it written, as it were, over the entrance of every Protestant conventicle, "PRIMITIVE CHRISTIANITY RESTORED HERE." But now it seems that the sin of Rome is hyperconservatism, that she has too scrupulously adhered to primitive usage, and too scrupulously preserved the sacred deposit committed to her charge from all alteration, from all the attempts of the innovators. So, on the authority of Professor Park, a child of the reformation, glorying in his parentage, we must say the reformers lied; said one thing and meant another; that, instead of restorers, they were innovators. It would be indecorous for us to contradict the professor on this point, on which his authority is so much better than ours. We presume him to be correct, and that the reformers were, as Catholics have always alleged, mere innovators, men who could no longer submit to primitive usage and worship, but wished to improve them, and to recast the Gospel in their own image. Hyperconservatism! We thank thee, Professor Park, for the word, and trust we shall hear no more about Roman corruptions, innovations, and departures from the faith. The Romish principle is that of hyperconservatism; the spirit of the reformation is that of improvement, that is, of change, of innovation,—for only by change and innovation is improvement effected. Was the professor prudent in saying this, and was he not in saying it thinking rather of the demands of Cambridge than of the pretensions of Andover?

But let us look the objection in the face. Catholicity checks the instinctive longings of the soul for progress. Progress in what? in what sense? and by what agency? The professor either admits that Almighty God has made us a revelation of truth to be received on the divine veracity, or he does not. If he does not, he is what all the world call an infidel, and his quarrel, as we have said or intimated more than once already, is not with us alone, but with all who profess to believe in divine revelation; and, moreover, if he denies all revelation, he gains nothing to progress, for the matters covered by revelation are matters which lie out of the range of natural reason, and therefore reason, however free, bold, vigorous, persevering, can of itself make no progress in them. If he admits that Almighty God has made us a revelation, he must believe that the revelation is perfect or imperfect, that is, complete or incomplete. If perfect, it requires and can admit of no progress; for progress is from the imperfect to the perfect, and is not predicable of what is already perfect. If he contends that it is imperfect, that is, that Almighty God has left it incomplete, unfinished, he must say its completion is to be effected by divine agency or by human agency. He cannot say it is to be effected by human agency, because the revelation is not only of things of God, but is made by God himself; and to assume that man can make it, take from it, or add to it, is to deny that it is divine revelation, and to assert that it is human revelation. Therefore, even admitting the revelation to be insufficient, incomplete, unfinished, *man* can do nothing towards completing, finishing it, or rendering it less insufficient. There is, then, no room in divine revelation for the instinctive longings of the soul for progress to express themselves. They are checked, we grant; not by Catholicity, but by the nature of things; because the progress, if progress there is to be, depends not on human will and effort, but on the divine will and bounty. We are taught in the Holy Scriptures to look not to ourselves, but to Jesus Christ as the author and finisher of our faith; and it depends wholly on God, not on our will nor on our merit, whether God shall reveal to us more truth or not,—for the simple reason, that revelation is a divine act, proceeding solely from the free will and gratuitous grace of God.

There can, we may assume, then, be no progress in divine revelation, as the object of faith, effected by human agency. Then progress here is not a thing we are to contemplate or labor for. If there are to be new and "greater Messiahs," as the progressists and transcendentalists blasphemously dream, it belongs not to us to raise them up, anoint, and send them forth, but to God alone. This, we presume, the professor will admit, and therefore we presume it is not progress in divine revelation that he contends for. In what, then, does he demand progress? In the extension of faith, and its more thorough application throughout the world to the government of the life and conduct of all men? But in this respect the church checks no instinctive longings of the heart for progress; for here she commands progress, and, by all her ministries and missionaries in all parts of the world, and by her unremitted efforts against all hostile influences, is constantly struggling to effect it. If this is what the professor means, his charge against Catholicity is false, —as the number and activity of Catholic missionaries, and the general zeal of Catholics to spread their faith, and to bring all men to it and under its influence, may abundantly prove.

But the professor says, "Progress in the *science* of divine things." The science of divine things is not faith, but theology, which, from conclusions obtained by reason from the articles of faith as first principles, seeks to produce, elucidate, strengthen, and defend faith, and also to determine its application to practical life, which takes in the whole science of morals, theoretical and practical. The assertion of the professor, then, is, that Catholicity checks the instinctive longings for progress in theology, speculative and practical, or dogmatical and moral. But if this is what he means, his assertion is false from beginning to end, and he offers, and can offer, not a single fact in the principles or in the history of Catholicity to give it even a coloring of truth.

Progress in the first principles of theology is not admissible, we grant; because the first principles of theology are articles of faith, that is, divine revelation, and in that we have just seen there is no progress to be looked for, at least from human agency, and for progress in them the professor cannot contend. But in the deduction of conclusions from these principles, in their scientific arrangement, illustration, and application, the church imposes no limits to our progress but those of the human mind itself. This the professor knows, and even admits. "We are, indeed, assured by Romish divines, that the science of theology may be advanced."—p. 454. "But Romanism (Catholicity) is so minute in its prescriptions, as to intersect the lines of advancement in almost every point, and whatever of expansion it does not prevent it leaves sickly and ill-shapen."—*Ib.* The only prescriptions of the church in relation to theology are articles of faith. She does not allow you to impugn an article of faith, either directly or indirectly; but so long as you do not do that, and proceed, not in a rash, but in a modest and reverent spirit, she leaves you perfect freedom. No prescriptions intersect the line of your advancement but the principles and definitions of faith; and these, if true, cannot hinder your progress, but must aid it, according to what the professor himself says,—"Truth is nature, and never enslaves the mind which it controls."—*Ib.* No injury, then, can come to the mind, and no check to progress, if these prescriptions be true, that is, the word of God, as the church alleges. Then they are not objectionable as prescriptions, but as *false* prescriptions. If, then, you object to them simply as prescriptions, your objection is without weight; if as false prescriptions, you beg the question.

"We are but mocked, when we are told that we have powers for research, and may exert them, and may use the multiplied helps of modern science in the pursuit of truth, still we must not cross a single boundary which the assembled bishops have prescribed; we may go on freely, so long as we are hemmed in by the canons and anathemas of Nice, Chalcedon, and Florence."—pp. 453, 454. Not at all, if the boundary prescribed by the bishops be such as truth prescribes; not at all, if the canons and anathemas are according to God's word. God's word is truth, and "truth never enslaves the mind which it controls." You must first show that the boundaries prescribed are false, and the canons and anathemas are not according to God's word, before your argument is any thing more than a *petitio principii.* Catholicity affirms that the bounds prescribed are bounds which the truth itself prescribes. If so, they are landmarks, guides to the traveler, first principles, *data,* furnished the theologian in the demonstration of truth, and are as useful to him as axioms and definitions are to the mathematician. They are injurious only on the supposition that they are false, which you are not at liberty to take for granted.

The professor's argument may be retorted. We are but mocked, when we are told we have powers, &c., still must not cross a single boundary prescribed by *divine revelation;* we may move on freely, so long as hemmed in by the canons and anathemas of *God's word.* If the professor admits revelation at all, be what may its organ, the principle of his objection bears as hard against himself as against Catholics. If he does not admit revelation at all, he should say so, tell us plainly that he stands on infidel ground, and objects to the church because she asserts that Almighty God has made us a revelation, which we must believe, and in no case disbelieve. *Qui crediderit, . . salvus erit; qui vero non crediderit, condemnabitur*—St. Marc xvi. 16. It is worthy of note, that the professor finds himself unable to bring an objection against Catholicity that is not equally an objection to Christian revelation itself. And yet we hear men, who think they are Christians, commending his Lecture! How short-sighted is error, and how hard it is for those who have departed from the truth to maintain consistency, to avoid arguments, which, if admitted, are as fatal to themselves as to their opponents!

The professor had no occasion to prove that bounds prescribed by men, restrictions imposed on thought by human authority, are injurious to the mind, fatal to its free and healthy action, and incompatible with progress in science. Catholics know this, and assert this, as well as he, and are far more strenuously opposed to all human authority in matters of faith than he is, or any of his Protestant brethren are or ever have been; for he, and even his brethren, if they carried out their principles, would allow us *only* a human authority for our faith, either the authority of our own minds, or that of others. What he should have proved, to have proved any thing to his purpose, is, that the church speaks with a merely human authority, and that the articles she imposes are not the word of God, and therefore not to be taken as articles of faith. That is, he should, as we told him in the outset, have raised the question of the authority and infallibility of the church. If the church be not authorized to speak in the name of God, if she have not from God the promise of infallibility, if, in a word, it be not God himself that speaks in her speech and decides in her decision, we grant all you contend for, and as much more as you please; but otherwise, we deny it, and you yourselves must deny it also; "for truth is nature, and never enslaves the mind which it controls."

III. The third charge alleged is, that Catholicity "exalts the traditions of antiquity above our own perceptions of truth, and degrades the mind by communion with triflers." —p. 454. The first part of this charge is false. The church does in no instance exalt the traditions of antiquity above our own perceptions of truth, or require us in any instance to deny or to doubt the truth of our perceptions;

for, if she did, she would exclude us from the number of teachable subjects. She teaches us truths which lie out of the range of our perceptions, and above them,—truths which we can receive only from supernatural revelation; but never any doctrine which contradicts or supersedes our own perceptions of truth, or in any sense weakens the certainty or importance of the truth we perceive naturally. To be above reason is not to contradict reason; and it is not easy to see how it can injure the mind to supply it gratuitously with first principles, by which its domain is almost infinitely extended, and which, except as supernaturally furnished, it has not and cannot have.

1. The church commands us to believe traditions of antiquity as the word of God, we admit. If these traditions be false, to command belief in them is to injure the mind; if they are true, really the word of God, it is not to injure the mind; for truth never injures. The professor must show them to be false, unauthorized, before, from the fact that the church commands us to believe them, he can conclude that she injures the mind. This he has not done, hardly even attempted to do.

If we object to the traditions of antiquity because they are *tradition*, we must object to the Christian revelation itself. A tradition of antiquity is something delivered, transmitted, or handed down to us from ancient times. The Christian revelation itself is, therefore, necessarily a tradition of antiquity, for it was made in ancient times, and could, in the nature of things, reach us only as delivered, transmitted, or handed down to us from ancient times. To contend, then, that the church injures the mind simply because she commands us to hold fast the traditions of antiquity is, in principle, to contend that she injures the mind in commanding us to receive the Christian revelation as the word of God, and forbids us to disbelieve or impugn it. Does it injure the mind to be required to believe and to be forbidden to disbelieve the word of God? If not, it cannot injure the mind to be required to believe and forbidden to disbelieve traditions of antiquity, simply because they are traditions.

But the professor will distinguish, we suppose, between tradition as contained in the written word, and oral tradition, insisted on by the church. The latter injures the mind, the former does not. But he cannot avail himself of this distinction; because, 1. His objection was not to the mode of transmission, but to traditions of antiquity as traditions; and because, 2. The oral traditions of the church can no more injure the mind than the written traditions, if they be equally true, equally portions of God's word. The question must turn, then, on the truth or authority of the tradition, not on the fact of its being written or unwritten.

But the professor may say, again, that the traditions he objects to are traditions of *men*, not of the word of God; and we cannot be commanded to believe the traditions of men, without injury to the mind. But this would be a plain begging of the question. The church concedes you, nay, teaches you, that the traditions of men are never to be taken as articles of faith, and that you cannot be rightfully required to believe them. She goes as far as, and even further than, you in condemning their authority. But who told you that what she commands us to believe *are* traditions of men? She denies it, and asserts that they are not traditions of men, but traditions according to Christ, divine revelations, which she received in the beginning, and is divinely commissioned to teach; you must prove, then, they are traditions of men, before, from the fact that the church enjoins them, you can logically infer, that, in so doing, she injures the mind. If human traditions, they *may* injure the mind, we grant; if divine, they cannot.

But, in point of fact, scarcely an article of faith, and not one of the primary or fundamental articles of faith, which the church teaches, depends on unwritten tradition alone, or is not expressed or implied in the Holy Scriptures. The church teaches nothing contradictory to the Holy Scriptures, and nothing not either contained in them or perfectly in harmony with their contents. What Protestants allege about Catholic disregard or neglect of the Bible is false and slanderous. Catholics hold the Bible in altogether higher veneration than does any class of Protestants, and make altogether more, as well as a better, use of it, in whatever relates to faith, morals, or devotion. Catholics are the only people that can afford to take the Bible throughout as the word of God, and understand its language in its most plain, easy, and natural sense; for it is only Catholics who can find in its teachings a uniform, connected, and consistent system of doctrines, without doing violence to its language. Interpreted on Catholic principles, the Bible, though not without difficult passages, can be received and venerated as the word of God. On the principles of any Protestant sect, it is a book of riddles, contradictions, and often of no meaning at all, or of a meaning remarkable only for its want of depth. Catholics are taught by the church that the Sacred Scriptures are the word of God, and they are excited to study them as the most abundant sources from which is to be drawn purity of morals and of doctrine, and are told by the highest authority, that, as such, they are to be left open to every one. Their interpretation is free, so long as the interpreter does not wrest them to teach what is incompatible with sound doctrine,—a restriction, in principle, which is put upon their interpretation by every Protestant sect; for no Protestant sect permits its members to interpret the Bible so as to impugn what it calls sound doctrine, or does not visit with its censures those of its members who chance to do so.

But the professor seeks to sustain his charge against Catholicity as injuring the mind, by alleging that she " lays down her instructions in a creed," and " elevates the digests of her councils to an infallible standard of truth."—pp. 454, 455. But, admitting the allegation, we deny the conclusion. The creed, if God's word, is true, and therefore cannot injure the mind, as we have agreed. It can injure the mind only on condition of its not being the word of God, or because not enjoined by the competent authority. But this is nothing to the professor's purpose; for he does not object to the creed that it is injurious because false, or imposed by incompetent authority, but simply because it is a creed; and he cannot do so without denying the authority and infallibility of the church,—which would be a mere begging of the question. A creed imposed by men injures the mind; but a creed imposed by God himself cannot injure the mind, for it is truth. You must prove, then, that the creed taught by the church is imposed by men, by human authority, as we said in the case of traditions, before from the fact that it is a creed you can conclude to its injurious influence.

But the professor either admits the Christian revelation, or he does not. If not, he is an infidel, and his quarrel, as we have before told him, is not with Catholicity alone, but with all who profess to receive that revelation as ultimate authority on the matters it covers. If he does admit the revelation, his admission of it is itself a creed, more or less definite, but still a creed; for he admits it as something he must believe, as authority in no case to be questioned or impugned. The idea of revelation itself, as a matter to be believed and obeyed, then, necessarily involves the idea of creed, a *credo*. You cannot, then, say that a creed, because it is a creed, injures the mind, without saying that the Christian revelation itself injures the mind, which no Christian will, or dare, say.

But, perhaps, the objection is not to a creed as such, but to its being condensed, methodical, compressing the faith within a narrow compass. This seems to be the gist of the professor's objection. But the revelation is made that it may be believed; condensing its substance into a few propositions, easily ascertained, and easily remembered, simply facilitates the apprehension and knowledge of what it is we are to believe. Is this an injury to the mind? Is it an injury to the mind to be able easily to seize the propositions which it is to believe without doubting, and in all its operations on divine things to take, as first principles, primitive *data?* If the professor is prepared to maintain the affirmative, we shall not take the trouble to contradict him.

But the professor, in what he says on this point, conveys a false impression. His language is vague, indeterminate, and may receive almost any interpretation the future exigencies of his argument may render expedient; but its natural interpretation is, that the church draws up a creed, into which she compresses the theological instructions of her fathers and doctors and her digests of the councils. But this is not the fact. In the first place, theological instructions, properly so called, are not embraced in the creed; for the creed embraces only what is of faith; and theology, whether of fathers or doctors, is not of faith. In the second place, the church denies that she does or has authority, properly speaking, to impose a creed. She teaches the creed, but she did not and does not make it. She received it from Almighty God through the apostles, and simply teaches what she has received, and been commanded to teach, and which she has no authority to alter, add to, or take from. She does not, then, condense her instructions into a methodical creed. She received them so condensed. The councils, again, do not give us digests of doctrine, but simply definitions of what is, and always has been, the creed, or the articles of faith on certain points on which controversies have arisen. They do not add to the creed, they do not take from it, nor in any sense alter it; they but tell us what it is and always has been. To this the professor cannot object, unless he carries his objection further back, and objects, not to the church for teaching the creed, or for requiring us to receive the decisions of councils as infallible truth, but to the church herself, that she has not received but has made the creed, and that her councils are fallible. But this he is not at liberty to do in his present line of argument, as we have shown him over and over again. He alleges the church does so and so, and thence concludes the church injures the mind. But if the church has from God authority to do so and so, what she does cannot injure the mind. Before her conduct can be alleged to be injurious to the mind, it must be proved that she acts from mere human authority, and when that is done, no Catholic will attempt to defend her conduct. The professor proves nothing till he proves that, and when he has proved that he has proved all.

But by what right does Professor Park inveigh against creeds? He belongs to Andover, not to Cambridge. He is a Protestant; and every Protestant sect, unless it be the Unitarians, and one or two minor sects, to which the professor would refuse to grant even the Christian name, it is well known, has its creed, a creed strictly enjoined, and which must be received on the pains and penalties of heresy. He is a Calvinist, and the Calvinists universally have a creed, or rather many creeds, professedly drawn up under the dictation of the Holy Ghost, and fitly emblemed by the weathercocks on their meeting-houses. He is a Congregational clergyman, and of that branch of the Congregational churches that have a creed, insist on a creed, and have been fighting for a creed with the Unitarians this last thirty years. And, finally, he is a professor in Andover Theological Seminary, which has a special creed, now lying before us, by the constitution of the Seminary "strictly and solemnly enjoined, and left in charge, that every article of it shall for ever remain entirely and identically the same, without the least alteration, addition, or diminution," and which the professor must subscribe, and promise "solemnly to maintain and inculcate in opposition to *Papists*, Arians, Pelagians, Antinomians, Arminians, Socinians, Sabellians, Unitarians, and Universalists, and to all other heresies and errors, ancient or modern." The constitution of the Seminary also adds,—" The preceding *Creed* and Declaration shall be repeated by every professor on this foundation, at the expiration of every successive period of five years; and no man shall be continued a professor on said foundation who shall not continue to approve himself a man of sound and orthodox principles in divinity agreeably to the aforesaid creed." And this man does not blush to arraign the Catholic Church because she teaches a creed! Whatever a Unitarian or an infidel might say against creeds, Professor Park is not—till he liberates himself and takes his stand with them—the man to open his mouth. He is bound hand and foot; and a sense of shame, if nothing else, should have restrained him from calling any other man a slave,—especially from calling freemen slaves.

2. To the second part of this third charge we have not much to reply. The "triflers," communion with whom, according to the professor, degrades the mind, are the fathers and schoolmen,—such "triflers" as St. Justin Martyr, St. Irenæus, Tertullian, before he became a Montanist, Clemens Alexandrinus, St. Cyprian, St. Ambrose, St. Basil, St. John Chrysostom, St. Peter Chrysologus, St. Gregory Nazianzen, St. Gregory Nyssen, St. Augustine, St. Jerome, St. Leo the Great, St. Gregory the Great, St. Anselm, St. Bernard, Albertus Magnus, St. Bonaventura, St. Thomas of Aquin, Duns Scotus, and hundreds of others hardly their inferiors! The only reply we have to make to the modern professor who can call such men as these "triflers" is to say, that he gives unequivocal evidence that his mind has not been *degraded* by communion with them. "To revere," says the professor, "their Gnostic or Platonic fancies, as a standard of thought, is a cause as well as the effect of a vitiated taste and unreasonable judgments."—p. 455. Very likely; but where or when does the church require us to revere "Gnostic or Platonic fancies?" The fathers, all with one accord, we had supposed, struggled against the Gnostics; and St. Justin Martyr, in his *Second Discourse to the Greeks*, gives us one of the most masterly criticisms on Plato extant. Very few of the fathers were Platonists before their conversion; and not one of them, so far as we recollect, retained, after his conversion, what may properly be termed a "Platonic fancy"; and furthermore, no father is held to be of authority any further than his teachings have been received by the church. The great charge usually urged against the schoolmen is, not that they were Platonists, but servile followers of Aristotle; and this is the charge urged by the professor himself. "Some of her

theories are literally made up of Aristotelianism."—*Ib.* But one cannot follow Aristotle, and, at the same time, revere the "fancies" of Plato "as a standard of truth." Moreover, the church has no *theories*, enjoins no *theories*. Theories belong not to the church, but to theologians, whose teachings are not of faith. The assertion, that even a theologian, of any consideration among Catholics, ever adopted a theory literally made up of Aristotelianism, would be false. No theologian of the church ever regarded either Aristotle or Plato of the least authority in theology; and when the fathers and schoolmen quote one or the other, it is as an argument *ad hominem,* or on a point, not of theology, but of philosophy.

Speaking of the schoolmen, the professor says, "They were *acute* rather than wise men."—*Ib.* We thought the professor began by commending acuteness of intellect, and making it a charge against the church that she hindered, or did not provide for, "sharpening the intellect." But now it seems her sin is that she sharpens the intellect too much, making men acute rather than wise. We wish the professor would agree with himself what is the real sin of the church, and not urge objections which overthrow one another, lest we be obliged to question both his wisdom and acuteness in urging them. If the church is unfavorable to acuteness of intellect, how did those schoolmen contrive to become such acute men? And, if to sharpen the intellect be a good, contemplated by Almighty God in adjusting the evidences of religion, why do you find fault with the schoolmen *because* they were acute? You should better digest your own doctrines, and become more consistent in your objections, before undertaking to pronounce *ex cathedra* on Catholicity.

IV. The fourth charge against Catholicity is, that it injures the mind by authorizing "a worship which presents a low standard of thought and feeling."—p. 456. If the church authorizes such a worship, she may not advance the mind much; but even then it does not follow that she injures it, unless the standard she presents is in the way of a higher standard. High and low are relative terms. If, without the church, the mind would have a higher standard than she presents, then she injures it; if, without her, it would have only a still lower standard, then she does not injure it, but benefits it. The professor, before he makes out his case, then, must not only prove that her standard is low in comparison with some ideal standard, but that it is substituted for a higher standard, which the mind, but for it, would have. But this he has not done; therefore his assertion, so far as he is concerned, remains an assertion, and nothing more,—an assertion which we have as good a right to deny as he has to affirm. As proofs of his assertion, the professor adduces,—1. The honor and invocation of saints; 2. The use of pictures and statues; and, 3. Certain miscellaneous charges, defying classification, but which can as well be arranged under the head of *Mere Externals of Catholic Worship*, as under any other.

1. The question is not now, whether the honor and invocation of saints are authorized by Almighty God or not, but whether honoring and invoking the saints tends to injure the mind. When we honor or invoke the saints, we are led to make ourselves acquainted with their lives and characters, to meditate on their heroic virtues, and to strive to imitate them. Where is the injury to the mind in this? What harm would it do our widows, wives, or daughters to meditate on the exalted virtues of the Mother of our Lord,— the Blessed Virgin,—or on the virtues of St. Catherine, St. Elizabeth, St. Monica, St. Bridget, or St. Theresa? Would it do them more harm than to meditate on the virtues of Aspasia, Laïs, Sappho, Madame Roland, Lady Russell, Caroline Fry, or Harriet Newell?

But this, the professor may say, is not to the point. He who communes directly with God himself communes with a higher standard of thought than he does who communes only with St. Nicholas, St. Xavier, and St. Cecilia. Admitted. But this is not the question. The real question is, Does communion with the great, the good, the saintly, made such by the grace of God, tend to divert the mind from God himself? The professor, to sustain his objection, may say that it does; but we tell him his assertion is contradicted by all experience. While in the flesh, we are obliged to commune with God through a veil, for we do not now see him face to face; and we are led to him by his manifestations of himself. Thus nature herself, as displaying his eternal power and divinity, leads us to acknowledge him, and to look to him as our beginning and end. But what brighter manifestation of the Divinity on earth than the lives of the saintly men and women who have lived in the most intimate communion with him permitted, and who in their lives exhibit nothing but continued miracles of his grace? When are we most thoughtful, most impressed with God's presence? and when send we forth the warmest ejaculations of prayer, praise, and thanksgiving? Is it not when in personal intercourse with, or when reading the life of, some truly good and saintly man or woman? Communion with such, instead of drawing off our minds and hearts from God, tends directly to lead our minds and hearts up to him, and we strive with new resolution and renewed energy to love and serve him as his saints do or have done. When is the young soldier fired for the battle, if not when communing with the renowned hero, listening to the recital of his dangers, trials, escapes, prowess, and victories? So is the soldier of the cross fired for the spiritual combat by contemplating the lives of those who have fought and won, by listening to their trials, their temptations, their struggles and their victories,—how God was always with them, even when hiding his face from them, his arm was always under them to uphold them, and his grace always sufficient for them. O God! let us imitate them! and ye who have ended your mortal combats, and now sing your songs of triumph around the throne of God, pray for us, that we too may fight on, overcome, and at last join your blessed throng!

On the same principle on which the professor condemns the invocation of saints and the honor we pay them, he should condemn all biography of great and good men and women; for the study of their lives would tend to draw off our minds from God, and to rest them on the creature, whose excellence was all borrowed from God. Yet we cannot much blame the Protestants for trying to find fault with the honor we pay to the saints; for they, alas! have no saints to honor. Luther, Calvin, Beza, Cranmer, Knox, even Cotton Mather and Jonathan Edwards, were at best but indifferent saints; and Henry Martyn, Brainerd, and Harriet Newell will hardly do to canonize. An eminent Congregational clergyman, a well known author, some of whose works are text-books in several American colleges, and who is himself a professor of Moral and Intellectual Philosophy in a New England college, informed a friend of ours, that he commenced, some time since, collecting the lives of eminent Christians. "When I began my collection," said he, "I thought I should find two or three in the Romish Catholic Church whom I might possibly insert in my list,— say Fénelon, and one or two others; but I have ended with the full conviction, that the highest type of Christian perfection is to be found exhibited nowhere out of the Roman Catholic Church." Such will be every man's experience, who, with some appreciation of what Christian sanctity is, engages in and prosecutes the same undertaking. The Roman Catholic Church is the only church that bears the note of sanctity. In losing unity, catholicity, and apostolicity, the sects lose also sanctity; and when—as most of them do—they profess to believe "*sanctam ecclesiam catholicam*," they must mean some church beside their own contentious body.

The professor has no occasion to talk to Catholics about the ennobling effects of spiritual communion with God. Just as if he could teach them any thing on this subject,— he whose sect has never produced even one respectable ascetic work, and whose best ascetic works are stolen and diluted from us! Just as if, because we pray to the saints, we pray to God less! All our prayers are directed to God; even those to the saints close always by ascribing the honor to the ever living and ever blessed Trinity.

Nor need he presume *quite* so much on the ignorance of Catholics. No Catholic is so ignorant, so poorly instructed in his religion, as to pay to the saints that worship which is due to God alone. We honor the saints for their heroic virtues, and, in so doing, honor God, to whose grace alone they owed their virtues. We pray to the saints, but not that they may do for us that which only God can do, not to perform for us what they cannot perform; but to assist us with their prayers, as the professor prays for his congregation at its request, or asks a brother or sister to pray for him. We make this request of sinful mortals like ourselves; how much rather of the saints who are freed from sin and stand near the throne! If, in the first case, we rob not God of his glory, why shall it be said we do in the last?

2. The use of "pictures and statues" cannot injure the mind, if communing with the saints does not; for they only serve to remind us of the saints, and to bring more vividly to our recollection their virtues and eminent sanctity. We honor them, indeed, as the professor honors a picture of John Calvin, President Edwards, or of his wife; as the patriot does the picture or statue of Washington; the soldier, of Alexander, Cæsar, or Napoleon; the Democrat, of Andrew Jackson; the Whig, of Henry Clay; the pious son, the picture of his mother; or the lover, the picture of his mistress;— not as material things, but for the sake of what they represent or bring to our minds and hearts. We see no injury to

the mind here. The statue or picture simply recalls to our minds and hearts a worth we delight to honor and which we ought to honor, or virtues which it is our duty to strive to imitate.

So the image of the crucifixion, the cross, the sign of the cross, serve to recall the mystery of the incarnation, the life, death, and sufferings of our blessed Saviour, the great work of the Atonement, to point us to the great Source of all merit, to remind us that we are to bear the cross, are to fight under it as our banner, and for it and in it to triumph. Where, in all this, is the injury done to the mind? Is it an injury to the mind to reflect on the great mysteries of man's redemption, or to have the attention, if but for a moment, directed frequently to their contemplation? The insinuation, that Catholics worship pictures, images, or the crucifix, is old, we admit, but is false. No Catholic believes there is any virtue in them, or ever addresses any prayer to them; for he is taught in his catechism, and he knows of himself, that they have no life or sense, and therefore no power to assist him. As well might we charge the people of Massachusetts with being fetichists, as the professor charge us with worshipping images. We go into the State House in Boston, into the Representatives' Hall, and right in front of the Speaker's chair we see suspended the carved image of a codfish. We watch; every time the Speaker rises, he bows gracefully, or ungracefully, to this image of the codfish; thus apparently paying it his reverence, and, as it were, asking its permission to put the motion, or to decide the question of order. "What stupid creatures these Massachusetts people are!" we exclaim; "what wretched idolaters! how they debase the mind! Why, they officially worship a carved codfish!" "O, no," says a grave legislator, "we do not worship the codfish, nor the image of the codfish. But we hang up that image there to remind the General Court of the great importance to the Commonwealth of the codfishery, and that they are to take care that in none of their legislative acts they injure it." "A mere Jesuitical refinement, intended to dupe the ignorant and unthinking; perhaps *you*, who are a man of some sense, may so understand it; but the mass of the members of the General Court do not and cannot." "But ask them; they will all give the same answer." "No matter for that; they have all been trained to give that answer, so as to screen the people of Massachusetts from the charge of worshipping a carved codfish. I know better. I tell you, you do actually worship the carved codfish. See there! the Speaker is even now bowing before it." Yet the answer of the legislator would be perfectly true and conclusive; and our reasoning and assertions would be false. The reason assigned for putting the image there is a good one. But if Massachusetts may, without idolatry, suspend in her State House the carved image of a codfish, to remind the General Court that it is not to sacrifice the codfishery, why cannot we, without idolatry, place on our desk before us, as we write, an image of the passion of our blessed Saviour, that, when we raise our eyes from the paper, we may be reminded of him who died for us, of what he suffered for us, whence our redemption comes, where is the source of all merit, whose virtues we are to honor and to strive to imitate, and for whose sake? If it be said, in return, this may do in our case, but that it will not in that of less instructed Catholics, for they will stop with the image and worship that instead of him who died on the cross, we answer, that too much is presumed on the ignorance of Catholics. Catholics are not quite so stupid as the professor imagines, and we assure him that we do not believe even the most ignorant class of Protestants themselves would be unable to distinguish between an image of the crucifixion and him who was crucified. But if so, the argument from their inability to that of Catholics would not be conclusive. If the professor, searching the world over, will find a Catholic, who has made his first communion, that does not know that supreme worship is due to God alone,—that is besotted enough to pay religious worship to any picture, image, or material thing, or to pay, even to a saint, that adoration which belongs only to God,—or that cannot, or does not, make all distinctions necessary to save him from the charge of idolatry in form or in substance,—we will yield him the argument. Produce, then, a Catholic that pays divine honors to an image or picture, to a saint or any created being, or for ever after hold your peace.

But be on your guard. No matter what strong language you may hear the devout Catholic use in addressing praises to the Blessed Virgin or to a patron saint, you are never from it alone to infer an idolatrous sense. The poet is permitted to call even a mortal woman, a sinful woman, who is little else than flesh and blood, divine; and the lover celebrates his mistress in terms as strong as any we can find in which to celebrate the praises of our Redeemer. And yet neither is accused of idolatry. If we would worthily celebrate her whom an angel pronounced "full of grace," who was found worthy to be the Virgin Mother of him "who is God over all,"—or if we would worthily celebrate the virtues of a beautiful saint, whom God himself delights to honor, we must use the strongest terms human language affords, and even then our language is too feeble for our thought. We can use no stronger terms when we celebrate the praises of God, for stronger terms we have not. It is not that we exaggerate the praises of the Blessed Virgin or of the saint, but that we fall lamentably short in the expression of our praises to God. No tongue can adequately praise him; no, not that of angel or highest archangel. The strongest terms that language furnishes, aided by the loftiest strains of soul-enkindling music, fall far below what the devout soul feels in the presence of her God, and are infinitely inadequate to their object. We cannot speak his praise;—we would do it; we would give the universe a tongue; we would touch its heart with fire from God's altar. We would bid it speak, and speak for us, but all too feeble; we fall prostrate, and speak only in our *silence*. Draw no inference from the language you may hear, for, if you do, you will deceive yourself. You must penetrate to the intent of the speaker. You must bring a Catholic, that, by his words and acts, intends to pay the honors to a creature due only to the Creator, and that cannot, or does not, when questioned, distinguish as clearly between what he pays to the creature and what he should pay to the Creator, as a Protestant can between the reverence due to a parent or magistrate and that due to God, or you bring not one we will acknowledge to be an idolater. Bring forward some such person, or stand convicted before the world of consummate ignorance or of consummate falsehood.

The professor is mistaken in his assertion, that Catholics attempt to shadow forth by pictorial representations the infinite, eternal, and invisible God, or to express by picture or statue his divine essence. They do no such thing, and they give pictorial representations of only such visible forms as God himself has been known actually to assume. If the Father is sometimes represented as the Ancient of Days, it is not because that form expresses his character, but because he so appeared to the holy prophet Daniel, and the representation is authorized by the Holy Scriptures. If the Holy

Ghost is represented by a dove, it is not because the dove emblems him, but because he himself chose that form and appeared under it at the baptism of our blessed Saviour. If the Son is painted in a human form, it is because, being man as well as God, that form is appropriate; and, moreover, it was in the form of a man that he appeared, suffered, died, and rose for us. But in no instance does the church authorize a pictorial representation as a likeness or emblem of the invisible God; for it is as well known among Catholics as among Protestants, that there is nothing unto which God can be likened. Protestants must not be quite so hasty to conclude, when by accident they light upon a truth, that it is theirs by right of first discovery. Some traveller may have been there before them; for they must remember they are not very old, and that it is only, as it were, yesterday that they set out on their travels. Considerable portions of the globe of truth had been discovered and occupied before they were even born. Brave men lived before Agamemnon. Luther and Calvin came too late to enjoy a monopoly of truth or virtue. The young think the old are fools, but the old know the young are fools.

3. We have no space to follow the professor through his long string of naked assertions concerning the mere externals of Catholic worship. We deny, in the outset, his competency to judge of Catholic worship; for it was designed to edify Catholics, and cannot produce its intended effect on infidels and heretics. He must be a Catholic, believe the Catholic creed, and love the Catholic Church as his spiritual mother, before he can be in the condition to appreciate the truth, beauty, or appropriateness of Catholic worship; for that worship must necessarily be altogether a different thing to the devout worshipper from what it is to the critical eye of the indifferent or hostile spectator.

We do not think, in a general way, the Catholic worship is very well calculated to edify those who go to *see* it and not to *assist* as worshippers. But this we do not regard as a reproach; it is a commendation. If, for instance, the Catholic worship could edify the infidel and the heretic as well as the Catholic, it would have no special adaptedness to Catholic faith, dispositions, and wants, and therefore would not answer the end for which it was intended. We ourselves were strongly prejudiced against Catholic worship. Our Puritan tastes and habits, our love of simplicity and dislike of every thing having the least appearance of being designed for mere show or stage effect, made us feel a real repugnance to Catholic worship, as we knew it when a Protestant. So strong, indeed, was our repugnance, that for some time, even after we had become pretty well convinced of the truth of Catholicity, we obstinately refused to assist at Mass; and when we did assist for the first time, setting aside the music and the sermon, which we could appreciate, we were only *not* disgusted. But now we seem to find the Catholic worship singularly simple, natural, and appropriate. We detect nothing in it not necessary, or, at least, highly useful. Protestant worship we find now to be formal, lifeless, and chilling. Not that we do not find it all that we ever did, all even that Protestants themselves find it; but the spirituality revealed by Catholicity is so much higher, so much truer and more refined than a Protestant ever conceives of, that Protestant spirituality itself ceases to be spirituality, and becomes a cold, lifeless formality, a mere shadow without a substance. This is, indeed, but the experience of an individual, and it is merely as such that we give it, to go for what it is worth. It is worth, at least, as much as the professor's bare assertions, proceeding as they do necessarily from Protestant ignorance and Protestant prejudice, which render it impossible for him to know what Catholic worship is, or the influence it is adapted to exert on the worshipper. If the Protestant reader will insist that he must make an allowance for our partiality to Catholicity, he must make at least an equal allowance for the professor's partiality against it.

The gist of the charge is, that Catholicity presents a low standard of thought and feeling in the worship it authorizes.

" When a Protestant enters the sanctuary, he is made thoughtful by the words of prayer and the reading of the Scriptures; and we are unable to measure the degree of mental improvement which he receives from services thus adapted to his understanding. But the Romanist [Catholic] is not instructed by the reiteration of his stereotyped observances. He hears the Bible read in a language which imparts to him none of its meaning, and in some churches he cannot even distinguish the words of the Scripture lesson, for these are drowned in the tumult of the ringing of bells, and the pealing of the organ, which are designed to honor the recital of what would be more truly honored if it were made intelligible, or even audible. The rational Protestant is *instructed* by the sacraments. They were intended to be sermons to the mind, and thereby to the heart. But the genius of Rome has transformed them from symbolical discourses into a species of necromancy. They are described as operating, not by rational appeal, but by a kind of talismanic influence. Protestantism would sanctify men by the truth which enlightens the intellect; but Romanism [Catholicity] depends on the mechanical working of rites that supersede our own activity. Protestantism insists, first of all, on faith, by which man is to be justified, and faith involves a vigorous exercise of reason; but Romanism lays the chief stress upon external ordinances which can renovate the soul without a rational contemplation of the truth addressed to it."— pp. 458, 459.

We have made this long quotation partly for the purpose of showing the professor's method of argument, which consists in following one bare assertion by another, without one particle of proof but what is supplied by the knowledge or the prejudice of his hearer or reader. If that knowledge or prejudice should happen not to be in his favor, he would establish nothing; and yet the *Christian Examiner*—a Unitarian periodical, which we have been accustomed to consider at least tolerably fair in its criticisms—says of this Lecture, that it "may be characterized as exhibiting a remarkable vigor and condensation of thought and *powerful argument*, with copious and apt historical illustrations and references. It is original, profound, and impressive, dealing in subtle analysis, and appealing to great principles of human nature." Nevertheless, the Lecture contains not even the semblance of an argument, from beginning to end; it has not a single apt historical illustration or reference, for it has not one that is not in a great measure, if not wholly, false; it has not a single original, striking, or profound remark, and makes not a single appeal to a great principle of either revelation or human nature, nor to any thing else but the ignorance and prejudices of the author's hearers or readers. All the author's strength, all his merit, lies in his simply saying what those he addresses are previously prepared to receive as truth. We concede to the author the merit of adapting his discourse to his audience, which, when a man's object is, not to vindicate the truth, or to promote the glory of God, but to carry his audience with him, is, perhaps, a merit,—a merit such as may be aspired to by a rhetorician or a demagogue; but not a merit very strongly coveted by one who has studied in the Christian school, and learned to value truth as " the pearl of great price," and to seek the praise of God rather than the praise of men.

Now, nothing can be more untrue than the general tenor and the particular statements of the extract we have made, so far as they bear on Catholicity; and nothing better can be desired to show how low and *unspiritual* are the author's own conceptions. In the first place, the bells do not ring nor the organ peal during the recital of the Scripture lesson; and, in the second place, the lesson for the day, the people, to a great extent, know by heart in their own language, and all have or may have it before them in a language they can understand.

But the passage extracted is worthy of notice as displaying a Protestant's conceptions of religious worship. It is remarkable how studiously the professor keeps God out of sight. Prayers are offered, not to obtain a blessing from God, but to make the hearer thoughtful and to improve his understanding. They are lectures addressed to the hearers, and are to serve as intellectual exercises. Hence, a newspaper in this city once complimented a prayer offered by a famous Protestant divine, by saying, "It was the most eloquent prayer ever offered to a Boston audience." The sacraments, again, are sermons, symbolical discourses, addressed to the understanding, and their efficacy is in their appropriateness, as intellectual addresses, to enlighten the mind; and yet, this same professor makes it a grave charge against the Catholic Church, that she observes, from the earliest antiquity, certain symbolical ceremonies in administering the sacrament of baptism! The whole thought which runs through the statement is human; and, according to the Protestant, the whole efficacy of divine worship consists simply in its being an intellectual exercise. Prayer does not benefit us by calling down a blessing from God, but by exercising our mind or affections; the sacraments impart no divine grace, but aid us only as an intellectual exercise. God, strictly speaking, answers no prayer; the worship he demands of us is the medium or condition of no grant from him, but an exercise, which, if performed, may have a tendency to strengthen the mind and warm the heart. Here is Protestantism; and it is easy to see that it embraces not a single religious conception, and acknowledges no principle which the veriest infidel might not admit; and yet it is commended for its sublime spirituality!

Protestant worship is, by the confession of Protestants themselves, mere formality, consists merely in empty ceremonies. Baptism with them is nothing but a ceremony.

It imparts no grace, impresses no character, is simply a ceremony of initiation into the church; and, in the case of adults, a mere ceremony initiating outwardly those believed to be already initiated spiritually. Ordination, as practised by Protestants generally, the laying on of the hands of the presbytery, is a mere ceremony, for it imparts no grace, no character, and no authority; but merely witnesses the fact that the recipient takes upon himself the office of teacher, or that the congregation has called him to be its pastor. At least, this is all it is among Congregationalists, of which sect the professor is a minister. Marriage, again, according to Protestants, is no sacrament, but a contract, and the solemnization by the minister is but a ceremony witnessing or declaring the fact of the contract. Hence Protestants call it "the marriage ceremony." So, also, what they call "the Lord's Supper" is purely a ceremony, the simple ceremony of taking a bit of bread and a sip of wine; for they insist, and in their case very truly, that it is nothing but bread and wine they partake. It is a shadow, a symbol; no real partaking of the Lord's body and blood, as they confess and contend. What is it, then, but a form, a ceremony, they observe, without any life or reality in itself? The Protestant has no altar, no victim, no real sacrifice, and therefore nothing which is distinctively divine worship. He has nothing to offer to God; and, according to his principles, he could worship God as well, as acceptably, as truly, and with as much benefit to himself, at home in his study, or abroad in the fields, and without a priest, as in the temple of God. But there is no worship of God where there is not a sacrifice, and no sacrifice without a priest, an altar, and the victim. The sacrifices of prayer and praise and of a contrite heart are, indeed, due to God, and are necessary, if we would have our offering upon the altar profitable to us; but they are not the distinctive act of divine worship, nor what distinguishes Christian worship from all others. They can be offered by a pagan or a Jew, and, if these were our only sacrifice, there would be nothing positive in Christian worship to distinguish it from the pagan or the Jewish; and yet the blessed Apostle Paul tells us, "We have an altar whereof they who serve the tabernacle cannot eat."—Heb. xiii. 10.

Now, in contrast with this Protestant view, the Catholic worship presupposes always and everywhere a real presence. Under the form you are always to look for a reality. Baptism is a sacrament; orders are a sacrament; marriage is a sacrament; and the Blessed Eucharist is a sacrament;—and sacraments are not mere forms, insignificant signs, nor mere symbolical discourses, designed simply to shadow forth some moral or intellectual truth to the understanding, but signs significant, which impart to the recipient the reality they signify. The sacrifice of the Mass is not a mere sacrifice of prayer and praise, nor the symbolical offering of the Lamb that was slain for us; but a real sacrifice, in which our blessed Lord, in a mystical, but in a real, manner, is actually present on our altars, and actually offered to God, himself being both priest and victim. The Communion, again, is not a symbolical communion, not the figurative reception of the body of our Lord, which our faith is to perform the miracle of converting into his real body; but an actual partaking of the real body and blood of our blessed Saviour. Here all is real, nothing merely figurative; substantial, not merely formal. The ceremonies usually observed in administering the sacraments, or in celebrating the most holy sacrifice of the Mass, are few, and only such as are well adapted to dispose the minds and hearts of those who receive the sacraments for their worthy reception, or those who assist at the most holy sacrifice to assist with proper affections and recollection. Now, take the Protestant view of Protestant worship, and the Catholic view of Catholic worship, and we ask, which is the least formal, and which presents the highest standard of thought and feeling?

"But the genius of Rome has transformed the sacraments into a species of necromancy." This remark betrays the Protestant thought, and shows that in the sacraments the Protestant looks for no virtue, believes in no efficacy, but what is supplied by the recipient. They, then, do not lead the Protestant directly up to God, nor bring God down to man. That is, they establish no direct communion with God, and therefore, according to the professor's own principles (p. 456), should be condemned. It shows, too, the infidel thought with which the author writes. To regard the sacraments as channels of grace, through which the Holy Ghost operates for our justification, growth, and perfection, is to "transform them into a species of necromancy!" How completely has the professor lost sight of God! How he sneers at the bare thought of expecting any thing from the Holy Ghost! A moment ago, he accused us of injuring the mind by separating it from communion with God; and now he accuses us of "necromancy," because we show him that we believe in communion with God!

"But Romanism depends on the mechanical working of rites that supersede our own activity." This is false. The Catholic in no sense believes in, or depends on, the "*mechanical* working of rites." The efficacy of the sacraments is not mechanical, but divine, and it is not the form, but the Holy Ghost operating through the form, that is efficacious; nor does this supersede our activity, for it demands the concurrence of our activity with the operations of the Holy Spirit. Yet, so little faith has the professor, so little does he understand of the genius of the Gospel, that, where any other agency than that of man is presupposed, he concludes it must needs be mechanical! A most learned doctor he, and a most devout believer! We may see here the real difference between the Protestant and the Catholic thought. According to the Protestant, God is nowhere present in Christian worship, save as he is present in nature, in every commendable affection or true thought; according to the Catholic, he is everywhere in the Christian worship, not only naturally present, but supernaturally present. By it we are brought into his presence in a supernatural manner, and therefore have a much more intimate communion with him than the Protestant even pretends to have. Consequently, according to the principles of the professor himself, the Catholic worship should have, as it actually has, a more elevating effect on the mind than Protestant worship.

Now, it is this supernatural presence of God that scandalizes our professor. He depends on the worshipper for the efficacy of the worship, or on the eloquence and skill of the minister, and does not once expect God to do any thing supernaturally. The Catholic differs from him in this. The Catholic expects all from God. He worships, that he may pay to God what he owes, and that God may grant him the help he needs. When he prays, he does not pray to himself, or regard the effect which the prayer, as a spiritual exercise, may naturally operate in himself, although this is an effect not to be despised; but he prays to God, and looks to God's bounty to answer his prayer, and confer on him the blessing he craves or needs. This is an important consideration, and shows that the Catholic believes in God's gracious providence, and that we may go to our God as children to a father, and not be sent empty away, or with no other benefit than the act of asking has produced within us.

Take this thought with you, and, for the "necromancy" of the professor, understand the grace of God; for "mechanical working of rites" of which he speaks, understand the operations of the Holy Ghost; and you may see that what Protestants object to Catholic worship is but the effusion of their own infidelity. The priest faces the altar, not the people, because he prays to God, and not to them; he speaks in a low, inaudible voice, or in a language they do not understand, because he speaks to God, not to them, and because his prayers are to benefit them, not by the edification which listening to them as popular harangues might afford, but by the blessings they obtain from God for them. They are *prayers*, not harangues,—and for the ears of Almighty God, not for the ears of the people. Here is the point. The prayer, in the estimation of the professor, appears to be thrown away, if only heard by Almighty God!

The use of the Latin language is no objection, for we may presume our Heavenly Father can understand Latin as well as English. It is used in the Latin Church because originally it was the language of the people, because her liturgy was originally composed in that language, because it is well that the church throughout the world should speak in one and the same tongue, and because all spoken languages are fluctuating and variable in the sense they give to their words, and, if the service were preserved only in them, the unity and integrity of the faith might be sacrificed. But every thing that is addressed to the people, every part of the service which it is necessary they should understand, is addressed to them in their own language; and, moreover, the whole Missal is translated into English, and the simply English reader can follow the priest whenever he chooses. If he does not choose, it suffices to join his intention with that of the priest, and engage in such special devotions as he finds most for his edification.

The ringing of bells, which the professor seems to object to, he would soon find, if a Catholic worshipper, is no idle ceremony. The bell does not ring to honor a recital, but to inform the worshippers, who are not presumed to be watching the motions of the priest, and many of whom are so placed as to be unable to see him, at what part of the most Holy Sacrifice he has arrived. Instead of a disturbance or a tumult, it is a very necessary thing. The professor is extremely hard to please. One moment, he objects that no respect is paid to the understanding of the people, and no pains taken to let them know what is going on; and the next moment, he finds an objection in what is specially designed to let them know what is going on. Why did he not object right out, that Catholicity is not Puritanism, and therefore is to be rejected? That would have been manly, and would have at least given a reason for finding fault with Catholicity.

But, after all, the real question to be answered is, Does the Catholic worship, taken as a whole, tend necessarily or naturally to lessen the importance of what is commonly called spiritual worship, that is, prayer, praise, meditation, and spiritual reading? Does it substitute for these internal exercises mere outward observances, or does it even tend to do this? The professor may say what he will, but to this we answer emphatically, No, and we appeal to experience for our justification. The central point with the Protestant in his public worship is the sermon. We readily admit the sermon does not hold so prominent a place in Catholic worship as it does in the Protestant. The central point of Catholic worship is the most holy sacrifice of the Mass. We do not go to church to hear Rev. Mr. Silvervoice, Rev. Mr. Prettyman, Rev. Mr. Greatman, or the Rev. Mr. Sonofthunder preach; but we go to assist at the adorable sacrifice of the Mass. But there is one means of instruction among Catholics of which the professor is ignorant, namely, the Confessional. In the sermon the preacher must necessarily confine himself to general instructions and exhortations; but in the Confessional the instructions, exhortations, or admonitions are particular, adapted to the precise case of the penitent, and therefore much more valuable, and not only because they are more appropriate, but because the penitent must take them to himself, and cannot distribute them among his neighbours. The Catholic Church, therefore, if she make less use of the sermon than do Protestants, provides, by means of the Confessional, much more amply for the spiritual instruction of her children.

In the next place, those among us who most abound in prayer, praise, meditation, and spiritual exercises generally, are precisely those among us who are most scrupulous in their attention to all external observances. Read the lives of the saints, those even whom the professor must admit to have been eminently holy men, and you will find they of all men were the most observant of the very things in Catholic worship which the professor condemns; and you may in general measure a man's inward piety by the degree of devotion with which he observes the external worship. Find a man who disdains the external observances, and you may be sure you find a man who is deficient in charity, in good works, and who neglects prayer, meditation, spiritual reading, and mortification. But the reverse of this would be the fact, if the professor's doctrine were true. Again, as a matter of fact, these exercises are much more abundant amongst Catholics than Protestants, as any one may know who has equal means of observing the practices of both. Take our servant-girls; the Protestant, if professedly pious, will run much oftener to evening meetings, camp-meetings, revival-meetings, and concerts of prayer; but the Catholic will spend much more time in private devotion, which, because private, may very often escape your observation. Spiritual or ascetic literature is almost exclusively Catholic. Protestants have no ascetic books worth naming. What is Doddridge's *Rise and Progress*, by the side of the *Exercitia Christianæ Perfectionis* of Rodriguez,—*Pilgrim's Progress*, by the side of *De Imitatione Christi*,—Baxter's *Call*, by the side of *The Sinner's Conversion* by Salazar,—Scougal's *Life of God in the Soul*, Hervey's *Meditations*, Williston *On the Sacrament*, Upham's *Interior Life*, by the side of *The Spiritual Meadow*, *The Garden of Roses*, *The Sinner's Check-rein*, by Father Lewis, or the *Introduction to a Devout Life*, and *Treatise on Love of God*, by St. Francis de Sales, or the *Visits to the Blessed Sacrament*, by St. Alphonsus, or the ascetic works of St. John Climachus, Pope St. Leo the Great, Pope St. Gregory the Great, or of St. Bernard, and so many others we could enumerate? But, if the Catholic worship tends to substitute external observances for inward piety, how happens it that the only works really spiritual, which indicate an intimate communion on the part of their authors with the Holy Spirit, and which raise the reader from all that is low and earthly, temporal and perishing, to an intense longing and striving after the spiritual, the divine, the permanent, and the eternal, are by Catholics, and Catholics eminently devout in the Catholic sense? Then, again, the ascetic books most popular among Catholics, those which circulate widest, and are most prized and most generally read, are precisely the books which breathe the purest spirituality, insist most strenuously on inward piety and intimate communion of the soul with God. How does this happen, if our worship tends to substitute external observances for inward practical piety? Facts as well as philosophy are decidedly against the professor. He has not looked so deeply into the subject as his friends seem to imagine. He has been misled by concluding from the effect which external observances, regarded as simple external observances, might have on a man without faith, to the effect they must have on one who has faith and believes in the supernatural presence and providence of God. He may also have been misled by not making sufficient allowance for the fact, that, while Protestants wear their piety on their faces, or hang it up for show, and take no inconsiderable pains to advise us of their devotions, Catholics are accustomed to obey the precept of their Master, to take heed when they pray not to be seen of men, and also to enter into their closet and to shut the door.

V. The fifth charge against Catholicity, as nearly as we can collect it, is, that the Catholic Church is deficient in candor, love of truth, and great philosophers and eminent preachers. In this the professor pretends to establish, by an appeal to facts, the conclusions he had in the previous charges obtained from reasoning.

To the charge, that Catholic writers are generally deficient in candor, it is hardly necessary to reply. The author sustains his charge by no facts. He names, indeed, "Moehler, Klee, and Wiseman as distinguished for ingenuity rather than fairness." Of Klee we cannot speak, for we are not acquainted with his writings. But of Moehler and Wiseman we can speak, and, though not enthusiastic admirers of either, we can testify to their singular candor and fairness towards their opponents. No Protestant writer ever showed so much fairness in treating of Protestant doctrines as Moehler has done; and though several attempts have been made to convict him of misrepresentation, not one of them, so far as we have seen, has been successful. A writer in *The New Englander* begins by charging him with misrepresenting Calvin, but is forced in the end to admit that he has not misrepresented him. Dr. Wiseman has a mind of singular fairness, and a heart of great tenderness towards those who differ from him. But perhaps the objection is not that these men misrepresent their enemies, but that they do not state the Catholic doctrines fairly; that is, do not state them as they have been stated by Protestants.* This is probably the complaint. Whenever a Catholic gives a fair and candid statement of Catholicity, the Protestant is obliged to do one of two things,—either admit that he has ignorantly or maliciously misrepresented it, or contend that the Catholic states it better than it is. His self-love and pride of sect, and perhaps his convictions, will not permit him to do the first; he is therefore compelled to do the latter, and to charge the favorable representation to the Catholic's ingenuity, want of candor, or readiness to sacrifice the truth. We can conceive nothing more uncandid or unjust

---

* This is, in fact, the real objection. " It is difficult," says the professor, in a note (p. 463), "to mention any modern work more ingeniously fitted to produce an impression which, upon the whole, is incorrect, than Moehler's *Symbolik*. Its sophistry consists, first, in concealing the more obnoxious phases of the Catholic doctrine; secondly, in the undue prominence it gives to such truths as have been defended by Romanists [Catholics] against the ill-judged attacks of Protestants; thirdly, in its appeal to the writings of individual Protestants with the same freedom as to publicly authorized Confessions of Faith; fourthly, in quoting the impassioned and extravagant remarks of Protestant controversialists, without attempting to modify those remarks by a reference to the circumstances or idiosyncrasies of the men who uttered them; and, fifthly, tacitly assuming that the creeds and standard treatises of Protestants are as authoritative as those of the Romanists." There is no want of candor, we suppose, on the part of the professor, in calling us *Romanists*, a name he knows we disown, and no insult in apologizing, as he does (p. 452), for now and then calling us by our true name. But this is a trifle. These charges against Moehler are unfounded. The first charge we deny; he, in no instance, practises any concealment. There are no "obnoxious phases of Catholic doctrine" to conceal. We do not like Moehler's Germanism, and sometimes he pushes philosophy beyond its province, and his theory of development is too broadly stated; but he has not stated the Catholic doctrine in too favorable a light, nor concealed any phase of Catholic doctrine which he could, consistently with his purpose, bring forward. He was not writing an exposition of Catholic doctrines in general, but of the particular doctrinal differences between Catholics and Protestants, and, so far as the Catholic doctrines are involved in these differences, he has kept no phase of them out of sight. To complain of him for not exhibiting the Catholic doctrines in the respect in which they did not concern the subject of his book is uncandid and unscientific. That he gives undue prominence to truths Protestants have attacked we should like to see proved. The professor admits that Protestants have made "ill-judged attacks" on truths. We will try to remember this; but we should suppose any attack upon truth at all would be *ill-judged*. The *third* objection is removed by the fifth. The creeds and standard treatises are known not to have the authority among Protestants that the authoritative expositions of Catholicity have for Catholics, and therefore Moehler does not rely wholly on them, but consults also the writings of prominent individual Protestants. But the charges of the professor are somewhat singular. He first accuses Moehler of sophistry, because he consults individual doctors as well as authorized Confessions of Faith, and then accuses him of attributing too

than this. Protestants misrepresent Catholics; Catholics expose the misrepresentation, and set forth their doctrines in their true light, as they are and always have been held; and forthwith they are charged with a want of fairness, of being ingenious, but uncandid! This is adding insult to injury.

2. Want of truth means, with the professor, in this charge, very much the same as want of candor. The charge comes with an ill grace from a Protestant. We have never met with a Protestant writer who states a single Catholic doctrine which he rejects, no matter on what point, correctly,

much authority to the Confessions of Faith; that is, of relying too much on them, and holding Protestants too strictly to them. But whoever knows any thing of Protestants knows, that, if individual doctors were not consulted, no fair or just view of Protestantism could be obtained; and we own we cannot see the sophistry, at least the unfairness, in assuming that Protestants really hold to what they solemnly profess in their Confessions. Do the Protestants regard us as sophistical, when we take them at their solemn profession? The *fourth* charge admits the reformers and Protestant controversialists made impassioned and extravagant statements. But does the professor forget that the reformers, Luther, and Calvin, and others, professed to be specially called of God, and to act under the immediate direction of the Holy Ghost, and that it was on this ground alone they attempted to justify their schism and heresy? When a man puts forth such a claim, and when, on the ground of such a claim, he founds a sect, we submit if his followers have a right to plead in arrest of judgment his idiosyncrasies. We owe something to truth and its slandered friends, and not all to misguided and factious heresiarchs or schismatics.

"Our faith," says the professor (*ib.*), "is the Bible." The Bible as you understand it, or as we understand it? As you, of course. Then which of you? for no two of you agree. How are we to determine what Protestantism is? How shall we be able to seize and delineate its features, so that every individual Protestant will admit that he sat for the picture? From your doctors?—which of them? None, you say. From your Confessions?—which of them, and which edition? None of them, you say; for these must not be assumed as authority. Where then? Is your Protestantism a definable thing? If not, why do you complain, if our statement of it, according to the highest authority you acknowledge, does not present it in the precise shape in which it presents itself to each individual Protestant, since in a precise shape or a definite shape it presents itself to no one?

We will take this occasion to inform the professor, that Paul Sarpi's account of the Council of Trent cannot be appealed to as authority. His history is denied to be authentic, and the professor might as well quote against us the recent publications of Hogan and Dowling. If he wishes to know the true history of the Council of Trent, he must consult Pallavicini. We reply to no argument based on the authority of Paul Sarpi, whose statements the professor knows, if he is at all acquainted with the controversy on the subject, are not to be relied on. This is all the answer we give to his charges against the Tridentine fathers.

—who in a single instance reproduces a Catholic argument in its full strength, or gives it a fair and logical reply. The unfairness, we will say the untruth, of Protestants, when engaged in controversy with Catholics, has been a constant theme of complaint with Catholic writers from Cajetan and Eck down to the present moment. It is notorious, and, if not notorious, it is really so flagitious that it would be incredible. When we first turned our attention to the controversy, and began to put Protestant statements to the usual historical tests, we were perfectly astounded. It is impossible to imagine grosser falsehood, or more outrageous injustice, than may be found in the pages of Protestant writers generally,—nay, the very best of them,—whenever they write against Catholics. It is not merely as a Catholic we say this; we say it as a fact of which we became fully convinced before we became a Catholic, and from consulting Protestant authorities themselves. Nothing can exceed the ferocity, falsehood, and wickedness of the books against Catholicity even now recommended by respectable religious journals and grave Protestant divines, and hawked about our streets. They are so barefaced, that they would carry their own refutation with them, if Protestants ever thought of pausing a moment to inquire into the internal probability of any thing said against Catholics or Catholicity. Never were a people so deceived, so gulled, as good, honest, simple credulous Protestants are by the getters-up and circulators of anti-catholic publications. We need but read for a few weeks the anti-catholic press of the country, to be satisfied of this. An editor lights somewhere upon a "mare's nest," cooks up a "startling incident," or a terrible tale of the "horrors of Popery," publishes it, and forthwith it is copied by all the editors of the same brotherhood throughout the country; pious deacons have more *vinaigre* faces than ever; pious old ladies are sure the end of the world is near; the politician screams out the country is in danger, and we must defend it against the pope, the cardinals, the bishops, the priests, and the Jesuits; and the double-distilled hypocrite, with his pockets gorged with the hard earnings wrung from the poor seamstress, the widow, and the orphan, "who puts a penny in charity's box and takes a shilling out," clasps his Bible, with eyes upturned, and a graveyard face, sets up a piteous howl, that the Bible is in danger, cries, "Down with the Pope, the Jesuits, and up with the Bible," and sets the whole community in commotion. A Catholic editor calmly contradicts and refutes the story; the Protestant editor takes no notice of the contradiction and refutation, but repeats it as before, or silently drops it. An anti-catholic writer, preparing an obscene book, lights upon it, copies it into his filthy pages as illustrative of "the horrors of Popery," and henceforth it is authentic Protestant history. This is but an unexaggerated statement of what passes before our eyes and in our own moral and enlightened country; and in this or a similar way Protestant history is manufactured, as some recent Protestant writers themselves, not being immediately concerned in putting down Catholics, have to some extent been forced to admit.*

On the other hand, without meaning to defend every Catholic writer,—for there may have been uncandid Catholic authors, although we know no such,—Catholic authors are singularly fair and candid towards Protestants. This is no merit in them, for they are required to be so. No Catholic would escape the rebuke of his director, if he should win a victory over an opponent by craft, cunning, evasion, misstatement, or sophistical reply. As Catholics, we are required to write in the presence of God, under a deep sense of responsibility,—not for our own glory, our own puny triumphs, but for the greater glory of God, which permits none but holy ends and holy means; and we are false to our religion, when we do not. In all the Catholic controversial works we have seen, we have found candid statements, and fair and logical arguments. In any "Course of Theology" we take up, we find the objections of opponents fairly and honestly stated, and not unfrequently with more clearness, force, and point than in the works of the opponents themselves. Take, as a specimen, Bellarmine, Sardagna, Billuart, Perrone, Bouvier. The man who could accuse such men as these of a want of candor or of love of truth,—of unfair dealing,—would only write his own condemnation.

The professor's own Lecture is a fair specimen of the Protestant mode of discussing the Catholic question. It is not without some cleverness, but, saving a half-candid remark on the Catholic doctrine of indulgences, it has not a single fair, candid, or truthful statement from beginning to end. With the exception named, and which is only half an excep-

---

* Consult Ranke's *History*, not *of the Reformation*, but *of the Popes*, Voigt's *St. Gregory the Seventh*, Hurter's *Pope Innocent the Third*, and especially Maitland's *Dark Ages*. Hurter wrote his work as a Protestant, but we rejoice to learn that he is now a Catholic.

tion, there is not a point of Catholic doctrine, or Catholic worship, or Catholic history, touched upon, on which the reader, relying on this Lecture alone, would not receive an impression directly the reverse of the truth. The ignorance of the professor in regard to Catholicity is indeed great, but his Lecture contains evidence enough that his perversions of truth, misstatements, and absolute untruths are not in all cases the result of misinformation or of defective information. Yet he does not appear to blush to come forward in open day and accuse the Catholic Church of being hostile to candor and love of truth. They were the blasphemous Jews, we believe, who accused our blessed Lord of blasphemy.

3. To the charge, that the Catholic Church is deficient in great philosophers and eminent preachers, we have not much to say. But, unless we have been wholly misinformed, the Gospel was not given expressly to make great philosophers or eminent preachers; but simple, docile, meek, humble, self-denying Christians, who, relying on God's goodness and promises, through the merits of Jesus Christ, hope and labor, by patient endurance and perseverance in well-doing, to attain, at last, forgiveness of their sins and life everlasting. It is better to be a good Christian than a great philosopher, and a true saint than an eminent preacher. The patient watchings, fervent prayers, and daily mortifications of the humble and devoted servant of God, whose name is never heard beyond the solitude in which he lives, avail more, both for himself and for others, than the profoundest treatises of your profoundest philosopher, or the most eloquent sermons of your most gifted divine.

The Gospel is not of man's device and does not stand in human wisdom. "Quid prodest tibi alta de Trinitate disputare, si careas humilitate, unde displiceas Trinitati? Vere alta verba non faciunt sanctum et justum; sed virtuosa vita efficit Deo charum. Opto magis sentire compunctionem, quam scire ejus definitionem. Si scires totam bibliam exterius, et omnium philosophorum dicta, quid totum prodesset sine charitate et Dei gratia? *Vanitas vanitatum, et omnia vanitas*, præter amare Deum, et illi soli servire. Ista est summa sapientia, per contemptum mundi tendere ad regna cœlestia."* The poor nun of Our Lady of Mount Carmel, whom the world knows not and dreams not of, may be doing more, as she recites her rosary, to build up the kingdom of

---

* *De Imitatione Christi*, Lib. I., cap. 1.

God on earth, and to advance the glory of God among men, than whole armies of your profound philosophers and eloquent divines. God loves the simple, the meek, the humble, who forget themselves and remember only him, and will grant almost any thing to their prayers. He does not need the great, the learned, the profound, the eloquent, and rarely makes use of them as his instruments; for they are rarely so humble as not to claim for themselves some share of the glory of what he does by them, and he will suffer no flesh to glory in his presence, or to rob him of the glory which is his, and cannot be another's. *Videte enim vocationem vestram, fratres, quia non multi sapientes secundum carnem, non multi potentes, non multi nobiles: sed quæ stulta sunt mundi elegit Deus, ut confundat sapientes; et infirma mundi elegit Deus, ut confundat fortia; et ignobilia mundi et contemptibilia elegit Deus, et ea quæ non sunt, ut ea quæ sunt destrueret, ut non glorietur omnis caro in conspectu ejus.*"—1 Cor. i. 26-29.

Nevertheless, the Catholic Church has a few men, besides Campanella, Descartes, Malebranche, Bossuet, Fénelon, Bourdaloue, Dupin, Döllinger, Hug, and Van Ess, that are not quite contemptible, and we had rapidly collected a list of several hundred names which we thought of inserting; but upon closer examination of the professor's assertions, we saw it would be of no use. He asserts the church is unfavorable to the mind; and if we should refute this by showing, that, in every department of mind, Catholics always have taken, and still take, the lead, he would reply, that it is in despite of the church. "We have no disposition to deny that many illustrious names are enrolled among the scholars of the church. The human mind will rouse itself to action in despite of all the sedative effects applied to it."—p. 464. What can we say? If we are deficient in great men, eminent philosophers and preachers, it is the fault of the church; if we are not deficient, but abound in them, it is in *despite* of the sedative effects of the church; —nothing is to be said to such reasoning. The argument, *post hoc*, ergo *propter hoc*, is conclusive against the church, but inadmissible if the church is to be defended. "The themes with which Catholic authors are most intimate are of inferior worth,"—"themes of external interest,—seldom of inward dignity." We can reply to this only by a smile, and the recommendation to the author to study the *Summa Theologica* of St. Thomas of Aquin, the commentary on it by Billuart, the *Moral Theology* of St. Alphonsus, the Theology of the Salamancan divines, the works of Bellarmine, especially of Suarez, or of Pope St. Leo the Great, of St. Gregory the Great, Benedict XIV, of Gerson, Thomas à Kempis, Rodriguez, Father Luis of Granada, Salazar, St. Bernard of Clairvaux, St. Anselm of Canterbury, St. Bonaventura, the *Prælectiones Theologicæ*, by Perrone, the volumes published by M. Carrière, of St. Sulpice, Paris, or even an ordinary prayer-book in the hands of our servant-girls, or the catechism we teach our children. The themes with which Catholic authors are most intimate are of inferior worth! Pray, tell us, what is of *superior* worth? Are there loftier themes than God, the sacred mysteries of faith, the Holy Catholic Church, the spouse of the Lamb, the soul,—its wants, weaknesses, depravities, trials, temptations, recovery, growth in Christian knowledge and virtue, its sanctification, and final beatitude? These are the themes with which Catholic authors are most intimate, and which they rarely leave, unless it be in condescension to the weakness of some pert objector, or to repel the sophistry and sneers of some scoffer, and even then only for the sake of these.

It is easy to sneer at the "niceties of the schoolmen," but not so easy to comprehend them. This sneer is on the lips and in the tone or the words of no man who has any knowledge or comprehension of the schoolmen. That the schoolmen are often "nice," we admit, but it is because they aim at exactness, at truth, and are not willing to favor falsehood by a loose expression. That they want comprehensiveness, or that they ever make a distinction without a difference, or which has no foundation *in re*, we have yet to learn. We have heard enough of sneers at the schoolmen,—sneers born of ignorance and the conceit which always accompanies it. Go and master the schoolmen, and then you may sneer at them, if you can. Saving some few matters pertaining to physical science, in which there may have been some progress since the fifteenth century, we stand ready to defend the schoolmen, and to prove to you that your sneers at them are the results of your own utter ignorance of them, or rather incapacity to comprehend theological and philosophical reasoning. We deny, positively deny, that in moral and intellectual science, properly so called, Protestants have made the least progress, or that their philosophers have ascertained a single fact or a single principle not known and recognized by the schoolmen. You know nothing of the schoolmen, if you know not enough not to sneer at them. They may have discussed with great labor and pains some questions of little practical importance, but there is not a single important question they have not also discussed, and well and ably discussed. You talk of "the Dark Ages,"—*dark*, forsooth, as Coleridge, one of your own number, tells you, because you have not light enough to read them.

We know something of your Protestant philosophers, and there are absolutely only four Protestant names that it is not discreditable to one's own knowledge to call a philosopher, and it is doubtful if any one of these was really a Protestant. We mean Leibnitz, Kant, Hegel, and Hobbes. Bacon was an able man, a man of some knowledge and considerable imagination. He discoursed, often eloquently, about philosophy, as it was said of Cicero, but he did not discourse it. Locke, Hume, Berkeley, Reid, Stewart, Fichte, Fries, Jacobi, Schelling, &c., were in some respects clever men, but no philosophers. Hobbes is the only English philosopher, and he was a downright infidel; Hegel has done little else than revive Buddhism, and lose himself in nihilism; Kant had a true metaphysical genius, but his system, as a system, is totally false, and is already exploded. Leibnitz was a man of a comprehensive mind, a boundless ambition, without, as one must believe, any real religious faith. The only portions of his philosophy which any one can now think of adopting were borrowed from the schoolmen. Protestants have no philosophy. If we ask, Where is the Protestant philosopher who has produced a philosophy even widely received by Protestants?—such a confusion of tongues will immediately be heard as will make us glad to stop our interrogatories. No, no, for shame's sake, say nothing about great philosophers.

In theology you are as badly off as you are in philosophy. You have no more respectable theological work than Calvin's *Institutes*, which none of you now accept,—unless with a qualification. There is no such thing as a Protestant systematic course of theology, properly so called. We will not except from this sweeping remark a single one of your famous *Glaubenslehren* of modern Germany, which studies all things, and some others, speculates, theorizes on all, and on none does more than erect a monument to its own folly, want of faith, and blasphemy. Even the boasted erudition of Germany is valuable only as it indicates the sources to be explored. It can in no case supersede the necessity of exploring them anew. Saving some branches of physical science, in which the progress effected is far less than is imagined, Protestants have really contributed nothing of any real importance to the progress of the human mind. We know the Protestant boasts, and we know what Protestants have done. Not one of the great inventions or discoveries, which have so changed the face of the modern world, with the exception, perhaps, of the mule and jenny, and a few other inventions in labor-saving machinery, all of which we look upon as a curse, are due to them. Every thing degenerates, except material industry, in their hands; and yet they have the singular impudence to accuse the Catholic Church of injuring the mind.

But who is this professor who brings this unfounded charge? He is a Puritan. But what have the Puritans done for the mind? In this country, including even the Presbyterians and Calvinistic Baptists, they have produced scarcely a single work in any branch of literature or science, that could receive honorable mention in a general history of literature and science for the last three hundred years. We know no Calvinistic work, or work proceeding from a Calvinistic source, produced in this country, which indicates that its author was master of the current literature of his subject, unless we must except Webster's *Dictionary*, and, perhaps, a geographical work on the Holy Land, by Dr. Robinson. The literature of our country, such as it is, and it is nothing at best to boast of, we owe to authors not of the Puritan or Calvinistic school. The profoundest works of the Puritan school in this country are Edwards *On the Will*, and *On the Affections*, Hopkins's *System of Divinity*, and Dwight's *Theology*. The school does little else than republish from England and Scotland, translate from the German, or compile from foreign scholars. And yet our Puritan professor, with the tail of a Dutch goose in his cap for plume, steps boldly forward, and gravely accuses Catholicity of being hostile to the mind, and seriously charges the Catholic Church with being deficient in great philosophers and eminent preachers!

"Rome has trained a smaller number of original thinkers, for the last three hundred years, than have arisen from even half the number of Protestant churches."—p. 464. If by original thinkers be meant mere dreamers, rash speculators, theorizers, founders of systems which die before their authors, or do not long survive them, we admit the assertion; if it be meant men of solid learning, sound judgment, of varied and accurate knowledge, just and comprehensive views of the subjects they treat, able to treat them in a clear, intelligible, and scientific manner, and to sustain their doctrines by profound erudition, and appropriate logical and conclusive arguments, we deny it, and pledge ourselves, after making all proper allowance for the excess of Catholic population over the Protestant, to produce ten Catholics to every one Protestant the professor will bring forward.

"Why, at the present day, are Lucerne, Friburg, and Uri so much less enlightened than Basle and Berne and Geneva?"—*Ib.* We deny that they are. True enlightenment is religious enlightenment, that which enlightens a man in regard to the end for which Almighty God made him,—both because this is the most essential, and because it most elevates the mind. Dare the professor deny this? If not, we assert the Catholic cantons of Switzerland are more truly enlightened than the Protestant. Moreover, when the Catholic cantons take measures to extend education, the Protestant cantons, with armed soldiery, attempt to arrest them, or assassinate their patriotic leaders, as in the case of the late M. Leu.

"Why is Spain so much more degraded than Holland, Portugal than Denmark, Ireland than Scotland?"—*Ib.* We deny the fact. The case of Holland is not fortunate, for half the population of the kingdom are Catholics. Spain is not more degraded than Holland, and her present afflictions are easily accounted for by her internal revolutions, fomented by anti-catholic influences either from within or from without. The same may be said of Portugal. The influence of the so-called "liberals," in all cases anti-catholic, joined with the protection and intrigues of England, will account for what we may have to deplore in either country, without accusing Catholicity. These nations have, indeed, fallen from their former grandeur; but it must be remembered that they attained their former grandeur under Catholicity, and were greatest, most renowned, when most truly Catholic. If Catholicity be hostile to national greatness and prosperity, how could these nations become so great and prosperous under Catholicity? And why do they decline, as they become less Catholic, and more affected by infidel and Protestant influences? If any man wishes to ascertain the true cause of the decline of some Catholic nations, he must seek for it in the causes which have made first Holland, then England, the commercial centre of the world. Here Catholicity will have nothing to dread or to be ashamed of. This is a subject we hope to be able to treat at length soon. Ireland is not so much more degraded than Scotland as the professor imagines. *Blackwood's Magazine* has given us some startling accounts of the rapid increase of crime in Scotland, and the professor may himself have heard of Glasgow lanes. That Ireland is not more degraded is owing entirely to the Catholic faith. It is this alone that has buoyed up her inhabitants, and enabled them to endure the untold sufferings to which they have been subjected. Not to Catholicity, but to the policy of England and the church by law established, must we look for Ireland's degradation. We would willingly let the question itself turn on the instance of Ireland. We want no better evidence to prove the superiority of Catholicity over Protestantism.·

In our turn, we ask the professor why the laboring classes are so much more degraded in England than they are in Austria, in Italy, or in Spain? Why crime is on the increase in all Protestant countries, but on the decrease in Catholic countries? Why Sweden is so much more immoral than Ireland or Belgium, Stockholm than Rome, London than even Paris? Why generally in Catholic countries are the provisions for the education of the people more ample than in Protestant countries, and a more advanced civilization found? Questions can be asked on our side as well as on the professor's.

"Why are the Austrian clergy so far inferior to the Prussian, the Bavarian to the Saxon, the French to the English?" — *Ib.* We deny that they are so in what constitutes the proper qualifications and true dignity and worth of a clergy. That they are inferior in pride, in vain learning, in rash speculation, and blasphemous doctrines, we admit; but inferior in solid piety, solid learning, true science, thorough knowledge of whatever pertains to their vocation, or in the faithful and diligent discharge of their numerous and painful duties, we deny. The professor, here as well as elsewhere, is liable to be deceived by concluding from Protestants to Catholics. We have no priests who introduce new doctrines, or gain notoriety by leaving old, well-beaten paths, attracting attention by their eccentricities. We have no Schleiermachers, DeWettes, or Strausses, and do not wish them. The Protestant minister lives in public, acts in public, and his qualities are displayed before the public, and noted. The Catholic priest does not act so much in public. His great duty is not to write books, nor his principal sphere the pulpit. His labors are chiefly by the side of the sick and the dying, in the hut of poverty, in succouring those who have no friend but God and the priest, and, above all, in the Confessional. No Protestant is qualified to judge of the ability, worth, or efficiency of the Catholic clergy. The Austrian clergy are not inferior to the Prussian, but they suffer, nevertheless, much in consequence of the *reformations* introduced by the half infidel, half Protestant Emperor Joseph II. To represent the present body of the French clergy, whether of the first or of the second order, as inferior to the English betrays an ignorance or a recklessness that we were not prepared for even in our Andover professor. The present clergy of France, of both orders, are a pious, able, learned, and faithful body of men, and their superiors, if their equals, are nowhere to be found. We love and honor the present French bishops and clergy. They are Catholic, and nobly, zealously, and, with God's blessing, successfully, are they laboring for the regeneration of their beautiful France. To think of comparing these with the indolent English clergy, with their fat livings and famished flocks, is an outrage upon common propriety. The professor must have been joking, or else he counted largely upon the ignorance and credulity of his countrymen.

The reason assigned by the professor for the superiority of the Protestant is ingenious; but, unhappily, he undertook, like a certain philosopher, to account for the phenomenon, before taking the pains to verify the fact. His sneer, that "Romanism is so contrived as to save men the trouble of thinking for themselves," does not greatly disturb us. We should prefer to have our thinking done vicariously, as the professor suggests, than to think to no better purpose than we have found our Protestant thinkers doing. We would rather look upward and outward for light, than into the depths of our own darkness; and we prefer to rely on the teachings of God's word, than on our own excogitations. If the professor thinks differently, perhaps it is not our fault, nor his merit.

VI. We come now to the portion of this Lecture which is specially devoted to the discussion of the *moral* influence of Catholicity, and, notwithstanding the interest of the subject, we are compelled to treat it with the greatest possible brevity; for we have but a few more pages at our command.

But we have already refuted, in principle, so far as they depend on any principle, the main charges which are urged. We must restrict ourselves to some brief observations on a few only of the professor's assumptions, misrepresentations, and false assertions.

The charge now before us is, that the Catholic Church injures the heart of man by holding doctrines which have "a peculiar tendency to be perverted."—pp. 465–467. It is not pretended that the doctrines are untrue or unimportant, but they are objected to simply on the ground of the ease with which they may be perverted. But is the injury done by the doctrines themselves, or by their perversion? If by their perversion, who is in fault,—the church who teaches the truth, or they who pervert it? The blessed apostle says,—" We are unto God the good odour of Christ in them that are saved, and in them that perish. To some, indeed, the odour of death unto death, but in others the odour of life unto life."—2 Cor. ii. 15, 16. Were the apostles guilty of injuring the heart of man, because they preached a doctrine which became to some, through their perversion of it, the odour of death unto death? And, in order to avoid such a result, was it their duty to withhold their doctrine, to modify it, or conceal some portions of it? The holy Apostle Paul did not think so; for he adds, in the following verse,—" We are not as many adulterating the word of God; but with sincerity, but as from God we speak in Christ." St. Peter (2 St. Pet. iii. 16) tells us, that St. Paul, in his epistles, has said some things hard to be understood, which the unstable and the unlearned wrest to their own destruction. Will the professor, therefore, charge St. Paul with injuring the heart of man? The wicked pervert, undoubtedly, the truth of the Gospel, the best gifts of God, for they pervert every thing; but the church cannot confine herself to the merely expedient. The true question for the Christian is never merely, What is expedient? but, What is the truth? and the truth he must speak, whether men hear or whether they forbear. To object to the church because she proclaims doctrines which may be perverted, and which may, therefore, be thought to be inexpedient, is objecting to her for adopting too high a moral standard, and not conceding enough to human weakness and perversity.

Moreover, the professor reasons on a false hypothesis. He assumes that the church, like Protestant sects, has full control over her doctrines, and may herself determine arbitrarily what she shall hold and teach, and what not. But this is not the fact. She does not make her own creed; she receives it, and can hold and teach only what she has received and been commanded to hold and teach. It is her duty to teach the whole word of God, and she must do so. While she is faithful to her trust, the responsibility of effects belongs to Him by whose authority she acts, and the guilt of the perversion of what she teaches belongs to those who pervert it. She cannot withhold the truth, because men may abuse it; nor deny her children the food they need, because perverse minds and hearts may despise it, or derive strength from it for their wickedness. Should she do so, there would be no end to the cry of Protestants against her for her timidity, temporizing, and unfaithfulness.

The professor falls again into the predicament of the philosopher to whom we have just referred him, of assigning ingenious reasons for facts not verified, and which do not exist. His statement of the errors into which Catholics are liable to fall is rather amusing; though after all lamentable, for the degree of ignorance of Catholic doctrine it betrays. "When a man," he says, "is bowed down under a thought of his sinfulness, and is therefore simply commanded to eat no meat for a month, he will not understand the nature of faith, and will misunderstand the nature of Christian works."—p. 466. We remember to have read somewhere of a young girl standing by a beautiful spring of water, bitterly crying and wringing her hands. Her mother came, and asked her why she cried. "I was thinking," said the poor girl, "If I should grow up and get married, and have a child, and the child should come to be able to run alone, and should be playing by this spring, and should fall in, and should be drowned, how very bad I should feel." Whereupon the mother burst out also a crying, and the father came, and heard the story, and he broke out a crying, and the grandmother came, and the grandfather, and the whole family came, and heard the story, and they all set to a crying, and it was truly a crying family. Now, there is this difference between the professor and the poor girl,— her apprehensions were of an evil which *might* possibly happen, but the professor's are of what *cannot* happen. The case he imagines is not even supposable. Such a command could never be given, and no Catholic could ever be simpleton enough to believe that simply refraining from eating meat can atone for sin. Mortification of the body, as a cure for its disorders, is enjoined by the Scriptures; and he who does not, in some way, mortify the flesh, will make little progress in Christian perfection. But for works of mortification to be worth any thing, they must be preceded by faith and repentance, be done in a state of grace, in a spirit of contrition and humility, and accompanied by charity. A few visits to the Confessional would teach the professor many things of which he appears to be now ignorant, and correct many of his false notions, as well as relieve him of certain imaginary fears which now affect his repose. It would do him no harm even to consult the instructions for penitents, which he may find in any of our ordinary manuals of piety.

The professor admits that "there is some truth in the Catholic doctrine of Indulgences," but blames the church for holding it, because "there is reason to fear that men who have made satisfaction for the temporal penalties of the law will consider themselves as having satisfied its eternal demands."—p. 466. The professor little imagines the ignorance of Catholic doctrine this statement betrays to a Catholic. Every Catholic knows that the eternal demands of the law are satisfied only by the death and sufferings of our Lord upon the cross, and that he must be *in a state of grace*, having repented of his sins, and received pardon of them from Almighty God, before his works of satisfaction can be acceptable, or he receive an indulgence.

"If their sins are cancelled for this life, they will presume on the life to come."—*Ib.* Nonsense! for there is no cancelling of sins, either for this life or for that which is to come, but through the infinite satisfaction made by our blessed Redeemer; and no way of escaping the penalty *temporal* or eternal, but by faith, which is always presupposed, sincere repentance, and the free pardon of Almighty God. It is only he who believes, repents, humbles himself before God, and performs acts of contrition and charity, to whom indulgences or works of satisfaction are available. Every Catholic knows this, and therefore the last blunder he could possibly commit would be the one the professor so gratuitously imagines. The professor is quite mistaken in his assertion of a difference between Catholicity "as cautiously and guardedly stated in the standards, and Catholicity as commonly taught and believed." He is equally at fault in his assertions as to what is Catholicity, as commonly taught and believed. He should be ashamed of his misrepresentations. No Catholic teaches, no Catholic believes, that the Blessed Virgin has divine attributes. In her own nature, by virtue of her own essential attributes, she is simply a human being, neither more nor less; and whatever the exalted rank above all creatures she is believed to hold, she holds it not in her own right, but by the appointment and free gift of God. Does it require rare sagacity, extraordinary powers, such as the professor seldom finds among his own people, to distinguish between a being holding, by its own nature, an exalted rank, and one holding an exalted rank solely by virtue of the supernatural gifts and graces of Almighty God? If so, intellectual culture must be sadly neglected among Protestants.

That "indulgences are a legitimate article of traffic," or in any sense an article of traffic at all, is not taught, never was taught, is not believed, never was believed, and never can be believed, by any Catholic. No money can purchase an indulgence; for an indulgence can be obtained only by faith, repentance, confession, absolution, prayers, and alms-deeds. Why did not the professor go a step further, and tell us indulgences are permits to commit sin? This is the general belief of Protestants, who know so little of what they speak as not to know that an indulgence cannot be granted till after the sin has been repented of, confessed, and its eternal guilt pardoned by Almighty God!

VII. "Romanism becomes injurious to the feelings by the *mystical* working of its machinery."—pp. 467–475. We have already answered this charge, in our remarks on the intellectual influence of Catholic worship. The *mystical* working here alluded to is the professor's way of stating the fact, that Catholicity teaches that the sacraments are efficacious through the power of God who instituted them, and the Holy Ghost, who operates in and through them. His first objection, under this head, is, that the church is held to be necessary as the medium of our relation to Christ. He himself would contend that communion with Christ should be proposed as the condition of communion with the church, not communion with the church as the condition of communion with Christ. He therefore regards communion with Christ as the means, and communion with the church as the end,— placing thus the church above Christ, and making Christ necessary only as the way into it. In this, he and the Catholic Church unquestionably differ in opinion. She proposes communion with Christ as the end, communion with her simply as the means of coming into relation with Christ,—thus subordinating herself to Christ, and not Christ to herself. We shall not undertake to say which is the sounder view, for we think St. Paul has done that effectually for all who are not without understanding (Eph. v. 22–32). Yet, if we can have full communion with Christ without the ministry of the church, we confess we see no reason for the church. Does the professor object to Catholicity because it is not no-churchism?

The second objection, under this same head, appears to be, that the church proposes Holy Communion as a condition of the Christian life, and not the Christian life as the condition of Communion. "It calls on us not first to live and then eat," but the reverse. The professor's doctrine, then, is, that we should live in order to eat, and not eat in order to live,—a very general Protestant doctrine. Yet the professor is mistaken, if he supposes the church does not demand life before eating; for a dead man cannot eat, any more than he can perform any other function. The communicant must have been born again, made alive in Christ by the sacrament of baptism, or, if he have sinned mortally after baptism, by the sacrament of penance, before he can worthily commune. He does not eat, then, as a dead man, that he may become a living man, but that he may have life more abundantly, that he may nourish, sustain, invigorate, and augment his divine life.

The professor is inexcusable for asserting that Catholicity "represents a sacrament as communicating rather than presupposing the fitness for receiving it," for he knows better; as also for saying, the only obstacle forbidden to be interposed to its operation "is not sin in general, but only a particular species of it,—sin against the church, and this is the sin unto death." We will not trust ourselves to characterize this statement as it deserves. The references the professor himself makes prove that he knew he was stating an absolute falsehood. No sacrament imparts the fitness to receive it, for no sacrament can be received with improper dispositions without sacrilege, and especially is this true of so great a sacrament as Holy Communion. We are everywhere admonished of the danger of eating or drinking unworthily; for he who does so eateth and drinketh condemnation to himself. In order to receive Holy Communion without eating or drinking our own condemnation, and being guilty of the

Lord's body, we must be free, not from one species of mortal sin only, but from every species of it (Conc. Trid. Sess. XIII., can. 11); and in order to receive the plenitude of its fruits, we must be free from even the affection to venial sins, and have a lively faith, a firm hope, and an ardent charity. The effect of the sacrament, indeed, does not depend on these dispositions as the *causa efficiens*, but it is not produced where these dispositions are wanting. They are not the efficacy of the sacrament, but the conditions without which it is not effectual in the recipient.

The objection, which the professor urges against Catholicity for teaching that the sacraments produce their effects *ex opere operato*, is one on which he will hardly dare insist. He himself, in the Andover creed, admits sacraments. The sacrament is intended to effect something, or it is not. If not, let it be dismissed, for it is an idle ceremony. If it is, then it must produce its effect in one of three ways:—1. *ex opere operantis;* 2. *ex opere suscipientis;* or, 3. *ex opere operato;* for these are the only conceivable alternatives. The first assumes the efficacy of the sacrament to be in the administrator. If you say this, you make the virtue of the sacrament depend on the priest; that is, you make the priest the efficient cause of the grace received in the sacrament. But this would be to put the priest in the place of the Holy Ghost, and to assert another source of grace than the merits of Jesus Christ, which is inadmissible. Moreover, the priest may be a sinful man, and to suppose a sinful man can be the efficient cause of grace is absurd. If, to obviate this, you assert that none but holy men can be legitimate priests, you fall into the old Donatist heresy of making the validity and efficacy of sacraments depend on the sanctity of the priest, —a fact which God alone can know.

If you adopt the second view, which supposes the virtue to be in the recipient, you deny that the sacrament, as a sacrament, has any virtue at all. If the efficacy of the sacrament depends on him who receives it, as the efficient cause, he, in receiving it, receives only what he gives it, and therefore nothing which he had not before receiving it; which is to say, he receives nothing at all. Cause, so far forth as cause, receives nothing from its effects. The creation does not react on the Creator, and augment his power. That which leaves us as it found us, or returns to us only what it receives from us, produces no effect in us. One needs to be no very profound metaphysician to know all this. The professor, we apprehend, is not aware of the consequences of making the virtue of the sacrament depend on the recipient. He contends, that the efficacy of the sacrament is in the faith of the recipient, and that it consists in strengthening faith, and thereby the life which is by faith. But, this involves a principle which may lead where the professor is not prepared to follow. If our faith be the efficient cause of the sacramental effect, to assert that by it there is an increase of faith, or an augmentation of the grace of faith, or of the effects of faith, implies that faith can be augmented from itself and by itself, or that of itself and by itself it can increase its power and fruitfulness; which implies the principle of self-growth, —an evident absurdity; for it implies that a given existence can, in and of itself and by itself, make itself more than it is,—that the possible is able to actualize itself,—*vacuum* to fill up itself and become *plenum*,—the precise absurdity of the modern progressists and of the old Buddhists. Is our professor prepared to accept this absurdity? If not, he must not say a thing can augment itself, or be augmented, save as it receives and assimilates somewhat *ab extra*, from a source foreign to itself. Then he must either admit in the sacrament a virtue not derivable from the recipient, or deny that it has any virtue at all.

Nothing remains, then, but the third supposition, namely, the virtue of the sacrament is *ex opere operato, non merito operantis vel suscipientis;* that is, that the virtue or efficacy of the sacrament is of God, who instituted it, and operates in and through it. The professor must admit this conclusion, or either assert another source of grace than the merits of Jesus Christ, or deny the sacraments altogether. The last is, in fact, what Protestants generally do.

These remarks on the sacraments contain a sufficient answer to all that the professor says of the influence of Catholicity on the clergy. The professor has become so enamoured of the modern German method of finding in human nature or in a philosophic theory the measure of all institutions, that he forgets that the church is to be judged not as a human, but as a divine, supernatural institution. He forgets, that, as a simple human institution, having its origin and cause in human nature, and operating only by human agencies and means, according to the simple laws of human nature, nobody proposes it, nobody pretends to defend it. His speculations, however ingenious, nay, however true they might be, were it a human institution, and to be judged as we should judge a temporal government, are valueless, and must count for nothing; because, as speculations, they proceed from a false assumption, and are not in return borne out by facts. To apply *a priori* reasoning, which might be legitimate to a natural, human institution, to a supernatural, divine institution, is an error which no man of any tolerable scientific attainments would willingly be guilty of.

The professor's objections all proceed from his overlooking one rather important fact, namely, the gracious presence of God. He reasons as if there was no grace of God. Here is his primal sin. If he chooses to deny that the church is a supernatural, divine institution, and that the grace of God operates in and through her sacraments, well and good; but then comes up the church question we began by stating. But till he does that, and ousts the church from her possession, by invalidating her claims, his present line of argument is illegitimate; and when he shall have done that, it will be unnecessary.

VIII. The eighth charge, that Catholicity has a tendency to separate religion from good morals, and to undervalue morality as distinct from religion (pp. 475, 476), is altogether unfounded. The basis of ethics, according to Catholicity, is theology; and ethics are uniformly treated by Catholic writers under the head of *Theologia Moralis*, or practical theology. Religion is always presented to us as the basis of good morals. The foundation and motive to the love of our neighbour is in the love of God. We are taught to love our neighbour for the sake of God, and throughout the whole range of morals the *propter quem* is God, who is our beginning and end; and every action not referred to him as the end or final cause, for the sake of which it is done, is always sinful, or at least morally imperfect. Here is the closest union between religion and morals conceivable. It is impossible to say more.

The assertion, that Catholicity places the fulfilling of the law in the external observances of the church, is false and inexcusable. The church can dispense from any of her own observances or laws, but she denies that she can dispense from a precept of the moral law. The professor knows this, if he knows any thing of the subject he pretends to treat. Where did he learn that it is, in the estimation of the church or of her doctors, "a comparatively humble virtue to speak the truth?" Do Protestants hold, that to speak the truth is a *virtue* at all? Judging from the professor's assertions against Catholicity, we should presume not. Catholic morality denies us the right, in any case, to speak what is not true, or what, in the plain, legitimate sense of our words, is false, though, in some restricted sense of our own, what we say may be true. No intentional falsehood, no intentional deception of any kind, in any case, or for any cause whatever, is allowed. This is Catholic morality. The author's assertions respecting Bossuet, Massillon, &c., and especially the general councils, that they divorce morality from piety, authorize pious frauds, teach that no faith is to be kept with heretics, &c., are barefaced falsehoods, and convict him of the very vice he is trying to fasten on others. He knows these charges have been denied and refuted over and over again,—unless his ignorance is more profound than even we believe it. Wherefore, then, does he not blush to reiterate them, and to reiterate them in the same breath in which he is trying to monopolize candor, fairness, and love of truth as Protestant virtues,—born, as it were, with Luther and Calvin?

"The spirit of mediæval piety was in too fearful a degree the spirit of robbery, and burnt-offering; of falsehood, and devotedness to the church; of an Ave Maria on the lips, and carnage in the heart."—p. 476. This from a man who is accusing the church of a want of candor, fairness, love of truth! The man is mad, and not "with much learning." The middle ages are not without their faults, but who knows any thing of them knows this—when intended to describe their predominating spirit—is false, totally false, as prove all the records of that glorious period of human history, on which he who loves God and man lingers, as the traveller on some green oasis in the sandy waste. But, even if true, a descendant of the Puritans, who robbed the Indians of their lands, then massacred the poor savages or sold them into slavery, while saying their long graces or interminable prayers, should, for shame's sake, hold his peace. A descendant of a class of men whose spirit was condensed in Cromwell's famous exhortation,—"Pray to God, my brethren, and mind and keep your powder dry,"—should not talk about Ave Maria on the lips and carnage in the heart. It is not for one who builds the tombs and garnishes the sepulchres of the canting, hypocritical, sour-visaged, greedy, arrogant, and cruel old Puritans, to accuse others of paying "tithes of anise, cummin, and mint, and of passing over justice and judgment, and the weightier matters of the law." The professor should know that there are some who have even Puritan blood running in their veins who do not remember to forget what the Puritans were. We know their history, and would be silent; but we may yet be driven to write it. These men of yesterday, these theologians not yet in shorts, who want ancestors, and whom their own children disown, may yet be summoned to answer for their presumption and pride, their cant and hypocrisy, their falsehoods and calumnies, before the bar of a public that will not consent to be forever duped. They have a terrible account to settle, and it will be no disadvantage to them to settle it now, before the books are opened for the last time.

"No faith to be kept with heretics." Where did the professor learn that this is a maxim of Catholicity? It is false. Catholicity knows no such maxim, and Catholic history authorizes no inference that she practically adopts or in the least conceivable manner countenances it. Individuals of bad faith may be found, no doubt, even among Catholics; but that Catholicity or Catholic doctors any where countenance any thing of the sort is a malignant falsehood. We are taught and required to keep our faith with all men, and faith plighted to a heretic can no more be broken without sin than faith plighted to a true believer. We would that Protestants would observe a tithe of the good faith towards Catholics that Catholics do towards Protestants; and when they shall do so, we give them free leave to abuse our morals to their full satisfaction.

"The end sanctifies the means." So the apostles were slanderously reported to teach,—" Let us do evil that good may come." "If they have called the master of the house Beelzebub, how much more them of his household!" No such doctrine is known among Catholics; we are not permitted to do evil that good may come. Both the means and the end must be holy. But on what principle do Protestants themselves act, when they lie about and calumniate Catholics? On what principle would Professor Park attempt to justify the misrepresentations, distortions of the truth, and downright falsehoods of his own Lecture, if not on the principle, that "the end sanctifies the means"? On what principle can your Brownlows, Sparrys, Breckenridges, Bemans, Kirks, Beechers, Dowlings, your famous anti-catholic lecturers, pamphleteers, editors, and colporteurs, pretend to justify their flagitious falsehoods and calumnies, but on the principle that Catholicity is so great an evil, that any means are lawful which will tend to destroy it,—that is, "the end sanctifies the means"? When have Catholics lied about or calumniated Protestants? When or where have they even exaggerated their errors, vices, or crimes? When or where have they combined by systematic misrepresentation and slander to overthrow Protestantism or to build up their own church? Facts, names, dates, Gentlemen, if you please,—which we hold ourselves ready to give in return, if those already given do not satisfy you, or if you presume to contradict us. No, no, dear Protestant friends, remember that he that is without sin is the one who has permission to cast the first stone. Your own morals are quite too questionable to allow you to rail at Catholics. Be so good as to practise a morality half as pure as we teach, before you think of reading us moral lectures.

IX. The ninth charge, touching the austerity of Catholicity and its influence on the emotions, we must pass over. The author converses on these matters as a rationalist, who forgets the grace of God may count for something, might be expected to converse on a subject of which he knows nothing, and which, in his present state of mind, he is as ill able to appreciate as a blind man is colors, or a deaf man harmony. The professor evidently has made no study of ascetic theology, nor ever devoted much time to prayer, meditation, and mortification; and this may account, in no small degree, for his hostility to Catholicity.

He might as well charge our blessed Lord with exerting a bad moral influence on the emotions and passions, in choosing his apostles from fishermen, publicans, and tent-makers, as to charge the church with a bad moral influence, because no small portion of her clergy are taken from the humbler classes of society. He thinks priests taken from the humbler classes, elevated suddenly to a higher condition of life, and invested with great power, must inevitably become proud, vain, servile towards those above them, and haughty and overbearing towards those below them. If they were to be Protestant ministers, this might perhaps be the case; for Protestants have not the grace of God to keep them humble. But we do not observe that the apostles became proud in consequence of their elevation and authority, nor as a fact is it often so with our Catholic clergy. The effects feared are guarded against by the religious training they receive, the influence of their religion on their consciences, and the grace of God imparted to aid them not only as Christians, but as Christian teachers and pastors. May we request the professor to remember that the grace of God is not regarded by Catholics as a fiction, and that Catholicity teaches us in all things to seek the glory of God, and to ascribe in all the glory to God?

X. The tenth charge, that Catholicity engenders an exclusive and persecuting spirit, we throw back on the professor. The Catholic Church is exclusive in the sense that truth is exclusive, but in no other. She never persecutes, never has persecuted, never authorizes or approves persecution. Legitimate authority may punish, but it cannot persecute. But the church herself inflicts only ecclesiastical punishments; and she has never authorized, or even tacitly approved, any *civil* punishment of heretics, when the heretic did not add to the sin of heresy, which St. Paul classes with murder and other deadly sins, the further sin of offences against the state, or of attacks on the very foundations of moral and social order, as in the case of the Albigenses, Wickliffites, Hussites, &c. The Catholic Church here, as well as elsewhere, is impervious to the shafts of her enemies.

But if you want to find persecution, genuine, unmitigated persecution, you must go out of the Catholic Church, among the reformers and their numerous bands of hostile sectaries; and especially among the Calvinists at Geneva, under Calvin's own reign of terror, where it was virtually a capital offence "to speak evil of M. Calvin," and where Calvin kept his grand inquisitor, Colladen, who applied the torture to the very point of death to whomsoever Calvin was pleased to designate; and where Calvin himself, in the coolest and most malignant manner conceivable, procured the judicial murder of the poor poet, Gruet, Michael Servetus, and others. Whoever would become familiar with *bona fide* persecutions must read the history of the reformers and their children.

XI. That Catholicity accepts the sneer of Hume, that "Religion rests on faith, not on reason," we admit, if regard be had to the intrinsic reasonableness of the mysteries; yet we deny that faith is unreasonable, for nothing is more reasonable than to believe God on his word. The rule the professor would introduce would be fatal to supernatural revelation. He contends for the principle, that we must judge the speaker by the word, and not the word by the speaker. This is a sound principle within the sphere of natural reason, in matters of which we have in ourselves a full knowledge, and therefore all the conditions of forming a correct judgment. But whoso adopts it in the sphere of religion is already an infidel or on the declivity to infidelity; for it cannot be adopted in the sphere of religion without first denying that in religion there is any thing to be believed which transcends natural reason; therefore it cannot be adopted without denying supernatural revelation; and to deny supernatural revelation is what is meant by infidelity.

We do not like to call a man an infidel, or to be continually telling him that his objections involve a denial of Christianity. We know how easy it is to say such things, and how very suspicious such charges usually are; but we confess, that, so far as we are competent to judge of the matter, the professor has not urged a single objection against us, not false in fact, which, if analyzed, reduced to its ultimate principle, does not imply a total denial of all revelation of the supernatural order. We have found in no professedly religious writer in this country, unless it be in Mr. Parker, so complete a rejection, in principle, at least, of all supernatural revelation. The whole Lecture is written from the humanitarian point of view, and proves that the author is far, very far, gone in German rationalism; and unless the Puritans of New England are much changed from what they were when we knew them better than we now do, he will yet be called to an account for his doctrines.

In this Lecture, his tendencies are not fully developed, and they show themselves to the Puritan reader only in their opposition to Catholicity, and therefore are not likely to be at once suspected of their real character. He will be allowed, without rebuke, to pursue a line of argument towards us, which, if he should adopt it in regard to his own creed, would not be tolerated for a moment. But whoso sows error sows dragon's teeth, and they will one day spring up armed men. They who countenance arguments false in principle, when directed against their opponents, will one day find them rebound, and with as much force as they were urged. We do not like Puritanism; we regard it as a deadly enemy to truth and religion; but we should be sorry to see it overthrown by the introduction of another error still greater, still more destructive. Bad as it is, it is not so bad as German rationalism, or even German supernaturalism, as represented by Schleiermacher, Neander, and De Wette, which is only rationalism sentimentalized.

We make these remarks with no ill-will towards Professor Park. We see his tendency, for it is a tendency we followed long before he was affected by it; we have followed it to its termination, and we know where it conducts. Would to God, that on this point the professor would place some little confidence in our words. We were bred in the same school he was, and we embraced the faith in which he was educated, and made what we thought was our first communion in a Calvinistic church. We sought, like him, to rationalize our faith, with less learning, less knowledge, and less advantages to begin with, we own; for we were a poor boy cast upon the world alone, to struggle our way as best we could. We wished to have a faith the intrinsic reasonableness of which we could demonstrate. Of the twenty years which followed we need not speak. They are not such as we are proud of, nor such as we can recur to, except for a lesson of humility; yet this have we learned,—had burnt and scarred into our very soul,—that there is no medium between a simple, meek, unquestioning faith in the sacred mysteries, as perfectly incomprehensible mysteries, on the sole authority of God revealing them, and absolute, downright infidelity; and that the first step taken for the purpose of rationalizing the Christian faith is a step downwards to the bottomless hell of unbelief.

The professor charges us with being unwilling to accept, or unable to delight in, goodness not in our own church. "The treasures of excellence that are spread out before us in Fénelon and Bossuet we, as Protestants, rejoice in; .... but when the amiable sentiments of a Zinzendorf or of a Spangenberg are presented to a Romanist, are they welcomed by him?"—p. 484. Yes, so far as truly amiable and good; and the Catholic is ready to acknowledge, and does acknowledge and delight in excellence, let him find it where he may.

1. But—and here is a point we beg the professor to remember—there is a difference between the amiable sentiments which are without grace, and the really amiable sentiments which are by grace. We admit amiable sentiments in men who are out of the church; but not that men, who are not, to say the least, *virtually* in the church, have or can have any truly meritorious sentiments; for no sentiments not proceeding from grace are or can be meritorious;

and we know no ordinary means of grace but the sacraments of the church.

2. The Catholic Church is older than any of the sectaries, and had examples of all the virtues long before Zinzendorf or Spangenberg was born, and purer examples than either of these gives us of any virtue. We find nothing in these men but feeble imitations of originals in possession of the church, and therefore we neither need them nor can profit by them.

3. These men were heretics and schismatics; and St. Paul classes heresy and schism with deadly sins. Moreover, we do not think it favorable to good morals to dwell with too much admiration on the few virtues individuals may have in despite of their moral sins. The tendency to compel us to do this is the crying sin of modern literature, as witness *The Corsair*, *Lucrèce Borgia*, *The Adventures of a Younger Son*, &c.

4. The blessed Apostle John says, "We are of God. He that knoweth God heareth us, and he that is not of God heareth not us. By this we know the spirit of truth, and the spirit of error."—1 St. John, iv. 6. Moreover, he says, again, *Si quis venit ad vos, et hanc doctrinam non affert, nolite recipere eum in domum, nec* AVE *dixeritis.*—2 St. John, 10. If the professor wants any further reply, we will give it, after he has settled his quarrel with the beloved apostle of our Lord.

If the Protestants rejoice in the treasures of excellence spread out in Fénelon and Bossuet, it is well, as far as it goes. They should do so; it is their duty; and it is also their duty to go further, and submit to the church of Fénelon and Bossuet, love and obey her as their spiritual mother; and even then they would have no right to put on airs; for when we have done our whole duty, our blessed Lord tells us to account ourselves unprofitable servants. We do not, we own, feel bound to be remarkably grateful to the would-be liberal Protestant, who thinks to say a kind thing to us, by saying, "O, yes, the Catholic Church has had some eminent men; there's Fénelon; I am a great admirer of Fénelon." We only do not take this as an insult, because no insult is intended. As well think to compliment a Christian by saying some of the apostles were very eminent men, that you are a great admirer of the virtues of the Founder of Christianity. Do you receive Jesus Christ as your master? Do you own the church as your mother? No?

Then you fall infinitely short of your duty. We are not Catholics because we admire Fénelon, or Bossuet, and we do not regard it as a compliment even to the Catholics you pretend to admire that you admire them, for you deride that to which they owed their virtues, and show your admiration is worth nothing by admiring also Luther, Calvin, Beza, Knox, and perhaps Cotton Mather. We do not thank you for praising our brethren, while you insult and calumniate our Mother. Speak evil of us, or of them, and we can forgive you. But call our Mother hard names, as you do, and nothing you can say in our favor or in theirs will enable us to forgive you. In the one case, you at worst only blaspheme men; in the other, you blaspheme the Holy Ghost, the eternal God, whose spouse she is; and even were we and our brethren to forgive you, it would avail you nothing.

XII. To the twelfth charge, that Catholicity "is fascinating to all classes," we will say not much. It is a charge we cannot retort upon Puritanism. That the Catholic Church is attractive to all men of all classes who would have faith, who feel that they are poor, helpless sinners, and would have the sure means of salvation; to the weary and heavy laden, who seek rest, and find it nowhere in the world; to those who would have confidence in their principles, and free scope and full employment for their intellectual powers; to those who are tired of endless jarring, and disgusted with shallow innovators, pert philosophers, unfledged divines, cobweb theories spun from the brain of vanity and conceit, vanishing as the sun exhales the morning dew which alone rendered them visible, and who would have something older than yesterday, solid, durable, carrying them back and connecting them with all that has been, and forward and connecting them with all that is to be, admitting them into the goodly fellowship of the saints of all ages, making them feel that they have part and lot in all that over which has coursed the stream of divine providence, that has been consecrated by the blood of martyrs, and hallowed by the ebb and flow of sanctified affection, and permitting them to love, venerate, and adore to their heart's content, or their heart's capacity;—to all these, of whatever age or nation, sex, rank, or condition, the glorious, sublime, God-inspired, guided, and defended Catholic Church is full of attractions, we admit, even fascinating, if you will. But in any other sense than this, or to any other than such as these, we deny it, and find the justification of our denial in the fact that the professor and his brethren are yet without her pale.—The thirteenth charge we shall consider in a separate article, designed to show the necessity of Catholicity to sustain popular liberty.

We here close our protracted review of this Lecture. The unchristian style of writing adopted by the author has prevented us from being briefer. But we have been as brief as we well could be. We have doubtless omitted some points which the author judges important, but we have touched upon all the main charges. For the most part, we have had nothing but assertions, unsupported by fact or argument, to combat. Where these were such as could, from the nature of the case, be met by argument, we have so met them; where they admitted no argument, we have met them by counter assertions, and put the author upon his proofs. If he shall attempt to bring forward facts to sustain any of his assertions which we have contradicted, or left uncontradicted, he will find us ready to meet him.

In some passages we have spoken plainly, perhaps severely. We are not in the habit of seeking for soft words, nor has the present case seemed to us to demand them. No Protestant can feel or understand the outrageous character of the Lecture we have had to combat. Its real flagitiousness is apparent only to a Catholic; and it were to be false to our brethren, false to the truth, false to our God, not to rebuke its author in the tones of a just severity. We have spoken calmly, sincerely, conscientiously, but strongly, and we hope to the point, and to the purpose.

THORNWELL'S ANSWER TO DR. LYNCH.*

[From Brownson's Quarterly Review for 1848.]

ARTICLE I.

SOMETIME in 1841, Mr. Thornwell, a Presbyterian minister, and "Professor of Sacred Literature and the Evidences of Christianity in the South-Carolina College," published, anonymously, in a Baltimore journal, a brief essay against the divine inspiration of those books of the Old Testament which Protestants exclude from the canon of Scripture. To this essay, as subsequently reprinted with the author's name, the Rev. Dr. Lynch, of Charleston, S. C., replied, in a series of letters addressed to Mr. Thornwell, through the columns of *The Catholic Miscellany*.† The volume before us is Mr. Thornwell's rejoinder to Dr. Lynch, and contains, in an Appendix, the original essay, and the substance of Dr. Lynch's reply to it. The rejoinder consists of twenty-nine letters, which cover nearly the whole ground of controversy between Catholics and Protestants, and, though written in a Presbyterian spirit, they are respectable for ability and learning. The work, though nothing surprising, is, upon the whole, above the general average of publications of its class.

The purpose of the essay was to "assert and endeavour to prove that *Tobit, Judith, the additions to the Book of Esther, Wisdom, Ecclesiasticus, Baruch, with the Epistle of Jeremiah, the Song of the Three Children, the Story of Susannah, the Story of Bel and the Dragon, and the First and Second Books of Maccabees* are neither sacred nor canonical, and of course of no more authority in the church of God than Seneca's Letters or Tully's Offices." (pp. 339,

---

The Apocryphal Books of the Old Testament proved to be Corrupt Additions to the Word of God.—The Arguments of Romanists from the Infallibility of the Church and the testimonies of the Fathers in Behalf of the Apocrypha discussed and refuted. By JAMES H. THORNWELL. New York and Boston: 1845.

†The Dr. Lynch here spoken of is the same who became Bishop of Charleston in 1858 and died in February, 1882.—ED.

340.) In the present work, the author attempts to maintain the same thesis, and to refute the objections urged by Dr. Lynch against it. He professes on his very title-page to have *proved* the books enumerated "to be corrupt additions to the word of God," and to have discussed and *refuted* "the arguments of Romanists from the infallibility of the church and the testimonies of the fathers in their behalf." The question very naturally arises, Has he done this? Has he proved that these books are uninspired, as he must have done, if he has proved them to be corrupt additions to the word of God; and has he refuted the arguments of Catholics, or rather of Dr. Lynch, in their behalf?

The arguments which Dr. Lynch adduces for these books are drawn from the infallibility of the church and the testimony of the fathers. If the church is infallible, the testimony of the fathers is of subordinate importance, for the infallibility alone suffices for the faithful; if the church is not infallible, it is of still less consequence what the fathers testify; for then all faith is out of the question, both for Catholics and all others. We may, therefore, waive all consideration, for the present, of the argument for the deutero-canonical books drawn from the testimony of the fathers, and confine ourselves to that drawn from the infallibility of the church. The argument from infallibility must, of course, be refuted, before the author can claim to have refuted Dr. Lynch, or to have proved his general thesis, that the books in question are "corrupt additions to the word of God."

The Catholic Church, undeniably, includes these books in her canon of Scripture, and commands her children to receive them as the word of God. This is certain, and the author concedes it; for he adduces it as a proof of her "intolerable arrogance." If she is infallible in declaring the word of God, as all Catholics hold, these books are certainly inspired Scripture, and rightfully placed in the canon. This is the argument from infallibility; and it is evident to every one who understands what it is to refute an argument that it can be refuted only by disproving the infallibility, or, what is the same thing, proving the fallibility, of the church. To prove the church fallible, moreover, it is not enough to refute the arguments by which Catholics are accustomed to prove her infallibility; for a doctrine may be true, and yet the arguments adduced in proof of it be unsound and inconclusive. It will, therefore, avail the author but little to refute our arguments for the infallibility, unless he refutes the infallibility itself; for so long as he is unable to say positively that the church is fallible, he is unable to refute the argument *from* her infallibility. It may still be true that she is infallible, and if she is, the books are not uninspired compositions, but infallibly the word of God.

Mr. Thornwell, who regards himself as an able and sound logician, appears to have some consciousness of this, and indeed to concede it. Accordingly, he devotes a third of his whole volume to disproving the infallibility of the church, or rather, to proving her fallibility. "I have insisted," he says in his preface, "largely on the dogma of infallibility,—more largely, perhaps, than my readers may think consistent with the general design of my performance,—because I regard this as the prop and bulwark of all the abominations of the Papacy."—(p. 8.)

But to prove the fallibility of the church, or to disprove her infallibility, is a grave undertaking, and attended with serious difficulties. The church cannot be tried except by some standard, and it is idle to attempt to convict her on a fallible authority. If the conviction is obtained on a fallible authority, the conviction itself is fallible, and it, instead of the church, may be the party in the wrong. The professor cannot take a single step, cannot even open his case, unless he has an infallible tribunal before which to summon the church,—some infallible standard by which to test her infallibility or fallibility. But before what infallible tribunal can he cite her? What infallible authority has he on which he can demand her conviction?

The only possible way in which the fallibility of the church can be proved is by convicting her of having actually erred on some point on which she claims to be infallible. But it is evident, that, in order to be able to convict her of having erred on a given point, we must be able to say infallibly what is truth or error on that point. Clearly, then, the professor cannot commence his action, much less gain it, unless he has an authority which pronounces infallibly on the points on which he seeks to convict her of having actually erred. But what authority has he? Unhappily, he does not inform us, and does not appear to have recognized the necessity on his part of having any authority. He sets forth, formally, no authority, designates no court, specifies no law, lays down no principles. This is a serious inconvenience, and affects both his legal and his logical attainments. His argument, let him do his best, must be *minus* its major proposition; and from the minor alone we have always understood that it is impossible to conclude any thing.

Mr. Thornwell denies the infallibility of the church, and he recognizes no infallible authority in any one of the sects, including even his own. He has, then no authority which he can allege, but the authority of reason, and his own private judgment. His own private judgment is of no weight, and cannot be adduced in a public discussion. The authority of reason we acknowledge to be infallible in her own province; but her province is restricted to the natural order, and she has no jurisdiction in the supernatural order, to which the church professes to belong. The church has the right to be tried by her peers. Reason is not, and cannot be, the peer of the supernatural, and is totally unable, in so far as the church lies within the supernatural order, to pronounce any judgment concerning her infallibility one way or the other.

Reason, undoubtedly, knows that God is, and that he can neither deceive nor be deceived. It knows, therefore, if he appoints the church, commissions her, as his organ, to declare his word, that she must declare it infallibly; for then it is he himself that declares in her declaration, and if she could either deceive or be deceived, he himself could either deceive or be deceived. If, then, reason finds sufficient or satisfactory grounds for believing that God has appointed or instituted the church to declare his word, to teach all nations to observe all things whatsoever he has revealed, it pronounces her infallible, and acknowledges its obligation to receive, without any questioning, whatever she teaches.

Reason, again, knows that God cannot be in contradiction with himself, and therefore, since both the natural order and the supernatural are from him, that he cannot establish principles in the one repugnant to those established in the other. On the authority of reason, then, we may always assert that he cannot teach one thing in the natural order and its contradictory in the supernatural order. If, then, it be clearly established, that the church, on matters on which she claims to teach infallibly, teaches what is in contradiction either to the supernatural or the natural order, it is certain that she is fallible. But as reason cannot go out of the order of nature, we can on its authority establish the fallibility of the church only on the condition of convicting her of having actually contradicted some law or principle of the natural order. If the church, in other words, contradict reason, reason is competent to conclude against her, but not when she merely transcends reason; for what is *above* reason may be true, but what is *against* reason cannot be.

It follows from this that the authority of reason in the case before us is purely negative, and that the professor can conclude from it against the church only on condition that he proves that she actually contradicts it. But it is necessary even here to bear in mind that the natural can no more contradict the supernatural than the supernatural the natural. When the motives of credibility have convinced reason that the church teaches by supernatural authority, her teaching is as authoritative as any principle of reason itself, and may be cited to prove that what is alleged against her as a principle of reason is not a principle of reason, with no less force than the alleged principle itself can be cited to prove that she contradicts reason. The professor must, then, in order to prove her fallibility, adduce a case, not of apparent contradiction, but of real contradiction,—a case in which what she teaches must evidently contradict an evident principle of reason,—so evident that it is clear that to deny it would be to deny reason itself.

The position, then, which the professor must take and maintain, in order to establish his thesis, is, that *the church, in her teaching on matters on which she claims to teach infallibly, has taught or teaches what contradicts an evident and undeniable principle of reason.* This he must do before he can prove the fallibility of the church, and he must prove the fallibility of the church before he can refute the argument drawn from it for the books enumerated. Has he proved this? Unhappily, he does not appear to have understood that this was at all necessary, or to have suspected that it was only by proving the church to be against reason that he could conclude her fallibility. He does not appear to have known that there are and can be no questions debatable between Catholics and Protestants but such as pertain exclusively to the province of reason. He labors under the hallucination, that he has something besides the reason common to all men which he may oppose to us, that he has the revelation of Almighty God, and that he is at liberty to attempt to convict the church, not on reason alone, but also on the word of God. This would be ridiculous, if the matter were not so grave as to make it deplorable. He has no word of God to cite against us, and if he cites the Holy Scriptures at all, he must cite them either in the sense of the church, or as simple historical documents; because it is only in the sense of the church that we acknowledge them to be inspired. We can cite them as inspired Scripture against him, as an *argumentum ad hominem;* for he holds them to be inspired Scripture as interpreted by private judgment. But he cannot against us; for the argument would not be *ad hominem*, unless cited in the sense of the church, since it is only in that sense, that, on our own principles, they are the word of God.

The fact is, Mr. Thornwell from first to last forgets in his argument that we are as far from admitting his authority as he is from admitting ours. He writes under the impression, that he has the true Christian doctrine, and is invested with ample authority to define what is, and what is not, the word of God. He assumes his Presbyterianism to be true, and when he has proved that Catholicity contradicts it, he concludes at once that Catholicity is false. But Presbyterianism is only his private judgment, and therefore of no authority. By what right does he erect his private judgment into a criterion of truth and falsehood, assume that it is infallible, and proceed to pronounce *ex cathedra* on the revealed word of God? We cannot recognize his authority as sovereign pontiff, unless he brings us credentials from heaven, duly signed and witnessed. His assumption we cannot admit. He is confessedly fallible, and his decisions we cannot even entertain. He does not come to us duly commissioned by Almighty God to teach us his word; he is simply a man, with no authority in the premises which may not be claimed and exercised by every other man as well as by himself. In an argument with Catholics he can be only a man, and is at liberty to adopt no line of argument that would not be equally proper in the case of a pagan, Mahometan, or any other infidel.

Protestant controversialists are exceedingly prone to forget this. They assume that they have the word of God, that they know and believe what God has revealed, and that they have in their opinions a standard by which to try the church. Yet they claim to be reasoners, and tell us that we have surrendered our reason! But whether the church be or be not commissioned to declare the word of God, it is certain that they are not. Certain is it, that, if she is not authorized to declare it, no one else is; and equally certain is it, that no one not so authorized has any right to adduce in an argument any thing he takes to be the word of God, save by the sufferance or consent of his opponents. It is a grave mistake to suppose that there is any other common ground between us and our adversaries than that of reason. It will not do for our adversaries to suppose, that, because we hold to the inspiration of the Scriptures, they may allege them in their own sense against us; for we admit their inspiration only on the authority, and in *the sense*, of the church. On her authority, and in the sense in which she defines their doctrines, we hold them to be the word of God; but in no other sense, and on no other ground. Independently of her authority and interpretations, there are no inspired Scriptures for us. This fact must never be lost sight of, and it would save Protestants an immense deal of labor, if they would keep it in mind, and govern themselves accordingly. If they cite the Bible against us, on any authority or in any sense but that of the church, it is not for us the word of God, but simply their private opinion, by which we are not and cannot be bound. Among ourselves, who admit the authority of the church, and therefore the inspiration of the Scriptures, it is lawful, on a point on which the actual teaching of the church is a matter of inquiry, to appeal to the written word, as also to the fathers and doctors of the church, and also to the analogies of faith; but it is never lawful for those out of the church, denying her authority, to make a like appeal against us; for the *authority* to which we appeal is resolvable into the authority of the church, which they deny.

The rule we here insist upon is that of common sense and common justice, and rests for its authority on the principle, that no man has the right to assume in his argument the point that is in question. We ourselves cite the Scriptures against our adversaries, but always either *ad hominem*, —because though we do not, they, admit their inspiration independently of the authority of the church,—or as simple historical documents, whose authenticity and authority as such documents, but not as inspired writings, reason is competent to determine. But we never assume our church and her definitions as the authority on which to convict those without of error; for to do so would be a sheer begging of the question. Undoubtedly, if our church is right, all her adversaries are wrong. It needs no argument to prove that. We, therefore, take our stand in the argument, either on what our adversaries concede, or on the common reason of mankind, and attempt to prove from the one or the other, or both, that every one is bound to believe and obey the church. Protestants must not expect us to allow them more than we claim for ourselves. They may need more in order to make out their case; but we are not aware that they have any right to special privileges, or to exemption from the common obligations of reason and justice. As there are no concessions of ours which can avail them, they must in their controversies with us take their stand on the reason common to all men, and, since common to all, alike theirs and ours. They must bring their action at common law, not on a special statute. Then they must restrict themselves to those questions which come within the jurisdiction of reason, and which she is competent to decide without appeal. Then they must waive all questions which pertain to the subject-matter of revelation; for these all undeniably lie in the supernatural order, and therefore without the province of reason.

We frankly concede that Mr. Thornwell has proved that Catholicity is not Presbyterianism, and that, if Presbyterianism is the revelation of God, Catholicity is not. But this amounts to nothing; Presbyterianism is neither proved nor conceded to be Christianity. He cannot, therefore, assume it against us. We concede him not one inch of Christian ground on which to set his foot. We demur to every argument he adduces or attempts to adduce from the convictions or prejudices of his sect, or from his own conceptions of the word of God. We listen to no arguments, we entertain no objections, we plead to no charges, not drawn from the common reason of mankind. We must, therefore, beg him to descend from his tripod, and meet us as a man with no authority but that which belongs to the reason of every man.

We must, in view of this state of the case, eliminate from Mr. Thornwell's arguments against infallibility, as not to be entertained, all that he urges on the authority of his own religious convictions or prejudices, and confine ourselves simply to what he adduces on the simple authority of reason. This last, all that is legitimately adduced, consists of an attempted refutation of Dr. Lynch's argument for the infallibility of the church, and certain philosophical, historical, and moral objections alleged against the church.

We might well pass over Dr. Thornwell's attempt to refute Dr. Lynch's argument for infallibility, because, if successful, it would accomplish nothing to his purpose. The argument he has to refute is the argument *from* the infallibility of the church, not the argument *for* it; for the question is not on believing that infallibility, but on denying it. It may, as we have said, be true, and yet the arguments by which we attempt to prove it be unsound and inconclusive. The defect of proof is a good reason for not believing but it is not always an adequate reason for denying. The thesis the professor seeks to maintain requires him to deny the infallibility of the church, or to assert her fallibility, and therefore the burden of proof devolves on him. He asserts that the disputed books are corrupt additions to the word of God, which he cannot possibly prove without disproving the infallibility of the church, which declares them to be inspired Scripture. But he claims to have won a victory over Dr. Lynch, and his friends have bound the laurel around his brows. We are, therefore, disposed to subject his claim to a slight examination, and to inquire if his shouts have not been a little premature, and if, after all, the victory does not remain with his opponent. If he has succeeded, he has gained nothing for his thesis; but if he has failed, we can conclude against it at once, at least so far as he is concerned.

Mr. Thornwell states Dr. Lynch's general argument for the disputed books to be,—

"Whatever the pastors of the Church of Rome declare to be true must be infallibly certain:

"That the Apocrypha [the books enumerated] were inspired, the pastors of the Church of Rome declare to be true:

"Therefore it must be infallibly certain."

This is stated in Mr. Thornwell's language, not in Dr. Lynch's, and is by no means so well expressed as it might be; but let that pass. Substituting the names of the books alleged by Mr. Thornwell to be corrupt additions to the word of God for the term *Apocrypha*, we are willing to accept it. To this argument, which he has shaped to suit the objections he wishes to bring against it, Mr. Thornwell's first objection is, that it is "vitiated by the ambiguity of the middle." The words "pastors of the church," may be understood either universally, particularly, or distributively, —to mean the whole body of the pastors, some of them, and every one individually.

Ambiguity of the middle is where the words are taken in one sense in the major, and in another sense in the minor; but where they are taken in the same sense in both the premises, although in themselves susceptible of several meanings, there is no ambiguity of the middle. In the argument as stated, the words, *pastors*, &c., are, in themselves considered, susceptible of the senses alleged, but as used in the argument they are tied down to one sense. The rule of construction is, to understand all words used in a general or universal sense, unless there be some reason, expressed or implied, in the context or the nature of the subject, for not doing so. There is, in the present case, no such reason in either premise, and therefore we must take the words generally, or universally, in both,—for the whole body of pastors. If so, there is no ambiguity of the middle.

But Mr. Thornwell asserts that Dr. Lynch does use the words in the three different senses mentioned. He accuses him of meaning by them, at one time, the whole body of pastors *collected or assembled* in council, at another time, *a part* only, and finally, *every one* individually; and alleges as proof, the fact, that in his Letter he predicates infallibility, 1. of the whole body of pastors in their collective capacity, 2. of the Council of Trent, in which only a part were personally assembled, and 3. of each single teacher or missionary.

1. That Dr. Lynch, when he predicates infallibility of the body of pastors in their collective capacity, means the whole body, takes the words, *pastors*, &c., universally, is conceded, but that he means the whole body *assembled in council* we deny. He speaks of them as a body of individuals in their *collective* capacity, not as a collected or congregated body; and that he does not mean the body of pastors assembled in council is evident from the fact, that he contends that the pastors of the church had decided the question of the inspiration of the books in dispute long before the Council of Trent, since, to do so, they did not need to assemble in a general council. Thus he says expressly,—" The doctrines of the Catholic Church can be known from the universal and concordant teaching of her pastors, even when her bishops have not assembled in a general council and embodied those doctrines in a list of decrees."—(pp. 370, 371.) It is evident, then, that Dr. Lynch holds the pastors of the church to be a body of individuals, to have a collective capacity, and the faculty of teaching infallibly in that capacity, even when not congregated. If Mr. Thornwell had recog-

nized a difference between *collective* and *collected*, or congregated, he would easily have surmounted this part of his difficulty, without any foreign aid.

2. The acts of the Holy Council of Trent, touching faith and morals, Dr. Lynch unquestionably holds to be infallible, not because he predicates infallibility of a part of the body of pastors, but because they were the acts of the whole church represented in it, or at least made so by subsequent adoption, as is evident enough from his language. The proof, therefore, that he takes the words in a partitive sense, is inadequate.

3. That each single pastor teaches infallibly in his *collective capacity*, as "member" of the body of pastors, is conceded, but that he does so individually or in his individual capacity is denied; for in his individual capacity he cannot teach at all. Dr. Lynch speaks of his teaching infallibly only in his capacity as member of the body. As member of the body, the only sense in which he is a teacher at all, he participates of its infallibility, and teaches by its authority, and infallibly, not because he is individually infallible, but because it is infallible. Consequently in representing the single teacher as teaching infallibly, Dr. Lynch does not use the words *pastors*, &c., in a distributive sense.

Mr. Thornwell is unfortunate in his proofs, notwithstanding he had shaped his statement of the argument with special reference to them. He fails to substantiate his objection of "ambiguity of the middle," and consequently all that he says, which is founded on it, falls to the ground. The beautiful argument he had constructed to prove that a Catholic can never know when and where to find the infallible authority on which he had expended so much labor, and lavished so many rare ornaments, falls to pieces through default of a foundation. Decidedly, it is an inconvenience to build without any thing to build with or to build on. It is worse than being compelled to make bricks without straw.

Mr. Thornwell, after his objection to the form of the argument, proceeds to deny and to refute its major, namely, the infallibility of the church. His first effort is to refute Dr. Lynch's argument for it. Dr. Lynch contends that "we cannot be called on to believe any proposition without adequate proof;" that "when Almighty God designed to inspire the works contained in the Holy Scriptures, he intended they should be believed to be inspired;" and that "therefore there *does* exist some adequate proof." Thus far all is evident enough, and the professor brings no objection to what is alleged. We may presume it, then, as conceded, that there *does* exist some adequate proof of their inspiration, that is to say, some authority competent to declare the fact. What is it? "It must be," says Dr. Lynch, "a body of individuals to whom, in their collective capacity, God has given authority to make an unerring decision on the subject." It must be such a body, because it can be nothing else. This body is composed of the pastors of the Catholic Church. Therefore the pastors of the Catholic Church have authority to make an unerring decision, that is, have infallible authority to declare the word of God.

Mr. Thornwell does not deny, that, if such a body exists, it is the pastors of the Roman Catholic Church. On this point he raises no question, and we may regard him as conceding it. He denies the necessity of any such body as Dr. Lynch asserts. He objects, first, to the form of the argument by which Dr. Lynch undertakes to prove it. The argument, he says, sins by an imperfect enumeration of particulars. It is a destructive disjunctive conditional, which must contain in the major all the suppositions which can be conceived to be true, and in the minor destroy all but one. But Dr. Lynch has not included all such suppositions in his major, and therefore, conceding that he has destroyed in the minor all he has enumerated save one, he is not entitled to his conclusion. Dr. Lynch has enumerated four methods: —1. Every individual, on the strength of his own private examination, is to decide for himself,—private judgment; 2. Every individual is to receive books as inspired, or reject them as uninspired, according to the decisions of such persons as he judges qualified by their erudition and sound judgment to determine the question,—the judgment of the learned; 3. We must take the inspiration of Scripture from some individual whom God has commissioned to announce this fact to the world; or 4. From a body of individuals to whom, in their collective capacity, God has given authority to make an unerring decision on the subject. But a *fifth* supposition is possible, says the professor, namely, "God himself by his eternal Spirit may condescend to be the teacher of men, and enlighten their understandings to perceive in the Scriptures themselves infallible marks of their inspiration." This supposition Dr. Lynch has "entirely overlooked," "strangely suppressed," and therefore cannot even by destroying the first three suppositions conclude the fourth.

But Dr. Lynch has not "entirely overlooked," "strangely suppressed," this fifth supposition, but expressly mentions it, and gives his reason for not including it in the number of supposable methods. Mr. Thornwell has generously furnished us the evidence of this. After enumerating the four methods stated, Dr. Lynch says (Appendix, p. 359):— "I might perhaps add a *fifth* method; that each one be informed what books are inspired by his *private spirit*. But I omit it, as, were it true, it would be superfluous, if not a criminal intrusion on the province God would have reserved to himself, to attempt to prove or disprove, when our duty would be simply to await in patience the revelation to each particular individual. You are not a member of the Society of Friends, and your essay is not an *exposé* of the teachings of your private spirit, but an effort to appeal to argument." With this passage before his eyes, we cannot understand how the Presbyterian minister could assert that Dr. Lynch entirely overlooked this fifth method, for undeniably the Catholic doctor means by the private spirit precisely the same thing the Presbyterian does by God condescending to teach men by his eternal Spirit. Moreover, the reasons assigned by Dr. Lynch for not including it in the list of supposable methods are conclusive, at least till answered. These reasons are two:—1. That, if assumed, all argument would be foreclosed, either as superfluous or as criminal; and 2. Mr. Thornwell evidently rejects it, because he appeals to argument, and therefore against him it cannot be necessary to include it. These are solid reasons, and Mr. Thornwell should have met them before accusing Dr. Lynch of having entirely overlooked the method of interior illumination, and especially before insisting upon its being supposable.

·Mr. Thornwell is apparently disposed to maintain that this fifth method is the one actually adopted, but this he is not at liberty to do. The method is private, not public, and cannot be appealed to in a public debate. In a public debate, the appeal must always be to a public authority, that is, to an authority common to both parties. If the authority to which the appeal is to be made is private, there can be no public debate; if private, interior, immediate, as must be the teachings of the spirit, there can be no argument. Argument in such a case would be superfluous and even criminal. When, therefore, a man resorts, on a given question, to argument, and to public argument, he necessarily assumes that the authority which is to determine the question is public, and denies it to be private. Mr. Thornwell in his essay made his appeal to argument, and wrote his essay to prove that the question he raised is to be settled, not by the private spirit, but by public facts, arguments, and authority. He therefore cannot fall back on the private spirit. Having elected public authority, he must abide by it. If he cannot now fall back on the private spirit, he cannot allege it as a supposable method; and if he cannot so allege it, he cannot accuse Dr. Lynch's argument of sinning by an imperfect enumeration of particulars, because it omits it.

Mr. Thornwell, furthermore, is very much affected by Dr. Lynch's supposed temerity in restricting the number of supposable methods to the four enumerated. He grows very eloquent, and manifests no little pious horror at what he calls an effort to set bounds to Omnipotence. All this is very well, but he himself excludes the method of private teaching, by writing his book to prove, on other grounds, that the books in question are uninspired, and he does not even attempt to suggest an additional method. Nobody, unless it be himself, seeks to limit Omnipotence; nobody, to our knowledge, denies that Almighty God might have adopted the private method, if he had chosen to do so. The question is not, as is evident from the whole train of Dr. Lynch's reasoning, on abstract possibilities, but on what is or is not possible *in hac providentia*. Nobody pretends that the private spirit is not supposable because it is metaphysically impossible, but it is not supposable because incompatible with other things which we know must be supposed, and which Mr. Thornwell undeniably does suppose.

The alleged *fifth* method not being supposable, unless Mr. Thornwell chooses to condemn himself for attempting to argue the question, and to confess that all his arguments are senseless and absurd, nay, profane and criminal, the objection raised to Dr. Lynch's major falls to the ground; and as he does not pretend that the conclusion is not logical, he must grant the conclusion or deny the minor. But he cannot grant the conclusion without conceding the infallibility of the church, which he seeks to disprove. He therefore asserts that "the minor is lame, and can at best yield only a lame and impotent conclusion." The minor is proved only by removing or destroying the first three suppositions. But this is not done; for the arguments by which Dr. Lynch seeks to do it apply with equal force against the fourth, which he must retain. But the legitimacy of this reply is questionable. One of the four suppositions must be true, for some adequate proof does exist. If the objections adduced are in themselves considered sufficient to remove the three, they cannot be urged against the fourth, for that would prove too much, namely, that there is no adequate proof. If sufficient, they must then be shown to be so on other grounds, or else we can always reply, one supposition is true, and it must be the fourth, because it cannot be one or another of the first three.

We deny the assertion, that the arguments against the three apply with equal force against the fourth. We begin with Dr. Lynch's argument against the first supposition,—that every individual is to decide for himself on the strength of his own examination. This is utterly impossible; for the bulk of mankind want the ability, the leisure, and the opportunity to acquire the amount of science and erudition necessary to enable them to come to an absolutely certain conclusion on the subject of the inspiration of the Scriptures. This is evident to every one who considers,—1. The controversies which have obtained respecting the canon; 2. The nature of the questions to be settled, and what it needs to enable one to decide respecting the fact of the inspiration of ancient books on intrinsic grounds; 3. That every one is required to believe the truth on the subject, not only after a life of inquiry, and historical and scientific investigation, but from the moment of coming to years of discretion; and 4. The actual condition of the generality of mankind in relation to science and erudition. These considerations are amply sufficient to disprove the first supposition; for every one is commanded to believe, and the proof, to be adequate, must be adequate in the case of every one,—of the ignorant slave and rude savage, as well as of the learned and gifted few,—of the boy or girl in whom reason has just dawned, as well as of the scientific veteran or the grey-haired scholar.

The professor replies: The learning asserted to be necessary, if necessary at all, must be so because the fact of inspiration in general is not determinable without it, and therefore must be as necessary in the body supposed as in the individual deciding for himself. But the body must acquire it either by investigation or by inspiration. If by investigation it has no advantage over the individual, and whatever proves his inability applies with equal force against its ability. If by inspiration, then it must have the same learning to be able to determine the fact of its own inspiration, and the people who are to receive its decision must also have it in order to be able to judge of its inspiration. Hence the professor sums up triumphantly,—"When you shall condescend to inform me how the fathers of Trent could decide with infallible certainty upon the Scriptures, without the learning which is necessary, in your view, to understand the evidence, if they themselves were uninspired; or how, if inspired, they could without this learning, either be certain themselves of the fact, or establish it with infallible certainty to the people, who, without your learning, must judge of the inspiration of the holy council,—when, consistently with your principles, you resolve these difficulties, one of the objections to your argument will cease." (p. 51.)

This is the argument in all its force. Its substance is, whatever difficulties there may be in the way of the method of private judgment, precisely the same difficulties are in the way of the body of individuals supposed, and can no more easily be overcome by it than by the individual himself. This is the common Protestant reply to our objections against the method of private judgment, and is tantamount to saying, that a man has just the same difficulties to overcome in simply declaring what he believes and always has believed as in determining by personal inquiry and examination what he ought to believe; or that it is as easy to ascertain and verify the truth we are ignorant of as it is merely to express with precision the truth we already possess and always have possessed from the first moment of our existence!

But let us examine this famous argument, which, in one form or other, is the great, and virtually the only, argument by which Protestants seek to evade the force of the objections of Catholics to their scheme of proof. Dr. Lynch asserts that a certain amount of science and erudition is necessary to enable an individual, on the strength of his own examination, to come to an absolutely certain decision on the fact of the inspiration of an ancient writing, whose inspiration is determinable, not on extrinsic, but mainly on intrinsic grounds. Then, says the professor, the same amount is necessary to enable an inspired individual to judge of the evidence of his own inspiration. But this conclusion can follow only from the assumption, that the evidence of inspiration must be the same for the inspired and the uninspired. If you make the evidence mediate in the uninspired, you must also make it mediate in the inspired; and if immediate in the inspired, then also immediate in the uninspired. But it is not mediate in the inspired; for, unquestionably, he who inspires immediately evidences the fact to the one he inspires. How, then, contend for mediate evidence in the uninspired? Grant this reasoning, and the author condemns himself. The evidence is immediate, and yet he has written a book to settle the question by argument and erudition, both of which are mediate. He has, on this hypothesis, evidently proved nothing; for he has offered inappropriate evidence, and must be mistaken when he says that he has proved the books enumerated to be "corrupt additions to the word of God."

Again; the professor asserts, that, if the learning alleged be necessary in the particular case, it is so because the fact of inspiration is determinable in no case without it, that is, that a thing cannot be true in the particular unless it be true in the universal,—as if one should say, some men cannot be black, because all men are not black; or, some are black, therefore all men are black! We presume Mr. Thornwell's servant is a black man; therefore, he himself is a black man. The principle the professor adopts is, not only that what is true of the *genus* must be true of the *species*, but, also, that what is true of the *species* must be true of the *genus*. Thus, man is an animal; but a goose is an animal; therefore, man is a goose;—or, a goose is an animal; but man is an animal; therefore, a goose is a man. But the principle, if adopted, carries us further yet. It is the denial of all *differentia*,—the fundamental error of Spinozism or pantheism. Thus, under the *genus* substance, God is substance; but a moss is substance; therefore, God is a moss, or reverse it, and a moss is God! Is this a principle to be adopted by a professor of " the Evidences of Christianity " in so respectable an institution as the South Carolina College? Has the professor yet to make his philosophy, as well as his theology?

But, evidently, there is a difference of species; for the professor would take it as unkind, nay, uncivil, in us, if, because he comes under the genus animal, as does every man, we should insist on including him in the species *goose*. It cannot therefore, follow, that, because a thing is true in the particular, it must be true in the universal. Consequently, Dr. Lynch may assert that a certain amount of science and erudition is necessary to decide on a particular fact by a particular agent, on particular grounds, and yet not be obliged to concede that the same amount is necessary in every case, whoever the agent, and whatever the grounds on which he is to decide. The amount alleged to be necessary may not be necessary in the case of the inspired themselves to determine the fact of their own inspiration; it may not be necessary in the case of the eyewitnesses of the miracles by which the inspired evidence the fact that God speaks to and by them; it may not be necessary to those who receive the fact immediately from the inspired themselves, or on the authority God himself has commissioned to declare it; and yet be indispensable in the case of a single individual who has, on the strength of his own examination, to decide whether a book written some two or three thousand years ago is or is not an inspired composition; as it needs no argument to prove.

The knowledge, be it more or be it less, necessary in the case, to determine what books are and what are not inspired, must be possessed by the body supposed, as well as by the individual, we concede; and if that body is destitute of it and has it to learn, it must learn it either from investigation or inspiration, we also concede; otherwise we deny it. But the body asserted in the hypothesis is, by the very terms of the supposition, already in possession of the truth, and of all the knowledge necessary to declare it, and, in deciding the question, has only to declare solemnly what it already holds and has held from the moment of its institution. Therefore, it has to acquire the knowledge neither by investigation nor by inspiration; for it has not to acquire it at all. Unless, then, the professor choses to maintain that to declare what one already holds directly from our Lord or his apostles is the same thing as for an individual ignorant of it to learn it by the examination of historical documents and scientific investigation, he must concede that the parity he seeks to establish between every individual deciding the fact of inspiration on the strength of his own examination, and the church, or body of teachers supposed, doing it on the authority of our Lord and his apostles, from whom it received it immediately, has no foundation except in his own fancy, and that the conclusions which depend upon it fall to the ground.

The professor's reasoning is vitiated by his supposing a

body of individuals totally different from that supposed in the hypothesis he is arguing against. The body he supposes is no body or corporation at all; but a simple aggregation of individuals who at any given time compose it. Between such a body and the apostles there must needs be all the distance of time and space, that there is between the apostles and the individuals themselves. It would and it could possess only what the individuals composing it should bring to it, and they could bring to it only what they acquire in their individual capacity. "The mere fact of human congregation," as the professor rightly contends, could confer no power, beyond the aggregate power of the individuals congregated. Hence the aggregate body, or collection of individuals, as well as the single individual, would need to obtain, either by investigation or inspiration, the knowledge necessary to come to an infallible decision. It needed no learned professor to tell us all this, which is by no means beyond the reach of any man of ordinary sense. Indeed, we feel humbled when we find learned men bringing such objections to us,—humbled for ourselves, that they can think so meanly of our understandings as to suppose us capable of holding any thing against which objections so obvious even to a child may be urged, and humbled for them, that they should imagine, that, in bringing such objections, they are telling something recondite, or that it is possible that such objections can have any power to demolish that lofty and spacious edifice, the church, founded upon the rock, firmly built and cemented, which has withstood all the assaults of wicked men and devils for eighteen hundred years, and against which the gates of hell shall never prevail, not even to loosen a single stone or to detach a single tile.

But *this* body, this aggregate of individuals, is not *the* body supposed by Dr. Lynch, and to prove that this has no advantage over the individual is nothing to the purpose, for nobody, certainly no Catholic, denies it. The professor's argument is a sheer paralogism, of that species which consists in proving what is not supposed in the question, and which is not denied by the adversary,—a sophism for which the learned professor has a peculiar fondness, and into which he falls with remarkable facility. The body supposed by Dr. Lynch is the church teaching; for he says, "the pastors of the Catholic Church claim to compose it." But the Catholic Church, as a body or corporation, the only sense in which it is alleged to have any teaching faculty at all, is not an aggregation of individuals who at any given time compose it,—a body born and dying with them; but the contemporary of our Lord and his apostles, in immediate communion with them, and thus annihilating all distance of time and place between them and us. She is, in the sense supposed, a corporation, and, like every corporation, a collective individual possessing the attribute of immortality. She knows no interruption, no succession of moments, no lapse of years. Like the eternal God, who is ever with her, and whose organ she is, she has duration, but no succession. She can never grow old, can never fall into the past. The individuals who compose the body may change, but she changes not; one by one they may pass off, and one by one be renewed, while she continues ever the same; as in our own bodies, old particles constantly escape, and new ones are assimilated, so that the whole matter of which they are composed is changed once in every six or seven years, and yet they remain always identically the same bodies. These changes as to individuals change nothing as to the body. The church to-day is identically that very body which saw our Lord when he tabernacled in the flesh. She who is our dear mother, and on whose words we hang with so much delight, beheld with her own eyes the stupendous miracles which were performed in Judea eighteen hundred years ago; she assisted at the preaching of the apostles on the day of Pentecost, when the Holy Ghost descended upon them in cloven tongues of fire; she heard St. Peter, the prince of the apostles, relate how the Spirit descended upon Cornelius and his household, and declare how God had chosen that by his mouth the gentiles should hear the word of God and believe; she listened with charmed ear and ravished heart to the last admonition of "the disciple whom Jesus loved,"—"My dear children love one another;" she saw the old Temple razed to the ground, the legal rites of the old covenant abolished, and the once chosen people driven out from the Holy Land, and scattered over all the earth; she beheld pagan Rome in the pride and pomp of power, bled under her persecuting emperors, and finally planted the cross in triumph on her ruins. She has been the contemporary of eighteen hundred years, which she has arrested in their flight and made present to us, and will make present to all generations as they rise. With one hand she receives the *depositum* of faith from the Lord and his commissioned apostles, with the other she imparts it to us. Such is the body supposed, between which and the individual Mr. Thornwell must establish the parity he contends for, or not establish it at all. What has this body to do, in order to decide what books are, and what are not, inspired? Merely to declare a simple fact which she has received on competent authority,—merely what our Lord or his apostles have told her. What needs she, in order to do it with infallible certainty? Simply protection against forgetting, misunderstanding, and misstating; and this she has, because she has, according to the hypothesis, our Lord always abiding with her, and the Paraclete, who leads her into all truth, and "brings to her remembrance" all the words spoken to her by our Lord himself personally, or by his inspired apostles, —keeping her memory always fresh, rendering her infallible assistance rightly to understand and accurately to express what she remembers to have been taught. Here are all the conditions requisite for an infallible decision; and all these must be supposed, because they are all asserted in the hypothesis.

Now we demand what parity there is between such a body, which has only to state what it believes and always has believed on the inspiration of Scripture, and which has the supernatural assistance of the Holy Ghost to state it infallibly, and an individual who has nothing but certain writings before him, and who has to determine, by the examination of documents and scientific investigation of the intrinsic evidences, whether they are inspired or not,—a fact which, since it is supernatural, lies out of the order of nature, and is therefore only extrinsically provable. Who so blinded by passion, by pride, by prejudice, or ignorance, as to pretend, that such a body, supposing it to exist, can no more come to a certain conclusion, is in no better condition for coming to a certain conclusion, on the fact of the inspiration of the Holy Scriptures, than an ignorant slave on our plantations, or a rude savage of our forests? Who is he? Indeed, it is the learned Presbyterian minister, the "Professor of Sacred Literature and the Evidences of Christianity in the South Carolina College!" It is evident to any man of ordinary sense, that such a body can decide the question infallibly, and equally evident that the ignorant slave or the rude savage cannot.

To the dilemma, therefore, in which the professor affects to have placed his Catholic opponent, we reply:—The Council of Trent could, uninspired, but simply assisted by the Holy Ghost, decide with infallible certainty upon the inspiration of the Scriptures, without the learning necessary in the case of the individual deciding for himself on the strength of his own examination, *because it had only to give an authoritative expression to the actual faith of the body of pastors it represented,*—and it could establish the infallibility of its expression to the people who were to receive it, because, to do so, it had only to establish that it did express the universal faith of that body, easily collected from its being received by the whole body as soon as made known. The other part of the dilemma falls of itself. We do not assume, nor are we obliged to assume, that the fathers of Trent were inspired. Inspiration is needed only where the truth to be promulgated is unknown and has to be revealed: where nothing is to be done but infallibly state the truth already revealed and believed, the infallible assistance of the Holy Ghost, without inspiration, suffices.

We have here shown that the difficulties suggested are resolvable on Catholic principles; the professor must therefore concede, according to his promise, that one objection to Dr. Lynch's argument ceases. But this one objection is his only objection to that argument, so far as it bears against the first-named method; and since this is removed, the argument, thus far, is not refuted. If not refuted, it, at least against the professor, is sound, and, then, the first method is destroyed, and Dr. Lynch is entitled to his conclusion against it.

There remain to be considered the second and third suppositions. The second, that of relying on the judgment of the learned, the professor passes over in profound silence, and therefore yields it up as indefensible. It is remarkable, however, that Mr. Thornwell should do so; for it is really the method actually adopted by the majority of Protestants, and abandoning it is virtually abandoning Protestantism itself. Undoubtedly, Protestants assert private judgment; but the private judgment on which they actually rely is not the private judgment of each individual, but the private judgment of those assumed to be learned and wise and prudent. Protestantism must never be taken at its word; for one of its essential properties is, to profess one thing and to do another, or to give us the name without the thing, —the sign without the thing signified. Whoever knows Protestants at all knows that they take their opinions, not on their own private judgment, but on the authority of their masters. Whenever they do not do so, we find them becoming downright rationalists, or absolute apostates from Christianity; and it is never, except as grouped around some leader, swearing by the words of some master, that we see them retain any thing of the form of religion, or present any compact appearance. The people are aware of their own inability to decide for themselves what they ought to believe, and they only decide what heresiarch they will follow,—what master they will have. Thus they say,—" So said Martin Luther, so said John Calvin, or George Fox;.so teach Edwards and Dwight, Owen and Gill, Wesley and Swedenborg, Murray and Ballou, Channing and Fourier, Emerson and Parker." It is not in himself the poor Protestant confides, but in some leader who seems to him, for his learning, wisdom, and sound judgment, worthy of confidence. If here and there a bold, energetic individual starts up with perfect confidence in his own judgment, and has the courage or the audacity to proclaim, as the truth of God, his own personal conceits or convictions,he either founds a new sect, or a new party or faction in the sect, to which he pertains; as we see in the instance of Muncer and George Fox, Brown and Sandeman, Wesley and Whitefield, Erskine and Irving, Southcote and Pusey, Campbell and Bushnell, Channing and Parker. If each judged for himself, we should see no sects, parties, or groups; each would stand alone, on his own two feet, acknowledging no master, and no fellow, saying always *I*, never able to say *we*.

This must needs be. How, except by relying on such men as Mr. Thornwell, could the great body of Presbyterians, for instance, come to any conclusion on the question discussed in the volume before us? In fact, they do not attempt to obtain a conclusion by any other means. " Mr. Thornwell is a godly man; he is a great and learned man; he has investigated the subject; he wont deceive us; and we will believe what he says." Here is the fact, disguise it as you will, and Mr. Thornwell knows it as well as we do. We must, therefore, regard his passing this method over in silence as a tacit confession that in his judgment Protestantism is not defensible.

Nevertheless, we cannot be much surprised that Mr. Thornwell passes this method over in silence. It is not a method to be avowed. Protestant ministers would have a short lease of their power, if they were to avow it. They would be pressed with a multitude of questions, which it would be very inconvenient to answer. "After all,"—the justly indignant people whom they have led might say,— "this private judgment you preached was only a pretext, a bait to catch gudgeons. You never meant it; you only meant that we must submit our judgments to yours! Is it true that you monopolize all the learning, all the wisdom, all the judgment, in the world? What guaranty can you give us, fallible men as you confess yourselves, that you yourselves are not deceived,—nay, that you are incapable of deceiving us? You deceived us, when you promised us the right of private judgment. What reason have we to suppose you do not deceive us in other things also?" Such questions might be put, and, if put, it is obvious that it would be very inconvenient to answer them.

The first method is disproved; the second is abandoned; only the third remains. This, that of a single individual duly commissioned by Almighty God to announce the fact of inspiration to the world, the professor does not attempt to defend as true, or as one which he does or can hold; but he maintains, that, on Catholic principles, it is probable, and therefore Dr. Lynch is entitled only to a probable conclusion, —not sufficient for his purpose, because he must conclude with absolute certainty. The professor concludes, that, on Catholic principles, this hypothesis is probable, from the fact, that, on Catholic principles, it is a probable opinion that the pope is infallible. But his argument involves a transition from one *genus* to another, and therefore concludes nothing. The single individual asserted in the hypothesis is commissioned in his individual capacity to announce the fact, and it is in this capacity that he is to do it. But such a commissioned individual is not the pope, or sovereign pontiff. No Catholic holds the pope in his individual capacity to be infallible. He is infallible, as we hold, and as we presume Dr. Lynch also holds; but only in his capacity of supreme head of the church, in which sense he is included in the fourth hypothesis, as joined to the body of individuals asserted, inseparable from it, and essential to it. Concede, then, the infallibility of the sovereign pontiff, nothing is conceded in favor of the third method; for in the sense in which he is infallible he is the church, or essentially included in the fourth method; since the head is not without the body, nor the body without the head.

The third method, then, is not the method. Then no one of the first three. Then the fourth is; because some method of proof does exist, and it can be no other. Mr. Thornwell, therefore, has not refuted Dr. Lynch's argument. If he has not refuted it, against him, it stands good. Then the method of proof is the body supposed. But this body has authority to make an unerring decision on the subject of inspiration, that is, to declare unerringly what is or is not the word of God, therefore infallible in declaring the word of God. But this body is composed of the pastors of the Catholic Church. Therefore the pastors of the church are infallible in declaring the word of God, the proposition Dr. Lynch undertook to prove. It would seem from this, that the learned and logical professor's shouts of victory were decidedly premature. It is clear, also, since we are not considering what is or is not possible in the abstract, but *in hac providentia*, that the whole controversy turns between the first method and the fourth; for the private spirit is not admissible, and the professor does not defend the second, and cannot, and would not if he could, defend the third. It is, then, either private judgment or the Catholic Church. So the professor virtually concedes or maintains. What, therefore, he further adduces in his Fourth Letter, namely, that it is as easy to prove the inspiration of the Scriptures as the infallibility of the church, cannot be entertained. There does exist some adequate proof; this is conceded. It evidently cannot be the method of private judgment; for it is absolutely impossible for a field slave, for instance, ignorant of letters, and with no time or ability to learn, to be able to decide for himself, on his own examination, whether *Tobias* or *Ecclesiasticus* is or is not an inspired composition. But, if not private judgment, it must be the infallible church, and therefore the church and its infallibility follow from the necessity of the case. This necessity overrides every possible objection. Bring as many objections as you please, and we dismiss them, as proving, if any thing, too much, and therefore nothing. *Quod nimis probat, nihil probat.*

Thus far we have confined ourselves, after stating the question, to showing that the professor has not refuted Dr. Lynch's argument for the infallibility of the church. This has been perfectly gratuitous on our part, for the burden of proof is on the professor. But having vindicated Dr. Lynch's argument for the infallibility of the church, we are now able to conclude it against Mr. Thornwell from the necessity of the case, the strongest argument that it is possible to use. Infallibility overrides all objections; and consequently, the professor, let him do his best, cannot prove the fallibility of the church. Here, then, we well might rest; but we find our author rather an amusing companion, and we should be sorry to part company with him so soon. We hope, therefore, to be able, in an early number, to consider the direct proofs of the fallibility of the church, which he has attempted to bring. In the meantime, we recommend him, since he must hold his logical reputation dear, to make himself acquainted with Catholicity, before attempting again to write against it, and review also his logic, before he again asks his opponent to reason in syllogisms.

ARTICLE II.

Mr. Thornwell begins his argument against the church (Letter IV.) by asserting, in substance, that we are unable to prove her infallibility, or if able, only by a process which supersedes the necessity of an infallible church to determine what is or is not the word of God. "It is just as easy," he says, "to prove the inspiration of the Scriptures as the infallibility of any church." The evidence for both "is of precisely the same nature." The infallibility of the church—"the inspiration of Rome," as he improperly expresses it—"turns upon a promise which is said to have been made nearly two thousand years ago; the inspiration of the New Testament turns upon facts which are said to have transpired at the same time. Both the promise and the facts are to be found, if found at all, in this very New Testament." You must prove its credibility, or you cannot prove the promise; and if you prove its credibility, you prove the facts. Therefore, "you cannot make out the historical proofs of papal infallibility without making out at the same time the historical proofs of Scriptural inspiration." Consequently, if you contend that the proofs are insufficient for the inspiration, you deny their sufficiency for the infallibility, and then cannot assert your infallible church; if you say they are sufficient for the infallibility, you concede their sufficiency for the inspiration, and then do not need your infallible church to determine what is or is not the word of God. (pp. 57–65.)

But Dr. Lynch proves, as we have seen in our former article, and as is sufficiently evident without proof to every one of ordinary reflection, that it is morally impossible to determine, with absolute certainty, what Scriptures are or are not inspired, except by the infallible church. To assert, after this, that the infallible church itself is provable only by proving Scriptural inspiration, is only asserting, in other words, that no adequate proof of what is or is not inspired Scripture exists. But some adequate method *does* exist, as Dr. Lynch proves, and Mr. Thornwell concedes. This method, if not private judgment, is the infallible church, as he also virtually concedes; for private illumination is not a method of proof, since, if a fact, it is not a fact that can be adduced in evidence; and the other two methods supposed, namely, the judgment of the learned, and the single individual commissioned by Almighty God to announce the fact of inspiration to the world, he either abandons or cannot assert. The method, then, is either the infallible church, or private judgment. It cannot be private judgment, if the objections urged against it be conceded. To attempt, without answering these objections, to show that equal objections bear against the church, is, for the purposes of the argument at least, to concede them, and therefore to prove, if any thing, that no adequate method of proof exists, which is not allowable. As long, then, as private judgment remains unrelieved of the objections which declare it an impossible and therefore an unsupposable method, the argument proves too much for the professor as well as for us, and consequently nothing.

This answers sufficiently Mr. Thornwell's reasoning, as far as it is intended to bear against Dr. Lynch's argument for infallibility from the necessity of the case. But we have a higher purpose in view than the simple vindication of Dr. Lynch, or the formal refutation of Professor Thornwell, and will therefore waive this reply and meet the reasoning on its intrinsic merits. Mr. Thornwell's conclusion rests on two assumptions:—1. That in order to establish the infallibility of the church, Catholics are obliged to establish the credibility of the New Testament; and 2. That the credibility of the New Testament, when established, is all that is needed to establish Scriptural inspiration,—that is, to settle the question what Scriptures are and what are not inspired. Both of these assumptions we deny.

1. In order to establish the infallibility of the church, it is not necessary to establish the credibility of the New Testament. All that is needed to establish the infallibility is the miraculous origin of the church. If she had a miraculous origin, she was founded by Almighty God; for none

but God can work a miracle. If founded by Almighty God, she is his church and speaks by his authority; therefore infallibly; for God can authorize only infallible truth. In order to make out the miraculous origin of the church, we are not obliged to recur to the New Testament at all; we can do it, and are accustomed to do it, when arguing with avowed unbelievers, without any reference to the authority of the Scriptures, either as inspired or as simple historical documents. We do it by taking the church as we find her to-day, existing as an historical fact, and tracing her up, step by step, through the succession of ages, till we ascend to her original Founder. The extraordinary nature of her claims, uniformly put forth, and steadily acted upon from the first; her various institutions, professing to embody facts, which could not in the nature of things have sprung from no facts, or from facts pertaining exclusively to the natural order; the external history which runs parallel to hers; the relation held to her from the beginning by the Jewish and pagan worlds, and by the various heresies in each succeeding age from the Gnostics down to the followers of the Mormon prophet;—all these combined prove in the most incontestable manner her supernatural character, and triumphantly establish the fact that her Founder must have had miraculous powers, and she a miraculous origin.

Undoubtedly, the infallibility of the church turns, in the argument, upon a promise made nearly two thousand years ago; but it is not true that the promise must necessarily be found only in the New Testament. A promise may be expressed in acts as well as in words, in the fact as well as in its record. The promise we rely upon is expressed in the miraculous origin of the church, and is concluded from it on the principle, that the effect may be concluded from the cause, if the cause be known. In the natural order, God, in giving to a being a certain nature, promises that being all that it needs to attain the end of that nature. So in the supernatural order, in creating a supernatural being, he promises it all the powers, assistance, means, and conditions necessary to enable it to discharge its supernatural functions, or to gain the supernatural end to which he appoints it. In supernaturally founding the church to teach his word, he therefore promises her infallibility in teaching it; because the function of teaching the word of God cannot be discharged without it.

2. But even if we were obliged—as we are not and can-

not be—to assert the credibility of the New Testament in order to make out our historical proofs, it would not be that credibility which would suffice to establish Scriptural inspiration, nor should we be obliged to make out any facts from which Scriptural inspiration could be immediately concluded. As all we have to make out is the miraculous origin of the church, and as this is made out, if the fact of the miracles of our Lord is established, all that, in any case, we could need to do, in regard to the credibility of the New Testament, would be to make out its credibility so far as requisite to establish this fact. We do not want the New Testament to prove the miraculousness of the facts, for that follows from the facts themselves; nor to accredit as teachers or witnesses those by or in favor of whom Almighty God performs the miracles, for that follows from the miraculousness; we can, at most, need it only for the purpose of proving that the miracles, in their quality of simple historical facts, actually occurred. For this simple historical testimony is sufficient, and consequently the simple *historical* credibility of the New Testament, as far as needed to authorize us to assert that the miracles actually took place, is all that it can even be pretended that we must make out. The New Testament is not one book, but a collection of books by different authors, each resting on its own independent merits, and the proof of the credibility of one does by no means establish the credibility of the rest. The most we can need for our purpose is the historical credibility of one of the Four Gospels, say the Gospel according to St. Matthew; for that Gospel records all the facts necessary to establish the miraculous origin of the church. Consequently, all the credibility of the New Testament we can, in any case, be required to establish, is the *historical* credibility of St. Matthew's Gospel.

This Gospel may be perfectly credible as an historical document, without being inspired. The facts to be taken on its authority, though supernatural as to their cause, are within the natural order as to their evidence, and as easily proved as any other class of historical facts. They fall under the senses, and require in their witnesses only ordinary sense and ordinary honesty. To the trustworthiness of their historian, who, in recording them, has only to give a faithful narrative of what has occurred before his eyes, or what he has collected from the testimony of eyewitnesses, nothing beyond the ordinary human faculties can be requisite. Hence, many

Protestants maintain the credibility of the Evangelical History, and yet deny the inspiration of the Gospels. We have by us a learned and elaborate work, in which the author, who, for learning and ability, ranks second to no Protestant theologian in the country, maintains, on the authority of the Pentateuch, the inspiration of Moses, and the divine origin of the Mosaic law, and yet denies the inspiration of the Pentateuch itself. Indeed, if none but inspired documents could be cited as credible authority for historical facts, human history would need to be closed at once, and Mr. Thornwell would find himself shut out from all means of establishing the *historical* objections he urges with so much zest, in the volume before us, against the church; for undeniably, he can cite no inspired Scripture for them. It is not prudent for an author to take a ground which must prove more fatal to himself than to his opponent.

This fact, namely, that we need only the historical credibility of the New Testament at most, seems not to have sufficiently arrested Mr. Thornwell's attention; or if it has, he must have too hastily concluded that the same order of credibility which is sufficient for the miracles is also sufficient for the inspiration. He proceeds, apparently, on the assumption, either that simple historical credibility is sufficient to establish the inspiration of the Scriptures, or that we need supernatural credibility to establish the miracles. Thus, he asks:—

"If the books of the New Testament are to be received as credible testimony to the miracles of Christ, why not on the subject of their own inspiration? Are you not aware that the great historical argument on which Protestants rely in proving the inspiration of the Scriptures presupposes only the *genuineness* of the books and the *credibility* of their authors? . . . . . They assert it [their own inspiration], and [if credible] are to be believed . . . . . I had thought that the only difficulty in making out the external proofs of inspiration was in establishing the credibility of the books which profess to be inspired. It had struck me, that, if it were once settled that their own testimony was to be received, the matter was at an end. But it seems now that . . . . . it is still doubtful whether, in the way of private judgment, a man could ever be assured that *credible* books are to be believed on the subject of their origin:"—pp. 62, 63.

This reasoning involves a transition *a specie ad speciem*. Credible books are certainly to be believed within the order of credibility which they are proved or conceded to possess, but not within an order which transcends or rises above it;

for nothing can transcend itself, and the conclusion must be in the order of the premises, or the argument is a fallacy. The credibility of the New Testament which we assert, or which it is contended we are obliged to assert, is simply historical credibility, or credibility in the natural order; but the credibility the professor needs, to establish the *inspiration*, is credibility in the supernatural order; for inspiration pertains, undeniably, to the supernatural order, both as to its cause and as to the medium of its proof. Therefore we may receive the books as credible testimony to the miracles, and not on the subject of their own inspiration.

Mr. Thornwell evidently reasons on the assumption, that we cannot assert the credibility of the New Testament in relation to the miracles without asserting it in relation to the inspiration. That is, a witness cannot be credible at all, unless he is universally credible, and he who receives his testimony in one order binds himself to receive it in every order; if he receives it in one respect, he must in every respect; in matters of fact, then also in matters of opinion! But this is too extravagant for any man in his sober senses seriously to maintain. If this were once admitted, there would speedily be an end to human testimony, and our Presbyterian friend would find himself in a sad plight; for his sole dependence is on private judgment, and he can pretend to nothing better than human testimony for his religious belief. No witness, unless absolutely omniscient, is or can be universally credible; and as no man is absolutely omniscient, it follows, if no one can be credible under one relation without being credible under every relation, that no one can in any respect be credible at all. But we cannot concede this. Every day, in every court of law, in all the practical affairs of life in which there is an appeal to human testimony, we act, and are obliged to act, on the supposition, that a man may be credible in relation to some things without being credible in relation to all things.

Everybody knows that a witness may be perfectly credible in testifying to facts which fall under the observation of his senses, and yet be deserving of no credit in relation to his opinions, his judgments, his views, or his explanations of the causes of the facts to which he testifies. Nothing hinders, then, a man from being a credible witness to the facts recorded in the New Testament, even though he should assert and believe himself inspired when in point of fact he was not; for in testifying to the facts he testifies to what has come under his senses, while in asserting his inspiration he is merely giving an opinion, or offering an explanation of certain facts or phenomena of his own internal experience. The erroneous opinion or explanation does not impair his credibility as a witness to the facts, if his error is one which he may innocently entertain. That a man can innocently believe himself divinely inspired when he is not can hardly admit of a doubt. A man so believing is, by the very terms of the supposition, uninspired. He is then, since inspiration is a supernatural fact, necessarily ignorant of inspiration, unacquainted with its phenomena, and destitute of the necessary criterion for determining what it is or what it is not. What more natural, then, than that he should mistake certain phenomena of his own experience, otherwise inexplicable to him, for those of inspiration, and thus honestly believe himself inspired, when in reality he is uninspired?

The professor argues on the assumption, common to all enthusiasts, that no man can honestly mistake the origin or cause of the phenomena of his own internal experience, and therefore, that, when one says he is inspired, we must believe either that he actually is inspired or that he is a liar, a *wilful* deceiver, whose word is to be received on no subject whatever. There is no reason for this assumption. He who is inspired, undoubtedly, knows the fact, and is as incapable of being deceived in relation to it as he is of deceiving others; but from this it by no means follows that a man who is not inspired must always know that he is not. Inspiration is, sometimes, at least, necessary to enable us to determine what is *not* inspiration, as well as to determine what is. He is little versed in the natural history of enthusiasm, who has yet to learn that honest men, men of rare gifts and inflexible principles, whose word on any subject within the range of sensible observation we should not hesitate a moment to take, not unfrequently labor under the impression that they hold immediate intercourse with the Almighty, are inspired, or divinely illuminated, when such is far from being the fact. Witness, for instance, Jacob Boehmen, George Fox, and Emanuel Swedenborg. These men are not inspired, nor are they liars. They do not *intend* to deceive, and are not even deceived themselves as to the facts of their internal experience, from which they infer their inspiration; they are deceived only in their opinions, their judgments of those facts, the explanations of them which they adopt, or the origin and cause which they assign them. Who dare pretend that this destroys their credibility in relation to simple matters of fact, evident to their senses? They do not mistake, they only misinterpret, the facts of their own consciousness; and who may not do as much? All men, however trustworthy they may be as witnesses to sensible facts, unless supernaturally protected from error, are liable, as is well known, to err in their judgments, in their explanations of phenomena,—in relation to the origin and causes of things, and in relation to the origin and causes of their own internal experience as well as of other things.

The professor falls into the common mistake of Protestants; that the inspiration of a genuine book, by an author proved to be historically credible, may be concluded from its own declaration. We say he falls into this mistake; for we cannot suppose that he falls into the still grosser one of supposing that we can prove the miracles only by a supernaturally credible witness, since that would deny that Christianity itself can be proved,—nay, that any thing supernatural is or can be provable, and therefore that man is or can be the subject of a supernatural revelation. If the miracles cannot be proved without a supernaturally credible witness, the supernatural credibility of the witness will in turn demand another supernaturally credible witness to establish it, and this another, and thus on *ad infinitum*. We should need an infinite series of supernatural witnesses in order to establish the supernatural. But an infinite series is an infinite absurdity.

As we cannot suppose the professor ignorant of the absurdity into which he would fall, if he contended for the necessity of any thing more than ordinary historical credibility to establish the miracles, we must suppose him to hold that ordinary historical credibility is sufficient to establish the inspiration of the Scriptures, in case they declare their own inspiration. But the inspiration of a genuine book, historically credible, cannot be concluded from its own declaration; because inspiration, being a supernatural fact, falling in no sense, as do the miracles, within the natural order, can be proved only by a supernaturally credible witness, which a merely historically credible witness is not. Before, from the declaration of the book, the professor can conclude its inspiration, he must prove its author a credible witness to the supernatural. But no witness is a credible witness to the supernatural, unless he is himself inspired or divinely commissioned. The witness is not credible, unless competent. In ordinary cases, a witness may be competent, and not credible; but in no case can he be credible, if incompetent. No witness, unless inspired or divinely commissioned, is competent to testify to the supernatural. The witness is not competent, unless he can intellectually attain to or take cognizance of that to which he is to testify. But no witness can intellectually attain to or take cognizance of the supernatural,—which, by the fact that it is supernatural, transcends all natural intellect,— without something more than natural intellect; that is, without supernatural illumination or assistance,—precisely what is meant by being inspired or divinely commissioned. Therefore the professor cannot conclude the inspiration from the mere historical credibility of the witness, and must prove the author to be inspired, or divinely commissioned, before, from its own declaration, he can conclude a given book is inspired Scripture.

Now, since in making out our historical proofs the most which it can be pretended that we must do is to make out the historical credibility of the books of the New Testament, or the credibility of their authors, in their quality of author, merely in relation to the natural order, it is not true, even in case we must appeal for our facts to the New Testament, that we cannot make out the historical proofs of the infallibility of the church, without making out at the same time the historical proofs of the inspiration of the Scriptures; for we are not obliged to assert the credibility of the New Testament in relation to the supernatural, the sense in which it must be asserted in order to be credible authority for its own inspiration.

Nor, waiving this, do we, in making out the credibility which we are supposed to be under the necessity of making out, establish any facts from which the inspiration of the New Testament can be immediately concluded. The professor himself says the Protestant argument "presupposes the *genuineness* of the books and the *credibility* of their authors." In addition, then, to the credibility of the authors, it is necessary, in order to establish the inspiration, to establish the genuineness of the books; that is, that they were actually written by the persons whose names they bear, and have come down to us in their purity and integrity. Now this, even if we must make out the credibility of the New Testament, we are not obliged to make out. An historical document may be authoritative without being genuine. If it contains a faithful narrative of facts as they occurred, it is sufficient for the ordinary purposes of history. That the Gospel according to St. Matthew, for instance, does contain such a narrative, is provable, without proving its inspiration, in the usual way of authenticating historical documents, by the nature of the narrative itself, the quality of the facts recorded, the circumstances under which it was published or first cited, the estimate in which it was held by those best qualified to judge of its authority, the manner in which it was treated by those who had an interest in discrediting it, and by reference to various contemporary or subsequently existing monuments, especially public institutions implying, founded upon, or growing out of, the facts which it professes to record. In this way we could accredit this Gospel as an historical document, even if it had come down to us without the author's name. Indeed, ancient historical works in general derive but little authority from the *names* of their authors, and, other things being equal, the works of Herodotus, Livy, and Tacitus would have no less authority than they now have, even if they had been anonymous productions. As the genuineness of the book is an essential element in any method of proof of its inspiration, except that by the infallible church, and as we are under no necessity, prior to the church, of proving it in the case of a single one of the books of the New Testament, it follows that we are not obliged, in making out the historical proofs of the infallibility of the church, to make out at the same time the historical proofs of the inspiration of the Scriptures.

We can now easily expose the fallacy of Mr. Thornwell's pretended dilemma. Assuming what we have just disproved, he says to Dr. Lynch, in his peculiarly sweet and delicate manner:—

"Now, Sir, one of two things must be true; either the credibility of the Scriptures can be substantiated to a plain, unlettered man, or it cannot. If it can be, there is no need of your infallible body to authenticate their inspiration, since that matter can be easily gathered from their own pages. If it cannot, then your argument from the Scriptures to an Indian or negro in favor of an infallible body is inadmissible, since he is incapable of apprehending the premises from which your conclusion is drawn. You have taken both horns of this dilemma, pushing Protestants with one, and upholding Popery with the other, and both are *fatal* to you. Now, as it is rather difficult to be on both sides of the same question at the same time, you must adhere to one or the other. If you adhere to your first position, that all human learning is necessary to settle the *credibility* of the Scriptures, then you must seek other proofs of an infallible body than those which you think you have gathered from the apostles. . . . . . A circulating syllogism proves nothing; and if he who establishes the credibility of the Scriptures, by an infallible body, and then establishes the infallibility of the body from the credibility of the Scriptures, does not reason in a circle, I am at a loss to apprehend the nature of that sophism. If you adhere to your other position, that the *accuracy of the Evangelists* can be easily substantiated, then your objections to private judgment are fairly given up, and you surrender the point, that a man can decide for himself, with absolute certainty, concerning the inspiration of the Bible. Take which horn you please, your cause is ruined; and as you have successively chosen both, you have made yourself as ridiculous as your reasoning is contemptible."—pp. 64, 65.

This argument evidently involves a transition from one genus to another. The professor confounds in the first part of his fancied dilemma the historical *credibility*, and in the second the *accuracy* of the Evangelists in their account of the miracles, with the *inspiration* of the Scriptures, and then concludes as if they were all facts of the same order; which is a sad blunder, and little creditable to the "Professor of Sacred Literature and the Evidences of Christianity in the South Carolina College." Dr. Lynch does not say that it requires "all human learning to settle the *credibility* of the Scriptures" in any sense in which he can need their credibility prior to the church; he simply maintains that all human learning, and perhaps more too, is necessary to settle, with absolute certainty, by private judgment, on intrinsic grounds, the *inspiration* of ancient writings,—which is a generically distinct proposition. The "accuracy of the Evangelists," which he asserts can be substantiated to the Indian or negro, is not the *inspiration* or the *supernatural* credibility of the Scriptures; but their accuracy as historians of the miracles, or that the miracles which they record actually took place. As this accuracy does not presuppose or necessarily imply the inspiration or the supernatural credibility of the Scriptures, nothing hinders Dr. Lynch from adhering to both of the positions he has assumed, "pushing Protestants with one, and upholding Popery with the other," however inconvenient it may be to his Presbyterian adversary.

"He who establishes the credibility of the Scriptures by

an infallible body, and then establishes the infallibility of the body from the credibility of the Scriptures, reasons in a circle," *if the credibility in both cases be taken in the same sense*, we concede; if in *different* senses, we deny. But Dr. Lynch does not establish the infallibility of the church from the credibility of the Scriptures at all; or if he does, it is not from their credibility in that sense in which he contends that their credibility can be proved only by the infallible body. The only sense in which he can be said to establish the infallible body from the credibility of the Scriptures is their simple historical credibility; the sense in which he asserts the infallible body as necessary to prove their credibility is their credibility as inspired writings. As they can have the former without having the latter, we may, without any *vicious* circle, take the facts we need to prove the infallible body from their historical credibility, and then take the infallible body to prove their inspiration, or supernatural credibility, although we are, as we have shown, under no necessity of doing so. Does the professor deny that we can do so? Does he contend that this would be to reason in a *vicious* circle? What, then, shall we say of his own reasoning for the inspiration of the New Testament? If he denies the distinction we have made, the historical credibility of the New Testament and its inspiration are one and the same thing,—convertible terms. Then we retort his argument. He says the infallibility of the church "turns upon a promise which is said to have been made nearly two thousand years ago,—the inspiration of the New Testament turns upon facts which are said to have transpired at the same time. *Both the promise and the facts are to be found, if found at all, in this very New Testament.*" Here it is positively asserted that the facts which prove the inspiration can nowhere be found but in the New Testament itself. Then they must be taken on its credibility. But credibility and inspiration, according to him, are one and the same thing, convertible terms. Then he must take the inspiration of the New Testament to prove the facts, and then the facts to prove the inspiration. If this be not to reason in a circle, we are "at a loss to apprehend the nature of that sophism."

Now one of two things must be true; either this reasoning is valid, or it is not. If it is, Mr. Thornwell cannot make out the inspiration of the Scriptures; for "a circulating syllogism proves nothing." If it is not, he fails to refute Dr. Lynch, and then is refuted by him, as we proved in our former article. In either case, he is refuted. "Take which horn you please, your cause is ruined." Although the professor says "it is rather difficult to be on both sides of the same question at the same time," yet he contrives to surmount the difficulty. He assumes that this reasoning is not valid, by urging, in spite of it, his own arguments for Scriptural inspiration, and that it is valid, by urging it against Dr. Lynch. We may, then, reply to him in his own choice language:—"Take which horn you please, your cause is ruined; and as you have successively chosen both, you have made yourself as ridiculous as your reasoning is contemptible."

But even this is not the worst. Mr. Thornwell's conclusion rests on the assumption that the Scriptures declare their own inspiration, that their inspiration "is a matter" which "may be easily gathered from their own pages." "They assert," he maintains, "their own inspiration, and, if credible, are to be believed." But, granting that they declare their own inspiration, we have shown that it does not necessarily follow that they are inspired, because, to render their own testimony sufficient for that, they must be proved to be supernaturally credible, since inspiration is a supernatural fact, provable only by a supernaturally credible witness, and the only credibility, if any, which the professor can claim for them is simple historical credibility. He binds himself to reason from our premises, because he says we cannot make out the historical proofs of the church without making out at the same time the historical proofs of inspiration. Consequently, since the *historical* credibility of the Scriptures is all that we, at most, can be obliged to make out, it is all the professor can have as the principle from which to reason against us. This is conclusive against him. But waiving this, waiving the objection to the order of credibility, and giving—what we do not concede—that we must make out the genuineness of the books it is pretended we must cite, still he cannot conclude Scriptural inspiration, *because no one of the books whose historical credibility we need or can need declares its own inspiration.* We have shown, that for our purpose it suffices, in any case, to establish the credibility of one of the Four Gospels as an historical document. But no one of the Four Gospels declares or intimates that it is inspired Scripture, or even asserts the inspiration of any other of the Scriptural books. Consequently, the professor has not even its own declaration for the inspiration of

Scripture, and must be mistaken in saying that Scriptural inspiration is a matter which "may be easily gathered from" the pages of the Scriptures themselves.

But, adds the professor, "you [Dr. Lynch] have yourself admitted that the teaching of the apostles was supernaturally protected from error, and if their oral instructions were dictated by the Holy Ghost, why should that august and glorious Visitant desert them when they took the *pen* to accomplish the same object when absent, which, when present, they accomplished by the *tongue*?"—(p. 62.) The question is irreverent and impertinent. We have no right to demand of the Holy Ghost the reasons of what he does or does not do. It is competent for him, if such be his pleasure, to inspire men for one thing and not for another, to inspire them to teach and not to write, to enable them to accomplish a given object by one method and not by another method; and the professor cannot say that he does not, because he sees no reason why he should. The Holy Ghost may have reasons not known to the learned Professor of Sacred Literature, &c., in the South Carolina College.

Dr. Lynch admits that the teaching of the apostles was supernaturally protected from error, and we must prove that it was, or not prove the infallibility of the church; but that it therefore necessarily follows that they were *inspired* as authors, or even as teachers, we neither admit nor are bound to admit. To be inspired, is, undoubtedly, to be supernaturally protected from error, but to be supernaturally protected from error is not necessarily to be inspired. Every Catholic believes his church supernaturally protected from error; but no one believes her to be inspired. As all Catholics make this distinction, Dr. Lynch's admission is no admission of inspiration even in the teaching of the apostles. Inspiration is necessary only when the mission is to reveal truth; when the mission is simply to teach a revelation already consummated, supernatural assistance, without inspiration, is all that is needed. If the mission of the apostles was simply to teach a revelation which they had received through their personal intercourse with their Master, while he was yet with them in the flesh,—and prior to the church, this certainly is all that we can be required to establish,— they had no need of inspiration, either as teachers or as writers, in order to be supernaturally protected from error. To concede or to assert such protection, then, is not to concede or assert their inspiration. We certainly cannot be required to make out for the apostles any thing more than we claim for the church, and since all we claim for her is supernatural protection from error in teaching a revelation already consummated, this is all that we can be obliged to make out for them.

Nor does the inspiration of the apostles or of their writings follow immediately from the facts on which we must rely in order to prove the infallibility of the apostles, or their supernatural protection from error. The facts on which we do and must rely are the miracles. These do not of themselves prove the inspiration, but simply the divine commission of him by or in favor of whom Almighty God works them, on the principle asserted by St. Nicodemus:— "Rabbi, we know thou art come a teacher from God; for no man can do the miracles which thou doest, unless God be with him." The divine commission follows necessarily from the miracles, and the supernatural protection from error, or the infallibility, follows necessarily from the divine commission. But the inspiration does not, because the teacher may be commissioned to teach, and may teach infallibly, without being inspired. Even apostolic inspiration, then, cannot be immediately concluded from the facts on which we must rely; then *a fortiori*, not the writings of the apostles. We say *immediately*, for to say it can be mediately is nothing to the purpose. We ourselves hold that the inspiration both of the Old Testament and the New can be mediately proved, that is, through the teaching of the church, proved by the miracles to be supernaturally protected from error.

But the professor continues,—"The apostles themselves declare their writings possessed the same authority with their oral instructions. Peter ranks the Epistles of Paul with the Scriptures of the Old Testament, which were confessed to be inspired; and Paul exhorts the Thessalonians to hold fast the traditions they had received from him, either by word or epistle."—(p. 62.) That the apostles anywhere declare their writings possess the same authority with their oral instructions, we have not found in any of the writings attributed to them with which we are acquainted; and if they did, it would not be sufficient, for the question at this moment relates, not to the authority, but to the inspiration, of the Scriptures, and it is not yet proved that even the *oral* instructions of the apostles were inspired.

The Epistles of St. Peter and of St. Paul are not admissible testimony, because, they are not included in that portion of the New Testament whose credibility we can, in any case, be obliged to make out. We can have no occasion for their testimony, prior to the church; and as the professor binds himself to the testimony we must use, or to what necessarily follows immediately from it, he cannot use it. The question now before us is, not whether he can or cannot, without the church, prove the inspiration of the Scriptures, but whether he can prove it from the facts which we must prove in order to prove the infallibility of the church.

St. Paul was not one of the twelve; his vocation was subsequent to the establishment of the church; and in no case can it be necessary for us even to establish his divine commission in order to establish the miraculous origin of the church, from which her infallibility immediately follows. But even if the professor could cite the authority of St. Paul, he would be obliged to make out, before his citation would avail him any thing,—1. That St. Paul's oral instruction was inspired; 2. That the Epistle to the Thessalonians is genuine; 3. That the Epistle to which he refers in it was *the* Epistles which we now have under his name; and, 4. That these Epistles are possessed by us precisely as he wrote them. Here are four facts not easy to make out, and which the professor must make out for himself; for we are under no obligation to make them out for him, and they do not follow necessarily from any thing we are bound to make out.

The divine commission of St. Peter as one of the apostles, we, of course, are obliged to make out; but *ubi Petrus, ibi ecclesia*—when we have done that, we have, in fact, made out our infallible church. Let this, however, pass for the present. Though we are obliged to make out the divine commission of St. Peter as one of the twelve, we are not obliged to make out his inspiration, or the authenticity or genuineness of the Epistles attributed to him. The Epistle the professor cites is no authority till its authenticity and genuineness are proved, and it happens to be precisely one of those books of the New Testament whose authenticity and genuineness Protestant theologians, at least many of them, call in question. But granting its genuineness, it avails nothing till the professor proves that the Epistles of St. Paul to which it refers are those we now have, and that we have them as St. Paul wrote them; for the professor is not merely to prove that there were inspired writings, but he is to prove what writings now possessed by us are or are not to be received as inspired Scripture. But even suppose this done, it does not follow that these Epistles are inspired. St. Peter does not, as the professor asserts, "rank them with the Scriptures of the Old Testament, which were confessed to be inspired," but simply with "the other Scriptures." What Scriptures these were, whether inspired or uninspired, the professor may or may not have some means of knowing, but St. Peter, in the writings attributed to him, nowhere informs him. That the Scriptures of the Old Testament were confessed to be inspired, we know from tradition and the church, but not from the New Testament. From the New Testament alone we can prove neither that the books of the Old Testament were inspired, nor of what books the Old Testament consisted. St. Paul tells us, indeed, that "all Scripture divinely inspired is profitable," &c., but he nowhere tells us what books or portions of books are divinely revealed Scripture. It is not true, then, that the inspiration of the Scriptures can "be easily collected from their own pages." Then the whole argument of the professor falls to the ground; for even if their own testimony were to be received, it would still be necessary to have the infallible body to prove their inspiration, since they themselves do not assert it.

We are not surprised that Mr. Thornwell should strive earnestly to convict his Catholic opponent of reasoning in a vicious circle. He must, as a Protestant, do so. Protestantism would abnegate herself, should she once concede that it is possible for us to prove the infallibility of the church, without having recourse to the supernatural authority of the Scriptures. It is with the Protestant, therefore, a matter of life and death. If he fails, it is all over with his cherished Protestantism. Her friends must follow her in long and sad procession to her final resting-place, howl their wild requiem, and leave the night-shade to grow over her grave, and return to their desolate hearths, with none to comfort them. What, indeed, is the essential principle of Protestantism, in so far as she pretends to be distinguished from the open and total rejection of all supernatural religion? What is it, but the assertion that the Bible is the original and only source or authority from which Christianity is to be taken? Everybody knows that this is her essential, her fundamental principle, in every sense in which she can even pretend to be a religion. To admit it to be possible for us to establish the infallibility of the church without the Scriptures, or without their supernatural authority, would be to surrender this principle, and with it Protestantism herself, as far as she can claim to be distinguishable from infidelity.

All Protestants know this, and hence they always assert that we do and must reason in a vicious circle. It would be so convenient, it is so necessary, for them, that we should, they have for so long a time so uniformly and so confidently asserted that we do, that it is hard for them now to admit, or even to believe, that we do not and need not. Like inveterate story-tellers, they appear to have come at last, by dint of long and continued repetition, to believe their own falsehoods,—the last infirmity of the credulous and the untruthful. Indeed, we can hardly doubt that the great body of Protestants really do labor under the hallucination, that we must, in order to establish the church, first establish, in the usual Protestant way, the authority of the Scriptures as inspired documents; and as we contend that the infallibility of the church is necessary to prove their inspiration, that we must prove the inspiration by the church, and the church by the inspiration,—a manifest vicious circle. But as a circle proves nothing, they think they may well say, that in proving the Christian religion we have and can have no advantage over them. Grant, say they, we must prove the credibility of the Scriptures before we can conclude their inspiration, from which we take our faith, you must prove the same credibility before you can conclude the infallibility of the church, from which you are to take yours, and you have and can have, prior to the church, no means of proving that credibility which we have not.

When the credibility is once established, our difficulties are ended, for the inspiration is easily collected from the express declaration of the Scriptures themselves; but the infallibility of the church is not. We have the express authority of the divinely accredited witness, but you have only your own interpretations or constructions of certain texts, in which you may err; and if you do not, you cannot assert that yours is the church intended, without making a full course of universal history for eighteen hundred years. How much simpler is our method than yours! With how many difficulties you encumber yourselves from which we are free! You have to make out all that we must made out, and in addition the fact of an infallible church, and the further fact that yours is it.

You may tell us that we may mistake the sense of Scripture, that our method is encumbered with difficulties, that it does not give us absolute certainty, and that something easier and surer is desirable. Be it so, what then? You have nothing to say, for you have nothing better to offer us. Suppose the church; what do you gain? You must take it from the Scriptures, and the Scriptures themselves from the same authority that we do, that is, private judgment. You must take it also from the Scriptures by your private interpretation of them; and you must take the fact that yours is the church from your private interpretations of history. Every step in your process of proof must be taken by private judgment, and we should like to know how private judgment is more certain in your case than in ours,—why it is to be condemned in us, and commended in you. Be it that it does not yield absolute certainty; what then? Absolute certainty,—who can have it? What presumption for such frail and erring mortals as we are to pretend to it! We do not need it. It is not in accordance with the intentions of Providence, nor compatible with our moral interest, that we should have it. "The true evidence of the Gospel is a *growing* evidence, sufficient always to create obligation and assurance, but *effectual* only as the heart expands in fellowship with God, and becomes assimilated to the spirits of the just. . . . . . Our real condition *requires* the possibility of error, and God has made no arrangements for absolutely terminating controversies and settling questions of faith, without regard to the moral sympathies of men."—(pp. 74, 75.) With such certainty as we have we study to be satisfied. It is not the characteristic of wisdom to aim at impossibilities, or of honesty to profess to have what it has not.

Thus they reason, and must reason, wise and honest souls! who assert that the Bible is the original and only source of Christian doctrine, and who define faith, with Professor Stuart of Andover, to be a species of probability, more certain, perhaps, than mere opinion, but less certain than knowledge, or ring the death-knell of their own system. If it be possible in the nature of things or the providence of God to bring an unbeliever to Catholicity without first converting him to Protestantism, they must forever shut their mouths, or open them only to give vent to their mortification and despair. But, happily for us, the reasonings which demand the principle of universal scepticism for their postulate are not apt to convince, and the assertions of men who deny all infallible authority, and confess to their own fallibility and want of certainty, are not absolutely conclusive. It is possible, after all, that these learned Protestants are mistaken, nay, laboring under "strong delusions," and that we poor benighted Papists have the truth. At worst, the authority on which we rely can be no more than fallible, while that on which they rely must be fallible at best. At worst, then, we are as well off as they can be at best.

But are these Protestants, who would have us regard them as full-grown men, strong men, the lights and support of the age, aware, that, in all this argumentation on which they pride themselves, and which they hold to be our complete refutation, they are merely reasoning against us from their own principles, and not from any principles common to them and us? Their reasoning, undeniably, rests on the assumption of the Bible as the original and only source, under God, of Christian doctrine,—a fundamental principle of Protestantism, and which we no more admit than we do the other fundamental principle of Protestantism, namely, private judgment. They are very much mistaken, if they suppose that we merely object to their rule of private judgment, if they suppose that they and we occupy common ground till we reach the limits to which the Bible extends, and that our only controversy with them, as far as the Bible goes, is one of simple exegesis, and after that merely a controversy in relation to certain points of belief not to be found in the Bible. Our main controversy with them is prior to the Bible, and relates to the origin or fountain and authority from which the faith is to be drawn.

Protestantism, taking it according to the professions of its most distinguished doctors, is resolvable into two principles, if principles they can be called, namely,—1. The Bible is the original and only source of Christian faith; and, 2. The Bible is to be taken on and interpreted by private judgment. . These are its two rules. It is nothing to us whether these two rules are or are not compatible one with the other, and we do not inquire now whether the latter does or does not necessarily and in fact absorb the former, and reduce Protestantism to sheer transcendentalism in principle, for that is a matter which we have already sufficiently discussed elsewhere; but we say, what everybody knows, that Protestantism professes these two rules as fundamental, and that they are essential to its very existence, and one of them as much as the other. Now we, as Catholics, reject and anathematize both of these rules, as Protestants ought to know. Consequently, for them to urge an argument against us which assumes either as its principle is a sheer begging of the question, or an assumption of Protestantism as the principle from which to conclude against Catholicity. Yet this is precisely the method of argument adopted in the brief summary of their reasoning which we have given.

This is not lightly said. Mr. Thornwell's whole reply to Dr. Lynch is a striking illustration and proof of it. Dr. Lynch states certain objections to private judgment; Mr. Thornwell replies, You cannot urge these objections, because, whatever their weight, they bear as hard against the church as against us. What is the proof of this? You must take the church from the Scriptures, or not take it at all; and if you take it from them, you must do so by private judgment, for you cannot use your church before you get it; and as you can get your church only subsequently to the Scriptures, you must take the Scriptures themselves on private judgment, or use a circulating syllogism, which proves nothing. But the proof that we must take the church from the Scriptures? Why you must take it from the Scriptures—because you have nothing else to take it from. But the proof that we have nothing else to take it from? The professor has no possible answer, but the assumption of the Bible as the original and only source of Christian faith. Consequently, at bottom, whether he knows it or not, he simply assumes one principle of Protestantism as the principle of his answers to objections urged against the other. That is, if we consider Protestantism in its unity, he attempts to prove the same by the same; if in its diversity, he reasons in a vicious circle,—proving private judgment by his Bible rule, and his Bible rule by private judgment! And yet Mr. Thornwell has the simplicity to accuse Dr. Lynch of using a circulating syllogism.

Undoubtedly, it is very convenient for Protestants, when hard pressed as to one of their principles, to resort to the other; but as both rules are denied, and are both directly or indirectly called in question in every controversy they have or can have with us, they would do well to bear in mind that the arguments they thus adduce are as illegitimate and worthless as if drawn from the very principle they are brought to defend. We really wish that our Protestant friends would study a little logic, at least make themselves acquainted with the more ordinary rules of reasoning and principles of evidence. It would save us some trouble, and themselves from the ridicule to which they expose themselves, whenever they undertake to reason. It is idle to attempt to convince a man by arguments drawn from the principle or system he is opposing, or to pretend to have refuted him by reasons which derive all their force from principles which he neither admits nor is obliged to admit. In reasoning, each party must reason from principles admitted by the other, or from principles proved by arguments drawn from principles which the other does not or cannot deny. Our Protestant friends ought to know this; for Mr. Thornwell very considerately informs us (p. 72) that they are not "prattling babes and silly women," but "bearded men."

Protestants seem to have inquired how it would be convenient for them that we should reason, and to have concluded, because, if we should reason in a given manner, it would be just the thing for them, that we of course do and must reason in that manner. If we admitted their doctrine as to the Bible, we undoubtedly should be obliged to reason in the manner they allege. If the road from unbelief to Catholicity lay through Protestant territory, if we could convert the unbeliever to the church only by first converting him to Protestantism, as Mr. Thornwell virtually contends, we should, of course, be obliged to make out the divine authority of the Scriptures, if at all, in the way in which Protestants attempt to do it, and then many of the objections we now urge and insist upon against private judgment we should be obliged to meet as well as they; but, surely, some other proof that such is the fact should be brought forward than this, that, if it be not so, then Protestantism must be false; for the conclusion is not one which we are not able to concede. In reasoning with Protestants, we are generally civil enough to take them at their word; and as we find them professing to hold the divine authority of the Scriptures, we draw our arguments against them from the Scriptures, because it is always lawful to reason against a man from his own principles; but in reasoning against unbelievers, we make no appeal to the Scriptures, unless it be sometimes as simple historical documents, proved to be such by general historical criticism, in which character we can legitimately appeal to them. The assertion, that we are obliged, by the nature of the case, to take the church from the Scriptures, is altogether gratuitous, and even preposterous. It rests, as we have seen, on the assumption, that the Bible is the original and sole authority for Christian faith. This is what Mr. Thornwell holds, what as a Protestant he must hold. The Bible, then, occupies the same place in his system that the church does in ours; for this is precisely what we say of the church. The Bible is for him the original and sole depositary of the faith,—its keeper, witness, teacher, and interpreter. He must, then, establish the divine authority of the Scriptures, as we the divine authority of the church; for only a divine authority is sufficient for Christian faith. To do this, as we have already established, we must have a supernaturally credible witness. Prior to and independently of the supernatural authority of the Scriptures, then, he must obtain such witness. This he can do, or he cannot. If he cannot, he cannot establish the divine authority of the Scriptures. If he can, then we also can; for prior to the Scriptures, we stand, at least, on as good ground as he. But such a witness is all we need for the divine authority of the church. Then either the professor cannot establish the divine authority of the Scriptures, or we can establish the divine authority of the church without the Scriptures. Where now are the professor's assumption and his triumph about reasoning in a circle?

Again. The divine authority of the Scriptures is itself an article of faith, because a supernatural fact, and a revealed fact, if a fact at all. This can be proved without the Scriptures, or it cannot. If it cannot, then it cannot be proved at all, for the Scriptures can authorize no article of faith till their own divine authority is established. If it can, it is false to say the Scriptures are the original and only authority for faith, for here is an article of faith not taken from them, but from some other source and authority. Or in another form: Either the supernatural witness supposed can be obtained, or cannot. If the professor says the latter, he abandons his Protestantism, by confessing to his inability to establish the divine authority of the Scriptures, from which alone he is to take it. If he says the former, he also abandons his Protestantism; for then he concedes the possibility of another authority for faith than the Scriptures, which Protestantism does and must deny, or deny itself. The professor may take which alternative he pleases; in either case, he must surrender his Protestantism, as far as at all distinguishable from sheer infidelity.

Thus easy is it to overthrow the strongest positions of

Protestants, and we confess that our only practical difficulty in refuting Protestantism lies precisely in its weakness, nay, its glaring absurdity. Our arguments against it fail to convince, because too easily obtained, and because they are too obviously conclusive. People doubt their senses, and refuse to trust their reason. They think it impossible that Protestantism, which makes such lofty pretensions, should be so untenable, so utterly indefensible, as it must be, if our arguments against it are sound. We succeed too well to be successful, and fail because we make out too strong a case. Indeed, Protestantism owes its existence and influence, after its wickedness, to its absurdity. If it had been less glaringly absurd, it would long since have been numbered with the things that were. *Fuit Ilium.* But many people find it difficult to believe it to be what it appears; they think it must contain something which is concealed from them, some hidden wisdom, some profound truth, or else the *enlightened* men among Protestants would not and could not have manifested so much zeal in its behalf,—forgetting that Socrates ordered just before his death a cock to be sacrificed to Æsculapius, that Plato advocated promiscuous concubinage, and that Satan, notwithstanding his great intellectual power, is the greatest fool in the universe,—a fool whom a simple child saying *credo* outwits and turns into ridicule. But they may be assured that it is not one whit more solid than it appears, and that the deeper they probe it, the more unsound and rotten they will find it.

Protestants would do well to study the Categories, or Predicaments, and learn not to contemn proper and necessary distinctions. They should know that they cannot conclude the supernatural from the natural; and that the historical credibility of the Scriptures does not, of itself, establish their divine authority in relation to the supernatural order. Historical credibility suffices for the miracles; and miracles accredit the teachers, but not immediately the teaching, whether oral or written. The teaching is taken on the authority of the accredited teacher. Consequently, between the miracles and the divine authority of the Scriptures the authority or testimony of the teacher must intervene, and whether it does intervene in favor of the Scriptures or not is a question of fact, not of reason.

Hence it is easy to detect the falsity of Mr. Thornwell's general thesis, that "it is just as easy to prove the inspiration of the Scriptures as the infallibility of any church"

The inspiration of the Scriptures and the divine authority or infallibility of the church are both supernatural facts, and therefore provable only by evidence valid in relation to the supernatural. In order to prove the inspiration of the Scriptures, the professor must prove their divine authority; for he is to take their inspiration from their own testimony, which is not adequate, unless supernaturally credible. But to prove the divine authority of the Scriptures, he must prove the divine commission of the apostles. The supernatural is provable in two ways,—by miracles, and by divinely accredited or commissioned teachers. The miracles accredit or prove the divine commission of the teachers, but, as we have just seen, not the divine authority of the writings. This must be taken on the authority of the teachers themselves, and the apostles are the only teachers supposable in the case; because all, whether church or Scriptures as a matter of fact, comes to us from God through them. Consequently, the professor must establish, in some way, their divine commission, or not establish the divine authority of the Scriptures, and therefore the supernatural credibility of their testimony to their own inspiration.

This we also must do, or not be able to assert the infallibility of the church. The divine commission is a point common to us both; both must make it out,—he without the authority of Scripture, and we without the authority of the church. If he can make it out, we can, and if we can make it out, he can; for we both, in relation to it, stand on the same ground, have the same difficulties, and the same, and only the same, means with which to overcome them.

The divine commission of the apostles is made out, if at all by the miracles historically proved to have actually occurred. These, thus proved, accredit the teachers, that is, the apostles, as teachers come from God, therefore commissioned by him; and if commissioned by him, what they teach as from him, must be infallibly true, because he cannot authorize the teaching of what is not infallibly true. Thus history proves the miracles, the miracles prove the divine commission, and the divine commission proves the infallibility. Thus far, we and the professor travel together. But—and this is the point he overlooks—when we have gone thus far, and obtained the divinely commissioned apostles, we have got the infallible church; for they are it, in all its plenitude and in all its integrity. Has the professor got his inspired Scriptures? No. He has not yet got even their divine authority, and does not as yet even know that there are any Scriptures at all, much less what and which they are; and he can know only as these divinely commissioned apostles inform him, that is, as taught by the infallible church,—precisely what we have always told him, and what he ought to have known in the outset.

Does the professor answer, that we have not yet proved the present existence of the infallible church, and that ours is it? Be it so. We must, of course, establish the fact of communion between us and the church of the apostles, or not be able to assert the infallibility of our church. But the professor has also to establish the fact of his communion with the same church, before he can assert the divine authority of the Scriptures; for he is to assert it on her authority, and this he cannot do until he proves that he has her authority. The simple question, then, between us is, whether it is as easy for him to establish the fact of the communion in his case, as it is for us to establish it in ours. He must prove, not only that it is *possible* in his case, but that it is as *easy* in his as in ours, or abandon his thesis.

As yet, the professor has only the point in common with us of the divine commission, or infallible church of the apostles. The authority of this church he must bring home to the sacred books with absolute certainty, and with so much exactness as to include no uninspired and to exclude no inspired Scripture. He must bring it home, not merely to some books, but to all whose inspiration is to be asserted; and this not in general only, but also in particular,—to each particular book, chapter, verse, and sentence. This, in the nature of the case, he can do only by proving the genuineness of the apostolic writings, and the identity, purity, and integrity of all those books which, though not written by the apostles themselves, are to be received as inspired on their authority. This he must do before he can establish the divine authority of the Scriptures, and be able to conclude their inspiration from their own testimony, in case he has it.

This is what the professor has to do, in order to make out the fact of apostolic communion in his case; but all we have to do, in order to establish it in ours, is to prove historically the continuance in space and time of the church of the apostles, and its external identity, or its identity as a visible corporation or kingdom, with our church. Now which is the easiest? Is it as easy to prove the authenticity, purity, and integrity of some sixty or seventy ancient books, written in different languages, and transcribed perhaps a thousand times, subject to a thousand accidents, as to establish the external identity of a visible corporation or kingdom, extending over all nations, the common centre around which, in one form or another, revolve all the significant events of the world for eighteen hundred years, and no more to be mistaken than the sun in the cloudless heavens at noonday? We are to prove, we grant, the external identity of our church with the church in the days of the apostles,—a thing, in its very nature, as easy to be done as to establish the continuance and identity of any civil corporation, state, or empire, ancient or modern. But the professor has to do as much as this, and more too, in the case of the Bible, and of each separate book, chapter, and sentence in the Bible,—a thing morally impossible to be done, as all the attempts of Protestants to establish the divine authority of the Scriptures sufficiently prove.

But even if this were done, the professor would not have established the inspiration of a single sentence of Scripture, as Scripture. The divine authority of the Scriptures does not prove their inspiration, unless they themselves declare it; for the professor must gather their inspiration from their own pages. He can assert no book to be inspired, unless, if it be a genuine apostolic writing, it clearly and unequivocally asserts its own inspiration, and if it be not an apostolic writing, unless it is clearly and unequivocally declared to be inspired by some book whose divine authority is established. And even this would not be enough for his purpose; for he must not only make out the inspiration of certain books, but he must establish by divine authority what books are, and what are not, to be received as inspired Scripture. He must bring divine authority to say, These, and these only, are to be so received. This last is impossible, for it is well known that Scripture nowhere draws or professes to draw up a list of the inspired books. This of itself is conclusive against the professor. The former, also, is impossible, for none of the apostolic writings, unless it be the Apocalypse, whose authenticity many Protestants deny, assert their own inspiration, and, with this exception, and some portion of the prophetic books, what is received as Scripture is nowhere in Scripture asserted to be inspired. Hence there are amongst us Protestant Doctors of Divinity, who, while professing to acknowledge the authority of our Lord and his apostles, and the general historical fidelity and authority of the Bible, deny entirely its inspiration.

The professor, therefore, must be decidedly mistaken in saying that, "it is just as easy to prove the inspiration of the Scriptures as the infallibility of any church." His meaning is, that, in the nature of the case, it must be as easy to prove the inspiration as the infallibility, which we see is by no means the fact, because, on no hypothesis, can he prove the inspiration of the Scriptures without first proving the infallible church, and the historical identification of the church in space and time is a thing infinitely easier to make out than the authenticity, identity, purity, and integrity of ancient writings. The latter can be done, if at all without a continued infallible authority, only with extreme difficulty, and by a few gifted individuals, who have ample opportunities and learned leisure for the purpose. The other is a thing easily done. It is, making allowance for the greater lapse of time between the two extremes, as easy to prove that Pius IX. is the successor of St. Peter in the government of the church, as that James K. Polk is the successor of George Washington in the presidency of the United States; and the fact of the succession in the former case as much proves that the church of which Pius IX. is Pope is the church of St. Peter, that is, of the apostles, as the succession in the latter case proves that the United States of which Mr. Polk is President is the same political body over which George Washington presided. Even the allowance to be made for lapse of time dwindles into insignificance, the moment we consider the more important part in the affairs of the world performed by the church than by the United States, or by any temporal state or kingdom of ancient or modern times.

To identify and to establish the purity and integrity of an ancient book, which has been subject to all the accidents of two or three thousand years, is by no means an easy task; but the identity in space and time of an outward visibly body, "a city set on a hill," the common centre of nations, and spreading itself over all lands and conducting the most sublime and the most intimate affairs of mankind, everywhere with us, at birth, baptism, confirmation, marriage, in sickness and health, in joy and sorrow, in prosperity and adversity, in life and death,—taking us from our mother's womb, and accompanying us as our guardian angel through life, and never leaving us for one moment till we arrive at home, and behold our Father's face in the eternal habitations of the just,—is the easiest thing in the world to establish through any supposable series of ages. You may speak of its liability to corruption; but far less liable must it be, even humanly speaking, to corruption than the Scriptures, and indeed, after all, it is only from its incorruptness and its guardian care, that even you, who blaspheme the spouse of God, conclude the purity and integrity of the Scriptures. Far easier would it be to interpolate or mutilate the Scriptures, without detection, than for the church to corrupt or alter her teachings, always diffused far more generally, and far better known than their pages. If publicity, extent, and integrity of the Christian people are to be pleaded for the purity and integrity of the sacred text, as they must be, then *a fortiori* for the purity and integrity of the church's teaching.

But passing over all this, supposing, but not conceding, that the professor could make out the inspiration of Scripture, it would amount to just nothing at all; for the real matter to be determined is, what is or is not to be received as the word of God, and till this is determined, or an unerring rule for determining it is obtained, nothing is done of any practical moment. To prove that the Scriptures are inspired, and therefore contain the word of God, is only to prove *where* the word, or some portion of the word, of God is, not *what* it is. Between *where* and *what* there is a distance, and, unless some means are provided for bridging it over, an impassable gulf. We are not told *what* the word of God is, till we are told it in the exact sense intended by the Holy Ghost, and this is not told us by being told that the word of God or some portion of it, is contained in a certain book. How will the professor tell us this?

The controversy turns on the means of evidencing the word of God to the Indian or negro. Suppose the professor goes to the Indian or negro, with his copy of the Holy Scriptures; suppose, *per impossibile*, that he succeeds in proving to him that the several books were dictated by the Holy Ghost, and in the exact state in which he presents them. What is this to him? He cannot read, and the book is to him a sealed book, as good as no book at all. What shall be done? Shall the Indian or negro wait till he has learned to read, and to read well enough to read, understandingly, the Bible,—which is out of his power,— and also till he has read it through several times, and some five or six huge folios besides, to explain its unusual locutions, and its references to strange manners and customs, and to natural and civil history, before hearing or knowing what is the message sent him by his heavenly Father? What, in the mean time, is he to do? Is he to remain a heathen, an infidel, an alien from the commonwealth of our Lord? If he needs the Gospel as the medium of salvation, how can he wait, as he must, on the lowest calculation, more than half the ordinary life of man, without peril to his soul? If he does not need it, what do you make the Gospel but a solemn farce? Suppose he does wait, suppose he does get the requisite amount of learning; what surety have you, even then, that he will not deduce error instead of truth from the book, and instead of the word of God embrace the words of men or of devils?

The pretence of Protestants, that they derive their belief, such as it is, from the Bible, is nothing but a pretence. If not, how happens it that, as a general rule, children grow up in the persuasion of their parents,—that the children of Episcopalians find the Bible teaching Episcopalianism, Presbyterian children find it teaching Presbyterianism, Baptist children Baptist doctrine, Methodist children Methodism, Unitarian children Unitarianism, Universalist children Universalism? Why is this? The professor knows why it is, as well as we do. He knows it is so, because their notions of religion are not derived from the Bible, but from the instructions of their parents, their nurses, their Sunday-school teachers, their pastors, and the society in the bosom of which they are born and brought up, and that, too, long before they read or are able to read the Bible so as to learn any thing from its sacred pages for themselves. He knows, too, that, when they come to read the Bible,—which may happen with some of them,—they read it, not to learn what they are to believe, not to find what it teaches, but to find in it what they have already been taught, have imbibed, or imagined. All Protestants know this, and it is difficult to restrain the expression of honest indignation at their hypocrisy and cant about the Bible, and taking their belief from the Bible,—the Bible, the precious word of God. The most they do, as a general rule, is to go to the Bible to find in it what they have already found elsewhere, and it rarely happens that they find any thing in it except what they project into its sacred pages from their own minds.

To hear Protestants talk, one would think they were the

greatest Bible-readers in the world, and that they believed every thing in the Bible, and nothing except what they learn from it. It is no such thing. Who among them trusts to the Bible alone? Where is the Protestant parent, pretending to any decent respect for religion, who leaves his children to grow up without any religious instruction till they are able to read and understand the Bible for themselves? Has not every sect its catechism? A catechism? What means this? With "the Bible, the whole Bible, and nothing but the Bible" on their lips, have they the audacity and the inconsistency to draw up a catechism and teach it to their children? Why do they not follow out their principle, and leave their children to "the Bible, the whole Bible, and nothing but the Bible?" Do you shrink, Protestant parents, as well you may, from the fearful responsibility of suffering your children to grow up without any religious instruction? Why not shrink also from the still more fearful responsibility of teaching them your words for the word of God? You tell us the Bible is your sole rule of faith, that there are no divinely appointed teachers of the word of God, and you sneer at the very idea that Almighty God has provided for its infallible teaching; and yet you, without authority, fallible by your own confession, draw up a catechism, take upon yourselves the office of religious teachers, and do not hesitate to teach your own crude notions, your own fallible, and, it may be, blasphemous opinions, training up your children, it may be, in the synagogue of Satan, keeping them aliens from the communion of saints, and under the eternal wrath of God! How is it that you reflect not on what you are doing, and for your children's sake, if not for your own, you do not tremble at your madness and folly? Who gave you authority to teach these dear children? Who is responsible to their young minds and candid souls for the truth of the doctrines you instil into them? O Protestant father, art thou mad? Thou lovest thy child, art ready to compass sea and land for him, and yet, for aught thou knowest, thou art doing all in thy power to train him to be the eternal enemy of God, and to suffer for ever the flames of divine vengeance!

But the catechism.—Who gave to you authority to draw up a catechism? Would you teach your children damnable heresies? Would you poison their minds with error and their hearts with lies? What is it you do when you draw up and teach a catechism? You deny the authority of the church to teach, yet here you are, Episcopalians, Presbyterians, Baptists, Methodists, Ranters, Jumpers, Dunkers, Socinians, Unitarians, Universalists, all of you, doing what you make it a crime in her to do,—drawing up and teaching a catechism, the most solemn and responsible act of teaching that can be performed; for in it you demand of confiding childhood simple and unwavering belief in what you teach! But the catechisms, you say, are for the most part drawn up in the language of the Holy Scriptures. Be it so. Who gave you authority to teach the Holy Scriptures? What infallible assurance have you, that, in teaching the words of Scripture, you are teaching the sense of Scripture? Is it a difficult thing either to lie or to blaspheme in the words of Scripture?

We confess that we can hardly observe any measure in our feelings or in our language, when we regard the profession and the practice of Protestants, when we consider how they lie unto the world and unto themselves, and how many precious souls, for whom our God has died, they shut out from salvation. One must speak in strong language, or the very stones would cry out against him. The professor, whom we have supposed going with his Bible in his hands, and holding it out to the rude savage or poor slave, ignorant of letters, saying, "Read this, my son, and it shall make you wise unto salvation,"—would he wait, think ye, till his tawny son or black brother had learned to read and become able to draw his faith from the Bible for himself, before instructing him? Be assured, not. He would hasten to instruct him without delay in his Presbyterian Catechism, the Westminster Confession of Faith, the Five Points of the Synod of Dort, or some modification of them. Never would he trust him to the Bible alone. So it is with all Protestant missionaries, and so must it be. No matter what they profess, in practice none of the sects place or can place their dependence on the written word to teach the faith without the aid of the living preacher. They all know, or might know, that they use the Bible, not as the source from which the simple believer is to draw his faith, but as a shield to protect the teachers of one sect from those of another; and that they assert its authority only as enabling each preacher to find some plausible pretext for preaching whatever comes into his own head. They place their dependence, not on a dead book, which when interrogated can answer never a word, which lies at the mercy of every interpreter, but, *nolens volens*, on the living teacher, and do without authority, and against their avowed principles, what they condemn us for doing, and what we do at least consistently, and in obedience to our principles.

There is no use in multiplying words or making wry faces about the matter. Whatever men may pretend, if they have any form of belief or of unbelief, their reliance is on the living teacher to preserve and promulgate it. The thing is inevitable. And since it is so, it is absolutely necessary, if we are to know and believe the word of God, that we have teachers duly authorized, divinely appointed to teach that word, so that we may not believe for the word of God the words of fallible men or of devils. Therefore, even if we could establish the inspiration of the Scriptures, as we cannot without the church, the church would still be indispensable, for without her we should still have no infallible means of knowing what is the word of God.

We have here refuted the professor's thesis in all its parts. We have shown him that he has no logical right to urge it; that if he is allowed to urge it, he cannot prove it, but that we can easily prove the contrary; and, finally, that if he could prove it, it would avail him nothing. We hope this will be satisfactory to him and his friends. He has been, even his friends must confess, singularly unsuccessful; but the fault has not been altogether his own. He has done as well as any Protestant could do. But it is an old and expressive proverb, if a homely one, that "nobody can make a silk purse out of a sow's ear." Nobody can make any thing out of Protestantism, and her defence must needs baffle the finest intellects. She is utterly indefensible. No man can construct an argument in her favor, or against the church, that is not at bottom a mere fallacy. Logic as well as salvation is on the side of the church, not with her enemies, and Protestantism is as repugnant to sound reason as she is to the best interests of man. Whoever espouses her must needs render himself an object of pity to all good men and good angels. Mr. Thornwell has naturally respectable abilities, even considerable logical powers, and some vigor of intellect. He wants refinement, grace, unction, but he has a sort of savage earnestness which we do not wholly dislike, and manifests a zeal and energy, which, if directed according to knowledge, would be truly commendable. But all these qualities can avail him nothing, for Protestantism at best is only a bundle of contradictions, absurdities, and puerilities. How a man of an ordinary stomach could undertake its defence would be to us unaccountable, did we not know to what mortifications and humiliations pride compels its subjects to submit. Pride cast the angels, which kept not their first estate, down from heaven to hell, and perhaps we ought not to be surprised that it degrades mortal men to the ignoble task of writing in defence of Protestantism.

The refutation of the professor's thesis gives us the full right to conclude the infallibility of the church with Dr. Lynch from the necessity of the case, and therefore to assert it, whatever objections men may fancy against it; because the argument for it rests on as high authority as it is possible in the nature of things to have for any objection against it. Nevertheless, we will examine in our next *Review* the professor's moral and historical objections to the church, and dispose of them as well as we can,—we hope to his satisfaction.

ARTICLE III.

IN the articles already devoted to Mr. Thornwell's book, we have vindicated Dr. Lynch's argument drawn from the necessity of the case for the infallibility of the church, and proved, unanswerably, if any thing can be so proved, that without the infallible church, the Protestant is utterly unable to prove the inspiration of the Scriptures. Since he concedes that if the infallible church exists at all, it is the Catholic Church, Mr. Thornwell must then, either acknowledge its infallibility, or give up the Christian religion itself. Having done this, which has been wholly gratuitous on our part, we proceed to the consideration of the professor's direct arguments for the fallibility of the church, or his direct attempts to prove that she is not infallible.

We have shown in our first essay, that the nature of the argument the professor is conducting does not permit him, even in case we should fail to prove the infallibility, to conclude the fallibility of the church. He denies that she is infallible, that is, asserts that she is fallible, and it is only by proving her fallible that he can maintain his thesis, that the books which he calls apocryphal are "corrupt additions to the word of God." The question is not now on admitting, but on rejecting, the infallibility of the church, and the *onus probandi*, as a matter of course, rests on him. He is the plaintiff in action, and must make out his case by proving the guilt, not by any failure on our own part, if fail we do, to prove the innocence of the accused; for every one is to be presumed innocent till proved guilty.

We have also shown, that in attempting to prove the fallibility of the church, Mr. Thornwell must confine himself to such arguments as an infidel may consistently urge. We have already dislodged him from every position he might be disposed to occupy on Christian ground. He has no magazine from which he can draw proofs against the church, but the reason common to all men. He can prove the church fallible only by proving that she has actually erred; and he can prove that she has actually erred only by proving that she has actually contradicted some principle of reason. It will avail him nothing to prove by reason that she teaches things the truth of which reason cannot affirm; for reason does not know all things, and things may be *above* reason, and yet not *against* reason. Nor will it avail him to prove that she contradicts his private convictions, or the teachings of his sect; for neither he nor his sect is infallible. Nothing will avail him but to prove some instance of her contradiction of a truth of reason, infallibly known to be such truth. The simple question for us to determine, then, in regard to what he alleges, is, Has he adduced an instance of such contradiction? If he has, he has succeeded; if he has not, he has failed, and we, since the presumption, as we say in law, is in our favor, may conclude the infallibility of the church against him.

1. Mr. Thornwell's first alleged proof that the church is not infallible is, that Catholics differ among themselves as to the seat of infallibility. It is uncertain where the infallibility is lodged. Then it is not apparent; and if not apparent, it does not exist; for *de non apparentibus et non existentibus eadem est ratio*. But this, supposing it to be true, though a good reason why we cannot assert the infallibility as a fact proved, is not a good reason for asserting that it does not exist. A thing may exist and yet not appear to us. Otherwise the stars would not exist when the sun shines, nor gems in the mine before being discovered. The point to be established is not the *non-appearance* of the infallibility, but its *non-existence;* and if the professor does not show that non-existence, he fails, for his own maxim then bears against him,—*de non apparentibus et non exis-*

tentibus eadem est ratio. But what is alleged is not true. Catholics do not disagree as to the seat of infallibility. Mr. Thornwell is mistaken, when he says (p. 76),—" There are no less than three different opinions entertained in your church as to the organ through which its infallibility is exercised or manifested." He confounds the three different modes in which Catholics hold that the infallibility is exercised with three different opinions as to its organ, evidently supposing that they who assert one of them must needs deny the other two. All Catholics agree, and must agree, for it is *de fide*, that the pastors of the church, that is, the bishops in union with the pope, their visible head, are infallible in what they teach, both when congregated in general council and when dispersed, each bishop in his own diocese; and the great majority hold that the pope alone, when deciding a question of faith or morals for the whole church, is also infallible. The only difference of opinion amongst us is as to the fact, whether the pope is or is not infallible, when so deciding. But as there is no difference of opinion as to the other two modes, whatever difference there may be as to this, it is not true that there are "three different opinions in our church as to the organ through which its infallibility is exercised or manifested."

2. The church cannot be infallible, because she requires a slavish submission of all her members, bishops, priests, and laity, to the pope. "The system of absolute submission runs unchecked until it terminates in the sovereign pontiff at Rome, whose edicts and decrees none can question, and who is therefore absolute lord of the Papal faith."—(p. 77.) We can see nothing unreasonable in making the pope, under God, the "absolute lord of the *Papal* faith." As to the submission, if the pope has authority from God as the supreme visible head of the church, it cannot be a *slavish* submission; for slavery is not in submission, but in submission to an authority which has no right to exact it. Reason teaches that we are bound to obey God, and to obey him equally through whatever organ it may please him to command us, or to promulgate his will. If he has commissioned the pope as his vicar in the government of the church, there is nothing repugnant to reason in submission or obedience to the pope. The professor must prove that the pope is not divinely commissioned, before, from the fact that the church obliges us to obey him, he can conclude that she errs or is liable to err. But this he has not proved.

3. The church makes the pope greater than God,—*Il papa è più che Dio per noi altri*,—and cannot assert his supremacy without asserting his infallibility. But if she asserts the infallibility of the pope, she denies that she is an infallible church; for, during the first six centuries, there was no pope.—(p. 78.) Where the professor picked up his scrap of Italian, he does not inform us; but if any one has made him believe that Catholics hold the pope to be greater than God, he may be sure he has been imposed upon. How can we hold the pope to be greater than God, when we believe him to be simply the *vicar* of Jesus Christ, receiving all that he is and has from God? Grant that papal supremacy necessarily carries with it papal infallibility,—a doctrine we by no means dispute,—the conclusion is not sustained; for it is not proved that during the first six centuries there was no pope. What the professor alleges as proof is not conclusive. His statements are either false or irrelevant. What he says that is true is not to his purpose; what he says that is to his purpose is not true. He alleges,—1. Till the seventh century, at least, the bishops of the church, not excepting the bishops of Rome, were regarded as officially equal; 2. According to St. Jerome, wherever there is a bishop, he is of the same merit and the same priesthood, and, according to St. Cyprian, the episcopate is one, and every bishop has an undivided portion of it; 3. St. Cyprian says to the African bishops in the great council at Carthage, that none of them makes himself a bishop of bishops, and that it belongs solely to our Lord Jesus Christ to invest them with authority in the government of his church, and to judge them; and, 4. St. Gregory the Great disclaimed the title of "Universal Bishop."—(pp. 78, 79.)

To the first we reply, that, not only as late as the seventh century were all the bishops of the church, not excepting the bishops of Rome, regarded as officially equal, but they are, as bishops, so regarded even now; and as the fact that they are now so regarded does not prove that there is now no pope, the fact that they were so regarded during the first six centuries cannot prove that there was no pope then. The equality of all bishops is a doctrine of the church. The pope, as simple bishop, is only the equal of his brethren; he is superior only as bishop of Rome, of which see the primacy is an adjunct, or prerogative. "Thus, a Roman council, in 378, says of Pope Damasus, that he is *equal in office* to the other bishops, and surpasses them in the prerogative of his see." *

To the second we give a similar reply. The unity of the episcopate, and that each bishop possesses an undivided portion of it, that is, that the bishops possess or hold it *in solido*, according to the felicitous expression of St. Cyprian, is held by the church now, and believed as firmly by all Catholics as ever it was. As the belief of this doctrine is not now disconnected with the belief in the papacy, it cannot follow, from its having been entertained in the time of St. Cyprian, that there was then no pope. This reply disposes of the citation from St. Jerome, as well as of that from St. Cyprian. But the professor argues, that, if the episcopate be one, and the bishops possess it *in solido*, there can be no pope. We do not see that this follows. Unity is inconceivable without a centre of unity, and how conceive the bishops united in one and the same episcopate without the pope as their centre of union?

To the third we reply, that, according to the fair interpretation of the language of St. Cyprian, in reference to its occasion and purpose, it has nothing to do with the subject. But let it be that St. Cyprian intended to deny, and actually does deny, the papal authority, what then? Before the professor can conclude that there was no pope down to St. Cyprian's time, he must prove either that St. Cyprian is a witness whose testimony we as Catholics, are bound to receive, or that he is one who could not err. As Catholics, we are bound to receive the testimony of single fathers or doctors only so far as their teaching is coincident with that of the church. The infallibility attaches to the church, and to single doctors only in so far as they teach her doctrine. Never, then, can we be bound to receive the testimony of any father or doctor which conflicts with her teaching. The testimony of St. Cyprian does thus conflict, if what it is alleged to be. Therefore we are not bound to receive it, and it cannot be urged against us, as an *argumentum ad hominem*. Then the professor must prove that St. Cyprian did not err. But, from the nature of the case, this he can do only by proving that he could not err. This he does not do, and cannot pretend; for he admits no infallible authority but that of the written word—(p. 84.) Consequently, let the testimony of St. Cyprian be what it may, it is not

---

*Ep. v. Apud Constant, T. I. col. 528, cited by Kenrick, *Primacy of the Apostolic See*, p. 106, 3d edition.

sufficient to prove that there was no pope down to his time. Moreover, if the alleged testimony of St. Cyprian refers to the papal authority at all, it refers to it only inasmuch as it denies the right of St. Stephen, his contemporary, whom Mr. Thornwell himself calls the pope, to exercise that authority. If St. Cyprian's language does not express *resistance* to the papal authority, it contains no reference to it. But resistance to an authority proves its existence. There was, then, in the time of St. Cyprian, an actual pope, that is, a pope claiming the right to exercise the papal authority; and the position of the professor, that there was no pope, is contradicted by his own witness. " But not according to the constitution of the church." That is a question, not of reason, but of authority, and therefore not debatable. The simple question, stated in the terms most favorable to the professor, resolves itself into this,—whether St. Cyprian is to be believed against St. Stephen, who claimed to be pope, and the church, who admitted his claim. To assume that he is, is to beg the question. The professor must, then, give us a valid reason for believing St. Cyprian rather than St. Stephen and the church, or he proves nothing by St. Cyprian's testimony, be it what it may. But he has given us no such reason. St. Cyprian was fallible, and fallibility is not sufficient to set aside the claim of infallibility.

To the fourth we answer, that St. Gregory the Great disclaimed through humility, as savoring of pride, the title of "Universal Bishop," we grant, but this is nothing to the purpose. The professor must prove that he disclaimed the papacy and the papal authority, or he does not prove his position. But this he does not and cannot do; for St. Gregory the Great, as is well known, on numerous occasions, asserted and exercised that authority; nay, it was in the exercise of it that he rebuked John Jejunator, Patriarch of Constantinople, for arrogating to himself the title of "Œcumenical Patriarch," a *title* which even the Bishop of Rome, though sovereign pontiff, forbore to assume.

The professor, it is evident from these replies, fails to prove that during the first six centuries there was no pope. His objection, founded on the assumption that there was none, falls, therefore, to the ground; and if it were required by our present argument, we could and would, prove an uninterrupted succession of popes from St. Peter to Pius IX.

4. The professor, taking it for granted that he had proved

that the infallibility of the church, if lodged with the pope, could not be asserted, proceeds to show that it cannot be maintained, if lodged either with general councils or with the *Ecclesia dispersa*. But these three ways are all the possible suppositions, and if in no one of these the church can be infallible, she cannot be infallible at all. But he has not, as we have seen, disproved her infallibility through the pope, and, for ought he proves, she may be infallible through her sovereign pontiffs. Consequently, as far as the argument to disprove her infallibility is concerned, it is no matter whether she is infallible in either of the other two modes or not.

But she cannot be infallible, if the infallibility be lodged with the general councils; for full two hundred years elapsed from the death of the last of the apostles before such a council was assembled.—(p. 79.) If her infallibility is expressed *only* through general councils, we concede it; but this is no Catholic doctrine; for we all, while we hold the general councils to be infallible, hold also that the bishops of the church in union with their chief, the pope, teach infallibly when dispersed, each in his own diocese, as well as when congregated in council.

But the councils cannot be infallible, because the early councils attributed the authority of the canons they settled to the sanction of the emperor.—(p. 80.) As this is asserted without any proof, it is sufficient for us simply to deny it. That the *civil* effect of the canons, or their authority as *civil* laws, depended on the sanction of the emperor, we concede,—for the church never assumes to enact civil laws; but that they depended on that sanction for their spiritual effect, or their authority in the spiritual order, we deny, and some better authority than that of one Barrow, an Anglican minister, which is no authority at all, will be needed to prove it.

The infallibility of the church, continues the professor, cannot be maintained, if lodged with the pastors of the church dispersed each in his own diocese; because it would then depend on unanimous consent, and the unanimous consent of all can never be ascertained.—(p. 81.) This unanimous consent could not be ascertained, if the pastors of the church were so many independent and unrelated individuals, like Protestant ministers, we concede; but, whether congregated or dispersed, Catholic pastors are ONE BODY, hold the episcopate *in solido*, and through the pope, the centre of unity and communion, they all commune with each, and each with all. Each is bound for all, and all for each, and each by virtue of this communion can give the unanimous faith of all. All that we need know is that the particular pastor to whom we are subjected is in communion with the pope; for if he is, we know he is in communion with the head, then with the body, and then with the members. If thus in communion with the head, with the body, and with the members, what he gives as the unanimous faith of the whole must be the unanimous faith of the whole, or that which has the unanimous consent of all.

5. But the church cannot be infallible, because she has contradicted herself. "Popes have contradicted popes, councils have contradicted councils, pastors have contradicted pastors, &c."—(p. 83.) This argument is good, if the fact be as alleged. But the fact of contradiction must be proved, not taken for granted. Does the professor prove it? Let us see. The first proof he offers is, that "the Council of Constantinople decreed the removal of images, and the abolition of image-worship, and the Council of Nice, twenty-three years after, re-established both."—(p. 84.) But, unhappily for the professor, no Council of Constantinople, or of any other place, recognized or received by the church as a council, ever decreed any such thing. There may have been, for aught we care, an assembly of Iconoclasts at Constantinople, collected by an Iconoclastic emperor, which made some such decree; but that no more implicates the church than a decree of a college of dervishes or of a synod of Presbyterian ministers.

"The second Council of Ephesus approved and sanctioned the impiety of Eutyches, and the Council of Chalcedon condemned it."—(*ib.*) But there was only *one* Council of Ephesus, and that was held before the rise of the Eutychian heresy! There was an Ephesian Latrocinium which approved the heresy of Eutyches, but it was no council, and its doings were condemned, instantly, by the church.

"The fourth Council of Lateran asserted the doctrine of a physical change in the Eucharistic elements, in express contradiction to the teachings of the primitive church, and the evident declarations of the apostles of the Lord."—(*ib.*) The professor is not the authority for determining what was the doctrine of the apostles or of the primitive church, and cannot urge his notions of either as a standard by which to try the church. He must adduce, on the authority of the church herself, the teachings of the primitive church contradicted by the decree of the fourth Council of Lateran, before he can allege that decree or assertion as a proof of her having contradicted herself. This he has not done.

"The second Council of Orange gave its sanction to some of the leading doctrines of the school of Augustine, and the Council of Trent threw the church into the arms of Pelagius." (*ib.*) Here no instance of contradiction is expressed. But it is not true, and the professor offers no proof, that the Council of Trent threw the church into the arms of Pelagius; and as a matter of fact, that council defines the doctrines of grace, which condemn the Pelagian heresy, in the very words of St. Augustine. The professor would do well to set about the study of ecclesiastical history.

"Thus, at different periods, every type of doctrine has prevailed in the bosom of an unchangeable church."—(*ib.*) Not proved, and would not be, even if the foregoing charges were sustained. False inferences and unsupported assertions are not precisely the arguments to disprove the infallibility of the church. We beg the professor to review his logic.

"The church has been distracted by every variety of sect, tormented by every kind of controversy, convulsed by every species of heresy." If this means that she has *sanctioned* every variety of sect and every species of heresy, we simply reply, that the professor has not proved it; if it means, that, first and last, she has had to *combat* every variety of sect and species of heresy, we concede it. But to adduce this as a proof of her having contradicted herself is ridiculous in logic, and monstrous in morals. You might as well argue that the church was once Lutheran, because she condemned Lutheranism, Calvinistic, because she condemned Calvinism, that St. John was a Gnostic, because he wrote his Gospel to condemn Gnosticism, or that Mr. Thornwell himself is a Catholic, because he anathematizes Catholicity; nay, that the judge, who, in the discharge of his judicial functions, condemns the crime of murder, must needs be the murderer, and that the eleven were guilty of the treachery of Judas, for they no doubt condemned it. Is this Protestant logic, and Protestant morality?

The church "at last has settled down on a platform which annihilates the word of God, denounces the doctrines of Christ and his apostles, and bars the gates of salvation against men."—(*ib.*) Indeed! How did the professor learn all that?

Here is all the professor adduces to prove the fact of the church having contradicted herself, and it evidently does not prove it. Then the argument founded on it against the infallibility of the church must go for nothing. For aught that yet appears, the church may be infallible. It is certainly a great inconvenience not to know ecclesiastical history when one wishes to reason from it.

From these objections, which the professor calls "historical difficulties in the doctrine of papal infallibility," we proceed to consider another class, in his Sixth Letter, which we may term philosophical difficulties. The charge under this head is, that the doctrine of the infallibility of the church—papal infallibility, as the professor improperly expresses it—leads to scepticism.—(p. 89.) The proofs assigned, as nearly as we can get at them, amidst a mass of speculations sometimes correct enough, but illustrating, when considered in relation to the argument, only the *ignorantia elenchi*,—a favorite figure of logic with the author,—are two, namely, the church enjoins dogmas which contradict reason, and holds that doctrines may be philosophically true, and yet theologically false.

1. The instance adduced to prove that the church requires us to believe what contradicts reason is the doctrine of Transubstantiation. It is a principle of reason that we believe our senses. But this doctrine denies the testimony of our senses, and therefore contradicts reason. "Upon the authority of Rome we are required to believe that what our senses pronounce to be bread, that what the minutest analysis which chemistry can institute is able to resolve into nothing but bread, what every sense pronounces to be material, is yet the incarnate Son of God, soul, and body, and divinity, full and entire, perfect and complete. Here Rome and the senses are evidently at war; and here the infallible church is made to despise one of the original principles of belief which God has impressed upon the constitution of the mind."—(p. 93.) What is here said about the minutest analysis chemistry can institute, &c., amounts to nothing, makes the case neither stronger nor weaker; for chemical analysis, however minute or successful, can give us only sensible phenomena. It never attains to substance itself. The simple assertion is, that the doctrine of Transubstantiation contradicts reason, because it contradicts the senses. But is this true?

There is no contradiction of the senses, unless the doctrine requires us to believe that what is attested by the senses is false. What is it the senses attest? Simply the presence in the sacred Host of the species, accidents, or *sensible phenomena* of bread. This is all; for it is well settled in philosophy, that the senses attain only to the phenomena, and never to the substance or subject of the phenomena. Does the doctrine of Transubstantiation deny this? Not at all. It asserts precisely what the senses assert, namely, the presence in the sacred Host of the species, accidents, or sensible phenomena of bread. Then it does not contradict the senses.

"But it is a principle of human nature to believe, that, where we find the phenomena, there is also their subject; that, if in the sacred Host all the sensible phenomena of bread are present, the substance of bread is also present." Undoubtedly, if reason has no authority, *satisfactory to herself*, for believing the contrary. In ordinary cases, reason has no such authority, and we are to believe that the sensible phenomena and their subject do go together. But reason cannot deny that God, if he chooses, can, by a miraculous exertion of his power, change the subject without changing the phenomena, and if in any particular case it be certified infallibly to her that he actually does so, she herself requires us to believe it. In the most holy Eucharist, it is so certified to reason, if the church be infallible, and therefore, in believing that the sensible phenomena of bread are there without their natural subject, we are simply obeying reason, and of course, then, do not contradict it. It is no contradiction of reason to believe on a higher reason what we should not and could not on a lower reason. In this doctrine, we are simply required to suspend the ordinary reason at the bidding of an extraordinary reason, which is not, and never can be, unreasonable. Consequently, there is in the doctrine nothing *contrary* to reason, and the church, in enjoining it, does not enjoin a dogma which contradicts either reason or the senses, though she unquestionably does enjoin a dogma which is *above* reason. The first proof, therefore, that the doctrine of infallibility "leads to scepticism," must be abandoned, as having no foundation for itself.

2. The second proof is no better. That certain infidel or paganizing philosophers, in the latter part of the fifteenth and early part of the sixteenth century, maintained that propositions may be philosophically true, yet theologically false, we concede; that this was the doctrine of the schoolmen, or that it was ever for a moment countenanced by the church, we deny. Indeed, Leo X. (*Concilii Lateranensis*

Sess. 8, 1513) condemns it, by declaring every assertion contrary to revealed faith to be false, and decreeing that all persons adhering to such erroneous assertions be avoided and punished as heretics,—*tanquam hæreticos.* It would not be amiss, if the professor would bear in mind that proofs which are themselves either false or in want of proof prove nothing, however pertinent they may be.

We cannot follow the professor in his declamatory speculations in support of his charge. His reasoning is all fallacious. He starts with the assumption, that the church is fallible, has no authority from God to teach, and then charges her with consequences which would follow, no doubt, if she were fallible, if she had no divine commission; for they are the precise consequences which do follow from the teaching, or rather action, of the Protestant sects. If the church were fallible, a mere human authority, arrogantly claiming to teach infallibly, we certainly should not defend her, or dispute that her influence would be as bad as Mr. Thornwell falsely alleges; but we do not recognize his right to assume the fallibility of the church as the basis of his proofs that she is not infallible; and we cannot accept as facts mere consequences deduced from an hypothesis which we deny, and which is not yet proved, far less receive them as proofs of the hypothesis.

There are in Catholic countries, no doubt, many unbelievers; but before this can be adduced as evidence that the church, by claiming to be infallible, leads them into unbelief, it is necessary to prove that she is not infallible. If infallible, she cannot have a sceptical tendency; because what she enjoins must be infallible truth, and scepticism, when it does not proceed from malice, results always, not from truth being present to the mind, but from its *not* being present. But it is worthy of remark, that the objections to Christianity on which unbelievers chiefly rely are not drawn from the distinctive teachings of the Catholic Church, nor from the Scriptures as she interprets them. They are nearly all drawn from the Scriptures as interpreted by private judgment, and hence, as we should expect, infidelity abounds chiefly in Protestant countries. Protestant Germany, England, the United States, are, any one of them, far more infidel than even France; and our own city cannot, in religious belief, compare favorably with Paris, infidel as Paris unhappily is. Modern infidelity is of Protestant origin; Giordano Bruno sojourned in Protestant England; Bayle was a Protestant, and resided in Holland; Voltaire, the father of French infidelity, did but transport to France the philosophy of the Englishman Locke, and the doctrines and objections of the English deists, Herbert of Cherbury, Tindal, Toland, Chubb, Morgan, Woolston, and others. Indeed, to England especially belongs the chief glory, such as it is, of infidelizing modern society. France and Germany are nothing but her pupils. Rightly do Protestants regard her as the bulwark of their religion; for in the war against the church, against the revelation of Almighty God, she, with her sanctimonious face and corrupt heart, has the chief command. It were easy to show, that, aside from the internal malice of unbelievers, the chief cause of infidelity in modern society is Protestantism, which asserts the divine authority of the Scriptures, and then leaves them to be interpreted by private judgment; but it is unnecessary. It is becoming every day more and more obvious, that, the more Protestants circulate the Bible, the more do they multiply scoffers and unbelievers.

In Letter VII. we come to another class of objections, which we may term *moral* objections. These are summed up in the assertion, The church cannot be infallible, because her "infallibility is conducive to licentiousness and immorality."—(p. 105.) The proof of this is, first, the unproved assertion, that the doctrine of the infallibility of the church leads to scepticism; and, second, the allegation that Catholicity and jesuitism are one and the same thing. The first assertion we dismiss, for we have just shown that the professor does not sustain it. As to jesuitism, we hardly know what to say; for we do not know, and the author does not inform us, what is meant by jesuitism. For aught that appears, the identity asserted may be conceded without prejudice to the church. The Society of Jesus is composed of Catholic priests, and we are not aware that these have any peculiar doctrines, either of faith or morals. Indeed, they could not have; for if they were to have any, they would be obliged to leave the order and the church. The notion among some Protestants, that the Jesuits are a *sect* in the bosom of the church, professing certain dogmas of faith or certain principles of morals different from those professed by other Catholics, is a ridiculous blunder. The church enjoins the same faith and the same principles of morals upon all her children, and no person, or class of persons, would be suffered to teach in her communion, who should add to or take from them. The Jesuits are Catholics, neither more nor less, and it is fair to presume that in faith and principles of morals they agree with all Catholics, and profess what the church teaches.

But that the Jesuits teach, or ever have taught, doctrines favorable to licentiousness or immorality is a matter to be proved, not taken for granted. What is the proof the professor offers? Here is all we can find:—"These three cardinal principles—of intention, mental reservation, and probability—cover the whole ground of jesuitical atrocity." —(p. 115.) The professor labors long and hard to identify Catholicity and jesuitism. He must, therefore, concede that these three principles cover the whole of what he holds to be atrocious in Catholicity. Catholicity, then, is "conducive to licentiousness and immorality," because it contains the three principles of "intention, mental reservation, and probability." But what is the meaning the professor attaches to these principles? Unhappily, he gives us no clear and explicit answer; for he writes with his head full of false assumptions.

"The detestable principles," he says, "of the graceless order [the Jesuits]........may be found embodied in the recorded canons of general councils. That the end justifies the means, that the interests of the priesthood are superior to the claims of truth, justice, and humanity, is necessarily implied in the decree of the Council of Lateran, that no oaths are binding—that to keep them is perjury rather than fidelity— which conflict with the advantage of the church. What fraud have the Jesuits ever recommended or committed, that can exceed in iniquity the bloody proceedings of the Council of Constance in reference to Huss? What spirit have they ever breathed more deeply imbued with cruelty and slaughter, than the edict of Lateran to kings and magistrates, to extirpate heretics from the face of the earth? The principle on which the sixteenth canon of the third Council of Lateran proceeds covers the doctrine of *mental reservations.* If the end justifies the means, if we can be perjured with impunity to protect the authority of the priesthood, a *good intention* will certainly sanctify any other lie, and a man may always be sure that he is free from sin, if he can only be sure of his allegiance to Rome and his antipathy to heretics. The doctrine of *probability* is in full accordance with the spirit of the papacy, in substituting authority for evidence, and making the opinions of men the arbiters of faith. And yet these three cardinal principles of intention, mental reservation, and probability, which are so thoroughly papal, cover the whole ground of jesuitical atrocity."—pp. 114, 115.

It would seem from this, that the professor understands by the principle of intention, that the moral character of the actor is determined by the intention with which he acts; by that of mental reservation, that no one can bind himself by oath to do that which conflicts with the advantage of the church; and by that of probability, the substituting of authority for evidence, and making the opinions of men the arbiters of faith. If this is not his meaning, we are unable to divine what it is.

That Catholicity teaches that the moral character of the actor is determined by his intention, or, in other words, that a man is to be judged according to his intention, may be true, but this must be morally wrong, or it cannot be adduced as a proof that the teaching of the church is "conducive to licentiousness and immorality." That this is morally wrong, the professor does not prove, or even attempt to prove. For ourselves, we are not now called upon to prove that it is right. It is for the professor to prove that it is wrong. But we own, that, from our boyhood, we have always supposed it a dictate of reason that the man is to be praised or blamed according to his intention. If you really intend to do a man evil, your unintentional failure to do him evil does not exonerate you from guilt; if you really intend to do him good, but, in attempting to do him good, unintentionally do him evil, you are not guilty. If you have killed a man in self-defence, the law excuses or justifies you; and it does not hold you guilty of murder, unless the killing has been done with a felonious intent. He who takes the life of a fellow-being through private revenge is a murderer; the public officer who does it in pursuance of a judicial sentence is no murderer, and does but a justifiable act. Whence the difference, if not in the difference of intention? That no act, in relation to the actor, is blameworthy unless done from a malicious intention, or praiseworthy unless done from a virtuous intention, we have always supposed to be the teaching of reason, and we must have high authority to convince us that we have been wrong.

"But on this ground the church erects her doctrine, that the end justifies the means." We cannot concede this; first, *because the church has no such doctrine*; and second, because the principle does not imply it. The assertion, that the church teaches, that any Catholic doctor teaches, or ever did teach, that the end justifies the means, is made without the faintest shadow of a reason, and the reverse is what she does teach, as every man knows who knows any thing of her teaching. The doctrine of intention objected to implies nothing of the sort. The church teaches, indeed, that the act for which we are accountable is the act of the will; but she teaches that no act is done with a good intention that is not referred to God as the ultimate end, and that *every one* of our acts is to be so referred. Now, in choosing the means, we as much *act* as we do in the choice of the end, and therefore must be, as to the means, bound by the same law which binds us as to the end; and then we can no more choose unjust means than we can unjust ends, and therefore can be allowed to seek even just ends only by just means.

The professor says that "the Jesuit Casnedi maintains in a published work, that at the day of judgment God will say to many, 'Come, my beloved, you who have committed murder, blasphemed, &c., because you believed that in so doing you were right.'" But he takes good care not to give us a reference to the work itself, and we hazard nothing in saying that no Jesuit ever published such a sentence, unless it was to condemn it, as containing a Protestant heresy. That invincible ignorance, if really invincible, excuses from sin, is, no doubt, a doctrine of the church; for she teaches that no one can sin in not doing that which he has no power to do. No doubt, involuntary mistakes, if unavoidable, springing from no malice in the will, from no culpable neglect of ours, are excusable; but no Catholic divine ever taught that invincible ignorance can extend to the great precepts of the natural law, to such as forbid murder, blasphemy, &c.; for they are engraven on the heart of every man, and are evident to every man by the light of natural reason. The professor has been misled, by relying on the authority of Pascal, and other writers of his stamp. He refers us to Pascal's *Provincial Letters* "for a popular exposition of the morality of the Jesuits." He might as well refer us to Voltaire's *Philosophical Dictionary* for a popular exposition of the morality of the Gospel. Pascal was a Jansenist, and Jansenists are heretics, not Catholics. The *Provincial Letters* are witty, but wicked,—a tissue of lies, forgeries, and misrepresentations, from beginning to end, as has been amply proved over and over again. If Mr. Thornwell is ignorant of this fact, he will have to search long before he will find a Catholic or a Jesuit doctor that will permit him to hold that his ignorance is excusable.

1. The principle of mental reservation happens to be no

Catholic doctrine. Protestants would, no doubt, be pleased to find that the church teaches that lying is sometimes justifiable, for such a doctrine is one they stand very much in need of; but she teaches nothing of the sort. She does not command her children at all times and on all occasions to speak *all* the truth they may happen to know, but she does command them never to speak any thing but the truth; and she teaches them, that, when they use words which by their natural force convey a false sense, they speak falsehood, whatever may have been their secret meaning, and that knowingly and intentionally to use language which is naturally calculated to deceive the hearer, to convey to him a false meaning, or a meaning different from that in the mind of him that uses it, is to lie, to sin against God. All who are acquainted with Catholic morality know that this is her teaching, and whoever asserts the contrary is guilty of the very offence he would fasten upon her, and has no excuse for his conduct. For if he is ignorant of her doctrine, he speaks rashly; if he is not ignorant, he is guilty of a wilful falsehood.

2. The facts which the professor alleges, granting them to be facts, do not prove the principle of *mental reservation.* We presume the professor wishes to maintain that the church teaches that it is lawful for her children to take oaths which conflict with her advantage, but that they must take them with the mental reservation, not to keep them; and that if so taken, it is no sin to break them. This is what he needs in order to make out his case. But this he does not prove. Granting that when he has rightly stated the doctrine of the Council of Lateran,—he does not tell us which council,*—all he proves is, that the church teaches that no oath taken to her prejudice is binding; but he does

---

* Dr. Brownson seems to have overlooked the second reference to the Council of Lateran in the extract just made from Professor Thornwell. Here the professor refers to the xvi. canon of the third Council of Lateran, which is what he intended in the first reference. But the xvi. canon is not at all to the effect supposed by Mr. Thornwell, and has not the slightest bearing on the subject of *mental reservations.* Neither does it declare that "no oaths are binding which conflict with the advantage of the church." The decree prohibits following the caprices of a minority of the younger members of the chapter where they assign no reason in their favor, and adds that no one shall excuse himself from obeying this decree by alleging that it has been the custom of the church in that place, and that he has made oath to preserve the customs of his church, for such an oath to act against the advantage of the church and the rules of the holy fathers would be perjury, not an oath. The coun-

not prove that she teaches that the reason why it is not binding is because it was taken with a mental reservation not to keep it in case it conflicted with her advantage. For aught that appears, the reason why the church declares that such oaths do not bind is because she holds them to be unlawful oaths,—oaths which no man has a right to take, and which therefore are void *ab initio*. The professor will hardly maintain the morality of robbers and cutthroats, that a man who has taken an unlawful oath is bound to keep it. He will hardly pretend that he who should swear to assist in a plot for blowing up the Presbyterian Assembly when in session, for instance, would be bound to keep his oath, or to refrain from revealing the plot, simply because he had sworn not to do so. The whole sum and substance of the charge, then, is, that the Jesuits and the church teach that unlawful oaths do not bind. Does this conflict with reason? Is this "conducive to licentiousness and immorality?" Is it immoral to teach that no man can bind himself to do wrong?

But in this the church teaches that "the interests of the priesthood are superior to the claims of truth, justice, and humanity; for she holds that all oaths which conflict with her advantage are unlawful." The conclusion is not necessary, for it may be that her interests, her advantage, are identical with the claims of truth, justice, and humanity; or that it is only by promoting her interests and seeking her advantage that it is possible to vindicate the claims of truth, justice, and humanity. If she be what she professes to be, this must be so; and that she is what she professes to be

---

cil speaks only of an unlawful oath already taken, and declares it unlawful and void. The following is the entire chapter xvi. :

Cum in cunctis ecclesiis, quod pluribus et senioribus fratribus visum fuerit, incunctanter debeat observari, grave nimis et reprehensione est dignum, quod quarumdam ecclesiarum pauci quandoque non tam de ratione, quam de propria voluntate ordinationem multoties impediunt, et ordinationem ecclesiasticam procedere non permittunt. Quocirca præsenti decreto statuimus, ut nisi a paucioribus et inferioribus aliquid rationabiliter fuerit ostensum, appellatione remota, semper prævaleat, et suum consequatur effectum, quod a majori et seniori parte capituli fuerit constitutum. Nec nostram constitutionem impediat, si forte quis ad conservandam ecclesiæ suæ consuetudinem juramento se dicat adstrictum. Non enim dicenda sunt juramenta, sed potius perjuria quæ contra utilitatem ecclesiasticam, et sanctorum patrum veniunt instituta. Si autem hujusmodi consuetudines, quæ ratione juvantur, et sacris congruunt institutis, irritare præsumpserit donec congruum egerit pœnitentiam, a Dominici corporis perceptione fiat alienus.—Labbe's Councils, X., 1517.—ED.

the professor must presume till he has proved the contrary. If she be the church of God, any oath to her prejudice is an oath against God, and no man can be mad enough to say that an oath against God can bind, or that the claims of truth, justice, or humanity can be prejudiced by not keeping it. But the professor cannot assume that she is not the church of God, for that she is not, is the very point he is to prove, and he cannot prove this by assuming it, and making the assumption the principle of his arguments to prove it. Such a procedure would simply beg the question. Granting, then, that the church does teach that oaths to her prejudice are unlawful, and therefore do not bind, nothing proves that she is not right in so doing, and therefore nothing proves that in doing so she favors "licentiousness and immorality." To condemn the church, on the ground the professor assumes, would be to assert the doctrine opposite to hers; namely, unlawful oaths are to be kept,—that, if we have been foolish or wicked enough to swear to do wrong, we are bound in conscience to keep our oath and do the wrong,—a monstrous doctrine, which strikes at the foundation of all morals. It is strange what blunders Protestants commit, in trying to get an argument against the church. It would seem as if it never occurred to them to examine the principle of the objections they urge. They seem to say, if the church should favor licentiousness and immorality, then she would not be the church of God; therefore she does favor licentiousness and immorality. The church forbids unlawful oaths.

3. The professor, evidently, is ignorant of the principle of *probability*, or probabilism, as understood by Catholic theologians. That principle, if he did but know it, is very nearly the contrary of what he supposes, and is little else than the well-known maxim of the Common Law, that, if there is a reasonable doubt, the accused is entitled to its benefit. But the principle, as the professor defines it, is not embraced by the church, nor defended by a single Catholic divine. He says, the church substitutes "authority for evidence, and makes the opinions of men the arbiters of faith;" but this, in principle, at least, is a mistake; for the church teaches that God alone is the arbiter of faith, and that nothing but his word, declared to be his word, by himself through his divinely appointed organ, can be of faith. His word divinely declared to be his word is the highest evidence reason can demand or receive; and if the church

is proved to reason to be his organ for declaring his word, reason has the highest evidence possible for believing that whatever she teaches as the word of God is infallibly true. She asserts that reason has the right to demand this evidence, and has no right to dispense with it. In principle, then, she denies the principle of probability as set forth by the professor. If she is what she claims to be, she denies it in her practice, and cannot possibly do as alleged. That she is what she professes to be the professor is bound, as we have already shown, to presume till he makes the contrary appear; which he does not do.

The professor identifies jesuitism with Catholicity, and resolves all that is atrocious in jesuitism into the three principles enumerated, and therefore all that is atrocious in Catholicity. But the first of these principles is a simple dictate of reason, and contains nothing atrocious. Then all that is atrocious in Catholicity, or all the atrocity that can be charged upon Catholicity, is resolvable into the other two principles, namely, mental reservation and probability. But these are not Catholic principles, and, however atrocious they may be, their atrocity cannot be charged to her. Therefore no atrocity can be charged to her, even according to the professor's own argument. But to be "conducive to licentiousness and immorality" is undeniably atrocious. Therefore the church is not conducive to them. So the professor does not sustain his assertion, that "Papal infallibility is conducive to licentiousness and immorality." Assuredly, the professor is ignorant of the laws of evidence.

The next proof offered against the infallibility of the church is, that "it is the patron of superstition and will-worship."—(p. 116.) This is a singular objection. How *infallibility* can patronize superstition and will-worship,— that is, *well*-worship, or the worship of wells, conceding them to be wrong, is more than we are able to conceive. Infallibility can be the patron of nothing wrong, and the professor, if he should prove his thesis, would prove that superstition and will-worship are right, not that the church is fallible. Can he mean that the assertion of her infallibility is the patron of superstition and will-worship? But this he would be troubled to prove, even if he should prove the existence of superstition and will-worship in the church; for they undeniably exist out of the church, in communities which lay no claim to infallibility. Does he mean that the church is not infallible, because she is the patron of superstition,

&c.? Why, then, did he not say so? If this is his meaning, his argument is valid, if the fact be as alleged. But, unhappily for his cause, the fact is not as alleged.* Catholics pay divine honors to God alone, as every one knows who knows any thing of Catholic worship. That we keep relics, pictures, and images, and pay them a relative honor as memorials of departed sanctity, we admit; that we venerate the saints, especially the ever-blessed Virgin, the most holy mother of God, we also admit; but that this is superstition or will-worship we deny, and the professor must prove, or not assert it.

The last proof of the fallibility of the church which the professor attempts to offer is, that she is not infallible, for "she is hostile to civil government."—(p. 143.) His argument is, when reduced to form,—the church that claims and exercises temporal authority is hostile to civil government; but the Roman Catholic Church claims and exercises temporal authority; therefore she is hostile to civil government. The church that is hostile to civil government is fallible; but the Roman Catholic Church is hostile to civil government; therefore, the Roman Catholic Church is fallible, that is, not infallible.

The church that claims and exercises supreme temporal authority is hostile to civil government, if she has received from Almighty God no grant of that temporal authority, we concede; if she has received the grant, we deny. No church which possesses, by the divine grant, temporal authority, can be hostile to civil government by claiming and exercising it, because she is herself, under God, the civil government. But the Roman Catholic Church, if she has received the grant, does thus possess the temporal authority. Therefore, if she claims and exercises that authority, she is not hostile to civil government.

The church that is hostile to all government in civil affairs is fallible, we concede; for the necessity of government in civil affairs is clearly evinced from reason; the church that is hostile only to distinct and independent civil government is fallible, we deny, for it may be that God has vested the government of civil as well as spiritual affairs in the same hands. The denial of civil government distinct from and independent of the church is a proof of fallibility

---

* The reader will find this objection replied to at length in *The Two Brothers*, ante pp. 337-352.

only on the supposition that such civil government exists by divine right. But if all government, civil as well as spiritual, is vested in the church, it does not so exist. Therefore its denial is no proof of fallibility. Moreover, the Roman Catholic Church, as we have seen, cannot be hostile to civil government, even if she claim and exercise the supreme temporal authority, if she has received it as a grant from God, the supreme ruler. But it is not proved that she claims or exercises it without such grant. Therefore it is not proved that she is hostile to civil government; and therefore, again, it is not proved that she is fallible. The professor labors to prove, that, according to Catholicity, "the pope is the vicar of the omnipotent God, invested alike with temporal power and ecclesiastical authority." (p. 147.) If so, the pope is the vicar of God in both orders, and is invested with the supreme authority in both. Then he is by divine appointment the temporal sovereign. But for the temporal sovereign to claim and exercise temporal authority is not to be hostile to the civil government, but to assert and maintain it.

But the claim of the church to "secular authority merges the state in the church. Kings and emperors, nations and communities, become merely the instruments and pliant tools of spiritual dominion."—(page 153.) What if the spiritual dominion be legitimate? All power is of God, and there is no legitimate authority not from him. Kings, emperors, nations, communities, have no right to exercise temporal authority, save as vicars of the omnipotent God, and it is only for the reason that they are such that we are under any obligation to obey them. If Almighty God has made the pope his sole vicar in both orders, obedience is due to him by all both in church and state, and then it is no objection to the church that she exacts the submission of kings, emperors, nations, communities, for they can, in such case, have no authority not derived from God through the pope. The professor, if he grant that the pope is the vicar of Almighty God in the temporal and in the spiritual order, cannot urge his objection, because in doing so he would resist the authority of the vicar of God, and therefore of God himself.

Again, if the pope be the vicar of God in both orders, the claim and exercise of the supreme temporal dominion do not merge the state in the church, for then the church is both church and state. The church could merge the state in herself by claiming and exercising temporal power, only on condition that she had received no special grant of temporal power, and claimed to exercise it solely by virtue of her grant of spiritual authority. But if she teaches, as the professor contends, that in the pope she has been invested with temporal *as well as with spiritual authority*, she does not do this, that is, does not claim the temporal as incidental to the spiritual. Therefore, even granting that she claims the supreme temporal authority, she does not and cannot merge the state in the church as a spiritual authority, which is the sense intended. This is evinced from the instance of the Papal States. The pope in regard to them is supreme in both temporals and spirituals, but they exist as a state, as a civil government, as much so as Tuscany or Sardinia.

The professor does not appear to understand the question he wishes to discuss. The spiritual order is undeniably superior to the temporal, and nothing can be legitimately concluded from the temporal to the prejudice of the spiritual. No man who has any knowledge of even natural morality can pretend that it is the prerogative of the temporal order to define or give law to the spiritual. It is not according to reason that the lower should rule the higher, the body the soul, for instance, or the state the church. To object to the church that she subjects the whole temporal order to the spiritual order, or that she makes the spiritual dominion supreme, is to make an objection which reason disavows, because it would be in principle the same as to deny the right of reason to rule the flesh, nay, the same as to deny reason itself. The church, if she is God's church, if she has received plenary spiritual authority as the vicar of the omnipotent God, must needs be superior to the state, and the state can have no authority to do aught she declares to be sinful or morally wrong, and must be bound to do whatever she declares to be required by the law of God. To allege that she subjects kings, emperors, &c., to her dominion is, then, to allege nothing against her.

The professor does not state the question properly. He begins with an assumption which he has no right to make. He assumes, that, if the church claims any authority in the temporal order, she is a usurper, and therefore cannot be infallible. He takes it for granted, then, that, if he proves that she has claimed such authority, he has disproved her infallibility. But we demand the proof from reason, that she has no authority in temporals. Till he proves this, he cannot conclude, from the fact that she claims it, that she is a usurper, and therefore fallible. It is certain from reason, since all power is of God, and there is and can be no rightful authority to govern in any order not derived mediately or immediately from him, that he *can* make the pope his sole vicar on earth in both orders, if such be his will and pleasure. If he does so, then it is also certain that the pope has the right to exercise the supreme authority in both orders, and then that, so far from his temporal authority being usurped, all authority not derived from God through him is usurpation. What the professor has to prove, then, in case he contends that the church claims the supreme temporal authority, is, not that she claims it, but that she claims it without having received it from God. If she asserts that she has received it,—since the legal presumption is in her favor, and the argument is not to prove, but to disprove, her infallibility,—he can prove that she has not received it only by proving that she has in the exercise of it violated some principle of natural justice.

We are far from conceding that the church has ever claimed or exercised temporal authority in the sense intended; but pass over that. Let it be supposed for the present that she has. What is the evidence that she has ever violated any principle of natural justice? You can arraign her only on the law of nature, before the bar of natural reason. Produce, then, the precept of the law of nature which she has violated or contradicted. We have looked carefully through all that the professor has urged, and we can find nothing that is immoral or unjust. All his proofs are reduced to this, that she claims and exercises temporal authority. Grant all this, what then? Where is your evidence that she has not rightfully claimed and exercised it? You offer none, and only work yourself up into a violent passion against her, because she has claimed and exercised it. Where is your evidence that the exercise you fancy you have proved has been contrary to the law of nature? You offer only two things; first, what you call the Jesuit's oath, and, second, the prohibition of duelling by the Council of Trent.

"Hence the Jesuit in his secret oath renounces all allegiance to all earthly powers which have not been confirmed by the Holy See."—(*ib.*) The Jesuit has no secret oath, and renounces no allegiance to the civil government. The charge is false.*

The Council of Trent condemns duelling, we grant; but is

---

*Like all members of a religious order, the Jesuits take the three it the condemnation of duelling, or duelling itself, that is contrary to the precepts of justice? Which is easier to defend,—duelling, or the church in condemning it? And who is in the wrong,—the church in condemning, or you in defending the base, cowardly, and detestable practice of single combat?

But the church does more than condemn it. According to the statute of the Council of Trent, in its twenty-fifth session, "the temporal sovereign who permits a duel to take place in his dominions is punished not only with excommunication, but with the loss of the place in which the combat occurred. The duellists and their seconds are condemned in the same statute to perpetual infamy, the loss of their goods, and deprived, if they should fall, of Christian burial, while those who are merely spectators of the scene are sentenced to eternal malediction."—(p. 152.) Well, what then? *What then?* Why, this proves that the church claims the right to exercise civil authority, nay, to inflict civil punishments; for such are the forfeiture of goods, and the loss of the place where the combat occurs. Yes, as you cite the statute, but not as it was passed by the Council of Trent.* But let that pass. If so, it is nothing to your purpose, unless the punishment prescribed is in itself unjust. Will you maintain that?

"In a conflict of power between princes and popes, the first and highest duty of all the vassals of Rome is to maintain her honor and support her claims."—(p. 153.) Suppose a conflict of power between the General Assembly of the Presbyterian Church in the United States and the civil authorities of the country, which party would the professor, as a Presbyterian minister and member of that church, support? The civil authorities? Then he either condemns his church, or raises the temporal order above the spiritual, which he expressly repudiates. Would he side with his

---

vows of perpetual poverty, chastity, and obedience; in addition to these the professed fathers, a fraction of the members of the society, make a fourth vow: "I promise, besides, especial obedience to the pope in what concerns the missions, as it is contained in the apostolic letters and in the constitution." This simply means that they bind themselves to carry the Gospel to any part of the world to which the supreme pontiff may direct; and that it has no other meaning is expressly explained by St. Ignatius in the *Declaration* annexed by him to the *Constitution*, Part V. It certainly cannot be called forswearing all allegiance to earthly powers not confirmed by the Holy See.—Crétineau-Joly, Histoire de la Compagnie de Jésus, Tome I. pp. 86, 87.—ED.

*Vide Conc. Trident. Sess. 25, cap. xix.

church, and maintain the independence of the spiritual order? Then he would recognize and act on the principle he objects to us, and we retort his objection. Suppose a conflict between an infallible church and a fallible civil government, we demand which of the two ought to yield. "But the church is not infallible." That is for you to prove. If she is infallible, she must be in the right, and then we are bound in reason to support her; if she is not infallible, we deny that we are bound to support her at all, for then she is not God's church.

"The Romish church, too, sets her face like a flint against the subjection of her spiritual officers to the legal tribunals of the state."—(*ib.*) Well, what if she does? Where is the proof that in this she is wrong? She "has positively prohibited the intolerable presumption of laymen, though kings and magistrates, of demanding oaths of allegiance from the lofty members of her hierarchy."—(*ib.*) *In case they hold nothing temporal of them*, conceded; but what then? Will the professor be good enough to demonstrate the right of the temporal authority to demand from a minister of religion an oath of allegiance in spirituals?

La Fayette is reported to have said, that, "if ever the liberties of this country should be destroyed, it would be by the machinations of the Romish priests."—(p. 154.) *Therefore* the church is fallible! La Fayette is *reported*, by whom? When? Where? What if he did say so? Was La Fayette infallible? And does it follow that the thing must be so, because La Fayette thought so? If he did once think so, it is possible that he changed his mind, for it is *reported* that he became reconciled to the church and died a Catholic, and it is well known that he was, when dying, exceedingly anxious for the services of a "Romish priest." He had probably had enough of French philosophism during his lifetime, without wishing to carry any with him into eternity.

"They are all of them [Catholic priests] sworn subjects of a *foreign* potentate."—(*ib.*) Not true. The authority of the church is catholic, not national, and can be no more *foreign* here than at Rome.

"There are peculiar principles in the constitution and polity of Rome which render it an engine of tremendous power."—(p. 159.) Who has more power than God? Because, if we admit the existence of God, we must admit his omnipotence, are we to be atheists? If the church be not God's church, she cannot possess the authority we claim for her, without danger, we concede; if she is his church, and the pope is his vicar, what have we to fear from her power more than we should have, if it were exerted immediately by God himself? We defend the church as God's church, and attempt no defence of her on the supposition that she is not his church. Prove to us that he has not instituted her, and we will abandon her; but remember that proving that she has a tremendous power is no proof to us that he has not instituted her; for it belongs not to us to say how much or how little power it is proper for him to delegate to her. The claim of similar power for a human or man-made church, like the Presbyterian, would unquestionably be dangerous, and has proved itself so in the whole history of Protestantism. But that it is dangerous in a divinely commissioned church, we know, and so does every man of common sense, is not and cannot be true; for God himself becomes our surety for the right exercise of the power, and that is sufficient.

"The doctrine of auricular confession establishes a system of espionage which is absolutely fatal to personal independence, and from the intimate connection between priests and bishops, and bishops and the pope, all the important secrets of the earth can be easily transmitted to the Vatican." This is ridiculously absurd. No priest can communicate to any person living the secrets of the confessional, and he can no more do it to his bishop or to the pope than he can to James H. Thornwell. He cannot speak, out of the confessional, of what has been told him in the confessional, even to the penitent himself. No instance of the secrets of the confessional having been betrayed has ever occurred. Even the vilest apostates have never been known to disclose what they had received under the seal of the confessional. The Catholic clergy do not record the confessions of their penitents in a book, making them a part of the records of the church, as did the former Puritan ministers of New England, as we had occasion ourselves to know from the inspection of the records of some of their churches, over which it was our misfortune to be settled as pastor.

As to the system of espionage, we all know that it was carried on to its perfection in the Congregational churches of New England; and it still existed in full vigor a few years ago in the Presbyterian churches in the Middle States, as we had personal means of knowing. In most Calvinistic churches, especially the Congregational, the Presbyterian, and the Methodist, the members are bound by a solemn covenant, a covenant frequently renewed, to *watch* over one another, which means, practically, that they shall be spies one upon another; and who that has had the misfortune to be brought up a Presbyterian has not felt that he was under perpetual surveillance, that every member, it might be, of the particular church to which he belonged was on the look-out to catch him tripping? We have ourselves had ample opportunities of learning the degree of personal independence allowed by Presbyterianism, and we never knew the meaning of personal independence till we became a Catholic. There is no comparison, in this matter of personal independence, between Catholicity and any form of Protestantism we are acquainted with, and that is saying much, if what is alleged concerning our frequent changes be not altogether untrue. Catholicity provides us all the helps we need in order to attain to Christian perfection; she exhorts, she entreats us to avail ourselves of them, and to attain to that perfection; but she throws the responsibility on our own individual consciences. Catholics, also, usually mind their own business, and attend rather to their own consciences than to those of their neighbours. Hence, you find among them very little hypocrisy. Their conduct is free, frank, natural, and, as far as we have had opportunities of observing, they generally wear their worst side outward. It needs a close and intimate acquaintance with them to know, or even to suspect their real piety and worth. This indicates any thing but the want of personal independence, and the presence of the system of espionage alleged. Indeed, the professor in bringing this charge must have argued against us from what he knows to be true of his own sect; but this is to pass from one genus to another,—not allowable in logic. Servility, slavishness, the want of personal independence, the fear to say that our souls are our own, though unquestionably characteristics of the Presbyterian, are no characteristics of the Catholic. There is a total difference between the mild and parental authority exercised by our clergy over us, and the harsh and severe tyranny notoriously exercised by Presbyterian ministers over their flocks; and it would take much to make Catholics believe it possible for a people to stand in such awe and dread of a minister of religion as Presbyterians do of their ministers. Our children are delighted to see a priest come into the house; we, when a boy, if we saw a minister coming, used to run and hide in the barn.

The professor has mentioned several other points, but they involve no principle not already met and disposed of. The great question of the mutual relation of the temporal and spiritual powers we have not discussed, for it has not lain in our way. In these essays we have not been laboring to establish the claims of the church, but to test the validity of the objections urged by the professor. We have shown that he has offered nothing that disproves, or tends to disprove, her infallibility. This is all that was required of us. That the church is hostile to civil government we deny, and could easily prove, if it were necessary. But the burden of proof is on the professor, and we are not disposed to assume it for ourselves. The church represents the spiritual order, and has exclusive jurisdiction under God, for her own children, of all questions which pertain to that order; but as the church, she has never enacted, or attempted to enact, civil laws. She asserts, undoubtedly, the independence, and if the independence, the supremacy of the spiritual order, because the spiritual order embraces every moral question, and the state is as much bound to obey the moral law as the individual; but as long as the civil government seeks the public good without violating any precept of that law, she leaves it, within its own province, free to adopt and carry out the economical or prudential policy it judges proper or expedient.

The professor alludes to the struggles which have at times occurred between the civil and ecclesiastical powers, and takes it for granted that in these struggles the civil power was always in the right, and the church in the wrong. It is singular how readily Protestants, when they wish to deny the infallibility of the church, assume it for individuals and for civil government. But civil government is confessedly fallible. The simple fact of a conflict between the two powers is, therefore, no evidence that the right is against the church. Indeed, the conflict itself is a presumption that the state is in the wrong; because the presumption is always in favor of the superior order. Do our Protestant friends ever reflect on the distrust which they manifest of their own pretended churches, when they assume that right must needs be, in every contest, on the side of the temporal authority? Do they remark that they prove themselves thus to be either courtiers or infidels? Even if the church were only a human institution, it would not follow that she would not be in the right in warring against political tyrants.

We certainly have no respect for Presbyterianism, and yet, if we should find the state, by virtue of its own authority, attempting to suppress it, we should side with Presbyterianism against the state; for we hold the utter incompetency of the state in spirituals, and we no more concede its right to sit in judgment on Presbyterianism than we do its right to sit in judgment on Catholicity. The question is one which belongs to the spiritual authority, and the state, in its own right, has and can have nothing to do with it.

It perhaps has never occurred to the professor that it might be profitable to investigate those struggles which afford him so much matter of virulent but foolish declamation against the church. In fact, the popes, in their contests with the civil powers, need no apology. Judged even as a human power, they were always in the right, on the side of justice and humanity, defending the cause of the oppressed, and putting forth their power only to vindicate the rights of conscience, to succor the weak, to console the afflicted, and to protect the friendless. We said all this, and even more, while yet in the ranks of Protestants and far from dreaming that we should one day be a Catholic. We grant that the pope has excommunicated princes and nobles, deposed kings and emperors, and absolved their subjects from their allegiance; but in this he has only done his duty as the spiritual father of Christendom, and what was required by humanity as well as religion. These princes were his spiritual subjects, amenable to his authority by the law of the church which they acknowledged, and by the constitution of their own states. He was their legal judge, had the right to summon them before him, and to cut them off, if he saw proper, from the communion of the faithful, and excommunication of itself worked virtual deposition. In absolving subjects from their allegiance, he usurped no authority, for he was the legal judge in the case; for whether the allegiance continued or had ceased presented a case of conscience, of which, as sovereign pontiff, he had supreme jurisdiction, and because he was by all parties the acknowledged umpire between princes and their subjects. But he never absolved from their allegiance the subjects of infidel princes, or of any princes not Catholic, or bound to be Catholic by the constitution of their states, as the kings and queens of Great Britain are bound, since 1688, to be Protestant.

But what, in fact, was the absolution granted, and in

what cases has the pope exercised, or claimed, the right to grant it? Has the pope ever claimed the right to absolve from their allegiance the subjects of a legitimate prince, who reigns justly, according to the laws and constitution of his state? Never. In every such case he impresses upon his spiritual children the duty of obedience. But the obligation between prince and subject is reciprocal. If the subject is bound to obey the prince, the prince is bound to protect the subject. This is implied in the very nature of the social compact. The people are not for the prince, but the prince is for the people. The authority of the prince is not a personal franchise or right, but a trust, and he is bound to exercise it according to the conditions on which it is committed to him. Government exists, not for the good of the governors, but for the good of the governed. The true prince is the servant of his subjects. Government is instituted for the common good, and the moment it ceases to consult the common good, or the public good, it forfeits its rights. The tyrant, the oppressor, has and can have no right to reign, and therefore no right to exact obedience. His subjects cease to be subjects to him, and are free—in a lawful manner—to resist, and even depose him; for resistance to tyrants, if the manner of the resistance be just, is obedience to God. When a prince becomes a tyrant, when he oppresses his subjects, and tramples on the rights of our common humanity, he breaks the compact between him and his subjects, and by so doing releases them from their allegiance. Hence our Congress of 1776 after having alleged George III. to be a tyrant, conclude,—" Therefore ...... these United Colonies are, and of right ought to be, free and independant states; and they *are absolved from all allegiance* to the British crown." Now suppose the subjects of a prince, feeling themselves aggrieved, oppressed, complain to the Holy Father, the judge recognized by both parties in the case, that their prince has broken the compact, violated his oath of office, and become a tyrant; suppose the Holy Father entertains the complaint, and summons both parties to plead before him, and, after a patient hearing of the cause, gives judgment against the prince, declares him to have forfeited his rights, and that his subjects are absolved from their allegiance, what would there be in all this to which reason could object? Well, this is precisely the kind of absolution the popes have granted, and never have they deposed a prince or absolved his subjects, except in cases precisely similar to the one here supposed. He merely declares the law, and applies it to the facts of the case presented. The absolution itself simply gives a legal character to a fact which already exists. The necessity of some such authority as that which Protestants complain of in the popes is widely and deeply felt in modern society, and various substitutes for it, such as a congress of nations, have been suggested or attempted, but without any favorable results. Having rejected the pope as the natural and legal umpire between the prince and his subjects, we find ourselves reduced to the dilemma, either of passive obedience and non-resistance to tyrants, or of revolution, which denies the right of government, renders order impracticable, and resolves society into primitive chaos. To deny the right to resist the tyrant is to doom the people to hopeless slavery; to assert it, and yet leave to each individual the right to judge of the time, the means, and the mode of resistance, is disorder, no-governmentism, the worst form of despotism. In the "dark ages," men were able to avoid either alternative. By recognizing the pope as umpire, who, by his character and position, as head of the church which embraced all nations, was naturally, not to say divinely, fitted to be impartial and just, they practically secured the right of resistance to tyranny, without undermining legitimate authority. It will be long before modern nations will be wise enough to recognize how much they have lost by what they call their progress.

For ourselves, we thank God that there was formerly a power on earth that was able to depose tyrants, and to step in between the people and their oppressors. We are not among those who are afraid to glory in the boldness and energy of those great popes who made crowned heads shake, and princes hold their breath. Our heart leaps with joy when we see St. Peter smite the oppressor of the church or of his people to the earth, and if we have ever felt any regret, it has been at the slowness of the Holy Father to smite, or at his want of power to smite with more instant effect. Even when a Protestant, we learned to revere the calumniated Hildebrands, Innocents, and Bonifaces, those noble and saintly defenders of innocence, protectors of the helpless, and humblers of crowned tyrants and ruthless nobles. O, how slow even we Catholics are to do them justice! How little do we reflect on the deep debt of gratitude we owe them! O, dumb be the tongue that would rail against the popes or apologize for their firm resistance to the usurpation of the temporal authorities! Alas! how often in the history of modern Europe have we seen them, under God, the last hope of the world, the only solace of the afflicted, the sole resource of the wronged and down-trodden! Alas! it is precisely because of their noble defence of religion and freedom, of their fidelity to God and to man, that they have been calumniated, and the world has been filled with the outcries of tyrants, and their minions and dupes, against them.

That the interposition of the sovereign pontiffs in temporal affairs often occasioned much disturbance, and even civil wars, we are not disposed to deny; but on them who made the interposition necessary must rest the responsibility. In this world, it often happens that right cannot be peacefully asserted and maintained, and tyranny proves a curse, not only while it is unresisted, but even when resisted, and successfully resisted. We cannot permit a band of depredators to go unresisted, because we must disturb them by resisting them. Injustice, iniquity, can never be redressed, the tyrant can never be deposed and the legitimate sovereign restored, without a combat, and often a long and bloody one. Even our Lord himself told us to think not that he had come to send peace on the earth, but a sword rather. But shall we, therefore, make no efforts to right the wronged, to save justice and humanity from utter shipwreck? Let no man who glories in the revolutionary principle, who boasts of being a lover of freedom and the progress of mankind, pretend it. We are no revolutionists; we hold ourselves bound in conscience to obey the legal authority; but we acknowledge no obligation to obey the oppressor, and let the competent authority but declare him an oppressor and summon us to the battle-field, and we are ready to obey, to bind on our armor, rush in where blows fall thickest and fall heaviest, let the disturbance be what it may. We are, thank God, Roman Catholics, and therefore love freedom and justice, and dare not, when called upon, to shrink from defending them against any and every enemy, at any and every sacrifice.

The professor contends that the church is hostile to civil government; we would respectfully ask him if he has reflected, that, without her, civil government becomes impracticable. How, without her as umpire between government and government, and between prince and subject, and without her as a spiritual authority to command the obedience of the subject and the justice of the prince, will he be able to secure the independence of nations, and wise and just government? Will he learn from experience? Let him, then, read modern history. The age in politics discards the church. Protestantism for three hundred years has been the religion of nearly a third, and, in politics, of the whole of Europe. Three hundred years is a fair time for an experiment. Well, what is the result? *Despotism* on the one hand, and *anarchy* on the other. There is not, at this moment, a single well-organized civil government on the whole Eastern continent, and only our own on the Western. The government of Great Britain may seem to be an exception for the Old World, but it is a perfect oligarchy; it fails to secure the common weal; enriches the few and impoverishes the many; and its very existence is threatened by a mob which the ever-increasing poverty of the industrial classes hourly augments, and grim want is rendering desperate. Our own government is sustained solely by the accidental advantages of the country, consisting chiefly in our vast quantities of unoccupied fertile lands, which absorb our rapidly increasing population, and form a sort of safety-valve for its superfluous energy. Strip us of these lands, or let them be filled up so that our expanding population should find its limit, and be compelled to recoil upon itself, and our institutions would not stand a week.

Here in the present state of the world, hardly to be paralleled in universal history,—when old governments are either all fallen or tottering ready to fall; when all authority is cast off, and law is despised; when the streets of the most civilized cities run with the blood of citizens shed by citizens, and the lurid light of burning cottage and castle gleams on the midnight sky; when saintly prelates bearing the olive-branch of peace are shot down by infuriated ruffians; when murder and rapine hardly seek concealment, and all civilization seems to be thrown back into the savagism of the forest,—here we may read the wisdom of those who discard the church, and denounce her as hostile to civil government,—the wisdom of the doctrine which a scoffing and unbelieving age opposes to the truth which Almighty God has revealed, and to the lessons of universal experience. Alas! how true it is, that God permits strong delusions to blind the impious and the licentious, that they may bring swift destruction upon themselves!

But it is time to bring our remarks to a close. We have

examined the principal arguments which Mr. Thornwell has brought forward to prove the fallibility of the church, and we leave our readers to judge for themselves whether we have not proved, that, in every instance, they are either unsound in principle or irrelevant, proving nothing but the professor's own malice or ignorance. The professor has made numerous assumptions, numerous bold assertions, but in no instance has he done better than simply to assume the point he was to prove. He has declaimed loudly against the church, he has said many hard things against her, but he has harmed only himself and his brethren. We now take our leave of him. We have done all we proposed. We have vindicated the Catholic argument for the disputed books drawn from the infallibility of the church, which is enough, without the testimonies of the fathers, although we have even these. We regret that the task of answering the professor had not been assumed by Dr. Lynch himself, who would have accomplished it so much better than we have done. Yet it was hardly fitting that he should have assumed it. He could not, with a proper respect for himself and his profession, have replied to such a vituperative performance as Mr. Thornwell's book. We were brought up a Presbyterian, and have been accustomed from our youth to the sort of stuff we have had to deal with, and therefore have been able to reply without feeling the degradation we should have felt, had we all our lifetime been accustomed to the courtesy and candor of Catholic controversialists.

LITERARY POLICY OF THE CHURCH OF ROME.*

[From Brownson's Quarterly Review for January, 1845.]

THE journal, the title of which we have placed at the head of this article, is the organ of the Episcopal Methodists of this country, and is conducted with considerable spirit and ability. If not remarkable for profound erudition and severe logic, it is at least quite commendable for its rhetoric; and if we miss in its pages the simplicity and unction of the earlier Methodists, we still find its papers characterized by a liveliness and freshness which contrast favorably with the more elaborate essays in religious periodicals of much higher pretensions. It is thoroughly Protestant, and holds the benighted Papists in due horror. Its number for July last contains an article against the Catholic Church, which, for its hearty hatred of Catholicity, and its vituperative character, if not for its strength and energy of expression, would have gladdened the heart of even Luther himself. Although the article is nothing but a string of false charges, or misrepresentations, from beginning to end, we have thought it would not be amiss to notice it, because its subject is one of great importance, on which the church of Christ is perpetually traduced by its enemies and persecutors.

"It is proposed in this paper," says the *Methodist Quarterly Review*, "to exhibit the proof that the church of Rome has ever waged a deadly warfare upon the liberty of the press, and upon literature, and that her expurgatory and prohibitory policy is perpetuated to the present hour, not only against the truth of revelation, but equally against the truth in nature and in science, both learning and religion having been the doomed victims of her perennial despotism."— p. 348.

The analysis of this passage gives us four distinct charges against the church of Rome, namely: 1. Hostility to the Liberty of the Press; 2. Hostility to Literature; 3. Hostility to Science; 4. Hostility to Revelation and Religion.

---

* *Methodist Quarterly Review, for July, 1844.* New York. Art. II. *Literary Policy of the Church of Rome.*

The first three of these charges, even if well founded, are urged with an ill grace by a Methodist. If we have been rightly informed, the Methodist press is itself under the strict surveillance of the bishops and elders, and the Methodist people have, we believe, great scruples about purchasing books, even of their own denomination, when not published by their own book society, which monopolizes the principal part of their publishing business. We even remember the time when the Methodist ministers were proverbial for their ignorance, and distinguished for their contempt for human science and learning. A better feeling is now, we are happy to admit, beginning to obtain among them, and the denomination has succeeded in establishing a few very respectable schools of its own; but we have not yet heard of a Methodist in this country of any remarkable literary attainments, and we are quite sure that no Methodist, clergyman or layman, has as yet made any valuable or permanent contribution either to literature or to science. It betrays, then, a great want of modesty, on the part of a Methodist editor, to bring charges of hostility either to literature or science against any portion of the community, however true in itself such a charge might be. We are commanded to cast the splinter out of our own eye, before we undertake to pull the mote out of our brother's eye. But this by the way. We proceed to take up and consider, in their order, each of the four charges preferred.

1. The *Methodist Quarterly Review* charges the church of Rome with having ever waged a deadly warfare upon the liberty of the press, and promises to exhibit the proofs which sustain it; but these proofs it seems to have forgotten. The editor has apparently presumed his readers prepared in advance to believe any thing which can be said against the Roman Church, and therefore ready to take the assertion itself for proof. He does not adduce a single fact to prove his assertion, and, more than all that, he cannot. We deny his assertion, and defy him to lay his finger on a single act of the Roman Catholic Church, which indicates the least hostility on her part to a free press. He tells us, and he enters into a long and labored argument to prove, that the church is now what she always was, and always was what she is now. For this we thank him. We not only concede, but we contend, that she is now what she always was, and always was what she now is, and always will be to the end of time. We hold the church to be immutable, like Him whom she

represents. Will it be pretended, that, prior to the sixteenth century, the church, as the church, ever waged war upon the liberty of the press? Prior to the invention of printing, there was no press, in the modern sense of the term; how could the church, then, be said to be hostile to its freedom? Is the Methodist reviewer acquainted with the writings of the fathers and monks of the middle ages? Does he find in them any want of freedom of thought or of expression? Prior to the invention of printing, the office of the modern press was mainly supplied by the pulpit. Did ever press speak freer than the old Catholic pulpit, when the humble priest dared address the monarch on his throne as a man and a sinner, and the cowled monk feared not to reprove even the pope himself? But the church has not changed, and therefore, if it was not hostile to the freedom of the press then, it is not now.

Printing itself was invented before the reformation, in good old Catholic times, and by a Catholic. Its glory belongs to Catholics, not to Protestants. And who were the first to welcome it, and to sustain the first printers? The dignitaries of the Catholic Church. The first printers in Italy, companions of Faust, were received and protected by the pope. The earliest patrons of Caxton, the first printer in England, were Thomas Milling, Bishop of Hereford, and the Abbot of Westminster Abbey, and it was in Westminster Abbey that he established his first printing office. It was by the aid of the Bishop of Holun, that Mathieson was enabled to introduce printing into Iceland, and whoever knows any thing of the subject knows, that the church of Rome has always encouraged literature and the free multiplication of books.

But the *Methodist Quarterly Review* adduces the instance of expurgatory indexes, &c., as proof of hostility on the part of the church of Rome to the liberty of the press. The existence of such indexes we of course admit; but so far as they concern merely the pope's own temporal dominions, they come not within the scope of our present argument. The temporal court of Rome is to be judged the same as any other court, and the church is no more responsible for its acts than it is for the acts of the court of France, of Spain, or even of England. The expurgatory indexes concern us, as members of the Roman Catholic Church, only so far as they are designed for the instruction of the faithful throughout the world. But what, after all, are these expurgatory indexes, about which we hear so much, and which are such frightful monsters to our Protestant brethren? They are simply matters of discipline, prepared by the highest pastoral authority in the church,—not to encroach on the liberty of the press, for no book is likely to find a place in the index, if not published,—but to guard the faithful against the destructive effects of the licentiousness of the press. This is all.

Nobody, we presume, no matter of what religious persuasion, can recommend to all persons the indiscriminate reading of all manner of books and tractates which may be published. There are books, and books even not without some value when read by persons prepared to profit by them, which no prudent parent would put into the hands of his children. It is not every book that is suitable for every person's reading. A full-grown man, well grounded in his principles, and strengthened and confirmed by divine grace, may perhaps read without injury almost any publication; but what Christian father would not tremble to find his son, some eighteen or twenty years of age, reading Paine's *Age of Reason*, Volney's *Ruins*, or Baron d'Holbach's *Système de la Nature?* or what Christian mother would willingly see her daughter reading Wolstonecroft's *Rights of Woman*, or the novels of Paul de Kock, Sir Bulwer Lytton, George Sand, or Eugene Sue, before experience, and maturity of thought and sentiment, had secured her against the subtle poison they contain? Books are companions, and bad books are as dangerous as any other species of companions. Evil communications corrupt good manners, and we may be corrupted by reading bad books as well as by frequenting bad company. Everybody knows this, and every father of a family, if he deserve at all the name, has virtually an *index expurgatorius*, which he does his best to enforce on all intrusted to his care. All admit its importance, so far as concerns children or young persons. Would the Methodist bishops and elders tolerate Universalist, Unitarian, *Papistical*, or infidel books in their Sunday-school libraries, or recommend them to the members of their flock for family reading? Do not the American Sunday-school Union alter, expurgate, or amend the books they publish, to make them conform to their standard of orthodoxy and propriety? Do not the laws of Massachusetts, New York, nay, of every state in the Union that has a public school system, institute an expurgatory index, by prohibiting all sectarian books from being used in the schools, or introduced into the common school libraries? And so far as relates to common schools in this commonwealth, what is our board of education, with its learned secretary, but a "congregation of the Index"?

In all communities there are large numbers who are children as long as they live. Every clergyman, no matter of what denomination, can point to not a few in his congregation, who are by no means qualified for reading with profit, or without detriment, all manner of books or publications which may be issued; and we know no clergyman that does not use his utmost influence to prevent the members of his flock from reading such works as in his judgment may prove injurious to them. Indeed, we see not how he could answer it to his conscience and to his God, if he should not. Is he not, by virtue of his office, set as an overseer, to watch over, guard, and promote their spiritual welfare? Our early acquaintance with the Methodists, with whom in a good measure we were brought up, has led us to believe that their ministers are by no means remiss in this duty. Indeed, all the sects, unless we must except Unitarians and Universalists, do their best to prevent their respective members from reading publications hostile to their peculiar tenets. The Methodists, Baptists, Presbyterians, and Congregationalists, are as strict in this respect as Catholics themselves. Each denomination has an expurgatory index, as much as the church of Rome,— only it does not publish it,—and an index equally exclusive, to say the least. What, then, but rank hypocrisy, is this outcry against the Catholic Church? Wherein is her peculiar offence? Is it in the fact, that she *publishes* her index for the guidance of the faithful throughout the world, and does not profess one thing and do another?

But, as we have said, the index is merely an affair of discipline, and simply points out the books not approved by the church, which are not sound in the faith, or which cannot be read without danger to piety or morals. Yet the reading of the books placed in the index is not absolutely prohibited; it is simply remitted to the discretion of the bishops or pastors, and may be allowed to any one, when any good reason can be assigned why it should be.

But we are told, or may be told, that the church of Rome establishes a rigid censorship of the press. Not the *church* of Rome, but the *court* of Rome; and not for the church universal, but for the pope's temporal dominions. How rigid this censorship may be we know not, nor does it concern us, who are not temporal subjects of the pope, to inquire. The pope, as temporal prince, is an independent sovereign, and is at liberty to govern his subjects in his own way, as much so as any other temporal prince. But it must be remembered that this question of the censorship of the press has two sides, or at least has something to be said in its favor; for there is no country on earth that tolerates the unlimited freedom of the press. There are some Protestant countries in Europe,—Prussia, for instance,—which subject the press to the most rigid censorship; so rigid, that the censors have been known to erase the word liberty, as " treasonable." England, indeed, boasts that her press is free; she establishes no censorship; and yet she restrains its liberty by treating as blasphemous libels the publications which contain certain doctrines. George Houston,—at present, we believe, one of the editors of the *New York Herald*,—was imprisoned two years and a half in London, for publishing an infidel work, entitled *Ecce Homo*. Robert Taylor, also, was long imprisoned in Oakham jail for writing certain infidel works. We, in this country, claim to have a free press; and yet Abner Kneeland, a few years since, was imprisoned in Boston for writing a certain newspaper paragraph; and one Dr. Knowlton was also, a short time before, imprisoned for publishing a certain infamous book. There are publications which no civilized people can tolerate, and which no Christian people can suffer to circulate freely. All have their *index expurgatorius*. Some place more works in it, others fewer. The question between them is not one of principle, but one of more or less. The only difference in principle, too, between those nations which profess to have a free press, and those which have a censorship, is, that the latter endeavour to *prevent* the mischief from being done, while the former only seek to punish the authors of it, after they have done it. Which is the wiser course we shall not undertake to decide. But one thing we will say, the licentiousness of the press should alarm every one who regards the moral and spiritual health of the people. The floods of obscene and corrupting novels and other cheap publications, which have of late inundated the country, are not to pass off without leaving terrible waste and destruction behind; and unless the moral portion of the community, especially the clergy, in the bosom of their several flocks, use their utmost endeavours, and exert all their pastoral authority, to prevent these works from being read by the young, the unsuspecting, and the impressible, the most frightful corruption of morals and manners will soon spread over the whole land. The *Methodist Quarterly Review*, instead of bringing false charges against the church of Rome, would do a much greater service to God and the country, if it would use its influence to guard our young community from the the blasting effects of the recent licentiousness of the Boston and New York presses. Here is an object worthy of all its holy zeal.

But the *Methodist Quarterly Review* seeks to establish its proposition by alleging that the church of Rome wages a deadly war upon liberty of mind and conscience. That the church of Rome teaches, that conscience needs to be enlightened by the word of God before it can be followed as a safe guide, we freely admit; and that she also teaches, that private judgment in interpreting the word of God or articles of faith should yield to the church, is by no means denied. Every Catholic believes the Holy Catholic Church infallible and authoritative. He believes that Christ has instituted a ministry which is competent to teach by authority, and competent because Christ is always with it, enabling it to teach the truth, and preventing it from teaching error. So far as submission to this authority is a restriction on freedom of mind, the Catholic Church undoubtedly restricts it. But this no Catholic feels to be any restriction at all; for to him the decision of the church is the highest conceivable evidence of truth; and it therefore guides him to the truth, instead of restraining him from embracing it. He feels it his blessed privilege to have an authority which cannot err, to decide for him, and set him right, where his own reason might lead him astray.

But must not this yielding to authority make one a mental slave, destroy all mental vigor, and tend to reduce or retain one in intellectual imbecility, in the most brutish ignorance? Certainly, if the authority be human, or that of any one of our sects. The full force of this reply can be understood by none but a Catholic. The Catholic Church is divine, it is a supernatural institution, and supernaturally sustained and protected. It teaches all truth, that is, all truth pertaining to religion and morals. It decides positively on no other subject. It leaves, then, necessarily, the human mind free to discover and defend the truth on all subjects; and both truth and *error* on all subjects but the fundamental principles of religion and morals. Is not this liberty enough to satisfy any sober friend of freedom? If you run athwart these fundamental principles, you are unquestionably arrested; but why arrested? Because the church will not tolerate your truth? Not at all. For all truth is homogeneous, and therefore, so long as you follow the truth, you cannot run athwart her decisions. You are arrested, then, because the church cannot tolerate your error. You are free to advocate *all* truth, but not free to advocate *all* error. Here is all the restriction placed upon you; and surely this leaves ample room for the freest thought, and the fullest investigation of all subjects.

But any such restriction, imposed by any one of the sects, would, we grant, have the effect supposed; because no sect is catholic, that is, no sect teaches all truth, and the authority of the sect is confessedly human. There are many religious truths which the Methodists, for instance, do not accept; and they have, moreover, no promise of the continued presence of the Holy Ghost to lead them into all truth. They do not even pretend that their decisions on matters of faith are the result of any but human wisdom. In subjecting us to them, they would subject us to *human* authority in matters of faith and conscience, which is the grossest tyranny; they would also debar us from entertaining and defending all truth not embraced within their defective symbols. We should then be really reduced to slavery, and brutish ignorance and mental imbecility would quickly follow. The government of God is freedom, that of man is tyranny.

But why all this clamor against the Roman Catholic Church as to freedom of mind? To hear our sectarians, one would think that they were the friends of freedom of thought and conscience. They talk of the right of private judgment, as if they really recognized it, and suffered every man to be his own judge of what is or is not true. All delusion! There is no religious denomination on earth, that allows unlimited freedom of mind, or the unrestricted right of private judgment. The Protestant rule is deceptive and self-contradictory. All Protestant sects professedly recognize the right of private judgment, but all in the same breath deny it. They affirm the Scriptures of the Old and New Testaments to be the word of God, and the sole rule of faith and practice. Now, here is an authority set up at once above private judgment; for no private judgment is permitted to decide against the word of God.

But "private judgment is free to interpret the word of

God." No such thing. The written word does not interpret itself, and is no rule till interpreted. Each sect puts its own interpretation on it; and that interpretation each member of the sect must accept or acquiesce in, on pain of heresy and excommunication. The Methodists excommunicate from their communion the member who lapses into what they call heresy, and so do all the other sects. We ourselves, many years ago, were excommunicated, and without even a hearing or a notice, by the Universalists, for having embraced views not quite in harmony with theirs. Even the Unitarians, who have, with us, no written creed, if they do not formally disfellowship the member of their denomination, who interprets the word of God differently from the interpretation which they tacitly adopt, excommunicate virtually, by turning the cold shoulder, by refusing ministerial intercourse, by nods, winks, hints, suggestions, private denunciations, &c., &c. Is it not so? That it is, many of our friends have had experimental proof. Nothing is more false than this hypocritical cant of Protestants about the right of private judgment. It means ever only that "you are free to judge that what I believe is true, and what I disbelieve is false." Nothing more. Every Protestant sect has persecuted those of its members who attempted to exercise practically the right of private judgment, and in every country where any one Protestant sect has been strong enough to establish its faith by law, it has done so. The first instance on record, we believe, of absolute civil liberty in regard to religious faith, is the Catholic colony of Maryland, founded by Lord Baltimore; and the Protestants no sooner gained the ascendency in that colony than they established the Protestant religion by law. The Puritans were notorious for their intolerance, and we have heard of their banishing, branding, imprisoning, and hanging persons, for presuming to exercise the right of private judgment. The Anglican Church has been from the first a persecuting church, and her history in this respect is the blackest page in the whole history of humanity; and even the evangelical bishop of the diocese of Vermont has recently proposed the establishment of a council, one part of whose duty it shall be to exercise a censorship of the press. Surely, Protestants, who are notorious the world over for their intolerance and their hostility to freedom of thought and conscience, should not talk about mental slaves and the liberty of the press. Let them give some proofs that they themselves comprehend and love even the first elements of freedom, before they bring railing accusations against others.

II. But, continues the reviewer, "the church of Rome has ever waged a deadly war upon literature." We do not know precisely in what sense the reviewer here uses the term, *church of Rome;* but we presume he will not object to our understanding by the church of Rome, the whole *Latin* Church, for at least one thousand years next preceding the reformation, and all particular churches which have since continued in communion with the see of Rome, and to acknowledge the pope as the visible head of the church. The charge, then, is, that the whole Latin Church, from the sixth century to the sixteenth, and the whole Roman Catholic Church since, as the church, has waged an unceasing and deadly warfare upon literature.

Now, the reviewer not only makes this charge, but he declares it the design of his paper "to exhibit the proofs" of it. Well, what proofs does he exhibit? Not a proof,— not the shadow of a proof; nor does he even attempt to bring any proof, but the assertion of hostility to a free press, which we have proved to be groundless. If the church has ever waged this war upon literature, how happens it that the reviewer can adduce no decree of council, universal, national, or provincial; no papal bull; nor, at least, some sermon, charge, letter, or other writing, of some cardinal or bishop, condemning literature and literary pursuits? It is strange, if this war has been unceasingly waged for at least thirteen hundred years, all over Europe, and in the face of all the world, that our reviewer can find no proof of the fact, but an unfounded assertion, and an unwarrantable inference from certain expurgatory indexes. Since he can find none, it is fair to presume none exists.

The simple truth is, as every one knows, who is at all acquainted with the literary history of Christendom, that the Catholic Church has been, from the first, the warm friend and generous patron of literature. A charge more false, more directly in the face and eyes of well-known truth, it is impossible to invent; and our Methodist friend, if he had knowledge enough of literature to be entitled even to take the sacred name upon his lips, would not have dared to make the statement he has; for we are not willing to consider him one of those who are given up "to believe a lie that they may be damned."

The early fathers of the church, St. Justin Martyr, Clemens Alexandrinus, Origen, Tertullian, St. Basil, Lactantius, St. John Chrysostom, the Gregories, St. Jerome, St. Augustine, and others, were not only the most learned men of their times, but can well take rank with the most learned men of the palmiest days of Greece and Rome. They loved learning, and encouraged it both by precept and example; and have always been held in the highest honor in the Roman Catholic Church, and, with one or two exceptions, of almost apostolic authority. It is idle to pretend that a church which reveres these noble and enlightened men as the glory of their race, and studies diligently their works, is hostile to literature. To a Christian heart and understanding, literature does not consist merely in an acquaintance with the poets, comedians, orators, and philosophers of pagan Greece and Rome. The Catholic has never condemned the study even of these, but he has always felt that the Christian literature of the early ages of the church was richer, and more befitting a follower of Jesus. And herein is the difference between Catholics and Protestants. With Protestants, the first names you hear are Homer, Virgil, Horace, Cicero, and Cæsar. With a Catholic, the first names you hear are the holy fathers, St. Jerome, St. Augustine, St. Basil, St. John Chrysostom, St. Gregory Nazianzen, St. Gregory Nyssen, St. Leo, and St. Gregory the Great. He has poets, orators, philosophers, of his own, who belong to the church, by whose labors the church, under God, was built up and sustained, and enabled to achieve its immortal conquests over Jewish prejudice, pagan darkness, idolatry, and corruption, and over pestilential heresies and destructive schisms. If he has preferred these to the Greek and Roman classics, it is to his honor, and proves that he has never been willing to sacrifice his faith as a Christian upon the altars of Jupiter, Apollo, Bacchus, or Cybele. It proves that the Christian life-blood has ever continued to circulate in his veins, and his heart to beat quicker at the mention of the cross of Christ. It proves that he has felt himself connected by one inner life to the whole army of martyrs, and, through the blessing of God, made one of the holy communion of saints. He needed not to wander to Greece or Rome, to linger in the Academy, the Lyceum, the Garden, or the Portico, to refresh his soul with the words of life. He inherited, in the sacred literature of his church, a wealth which made all that pagan antiquity had to offer appear poor, mean, and contemptible. Of all this our poor Protestants know nothing, feel nothing. Having left their father's house, and spent their portion of the heavenly inheritance in their riotous living, sectarian jars, and theological janglings, ready to starve, they would fain feed their famished souls with the husks of heathenism. O, would they could once remember that in their father's house there is bread enough and to spare!

But there never has been a period in the history of the church, when the valuable literary works even of Greece and Rome were not studied, and appreciated at their full value. We are indebted to the old monks, in their cloisters, for the preservation of all that remains to us of Greek and Roman literature. The monks and the secular clergy, though they never placed this literature above the Sacred Scriptures and the writings of the fathers, yet made themselves acquainted with it, and probably even in the "Dark Ages" appreciated it more justly than we do. But even if they did not, does it follow that they were hostile to literature? Cannot a man love and encourage literature, without loving and encouraging the study of the Greek and Roman classics? Is there no literature for us, but that of Greece and Rome? Even admitting this gross absurdity, who, we ask, revived the study of Greek and Roman letters? We hear of the dark ages, and then of the revival of letters. But when was this revival, and by whom was it effected? It took place about a century before the birth of Protestantism, and was effected by the encouragement and patronage of the Roman Catholic Church. It was the pope who provided an asylum at Rome for the Greek scholars who fled from the Mahometan conquerers of Constantinople. Very little has been learned of ancient Greek and Roman literature, which was not well known in Western Europe long before the reformation.

But we do not rest here. We will not resign the so-called "Dark Ages." We dare affirm that no period in the history of our race, of equal length, can be pointed out, so remarkable for its intellectual and literary activity, as the thousand years dating from the beginning of the sixth century, and extending to the commencement of the sixteenth. These are the thousand years of what Protestants would call the peculiar reign of Popery. This period opens with the entire dissolution of the old world. The northern barbarians have overthrown the western empire, and seated themselves permanently on its ruins. The old world has disappeared, and nothing remains standing to connect the present with the past, but the ecclesiastical society. Greek and Roman civilization, its arts, sciences, and refinements, save what are retained by the church, are swept away. Ignorance and barbarism have resumed their ancient dominion. In the midst of this ignorance and barbarism, on the ruins of a past world, when all is to be begun anew, the church takes her stand. Now, in order to judge fairly of what the church has done for the human race, whether in reference to religion, morals, literature, or science, we must ascertain what she attempted with the rude materials on which she was obliged to work, and what she actually effected. We must compare the state of European society at the beginning of the sixth century with what it was at the beginning of the sixteenth. The question to be decided is not, whether, during this period, the state of society, morally or intellectually considered, was perfect, or all that could be desired; but whether the church constantly exerted herself for its advancement, and whether, at the end of the period, an advance had been effected as great as under the circumstances could be reasonably expected. Judged in this way, the church, to say the least, has nothing to fear. During those thousand years, nearly all was effected that has been effected for modern society, and we fearlessly assert that there is not a Protestant country in Europe that can at this moment show a social state in advance of what had then been reached.

But our concern is now more especially with literature. It must be remembered that literature in Greece and Rome, in their palmiest days, was but slightly diffused. Even under the Roman Empire, when some schools were established by the public, there was nothing like a public system of education. At the commencement of the sixth century, as we may learn from Guizot and others, the civil schools of the empire were nearly all destroyed, and theological schools had not yet been established. Now, if the church had been hostile to literature, here was the precise state of things she would have desired. If ignorance was what she loved and wished to perpetuate, here was ignorance to her heart's content, and the condition of its perpetuation. But what is the conduct of the church? She immediately sets to work to establish schools, the great monasterial schools, cathedral or episcopal schools, and parochial schools.

So early as 529, we find the Council of Vaison in France urging the establishment of country schools.* In the beginning of the sixth century arose the cathedral schools in Spain, where children, offered by their parents, were to be educated under the eye of the bishop, and to dwell under one roof.† In the same century arose, too, the schools of the Benedictine monks, which soon spread themselves over the whole Western Church. Of these, the most celebrated was that of the island of Lerins, founded by St. Honoratus, and which produced Maximus, Faustus, Hilary, Cæsarius, Vincent, Eucherius, Salvius, and many other eminent men and scholars. The school of Seville, in Spain, was justly renowned. Of this school, Mariana, the Spanish historian, says, "that, as if from a citadel of wisdom, many came forth illustrious, both for probity of manners, and for learning. St. Isidore gave this precept for this and all similar schools in Spain,—'*Cura nutriendorum parvulorum pertinebit ad virum, quem elegerit pater, sanctum sapientemque atque ætate gravem, informantem parvulos non solum studiis literarum sed etiam documentis magisterioque virtutum.*'" ‡ Before the close of the fifteenth century, nearly all Western Europe was covered over with schools. This is especially true of England and many parts of Germany. All the great renowned universities of Europe were founded prior to the reformation, such as the universities of Bologna, Paris, Oxford, and Cambridge. In England, the monasterial, cathedral, and parochial schools, nearly all of which were destroyed by the reformation, brought education within the reach of the great mass of the people. Nor less solicitous was the church for the multiplication of books and the establishment of libraries. Cassiodorus had early set the example to the monasteries, by placing his own splendid library in Monte Cassino. Nearly all the monasteries were graced and enriched by valuable libraries. In each monastery was a *scriptorium*, and a number of monks employed in copying and binding manuscripts. Mabillon speaks of the immense manual labor exercised by the Cistercians and Carthusians in copy-

*Conc. Vasens. II. Can. i.

†Concil. Toletan. II. Cap. i.

‡See *Mores Catholici*. Mr. Digby has collected, in his second volume, ample proofs of the position we are endeavoring to maintain; and we refer the reader generally to the work, for a reference to the authorities on which we rely for many of our own statements.

ing manuscripts and in writing them out for the public. "Be not troubled at the labor through fatigue," says Thomas à Kempis, in addressing youth; "for God is the cause of every good work, who will render to every man his recompense, according to his pious intention, in heaven. When you are dead, those persons who read the volumes which were formerly written beautifully by you will then pray for you: and if he who giveth a cup of cold water shall not lose his reward, much more he who gives the living waters of wisdom shall not lose his recompense in heaven." Estates and legacies were often bequeathed for the support of the scriptorium in abbeys. At Montrouge, indulgences were often given for a supply of books. The pope, by his bull, in the year 1246, requests the monks and other persons to send, at their own expense, books to the churches of Prussia and Livonia, which were unprovided. One can hardly restrain his indignation, when he recollects that the rich libraries of the universities and abbeys of England, collected by the pious and learned churchmen through so many ages, were nearly all destroyed by the *enlightened* reformers in the sixteenth century; or repress his disgust at the Protestant journalist, who, after his brethren have done their best to obliterate every literary monument of Catholic antiquity, has the effrontery to come forward in open day and charge the Catholic Church with having "ever waged a deadly war upon literature." Alas! none are so blind as those who *will* not see.

The period of which we speak was no less remarkable for the number and ripeness of its scholars. The scholars at the universities, unless we must discredit all accounts, numbered, taking into consideration the difference of population, as fifty to one to what they do now. It must be remembered, that, in those days of Popish ignorance and superstition, the schools were open to the poorest, and in most cases nearly free of expense. Hence it was that the great body of the clergy, and the majority of the eminent prelates and dignitaries of the church, were from the lowest ranks of social life. This, too, may account for the number of scholars, and the general diffusion of education. History informs us of the thousands of scholars that flocked from all parts of Europe to attend upon the lectures of the famous Abélard, and that, when he retreated to a solitary spot at some distance from Paris, they flocked around him, and actually built up a not inconsiderable village, solely for the purpose of residing near him. At Oxford, in England, one thousand scholars were annually educated *gratis*. One writer informs us, that, at the same university, there were above fifteen thousand students in 1264, of those only whose names were entered on the matriculation books. We are told, that, in 1300, the number there was thirty thousand, which also was the number in 1340. The university of Cambridge was also crowded to a degree which seems at the present time almost incredible. "At the reformation, all these things were altered. A great part of the houses of both universities went to ruin; all the schools attached to the monasteries were destroyed; most of the cathedral schools and colleges were converted to private purposes; education was discouraged in every possible manner,—was allowed only to the rich, and positively forbidden to the poor, as a most dangerous and pernicious article. At the period of the English revolution, in 1688, the mass of the English people were buried in the grossest ignorance; even long after, when the Wesleys first started, they talked almost in the same style of the ignorance of the people of Cornwall,—nay, of the people in the very heart of London, —as they would of the South Sea islanders; and the correctness of their description was allowed to be but too faithful." * And yet one of the spiritual sons of Wesley has the temerity to come forward and charge the Catholic Church with hostility to learning! Really, this is too bad. After the Protestants, a new race of Goths and Vandals, have swept over half of Europe, destroyed the schools Catholicity had founded, dispersed or burned the libraries which she had with immense labor and expense been collecting for ages, and succeeded in reducing the mass of the people to a state of grovelling ignorance, it is too bad for a descendant of these same Goths and Vandals to turn round and charge this very ignorance upon the Catholic Church. And this is what the maligners of the Roman Catholic Church are continually doing; and if the outraged Catholic attempts to repel the charge by quoting facts, the mob stands ready to shoot him down in the street, or to enlighten him by the blaze of his church or his dwelling in flames! Well did the bluff old Samuel Johnson say: "Sir, the Catholic Church is the most calumniated church in the world."

---

* *Arbitrary Power, Popery, Protestantism.* Philadelphia. 1842, pp. 99, 100.

We have not room to speak of what was taught in the schools to which we have referred, but in the more renowned was taught at least what were called the seven liberal arts, which embraced as wide a range of studies as is common in our schools and colleges now. The number of literary men in the period of which we are speaking was proportionally much greater than it is now in Protestant countries. Of their eminence, of the value of their attainments, doubtless, different opinions may be formed. Guizot, an unsuspected authority, Protestant and philosopher as he is, commends the poetry of St. Fortunatus in the sixth century, and institutes a comparison between the poems of St. Avitus, Bishop of Vienne, in the same century, on the *Creation*, the *Fall*, and *Expulsion from Paradise*, and the *Paradise Lost* of Milton, and even in some respects awards the palm to the Catholic bishop. Speaking of the literary state from the sixth century to the eighth, he says, indeed, that the literature was then religious and practical, but he is astonished at the wonderful intellectual activity and development, at the immense number of literary works which were produced, and which *form a veritable and rich literature.**

In the seventh and eighth centuries, learning, we all know, flourished in England. In the ninth century, it suffices to mention the great Alcuin, Scotus Erigena, and the celebrated Raban Maur. Scotus Erigena was a native of Ireland, and flourished as chief of the *School of the Palace* under Charles-le-Chauve of France. As a speculator, he fell into some errors; but he was a man of extensive learning, had traveled in Greece and the East, was a profound Greek scholar, and was probably acquainted with Hebrew. He was familiar with the philosophers, especially Plato and Aristotle. In the eleventh century, literary studies and intellectual activity strike us everywhere throughout the Latin world. It is enough for us to mention St. Anselm, an Italian, and Archbishop of Canterbury. His *Monologium*, to say nothing of his other writings, is sufficient to immortalize his name as a writer and philosopher. It is the most successful effort to demonstrate the existence of God we have ever seen. That single work were more than enough to redeem the age in which it was written.

***Civilization en France*. Leçon xvi. Paris: 1829.

From the eleventh century down to the sixteenth, literature and science received no check. The four hundred years which preceded the reformation were ages of prodigious activity. In them we meet with the great names of Abélard, under whom Héloïse studied philosophy, Greek, and Hebrew,—St. Bernard, Albertus Magnus, whose works make up twenty-two huge folio volumes,—Vincent de Beauvais, St. Thomas Aquinas, the prince of the scholastics, and who, as a metaphysical writer, has never been surpassed,—St. Bonaventure, Roger Bacon, Petrarch, Dante, &c. All these were Catholics, many of them Italians, men who stand out as the great men of the race; and yet the church that produced them, and reveres their memory, has ever warred upon thought and intelligence, and sought to produce and perpetuate ignorance!

If we come down to the period since the reformation, we shall find the church of Rome the steadfast friend of literature, and in every department maintaining at least an equality with her Protestant rivals. Italy was distinguished in the sixteenth century for her literary preëminence over all the rest of Europe. German literature slept from the reformation, till awakened about the middle of the last century; English genius half expired with the establishment of the Protestant religion. Shakspeare belongs to the Catholic world, not to the Protestant; for **not a** thought or expression can be detected in all his works which indicates even a Protestant tendency, and, if not technically a Catholic, he was at least formed under Catholic influences and nourished by Catholic traditions. Milton was a strange compound of heathenism and Catholicity, with a dash of Puritanism. But the most successful portions of his great poem are those in which he remains true to Catholic tradition. What was the boasted literature of England in the days of Queen Anne, but a feeble imitation of the French school of Louis Quatorze? Dryden and Pope were both Catholics. The Society of Jesus, founded by Ignatius Loyola, has always been considered as peculiarly dear to the popes of Rome; and the members of this society, we all know, have not been more remarkable for their missionary zeal and enterprise, than for their literary and scientific attainments. Yet the church of Rome has ever waged a deadly war upon literature!

The northern nations of Europe are Protestant; the southern are Catholic. Which are really the most distinguished for literary attainments, even at this moment? Surely, France and Italy will not be obliged to yield the palm to England and Germany. In simple erudition, Germany may rank respectably; but Italy or France can boast scholars at least the equal of her own. And Catholic Germany is no longer behind Protestant Germany. England is out of the question. She is distinguished only for her industrial enterprises, her commercial ambition, her overgrown wealth, and the ignorance and destitution of the immense majority of her population.

The fatal influence of the reformation on literature is well known, and is admitted by many Protestant writers, as the following passage from *Blackwood's Magazine* may testify.

"The pontificate of Leo the Tenth commenced in 1513. His patronage of literature is too well known to be long dwelt upon; yet, during his life, literature was fated to receive the severest check it had ever yet received. This was occasioned by the Reformation, whose dawn, while it shed light upon the regions of theology, looked frowningly upon those of profane learning. In fact, the all-important controversy then at issue so thoroughly engrossed the minds of men, as to divert them for a while from other studies. The quick eye of Erasmus saw this; and, casting down the weapons of theological strife, which he had grasped in the first onset, he left the field, exclaiming, in a tone of heartfelt anguish, *Ubicumque regnat Lutherismus, ibi literarum est interitus:* Wherever Lutheranism prevails, there learning perishes."

As to the present state of education in Catholic countries, we quote the following from Mr. Laing's *Notes of a Traveller*, which have just appeared. He says:

"In Catholic Germany, in France, and even Italy, the education of the common people in reading, writing, arithmetic, music, manners, and morals, is at least as generally diffused and as faithfully promoted by the clerical body as in Scotland. It is by their own advance, and not by keeping back the advance of the people, that the Popish priesthood of the present day seek to keep ahead of the intellectual progress of the community in Catholic lands; and they might perhaps retort on our Presbyterian clergy, and ask if they too are in their countries at the head of the intellectual movement of the age. Education is in reality not only not repressed, but is encouraged, by the Popish Church, and is a mighty instrument in its hands, and ably used. In every street in Rome, for instance, there are at short distances public primary schools for the education of the children of the lower and middle classes. Rome, with a population of 158,687 souls, has three hundred and seventy-two [381, at least] primary schools, with four hundred and eighty-two teachers, and fourteen thousand children attending them. Has Edinburgh so many schools for the instruction of those classes? I doubt it. Berlin, with a population about double that of Rome, has only two hundred and sixty-four schools. Rome has also her University, with an average attendance of six hundred and sixty students; and the Papal States, with a population of two and a half millions, contain seven universities. Prussia, with a population of fourteen millions, has but seven."

After this Protestant testimony, showing that education is much better provided for in the Papal States than in either Scotland or Prussia, the two boasted countries of common schools, shall we still be told that "learning has ever been the doomed victim of the perennial despotism" of the church of Rome? The doomed victim! It is to Rome and her general policy we owe it, that learning has *not* been a doomed victim; and the generous encouragement which she has never ceased to bestow on literature and the arts should command our respect and gratitude, whatever may be our estimate of her theology. We may remark, in concluding this division of our subject, that these *Popish* schools are, many of them, supported by private charity, while those of Protestant countries are supported only by burdensome taxation.*

III. "The church of Rome has ever waged a deadly war upon science." The only proofs of this charge adduced by the reviewer are two,—the case of Virgil, Bishop of Salzburg, in the eighth century, and that of Galileo in the seventeenth. He says:

"Who can recount the number of the papal bulls which have been fulminated against successive discoveries in science, when announced in Romish countries? Pope Zachary uttered his anathemas against Virgil, a bishop of his own church, for daring to think and speak the awful heresy, that there were men living on the opposite side of the earth. 'If,' says the infallible pope, 'he persist in this heresy, strip him of h s priesthood, and drive him from the church and the altars of his God!' The venerable Galileo shared a still worse fate for presuming to think and teach that the earth was a sphere, turning on its axis and moving round the sun. Pope Urban and the Inquisition—*infallible authority*— decreed that his doctrine was false and heretical, and then doomed him

---

* See *D'Aubigné's History of the Great Reformation reviewed.* By M. J. Spalding, D. D. Ch. xiv. We cannot too earnestly commend this work to our readers. It is the work of a scholar, of a man of learning and ability; though, for aught we know, he may have been educated at Rome.

to a dungeon for daring to think contrary to Holy Mother Church. One can almost excuse the righteous indignation of the bosom friend of this aged philosopher, when he exclaimed concerning Pope Urban, and the other despots who condemned Galileo, '*I shall devote these unnatural and godless hypocrites to a hundred thousand devils.*'"—p. 353.

Before proceeding to comment directly on these statements, we have one or two remarks to make on the *infallible authority* about which the reviewer has so much to say; for this is a matter, though simple enough in itself, which Protestants do not seem ever to comprehend. Do Catholics recognize an infallible authority? If so, what, where, and when is it? The Catholic undoubtedly believes the church, as the church, is infallible; but his belief is not grounded on any supposed infallibility in the individuals composing the church,—although there is undoubtedly a spiritual illumination, proper to every living member of Christ's body, not possessed by those separate or separated from it,—but solely on the fact, that Christ has promised to be with his church all days unto the consummation of the world. The Catholic, therefore, believes, that, when the church is called upon to act, as a church, Christ is with it, and, by his supernatural interposition, protects its decisions from error, and guides it into all truth. He really predicates infallibility only of Christ, and regards the decision of the church as infallible only because he believes it is Christ that really and truly decides in the church. Let it be understood, then, that the Catholic holds the church to be infallible only by virtue of the supernatural protection and guidance of its invisible Head, according to his promise. But this promise was made to the church, the *whole* church,—not to any particular portion of the church, nor to any given number of individuals in the church. Consequently, the Catholic regards no act of the church, even of the highest dignitaries of the church, as infallible, unless the act of the whole church. There are only two ways in which the church is assumed to act as the whole church,—that is, in a universal council, or, what is the same thing, the unanimous, or the morally unanimous, assent of all the bishops or pastors of the church, and through the pope, deciding *ex cathedra*, as the representative of the church; and a man may be a Catholic, without believing that the decision of the pope, unless assented to by the body of the bishops, is to be regarded as infallible. But we, for ourselves, hold the decision of the pope, when he represents, or decides for, the church universal, to be infallible.

Now, the pope acts in three separate capacities,—as temporal prince, as bishop of the particular church of Rome, and as head of the church universal. If he was regarded as infallible as a man, if infallibility was regarded as inhering in him as a personal attribute, he would be held, inasmuch as he is one and the same man in whichever capacity he acts, equally infallible in all three of these capacities, as Protestants commonly suppose Catholics do hold. But Catholics do not hold the pope to be infallible as a man; as a man, or when acting in any case in which he has not the express promise of Christ to protect him from error and to guide him to the truth, they believe him just as liable to err, after becoming pope, as he was before. The promise of Christ, which is the pledge of infallibility, is made, as we have said, only to the church universal, and therefore to the pope only when representing, and only in so far as he represents, the universal church. But the pope, as temporal prince, as the civil ruler of the ecclesiastical states, or as the bishop of the see of Rome, does not represent the universal church, and therefore in these capacities has no promise of inerrancy.

These distinctions made, it will be proper and necessary to ask, when any particular act assumed to be reprehensible is alleged to have been done by the Catholic Church, and therefore by infallible authority, Has it been done or sanctioned by a universal council, or the great body of bishops? or has it been done or sanctioned by the pope, deciding *ex cathedra*, as the representative of the church universal? If not, it has been done, has been sanctioned, by no authority held by a Catholic to be infallible; and, if bad, it must, as in all other cases, be charged to human fallibility or depravity.

Now, the reviewer alleges, or virtually alleges, that the heliocentric theory has been condemned as a heresy by an authority which Catholics hold to be infallible; for this is the real purport of his allegation. But this we deny. First, because it is not the principle of the church to pronounce dogmatically on questions of pure science; and second, because no instance ever has been or can be adduced of her having so pronounced. The Catholic recognizes no authority but that of the universal church, expressed in one or the other of the two ways we have specified, as competent to declare what is or not a heresy, or to declare an article of faith, or any question whatever; and there is no purely scientific question on which this authority, in either of the ways specified, has ever spoken. Individuals in the church, eminent doctors and high dignitaries, may have spoken, some condemning one doctrine, and some another; but never any authority believed by any Catholic to be infallible, or which, according to the principles of his church, he is required to believe infallible. And furthermore, the theory in question has never been condemned at all as a heresy.

We turn now to the direct consideration of the two cases alleged by the reviewer. The case of Virgil, Bishop of Salzburg, we dismiss, as not authenticated. The extract said to be from a papal bull bears on its face unequivocal evidence of being supposititious. It is not the style in which the pope is accustomed to speak, when declaring the decision of the church universal. We are not acquainted with the particulars of the case, but it appears that Virgil did speak of there being inhabitants on the opposite side of the earth, and that this gave offense to some bigoted churchmen, who made an application to Pope Zachary to condemn him; "but it does not, however, appear," says Mr. Whewell, in his *History of the Inductive Sciences*, (Vol. II. p. 256, London, 1839,) "that this led to any severity; and the story of the deposition from his bishopric, which is circulated by Kepler and some more modern writers, *is undoubtedly altogether false.*" This is good Protestant authority, and all that it is necessary to adduce in the case of the Bishop of Salzburg.

But the case of Galileo is in point; and, surely, you are not about to deny that? Surely, you will not pretend to deny that Galileo was imprisoned in the dungeons of the Inquisition for teaching that the earth turns on its axis, and moves round the sun,—that his doctrine was pronounced by the church of Rome to be a heresy, and that he himself was forced to retract it,—and that the venerable old philosopher, rising from the posture in which he had made his abjuration, stamped his foot upon the ground, and exclaimed, "Nevertheless, it *does* move?" The story is so well told, has been so often repeated, and has proved so serviceable to numerous pretenders, wishing to palm off their stupid dreams for some new discovery in the science of man or nature, especially to our phrenologists, neurologists, and Fourierists, that, we own, it seems almost a pity to spoil it by contradicting it; yet it is false, totally false from beginning to end, with not one word of truth in it. We make this assertion on indubitable authority.

The heliocentric theory was publicly taught in Rome by the great Cardinal Nicholas Cusanus, who was born in 1401, and died in 1464, just one hundred years before the birth of Galileo; it was taught in the same city, in public lectures, by Copernicus, a Catholic canon, educated at Bologna, in Italy, and professor of astronomy at Rome, in 1500; and Leonardo da Vinci, in 1510, "connects the theory of the fall of bodies with the earth's motion, as a thing then generally received." Cusanus was never disturbed for asserting "the earth moves, the sun is at rest," but was created Cardinal by Nicholas V., who conferred on him the bishopric of Brixen; and he enjoyed the favor and confidence of four successive pontiffs, till the day of his death. Copernicus was invited by the pope to assist in reforming the calendar, which he did; and, on his retiring from his professorship, the dignitaries of the church charged themselves with providing for him a safe and honorable retreat, where, above the wants and distractions of life, he might devote the undivided energies of his great mind to the reconstruction of the whole fabric of astronomy. When it is known at Rome that his system is prepared, Cardinal Schomberg writes to him, urging him to publish it, and generously offers to advance from his private purse the necessary funds. The cardinal unhappily dying before the publication, another dignitary of the church, Gisius, Bishop of Kulm, steps forward to replace him; and when the work is brought to light, it is dedicated to Pope Paul III., with the pope's approbation. Thus did Rome originate, foster, and mature this *heretical* theory, and thus did she treat its advocates for more than eighty years before Galileo. If it was a heresy, why was it so long tolerated? If Rome was opposed to science, why did she protect and honor its cultivators? And how happens it, that in the case of Galileo alone, who broached no novelty, who brought out no new theory, she suddenly became a persecutor? The fairer presumption would be, that Galileo, if condemned at all, was condemned for something extraneous to his simple promulgation of the heliocentric theory, so formally taught, eighty years, nay, a hundred years, before, by Copernicus, in Rome herself.

But Galileo was not condemned for teaching this theory, nor was the theory itself condemned, nor was Galileo ever imprisoned, or required to retract his doctrine. What, then, are the real facts in the case? It appears, that Galileo, by the manner in which he proclaimed his theory, his intemperance in advocating it, and his attempt to reconcile it with the Scriptures, created him many enemies, who sought, in 1615, to get him cited before the Inquisition, but without effect. No censure was passed upon him or his doctrine; he was simply required to speak as a mathematician, to confine himself to his discoveries and his scientific proofs, without meddling with the Scriptural question. But with this Galileo was not satisfied. He insisted on two things,—first, that his doctrine was demonstrated, and second, that it was supported by Scripture; and he came of his own accord to Rome, in 1616, to obtain a decision of these two points in his favor. There was no charge against him, he was not *cited* to appear, but he came of his own accord, because he wished to obtain the sanction of Rome to his theories. The court of Rome was unwilling to interfere; but, at length, yielding to the importunities of Galileo and his friends, the pope finally referred the question to the Inquisition, who decided the two points against Galileo; that is, they decided that the doctrine was not demonstrated and not supported by Scripture,—for these were the simple points before them,—and enjoined it upon Galileo not to teach it henceforth as a theory demonstrated, and to observe silence as to the Scriptural question. This would still have left him free to teach it as an hypothesis, and to have adduced every mathematical proof in its favor in his power. But Galileo was not content with this, which left him full liberty as a scientific man, and he was therefore forbidden to teach the doctrine at all. This, as nearly as we can seize it, is the purport of the decision of the Inquisition in 1616. But there was in this no positive condemnation of the doctrine, and no retraction of it required. Galileo was still honored at Rome; and when his friend, Cardinal Barberini, became Pope Urban VIII., he came to Rome again, was received with the highest honors, and the pope bestowed a pension on him and his son.

For seventeen years after this decision in 1616, Galileo continued his mathematical pursuits, undisturbed, with the greatest success, receiving everywhere honor and applause, and nowhere more than at Rome. Cardinal Barberini, who dissented from the decision of the Inquisition, became Pope Urban VIII. He was the friend of Galileo, and not opposed to the heliocentric theory. Galileo's friends under this pope were everywhere encouraged and promoted, and it seemed that one needed only to advocate his doctrine to be sure of the pope's favor. Galileo was elated, and published his *Dialogues*, in which he brings out the theory, contrary to the obligation he had taken, and in a manner the most intemperate, and the most satirical and contemptuous to authority. He was accordingly cited in 1633 to appear at Rome, and was condemned,—the question turning on his contempt for authority, and not at all on the truth or falsity of his doctrine. What punishment was imposed upon him we do not know. But he was not imprisoned. While at Rome, he resided in the palace of his friend, the Tuscan ambassador, and during the trial was subjected, at most, to a nominal confinement,—as Mr. Drinkwater, in his *Life of Galileo*, and Mr. Whewell admit, —for four days, in a splendid apartment in the palace of the Fiscal of the Inquisition. Such are the main facts in the case, as simply and as briefly as we can narrate them.*

The whole treatment of Galileo, so far as Rome was concerned, appears to have been singularly lenient and respectful. All that was ever asked of him was, that he should be content to teach his doctrine as an hypothesis, not as a doctrine demonstrated, and confine himself to mathematical arguments and proofs of it, without meddling with the Scriptural bearings of the doctrine. Had he been content to pursue a straightforward course as a scientific man, no complaint would ever have been entertained against him, and no official action would ever have been taken. His troubles all arose from his rashness; from his insisting that authority should sanction, as demonstrated, what was as yet only a probable hypothesis; for we must remember, that, in 1616, the heliocentric theory was very far from being demonstrated. It is true, Galileo's own discovery of the phases of Venus went far towards demonstrating it; but these he himself did not insist upon, and he relied for his demonstration almost solely on the flux and reflux of the tides. Bacon, the contemporary of Galileo, rejects the doctrine; and Milton, at a later period, seems to entertain, to say the least, strong doubts of its truth. Tycho Brahe re-

---

* Our limits do not allow us to cite at length our authorities, but our readers will find them in a remarkable article in the eighth number of the *Dublin Review*, which has been republished separately in this country, in a pamphlet, entitled, *Galileo; the Roman Inquisition; a Defence of the Catholic Church from having persecuted Galileo for his Philosophical Opinions. From the Dublin Review, with an Introduction by an American Catholic.* Cincinnati: 1844.

jected it, and constructed another theory, on Scriptural grounds, in opposition to it, which was for a time very popular with Protestants, but is now universally exploded; and the historians of astronomy will tell us, that it was nearly a hundred years after Galileo before any one had a right to say the theory was demonstrated. But was not the doctrine condemned as heresy? No. The words "*heretical,*" "*heresy,*" in the condemnation of 1633, are, says the *Dublin Review,* but the *stylus curiæ*; the evidence is most decisive, that of the pontiff in whose name it issued, and of the person condemned addressing his very judges. " No !" says Urban, "the church has not condemned that system, nor is it to be considered as heretical, but only as rash." Galileo himself, standing before the Inquisition in 1633, speaks of it with the approbation of the court, as of a doctrine condemned *ad interim,* that is, not to be taught in its absolute form till proved to be true. Moreover, the Inquisition which uses the terms *heretical,* &c., in the decision in 1616, which is merely recited in the condemnation of 1633, is not an institution supposed by Catholics to be infallible, and its decisions have no promise of exemption from error. It is merely a court of inquiry. It has no power to make the law, nor even to declare what the law is, but simply to inquire whether, in a given case, the preëxisting law has been violated. Its having termed the doctrine *heretical* would not have made it so, unless it had been previously declared to be a heresy by the authority of the church, which it had not been; because heresy never consists in maintaining a false scientific theory, but in wilfully departing from the faith. It was never an article of faith in the church, that the earth is at rest and the sun moves. Consequently, to maintain the contrary never was and never can be a heresy. Furthermore, if the doctrine had been condemned as a heresy, the teaching of it as a mere hypothesis, even, could not have been permitted; for the church does not permit what she has declared to be heresy to be taught at all. Yet the teaching of the doctrine as an hypothesis was permitted, as we have seen, in the case of Cusanus; as a scientific theory, in the case of Copernicus; and at the very moment Galileo was condemned, it was taught by the professor of astronomy, we believe, in the pope's own university of Rome. Evidently, therefore, it was not condemned as a heresy. The sole difficulty concerning the question grew out of

Galileo's insisting on interpreting the passages of Scripture, which seem to teach the geocentric theory, so as to make them harmonize with the heliocentric. This was deemed by his judges to be premature, to say the least, for it was unnecessary to disturb the received interpretation of these passages, till the theory itself was fully demonstrated on scientific grounds; and the attempt to do it could only scandalize those who rejected the theory, as they supposed, for scientific reasons. They said to Galileo, Go on and establish your theory on scientific grounds, and when you have succeeded in demonstrating it as a science, it will be time enough to consider the Scriptural question; but till then, let the Scriptural question alone. Had he followed this advice, which was recommended by his friends, and was all that his enemies asked, no difficulty would have occurred. The troubles Galileo had did not, then, grow out of his advocating his scientific doctrine, but from the manner in which he advocated it, and the extraneous questions he mingled with it. This condemnation by the court of Rome is, then, no evidence of hostility on the part even of the court of Rome, much less of the church of Rome, to science. With these remarks, referring for details and references to authorities, to the pamphlet which we have cited, we dismiss the case of Galileo. Had we room, we would retort the charge upon Protestants, which they have brought against Catholics. Kepler was a Lutheran priest; but the Lutheran University of Tübingen, as Menzel informs us, condemned his doctrine as repugnant to the language of Scripture, and he was obliged to flee his country; and where did he find refuge? *As professor of astronomy*, all Lutheran as he was, *in a Catholic university.* The devotion of Protestants to science, and their readiness to adopt scientific discoveries, are admirably evinced in the case of the reformed calendar of Pope Gregory XIII., in 1582. England refused to adopt it for one hundred and seventy years, until 1752; Sweden adopted the new style one year later, in 1753; and the German States not until 1776; preferring, as some one says, "warring with the stars to agreeing with the pope."

The *Methodist Quarterly Review* adds, "Except painting and sculpture, no one of the arts or sciences has escaped the anathemas of Rome." When and where has Rome ever anathematized any art or science? Music is both an art and a science; has Rome ever anathematized it? Architecture, whether as an art or a science, when has Rome ever anathematized it? We have heard of the Gothic architecture, the admiration and despair of our modern architects, which sprang up in the middle ages, and which we have been accustomed to regard as Catholic. Perchance the glorious old cathedrals, of which European tourists tell us so much, were all built by Protestants, and our modern meeting-houses have been designed by Catholic architects! Mechanics is a science; has Rome ever anathematized it? According to the confession of Mr. Whewell, it was completed, so far as it remained for moderns to complete it, by Leonardo da Vinci and Galileo,—for DaVinci anticipated the discoveries of Stevinus,—both Catholics, and honored at Rome, and the latter a pensioner of the church. Astronomy, we have seen, owes to Rome its principal discoveries and encouragement. Metaphysics is almost exclusively a Catholic science. Bacon is more than matched by Campanella or Descartes. Leibnitz owed his eminence to his acquaintance with the scholastics, and St. Thomas Aquinas alone will weigh down the whole race of modern German metaphysicians. Italy and France early took the lead in history, and still keep it. In poetry, the Catholics are more than successful rivals of the Protestants. Shakspeare is no Protestant. Dante, Petrarch, Boccaccio, Tasso, Ariosto, are all Catholics and Italians. The Spanish and Portuguese poetry is not to be despised; and take away from the poetry of Germany and England what is not Protestant, and neither surpasses France in this department, in which France is poorest. Has Rome ever anathematized logic? If the reviewer believes it, we ask him to read a Catholic course of theology,—no matter what one, but any one prepared for young theological students,—and he will very soon change his mind. The truth is, all the great, leading scientific discoveries and inventions of which we boast, Christendom owes to Catholics. Parchment and paper, printing and engraving, improved glass and steel, gunpowder, clocks, telescopes, the mariner's compass, the reformed calendar, decimal notation, algebra, trigonometry, chemistry, counterpoint, equivalent to a new creation in music, are all possessions inherited from our Catholic ancestors. The great maritime discoveries, the discovery of the Cape of Good Hope, and the New World, were all made by Catholics before Protestantism was born. The principle of the steam-engine was discovered by Roger Bacon, and the application of steam to navigation was first made by a Spanish Catholic in the early part of the seventeenth century. The application of the sciences to the industrial arts received its principal developments in Catholic countries, and has made any considerable progress in Protestant countries only since the middle of the last century, that is, since the obvious decline of Protestantism in those countries. And yet, a writer who probably never read a Catholic book in his life, and who, we will venture to assert, cannot state correctly a single distinctive dogma of the Catholic Church, and who proves himself by his reckless assertions utterly ignorant of her history, has the impudence to say, that, excepting painting and sculpture, "no one of the arts or sciences has escaped the anathemas of Rome; and these have only been fostered because they could be made tributary to the idolatrous ceremonies of the church!"

But our limits do not permit us to proceed. Having, as we trust, sufficiently vindicated the church from the charges of hostility to literature and science, we must reserve to a future number the reply to the charge of hostility to revelation and religion, which we suppose means an unwillingness to accept King James' Bible as the pure word of God. The Catholic policy in regard to the Bible we will endeavour to explain in our next.

The Edinburgh Review for October, 1883, in an able review of Leopold Prowe's first volume on Copernicus, lately published at Berlin, says (pp. 180, 181, Am. Ed.):

"Widmannstad, in 1533, derived from this source [the *Commentariolus* of Copernicus] the substance of a lecture which Clement VII. recompensed with the gift of a rare Greek text; Calcagnini was encouraged to denounce the absurdity of attributing a diurnal rotation to the sphere; and Cardinal Schönberg transmitted to Copernicus a formal request for the full publication of his system. There was, indeed, a counter current. The doctrine of the earth's motion was made the subject of a farce put upon the stage at Elbing during the Carnival of 1531, or 1532; Luther pronounced it contrary to Holy Writ, and stigmatised its chief advocate as 'a fool who thought to turn the whole art of astronomy upside down' (*Tischreden*, Ed. Walch. p. 2260, quoted by Prowe, Th. ii. p. 232); and Melanchthon went so far as to desire the suppression by the secular power of such mischievous doctrines," and in a note it adds: "Beckmann has conclusively shown (*Zur Geschichte des Kop. Systems*, Zeitschrift für die Geschichte Ermlands, Bd. ii.) that in the sixteenth century, no serious theological objections were made to the Copernican system save from the Protestant side. Catholic ecclesiastics were, in general, extremely well disposed towards it, so that Giordano Bruno's advocacy of it cannot be held responsible for his tragical end. A full discussion of the reformers' attitude towards the new astronomy will form part of Dr. Prowe's third volume."—ED.

METHODIST QUARTERLY REVIEW.*

[From Brownson's Quarterly Review for January, 1846.]

THE *Methodist Quarterly Review* for July, 1844, contained a paper on the literary policy of the church of Rome; the avowed purpose of which was "to exhibit the proofs that the church of Rome has ever waged a deadly warfare upon the liberty of the press, and upon literature; and that her expurgatory and prohibitory policy has been continued to the present hour; not only against the truth of revelation, but equally against the truth in nature and in science, —both learning and religion having been the doomed victims of her perennial despotism." To this paper, so far as concerned hostility to the press, literature, and science, we replied in our *Review* for last January. To this reply of ours the article before us is a rejoinder, attempting to make good the original charges, notwithstanding what we alleged against them.

In our reply we retorted the charge of unfriendliness to literature upon the Methodists themselves, who, we said, had originally manifested a great contempt for human science and learning, and cannot, in this country at least, boast of having made a single permanent contribution either to literature or science. The *Review* thinks this charge is not true, for one Mr. Elliot has written *A Delineation of Roman Catholicism*, which has even been republished in England. We confess, when we wrote, we had not heard of this work, and we have not yet seen it; but we will engage before hand that it is nothing but a tissue of falsehood, misrepresentation, ignorance, impudence, sophistry, and malice; in the main, a mere repetition of what Protestants have been constantly repeating from the first, and which has been refuted time and again. We are always safe in saying this of any work written by a Protestant against Catholicity, and, *a fortiori*, of a work written by a Methodist. Yet if the author or reviewer will send us a copy of the work, and we find on actual examination that we are

---

*Methodist Quarterly Review for July, 1845. Art. VII. *Brownson's Quarterly Review*, No. V. 1845.

mistaken as to its real character, we will make all necessary retractions. We stated that "the Methodist press is, if we are rightly informed, under the strict surveillance of the bishops and elders." The reviewer says we are wrongly informed, for the bishops and elders have no power over it whatever. Yet he tells us the editors and agents are appointed by the conferences, and are aided by the advice of a council. The conferences are composed of "bishops and elders." The bishops and elders, then, appoint the editors and agents, and we presume also the council of advice. We should think this were exercising *some* power over the press. Furthermore, in the intervals of the general conference, these editors and agents are accountable, the reviewer tells us, for their *official* conduct, "to the book committee, who have power, after due forms of trial and conviction, to *displace* them for malpractice." The book committee must be appointed by the particular conferences, or by the general conference, and in either case by the bishops and elders. The bishops and elders, then, through the book committee, exercise a strict surveillance over the Methodist press. The point on which we were intent was, that the Methodist press is not free, and we find, by the reviewer's own admissions, it is less free than we had supposed. There is a power which appoints the editors and agents, furnishes them a council of advice, and then there is a tribunal to which they are accountable, before which they can be tried and convicted, and which has power to *displace* them for malpractice; that is, should they publish what their masters disapprove. Surely, this is subjecting the press to a very stringent control, and we must still retain our opinion that the charge against the Catholic Church of hostility to a free press comes with an ill grace from a Methodist.

We stated, also, that "the Methodist people generally have great scruples about purchasing books, even of their own denomination, when not published by their own book society." The reviewer says this is not true. We know from our own knowledge that it *was* true a few years since to some extent, and we know, and the reviewer admits, that the Methodist elders do "urge their people to patronize their publishing establishments." It seems, however, we were wrong in speaking of their "book *society*," for they have no book *society*, but a "book *concern*." We acknowledge our mistake. The simple fact is, the Methodist denomination is itself, properly speaking, a huge society, and this society carries on a large book concern, and seeks as far as possible to monopolize the whole publishing business of its members.

We denied that the Catholic Church has ever been hostile to the liberty of the press, and asserted that the reviewer had not adduced a single fact in proof of his charge. In the article before us, he appears to think we were wrong in this; for he adduced some extracts from the encyclical letter of the Holy Father, bearing date August 16 (15), 1832, which goes far at least to prove it. We had, and now have, that letter before us, but it does not sustain the charge we denied. The reviewer misquotes and perverts the sense of the passages he professes to give. The Holy Father does not declare, "Liberty of conscience is an absurd and erroneous opinion, or rather a mad conceit," as the reviewer asserts; but that the opinion, that liberty is to be asserted and maintained for the conscience of each one, is absurd and erroneous, or rather a madness. *Atque ex hoc putidissimo indifferentismi fonte absurda illa fluit ac erronea sententia, seu potius deliramentum, asserendam esse ac vindicandam cuilibet libertatem conscientiæ.* What is condemned is not liberty of conscience, rightly understood, but that false view of the liberty of conscience which releases conscience from all obligation to conform to the truth, and which makes the conscience of each the sovereign arbiter in all cases whatsoever. Conscience is free, has all its rights, when subjected only to the will of God; but that its freedom demands that it must in no instance be restrained,— that the individual, under plea of conscience, must be free to conform or not to conform to the law of God,—free to run into any and every excess of error and delusion, to subvert all religious, social, and domestic order, is indeed an absurd and erroneous opinion, a real delusion, which every rightminded man must condemn. That the Holy Catholic Church does not allow liberty of conscience in this sense, which is not liberty, but license, we have never denied, and trust we never shall. The church leaves the conscience all the liberty, that is, all the rights, it has by the law of God. If the reviewer is not satisfied with this, he must bring his complaint against his Maker, not against the church.

In fact, this notion of the unbounded license of conscience no man in his sober senses can undertake to defend. We remember to have read some years ago, in one of the

Protestant missionary journals, of a pious Protestant convert among the heathen, who, on her dying bed, having but a poor appetite, thought she might, perhaps, eat the *little finger of a very young child, if nicely cooked!* This her conscience permitted. Was the liberty of her conscience to be respected? The conscience of the Anabaptists required them to run naked through the streets, and that of the early Quakers required them, especially the women, to go naked into the religious assemblies and prophesy. Was their conscience to be respected at the expense of public decency? There is, or at least was two or three years ago, a new religious sect in Western New York, who reject marriage, allow promiscuous sexual intercourse, and practise various obscene and filthy rites which we dare not name. Is the liberty of their conscience to be respected? There was, too, Matthias, the famous New York prophet, whose queer conscience commanded him to claim his neighbour's property and his neighbour's wife as his own. Was the liberty of his conscience to be allowed? We have a friend who is conscientiously opposed to paying taxes to the government. Shall the government respect his conscience, and exempt him from the payment of taxes? We have another friend who believes it decidedly wrong to use money. So, when he steps on board the steamboat at New York for Boston, he insists on having a free passage, because his conscience will not let him pay for it. Shall he go scot-free through the world? One man is conscientiously opposed to the observance of Sunday; do you respect the liberty of his conscience? Another is opposed to the employment of chaplains by legislative assemblies; do you respect his liberty of conscience? Not at all.

It is evident from what we have advanced, that some bounds are, and must be, set to the license of conscience,—that there must be somewhere a limit beyond which the plea of conscience is not to be entertained. But where is this limit? Where are these bounds? Who shall determine? The individual for himself? No; for that would be to leave conscience without any restraint whatever; because *conscience is each man's own judgment of what the law of God commands or permits.* If you leave the individual to determine for himself, you leave conscience without law. You must, too, respect the determination of one as much as that of another. Individuals as such are all equal, and you have no right to prefer the judgment of one to that of another. The judgment of the Libbeyite of Western New York, of Matthias, the prophet, of the anti-Sabbatarian, of the anti-chaplainite, must be held as respectable as your own. This, then, will not do. If any bounds are to be set to conscience, it must be by an authority above the individual, and which may command the individual, and enforce its commands on the individual. What is this authority? The civil government? We deny it; for the civil government, except as the executive of the commands of a more ultimate authority than its own, has no right to meddle with conscience. Shall it be the authority of some one of the sects? Which one? Why one rather than another? Of all the sects combined? That is impossible; because one will insist that the law of God allows a latitude to conscience which another denies, and their agreement is out of the question. But waive this; we still say no; because the sects are all, taken singly or together, by their own confession, fallible, and may, therefore, misjudge, allow what the law of God prohibits, and forbid what the law of God permits. Moreover, conscience is accountable only to God, and to subject it to any fallible authority is intolerable tyranny. If, then, there be not on earth an authority through which Almighty God speaks, and interprets infallibly his own law, you have and can have no authority for restraining the licentiousness of conscience. But, if you have such authority, whatever restraints it imposes on conscience will be restraints imposed by the law of God, and therefore restraints perfectly compatible with the liberty of conscience. The authority of the Catholic Church is such authority, and therefore her control of conscience is not, and never can be, an attack on the liberty of conscience. It leaves it all the freedom Almighty God gives it, and that is all it has a right to demand.

The same or similar remarks may be made in reference to the freedom of opinion. The unrestricted freedom of opinion is no more permitted by the law of God than is the unrestricted freedom of conscience. The Holy Father condemns not the liberty of opinion, properly so called, but the *immoderata libertas opinionum*, that is, the licentiousness of opinions. If there be any truth in Christianity, the mind is as accountable to God as the body, and licentiousness of mental action is as reprehensible as the licentiousness of bodily action. We are as accountable for our opinions as we are for our deeds. Else what means the confession we all make, that "we have sinned in *thought*, word, and deed"? If there is no law to which the mind is accountable, there can be no sin in thought, for sin is the transgression of the law; and where there is no law, there is, and can be, no transgression of the law. If there be a law to which the mind is accountable, then are we bound to conform to it, and are not free to do what it prohibits. Then the liberty of mind, of thought, of opinion, as well as the liberty of conscience, has its limits. And is it not so? Is there a Christian who dares assert that we are free to think and form opinions which are repugnant to the law of God? No; and we dare tell even this godless generation, let it declaim as grandiloquently as it pleases about the inalienable rights of the free-born mind, that the mind has no rights but what Almighty God gives it, and we have no right to think what he forbids. We are bound to submit our very thoughts and imaginations to his divine law.

We say the same as to freedom of speech. We may sin in *word* as well as in *deed*. Speech, then, is subjected to the law of God; and the liberty of speech is only the liberty to say that which the law of God permits. We shall be called to account before God for our words, as well as for our thoughts and deeds. There is, then, a limit beyond which the liberty of speech does not and cannot extend. To prohibit beyond that limit is not to abridge the freedom of speech, nor to make war upon it; because, beyond that limit, Almighty God has given man no freedom of speech.

The principle here asserted is applicable to the press. The press is nothing but public speech, and its liberty must be subject to all the restrictions to which the law of God subjects thought and speech in general. The press has no liberty to publish what is contrary to the law of God, and when it is forbidden to publish what is contrary to the law of God, its license is indeed restrained, but its liberty is left untouched. We are not ignorant that this question of the press is a delicate question, and one on which it is impossible to speak as a Christian man should speak, without giving to the ill-natured and wicked an opportunity to pervert your meaning, and make the great mass of the people believe you mean what you do not mean. But it is a question that presses home upon every parent, every citizen, not to say every Christian. The licentiousness of the press at home and abroad has become so great as to threaten all that is dear and sacred. Every thing venerable, every thing sacred in religion, in the state, in the family, is attacked with remorseless fury. Our youth grow pale over publications which pervert their understandings, extinguish every virtuous sentiment, and excite to terrible activity every evil propensity. Respectable booksellers keep, if not on their counters, at least on their back shelves, books which the Christian father or mother would be filled with horror to see in the hands of a son or a daughter. And those mischievous works are sent out at a price that places them within the reach of even the poorest. The infection becomes universal. No rank, no age, no sex, no condition, escapes it. Is this a time to talk of the blessings of a free press? Books are companions, and bad books are bad companions, the very worst species of companions. They are made by the base and remorseless the vehicles of corrupting the innocent and unsuspecting. The licentious and designing have only to send a selection from the cheap publications of the day before them, and the way is prepared for them to follow. They have, too, books of all kinds, adapted to all dispositions. Our homes are no longer sacred. Corruption steals in by our very firesides, and we close our eyes and ears, lest we discover it in those nearest and dearest to our hearts. Will you tell us this is the inevitable consequence of a free press, and that, if you touch the freedom of the press, you take away the palladium of our liberty? Liberty! What is liberty, where the moral health of the people is gone, where virtue ceases to exist, and your community is nothing but a mass of rottenness?

Some restraint on the licentiousness of the press is unquestionably necessary. This the Methodist reviewer admits in admitting that Protestant sects make the reading of books "of an irreligious tendency" a matter of discipline. What restraint is necessary, or by whom it shall be imposed, is another question. Religion is the only basis of morals, and it is idle to expect good morals where there is no religion. Every book which attacks religion, which tends to undermine faith in divine revelation, or which gives a false view of the dogmas of faith, is a bad book, an irreligious book, and repugnant to good morals,—a book no man has the right to produce, no press to publish. No restraint on the licentiousness of the press will be effectual which does not extend to all books which tend to undermine or corrupt the faith of the people in the one only true religion. But who shall impose such a restraint? Evidently no authority is competent to impose such a restraint but an authority which is competent to say *infallibly* what is and what is not the true religion. This cannot, as we said in the case of freedom of thought, be the civil authority, for the civil authority is not infallible; and, moreover, has no jurisdiction in the case, since its jurisdiction does not extend to spiritual matters. It might misjudge and suppress good books, under pretence of suppressing bad books; and through its control of the press it would consolidate its tyranny and screen its oppressions from animadversion. Nor can it be the authority of any one of the sects, nor of all the sects combined; because the sects are all by their own confession fallible, and may err as to what is the proper degree of restraint, may permit books which ought not to be permitted, and suppress books which the well-being of individuals and of society requires to be published.

In this state of things, what is to be done? Do not answer us with Milton and Jefferson, that "error is harmless where reason is free to combat it." No such thing. "Error," says the Chinese proverb, "will travel over half the globe, while truth is pulling on her boots." The doctrine of the harmlessness of error assumes two things which are not true; first, that the mass of mankind are capable, *in all cases*, of distinguishing between truth and error; and, secondly, that they have no natural inclinations or prejudices which warp their judgments and lead them to prefer the error to the truth. If the first were true, we should not find men equally great, wise, and good, embracing opposite doctrines; the second is contradicted by all experience. No matter how free reason may be, no error ever yet was harmless, or ever can be harmless. Error puts on a thousand disguises, appears in a thousand specious shapes, corrupts the simple, the young, the unsuspecting, does the mischief before reason detects her and exposes her in her true character. What capacity to distinguish between truth and error have the mass of our youth of either sex, who in hotels, steamboats, and elsewhere, pore over the prurient pages of Byron, of Moore, of Eugene Sue, George Sand and Paul de Kock? We repeat it, *some* restraint is necessary. That it is difficult to say, as matters are with us, what restraint is practicable, or by whom the restraint should be imposed, is undoubtedly true. For ourselves, we see no way of disposing of the question, but to leave to the state the power to suppress such publications as are grossly and palpably immoral and blasphemous, and to each denomination such supervision over the reading of its members as it judges proper. This is as far as the church goes or ever has gone. She never restrains the liberty of the press, but seeks to restrain its licentiousness, or to guard against its licentiousness by exercising a careful supervision over the reading of her children. This she does by examining from time to time the books which are published, and placing in the index such as are hurtful, dangerous, or unprofitable.

If the reviewer attends to what we have here advanced, he will understand why we denied, in the most positive terms, that he had, notwithstanding his quotations from the encyclical letter of the Holy Father, adduced a single fact in proof of his assertion, that the church of Rome is hostile to a free press. The "execrable liberty of booksellers" the Holy Father condemns is not the legitimate freedom of the press, but its license. We do not war against freedom when we war against license. Liberty is freedom to do whatever is permitted by the law of God, that is, whatever Almighty God gives us the right to do; license is freedom to do what the law of God does not permit, what Almighty God does not give us the right to do. Liberty is violated only when one's rights are denied or abridged. But in forbidding a man to do what the law of God gives him no right to do, we do not deny or abridge any one of his rights; therefore do not violate his liberty. The government does not violate the liberty of the subject when it commands him not to steal or to murder, or when it imprisons the thief or hangs the murderer; for no man has the right to steal or to murder.

But the Holy Father in his encyclical letter goes no further in principle than our Protestant countrymen go. We read, but a short time since, in one of our city newspapers, that the grand jury of this county had made inquiries concerning the conduct of our booksellers, and threatened to present some of our *respectable* booksellers, in case they should not speedily clear their shops of certain infamous and immoral publications. Even while we are writing, the Rev. Mr. Kirk, the commander-in-chief of the *Christian Alliance*, and his friends, are denouncing in the city of New York the cheap publications of the day, and declaring they must be suppressed. What is this but making war on the "liberty of booksellers"?

The main fact, however, on which the reviewer relied for proofs of the hostility of the church of Rome to the freedom of the press was "the expurgatory and prohibitory indexes." We have stated that these indexes are a mere matter of discipline. The church examines the books published, and places in the index those she forbids or cannot recommend her children to read. She publishes the index for the guidance of all her children throughout the world. But in this she does no more than the reviewer admits the Methodists themselves do. He admits the Methodists make the reading of books of "an irreligious tendency" a matter of discipline, and goes so far as to admit by implication, that the author who publishes a book "that would injure the morals of the community, and subvert the whole social compact," may be visited with legal penalties. This is going full as far as the church goes, even admitting that she goes as far as the reviewer contends. The only thing, then, he can complain of is that she publishes beforehand what books she holds to be of an irreligious tendency, that the faithful may know the law before being summoned to answer for its breach.

But it appears that the church puts in the index certain books which the reviewer does not regard as of an irreligious tendency. If she prohibited only "such books as Paine's *Age of Reason*, Volney's *Ruins*, &c., no one would have cause to complain;" but she goes further, and claps in the index some of the admired *chefs-d'œuvre* of Protestantism. This is, no doubt, provoking to our Protestant friends. But we suppose the Methodists claim the right to determine the books the reading of which shall or shall not be made a matter of discipline in the case of a Methodist; will the reviewer, then, tell us why the church has less right to determine what is suitable reading for a Catholic? Will the Methodist ask the church what a Methodist may read? Of course not. Why, then, shall the church be required to ask the Methodists what a Catholic may or may not read? The judgment of the church, on any hypothesis, is as respectable as the judgment of the Methodists, and we are not aware of her having ever condemned a book which, even in our private judgment, did not in some way or other tend to undermine faith or morals. Protestant books are rarely suitable reading for Christian men or women.

In our reply to the reviewer, we said, "The Catholic regards no act of the church, even of the highest dignitaries of the church, as infallible, unless the act of the whole church. There are only two ways in which the church is assumed to act as the whole church,—that is, in a universal council, or, what is the same thing, the unanimous or morally unanimous consent of all the bishops or pastors of the church, or through the pope, deciding *ex cathedra* as the representative of the church; and a man may be a Catholic without believing the decision of the pope, unless assented to by the body of bishops, is to be regarded as infallible. But we, for ourselves, hold the decisions of the pope, when he represents or decides for the church universal, are infallible."

The reviewer contends that in this we do not state the Catholic doctrine correctly. "Mr. B.," he says, "is but a novice in Romanism. . . . . . We heard Bishop England preach upon the peculiar dogmas of Rome in the Cathedral in Baltimore, in 1840, and he asserted that infallibility was lodged in the church collectively. He said a bishop might err, a council might err, and the pope might err; but the whole church could not err."

Our own statement is substantially correct. It was written some months before we became a Catholic, and we should use somewhat different terms were we to write it now, yet we should not alter its sense. The only objection we make to it is, that we seem to resolve the assent of the bishops dispersed abroad and congregated in council into one and the same mode of expressing the assent of the church. This is not correct. They are two different modes. We should therefore have said there are *three* ways, instead of only two, in which the church is assumed to act as the whole church. This, however, is a mere formal correction, and does not affect at all the substance of the statement.

We pay, as we are in duty bound, great respect to any assertion concerning the Catholic faith made by so eminent a prelate as the late Bishop of Charleston. But we may be permitted to doubt if he ever used the precise language ascribed to him. We had on a certain occasion, as the reviewer will remember, full proof that our Methodist friend could not well trust his own eyes; and we have no assurance that his ears are better than his eyes. But if the bishop actually used the language ascribed to him, he used it in a sense different from the one the reviewer imagines. He may have said a single bishop can err, for that nobody denies; but that all can, or any considerable number can, in what pertains to faith and morals, no Catholic can assert or admit. If he said a council might err, he meant a particular council, that is, a provincial or national council, not an œcumenical council; for every Catholic holds as an article of faith the infallibility of œcumenical councils. He may have said the pope can err in matters of administration, acting on misinformation or as a private doctor; but, if he said he might err as visible head of the church, when deciding for the whole church, *ex cathedra*, a question of faith or morals, he uttered a private opinion, which few Catholics share with him. The difficulty the reviewer has conjured up is one which has no real existence. The sense of the church is easily ascertained on any point of faith or morals.

"Upon Mr. B.'s theory," says the reviewer, "all we would have to do would be to consult the 'Holy Father' at Rome, and implicitly submit to his decisions." Not on *our* theory, but on the Catholic theory, for we have no theories of our own. Certainly, when the pope decides, we submit, for we recognize his right to decide, and we believe his decisions are infallible. "But," continues the reviewer, "when the decisions of one pope contradict those of another, and especially when the same pope decides different ways at different times, it is a little difficult to determine which is right, or to see the signs of infallibility anywhere." Unquestionably. But we deny the supposition. One pope has never in his decisions contradicted those of another, and no pope has ever decided different ways at different times. Protestants make the assertion, but why do they not adduce the instances, at least one instance, of such contradiction? Show us from ecclesiastical history one single well authenticated instance of such contradiction, and we are for ever silent. Bring forward, then, the instance, or never again make the assertion.

The reviewer tries to be quite witty in relation to the degree of liberty which, according to the view we gave, Catholics must enjoy, which he defines to be "the "liberty to hold and teach what his Holiness the Pope says they may." But wit is not our friend's forte. Nevertheless, we have no objection to his definition. Liberty to hold and teach what the sovereign pontiff says we may is all the liberty we ask; for it is liberty to hold and teach the word of God in its purity and integrity,—"the faith once delivered to the saints,"—which is all the liberty Almighty God allows to any man. The reviewer, we presume, holds that he is amenable to law, and that he is at liberty to do only what the law permits. Why should not we ridicule him for this? Has he yet to learn that law is the basis of liberty, and that where there is no sovereign authority there is no law? Liberty is not in being free of all law, but in being held only to the law. We believe the church, and the pope as visible head of the church, is the organ through which Almighty God promulgates the law. Consequently, in our own estimation at least, in submitting to the pope, we find, instead of losing, our liberty. At any rate, we have all the liberty we want. We know from experience what Protestant liberty is. We know all that it has to attract, but we never conceived of true liberty till we became a Catholic. In the absolute surrender of ourselves to Jesus Christ, in becoming his *slaves*, we become true freemen. "If the Son shall make you free, you shall be free indeed." It is idle, so far as we are concerned, to sneer at us for our submission to the pope. Call us slaves, if you will, you will not move us. We know your slavery and our freedom. We ask no other freedom than that of absolute obedience to God in his church; and you, if you knew any thing of the glorious Gospel of him whose name you bear, "to take away your reproach," would also ask no other. Did not St. Paul glory in being the *slave* of Jesus Christ?

But it seems, after all, that we mistook in our reply the thesis of the reviewer. He did not mean to say that Rome had produced no literary men, or that she had really warred upon literature as such, but only upon "every species of literature which could not be made tributary to her hierarchy." All we have to say in our defence is that we took the author's thesis according to his own formal and official statement of it. If he stated his design to be to prove one thing, but really attempted only to prove another thing, that was not our fault. If men will write without method, in a loose, declamatory style, paying no attention to the relation there may or may not be between their positions and their proofs, their premises and conclusions, they must be answerable for the consequences. The reviewer stated positively that his design, among other things, was, "to exhibit the proofs that the church of Rome had ever waged a deadly war upon literature." The proposition here set forth we denied, and we asserted that the reviewer had not adduced a single fact in proof of it. In this we were right. Whether he had or had not proved something else, and some things not at all to his own credit, we neither asserted nor denied.

But take his thesis as amended, we are ready to meet it. Fairly translated, it means that the church of Rome has never encouraged, but has done her best to discourage, every species of literature not consistent, or at war with the religion of Jesus Christ, as she had received the authority and the command to hold and teach it. So understood, we are far from controverting the thesis of the reviewer. If the church has so done, it is only another proof of her fidelity to her sacred trust. We hold religion before literature and science, and are barbarian enough to say that we have not the least conceivable respect for any literature or science not directly or indirectly enlisted in the service of religion, or, if you prefer, in the service of the Roman Catholic Church. Infidel literature, or science pressed into the service of infidelity, or even into the service of mammon, we grant, has no attractions for us, and, in our judgment, contributes nothing not really injurious to the best interests of mankind. If the reviewer thinks differently, we thank God the church does not think with him. What benefit to mankind does the reviewer think has accrued from the writings of Hobbes, Tindal, Collins, Morgan, Mandeville, Voltaire, Rousseau, Helvetius, D'Holbach, Dupuis, Cabanis, Destutt de Tracy, Goethe, Schiller, Kant, Schelling, Hegel, Heine, Eichhorn, Gesenius, Paulus, Strauss, Feuerbach, Godwin, Byron, Shelley, Bulwer, Victor Hugo, De Balzac, George Sand, Paul de Kock, Eugene Sue, and hundreds and hundreds of others we might mention had we room? Genius, talent, learning, are never respectable unless enlisted in the cause of religion, unless they bow low at the foot of the cross, and lay their offerings on the altar of the crucified God. Is the reviewer prepared to deny this? If not, let him say no more against the expurgatory and prohibitory indexes of the church. The church was not instituted to foster literature or science, but to train men up for God. Yet she has never ceased to honor men of science, to patronize men of literature, and of every species of literature, when they did not seek to abuse their gifts and prostitute their genius, ability, and acquirements to the injury of religion, to the corrupting of men's minds and hearts, to leading them into doubt and darkness to their everlasting ruin. This was all that she had a right to do, and all that could be asked of her. If the church in her relations with literary and scientific men has erred at all, it has been in the fostering care she has extended to them, and in the leniency with which she has viewed their aberrations. She has always proved herself a kind, affectionate, and forbearing mother to them.

The reviewer abandons the case of Virgil, Bishop of Salzburg, which he had before adduced as proving the hostility of the church to science, but holds on to the case of Galileo. He makes two points against us. 1. That Galileo's doctrine was actually condemned as a heresy; and 2. That the Inquisition, which condemned him, claims infallibility for its decrees. In proof of the first he cites at length what he asserts is the *sentence* of the Inquisition. But as he does not tell us whence he obtained this document or where it may be found, and as he cites it in English, not in the original Latin, it is not admissible testimony. That in the sentence of the Inquisition the doctrine of the earth's motion is declared to be a *heresy*, we have not denied, and do not now deny. But this is the language of the theological *qualifiers* who examined the case in 1616, and is merely recited in the sentence in 1633. In 1616, the case, at the request of Galileo and his friends, was sent to the Inquisition, and the theological qualifiers to whom it was commited qualified the doctrine as heresy; but, in consequence of Galileo's promise to refrain from teaching the doctrine, no final action was had on the subject, and the fact whether the doctrine was or was not a heresy was not decided, but remained as the report of the qualifiers. In 1633, when Galileo was finally condemned, the question did not turn on the point whether his doctrine was or was not heretical, but on the point whether he *had* actually taught the doctrine after he had been forbidden to teach it. The Inquisition merely cites the report of the *qualifiers*, without passing upon the question of the heretical character of the doctrine itself, and condemned Galileo not because his doctrine was a heresy, but because he had continued to teach it in contempt of authority. The fact, then, that the Inquisition employs the terms *heresy* and *heretical* does not prove that it adjudged the doctrine itself to be heretical. In order that it should prove this, the character of the doctrine should have been the precise question before the court. Any lawyer will inform the reviewer that the court decides only the precise point or points before it. What else it may allege is an *obiter dictum*, or the mere private opinion of the judge, and without authority. The terms *heresy* and *heretical* also prove nothing, because they are the mere *stylus curiæ*, and are frequently adopted by the Inquisition where it is manifest the offence is not, strictly speaking, heresy. That Galileo was condemned for teaching, or rather, for the manner in which he taught, the doctrine of the earth's motion, we did not deny; but that the doctrine itself was condemned as heretical we did, and do still, deny. We quoted, in proof of our denial, the words of the pontiff under whose reign he was condemned, and of Galileo himself. We also showed that the reigning pontiff was himself favorable to the doctrine, and that at the very moment of the condemnation of Galileo it was publicly taught in Rome by the professor of astronomy in the pope's own college. It is idle, then, to pretend that it was condemned as a heresy.

The doctrine of the motion of the earth as a scientific hypothesis had long been promulgated at Rome, and Galileo might have taught it undisturbed, if he had chosen to observe certain very proper restrictions. The difficulty was in the fact, not to be denied, that the doctrine of the earth's motion is repugnant, or apparently repugnant, to the literal sense of the Holy Scriptures. It was never held that the literal sense of Scripture might not be set aside on competent authority, and a less literal construction adopted. But this can never be done to make way for a conjecture or an hypothesis. Science and revelation can never be in contradiction; but what you allege as science must be science, must be absolutely demonstrated, before it can be taken into the account in the interpretation of the Holy Scriptures. Now, in the time of Galileo, the doctrine of the earth's motion was not demonstrated, was at best a mere hypothesis; and therefore to have undertaken to explain the texts which seemed to contradict it, and which, as they had hitherto been understood, did contradict it, so as to make them conform to it, was, to say the least, rash, and implied an heretical disposition on the part of him who should so undertake. Here was the rock on which Galileo split. He undertook to explain the Scriptures in accordance with his theory, and treated the Scriptural objections with a degree of levity and contempt incompatible with a becoming respect for the language of the inspired writings. Had he followed the direction of Cardinal Bellarmine, who suggested that it would be time enough to take into consideration the interpretation of the texts which seemed to oppose the theory after the theory should be proved to be demonstrated, no one would ever have disturbed him.

As to the second point, we would remind the reviewer, that, while we accept his authority on any question of the constitution of the Methodist society, we do not recognize it where he assumes to speak as a Catholic doctor. We told him, and we tell him again, that the Inquisition is not an institution of which Catholics predicate infallibility. It is no essential part of the church, and its decrees have been and may be set aside by a higher authority. "It is sufficient for us to know," says the reviewer, "that the decrees of that court claim to be infallible, and are enacted with that claim with the pope's knowledge and approbation, and the condemnation of heretical books and persons by the holy officer are as much the act of the church of Rome as any act of the supreme pontiff." Here are many things jumbled together that should be kept distinct. We have no time or space to disentangle them. The Inquisition without the pope is evidently not infallible, according to Catholic principles. Admit its decrees, when formally approved by the pope, and thus made his, are to be held by Catholics as infallible, it still will not affect the case before us; for the approbation of the pope was not thus given to the condemnation of the doctrine in 1616, and in 1633 it was not, as we have seen, in question. The act which received the pope's approbation was the condemnation of Galileo in 1633, when the question turned not on the doctrine, but on Galileo's contempt of authority.

"And whatever Mr. B. may say, this has been the opinion of abler and better informed Roman Cotholics than himself." If the reviewer means that it is the opinion of abler and better informed Roman Catholics that the Inquisition is an institution of which Catholics predicate infallibility, we deny it, and challenge him to prove his assertion. If he means simply that some Catholics as well as Protestants have taken a different view of the condemnation of Galileo from the one we have given, we do not deny it, and have no wish to deny it, for Catholics are not infallible, and may err in their version of historical facts.

"And in the preface of the Jesuits' edition of Newton's *Principia*, we have the clearest evidence that the editors supposed his system under ban of the church. This is the language:—'Newton in his third book supposes the motion of the earth. We could not explain the author's propositions otherwise than by making the same supposition. We are therefore forced to sustain a character not our own;

but we profess to pay the obsequious reverence which is due to the decrees pronounced by the supreme pontiffs against the motion of the earth.'" This would seem to be conclusive; but, unhappily for the reviewer, this Jesuits' edition of Newton's *Principia* is a pure fiction. The Jesuits never published such an edition, and the language quoted never was written by a Jesuit. The language betrays at a single glance its origin. There are no decrees, and there never were any decrees, pronounced by the supreme pontiffs against the motion of the earth. The Jesuits never published an edition of Newton's *Principia*, except the edition by Father Boscovich, and that is not the edition referred to. The edition cited was got up by a couple of infidel editors, in France, we believe, and was palmed off as an edition of the Jesuits. The extract the reviewer quotes from the preface bears the living impress of the French infidel of the last century. No Jesuit could ever have spoken thus ironically of what he held to be a decision of the sovereign pontiff. It would be even more out of character than for the reviewer to invoke the Blessed Virgin, or to officiate at High Mass.

We here take our leave of the *Methodist Quarterly Review*, by simply reminding the editor that he is not qualified to be our biographer. His assertion, that there "are hundreds of living witnesses who heard our atheistical lectures in the city of Boston," is absolutely and unqualifiedly false; for we never gave an atheistical lecture in the city of Boston or elsewhere in our life. We never were, properly speaking, an atheist, a transcendentalist, or a pantheist, the assertion of the reviewer to the contrary notwithstanding. For a few months, some years ago, we had, it is true, some doubts as to the existence of God; but, since the latter part of the year 1830, we are not conscious of having had, even for a moment, a single doubt cross our mind of the existence or the providence of God. It is true that we fell unconsciously into some speculations which had a transcendental and pantheistic tendency; but, the moment we discovered that they had that tendency, we renounced them, and for the very reason, that they had it. We have been, ever since we resided in Boston, or for the last ten years, constantly writing and publishing against both transcendentalism and pantheism. We have had errors enough, without having laid to our charge errors we have never entertained.

HOPKINS'S BRITISH REFORMATION.*

[From Brownson's Quarterly Review for January, 1845.]

WE agree entirely with Bishop Hopkins, that "the aspect of the religious world, at this moment, presents the same elements of controversy, only under varied forms of practical application, which agitated all Europe three hundred years ago." A little over three hundred years ago, under pretence of religious reform, and of reviving the faith and worship of the primitive Christians, a portion of the nominally Christian world seceded from the Catholic Church, and set up new establishments for themselves, with such forms of worship, such symbols of faith, and under such systems of government, as they judged most advisable. The church then existing,—and which had been regarded by the whole Christian world, condemned heretics and schismatics excepted, for fifteen hundred years, as the one Holy Catholic and Apostolic Church,—as was to be expected, condemned them as heretics and schismatics, declared them out of the pale of the church and severed from the communion of Christ.

For three hundred years, these seceders and their successors have been laboring to effect a reversal of the sentence then solemnly pronounced against them, and to convince the world that they were wrongfully condemned; that their private establishments are really living members of the church of Christ, and that they, in founding them, acted by the authority of Christ himself, and did not break the unity either of the orthodox faith or of the Lord's body. They have been zealous and diligent, have had learning, talents, genius, and power on their side, but they have labored without success. The sentence has not been reversed; their claims have not been admitted; and never has the necessity of their undertaking to defend themselves been greater than now. The religious world at this moment seems further than ever from reversing the sentence recorded

---

*Sixteen Lectures on the Causes, Principles, and Results of the British Reformation. By J. H. Hopkins, D. D., Bishop of the Protestant Episcopal Church in the Diocese of Vermont. Philadelphia: 1844.

against them. The church from which they seceded is now, if possible, more vigorous than ever, and counts a larger number of members than at any former period of her existence. Her missionaries have penetrated to almost every nook and corner of the globe. She is rapidly regaining the ground she had lost in France, England, and Germany, and has obtained a new empire in America; while, on the other hand, the Protestant churches, cut up into innumerable sects, are everywhere languishing and disappearing. Nowhere do they gain on Catholicity; nowhere have they gained on Catholicity for the last two hundred years. In fact, they everywhere lose ground. They have lost it in Ireland, in France, in Germany, and are losing it in our own country and even in England. And, what is perhaps more discouraging still to their cause, in the bosom of each and all of their communions there is a wide and deep feeling that the separation from the Catholic Church, if not absolutely unauthorized, was unnecessary and ill-advised; that what was substituted for the church does not and cannot supply her place; that Protestantism has proved a failure; and that nothing remains for us but either to return to Catholicity, or to lapse into complete infidelity.

The seceders, through their successors, are, therefore, unquestionably under the necessity either of abandoning their cause or of renewing the controversy. It is no time for them to be idle, no time for them to sleep, and to dream that the controversy is over. The church has abandoned none of her claims, and never will abandon any of them; for her authority she has inherited from the apostles, and her faith she holds as a sacred deposit from Christ the Head. She has made, and will make, no compromise with error and schism. She must be all or nothing. She has not ceased, and she will not cease, to exert herself with all fidelity, zeal, and diligence, to recover every revolted province, and to secure the heathen and the ends of the earth to God's dear Son for his inheritance. The church does not sleep; she does not cease from her mission. Everywhere does she bear witness for her Lord; everywhere is she ready to combat for the truth, and shed the blood of her martyrs for the salvation of souls. She will give no rest to heretics and schismatics. If, then, they mean to defend themselves, to maintain the ground they have acquired, they must be vigilant and active. Nay, they must do more; they must meet the question fairly, in open and rational debate. They can no longer call on the civil power to secure them the advantage; they can no longer rely on penal enactments to stifle the voice of truth. They can no longer maintain their cause by false charges and misrepresentation. They must now debate the question, and debate it fairly; and yield, if they cannot sustain themselves by good and sufficient reasons.

We regard it as a happy day for the church, that she has, at length, secured in most Protestant countries the liberty to speak and write in her own defence. This is all she needs. She asks no other advantage of Protestants. She knows the strength of her own cause and the weakness of theirs; and if she can only be met in fair discussion, she fears not the result. All she asks of Protestants is, that they consent to reason, instead of declaiming, and confine themselves to facts instead of falsehoods.

All appearances indicate that in this country the great debate is coming on, and is likely soon to absorb the attention of the American people. The better portion of the community are daily losing their interest in political disputes,—their confidence in the ability of government alone to secure even the temporal well-being of a people; and are beginning to feel the necessity of a religion, fixed and firm, immovable amid the fluctuations of time, and able to command the passions, subdue evil propensities, wean the affections from things of the earth and place them on things above, and direct all our energies to gaining the kingdom of God and his justice. Our sects are breaking up. Puritanism has exhausted itself, and Congregationalism totters to its fall. The Presbyterian Church is divided into hostile factions, and the powerful sect of the Methodists is torn by schisms and internal divisions. The Baptists must follow the fate of their Calvinistic brethren. The Episcopalians, boasting of their "admirable liturgy," and pretending to be "a branch" of the Catholic Church,—divided between high and low church into two parties, one seeking to get rid of the name of Protestant, the other to retain it,—having the form of godliness without its reality, must erelong fulfil the prophecy, that a kingdom divided against itself cannot stand. Union in the bosom of any of these sects is out of the question, much more the union of them all in one body. What have they, torn with intestine divisions, cut up into cliques and coteries, each armed against each, each controverting and confuting what each advances, to offer to satisfy the religious wants of the American people? Do they not see that their power is gone? How are they to recover it? They may exhort one another to union and peace. But what principle, save the negative principle of hatred to Catholicity, have they on which to unite, or which can be the principle of peace? Do they not see that their contentions are inevitable, their divisions impossible to be healed? They deserted the principle of unity, the ground of peace, when they left the church. They have foolishly, like the rash builders in the plain of Shinar, attempted to build a tower which should reach to heaven, and God confounds their speech, and disperses them abroad.

In this state of things, the great question of Catholicity necessarily comes up. The Catholic Church steps forth in the majesty of ages, splendid with the robes of light, and beautiful with the beauty of holiness, and offers to a distracted people, worrying and devouring one another, the olive-branch of peace. She has a faith, once delivered to the saints, which she has preserved unimpaired through all the changes of time, to offer them; she has a worship consecrated by a long line of saints and martyrs, now reigning with Jesus in heaven, to offer them; she has a church, which, like the ark of Noah, rises sublime on the deluge of waters, in which are the chosen of the Lord, and safety for all within, to offer them; and will the distracted mind and the wearied heart slight her offer? "Come unto me," she says, in the name and tones of her Master, "ye who labor and are heavy-laden, and I will give you rest." And is her invitation one not likely, in these days, to be heeded? We have sought repose, we have found it not; we seek it everywhere, and we find it not; we seek it in this sect or in that, —it is not there; we seek it in infidelity or indifference,— it is not there, for there is only the repose of the charnel-house. Where, then, shall we seek it? To whom, then, shall we go? To whom, but to the blessed Jesus in the church which he has founded as the medium of access to him, who only has the words of eternal life?

We do assuredly look upon the times as auspicious for the church. We do assuredly look upon the spread of Catholicity in this country, as likely to be speedy and extensive. Its adversaries must, then, meet it, must renew the debate, and defend themselves if they can. That they will, there can be no doubt. They will go over the old ground, and free themselves, if in their power, from the old charges of heresy and schism. For with the spread of Catholicity revives faith in God, faith in Christ, faith in the church; and with the revival of this faith, men cease to sit down easy under the charge of heresy or schism. Heresy and schism become again words full of meaning, and of a terrible meaning, which cannot be looked in the face. Orthodoxy recovers its old sense, and men feel, that, without the true faith and the true church, they are without Christ, and without Christ they are without God. The sects must prove that they, as sects, are members of the Lord's body, and that they maintain the true faith; or else abandon their pretensions, and acknowledge themselves to be rightfully condemned as heretics and schismatics, and therefore as dead branches, severed from the vine, whose end is to be burned.

Something of all this appears to have been felt by the learned and accomplished author of the Lectures before us. And he has come forward to do what he can to justify the reformers in their separation from the Roman Catholic Church, and to free at least the Protestant Episcopal Church from the charge of schism. The question is one of fearful import for him and his brethren; for if he fails to free his church of this charge, he fails to prove that it is, in the Christian sense, a church at all,—fails to vindicate the legitimacy of its ministry and sacraments; and compels himself to admit, that, if he continue in its communion, he is out of the communion of Christ, and that he is guilty, not only of usurping an honor to which he has not been called of God, as was Aaron, not only of breaking the commandments of God and the unity of the Lord's body, but of teaching others to do the same, of leading others astray, of confirming them in error, and perilling their salvation. His is a position fearfully responsible; and he has need, not only to be firmly persuaded that he is not wrong, but to know positively and infallibly that he is right,—not only to show that the reformers were *possibly* excusable, but that they were positively and infallibly right and justifiable, and that the churches they founded are the one Holy Catholic and Apostolic Church, which our blessed Saviour said he would build on a rock, and against which the gates of hell should not prevail.

In proceeding to remark on these Lectures, we shall consider them solely in their bearing on this question of schism. The church of which the author is a high dignit-

and has lain from its origin, under the charge of schism, and these Lectures concern us only so far as they are designed to free it of that charge. We ask, then, has the author succeeded in vindicating the British reformers, and in proving that the Anglican Church is not rightfully regarded as a schismatic church? This is the question before us, and to this question we shall confine ourselves as strictly as possible.

Now, it is evident, at first sight, that, before proceeding to answer this question, the bishop should allege some principle or ground of defence, on which he relies, to show that the secession of the reformers was not schism. He himself professes to believe in the unity and catholicity of the church, and must then, of course, admit that separation from the church is schism. Now, the body from which the reformers separated had been regarded by the whole Christian world, condemned schismatics and heretics excepted, from time immemorial, and was still regarded by the great majority of the Christian world, as the church of Christ. The reformers themselves had so regarded it, had received from it their Christian birth, and their mission, so far as they had any. Their secession was, then, *prima facie*, schism, and must be taken and deemed to be such, till they show good and sufficient reasons why it should not be. The church stands on the *olim possideo*, the *prior possessio*; and cannot be ousted from her inheritance, nor summoned even to plead, till good and sufficient reasons, in case they are sustained, are adduced to invalidate her title. These reasons must be adduced as the grounds of the reformers' claim, and, till they are adduced, we cannot argue the question, whether the reformed churches are schismatic, for till then the simple fact of secession convicts them of schism.

We have looked through these Lectures to ascertain the ground on which the bishop rests the defence of the reformers, but very nearly in vain. He does not meet the question manfully; he does not proceed in an orderly and logical manner; and, we are sorry to see, nowhere states clearly and distinctly the principles from which he obtains his premises. He lays down no rules for the admission of testimony, and none for testing the value of the testimony admitted. All is loose, confused; and, whether true or false, so adduced, that one cannot say what it proves or does not prove to his purpose. Yet, by much searching, by much guessing, and borrowing largely from the general arguments of Protestants elsewhere, we conjecture that he means to contend that the church is composed of all who maintain the orthodox faith, and that, since the reformers, in separating from the communion of Rome, retained the orthodox faith, they did not separate from the Catholic Church, and therefore were not schismatics. He reasons, then, in this way.

1. The Catholic Church is composed of all who maintain the orthodox faith.

But the reformers maintained the orthodox faith; therefore, the reformers were members of the Catholic Church.

2. They only are schismatics who separate from the orthodox faith.

But the reformers did not separate from the orthodox faith; therefore the reformers were not schismatics.

But this definition of the church is defective, for it does not embrace the idea of the church as a teaching and governing body, asserted by the bishop's own church, and in fact contended for by the bishop himself. It also destroys all intelligible distinction between schism and heresy. Heresy is a wilful departure from the orthodox faith; schism is a wilful separation from the ministry or authority of the church. All heresy is schism, and all schism may conceal heresy at the bottom; but all schism, as such, is not necessarily heresy. Consequently, if the church be defined so as to embrace all who maintain the orthodox faith, schism, as a distinct sin from heresy, is denied. Consequently, separation from the legitimate ministry of the church, the formation of new and distinct congregations, with a new ministry, not deriving from the apostles, would not be schism, would not break the unity of the body, in case the seceders maintained the orthodox faith. Nay, these new congregations would be integral members of the Catholic Church, although they should have no ministry, no sacraments, no worship; for nothing is essential to the church but the orthodox faith. This would be giving to the doctrine of salvation by faith alone a very convenient latitude. But congregations without a ministry, without the sacraments and worship, cannot be called members of the church; for the bishop's own church defines the church to be " a congregation of faithful men, in which the pure word of God is preached, and the sacraments be duly ministered according to Christ's ordinance, in all those things that of necessity are requisite to the same." Art. XIX. Here something beside the orthodox faith is made essential to the church,—namely, the sacraments duly administered. The bishop is therefore precluded by his own church from insisting on his definition. But if the due administration of the sacraments be, as here declared, necessary to the very being of the church, then is necessary to the being of the church a ministry authorized to administer them; and separation from this authorized ministry must be separation from the church, and therefore schism, as much as separation from the orthodox faith itself. The reformers, as is well known, did separate from the ministry authorized to administer the sacraments; therefore were schismatics, even admitting they did not cease to be orthodox believers.

But even conceding that all orthodox believers are members of the church, we must still ask, Who or what keeps, propounds, and defines the orthodox faith? This faith does not keep, propound, or define itself. It must have a depositary, a propounder, and a definer, or else we can never know what it is, who embrace it, and therefore who are or are not of the church. "I do indeed," says the bishop, "profess myself a believer in the one catholic or universal church of the Redeemer, which forms a distinct article in the primitive creed; but I have long cherished the opinion, that all orthodox believers are members of that church, whatever may be the diversities of their particular communion."—p. 2. But who *are* orthodox believers? What *is* the orthodox faith? There must be a standard of orthodoxy, and somewhere an authority competent to say what does or does not conform to it. What is this standard? What is this authority?

According to the bishop, the standard is the word of God contained in the Scriptures of the Old and New Testaments. The Bible he holds to be the depositary of the word of God;. belief of which is the orthodox faith. But it is essential to the orthodox faith that it be belief of the *whole* word of God; for God reveals nothing superfluous, and he who refuses to believe any portion of God's word, refuses to believe God just as much as he who refuses to believe the whole. Before the Bible is assumed to be the standard of orthodoxy, it must, then, be proved to contain the *whole* word of God. But how is this to be proved? It cannot be proved by natural reason; because the question, how much or how little is revealed, is not a question of natural reason, but must be determined by a supernatural authority. It cannot be proved from the Bible, for the Bible nowhere professes to contain the whole word of God; nay, it does not even profess that the whole word of God has been written, but contains several passages which indicate very clearly to the contrary. How, then, will the bishop prove that the Bible contains the whole word of God? But if he cannot prove that the Bible contains the whole word of God, how can he prove that he who believes it, or conforms to all that it teaches, is an orthodox believer?

Will it be said, that the orthodox faith is that faith which is necessary to salvation; that the Bible contains all that is necessary to be believed for salvation; and, therefore, he who believes what it contains is an orthodox believer? We grant that he who believes all that is necessary for salvation is an orthodox believer; but how know we that the Bible contains all that is necessary to be believed for salvation? The Bible itself nowhere says so, and by an authority below that of the Bible the fact cannot be established. The whole question lies out of the jurisdiction of natural reason. Reason by its own light can never know that a supernatural faith is at all necessary to salvation. The necessity of such faith we know only by supernatural revelation; consequently, supernatural revelation is as necessary to determine the extent as the subject-matter of the faith itself. With nothing but the Bible and natural reason, no man can say that the Bible contains all that is necessary to be believed for salvation. Consequently, the conclusion, that he who believes all the Bible contains is an orthodox believer, is not proved. But, according to the state of the argument, the presumption is against the bishop; therefore, he is bound to prove that the Bible positively does contain the whole word of God, at least, all that is necessary to be believed for salvation, before he can assume it as the standard of the orthodox faith.

But, waiving this question, conceding for the moment that the Bible contains the whole word of God, one must believe that word in its *genuine sense*, or he is not an orthodox believer. The Bible does not interpret itself. It must be interpreted, and its genuine sense determined. But who or what is the interpreter? According to the bishop, the interpreter, save exceptions in favor of private reason, hereafter to be noticed, is the church. This he is bound to hold; because the twentieth article of his church expressly declares the church to have "authority in controversies of faith," and therefore must have authority to declare what the faith is. He also insists (p. 18) that the church is the court for expounding and applying the law. The court expounds and applies the law authoritatively. So also must the church, if the analogy is to hold good. Then the church must be an authoritative body,—not to make the law, for that nobody ever pretended, but to expound and apply it.

This is a point gained. It is no longer sufficient to define the church to be simply the great body of believers in the orthodox faith ; for we must now add that it is an *authoritative* body, having the authority to declare what the orthodox faith is. Now, this authority is either legitimate or it is not. If the latter, it is usurped, and therefore really no authority at all, for nobody is bound to regard it. If the former, then it is from Christ, the source of all legitimate authority in the church ; then it is obligatory on all, and can be resisted by no one without sin, without rebellion against Christ, which is schism. If, then, the reformers resisted this authority, as it is well known they did, or separated from it, they were schismatics, and the churches they founded are out of the communion of Christ.

The bishop concedes the church to be an authoritative body. But the church is not *many*, but *one*. Therefore the authority is one. The court to expound and apply the law, then, is the universal church, not a particular church. The authority that declares the law must be the authority of the whole, and not of a part. This is evident from the fact, that, if the authority of the church be an unitary authority, the authority of a part, or of some particular portion of the church, must be inferior and subordinate to the whole, on the principle that the whole is greater than a part. The decision of a part can never be final, and the case may be carried up and argued before the full bench.

The bishop professes to believe in the *one* Catholic Church. He then must admit the unity of the church. This unity must extend to all that is embraced within the definition of the church. This we now see, from the bishop himself, is not only the orthodox faith, but the authority competent to declare what that faith is. The church, then, must be one in its faith, and one in its authority. That is, its unity is not only the unity of faith, but the unity of authority. Now, whoever breaks the unity of this authority breaks the unity of the church, as much as he who breaks the unity of the faith. But the reformers did break this authority, and therefore were schismatics.

This conclusion we do not understand Bishop Hopkins to controvert, so far as it concerns the German and Swiss reformers, (pp. 26, 27,) but only in the case of the *British* reformers. The British reformers were not schismatics, because they did not proceed on their own individual authority, but on the authority of a national church. His argument is, they who separate from the Catholic body by authority of the national church, of which they are members, are not schismatics; but the British reformers separated by authority of the national church; therefore, they were not schismatics.

To this we reply, 1. That the British reformation, in point of fact, was not effected by the authority of the British Church as such, but by authority of the king and parliament, as is notorious,—an authority which the British Church herself declares incompetent to do any thing of the sort; for she declares that "the civil magistrate hath no authority in things purely spiritual." Art. XXXVIII.

We reply, 2. That, even if the reformers had proceeded by authority of the national church, they would have been none the less schismatics; because no national church is a complete church polity in itself, but merely a part, and therefore subordinated to the whole. The church of Christ is catholic, and knows no geographical limits, or national distinctions. It is one, and, as we have seen, one in its authority as well as in its faith. The authority of the national church could be sufficient for the reformers only on condition of its being a complete polity in itself, and, as to authority, independent of all other ecclesiastical bodies. But to assert this completeness and independency of the national church would be to deny the unity of the Catholic body, and to assert as many distinct, separate, and independent churches as there are nations in which there are churches. To call these several distinct, separate, and independent churches all one church would be as false and as absurd as to call all the nations of Europe and America one and the same nation.

Again, the bishop's argument presupposes the right of each national church to expound the law in its own sense, and to differ as it judges necessary from all others. Consequently, he denies the obligation of the national church to maintain the unity and integrity of the Catholic faith. For there may be rightfully as many different interpretations of the law, and therefore as many different faiths, as national churches. He goes further; he even lays down the doctrine, that "the church," meaning the national church," hath authority in controversies of faith." If the church hath authority in controversies of faith, the faithful must be bound to submit to it; for the right to command involves always the obligation to obey. The faithful, then, in each nation are bound to receive the interpretations of the national church. The authority of the church is divine, and the church therefore commands in the name of God. The faithful are commanded, then, in the name of God, in each nation, to believe what the national church teaches. * Consequently, the faithful may be commanded in the name of God to believe one doctrine as orthodox in one country, and another doctrine in another. So that the bishop's doctrine of the independence of national churches not only breaks the unity of the ecclesiastical authority, but even the unity of faith. But we have already established both unity of faith and of authority to be essential to the unity of the church. Therefore this doctrine of independent national churches is inadmissible; therefore the authority of the national church could not justify the reformers in seceding from the Catholic body. Therefore their secession was, as we have said, schism.

Moreover, if we should admit this doctrine of the absolute independence of national churches, we should be obliged to deny the possibility of a national church ever becoming heretical or schismatic. It cannot become schismatic; for it can become so only on condition of wilfully separating from its own authority, which is absurd. It cannot be heretical; because it is itself the supreme judge of the law and propounder of the faith. Orthodoxy is what it declares to be orthodoxy. It is impossible for it, then, to be heterodox; for heterodoxy is the doctrine repugnant to what it declares to be orthodox. It can be heterodox only on condition of denying what it declares, and even in declaring it. But a national church may be both schismatic and heretical; for the Church of England herself declares, that, "as the Church of *Hierusalem, Alexandria,* and *Antioch* have erred, so also the Church of *Rome* hath erred, not only in their living and manner of ceremonies, but also in matters of faith." Art. XIX.

But the bishop also seeks to justify the reformers by asserting the right of private judgment. His doctrine is, that the church is indeed authoritative, that the authority of the smallest sect is superior to that of the individual, that the authority of the national church is still greater, and that of the universal church is the greatest of all. Where the universal church is unanimous, its authority is complete; but where it is not agreed, but divided, individual reason, private judgment, must decide for each one as well as it can. We shall not smile at the bishop's simplicity, in supposing that this reservation in favor of private judgment amounts to any thing. All Catholics allow full scope to private judgment, reverently exercised, on all matters not decided by the church; and this is all the bishop himself asserts or implies. He admits the authority of the church, and of course must deny the authority of private judgment in all matters coming within the jurisdiction of that authority; for it is absurd to contend for the right of private judgment in regard to those matters covered by the ecclesiastical authority. The two authorities may, indeed, coexist, but not in regard to the same matters; for one is the negation of the other. But the church, it is conceded, hath authority in controversies of faith. Art. XX. Consequently, in matters of faith private judgment has not authority. Whatever authority, then, it may have, it can have none to justify the reformers in those matters they stand accused of, for those are really, directly or indirectly, matters of faith; since the authority of the church itself, which they resisted, is an article of faith, professed in the creed, "I believe the Holy Catholic Church,"—not, I believe *in* it, that is, that there is a Holy Catholic Church, but that I believe it, what it teaches, and observe what it commands.

But the bishop says, where the church is unanimous, its authority is complete and final; where it is divided, it is not authoritative, and private judgment is. Is it possible for the church to be divided? The church is an authoritative body, as already proved, and as the bishop contends earnestly (pp. 26, 27). But can authority be divided against itself? The church either decides or it does not. In any matter decided, it cannot be said to be divided; for the decision itself is proof to the contrary. Matters not decided are not decided, and are not articles of faith. The church cannot be said to be divided about these, for she has taken no action on them. Individuals may be divided about them, but not the church. Moreover, if the church could be divided on any matter, it would be a kingdom divided against itself, and therefore must fall; but we have the promise of him who cannot lie, that it shall not fall, for it is built on a rock, and the gates of hell shall not prevail against it.

Furthermore, when the church has decided, those, be they few or be they many, who refuse to submit, are *ipso facto* schismatics, out of the communion of the church, and no part of it. The dissent of these, therefore, makes nothing against the unanimity of the church. Here, we apprehend, is the great difficulty of our Protestant bishop. When he talks of divisions in the church, we suspect he has reference to divisions, not in the church, but out of it. Bishop as he is, he does not appear to have any clear notions of ecclesiastical authority. He admits the authority of the church in one breath, and denies it in the next, and then apparently both admits and denies it in the same breath. We, however, hold him to the Thirty-nine Articles, which declare, "The church hath authority in controversies of faith." Then he must admit that there is somewhere in the church an authority competent to decide such controversies. Then he must also admit, that, when that authority has decided, they who refuse to submit to the decision are rebels, and by their rebellion placed out of the church. In demanding unanimity as essential to complete the authority of the church, does he demand the unanimous assent of all, both the church condemning and the adherents of the doctrine condemned? The Council of Nice condemned the Arians, but certainly not with the consent of the Arians. Was it after that condemnation lawful for a member of the church to question its justice, and to attempt to decide for himself, by his private judgment, the subject-matter of the original controversy, on the ground, that the whole body of professed Christians, or of professed Christian pastors, had not been unanimous in condemning Arianism? If so, where was the authority of the church in controversies of faith? The adherents of the heretical doctrine, of course, cannot be unanimous in condemning it; and if their assent to its condemnation must be obtained, before the condemnation can be pronounced by a competent authority, we should like to be informed how any doctrine can ever be condemned as heretical!

The church either has authority to condemn doctrines as heretical, or she has not. If not, then it is idle to talk of her *authority* in controversies of faith. She has no authority, and the whole question is left to private judgment; and each individual, from the best evidences in the case, is free to form his own opinions, and to abide by them, whether agreeing with the great body of believers or not. The fathers, the decisions of councils, &c., may have great weight with him, and be, in fact, the *data* from which he reasons, but they cannot bind him. He is free to read the Bible for himself, and form his own creed. Is the bishop prepared to admit this conclusion? Of course not, for he contends that the church has authority in controversies of faith, holds dissent to be a sin, and censures severely the German and Swiss reformers for asserting the *dangerous* principle which leads to it.

If we take the other alternative, and say that the church *hath* authority to condemn doctrines as heretical, then the question is not, whether all who profess to belong to the church consent to the condemnation, but whether the condemnation has been really pronounced by the government of the church. If the government has pronounced the condemnation, it is unquestionably authoritative, and all who refuse to consent are by that fact rebels, and to be condemned as schismatics. In determining, then, on what matters the church is agreed, we have not to inquire on what matters all who bear the Christian name are agreed; but simply, what matters the church has decided. The decision is, *ipso facto*, proof of unanimity; for whoso refuses to submit to it is, *ipso facto*, a schismatic, and out of the church, as says our blessed Saviour: "If he will not hear the church, let him be to you as the heathen and the publican." This must be admitted, if we admit the church to be authoritative at all.

But the reformers are accused of schism, only for rejecting the authority of the church on those matters it had decided, and on which its unanimity is to be presumed. Since, then, the authority of the church, in all matters on which it is agreed, is conceded to be ultimate, the right of private judgment on other matters cannot be pleaded in justification of the reformers. Consequently, the reservation in favor of private judgment cannot free them from the charge of schism.

It is true, the bishop himself would seem to extend the right of private judgment beyond the limits we have assigned it, and give it, in some sense, a coördinate jurisdiction with that of the church, and of the same matters. To this end he quotes several passages from the Sacred Scriptures. But to assume the authority of both private judgment and the church on the same matters is, as we have said, absurd. One authority necessarily excludes the other. If it is private judgment, then not the church; if the church, then not private judgment. If it is private judgment, private judgment can override the decision of the church, and then the authority of the church is null; if it is the church, then the church can override private judgment, and the authority of private judgment is null. Obviously, then, the two authorities cannot have coördinate jurisdiction of the same matters. If the two authorities be admitted, it must be in relation to different matters.

The passages quoted from the Holy Scriptures are not to the bishop's purpose. They undoubtedly recognize man as a reasonable being, and call upon him to exercise his reason; but not in relation to those questions which are subjected to authority. Almighty God calls upon us to reason, we admit,—to exercise our private judgment, we cheerfully concede; but not in regard to the intrinsic truth of the mysteries of faith, nor in regard to the genuine sense of the word of God; but solely in regard to the motives of credibility. He calls upon us to reason on the question, 1. Whether his providences do not harmonize with our natural sense of justice; 2. Whether we have not sufficient motives for believing his word, that is, to believe him when he speaks, on his own veracity; 3. Whether we can justify to ourselves our refusal to trust his veracity, and to obey his commands; 4. Whether the witness to his word is not altogether credible; and 5. Whether the interpreter whose interpretations we are commanded to take has not received ample authority to interpret the word of God. All these are questions addressed to reason, and come within the jurisdiction of private judgment; for otherwise our faith would be blind and irrational, even if true, and faith without reason is not what God demands of us. But the admission of the right of private judgment on these questions is one thing,—the admission of the right of private judgment in regard to the intrinsic truth of the mysteries of faith is another and a very different thing. The mysteries are inevident to reason, because they transcend it, and are taken, not on the authority of reason apprehending their intrinsic truth,—for, if they were, they would be matters of science, and not of faith,—but on the simple veracity of God revealing them; and the fact that God has revealed them is not taken on their intrinsic reasonableness, or any perception of their intrinsic reasonableness, but on the authority of the witness for God which he himself hath appointed.

We accept private judgment, as well as the bishop, and give full scope to individual reason, but only within its legitimate province. We reconcile reason and authority by ascertaining the province of reason, and confining it within its legitimate province. Questions of reason are to be decided by reason, but questions of faith are to be decided by authority; for all faith rests on authority, and would not be faith if it did not. The bishop does not seem to have been aware of this fact; for he does not seem to have ever clearly distinguished in his own mind, on the one hand, between faith and science, and, on the other, between faith and opinion.

The bishop seems to fancy that he escapes our conclusion, that the right of private judgment does not relieve the reformers from the charge of schism, on the ground, that the church may be divided on matters of *faith*. If we understand him, he holds that on some articles of faith the church is unanimous, but on others it is divided. In regard to all those articles on which it is divided, the exercise of private judgment is our right. That the church is agreed on some questions, and divided on others, we concede; but that the questions on which it is divided are matters of *faith* we deny. His error arises from not making this distinction. The church cannot be divided on articles of faith; for the bishop himself contends, as well as we, for the unity of the faith. Faith is and must be one, and they who embrace not the one faith are no part of the church; for the bishop himself defines the church to be composed of all who embrace the orthodox faith, and of course of no others. The questions on which the church is divided, or can be divided, without breaking its unity, must be simply questions of science or of opinion, and not questions of faith. The freedom of private judgment in relation to all these questions the church fully recognizes.

But the bishop would seem (p. 3) to rest his defence on the distinction between fundamentals and non-fundamentals. The church, he would probably say, cannot be divided on fundamentals, but it may be divided on non-fundamentals.

This is the usual resort of Protestants. But to this we reply : 1. The non-fundamentals are either matters of faith or they are not. If not, they are out of the question ; for the question concerns matters of faith only. If they are matters of faith, we ask on what authority are they declared to be non-fundamental? Not on the authority of reason, for the question is not a question of reason. On the authority of the Sacred Scriptures? But there is no passage of the Sacred Scriptures which declares or implies that a certain portion of the faith is not fundamental. On the authority of the church? But the Protestant cannot admit the authority of the church without condemning himself, for he resists that authority; and moreover, the church never regards any portion of the faith as non-fundamental. What is not fundamental she does never propose as an article of faith, for she always teaches that it is equally necessary to believe all that she teaches. There is, then, no authority for making the distinction between fundamental and non-fundamental.

2. The matters assumed to be non-fundamental are either matters divinely revealed or not. If not, they are not articles of faith in any sense ; for nothing can be made an article of faith, except what is divinely revealed. If divinely revealed, they cannot be non-fundamental; for it is essential that all which God reveals should be believed. It is repugnant to reason to suppose that God would reveal to us, supernaturally, what might be rejected without detriment to salvation. Moreover, he who rejects any portion of God's word makes God a liar ; because he refuses to rely on the veracity of God, which is as good authority for believing one article as another.

3. Admitting that some articles are fundamental and others non-fundamental, still the bishop has no rule for distinguishing the one from the other. Private reason cannot, as we have seen ; because what articles of supernatural faith are fundamental, and what not, is not a question of reason, but itself a question of faith, and therefore must rest on supernatural authority. Not the Sacred Scriptures; because, in nearly all cases, the question turns on what the Scriptures do really teach, or what is the faith they enjoin.

Will the bishop say, that fundamentals are those articles in which all Christians agree, and non-fundamentals are those about which they dispute ? Understanding by Christians all who bear the name, we ask him what these fundamental doctrines are, in which they all agree? We are ignorant of all such doctrines, and think he will find it difficult to adduce a single doctrine the contrary of which has not been maintained by some portion of the Christian world. Will he, abandoning this ground, say, fundamentals are only those doctrines which are clearly and expressly taught in the Sacred Scriptures? Be it so. The Scriptures, unquestionably, make faith in Jesus Christ, the Son of God, indispensable to salvation; but is it equally express as to what is to be believed concerning Jesus Christ? Certainly not. For nothing can be said to be expressly taught in the Scriptures, about which men, equally able, learned, honest, and sincere, who take them for their rule of faith, continue to dispute. Has it ever been settled from the Bible alone, interpreted by private reason, whether we are to believe the Son of God is consubstantial to the Father, as teaches the Nicene Creed; or created out of nothing, as the Arians contended? Whether he is the second person in the ever-adorable Trinity; or merely the Son of Joseph and Mary, as allege our modern Unitarians? Whether he saves the world as a grand expiatory sacrifice, dying to redeem men from the curse of the law, and raising them to newness of life by the communication of himself; or merely as a teacher of wholesome truths and an exemplar of a holy life? Are not these, and many more like them, fundamental questions? Can they be settled by an appeal to the Scriptures alone? If so, why have they not been? Why are not all sincere and honest Protestants, whose rule is the sufficiency of the Scriptures, agreed respecting them? If all that is fundamental is expressly taught in the Scriptures, why have not our Protestant brethren, long before this, hit upon certain articles of faith which they can all adopt? At least, why have we not seen, after three hundred years of experiment, some approximation to unanimity among them? Yet we see nothing of all this. They divide and sub-divide more and more; and if at the present moment they appear less widely separated, and to fight one another less fiercely than formerly, it is because they have fallen into indifference, and are gradually coming to believe that one creed or one sect is about as good as another, and perhaps none nor all are worth troubling one's head about. No, this ground is untenable. Strike from the creeds of our Protestant sects all articles concerning which there is a difference of belief, and take the residuum, as we must, as the sum of what is clearly taught in the Scriptures, and we should have a faith which would be unanimously, by all parties, declared altogether insufficient,—too meagre to satisfy even Socinians.

It seems to us, on attentively reading Bishop Hopkins's Lectures, that the singular confusion which runs through them arises from his never having clearly conceived of the Church of Christ as an authoritative body. The *Ecclesia docens et gubernans* appears to have remained to him in profound obscurity, or to have been confounded in his mind with the *Ecclesia credens*. He believes Jesus Christ founded a church, but, one is tempted to think, merely a church of believers. He does not appear to be fully aware, at least theoretically, that our blessed Lord has set in this church of believers some " to be apostles, and some prophets, and others evangelists, and others pastors and teachers, for the perfection of the saints, for the work of the ministry, unto the edification of the body of Christ; till we all meet in the unity of the faith, and of the knowledge of the Son of God, unto a perfect man, unto the measure of the age of the fulness of Christ,—that we may not now be children, tossed to and fro, and carried about by every wind of doctrine, in the wickedness of men, in craftiness by which they lie in wait to deceive," (Eph. iv. 11–14,) and that to these, who constitute the ministry of the church, is given authority to teach and to rule the church. It is true, he holds episcopacy to be of divine appointment; but he holds it to be necessary, not to the *being* of the church, but simply to its *order*. Hence, he really believes it possible to retain *the unity of the church under a diversity of ecclesiastical governments*. Here, it seems to us, is his primal error. Our blessed Lord, in constituting his church, did constitute an authoritative ministry, and made communion with that ministry the indispensable condition of communion with his church. " Go ye, therefore, and teach all nations; baptizing them in the name of the Father, and of the Son, and of the Holy Ghost; teaching them to observe all things whatsoever I have commanded you; and behold, I am with you all days, even unto the consummation of the world." (Matt. xxviii. 19, 20.) Here was instituted the *Ecclesia docens*; here was instituted a perpetual ministry, with authority to teach; and whoso rejecteth this authority rejecteth Christ himself. Now, if this ministry has authority to teach, then all are bound to believe what it teaches; for there is no authority to teach, where there is no obligation to believe.

The authority here given, the bishop concedes, was not given to the apostles personally, but to them and their successors. But it was given to them and their successors, not separately, but collectively, as one ministry, to be possessed by each only as he remained in the unity of the body,—in the unity of the teaching body, not merely of the believing body. Then this ministry, the apostles and their successors, are to be regarded as a body corporate, endowed with the attributes of individuality and immortality. Its authority must be one, not merely one in the sense that he who confers it is one, but in the sense that the body exercising it is one body, as a state, a town, or a banking corporation is one body. This must not be overlooked. We suspect the bishop, however, does overlook it, and thinks he maintains the requisite unity by asserting the unity of authority in Christ the invisible Head. That Christ is the fountain of all authority in the church is admitted; that he is the real governor, and the only governor in the church is also admitted; but this is not the question. The question is as to the ministry which he has commissioned to exercise his authority, or through which he governs the church. The ministry is instituted, because Christ chooses to govern by an outward visible agent. The question relates, therefore, solely to this visible agent. If the great Head of the church had chosen to govern without a visible ministry, doubtless he could. But he has not so chosen. He has instituted a ministry, and being himself one, the ministry must be one. The ministry, like the human body, may have many members; but all these members must be members of one and the same body, and members one of another, or else we must adopt the monstrous supposition, that Christ has a multiplicity of bodies. The ministry is instituted to be the visible organ of the invisible authority of Christ. If Christ is one, his authority must be one; if his authority is one, the visible organ must be one; for a visible organ which is manifold cannot express an authority which is one. The ministry, also, must be one; for if not, we shall be perplexed, and at a loss to distinguish the true ministry from the false. Assume a multiplicity of true ministries, and a variety of false ministries, as there has been, is, and always will be so long as the corruptions of human nature remain, and how shall the young, the simple, and the unlettered, all of whom have souls as precious in the sight of God as the soul of the bishop himself, know which is the true ministry to which they owe obedience, and on which they may rely with confidence and safety? We have already proved, that unity of authority, and therefore of the ministry, is necessary as the condition of unity of faith. Unity of the body teaching—*Ecclesia docens*—becomes as necessary as unity of the body believing—*Ecclesia credens*. As unity of faith, according to the bishop himself, is essential to the being of the church, it follows that unity of the ministerial authority is necessary to the *being* as well as to the *order* of the church. Any split or division in the ministerial authority is as much a schism in the church as a split or division in the faith believed.

If these considerations deserve any weight,—and we hold them to be conclusive,—the unity of the church under a diversity of ecclesiastical governments is impossible. It cannot coexist with a divided authority. As well might we say that a state can exist as a single state under two distinct, separate, and independent governments. Here is the rock on which our Anglican divines seem to us to split. They all profess to believe in the unity of the church; but they all assume that its unity may be, and is, retained under distinct, diverse, and independent governments. Hence, they call their church—which, as an ecclesiastical polity, is as isolated and independent as the government of Great Britain itself—" a branch " of the one Catholic Church, and, with a marvellous simplicity, speak of it as "*our* branch of the Catholic Church." A branch is incomplete in itself; but the Anglican Church, if a church at all, is not incomplete in itself. It claims to be an independent body, and participates in the authority of no other body; nor does it depend on any other body for its life or any portion of its life. It is therefore false and absurd to call it a *branch*. It is no branch. It is the whole tree, or no part of it. It is an island church, and nowhere joined to the continent. Can these divines fail to perceive this? Alas! when one has strayed from the fountain of living waters, and lost the path which leads to it, there is apparently no absurdity too gross for him to believe, no truth too obvious and palpable for him to overlook. So we doubt not but our Anglican divines honestly believe their church is a *branch*, although there is never a trunk of which it is a branch,—their church a *member*, although there is never a body of which it is a member.

It is this false view of unity, of the unity of the church under a diversity and independence of government, that has led Bishop Hopkins to contend, in these Lectures, that individuals are free to select what church they will join. Strange unity of the church, which is compatible with the existence of different churches and different communions, and allows it to be a matter of at least comparative indifference which one a man joins; just as if a man can be saved in any other communion than that of the one Holy Catholic and Apostolic Church! We own individuals are free to join the church, or to unite with such one of the sects as they choose, but only as a man is free to choose life or death; and so would the bishop himself say, if he only clearly perceived the unity of the Catholic Church, and that out of unity there is no life.

But the bishop can justify the reformers in seceding from the communion of the Catholic Church only on condition of its having ceased to be the communion of Christ; for to secede from a church which is in communion with Christ is to secede from Christ himself. Now, will he deny that salvation is possible in the Roman Catholic Church? Will he deny that it was possible in that church in the beginning of the sixteenth century? The Roman Catholic Church was then what it had been for many ages before, and what it is now. It embraced at that epoch, and had for many ages, nearly the whole Christian world. If we say that salvation is not possible in its communion, we pronounce a fearful sentence on the millions who lived and died in its communion prior to the reformation, as upon the many millions who have lived and died in its communion since. But the bishop will not say this; Protestants generally do not say it. Were they to say it, what should we say of the piety of our English ancestors? England herself was converted from heathenism by missionaries from this very church of Rome; and she has not, we believe, a saint in her calendar, who did not belong to the period of her communion with Rome. It was during that period that all that makes her glory took its rise. Then were founded her institutions of learning; then was laid the foundation of her real national greatness. Then was she renowned for her piety, and her land was filled with the pure, faithful, self-denying servants of God. Shall we say that all her saints, martyrs, and confessors have gone to hell? Of course not. No Protestant really doubts the possibility of salvation in the Roman communion, and the bishop does not himself seem to think that communion with Rome endangers salvation. In his first Lecture he plainly recognizes the Roman Catholic Church as still having all the essential elements of the church of God. He concedes her orthodoxy and her catholicity. He does not even seek to unchurch her. He admits her to be a church of Christ; and states, that the question was not, whether she was Catholic or not, but whether she had an *exclusive* claim to the title of Catholicity. "The Church of Rome," he says, (p. 6,) "claimed the exclusive title of Catholic, and branded all without her pale as cut off from Christ as heretics, as guilty of mortal sin. The reformers denied that she had the *exclusive* right to the name of Catholic." That is, the reformers admitted her to be Catholic, but contended that they were Catholic as well as she, and perhaps more so; because, as they alleged, they were more in harmony with the church in primitive times.

Now, if he concedes salvation to be possible in the Roman Catholic Church, he concedes her to contain in herself all that is necessary to salvation. Belief in the true orthodox faith is necessary to salvation, as all must admit; for "without faith it is impossible to please God," and "he that believeth not shall be condemned." Then the Roman Catholic has the true orthodox faith, and this the bishop also seems to admit. Then the reformers had no reason to secede for her on account of any supposed corruptions of the faith. But if salvation was possible in her bosom, she must have been in communion with Christ; for "there is no other name given under heaven, among men, whereby we must be saved." But if she was in communion with Christ, she was the church of Christ; and as the church is but one communion, she and such particular churches as were in communion with her were the only church and the whole church of Christ. To separate from her communion, then, was to separate from the communion of Christ. The reformers did separate from her communion, and therefore separated from the communion of Christ, and were schismatics. No man can be saved, unless he abide in the communion of Christ. The reformers did not abide in his communion. We leave the conclusion to be drawn by the bishop himself.

Here is the necessary conclusion, if it be once admitted, as it is and must be, that salvation is possible in the Roman Catholic Church. This is a terrible conclusion, and worthy of the serious consideration of those who talk so loudly and arrogantly of the "corruptions," "errors," and "usurpations of modern Rome"; especially of those who form Protestant leagues and missionary societies for the conversion of the benighted Papists of Italy, France, and Spain. It will be well for them to look at their own foundation. They must muster courage enough to deny the possibility of salvation in the Roman Catholic communion, or else admit that salvation is not possible in their own. If they conclude to deny that salvation is possible in the Roman Catholic communion, we will thank them to agree in which of their own party-colored communions it is possible.

But what! do you mean to say that none in these various Protestant sects can be saved? We mean to say that no man can be saved who is not actually or virtually in the church which is in communion with Christ; and if the Roman Catholic Church is in communion with him, Protestant sects are not, for they are not in communion with it. That individuals who are outwardly in Protestant sects may be saved, we do not deny; because they may be there through invincible ignorance, but would not be there, if it were in their power to unite with the true church. God does not exact impossibilities. Where the deed is impossible, he takes the will for the deed. All who believe the orthodox faith, without which no one can be saved, and have the desire and intention which would accept the Catholic Church were it presented, will be saved; but not because they are in this or that sectarian communion, but because they are virtually, *in voto animique dispositione*, out of it, and in the Catholic communion.

There are various other matters in these Lectures, on which we should like to remark; but we pass them over, because we have in the present article wished to confine ourselves to a single point. We think we have shown, that, on the grounds assumed by the bishop, the British reformers are not cleared of the charge of schism. So far as we can see, he has brought forward nothing which takes their secession out of the category of schism, or in the least removes the presumption we began by saying is against them. Till this is done, the Catholic Church stands secure in her ancient possession, and has no occasion to enter upon the defence of her title.

END OF VOLUME VI.